THE ENCYCLOPEDIA OF
CLASSIC CARS

THE ENCYCLOPEDIA OF
CLASSIC CARS

GENERAL EDITOR: DAVID LILLYWHITE

THUNDER BAY
P·R·E·S·S

San Diego, California

Thunder Bay Press
An imprint of the Advantage Publishers Group
5880 Oberlin Drive, San Diego, CA 92121-4794
www.thunderbaybooks.com

Library of Congress Cataloging-in-Publication Data

The encyclopedia of classic cars / general editor, David Lillywhite.
    p. cm.
  ISBN 1-57145-990-1
   1. Antique and classic cars--Encyclopedias. 2. Automobiles--History. I. Lillywhite, David.

TL9.E52353 2003
629.222'03--dc22

2003061781

Printed in Singapore

2 3 4 5 6 08 07 06 05 04

Authors: Craig Cheetham, Ian Cushway, Richard Dredge, Richard Gunn, David Lillywhite, James Ruppert
Project Editor: James Bennett
Editor: Conor Kilgallon
Design: www.stylus-design.com
Picture Research: Lisa Wren, Natasha Jones

CONTENTS

The Bugatti Type 23 Brescia was a long-wheelbase variant of the original Type 13. The Brescia name was adopted after Bugatti's great success at the 1921 Italian Grand Prix at Brescia.

The Singer SM Roadster, also known as the 1500 Roadster, was launched in 1951 to compete with the MG TD. It was little more than a revamped 1939 Nine Roadster, and offered lacklustre performance.

The Pontiac Chieftain was one of the most stylish and dramatic cars of the early 1950s. This is a 1951 Chieftain De Luxe model.

CONTENTS

Considered to be the epitome of classic car design, and with a hood that stretches almost half its length, the Mercedes 540K was a truly extravagant way to transport just two passengers.

The world's fastest production car when it was unveiled in 1987, Porsche's 959 was surprisingly easy to drive compared with other supercars.

INTRODUCTION

This isn't just a book just about cars. It is about the imagination, technical innovation, perseverance, belief and, above all, the passion that went into creating them. People from all backgrounds and all trades have become involved with the evolution of the motor car from its very humblest beginnings, and it is their optimism and vision that has provided us with the richly diverse variety of cars in this book. To them, the engineers, designers and entrepreneurs, we should be eternally grateful.

Ignoring the very first pioneering vehicular contraptions for a moment, in its purest, commercial sense the motor car has always existed as a means of making money – usually involving some kind of manufacturing activity, followed by a sales transaction resulting in, hopefully, profit. Yet, with its unrivalled ability to stir the emotions, the motor car is truly unlike any other consumable. People worship the car. Some sit in bars arguing about them; some even fight over them. When it finally becomes too much of an obsession, happily-married couples even get a divorce over them. Then there are those that hate the car. They hate everything it stands for and in particular what it has done to the environment: congestion, tracts of land ruined by road building, pollution. Love it or hate it, the car has always been controversial, but putting prejudices aside, it has undoubtedly done more good than harm.

Being an emotive subject, you will notice the emotions of our authors, each of whom are specialists in their field, reveal themselves in the entries. That is only natural – without it you would have pure facts and rather dry reading.

COVERAGE

From the diverse pageant of motor cars produced, this book covers the most significant and interesting marques. The earliest car we have included is the Panhard-Levassor dating from 1891, and among the latest is the Aston Martin Virage, which was introduced in 1988 and is still in production. Some cars were sold in huge numbers, others barely made double figures, but generally all were intended for the road, so there are no competition-only cars here.

We have tried to be as objective as we can about how much coverage each car receives – and we have afforded more space to those that have gone on to become icons in their own right, like the Jaguar E-type. Others have won themselves larger coverage by virtue of their interest from a technical point of view or due to some ground-breaking innovation. Cars or manufacturers that had a short lifespan, were particularly obscure or otherwise less significant than others have shorter entries. Either way, we have included all the cars we felt appropriate to provide a full and concise representation of all the cars ever produced. There are bound to be omissions and some inconsistencies in this selection, and for this we apologise in advance.

TECHNICAL DATA

When deciding what facts were important concerning a particular car, we hit upon a dilemma. If we were to include the full gamut of technical detail about each car, our coverage would have been less catholic. That is why we chose to only quote the most important statistics while retaining our original, extensive list of cars for inclusion. Then as soon as we solved one problem, another came rushing up. Because usually each car was produced in more than one model or engine size, how would we be able to cover them all? Again, there was nothing for it but to be ruthless if we were to include as many different manufacturers and cars as we could. The decision was made, therefore, to quote only specifications for the most successful, most iconic derivative in the range. So, using the famed E-type as an example again, we quote specification figures for what we consider the finest car in the range, the Series 1 4.2-litre (258 cu in) model which retained all the purity of the original and equally fine 3.8-litre (232 cu in) car but with a smoother, more flexible engine. However, rest assured that the overwhelming majority of entries will also have a full account of the other engines available in the range to ensure that you get the full picture.

There may be some confusion over the naming of some pre-war cars using the RAC rating of horsepower in their title. The Singer Nine, for example, was so-called because it had a 9HP rating according to the RAC

In the 1960s, the Jaguar E-type was one of the most famous sports cars in the world. It was stylish, sensationally fast, and had obvious connections with earlier racing Jaguars such as the D-type. The E-type was also great value – in 1961, a roadster could be yours for just £2098.

scale. That doesn't mean it had a 9bhp (7kW) engine! The Citroën 2CV is so called because it had a 2HP engine (the name stands for *Deux Chevaux*, or Two Horses) using the old, and now thankfully obsolete, rating system – but it actually had 9bhp (7kW) in original form. Such reckoning, calculated only from the square of the car engine's cylinder bore in millimetres multiplied by 1,613, was wholly inaccurate and only used for taxation purposes in the U.K.

Regarding production figures, you will no doubt notice that there are a number of entries with 'n/a' or 'not available' against them. This isn't an omission or laziness on our part, simply a consequence of the fact that no record of the actual quantity of cars produced exists in the public domain. By way of explanation, where a figure is quoted it may be taken to represent the total production of all models throughout the entire lifespan of that vehicle.

Researching the cars featured here proved to be an interesting and wholly satisfying experience, but sadly where secondary sources are used there is always the risk of errors being perpetuated. That is why our authors took the time and effort to seek out contemporary road tests, sales literature, museum archives and other primary sources wherever it was available to ensure that the information remained as accurate as possible. Having said that, there will always be some discrepancies – especially when referring to something as controversial as top speeds. Obviously manufacturers wanting to impress are more likely to err on the side of optimism; sang-froid road testers will establish more 'accurate' data. So which do you quote? The answer is the source that, by experience, you have learnt to trust the most.

A further potential area for confusion concerns the dating of a particular model. Typically, a company will produce a prototype, present it at one of the big motor shows such as London, Geneva or Paris, start production soon after, then continue for further period. Rarely is the demise of a model given the same publicity as its launch, so quoting the precise date when production started and finished is fraught with problems. Moreover, it can commonly take several years for a manufacturer to 'dispose' of made-up cars from its production line as the company tries to put off the inevitable.

In 1974 Caterham reintroduced the obsolete Lotus Seven S3 as the Caterham Super Seven. A variation of the model is still produced today.

Enough of the preamble – let's get on with the cars themselves. But first an insight into how it all began.

EARLY RUMBLINGS

By his very nature, man is a nomadic beast, and historically he did whatever he could to make travelling from one place to another less taxing. Getting other animals to do the work for him was the obvious solution, but he was soon eager to harness a more controllable and reliable source of energy.

The first 'horseless' carriages were human-powered using treadmills, cranks and primitive gearing, but unsurprisingly these were not particularly popular with the men dragooned into propelling these heavy machines, and attention was drawn to other sources of energy, including wind power and even clockwork.

It wasn't until the advent of steam power that the self-propelled carriage truly became a realistic proposition, with Swiss engineer Nicholas Joseph Cugnot being generally credited with making the first full-scale vehicle to be moved by mechanical power in 1765. Funded by the French government, his first experimental vehicle is said to have carried four passengers on its inaugural trip and to have travelled at around 5km/h (3mph). The second machine he made is still preserved in Paris.

The mantle was then passed to Cornish engineer Richard Trevithick who produced a steam carriage in 1801 that was capable of a sprightly 19km/h (12mph), and even had an arrangement of spur gears to provide a high ratio for the flats and a low ratio for hills.

The Industrial Revolution forged ahead in Britain, and it was here that steam road vehicles continued their development throughout the mid-nineteenth century until the arrival, finally, of the internal combustion engine – patented by Etienne Lenoir in 1860. A year later, to demonstrate just what his engine was capable of, Lenoir constructed a crude motor car; but travelling between Paris and nearby Joinville just 10km (6 miles) away took an exhausting six hours. Woefully inefficient, his pioneering engine did however stimulate other engineers to create more efficient devices. The most significant of these was the four-stroke engine designed simultaneously and quite independently by Gottlieb Daimler in 1876 and Karl Benz of Mannheim, who in 1885 famously united his engine with a

The Ferrari 212, which was produced from 1951 to 1953, was available in an array of chassis lengths and engine specifications, with bespoke bodywork.

With the Model T, Henry Ford set out to build a 'motorcar for the great multitude' which was light, powerful, affordable and easy to drive. In almost twenty years of manufacture, over 15 million cars were produced, the longest run of any single model apart from the Volkswagen Beetle.

tubular-framed three wheeled chassis to produce the first limited-run production motor car.

The story continues with two French engineers, Panhard and Levassor, who began manufacturing Daimler's four-stroke engine in 1890 and, predicting no future in the motor car, subsequently sold the rights to use the engine in motor vehicles to the French ironmongery and cycle-manufacturing firm Peugeot. By 1891 they had sold five cars, which rocketed to 29 the following year.

Meanwhile Benz had also started selling his cars in France, but it was not until the four-wheeled Viktoria of 1893 that serious production started.

Such was Peugeot's success that Levassor reconsidered his earlier decision not to make cars and after a couple of crude automotive attempts devised the famous Système Panhard, with the engine at the front driving the rear wheels via a sliding pinion gearbox – a method used on the majority of cars ever since.

By the end of the 1890s, demand for the motor car was growing rapidly and the British motoring lobby showed its strength by forcing the repeal of the ludicrous law which insisted that motor cars should be preceded by a man on foot, waving a red flag (a legacy of the old Locomotives on Highways Acts of 1865 and 1878). A commemorative run was organised to Brighton on November 14, 1896 to celebrate the raising of the speed limit to 19km/h (12mph).

As the decade drew to a close Benz had produced his 2000th production vehicle. Motoring, however, remained the preserve of the privileged rich and eccentrics, and few people had yet to set eyes on the new contraption. This, however, was all about to change.

COMMERCIAL PIONEERS: 1901–1914

Daimler's engineer Wilhelm Maybach opened the new century with a bang, having taken an order from the wealthy Austro-Hungarian Consul at Nice, Emil Jellinek, for a batch of 30 cars which he insisted be named after his daughter Mercédès. All German Daimlers were to adopt the name thereafter.

The Mercedes took the design of the motor car to new heights with its honeycomb radiator, pressed steel chassis and gear selection made via a gate rather than a quadrant, and the layout became the template that other manufacturers would follow.

These cars, however, with their high price tags, didn't represent the growing motor car movement at the start of the century. This was the

With a top speed of 120 km/h (75mph), the Vauxhall Prince Henry was one of the best sports cars of its day. Original cars had four seats but no doors.

preserve of the smaller, cheaper runabouts like the single-cylinder De Dion and Renault which, in turn, were also widely imitated.

In the United States, the development of the motor industry was hindered by legal wrangling concerning an earlier patent of the gasoline combustion engine by patent lawyer George Baldwin Selden, but maverick entrepreneur Henry Ford finally took matters into his own hands by founding his own Ford Motor Company in 1903. Basing his design on Lenoir's engine (not Selden's) by 1908 he had fought off the legal profession and introduced the immortal Model T.

Such was the instant popularity of the T that Ford created the first moving production line in order to build enough cars to satisfy demand.

Ford's 'Universal Car' changed the complexion of motoring – and society for that matter – overnight and by the time production ended in 1927, over 16.5 million had been built.

With motoring finding a new mass market in the United States, increased automation produced an array of cheap new models and, as a result, some of the more ostentatious marques went into decline. In Europe, however, it was the motorcycle that fuelled the insatiable appetite for motoring, providing a source of cheap engines that could be crudely bolted onto a chassis to create what became known as 'cyclecars'. Thankfully, their popularity was short-lived, as new and affordable cars appeared on the horizon.

THE DAWN OF A NEW ERA: 1915–1930
Optimism flourished in the immediate aftermath of World War I, and everyone wanted to get behind the wheel of a motor car. The 'world on wheels' was about to become reality. The sudden boom had existing manufacturers working flat out, while new companies run on a shoestring and working from inadequate backstreet premises producing the most basic light cars and cyclecars emerged from nowhere to satisfy demand.

It was not to last. Strikes, shortages of raw materials and new taxes bludgeoned confidence in the industry and, following a collapse in 1920–21, only the fittest and most profitable companies survived. Ford's lead in cutting prices to boost sales was followed by numerous other European and U.S. manufacturers and, a year later, the industry successfully emerged from the doldrums bringing with it a new, exciting generation of cars including the famous Austin Seven.

Throughout this period cars were to benefit from advances made in the aviation industry, most notably the use of overhead camshaft engines such as those in the Hispano-Suiza V8, later built by Wolseley and used by Morris after their takeover in 1927 in their coveted MG sports cars. Such engine design would later became commonplace on most modern cars.

Bentley, too, made use of their aero engine experience, developing an in-line four-cylinder 3-litre (183 cu in) engine with an overhead camshaft which went into production in 1921 – and powered one of the most evocative sports cars of its time.

Meanwhile, cheaper cars developed four-wheel brakes and other technical innovations such as windscreen wipers, electric starters and low-pressure rubber tyres became commonplace, making motoring safer and more comfortable.

A QUEST FOR MORE REFINEMENT: 1930–1944
Throughout the 1930s motorists sought even more refinement, demanding covered saloon bodies to replace the open tourers that dominated the previous decade. Economic problems meant people wanted smaller engines, too, which inevitably had to be geared appropriately to cope with the increasing weight of the car bodies.

The Land Rover might have been basic, but that was part of its appeal. Reliable, easy to service and able to go almost anywhere, it became a legend.

Design changed too. The public demanded more space inside the car, so the engine was pushed forward over the front axle, and cars became more elegant and more streamlined to reflect current fashion. The angularity of the 1920s cars was smoothed out by the introduction of flowing wings and contours, and the most modern cars even had a luggage compartment to satisfy the motorist's increasing desire to cover greater distances.

Such cars were increasingly the work of the stylist rather than the engineer, and handling suffered as a result – despite the development of independent suspension by this time.

Morris, Austin and Ford continued to be household names, while cars like the front-wheel drive Citroën of 1934 began to make their mark in terms of technical innovation. During this period the first Jaguar emerged, as did Ferdinand Porsche's prototype for the Volkswagen or 'people's car'.

The 1930s acted as a watershed to some extent, with some of the luxury manufacturers such as Hispano-Suiza, along with smaller concerns and coachbuilders making cars in limited numbers, becoming victims of the ever-increasing move towards mass, low-cost production.

The impending war, however, was about to change things forever.

POSTWAR GLORY: 1944–1959
After the celebrations at the end of World War II finally died down, a new optimism spread across Europe and the United States, fuelled by promises that new technology gained during the wartime years would be put to use in motor car construction. However, the shell-shocked car industry was plagued by shortages of raw materials and bomb-damaged factories, and instead of launching exciting postwar models festooned with new goodies and gadgets it merely re-used prewar technology, giving it a slightly more modern spin to lure customers. Across Europe cable brakes, sidevalve engines and running boards lingered on, and it was left to car makers in the United States to make real headway with the general adoption of automatic transmission and hydraulic suspension.

German manufacturers such as Volkswagen rose from the ashes and received much-needed funding to develop the Beetle, while other memorable postwar classics of this era included the fabulous Jaguar XK120, Morris Minor and Citroën 2CV – all of which debuted in 1948.

It wasn't until the 1950s that true confidence in the motor industry was finally regained, and this decade proved to be one of the most significant and imaginative periods of car development. Slowly but surely designs became more rounded with the adoption of the full-width body, integrated headlamps and at long last the death of the running board. Most important of all was the new method of unitary or monocoque construction, where the car's body provided structural

In 1953, General Motors launched its homegrown competitor to the European sports car, the Chevrolet Corvette. With a fibreglass body and powerful acceleration, the 'Vette became an American legend. This is a 1956 model, with a 4343cc (265 cu in) V8 engine and 'scooped out' sides.

integrity, removing the need for a separate chassis and side members. The knock-on effect was that there was no longer a place for the specialist coachbuilders, and many faded into obscurity.

Jaguar demonstrated their disc brakes at Le Mans in 1953 and introduced them to their production cars a few years later. Today they are standard on most cars.

In America the big three – Ford, General Motors and Chrysler – killed off smaller manufacturers like Kaiser's brave attempts at gaining a foothold, while in Europe the merger between Austin and Morris would ultimately sow the seeds for the formation of the British Motor Corporation, which in turn would later become British Leyland. Their aim to supply small family cars to the populace proved successful for many decades to come.

The Suez crisis of 1956 sent shockwaves across the world, and in the face of increasing pressure on resources the American manufacturers followed the European lead and started producing smaller 'compact' cars towards the end of the decade. Gradually the public began voting with their pockets, phasing out the gargantuan, grotesquely styled gas-guzzlers, cars that represented the height of fashion just a few years earlier.

A new trend for even smaller, more thrifty cars emerged in Europe pioneered by German companies such as Heinkel and Messerschmitt who started making 'bubblecars', while in Britain the revolutionary Morris Mini appeared in 1959 with its inspirational front-wheel drive, decent build and sporty handling. Fiat followed a similar path with its 500 model.

The decade also had its more glamorous elements too in the form of the streamlined MGA, Triumph TRs and Healeys. More exotic still were offerings from Ferrari and Mercedes (with their distinctive 300SL 'gullwing'), while Citroën were busy experimenting with the bizarre with their complex and technically advanced DS model with its hydropneumatic suspension. The motor car had finally come of age.

SIGN OF THE TIMES: 1960–1972

The 1960s, more than any other decade, saw the car becoming a fashion statement, a declaration of identity and a visual demonstration of its owner's individual aspirations. The Jaguar E-type typified the spirit of the time with its sensuous styling, playboy image and devastatingly impressive performance.

The beginning of this period was dominated by mergers, with several European manufacturers, seeing the potential economies to be made from working in co-operation with each other making engines and running gear, quickly joining ranks.

'The Times They Are A-Changin'' sang Bob Dylan and he wasn't wrong. Four-wheel drive with anti-lock brakes was demonstrated by Ferguson Formula and first appeared on the Jensen FF in 1966. Overhead-camshaft engines, which first appeared on the groundbreaking Jaguar XK120 in 1948, quickly became commonplace, with manufacturers realizing the potential for double overhead camshafts and multivalve engine layouts.

When Ford's bid to buy Ferrari failed, they turned to British endurance motoring expertise to build the Le Mans-winning GT40.

Hydraulic suspension, pioneered by Citroën on their 1955 DS model, was used by BMC, while the Mini's front-wheel drive configuration also became universally adopted.

Styling-wise, by the mid-1960s fintails had largely disappeared, and in came cleaner, less cluttered designs. The move was towards lower, wider cars; chrome was still used but in less abundance, and glass area was increased to improve looks and driver visibility.

In the liberated '60s, stylists such as Bertone were given a free hand – frequently with stunning results such as the Lamborghini Miura, unveiled in 1966.

There was to be another significant change on the motoring landscape with the emergence of car manufacturing activity in Japan. Japanese cars would soon become a common sight on every street in every country of the world.

Throughout the 1970s, '80s and '90s car design and technology continued to evolve – though it was a rollercoaster ride at times, with cars like the infamous Austin Allegro proving that even the most talented stylists could get it wrong sometimes. Increasing emphasis was placed on practicality, leading to the increased use of the hatchback design (first appearing way back in 1964 on the Renault 16), safety, and further automation. By the mid-1990s even the most mundane family hack would come with power steering, air conditioning, anti-lock brakes, airbag restraints and hi-fidelity in-car entertainment as standard.

ECOLOGY AND EVOLUTION: 1973–PRESENT

Since the oil crisis of 1973 and increased speculation a decade later about the effect of exhaust fumes on the earth's ozone layer, car engines have become more efficient and less polluting. Plastics are being used more and more in place of steel for body panels, to reduce weight and further increase energy saving, while wind-tunnel technology to reduce drag has had the effect of making all cars look broadly similar.

The public quickly rebelled against this ever-broadening anonymity, expressing a longing for cars with personality or some kind of individuality, and manufacturers like Volkswagen and BMW have responded by producing 'retro' models like the new Volkswagen Beetle and the MINI.

Key to the evolution of the car in recent years has been the ever more demanding requirements of buyers. People want a single car to perform a

The 1960s saw the birth of the muscle car – and few turned more heads than the 272kW (366bhp) Pontiac GTO Judge.

variety of tasks: to be practical, stylish and economical to run, while feeling like a sports car to drive. Needless to say, manufacturers have drawn upon every bit of inspiration and technical innovation to create vehicles that satisfy all these needs.

Meanwhile, experimentation with various sources of power is progressing, with hybrid cars using both conventional fuels and electricity now a common sight on our highways, and the use of alternative sources of energy such as hydrogen not far away.

What the future holds for the car is uncertain. While we all love the freedom it brings, our ever more congested roads groaning under the sheer density of traffic must one day reach breaking point. One thing is for sure, however: the optimism and true spirit of motoring that has powered the last hundred years of evolution isn't about to lay down and die. Watch this space, and look forward to the new and exciting motor cars yet to be created.

Until then, let's enjoy the heritage that has been left to us and marvel in our grand and illustrious motoring past.

Ian Cushway

Originally introduced in 1964, the Porsche 911 has been gradually modified over the decades. The 1998 Porsche 911 Coupé shown here consolidated the 911's position as one of the world's most coveted supercars, due to its superb handling, unforgettable engine note and classic looks.

ABARTH-FIAT 850/1000

1960–70

Engine: 982cc (60 cu in), 4-cylinder
Power: 45kW (60bhp)
0–96km/h (60mph): n/a
Top speed: 201km/h (125mph)
Production total: n/a

Carlo Abarth was a self-taught engineer who had worked with many of the automotive greats, including Ferdinand Porsche. In 1949, he set up his own company from the remains of Cisitalia (see separate entry) and planned to develop their 1100s for racing. He also developed a line of performance tuning parts and moved on to modifying production cars.

The conversion that really made Abarth successful was his modification work on the little Fiat 600. The first of these came in 1956, followed by a 747cc (46 cu in) version in 1959, but the best came when the Fiat engine was bored out to 847cc (52 cu in).

The resultant 850TC was a true buzz-box, a fun combination of light weight, diminutive size, go-kart handling and a high revving engine. It had disc brakes at the front and an extra radiator and

modified suspension. The basic version came with 39kW (52bhp), but there was also an 850S with 41kW (55bhp) and an 850SS with 42kW (57bhp). Compare this to the standard 600 which produced only about 15kW (20bhp).

Other cars followed, including the 1000, and then twin-camshaft versions of both the 850 and 1000. The most potent version was the 1000TCR, with 83kW (112bhp), an extended front valance and an engine lid on stilts for cooling.

The massive bodywork appendages signal that this is an example of the ultimate Abarth-Fiat 850/1000 range, the 1000TCR. The TC stood for twin-camshaft and the R for race version. Genuine examples are now highly sought after.

ABARTH-FIAT 595/695

1963–71

In the UK the Mini Cooper was the tiny car with big performance, but in Italy it was Carlo Abarth's Fiat-500-based models. They're still cult cars today, often seen in saloon car races against much larger machines, losing out on the straights but nipping through gaps on the corners.

Before the great success of the 600 and the 1000, Carlo Abarth had started by modifying the Fiat 500, producing his famous 595 and 695 models. These were based on Fiat's updated version of its tiny 500, named the 500D. Abarth took the Fiat and managed to turn it from a basic and highly economical run-around to a mighty little pocket rocket that could easily challenge the performance of many larger and more expensive sports cars.

The two-cylinder engine was tuned and bored out to 593.7cc (36.2 cu in) and power went up to 20kW (27bhp). This was hardly a large amount, but was more than enough in such a tiny, lightweight machine. Little else was changed for this new

model which was named the 595.

Then came the Abarth-Fiat 595SS, which gained more power through the incorporation of a bigger carburettor, This produced 24kW (32bhp). By enlarging the Fiat engine still further, Abarth managed to obtain 22kW (30bhp) from a 689.5cc (42 cu in) unit (in the 695) and 28kW (38bhp) for the 695SS.

Handling options also became available, while the Abarth-Fiat 695SS could be bought fitted with front disc brakes and much wider wheelarches. These cars were to become so widely sought-after by enthusiasts that they are still made to this day by enterprising replica manufacturers, who incorporate Abarth stripes and the distinctive Abarth scorpion badge.

Engine: 689.5cc (42 cu in), twin-cylinder
Power: 28kW (38bhp)
0–96km/h (60mph): n/a
Top speed: 142km/h (88mph)
Production total: n/a

SIMCA-ABARTH 1150

Fiat cars were tuner Carlo Abarth's usual choice of machine for modifying. In 1961, however, he added a surprising choice to his line-up. This was a conversion which was based around the Simca 1000. This was a new model, from the French company, which was a box-like, rear-engined saloon with somewhat ugly appearance and suspect handling.

There wasn't really that much to the Simca-Abarth conversion other than a bigger engine – enlarged to 1137cc (69 cu in) – and a new Abarth grille. But the Abarth conversion spiced up a boring car nine years before Simca managed to do the same thing with their Rallye version.

More importantly, the Simca-Abarth 1150 set the tone for the Corsa, a beautiful coupé built on a Simca floorpan, and numerous other larger-engined Abarth-Simcas. These included a 2-litre (122 cu in) vehicle which could achieve more than 241km/h (150mph) – not what you would expect from a Simca.

Engine: 1137cc (69 cu in), 4-cylinder
Power: 41kW (55bhp)
0–96km/h (60mph): n/a
Top speed: 151km/h (94mph)
Production total: n/a

AC 10HP

The AC name is now generally associated with fire-breathing sports cars. But in its very early years, starting in 1904, the company made strange little three-wheelers, called AC Sociables, and cyclecars – these were lightweight economy cars that were designed to replace the motorcycle and sidecar combination.

The AC 10hp was one of the first cyclecars to look like a full size car. Its engine was a French-built four-cylinder unit, while the chassis was cleverly made from pressed sheet steel made into U-shapes, providing strength and light weight – an idea that was soon taken up my many other manufacturers.

In fact, the 10hp was initially too heavy to be counted as a true

As the oldest existing UK car manufacturer, AC's history began with lightweight 'cyclecars' – this 10hp was the first to deserve to be taken seriously and was good enough to begin a long tradition of ACs competing in motorsport.

cyclecar by the tax-led categories of the day, but a redesign of the transmission soon brought it back under the 508kg (10cwt) threshold. It was ready just in time to take part in the first cyclecar trial, organized by the ACU, Auto Cycle Union, organizers of motoring events, in which the new model won several awards.

The 10hp vehicle was followed by a 12hp version which ensured that the precariously financed AC company could look forward to a much more certain future, despite the long interruption to production caused by the outbreak of World War I. During the Great War, AC designed their own four-cylinder engine, but it was never quite as good as the French unit. However, by then, the company had its eye on bigger machines.

Engine: 1315cc (80 cu in), 4-cylinder
Power: n/a
0–96km/h (60mph): n/a
Top speed: n/a
Production total:

AC 12/24

After the end of World War I, AC found that they were unable to use the French engine that had powered the earlier 10hp model. To replace the 10hp engine, they chose a British-built Anzani four-cylinder unit, which was highly reliable and powerful for its time. It also has the advantage of being extremely light in weight.

One of the three Anzani-engined models built was the 12/24, which was so named because the RAC tax rating of this particular engine was 12hp, while the true power was 18kW (24bhp). It was a more sophisticated model than the previous 10hp and it gained a modest sporting reputation, with some owners stripping them of wings, running boards and windscreen to run them in as many competition classes as possible, mostly at Brooklands.

From the mid-1920s, brakes on all four wheels became an option.

Engine: 1496cc (91 cu in), 4-cylinder
Power: 18kW (24bhp)
0–96km/h (60mph): n/a
Top speed: 76km/h (47mph)
Production total: n/a

AC SIX

The AC Six was an enduring model produced in several versions over the years. All of these versions were classified according to engine power. To add even more complication to this model's history, the AC Six also came in a wide variety of body styles, including a drophead coupé called the Aceca, a name reused by AC many years later.

However, the fundamental design of the Six remained the same, with a highly advanced overhead camshaft six-cylinder engine, which started out with a capacity of 1.5 litres (92 cu in) unit but was later to be changed to 2 litres (122 cu in) capacity. The engine was developed by AC and was often used in racing and in the attempt to break records.

The gearbox was a three-speed unit and the suspension was by quarter-elliptic springs. The AC Six's standard brake set-up was for rear wheels only, although front brakes were to become an option. From 1927, front brakes became standard equipment on this vehicle.

The first versions developed 26kW (35bhp) but that was increased to 30kW (40bhp) for the 16/40 version. A 16/56 version of the AC Six followed, which itself was to be replaced by the triple carburettor 16/66.

Engine: 1992cc (122 cu in), 6-cylinder
Power: 49kW (66bhp)
0–96km/h (60mph): n/a
Top speed: 137km/h (85mph)
Production total: n/a

AC ACEDES MAGNA

AC's staple product during the 1920s was the Six. But by the end of the decade this successful vehicle was becoming very obviously an obsolete product. The solution was to revamp the 16/56 version of the Six, which resulted in the Acedes Magna.

The updated model was significantly larger than the previous Six models, which was both good and bad – good because it enabled the car to be much better-equipped and more refined than the Six, but bad because it added lots of extra weight and

slowed the car down. This was a problem, since ACs of this period were famous for their race and speed record successes.

However, the Acedes Magna was a much more modern machine than many of its competitors. It had hydraulic brakes on all four

wheels as standard and its ignition was by coil, rather than magneto.

Engine: 1992cc (122 cu in), 6-cylinder
Power: 42kW (56bhp)
0–96km/h (60mph): n/a
Top speed: n/a
Production total: n/a

AC 2-LITRE

Even before World War II, AC had been struggling to keep its costs low enough to stay in business. When the war ended, the company was in desperate need of a new model to capitalize on the rising demand for cars but it deemed it too risky financially to develop an all-new model.

Thus for the 2-litre model, the chassis that AC had used to good effect in the 1930s gained a new lease of life. The engine in the new

offering had an even longer history, being basically the six-cylinder long-stroke engine that AC had developed in the 1920s.

As for the body, a wide range of labour-intensive coachbuilt designs were out of the question initially, mostly because manpower costs had risen since pre-war days. Instead, AC designed a two-door saloon body using the traditional construction of aluminium over an ash frame, with little in the way of

styling embellishment.

The interior, too, was initially more basic than would have been expected in pre-war days. Later, the 2-litre got higher specification trim and also the option of four doors, but the first models were successful enough to firmly re-establish the AC name. Surprisingly, considering their aging components, several were raced and rallied at Silverstone and in the RAC and Monte Carlo events.

Engine: 1991cc (121 cu in), 6-cylinder
Power: 55kW (74bhp)
0–96km/h (60mph): 19.9 secs
Top speed: 132km/h (82mph)
Production total: 1284

The sleek-looking radiator grille of the 2-litre was easily its most impressive styling feature. But although the front looks elegant, the roof was too high in proportion to the rest of the body even by the saloon standards of the day.

AC BUCKLAND TOURER

1949–54

While the 2-litre saloon kept AC in business after World War II, it became obvious to the company's management that there were niche markets to be exploited using more specialized versions of the model – and every order helped.

So as many variants as possible of the 2-litre (122 cu in) were produced, including four-door saloons, drophead versions of the saloon which were almost unchanged from the waistline down, estates to exploit a loophole in the tax laws, and a proper four-seater sports tourer – the Buckland.

The Buckland was so-called because the body was built by the Buckland Body Works located in Cambridgeshire, well away from AC's Thames Ditton factory. The chassis were sent to the Buckland workshops and emerged with a swooping (but slightly bulky-looking) body made with the same aluminium-over-ash frame construction as the saloon.

This model's doors were much smaller than those on the saloon version, with curvy cutaways along their top edges. The windscreen was designed to fold flat and the hood folded away into

a recess behind the rear seats. The idea behind this design was to generally enhance the sporty feel of the model – although its weight and slightly antiquated feel did much to offset that.

Despite post-war austerity, there was a market for large sports tourers, which is why AC built the Buckland. Despite stiff competition, the Buckland sold reasonably well for a low-volume manufacturer.

Engine: 1991cc (121 cu in), 6-cylinder
Power: 55kW (74bhp)
0–96km/h (60mph): n/a
Top speed: 136km/h (84mph)
Production total: 70

AC ACE

1953–63

The Ace redefined AC almost overnight. Until the 1953 London Motor Show, the company was known as a maker of sports saloons that were clearly high quality but outdated in the fast-changing world of post-war motoring.

And then, to the surprise of the press and public, AC exhibited its new Ace sports car at the show. The saloons were forgotten in favour of this exciting new model.

The Ace had been inspired by specialist builder John Tojeiro, who had produced a number of highly successful racing cars using transverse leaf spring independent suspension front and rear. AC did a deal with Tojeiro and worked quickly to slot the 2-litre (122 cu in) saloon's six-cylinder engine into his chassis and adapt the aluminium bodywork for production.

By 1954, the Ace was ready for sale and already attracting glowing reviews. A remarkable (at least for

AC) 60 units were built in the first year and the model continued to sell well into the 1960s. Bristol's excellent 2-litre (122 cu in) engine was offered as an option in 1956 and a Ford Zephyr 2.6-litre (156 cu in) engine, in various states of tune, was added to the line-up in

1961. AC had reinvented itself as a sports car manufacturer.

Engine: 2553cc (156 cu in), 6-cylinder
Power: 127kW (170bhp)
0–96km/h (60mph): n/a
Top speed: 210km/h (130mph)
Production total: 723

The great second wave of open-top two-seaters began in the 1950s with a new breed of sports car, like the MGA, the Austin-Healey 100 and the Triumph TR2. But the most exclusive and most competent was the Ace. Buying an AC marked you as someone with exceptional taste.

AC ACECA

Engine: 1971cc (120 cu in), 6-cylinder
Power: 93kW (125bhp)
0–96km/h (60mph): 9 secs
Top speed: 189km/h (117mph)
Production total: 328

When a company produces a successful model, it invariably tries to sell more versions on the back of the original. Initially, AC experimented with fitting a glassfibre hardtop to the Ace but all it succeeded in doing was exaggerating the heat build-up and noise inside the car. The company might have given up there but instead embarked upon an extensive re-engineering project that gave birth to the Aceca.

The basic tubular chassis of the Ace was retained for the new model, as was much of the bodywork, but the doors were enlarged and strengthened with ash framing, and a new fastback roof was fashioned out of aluminium and supported by an extra tubular framework.

To reduce the noise, heat and fumes the company's engineers developed a full-width bulkhead

from glassfibre to sit between the engine bay and the cockpit. The differential was mounted on rubber isolators, the steering column was made adjustable and the interior was fitted with trim that would

have been deemed too luxurious for the simple Ace, featuring Wilton carpet, excellent ventilation and demister systems, leather upholstery and wood trimmings. A true grand tourer.

Sports cars were easy fodder for small manufacturers, because little time had to be spent worrying about creature comforts. The Aceca was different, being more luxurious and much more work for AC.

AC GREYHOUND

After the success of the Aceca, AC decided to build a more luxurious four-seater version of the car – the Greyhound.

It didn't just squeeze two back seats into the Aceca though. AC had to lengthen the Aceca's wheelbase and do away with the old transverse leaf suspension, which took up valuable space for

the engine in the front and the rear passengers at the back. In its place was fitted independent coil spring suspension.

The car's chassis had to be

comprehensively engineered to cope with the extra weight and length of the car. But the Greyhound still didn't handle nearly as well as the Ace and Aceca and the extra weight dulled performance, whatever the engine choice (AC, Bristol or Ford). All this development work was a drain on the company's resources and the car still really needed further work. But then the Cobra came along, and the Greyhound ended up on the sidelines.

Engine: 1971cc (120 cu in), 6-cylinder
Power: 78kW (105bhp)
0–96km/h (60mph): 11.4 secs
Top speed: 167km/h (104mph)
Production total: 83

A majority of the Greyhound's competitors had more powerful engines, which gave performance to match the aggressive looks. With such rakish style and that snout on the bonnet, the Greyhound's 2-litre engine just wasn't enough – but AC didn't have anything else available.

AC Cobra 289

Engine: 4727cc (289 cu in), V8-cylinder
Power: 224kW (300bhp)
0–96km/h (60mph): 5.5 secs
Top speed: 250km/h (155mph)
Production total: 673

The legend of the AC Cobra is one of the great automotive tales. A Texan chicken farmer (and racing driver), Carroll Shelby, takes the quintessentially English AC Ace and shoehorns a huge US V8 engine into the engine bay, thus forming the fire-breathing Cobra.

If may sound far-fetched but it really is the truth. The US engine was the then-new Ford small-block V8, which was built first as a 2.6-litre (156 cu in) unit, swiftly followed by a 4.2-litre (260 cu in) version. The 4.2-litre (260 cu in) unit was the one first squeezed into the Ace and it weighed only a little more than the existing engines used by AC.

AC were so impressed with the V8 and Shelby that their contract with Ked Rudd, until then the supplier of the Ace's Ford six-cylinder, was terminated.

After a year of production, the 4.2-litre (260 cu in) engine was swapped for a 4.7-litre (289 cu in) version: the resultant Cobra 289 is now the second best-known AC of all time. The wheelarches were left unflared, so there was little to distinguish a V8 Cobra from an Ace, except for the scintillating performance of course.

The last Cobra 289s were designated Sports and these came with the flared arches of the later 427 model (featured on page 20).

Despite playing second fiddle to its big brother, the Cobra 427, the 289 was in many ways the more useable car, and you will often find the true AC aficionados generally prefer it. Its smaller wheelarches are less 'in-your-face', the power more useable.

AC 428

Just as it does now, the AC name meant 'Cobra' by the mid-1960s. Unfortunately, the Cobra name also meant limited market appeal – too limited even for a small production company like AC. So AC had to develop a new model to supplement Cobra sales.

The obvious way to develop a new model was to base it on the coil-spring Cobra chassis, which had been developed by Carroll Shelby and Ford US at no real cost to AC. Ford had already

The AC 428 was a grand tourer with the heart of the fire-breathing Cobra sports car, similar to the later Jensen Interceptor in concept. Note the typically Frua treatment of the nose and headlights – similar to Maseratis of the period.

ordered a lengthened version of one of these chassis, and had it bodied by Ghia as a convertible show car.

So AC decided to follow suit, but went to another Italian styling house, Frua, for the body. The result was the 428.

There were two body styles developed by Frua, a coupé and a convertible. Both were sleek and good-looking, with more than a nod to a previous Frua model, the Maserati 3500. The bodies sat on a lengthened, more well-behaved version of the Cobra chassis, with a 7-litre (427 cu in) Ford US V8 engine up front.

The 428 was not only a very fast car, but was also remarkably luxurious – it was a true grand tourer. To this day it remains an underrated great.

Engine: 7014cc (427 cu in), V8-cylinder
Power: 257kW (345bhp)
0–96km/h (60mph): 5.45 secs
Top speed: 234km/h (145mph)
Production total: 81

AC COBRA 427

After Aston Martin had set the benchmark for performance by accelerating from 0–161km/h (100mph) then back down to a standstill in 25 seconds, the Cobra showed what it was made of almost immediately – by doing the same trick in just 13.8 seconds!

This was incredible stuff. Tyre technology has since progressed a long way, yet few cars can achieve such figures even now. The 427 even made a mockery of the earlier Cobra 289.

The 289 had been born when Texan Carroll Shelby decided that the future of racing lay in using one of the new generation of powerful American V8 engines in a British sports car. He didn't seem to care which British sports car this was to be – they were all smaller and lighter than their Stateside counterparts, and well-loved by Americans. But he happened upon the AC Ace. Perhaps he realized that AC would be more open to his ideas than the higher-volume manufacturers.

The Ford V8 engine sits so perfectly in the Cobra that it's easy to forget that this chassis and body design was meant for milder motors. Here, the circular air filter is shielded from the heat of the engine so only cold air from the bonnet scoop finds its way into the engine.

So the little AC factory was hit with the full force of the Shelby ideas machine, and a monster was created – the Cobra 289. In the early 1960s, the 289 achieved plenty of competition success around the world, but it was gradually overtaken by Ferrari. At the same time, the long-rumoured 7-litre (427 cu in) Chevrolet Corvette was threatening to usurp the Cobra as the king of performance cars. Worse still, Ford seemed to be losing interest in the Cobra 289, and looked unlikely to finance another season of racing (we now know that Ford's time and money was going into the car that would become the GT40).

However, there was really no way to increase the power of the racing 289s without seriously compromising reliability. Then, one evening in December 1963, someone at Carroll Shelby's racing shop suggested that fitting the 7-litre (427 cu in) big-block V8 from a Ford Galaxie NASCAR racer in the garage might be the solution.

In fact, Shelby had been wondering about the possibilities offered by the new big-block engine some months before, but this was the first time there had been an opportunity to try one out for size. So in went the engine, a larger radiator and uprated leaf springs, along with a set of wider wheels and oversize tyres. The prototype Cobra 427 had arrived.

Not long after, Shelby's team tried out the 427 on a track. The chassis was still the transverse leaf design which had served the AC Ace well enough, and had just coped with the Cobra 289's power, but it couldn't handle the weight, power and torque of the 427.

The Shelby team, with assistance from Ford (who'd become interested again), put together a new chassis instead, with coil springs instead of the old leaf design. The model was then handed over to AC to build, using stronger, wider-spaced chassis tubes and extra bracing. Rather

The 427's engine needs serious cooling, so the nose is just a hole for unhindered airflow. The immense power demands massive tyres for traction, so the wheel arches are simply extended to fit. And the exhaust was required to be a large diameter for maximum power.

than create a whole new body, the old 289 body simply received massively flared wheelarches to accommodate the wider track and fat wheels.

The response to the new Cobra 427 was overwhelming, with magazine road tests instantly recognizing it as a fearsome, single-minded machine. Soon, everyone knew about the Cobra 427, but sales weren't very good. Perhaps the ferocious power scared prospective customers away. Even in the US, few road-going Cobra 427s were sold, although the 427 S/C (a road-legal racer) was more popular. But the legend of the Cobra 427 gets stronger every year, and has spawned an unrivalled number of kit car replicas, as well as a rebirth of the real thing from AC themselves.

Engine: 6984cc (427 cu in), V8-cylinder
Power: 317kW (425bhp)
0–96km/h (60mph): 4.2 secs
Top speed: 266km/h (165mph)
Production total: 306

AC 3000 ME

1979–84

With a very powerful Ford V6 mid-mounted engine in a tough sheet-steel chassis and an aggressive-looking glassfibre two-seater body, the 3000ME should have returned AC to the greatness that the company had achieved in the 1960s.

But instead, it was a disaster. The car (based on a prototype called the Diablo) was first shown at the 1973 London Motor Show, and was due to start production in 1974 and sell for between £3000 and £4000. Instead, development dragged on, hindered by new legislation, and it wasn't until 1979 that the 3000ME finally went on sale – at £13,300.

By then it was outdated. Magazine road testers discovered nasty handling quirks, and criticized its performance, especially compared to rivals such as Lotus, Porsche and TVR. Even so, they liked the way it looked and praised its practicality.

Later, problems with the gearbox added to the 3000ME's

woes. It was only in the 1990s that the specialists really managed to get to grips with the handling and gearbox weaknesses in the AC 3000ME, as well as perfecting

Even three decades since the prototype Diablo was first shown, the 3000ME could be mistaken for a new sports car. Indicators, covered auxiliary lamps and the side repeaters, as well as Wolfrace slot wheels, are the only clues to its age.

turbo conversions that gave the car the performance it needed. Now, a good 3000ME is a great classic to own, and a rare sight on the roads.

Engine: 2994cc (183 cu in), V6-cylinder
Power: 103kW (138bhp)
0–96km/h (60mph): 8.5 secs
Top speed: 202km/h (125mph)
Production total: 82

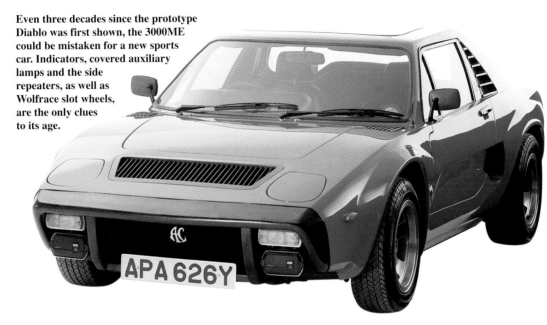

AJS Nine

1929–33

Engine: 1018cc (62 cu in), 4-cylinder
Power: 7kW (9bhp)
0–96km/h (60mph): n/a
Top speed: n/a
Production total: 3300

The Wolverhampton-based AJS company, named after its owner AJ Stevens, began life like many other car manufacturers at the time by making motorcycles, before

building Meadows-powered light cars in 1923. However, in the face of competition from the likes of Austin and Morris, and the subsequent demise of so many

Most of the Nine's engines were made by Coventry Climax; the car's overall build and fittings were considered above average quality at the time. Many had the 'fashionable' fabric bodywork which didn't age well.

other small car companies, AJS quickly suspended production.

In 1929, the company tried again by making a series of high-performance coach chassis powered by Coventry Climax engines, which included the Nine. Available as a two-seater or a fabric-hooded saloon, the car had a single dry plate clutch mated to a three-speed, and later four-speed, gearbox and featured a semi-elliptic suspension. The engines were mostly made by Coventry Climax, and the general quality of the parts and manufacture were above average for the time.

Many cars were fitted with the fabric bodywork, which was fashionable in this period. Because it looked worn quickly, a great number of Nines were prematurely relegated to the scrapheap.

ALFA ROMEO 24HP

1910–11

Engine: 4084cc (249 cu in), 4-cylinder
Power: 31kW (42bhp)
0–96km/h (60mph): n/a
Top speed: 100km/h (62mph)
Production total: 50

No two words in the world of motoring are more evocative than

Alfa Romeo. The origins of the company date back to 1906 when the French Darracq works were bought out by a group of Italian car enthusiasts known as Anonima Lombardo Fabbrica Automobili. This tongue-twisting name became abbreviated to ALFA.

The 24hp model was the new company's first car and featured a four-cylinder 4084cc (249 cu in) engine with a peak power output of 31kW (42bhp). When this engine was mated to a four-speed gearbox, this was enough to forcefully propel the vehicle's huge chassis,

fitted initially with a six-seater body, at a truly impressive speed.

Central to the Alfa Romeo 24hp's success was its consistent reliability. For this reason, a stripped-out racing version appeared in 1911 and entered the legendary Targa Florio race.

ALFA ROMEO 6C1750

1929–33

Engine: 1752cc (107 cu in), 6-cylinder
Power: 48kW (64bhp)
0–96km/h (60mph): n/a
Top speed: 109km/h (68mph)
Production total: n/a

During World War I, Alfa was taken over by engineer and racing enthusiast Nicola Romeo, thus completing the now world-famous company name.

The 6C was the brainchild of chief designer Vittorio Jano, who was asked to develop a lighter

version of a model called the RL, which ran from 1923. The first car in the new series, the 6C1500, originally had a massive six-seater body. This was soon replaced by the Sport version (which featured a twin-camshaft engine) and later the Super Sport in 1929, which used a special lightweight alloy body on a wooden frame with the option of a supercharger.

The year 1929 also saw the appearance of the famed 6C1750 which, although little different

visually, used bored out engines and became renowned for its magical mix of speed and agility. As well as featuring specialist bodies by coachbuilders Touring, a beautiful open-top two-seater version was offered. This was made by Zagato.

The car utilized a conventional chassis with an in-line six-cylinder engine with a cast-iron block and light-alloy crankcase. An optional Roots-type supercharger boosted power to 63kW (85bhp).

The elegant 6C1750 was available in three body styles; the six- and four-seater tourers and a two-seater to special order. Heavier than its predecessors, the car's strength and competition prowess came from its immense torque. Of the 112 Super Sports made in 1929, 52 were fitted with Roots-type superchargers (with a pair of contra rotating figure of eight shaped rotary pistons) which pushed power output from 48kW (64bhp) to 63kW (85bhp).

ALFA ROMEO 8C2900

1935–39

Following the success of the 6C, Jano embarked on a new range of cars featuring the legendary straight-eight twin-camshaft engine with its two four-cylinder blocks and twin-cylinder heads joined to a common crank, with camshaft drive up the centre of the unit. The engine was installed in chassis of two different lengths. The shortest (Corto) was used for Grand Prix racing in a car known as the

Monza, and the longer (Lungo) was used in a rakish two-seater sports car. Since it was agile and light, the racing 8C2300 displaced Britain's big Bentleys at Le Mans, winning the classic 24-hour event from 1931 to 1934.

Engine capacity grew to 2.6 litres (159 cu in) and then 2.9 litres (177 cu in) before a batch of twin-supercharged units appeared in 1935, fitted to an all-new chassis

Despite its size, the 8C2900 was well proportioned and had first-class handling due to independent suspension inherited from Grand Prix cars. As well as the coupé, there was this elegant two seater.

with Grand Prix-type fully independent suspension. Three prototypes took the first three places at the 1936 Mille Miglia event and a production model, the

8C2900B, was marketed from 1937.

The car, the world's fastest pre-war production sports machine, was available with a number of handcrafted bodies from the likes of Touring and Pininfarina.

Engine: 2905cc (177 cu in), 8-cylinder
Power: 134kW (180bhp)
0–96km/h (60mph): n/a
Top speed: 184km/h (115mph)
Production total: 30

ALFA ROMEO 1900

1950–58

Engine: 1884cc (115 cu in), 4-cylinder
Power: 67kW (90bhp)
0–96km/h (60mph): 17.8 secs
Top speed: 149km/h (93mph)
Production total: 17,423

Compared with the 6C2500, which was largely a pre-war design without much sporting performance, the 1900, with its unitary body and twin-camshaft engine, was a

revelation. It was the work of a new member of Alfa's design team, the brilliant Dr Orazio Satta Puliga, known universally as 'Satta'.

The car, the first true mass-market Alfa Romeo, featured a simple monocoque body with four doors and an understated styling. For the very first time, however, it featured an attractive aerodynamic body which was developed using

Satta's aeronautical engineering knowledge. With bench seats in the front and the rear, and with column gearchange, the new car could seat a maximum of five people, and the all-new engine was designed with performance, efficiency and reliability in mind.

While pre-war production Alfas borrowed fully independent suspension from their racing cars,

the 1900 reverted to coils at the front and a solid rear axle at the rear to provide safe, controlled handling. The little Alfa was an exhilarating drive with pin-sharp handling and a responsive engine – quite out of keeping with its mundane four-door saloon styling. The Super from 1953 boasted a 1975cc (121 cu in) engine and 86kW (115bhp).

ALFA ROMEO GIULIETTA

1954–65

Engine: 1290cc (79 cu in), 4-cylinder
Power: 48kW (64bhp)
0–96km/h (60mph): 13 secs
Top speed: 154km/h (95mph)
Production total: 258,672

The coupé version of the Giulietta, launched in 1954, heralded the first in a line of cars that included a saloon, the Spider and several other bespoke derivatives based on the same floorpan. The coupé featured 2+2 bodywork, designed and built by Bertone, using a twin-camshaft 1290cc (79 cu in) engine which was later increased to 1570cc (96 cu in) on the Giulia Sprint version from 1962. A Sprint Veloce version was also offered which incorporated a 1290cc (79 cu in) unit tuned to produce 67kW (90bhp) or 75kW (100bhp) (as the twin-carburettor Speciale) and part-alloy bodywork and sliding perspex side windows.

The Berlina saloon arrived in 1955 and was very spacious and enjoyable to drive, especially in 55kW (74bhp) TI guise from 1957. This was joined by the Spider which featured attractive open-top bodywork by Pininfarina.

The 1.6 Giulia Spider replaced the Giulietta Spider in 1962, and offered a much improved torque and a five-speed gearbox. Much faster Veloce versions of both the Giulietta and Giulia were offered as significantly faster twin-carburettor Veloce versions, though these were very rare and highly sought-after.

It is a sad reality that only a small fraction of the numerous Giuliettas that were manufactured between 1954 and 1965 are still in existence today. This is due mainly to severe rust problems.

The Giulietta was named after Juliet, the Shakespearean tragic heroine and would-be partner to the fated Romeo. Rather unusually, the company decided to debut this particular range with the sporty Sprint coupé rather than a more conventional saloon.

ALFA SPIDER 2000/2600 SPIDER

1958–65

The 2000 Spider range used a reworked version of the old 1900 model's engine and chassis, but with elegant open-top bodies made by coachbuilders Touring of Milan.

Brakes were drum all-round and the car had a traditional floor-mounted gearshift, five gears and a detachable hardtop, which complemented the more usual fabric hood. Meanwhile, two additional 'token' seats made it possible to squeeze in children or an adult sitting sideways in the rear.

In 1962, the Spider received new front-end styling, with a full-width bumper, a single chrome strip along the side (instead of the previous two) and no air vents behind the front wheels. More significant, however, were the changes under the bonnet, with a new twin-camshaft six-cylinder 2584cc (158 cu in) engine developing 108kW (145bhp) and capable of propelling the car to a top speed of 200km/h (125mph).

Despite all the extra power and sporting looks, neither version was particularly lightweight, so handling left much to be desired. Nevertheless, the Spider remains very collectable today thanks to its classic looks and thoroughbred Alfa Romeo pedigree. Of the 5698 cars made, 3443 had the 1975cc (120 cu in) engine.

Engine: 1975cc (120 cu in), 4-cylinder
Power: 86kW (115bhp)
0–60mph (96km/h): 14.2 secs
Top speed: 179km/h (112mph)
Production total: 5698

The 2000's elegant bodywork was crafted by coachbuilders Touring of Milan. The car was made famous by its appearance in the 1967 film *The Graduate*.

ALFA ROMEO GIULIA

1963–78

Engine: 1290cc (79 cu in), 4-cylinder
Power: 41kW (55bhp)
0–96km/h (60mph): 15.3 secs
Top speed: 138km/h (86mph)
Production total: 486,801

The box-like 105 series Giulia was really nothing much more than an up-to-date version of the 1950s Giulietta Berlina, with its somewhat dull-but-worthy four-door saloon body hiding a more sporting character underneath.

Initially, the Giulia was available with a 1600cc (98 cu in) engine, a five-speed gearbox, column gearshift, front bench seats and the traditional Alfa rigid rear axle. The 1290cc (79 cu in) engine arrived in

1964, distinguished by its single headlights and downgraded four-speed gearbox. However, throughout its long production lifespan, the car's specification was gradually improved; all-round disc brakes replaced the drum items and all models got five gears. The Giulia Nova of 1974 featured a slightly revised body, but otherwise the shape remained much the same until 1978.

Styled by Alfa's star designer Dr 'Satta' Puliga, the idea was to create a car that was small on the outside, but with the spaciousness of a bigger car on the inside.

The design proved to be highly successful and the Giulia sold in

enormous numbers in both Italy and across the rest of Europe. The company made their first foray into diesel power with their oil-burning Giulia in 1976.

Common in Europe during the 1960s and 1970s, the upright, boxy Giulia changed little in appearance during its production lifespan which lasted from 1963 to 1978.

ALFA ROMEO 33 STRADALE

1967–69

Raced for the first time in 1967, having been produced two years earlier, the Alfa Romeo 33 met with instant competition success. As well as the racing version, a road-going 33 Stradale was made with a 10cm (4in) longer wheelbase and a breathtakingly beautiful two-door coupé body styled by ex-Bertone designer

Franco Scaglione. The bodywork itself was made from a special light alloy and was built at Scaglione's works in Turin. Its shape was reminiscent of Pininfarina's classic Ferrari Dino design.

The double overhead camshaft V8 engine used in the racing version was detuned for use on the road but this still provided plenty

of performance. With a six-speed gearbox fitted, it was capable of 259km/h (162mph), making it one of the fastest production cars on the road at that time.

Several of the 18 cars made had bodies made by independent coachbuilders. Bertone created the low, wedge-shaped Carabo, Giugiaro built the 33 Iguana, which

looked like a squashed Alfetta GTV, and Pininfarina made two open-top versions, the P33 Roadster and the wedge-like 33/2 of 1971.

Engine: 1995cc (122 cu in), 8-cylinder
Power: 171kW (230bhp)
0–96km/h (60mph): n/a
Top speed: 259km/h (162mph)
Production total: 18

ALFA ROMEO DUETTO

1966–67

The Duetto was created by Italian design house Pininfarina and had distinctive 'boat-tail' rear end styling. It set a styling trend that would evolve into the Spider range that lasted until 1993 (background).

following a bizarre international competition in which the person who came up with the name won a free car.

While the Duetto's mechanicals were almost indestructible, the body wasn't and over time many fell victim to severe corrosion problems. These were partly due to poor anti-corrosion protection and partly due to the car's paint finish and build which weren't meant for harsher climates.

The pretty Duetto, in production for just one year between 1966 and 1967, was introduced as a replacement for the earlier Spider and was the last true member of the Giulia 105 series of cars. Designed by styling house Pininfarina, it incor-

porated a streamlined body with enclosed headlights and a 'coda lunga' or 'long end' reminiscent of a boat – a shape which became known as the boat-tail.

Power came from a responsive twin-camshaft 1570cc (96 cu in)

unit and with 81kW (109bhp) available, it was a lively performer with precise steering, great balance and nimble handling. Disc brakes all-round also made it reassuring to drive quickly. The name Duetto was applied to the sporty two-seater

Engine: 1570cc (96 cu in), 4-cylinder
Power: 81kW (109bhp)
0–96km/h (60mph): n/a
Top speed: 187km/h (116mph)
Production total: 6325

ALFA ROMEO SPIDER

After just 18 months of Duetto production, Alfa changed the car's name to Spider and installed a 1779cc (109 cu in) engine.

Officially called the 1750 Spider Veloce, it was joined a year later, in 1968, by the 1300 Spider Junior.

This was distinguishable from its bigger brother by its lack of transparent headlight covers.

In 1970, the boat-tail rear end was elongated even further. The 1750 was replaced by the 2000 in 1971, although, arguably, the 1750

was perhaps the smoother of the two engines.

With the 2000cc (122 cu in) unit came larger brakes and high power outputs – as much as 99kW (133bhp) – although later cars largely meant for the US market

Duetto reverted to the Spider name in 1967, with the introduction of Alfa's wonderfully flexible 1779cc (109 cu in) engine and a chopped-off Kamm-tail rear end. The 2000 model lasted right up until 1993, although with more body kit and a less delicate styling.

were restricted by emissions regulations. These cars also had a raised ride height and, after 1975, included much bigger rubber bumpers in order to meet US Federal safety regulations.

Later cars, specifically those made between 1983 and 1986 were called the Aerodynamica and featured body-coloured spoilers front and rear and plastic bumpers. The Series III from 1986 had a much improved interior and the final 1989 to 1993 model received a minor cosmetic facelift by Pininfarina.

Engine: 1779cc (109 cu in), 4-cylinder
Power: 84kW (113bhp)
0–96km/h (60mph): 9.2 secs
Top speed: 189km/h (117mph)
Production total: 104,958

JUNIOR ZAGATO

Engine: 1290cc (79 cu in), 4-cylinder
Power: 65kW (87bhp)
0–96km/h (60mph): n/a
Top speed: 168km/h (105mph)
Production total: 1510

Using the chassis from the Spider and the engine and five-speed gearbox from the Giulietta, Italian stylist Zagato created a mildly attractive, but somehow clumsy-looking coupé which made its debut at the Turin Motor Show in 1969. Key features were a drooping front bonnet, a curved roofline that ended at a cut-off fastback rear end and a seemingly large side glass area. What it lost in terms of aesthetics, however, it gained in practicality, offering accommodation for four people – albeit at a squeeze.

Combining lightness and strength with clever aerodynamics the Junior Z, as it became known, incorporated a number of interesting design features, including headlights cleverly hidden behind a transparent panel

running the width of the car.

Initially offered with a 1290cc (79 cu in) engine capable of 168km/h (105mph), a 1570cc (96 cu in) version arrived in 1972 along with a slightly longer wheelbase.

Being built by Zagato rather than Alfa Romeo, production was limited and in terms of sales, the car was never particularly successful because of its price which was higher than both the Spider and 1750 GTV.

Hardly harmonious, Zagato's modern coupé body on Alfa's Spider floorpan did little to stir emotions at the time. Its prohibitive cost didn't help matters – it was pricier than both the Spider and the 1750 GTV.

ALFA ROMEO 1750/2000 BERLINA

1967–77

Engine: 1779cc (109 cu in), 4-cylinder
Power: 84kW (113bhp)
0–96km/h (60mph): 10.8 secs
Top speed: 179km/h (112mph)
Production total: 191,720

Resuming where the Giulia left off (there was actually a one-year overlap in production), the Berlina looked almost the same as its predecessor with its boxy, upright shape. It was just a bit bigger, but with a bloated, more rounded body, all the character and sharpness of the original car was lost, despite being tweaked by Pininfarina. It was also 70kg (154lb) heavier than the Giulia.

The saving grace was the car's engine. The lively twin-choke, twin-carburettor 1779cc (109 cu in) powerplant provided impressive performance, and the power-assisted all-round disc brakes made it a real driver's car.

In response to bigger-engined competition from German manufacturers, Alfa introduced a 2-litre (122 cu in) version in 1970. Now with 98kW (132bhp) and a top speed of 189km/h (118mph), the new car sported a wider grille and a facelifted facia, though both new and old models were on sale at the same time for a while.

With the increased power, deficiencies became noticeable in the Berlina's chassis which lead to its replacement in 1977.

The plain Berlina sold well and its 1779cc (109 cu in) twin-choke twin-carb engine provided typically energetic Alfa Romeo performance.

ALFA ROMEO MONTREAL

1970–77

Engine: 2593cc (158 cu in), 8-cylinder
Power: 149kW (200bhp)
0–96km/h (60mph): 7.6 secs
Top speed: 218km/h (136mph)
Production total: 3925

Based on a modified Giulia GTV chassis and fitted with a sporty Bertone-styled fastback 2+2 coupé body, a prototype of this car was first shown at the 1967 Montreal Expo. In 1970, the company started a limited production run and called the car, appropriately, the Montreal, to offer cheap competition for the likes of more exotic marques like Maserati. But instead of the sleek lines of the show car, the Montreal looked clumsy and overdetailed, and was never particularly successful in terms of sales.

It used a detuned version of the 33's twin-camshaft V8 powerplant, tamed further by the use of fuel injection which blunted power and made it docile and more manageable to drive. But that's not to say it wasn't exciting, as it had great acceleration and an exhilarating top speed of 218km/h (136mph). An interesting design feature was the front headlights, which were partially hidden behind slatted grilles, making them almost invisible during daylight hours.

Despite being the flagship car of the company for several years, it was over-complicated and the engines were difficult to maintain properly.

Montreal was a failed attempt at making a budget supercar. Fuel injection blunted its power and proved horrendously unreliable.

ALFA ROMEO ALFASUD

1972–84

Built in the south of Italy to promote economic growth, the Sud was celebrated for its superb handling, modern styling and distinctive flat-four engine which was particularly potent in Ti guise.

Engine: 1186cc (72 cu in), 4-cylinder
Power: 47kW (63bhp)
0–96km/h (60mph): 14.1 secs
Top speed: 149km/h (93mph)
Production total: 567,093

Marking an exciting and completely new chapter in Alfa Romeo's history, the Alfasud featured front-wheel drive for the first time and an entirely new range of engines.

In line with government initiatives to aid economic regeneration in southern Italy, Alfa Romeo located production of the car in a new factory on the outskirts of Naples, hence the name, Alfasud. In charge of the project was Austrian engineer Rudolf Hruska who helped develop the VW Beetle, so it was no surprise that the new Alfa used a flat-four engine to provide space to accommodate the front-wheel drive and allow a low bonnet line for good aerodynamics and visibility.

As well as being spacious inside, the Alfasud carried on the company's tradition of being involving to drive, with pin-sharp steering and spirited handling. After 1981, it even gained a practical opening rear hatch.

Engine size was increased to 1286cc (78 cu in) in 1977, and 1350cc (82 cu in) and 1490cc (91 cu in) versions arrived a year later. The sporty Ti version was available from 1974.

ALFA ROMEO ALFETTA

1972–84

Deriving its name from Alfa's post-war single-seater Grand Prix car, the Alfetta also inherited the racer's De Dion rear suspension which inspired handling of this mid-range saloon. At the same time, the gearbox and clutch were located on the rear differential to balance weight distribution, thus making the car handle better along with lighter steering.

Styling was developed in-house under the auspices of Alfa's renowned Dr Orazio Satta Puliga, his last project, and the car had none of the box-like looks of Alfa's earlier saloons. There was also a hint of sportiness in the design.

It used the classic Alfa twin-camshaft engines, initially with 1800cc (109 cu in), then 1600cc (96 cu in) from 1975 and 2000cc (122 cu in) from 1977, when power peaked at 97kW (130bhp). Production problems dogged the Alfetta early on and it struggled to match the popularity of earlier Alfa saloons. Criticisms of the imprecise gearchange didn't help and while selling in reasonable numbers, the Alfetta never realized the success that its pedigree and development should have produced.

Engine: 1570cc (96 cu in), 4-cylinder
Power: 80kW (108bhp)
0–96km/h (60mph): 11.5 secs
Top speed: 174km/h (108mph)
Production total: 450,000

Dumpy styling hid a real racer beneath with its fully independent suspension, finely tuned chassis and feisty engines. Four headlamps on the 1.8 (109 cu in), two on the 1.6 (96 cu in) and rectangular units on the 2-litre (122 cu in).

ALFA ROMEO ALFASUD SPRINT

Giugiaro's sharp-looking coupé body grafted onto the superb Alfasud floorpan was a sure recipe for commercial success, and production of the Alfasud Sprint lasted until 1990. Style and handling were plus points, but rust was a definite negative.

A baby version of the GT/GTV, which had appeared two years earlier, the Alfa Romeo Alfasud Sprint was based on the Alfasud floorpan and used the same engines and suspension. Giugiaro's clean

coupé design for the Sprint featured a twin-headlight grille and a steeply raked fastback back end with a useful opening rear tailgate.

Initially sold with a lively flat-four 1.3-litre (78 cu in) engine, a

1.5-litre (91 cu in) unit arrived in 1978, which was also available as a tuned-up Veloce version producing 71kW (95bhp).

One of the Alfasud Sprint's many qualities was its great agility

and light handling which made it a very responsive car to drive. It was also reasonably spacious on the inside. As time went by, the uncluttered design of the early cars was spoilt by ever more stringent safety regulations, and a facelift in 1983 introduced a chunkier nose, deeper section bumpers and additional matt black trim on some of the body panels.

Like the Alfasud itself, the Sprint was also particularly prone to rust and, despite a long production run, relatively few good original examples exist today.

Engine: 1286cc (78 cu in), 4-cylinder
Power: 57kW (76bhp)
0–96km/h (60mph): 13.1 secs
Top speed: 158km/h (99mph)
Production total: 96,450

ALFA ROMEO ALFASUD GT/GTV

While still working at Italian styling house Bertone, designer Giugiaro was responsible for the sleek coupé version of the Alfetta which first appeared as the Alfetta GT in 1974, then as the GTV in later years.

It used a shorted floorpan from the Alfetta with the same 1779cc (109 cu in) engine, before being offered with the old 1570cc (96 cu in) Giulia unit and then the 1962cc (120 cu in) engine in 1976. From 1981, there was also the spectacularly fast GTV6 with its 2492cc (152 cu in) fine alloy V6, capable of 0–96km/h (60mph) in 8.8 seconds and a top speed of 203km/h (127mph).

More spacious than previous coupés from Alfa, the GT/GTV initially featured a strange instrument configuration where all the instruments, except the rev counter, were placed centrally on the dashboard. A proper tailgate aided practicality, but luggage space was limited.

Persistent rumours that a Spider

version of the car was going to be made never came to fruition, despite the appearance of a prototype open-top version designed by Pininfarina.

GT/GTV was the epitome of what a sporting Alfa coupé should look like with its rakish roofline, eagerly poised four-headlamp grille and its steeply sloping back end.

Engine: 1962cc (120 cu in), 4-cylinder
Power: 97kW (130bhp)
0–96km/h (60mph): 8.7 secs
Top speed: 192km/h (120mph)
Production total: 120,000

ALFA ROMEO GIULIETTA

1977–85

While bearing an Alfa name from the past, the rakish Giulietta also borrowed from a past model – the Alfetta, using its De Dion rear axle and rear-mounted gearbox.

Although it was dull to look at, it was a surprisingly spirited car

powered by a 1357cc (83 cu in) engine which was nothing more than a bored-out version of the old 1290cc (79 cu in) unit. A 1.8-litre (109 cu in) version arrived in 1979 and a 2-litre (122 cu in) version joined the line up a year later.

Referred to by the company as the Nuova Giulietta, the numerous facelifts that it received in 1981 and 1983 improved the angular appearance of this otherwise uninteresting car, whose only distinguishing feature in terms

of styling was its high-tail rear end.

Engine: 1570cc (96 cu in), 4-cylinder
Power: 81kW (109bhp)
0–96km/h (60mph): 10.5 secs
Top speed: 168km/h (105mph)
Production total: 379,689

ALFA ROMEO SIX

1979–87

This rather clumsy attempt at making an executive car to compete against competition from German manufacturers such as BMW and Mercedes did nothing to enhance the Alfa Romeo name.

Its boxy and unimaginative four-door styling by Bertone (which was based on the smaller Alfetta),

was dynamically poor from the beginning, while the build quality and the car's finish proved to be substantially inferior to that found its rivals.

Its only true, positive quality was its tremendous, silky smooth V6 engine. This was almost the same engine unit as was used in

the GTV6. A 2-litre (122 cu in) version was offered along with a turbodiesel engine, but these models only served to actually lessen the car's appeal to an executive market.

The Quadrifoglio Oro (Gold Cloverleaf) had fuel-injection (replacing the three twin-choke

carburettors in 1985), square headlights and more substantial bumpers front and rear.

Engine: 2492cc (152 cu in), 6-cylinder
Power: 118kW (158bhp)
0–96km/h (60mph): 11.4 secs
Top speed: 194km/h (121mph)
Production total: 12,288

ALLARD P1

1949–52

Motor trader Sydney Allard started business as Adlards Motors (taking the name from his father's building firm) during the 1930s. After World War II, Sydney Allard started a new company, Allard Motor Co Ltd.

The two-door P1 took the distinctive curved grille from the

first of these postwar cars, but with full-width bodywork and seating for at least four people. The use of aluminium bodywork enabled it to retain a modicum of performance, though an awkward column-mounted gearchange did away with any sporting pretensions.

Power came from either a Ford

3622cc (221 cu in) unit or a modified Mercury 4375cc (267 cu in) engine, both of which were V8s.

Engine: 3622cc (221 cu in), 8-cylinder
Power: 63kW (85bhp)
0–96km/h (60mph): n/a
Top speed: 144km/h (90mph)
Production total: 559

The use of aluminium panels helped kept the P1's weight down and helped performance of the four/five-seater, two-door saloon which featured full-width bodywork at the rear. Possibly the most popular of all the Allard Cars, Sydney Allard drove a P1 to victory in the 1952 Monte Carlo rally.

ALLARD J2

1949–54

The J2 was a new design featuring a rigid, tubular-braced ladder chassis and minimal alloy bodywork that incorporated cycle wings at the front. It was the archetypal Allard and motoring at its most extreme. The car was brutally quick with little in the way of creature comforts, an aero screen being the only protection afforded to the driver.

At the rear was a De Dion axle and at the front was split-axle independent suspension. Power came mostly from a bored-out Mercury V8 unit, which propelled the fragile J2 to 96km/h (60mph) in a fraction under six seconds – sensationally quick for 1949. However, performance could be even more spectacular with the Ardun overhead valve conversion for the Ford V8 unit, though this compromised reliability.

The majority of J2s sold to the US, however, were supplied without engines, as the chassis could take many different types of V8 powerplants. Among the most scary were the Cad-Allards, which used Cadillac engines producing

an incredible 223kW (300bhp). One such car, fitted with a 5.4-litre (331 cu in) Cadillac engine, powered Sydney Allard to third place at Le Mans in 1950.

Evocative, sensationally quick and extremely rare, a number of J2 replicas have been built recently.

Engine: 4375cc (267 cu in), 8-cylinder
Power: 82kW (110bhp)
0–96km/h (60mph): 5.9 secs
Top speed: 175km/h (110mph)
Production total: 90

Almost brutally quick with its Mercury bored and stroked 4375cc (267 cu in) engine, the speedy Allard J2 could accelerate to 160km/h (100mph) in 23.6 seconds. It could exceed 176km/h (110mph) in road trim.

ALLARD JR

1953–56

Based largely on the mechanicals of the Allard Palm Beach roadster launched a year earlier, the JR series was meant for competition use, hence the austere windscreens and the lack of bumpers.

Instead of the rigid rear axle used in the Palm Beach, however, the JR used the J2's De Dion set-up at the rear to provide better handling on the track. There was a wide choice of engines to fit the

JR's chassis, but the most popular was the 5.4-litre (331 cu in) Cadillac V8 which was capable of 224km/h (140mph) and gained Allard provisional pole position in the 1953 Le Mans 24-hour race.

Allard's fortunes waned as more sophisticated competition from the likes of Jaguar's stunningly successful XK120 finally caused the company to stop production in 1962. However, the Allard name continued, being associated with tuning, supercharging and sunroofs. Following Sydney Allard's death in 1966, his son, Allan, also became involved in the business, operating a factory in Daventry, before moving to Ross-on-Wye.

Engine: 5420cc (331 cu in), 8-cylinder
Power: 186kW (250bhp)
0–96km/h (60mph): n/a
Top speed: 224km/h (140mph)
Production total: 17

The JR series was the most fierce of all Allards with its huge 'Caddy' or Chrysler powerplants making it a real white-knuckle machine. It followed a similar specification to their more civilized Palm Beach model but with a de Dion rear axle and a wider engine choice.

ALPINE A110

1962–77

When successful rally driver and Renault dealer Jean Rédélé began to modify his competition cars to overcome their shortcomings, he equipped a few with lightweight aluminium bodies. In the early 1950s, he even drove these cars at Le Mans and Sebring.

People started to notice how well Rédélé's cars performed, which prompted him to form a proper company to build them, in 1954. The company was called the Société Anonyme des Automobiles Alpine, but the use of the Alpine name caused many problems with Sunbeam Talbot, who had already used it.

Rédélé's first production car was the A106, followed by the A108. Then came the definitive Alpine, the A110. All had glassfibre bodies and a stiff tubular backbone chassis, which featured on all subsequent Alpines. The A110 was powered by Renault R8 mechanicals.

These were competition-orientated cars, with very few concessions to comfort. However, this allowed Alpine to keep weight low, while the strength of the chassis was renowned. Over the years, larger, much more powerful engines were fitted. But in 1974, unfortunately, the company hit financial trouble and was taken over by Renault.

Natural territory for an A110, hard-charging on an international rally. These cars were conceived by a rally driver for rallying, and so it's no surprise that they were supremely successful. Now, A110s fetch high prices and an extremely high proportion of them are still in competition specification for historic rallying. Only the relatively delicate Renault mechanicals let them down now.

Engine: 1647cc (101 cu in), 4-cylinder
Power: 103kW (138bhp)
0–96km/h (60mph): n/a
Top speed: 214km/h (133mph)
Production total: 8139

ALPINE A310

1971–85

In the 1970s, Renault saw the success of Porsche's 911, and decided to try and compete with it. A 911 competitor was never going to sell badged as a Renault, but the company did have the Alpine name, already used on the stripped-out A110.

So Alpine Renault launched the A310, using the same backbone chassis and rear-mounted engine configuration as the A110, but with a 2+2 cabin and more luxurious trim. The first A310s came with the Renault 17TS four-cylinder engine but this lacked the specification needed for the market, despite its 104kW (140bhp) output. To remedy this, in 1976, the A310 gained a 2.6-litre (163 cu in) V6 engine with greatly improved torque and refinement.

In 1978, the A310 was fitted with a five-speed gearbox as well, which improved the car still more. It was never as good a car as the 911, but it sold reasonably well in mainland Europe until the mid-1980s. However, It was never sold in the UK because of legal trouble with Sunbeam Talbot over the Alpine name.

Eventually, the A310 evolved into the GTA, which was sold in the UK as a Renault. When the GTA was turbocharged, it finally achieved supercar status and is now looked upon as one of the unsung heroes of the 1980s.

An unpromising start for a model that was meant to compete with the stylish Porsche 911. The heavy rear flanks look at odds with the slim nose, an effect which is exaggerated by the darker combined bumpers and valances front and rear.

Engine: 2664cc (163 cu in), V6-cylinder
Power: 112kW (150bhp)
0–96km/h (60mph): n/a
Top speed: 221km/h (137mph)
Production total: 11,616

ALVIS 10/30

1920–22

Although one of the great names of British motoring, the name Alvis has no meaning and was just used to describe an aluminium piston designed by GPH de Freville who, along with TG John, designed the first 10/30 car in 1920. The word Alvis was just intended to be easily pronounceable in any language.

The 10/30 was ahead of its time when it appeared, with a four-speed gearbox and force-feed lubrication system. The lightweight two-seater used a 1.5-litre (89 cu in) engine designed by de Freville and the simplistic bodies were built by outside coachbuilders. Most of the engines were side-valve, but a

Alvis's most well-known logo was the red triangle badge, but the earlier cars – like the 10/30 tourer pictured – also featured a hare mascot on top of the radiator.

few more sporting examples were fitted with overhead valve engines, and known as Super Sports models. They were around 32km/h (20mph) faster than their side-valve sisters.

Despite a relatively high price tag of between £750 and £870, sales were impressive since many customers were attracted by the 10/30's willing performance and neat looks. Most cars came in blue and grey paintwork as standard, complemented by a matching leather interior.

A slightly modified version, the larger-engined 11/40, appeared in 1921, but was only made for six months before being dropped.

Engine: 1460cc (89 cu in), 4-cylinder
Power: 22kW (30bhp)
0–96km/h (60mph): n/a
Top speed: 97km/h (60mph)
Production total: 770

ALVIS FD/FE

1928–30

Alvis was one of the European pioneers of front-wheel drive cars. It built a sprint car in 1925 and an eight-cylinder racing model in 1926, both of which used this new configuration. In 1928, two Alvis front-wheel drive cars finished sixth and ninth at Le Mans.

That same year came the FD/FE series, an attempt to adapt the racing technology for mainstream production. Chief engineer TG Smith-Clarke and chief designer WM Dunn ensured that the entire car was a technical marvel throughout. As well as front-wheel

The front-wheel drive FD/FE was a major technological step forward, but in sales terms, it was a failure. This was partly due to suspicious insurance companies, who refused to meet accident claims just because the cars weren't conventional rear-wheel drive.

drive, the car featured all independent transverse leaf suspension, an overhead camshaft (although the standard engine was just a four-cylinder unit), a four-speed gearbox, inboard front brakes and the option of a Roots supercharger. For those wanting even more power, an eight-cylinder engine (with the same capacity as the four) could be specified. Body styles were a two-seater sports, a four-seater sports and a sports saloon.

Alvis was unfortunate that the general public was unwilling to accept so much mechanical innovation in one package. Sales were disappointing, leading to the model being dropped after two years and the firm returning to more conventional engineering principles.

Engine: 1482cc (90 cu in), 4-cylinder
Power: 56kW (75bhp) at 5500rpm
0–96km/h (60mph): n/a
Top speed: 137km/h (85mph)
Production total: 155

ALVIS 12/50

1931–32

The 12/50 first appeared in 1923, an evolution of the overhead valve-engined 10/30. It was gradually developed as the 1920s progressed, appearing as several slightly differing versions until 1931, when the Series TJ 12/50 was launched.

It differed from its predecessors in a number of ways. Coil ignition (previous models had magnetos) was used and a separate radiator shell, where there had previously been a one-piece block, appeared. Also featured was a 1645cc (100 cu in) overhead valve engine, in place of the original 1496cc (91 cu in) unit used in the early and mid-1920s. The transmission was a four-speed manual gearbox, with both the hand brake and the foot brake working on all four wheels. Customers could order their cars with two-seater, tourer, drophead coupé and saloon bodies.

For Alvis, the 12/50 was a significant model. It came to be regarded as one of the best of all British lightweight cars from this era, compiling a very good racing record. Its most impressive achievement was a win in the 1923 Brooklands 200 mile (322km)

race, where it beat two faster supercharged Fiats.

A more sporting 12/60 model, with twin carburettors, was also available at the same time.

Engine: 1645cc (100 cu in), 4-cylinder
Power: 39kW (52bhp)
0–96km/h (60mph): n/a
Top speed: 115km/h (71mph)
Production total: 642

By the 1930s, the Alvis 12/50 was outdated. The TJ model was the final flowering of the original design, although updated with better components and extra power.

ALVIS SPEED 20

1932–36

One of Britain's most impressive and well-known vintage models was the Speed 20. In specification, performance and appearance, it was comparable to products from manufacturers such as Bentley, Lagonda and SS (Jaguar), yet it undercut them all in terms of price.

The Speed 20 was an imposing car, characterized by a long bonnet concealing the large six-cylinder triple-carburettor 2511cc (153 cu in) overhead valve engine. As well as standard sports tourer, drophead coupé and sports saloon bodies, several attractive special bodies by

coachbuilders such as Cross & Ellis and Vanden Plas were offered. What really made the Speed 20's reputation was the introduction of the SB, SC and SD models from 1934 onwards. These pioneered new innovations, with their four-speed all-synchromesh gearboxes

and independent transverse leaf suspension at the front. Its impressive appearance was helped by the addition of large P100 headlights. The SC version of 1935 was fitted with a 2762cc (169 cu in) engine to cope with increased weight and also gained a slightly longer wheelbase as well.

As suggested by its name, the Speed 20 had a major career in racing, as well as being a luxurious grand tourer.

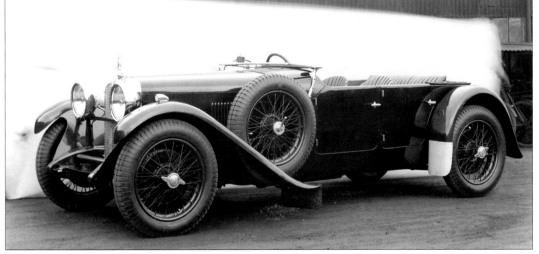

Engine: 2511cc (153 cu in), 6-cylinder
Power: 65kW (87bhp) at 4200rpm
0–96km/h (60mph): 22 secs
Top speed: 143km/h (89mph)
Production total: 1165

The Speed 20 helped to cement Alvis's sporting marque reputation. It was very handsome, with its appearance matched by superior performance and technical cleverness. Gentleman racers of the period loved it, making it a regular on the British motor sport scene.

ALVIS TA21

1950–53

Engine: 2993cc (183 cu in), 6-cylinder
Power: 67kW (90bhp) at 4000rpm
0–96km/h (60mph): 19.8 secs
Top speed: 138km/h (86mph)
Production total: 1313

Alvis struggled to recover after World War II since its Coventry factory was almost completely destroyed in the blitz. It started post-war production with the TA14, based on the pre-war 12/70, before offering the all-new TA21, launched at the Mach 1950 Geneva Motor Show.

The TA21 kept the traditional and aristocratic big Alvis look, although it was much more streamlined, with the headlights now incorporated into the front wings and the rear wheels partially concealed behind spats.

Saloon bodies came from the Mulliner coachbuilding firm, while Tickford supplied the coachwork for the appealing drophead coupé versions, of which only 302 were built. Wood and leather furnished the interior, with sun visors and a sliding roof fitted as standard, although somewhat strangely, a heater cost extra.

Power was provided by a new 2993cc (183 cu in) six-cylinder engine, leading to the car's public designation as the 'Alvis Three-litre'. Its hydraulic brakes were a tremendous improvement over those used on previous Alvis models, and the TA21 also boasted coil sprung independent front suspension.

The first cars came with a single SU carburettor, but within just a year, this had been changed for twin carburettors.

Post-war production proper got under way for Alvis with the TA21. The rakish, straight-cut lines of the pre-war cars were replaced by curves, although the new Alvis could look positively bulbous. It was an expensive, high-class car.

ALVIS TC21

1953–56

The TC21 wasn't a new model, just a 1953 designation change for the existing TA21. There were some minor alterations to the mechanics as well as a subtle facelift which included narrower window frames and a slimmer central pillar (on which the two doors were hung).

More updates were made later that year, with the introduction of the higher performance TC21/100, known as the Grey Lady. The '100' designation came from its 100bhp (75kW) output, as well as the fact it could top 100mph (161km/h), while the 'Grey Lady' name came from the colour of the 1953 Earls Court Motor Show display vehicle. The extra performance was provided by a higher engine compression and rear axle ratios.

Higher specification versions of the Alvis TC21 were all known as Grey Ladies, whatever their colour was. Two-tone paint schemes always suited the flowing lines of the car.

Visually, only small changes characterized the 'new' Alvis. Twin cooling bonnet scoops were fitted, along with louvres on the side of the bonnet doors, while Dunlop wire wheels were the most noticeable change. As with the TA21, Mulliner built the saloon bodies, while Tickford built the drophead coupés. The Swiss coachbuilder Graber also produced some stylish versions.

Production came to an end when Mulliner agreed to work solely for Standard-Triumph and Tickford was taken over by Aston Martin.

Engine: 2993cc (183 cu in), 6-cylinder
Power: 75kW (100bhp)
0–96km/h (60mph): 16.5 secs
Top speed: 163km/h (101mph)
Production total: 805

ALVIS TD21

Engine: 2993cc (183 cu in), 6-cylinder
Power: 86kW (115bhp)
0–96km/h (60mph): 13.9 secs
Top speed: 171km/h (106mph)
Production total: 1070

With Mulliner and Tickford now unable to supply bodies (see above), Alvis turned instead to coachbuilder Graber. The Swiss firm produced sleek, modern and very elegant saloon and drophead designs to fit to the TC21 chassis.

As it was impractical for bodies to be made in Switzerland and shipped to Britain, the design was built by Willowbrook of Loughborough instead.

Problems with production standards at Willowbrook lead to work being transferred to the more reliable and experienced Park Ward of London. Its facelift of the TC108G (as the cars were known) was called the TD21. Various improvements included a single-

piece rear window and more room in the boot and the back seat.

An automatic gearbox became available and power was boosted from 77kW (104bhp) to 86kW (115bhp), with front disc brakes to cope with the extra power. The Series II from 1962 had disc brakes on all four wheels, a five-speed gearbox and recessed spotlights either side of the grille.

The TD21 evolved into the TE21 and TF21 (with vertically stacked

Alvis modernized the look of its range with the TD21. The look may have been British, but it was actually penned in Switzerland. The final evolution of the body would see the single headlamps replaced by stacked twin units.

twin headlights) until 1967 when the company's new owner, Rover, stopped Alvis car production so the marque could concentrate on manufacturing military vehicles.

AMC RAMBLER

AMC – which was short for the American Motors Corporation – was formed in 1954 when the companies of Nash and Hudson merged. The Nash and Hudson names were dropped in 1958, with the Nash Rambler continuing as an AMC model.

By the time the 1966 Rambler models were introduced, the name had become a generic term for a number of different vehicles in

the AMC catalogue, including the compact Rambler American (which was also available as the attractive Rogue two-door hardtop coupé) and the bigger Rambler Classic and Ambassador.

Catering for the sporting market – or what was left of this market once Ford's Mustang had gone on sale – was the Rambler Marlin fastback coupé. All were strictly conventional Detroit-style cars,

with well-proven underpinnings and the usual choice of straight-six or V8 engines.

Changes to the Rambler range came yearly, with the degree of alteration depending on the car. From 1967, the Ambassador became a model in its own right, but the Marlin was dropped a year later.

By 1969, the compact American was known simply as the Rambler

and was a last effort to generate sales for this long-established car before it disappeared after almost 20 years in production. Between 1950 and 1969, 4,204,925 Ramblers were built.

Engine: 4752cc (290 cu in), V8-cylinder
Power: 149kW (200bhp)
0–96km/h (60mph): 9.9 secs
Top speed: 171km/h (106mph)
Production total: n/a

AMC REBEL
1967–70

Engine: 5619cc (343 cu in), V8-cylinder
Power: 209kW (280bhp)
0–96km/h (60mph): 9 secs
Top speed: 177km/h (110mph)
Production total: 284,326

There were two sides to the Rebel. Ordinary versions were worthy, but dull. But the SST range-topper pictured here had a wilder side to its character, the performance engine and cosmetic bolt-ons giving it an extra dose of attitude.

The Rebel started life as the Rambler Rebel, a 1967 replacement for the Classic, marketed between the larger Ambassador and the smaller American. These cars were big, box-like undistinguished designs, with two-door hardtop fastback styling, although station wagons and convertibles were also available. Top of the range was the SST, the initials standing for Super

Sport Touring. As with other Ramblers, buyers had a choice of straight-six or V8 engines.

For 1968, the Rambler prefix was dropped and the car underwent a subtle restyle. The Rebel convertible was also the only open-topped AMC available, but this only lasted for another year before it, too, disappeared. For 1969, only a sedan, hardtop and a station

wagon were offered, available in base series or as the SST.

1970 was the final year of Rebel production, and saw the creation of the most flamboyant version of the model, the aggressive-looking Rebel Machine. It had the most powerful V8 engine ever offered on an AMC, producing 253kW (340bhp), but like the rest of the range, it had been dropped by 1971.

AMC JAVELIN
1967–74

Engine: 6392cc (390 cu in), V8-cylinder
Power: 235kW (315bhp)
0–96km/h (60mph): 7 secs
Top speed: 174km/h (108mph)
Production total: 235,497

Since every other manufacturer had a Ford Mustang competitor on the market by the end of the 1960s, AMC needed one too. It launched the Javelin, a car that seemed to have the right mechanical

specifications, but failed to excite the public in the same way as cars from rival makers did.

Although handsome, with smooth, clean-cut lines, sales never reached AMC's expectations,

despite a wide choice of customer options, as well as in-line six or V8 engines. These ranged from 3799cc (238 cu in) to 6392cc (390 cu in), with power outputs from 75kW (100bhp) to 235kW (315bhp).

As was usual with American cars of this era, the Javelin was subtlety restyled every year up until the end of production. Most alterations were very superficial, but, in 1971, a very unusual feature was added. Bulging curved wing lines were added above each wheel, which left the car looking very strange.

This, and the car's increasing bulk, failed to reverse falling sales and the Javelin disappeared in 1974. Nowadays, enthusiasts regard it as one of the more interesting and better pony cars.

1971's Javelin revamp was a concoction of conflicting curves and straight-edges, but it was at least more individual than rivals. Intended to steal the crown from Ford's Mustang, the Javelin never flew high enough to trouble the pony car king.

AMC AMX

1968–71

Complementing the Javelin was the AMX, unveiled in February 1968. The name stood for 'American Motors Experimental', the experimental designation referring to the fact that this was the first two-seater, steel-bodied sports car to go into mass production since the original 1955 Ford Thunderbird.

In appearance, the AMX bore similarities to its bigger sister, but the resemblance to the Javelin stopped towards the back, with a sharply cut-off coupé rear end. The platform was a short wheelbase version of the Javelin, sharing the mechanicals and most of the same V8 engine options as well.

Despite having sharper handling and better performance than the longer car, the American public were unconvinced by the AMX. It wasn't as exotic as other the two-seaters around, and customers weren't sure that being charged more money for fewer seats than in the Javelin was such a good deal.

There were no major changes for 1969, but the front was restyled for 1970. The car itself was dropped the following year, although the name lived on as a designation for performance versions of the Javelin and the Hornet.

Engine: 6392cc (390 cu in), V8-cylinder
Power: 238kW (319bhp)
0–96km/h (60mph): 7.2 secs
Top speed: 177km/h (110mph)
Production total: 19,134

Only two seats and a steel coupé body, but the AMX was no successor to the 1950s Ford Thunderbird. The close likeness to the Javelin was very noticeable and contributed to poor sales of AMC's sporting two-seater.

AMC Gremlin

1970–78

Engine: 3802cc (232 cu in), 6-cylinder
Power: 108kW (145bhp) at 4300rpm
0–96km/h (60mph): 12.5 secs
Top speed: 153km/h (95mph)
Production total: 650,000 approx

The AMC Gremlin appeared on April Fool's Day, 1970 – its terrible styling resulted in it becoming a national joke. Yet the theory behind America's first attempt to build a modern Mini-type car was sound, even if its execution wasn't.

The small car may have been novel to US manufacturers, but the Gremlin itself wasn't completely new. From the front doors forwards, it was nothing more than a Hornet, with an unattractive slab-shaped

hatchback grafted on, all mounted on a short chassis. Despite looking tiny compared to other American cars, the Gremlin was longer than a VW Beetle, and less attractive too.

Two models were launched, a two-seater car and a cramped four-seater with a fold-down rear seat. There were 30 accessories and seven performance packages for those who wanted to individualize their car. Despite the car's economy-motoring selling point, a 4979cc (304 cu in) V8 was an option, although its power output wasn't high. Six-cylinder engines were more usual though, and from 1976, an Audi 2-litre (122 cu in) four-cylinder engine was also available.

Attack a Hornet with a can opener, and you get a Gremlin. AMC's first foray into small cars used the Hornet as a base, but lost some of the bodywork and lots of the appeal. Still, it was handy for shopping.

AMC Pacer

1975–80

Not since the Edsel has an American car been so universally derided. The Pacer was another economy sub-compact, built to fight the tide of more efficient, smaller European and Japanese imports. Styling was unusual, with huge amounts of glass mounted on a rotund body. Marketed as 'the first wide small car', its extensive girth didn't help its looks. Even the doors were unusual, being of different lengths on each side.

Intended originally for GM's abandoned rotary engine, the Pacer instead appeared with 3799cc (232 cu in) and 4229cc (258 cu in)

straight-six engines, and a 4979cc (304 cu in) V8 unit, all of which defeated the purpose of this 'economy' model, which also was not particularly pleasant to drive.

The Pacer has now achieved cult status, as whatever it lacked in appeal originally is now seen as quirky and fascinating. Indeed, the world would be a less interesting and amusing place without it.

Engine: 4229cc (258 cu in), 6-cylinder
Power: 75kW (100bhp)
0–96km/h (60mph): 15.8 secs
Top speed: 142km/h (88mph)
Production total: 280,000 approx

It had an engine the size of an E-type Jaguar, yet the Pacer struggled to 142km/h (88mph) and had under half the power. America's sub-compact was eccentric, induced by AMC's fuel crisis and foreign imports panic.

AMPHICAR

Engine: 1147cc (70 cu in), 4-cylinder
Power: 28kW (38bhp)
0–96km/h (60mph): 42.9 secs
Top speed: 113km/h (70mph)
Production total: 3878

What could be more bizarre than a car that was also a boat? This was exactly what the Amphicar was. It was the brainchild of Hans Trippel, who had developed amphibious vehicles for the German Army during World War II.

Using a Triumph Herald engine, mounted in the back, and a VW Beetle-type four-speed transmission, the Amphicar could reach 113km/h (70mph) on the road. But in the water, a special unit made by Hermes (the makers of Porsche transmissions) could be used to switch to the two-speed water transmission, powering twin propellers. These allowed the Amphicar to reach up to 11km/h (7mph) in the water.

The Hermes unit could even allow both driving wheels and propellers to drive at the same time, to help entry and exit to and from the water. Once floating, the front wheels acted as rudders. Predictably, the Amphicar was not particularly good either on road or in water but nevertheless the car was fun and innovative and remains the only civilian amphibious vehicle to ever be mass-produced.

Most Amphicars were sold to the United States. But unfortunately, it was this dependence on the US market that eventually killed the Amphicar as, in 1968, some new regulations were introduced which effectively prevented the vehicle from being sold.

Find a slipway, drive down, switch from wheels to twin propellers and car turns into boat. The Amphicar wasn't great in either role, but the concept is nevertheless great fun.

ARAB SPORTS

Engine: 2000cc (122 cu in), 4-cylinder
Power: 48kW (65bhp)
0–96km/h (60mph): n/a
Top speed: 145km/h (90mph)
Production total: 12

Long, low, sleek and blessed with good performance, the good-looking Arab Sports deserved better than its limited five-year production run, which saw only 12 models built. A bigger manufacturer could have scored a major success with this exciting looking model.

In 1920, the star of the London Motor Show was the Leyland Eight. At the time, it was the most powerful and expensive car ever to be produced in Britain. Yet while it was undoubtedly an outstanding vehicle packed with technical innovation, it proved a failure in the market place due to its high price and Leyland's lack of upper class appeal.

Behind the so-called 'Lion of Olympia' were two prominent engineers, Reid Railton and J.G. Parry Thomas. When the Eight

went out of production in 1923 (after just 18 were built), Railton left Leyland to form his own marque. His Arab company came into being in 1925. The reason behind the choice of name has been lost in the mists of automotive history, but during the career of this short-lived marque, its only product was the Sports. As the moniker suggested, this was a high-performance model, with a stylish open body on a low-slung chassis.

The two-litre engine in the Arab Sports was closely related to that used in the Leyland Eight, featuring an unusual system of leaf valve springs (designed by Parry Thomas), as well as an overhead camshaft with adjustable

drive train and very robust two bearing crankshaft. A Moss four-speed gearbox was standard. The cars were built at a factory in Hertfordshire, and sold for around £500 to £550.

Performance was impressive, and in July 1927 one beat a theoretically superior eight-cylinder Bugatti up the famous Shelsley Walsh Hill Climb in England.

Like the Leyland before it, the Sports didn't prove to be a soaraway success, with only

around 10 built in five years. However, the reason for the demise of both the car and the firm was not financial. Parry Thomas was killed during a land speed record attempt in 1927, and Railton and his fellow Arab directors lost enthusiasm for the company as a result. A few were made by another firm, Thomson and Taylor, after Arab was wound up, but by 1930, it was all over for one of the more interesting sports cars produced in Britain during the 1920s.

ARGYLL TWELVE

1922–30

Scotland's only homegrown car manufacturer was one of Britain's biggest car firms before World War I, but it went bankrupt in 1914. It was bought by its repair works manager, JA Brimlow, and started building cars after the Great War based on pre-war designs.

The Argyll Twelve, which was introduced in 1922, was available with 1496cc (91 cu in) and, from 1926, 1640cc (100 cu in) engines, employing single sleeve-valves.

This was simpler than a conventional poppet valve engine, with fewer moving parts to maintain. The smaller-engined Twelves could boast 22kW (30bhp), while the bigger 12/40s mustered 30kW (40bhp).

They were big, impressive-looking cars but came with a high price tag, and it was this that caused the company's demise. When the Great Depression hit on both sides of the Atlantic, Argyll gradually found very few buyers for its cars, and the firm quickly faded away again at the beginning of the 1930s.

Engine: 1496cc (91 cu in), 4-cylinder
Power: 22kW (30bhp)
0–96km/h (60mph): n/a
Top speed: n/a
Production total: Approx 250

ARIEL NINE

1922–29

This Birmingham-based cycle firm was one of the early British automobile pioneers, building its first car in 1902. During its short and rather turbulent history as a car manufacturer, Ariel changed hands several times. One revival of the name, in 1922, saw the introduction of the Ariel Nine. This vehicle was intended by the company to compete in the small car market.

Its diminutive flat-twin engine had a capacity of 996cc (61 cu in), but it was an unsophisticated, unrefined unit. Its roughness, coarseness and excessive noisiness led many people to believe it was air-cooled. But, in reality, the Ariel Nine's engine was actually cooled by water.

With cheapness firmly in mind, the Nine was available with only one colour as standard. This was an austere grey. Despite the fact that it had an attractively low price and impressive fuel economy, which were combined with an energetic and entertaining performance, only around 700 were sold before the model was dropped in 1925, and Ariel concentrated on motorcycle production instead.

Engine: 996cc (61 cu in), twin-cylinder
Power: approx 15kW (20bhp)
0–96km/h (60mph): n/a
Top speed: 85km/h (53mph)
Production total: 700 approx

ARMSTRONG-SIDDELEY THIRTY

1919–31

Formed when aircraft engineers Armstrong-Whitworth bought car maker Siddeley Deasy in 1919, Armstrong-Siddeley went on to successfully build aircraft, aero engines and agricultural machinery. But while Armstrong-Siddeley was most famous for its aircraft, the company also made a range of quality saloon cars for almost four decades. These were recognizable by their famous Sphinx motif bonnet mascots.

The first model from Armstrong-Siddeley was the Thirty. This vehicle was a huge saloon that proved to be equally as popular as a taxi carriage as it was with the more discriminating upper-class buyers. It was mechanically very simple, with a 4960cc (303 cu in) six-cylinder engine developing 45kW (60bhp).

The Thirty was a highly sedate car to drive and its relaxed nature gave it a well-earned reputation for longevity – the engines were rarely stressed and suffered very little wear and tear. Production of the Armstrong-Siddeley Thirty lasted for an impressive 12 years – quite an achievement in an era when other manufacturers changed styles almost every year.

Engine: 4960cc (303 cu in), 6-cylinder
Power: 45kW (60bhp)
0–96km/h (60mph): n/a
Top speed: 110km/h (68mph)
Production total: 2700

ARMSTRONG-SIDDELEY FOUR-FOURTEEN

1923–29

The Four-Fourteen was a more downmarket car from Armstrong-Siddeley. This particular model was the first of the company's cars to feature a four-cylinder engine, and the 1852cc (113 cu in) unit was unimpressive. The Four-Fourteen's overall reliability was only average, while performance and fuel economy suffered badly as the motor struggled to power what was a heavy car.

Simple six-volt electrics and front brakes only until 1925 distinguished the Four-Fourteen from more upmarket Armstrong-Siddeleys, and it was immediately identifiable by of its plain, flat radiator grille.

The car's name was changed in 1925 to 14/30 with the launch of the Mk II. This model had brakes on all four wheels and better fuel economy. Various body styles were offered, although most came with saloon coachwork.

Engine: 1852cc (113 cu in), 4-cylinder
Power: n/a
0–96km/h (60mph): n/a
Top speed: 81km/h (50mph) approx
Production total: 13,365

ARMSTRONG-SIDDELEY 20

1926–36

The best-selling Armstrong-Siddeley of the late 1920s and the early 1930s, the Armstrong-Siddeley 20 was a conventionally engineered but supremely well-built machine.

Two chassis were offered. This first was a short version for family motorists which allowed seating for five people with excellent rear legroom. The second was a long chassis version which could be specified as a seven-seater saloon or limousine, although it was much smaller than most other manufacturers' luxury models.

Two further cars were offered by Armstrong-Siddeley on the 20's chassis, but with side-valve engines in place of the 20's overhead valve unit. The Fifteen was sold as a budget family model, while the Twelve, built between 1929 and 1937, had a tiny 1.2-litre (73 cu in) six-cylinder engine and was aimed at younger drivers.

Engine: 2872cc (175 cu in), 6-cylinder
Power: n/a
0–96km/h (60mph): n/a
Top speed: n/a
Production total: 4997

ARMSTRONG-SIDDELEY LANCASTER

The Armstrong-Siddeley Lancaster, named after the famous bomber, went on sale in May 1945, just six days after the end of World War II.

The Lancaster was effectively a pre-war design, but didn't enter production until the end of World War II, when it became Britain's first all-new post-war car. Armstrong-Siddeley were quick to launch it – the car appeared in May

1945, in exactly the same week as the war in Europe officially ended.

The Lancaster set a trend for Armstrong-Siddeley, sharing its name with the famous bomber aircraft. It was initially offered with a 2-litre (122 cu in) engine developing 52kW (70bhp), although a 56kW (75bhp) 2.3-litre (140 cu in) unit replaced this in 1949.

It was a solid car to drive, with a good ride thanks to torsion bar

front suspension, hydromechanical brakes and a four-speed all-synchromesh gearbox.

The interior was spacious and well-equipped, while rear legroom was on a par with many much larger cars. A great export success that helped Britain's post-war recovery, the Lancaster was replaced in 1952 by the all-new Sapphire, although the chassis remained in production for a

further two years for use on the Hurricane and Whitley models (see below). Most Lancasters were long-lived, but had a reputation for rust-prone bodywork if they were not properly looked after.

Engine: 1991cc (121 cu in), 6-cylinder
Power: 52kW (70bhp)
0–96km/h (60mph): n/a
Top speed: 113km/h (70mph)
Production total: 12,470

ARMSTRONG-SIDDELEY HURRICANE

The Armstrong-Siddeley Hurricane was launched alongside the Lancaster and shared the same chassis, although it was offered as a two-door drophead only. Front end styling was identical to the saloon, with flush-fitting headlights and fared-in front wings, plus

wide-opening backward-hinged doors. A budget offering – the Typhoon – appeared in 1946 and had a cheaper fabric hood and a more spartan interior.

Just like the Lancaster, the Hurricane and Typhoon got a larger 2.3-litre (140 cu in) engine

in 1949, although the Typhoon version was dropped shortly after this engine was introduced, so only a handful were equipped with the larger unit.

Despite their sporting looks, the Hurricane and Typhoon weren't involving to drive, although they

were comfortable touring machines.

Engine: 1991cc (121 cu in), 6-cylinder
Power: 52kW (70bhp)
0–96km/h (60mph): n/a
Top speed: 121km/h (75mph)
Production total: n/a

ARMSTRONG-SIDDELEY WHITLEY

1949–54

The Whitley was built with export markets in mind and featured more extravagant styling than the standard Lancaster saloon, with a wider, more angular nose and a taller rear roofline which allowed for extra headroom and leg space for rear seat passengers.

The car was only offered with the 2.3-litre (140 cu in) engine used in later versions of the Lancaster, which gave reasonable performance. A comfortable car, it was available as a five-seater saloon, a long wheelbase limousine, a Station Coupé and a utility pick-up. All versions were built in very limited numbers and were seldom seen from the end of the 1950s. Production ceased in 1954, and Armstrong-Siddeley concentrated its efforts on smaller models.

Engine: 2309cc (140 cu in), 6-cylinder
Power: 56kW (75bhp)
0–96km/h (60mph): n/a
Top speed: 121km/h (75mph)
Production total: n/a

ARMSTRONG-SIDDELEY SAPPHIRE 346

1952–60

Aimed at buyers of cars such as the Jaguar Mk VII, the Sapphire was too slow and unwieldy to have mass appeal. It was an elegant and well-appointed machine, however, and was far superior to the 234 and 236 models that replaced it.

While it was immediately identifiable as the Lancaster's replacement because of its similar styling, the Sapphire 346 was an entirely new car. It came with an all-new chassis, featuring coil sprung suspension at the front and leaf springs at the rear. Power came from a 3.4-litre (210 cu in) six-cylinder engine that was capable of 154km/h (95mph), while later Star Sapphire versions, from 1958, were fitted with a 4-litre (244 cu in) six-cylinder unit which could cruise at over 161km/h (100mph).

Two gearboxes were offered – a four-speed all-synchromesh manual, or a Rolls-Royce supplied Hydramatic automatic, while power steering was offered as an option – a first for a UK market car. A long-wheelbase limousine variant appeared in 1955 and was available with automatic transmission only.

1955 also saw the launch of the Sapphire 234 and 236, which shared the same name as the 346, but were different machines. Using the Lancaster's old 2.3-litre (140 cu in) six-cylinder engine and rather obscure styling, they were a sales disaster and were dropped after just three years. Less than 1500 were made and the financial loss suffered was severe enough to cause Armstrong-Siddeley to stop producing cars entirely in 1960.

Engine: 3435cc (210 cu in), 6-cylinder
Power: 93kW (125bhp)
0–96km/h (60mph): 13.9 secs
Top speed: 154km/h (95mph)
Production total: 8777

ARNOLT BRISTOL

Engine: 1971cc (120 cu in), 6-cylinder
Power: 98kW (132bhp)
0–96km/h (60mph): n/a
Top speed: 181km/h (112mph)
Production total: 142

Stanley 'Wacky' Arnolt's first venture in car building had been based around the MG TD, with Bertone bodywork, but he soon realized that he needed to base his cars around more powerful mechanicals. As he was not only an importer for MG but also for Bristol in the USA, he had an obvious source.

Wacky persuaded Bristol to supply their new 404 chassis, which had been overproduced. Bristol shipped out chassis, engine and running gear from its factory at Filton to Turin, where Bertone clothed them in sports bodies.

These bodies were mostly open-top, in steel, although a few aluminium versions were made for competition work, as well as a handful of coupés. Arnolt was a director of Bertone, so there was no chance of the work going elsewhere.

The resultant Arnolt Bristol cost

You only need to turn to the section on Bristol saloons to note how radically different Wacky Arnolt's Bertone-bodied sports cars were from the models they were based around. The lack of trimming, both interior and exterior, and the simple (though outrageously curvaceous) body meant that the Arnolt Bristol was, however, far cheaper than the Bristol saloon. Ironically, that price difference led to the Arnolt's demise.

less than half the price of the Bristol 404, and it's thought that Wacky Arnolt lost money on every single one built. That didn't necessarily matter to him: this was a vanity project and his other business enterprises were successful enough to allow him such indulgence. The Arnolt Bristol was a fair

success in terms of number sold, and many were raced. Wacky took three Arnolt Bristols to race at Sebring, finishing second, third and fourth. Production ended only because Bristol stopped supplying the chassis, possibly miffed because of the massive price difference between its own cars and the Arnolt.

ARNOLT MG

1952–56

In the early 1950s, the Bertone coachbuilding company produced two special-bodied MG TDs with the last of Bertone's cash resources. These appeared on the company's stand at the 1952 Turin Show, where American industrialist and US MG importer Stanley 'Wacky' Arnolt spotted them.

Wacky was very impressed and immediately ordered 100 roadsters and 100 cabriolets. The order saved Bertone, while Arnolt himself became a director of Bertone as part of the deal.

The Arnolt MGs looked years ahead of the cars they were based on, but unfortunately the all-enveloping bodywork was too heavy for the TD mechanicals. Performance just didn't match the car's looks and so sales were disappointing.

In the end, just half the original order was completed, but the energetic Wacky Arnolt didn't give up – instead the industrialist went on to build other models, such as the Arnolt Bristol and the Arnolt Aston Martin.

Engine: 1250cc (76 cu in), 4-cylinder
Power: 41kW (55bhp)
0–96km/h (60mph): n/a
Top speed: 121km/h (75mph)
Production total: 100

ASA 1000GT

1962–68

This could be a tourer of the 1960s, but the passenger compartment seems large for the rest of the bodywork. That's because the ASA is a mini-GT, scaled-down in size.

The ASA 1000GT is often referred to as a 'Ferrarina' because it started out as a pet project of Enzo Ferrari. Enzo had always wanted to build a small sports car, and so the engine and running gear were designed at the Ferrari factory by Giotto Bizzarrini (who went on to build his own Ferrari competitor).

The body was produced by Bertone, with its design by an up and coming car stylist, Giorgetto Giugiaro (who was working for Bertone at the time). The prototype for the car was displayed at the 1961 Turin Motor Show and attracted plenty of attention, but Enzo Ferrari had lost interest and made it clear that his company wouldn't be producing it.

Instead, the design was sold to the affluent De Nora family, who formed ASA to build it. The production version was called the 1000GT and was joined by a glassfibre-bodied convertible. The cars were a joy to drive and fast, but were also very expensive.

Engine: 1032cc (63 cu in), 4-cylinder
Power: 63kW (84bhp)
0–96km/h (60mph): n/a
Top speed: 185km/h (115mph)
Production total: 101

ASTER 20/55
1924–29

Although few people will recognize the name Aster, in its heyday it was regarded as a maker of some of the finest cars in the world. Established in Wembley, London, in 1898, the firm originally started making engines for a French carmaker of the same name.

UK Asters became independent designs in 1922, when the factory occupied 18 acres of industrial land that is today occupied by London's North Circular road. The first UK-designed and built car was the 18/50 – a luxury saloon with a 113km/h (70mph) cruising capability. This was superseded in 1924 by the hand-built 20/55, described in Aster's corporate literature as 'transport for those that know most about motor cars and for the connoisseur'.

The Aster 20/55 was powered by a six-cylinder engine unique to the model and could be ordered as a saloon or an open-top tourer. Famous clientele included the Duke of York, who bought one to replace his Armstrong-Siddeley Thirty in 1924.

Engine: 2890cc (176 cu in), 6-cylinder
Power: n/a
0–96km/h (60mph): n/a
Top speed: n/a
Production total: 52

ASTON MARTIN INTERNATIONAL
1929–30

By the time the International was introduced, the Aston Martin company had been in existence for more than a decade, and had already been through one major financial crisis.

The company was founded by Lionel Martin and Robert Bamford just before World War I. The Aston part of the name was taken from a hillclimb venue, Aston Clinton, near Aylesbury, England, and the company soon settled into making 1.5-litre (91 cu in) and 2-litre (122 cu in) sports cars.

Although the International was one of the 1.5-litre (91 cu in) models, what made it particularly special were the bodies, which were designed by Enrico Bertelli and were available in a choice of either a two-seater sports, a four-seater sports, a fixed-head coupé or a drophead coupé.

The Internationals had Aston's chain-drive overhead camshaft four-cylinder engine. This had a pump-cooled cylinder head but relied on the less advanced thermo-syphon method of cooling for the cylinder block. Behind the engine was a separate gearbox and a worm-drive rear axle, which distinguished these cars from the model that followed, the International Le Mans.

Engine: 1495cc (91 cu in), 4-cylinder
Power: 42kW (56bhp)
0–96km/h (60mph): n/a
Top speed: 129km/h (80mph)
Production total: 81

There's little elegance to the lines of this early Aston, but there are signs that the International is a driver's car. It is low-slung with the engine set well behind the front wheels for optimum weight distribution.

ASTON MARTIN LE MANS

With just a very few styling improvements over the Aston Martin International, the Le Mans managed to look more purposeful, typifying the good looks of the best sports cars of the 1930s.

There were three bodies available in the line-up, a two-seater sports, a four-seater sports and a long-wheelbase four-seater sports. The Le Mans also gave birth to a more staid model, the 12/50 Standard, which had the mechanical specification of the Le Mans but with a heavyweight four-door saloon body.

The Short model was closely related to the Le Mans but came with its exhaust headers emerging from the sides of the bonnet, which made it look even more sports-like than the Le Mans itself.

Of all the pre-World War II Aston Martins, the Le Mans is arguably the finest, challenged only by the more racer-like Short model that followed it. The car evolved from the International, via the interim International Le Mans.

It greatly improved upon the International's specification by having the same Moss gearbox and bevel back axle as the International Le Mans, as well as using its predecessor's four-cylinder overhead camshaft engine. But the Le Mans was better-looking than the models that had gone before it, by virtue of its lower-slung radiator and its purposeful outside exhaust.

Engine: 1495cc (91 cu in), 4-cylinder
Power: 56kW (75bhp)
0–96km/h (60mph): n/a
Top speed: 129km/h (80mph)
Production total: 72

ASTON MARTIN ULSTER

For much of its life, the Aston Martin company has spent periods in deep financial trouble. The mid-1930s was no different. One of the company founders, Lionel Martin, had a serious diagreement with a major company investor and then the Bertelli brothers, who had been crucial to the design of the best Aston models, left the company as well.

Amid all acrimony, the Ulster was born, arguably the last good Aston Martin before the DB range commenced after World War II. It was a road-race model, born from the factory's racing campaigns and was extremely fast.

The Ulster's engine was the usual 1.5-litre (91 cu in) four-cylinder unit but with larger-than-usual valves and heavy duty springs, a Laystall crankshaft, a high compression ratio and large SU carburettors. This car was able to produce far more power than the typical 1.5-litre (91 cu in) units found in the other Aston models at the time.

Using the right axle ratio, the extra power meant that the Ulster could achieve 161km/h (100mph), a highly impressive feat in the mid-1930s. The Ulster is now one of the most desirable of the pre-war Aston Martin models.

Engine: 1495cc (91 cu in), 4-cylinder
Power: n/a
0–96km/h (60mph): n/a
Top speed: 161km/h (100mph)
Production total: 24

A motorsport-derived 1930s model was not complete without a fold-flat screen, leather straps holding down the bonnet, and an exhaust that endangered one's health.

47

ASTON MARTIN DB2

The DB series of Astons actually started with the 2-litre (122 cu in) Sports model just after the company had been bought by David Brown (hence the DB initials) and then merged with Lagonda to become Aston Martin Lagonda. Now the 2-litre (122 cu in) Sports is known as the DB1, simply because it acted as a test bed for so many of the models that followed it. Just 14 DB1s were made and it wasn't the best car made by the company.

The DB2 followed in 1950. This

For purity of design, the DB2 is hard to beat. The bumpers are elegant and the rear roof pillars blend into the curves of the rear wings. The front end is one-piece, with combined bonnet and wings.

really was a special machine, despite early problems. Its bulbous but elegant styling was the work of Frank Feeley, previously a stylist for Lagonda, while the well-braced chassis came from Claude Hill's DB1 design. Hill had also designed an engine for the new model but

when he found out it wasn't going to be used, he resigned.

Instead, the DB2 used an unproven 2.6-litre (157 cu in) engine design, mainly because it was much better-looking than Hill's engine – after all, Jaguar's XK unit had just set the standard for engine appearance. Early engines tended to self-destruct but they did at least endow the DB2 with good performance.

What really made the DB2 stand out among its rivals, though, was its sheer quality. Unlike their

Italian contemporaries, Aston produced body panels separately on rolling machines for a near-perfect fit, while the Italians beat their panels out with hammers. And the DB2's interior was stylishly simple, with leather seats, Wilton carpet and a wooden dash – all very English.

Engine: 2580cc (157 cu in), 6-cylinder
Power: 78kW (105bhp)
0–96km/h (60mph): 11.2 secs
Top speed: 187km/h (116mph)
Production total: 411

ASTON MARTIN DB2/4

The DB2 was a great car but needed further refinement, so it was replaced after three years by the DB2/4. Most of the DB2's short-comings were addressed – the split windscreen became a one-piece item, an opening boot was added and tiny rear seats were squeezed in to turn the model into a 2+2.

However, the new boot made the DB2/4 look more bulbous, although this effect was reduced by adding

proper bumpers to effectively lengthen the car. Also, predictably, the car's weight rose.

The DB2 had been available in a higher output 'Vantage' tune, so the obvious answer to the weight problem was to adopt the Vantage tuning for all DB2/4s. Later the 2.6-litre (157 cu in) Vantage engine was increased to 2.9-litre (177 cu in), which helped still further.

Like the DB2, the DB2/4 could

also be bought in drophead form, although the majority were sold with fixed heads. With its added refinement (noise and vibration were reduced), the DB2/4 sold well at the time, with 565 being built in two years compared with 409 DB2s in three years. But Aston couldn't resist updating the design, and produced the DB2/4 Mk II in 1955.

The Mark II had a separate bonnet (previous models' bonnets

were combined with the front wings) and a higher roofline, as well as some unnecessary exterior trim. Aston enthusiasts don't regard the Mk II version as a great model, but in fact, it's a fine car.

Engine: 2900cc (177 cu in), 6-cylinder
Power: 104kW (140bhp)
0–96km/h (60mph): 10.5 secs
Top speed: 192km/h (119mph)
Production total: 764

ASTON MARTIN DB MK III

1957–59

Logically, the DB3 should have been the next car to follow the DB2 (or the DB2/4). But Aston had already produced a DB3 – a lovely racing car that was then updated to become the successful DB3S and the legendary DBR1.

So when it came to further improvements to the DB2/4 road car, Aston had to use the clumsy DB Mk III moniker. The new car, though, was anything but clumsy. The cluttered exterior trim on the

DB2/4 Mark II was dropped, while long, vertical rear lights replaced the ugly round lenses of previous models. Most obviously, though, the front grille design was improved and its shape was echoed by the instrument binnacle inside the car.

Perhaps the looks alone were enough for the DB Mark III to be chosen as the first James Bond Aston Martin. But the real innovations on the DB Mark III were the introduction of front disc

brakes and an updated version of the previous models' engine.

The new version of the old 2.9-litre (178 cu in) unit was much stronger and more efficient, with much-improved power outputs – up to 159kW (214bhp) if you believe Aston's claims for the top-specification 'Competition' tuned engine. This was probably an exaggeration, but it is certainly true that the DB Mark III was a massive improvement over the DB2/4.

Engine: 2922cc (178 cu in), 6-cylinder
Power: 121kW (162bhp)
0–96km/h (60mph): 9.3 secs
Top speed: 192km/h (119mph)
Production total: 551

The DB Mk III is a stepping stone in design between the rounded DB2 and the more elegant DB4. The shape of the front grille and of the rear light panel led the way, while the rear side windows are heading for DB4 territory.

ASTON MARTIN DB4

1958–63

In 1958, a new Aston was revealed – the DB4. The old square section chassis was replaced by a massive base unit structure made from sheet steel with 15cm (6in) box section sills welded to either side. A steel plate cradle at the front supported the engine and suspension. Around this base unit was a lightweight aluminium body, supported by a network of steel tubes (a Superleggera construction), designed by Italian coachbuilders Touring.

The engine was designed by Aston Martin Lagonda engineer Tadek Marek. He deliberately over-engineered it, leaving plenty of room for it to be expanded from its initial 3-litre (183 cu in) capacity. The unit had six cylinders and double overhead camshafts, built around a cast alloy cylinder block.

At first glance, the DB4 could be assumed to be a mere re-design of the DB MK III. But its construction is quite different and the engine was all-new at the time. This style of DB Aston is still the best-loved.

In fact, Marek had wanted to use a cast-iron cylinder block, but the foundry chosen to build the engine found it had no spare cast iron production facilities, so the alloy design was used instead.

The DB4 was a massive success. It was much more impressive to drive than the previous Astons, and

was more reliable as well. Like the previous generation of cars, it evolved gradually from the original 1958 Series 1 through to the 1962 Series 5, by which time it had grown in length and height and had gained power – especially in high-specification Vantage form. The DB4 also gave birth to the

shortened, high-power DB4GT and the fantastic DB4GT Zagato, which are now the ultimate classic Astons.

Engine: 3670cc (224 cu in), 6-cylinder
Power: 179kW (240bhp)
0–96km/h (60mph): 8.5 secs
Top speed: 227km/h (141mph)
Production total: 1213

ASTON MARTIN DB5

1963–66

Today, most people idolize the DB5, especially in silver livery, thanks to James Bond. But when it was launched, it went almost unnoticed in the motoring world, because it seemed so similar to the older DB4. In fact, there were plans to call the new model the DB4 Series 6.

However, the DB5 was soon recognized as a fine model in its own right. It replaced the two factory DB4 models, the DB4 and DB4GT, by incorporating many of the features used on the GT, including Girling disc brakes front and rear, a 4-litre (243 cu in) engine, triple SU carburettors and fared-in headlights.

But once again the new model had gained weight and had become less demanding, so the cabin was quieter and the ride more comfortable, but less sporting. At least the Vantage option, which used triple Weber carburettors, added performance, while a five-speed ZF gearbox gave the car better high-speed cruising – something the DB5 was perfect for.

A convertible version of the DB5 was also launched, in line with the previous models which had also been available as soft-tops, but unusually, an estate version was also offered. These were made by the high-quality conversion company Radford, which built 12 'shooting brakes' to special order, replacing the rear sections of the Superleggera bodywork with a new steel framework to take the estate panelwork. They looked surprisingly good.

Engine: 3995cc (243 cu in), 6-cylinder
Power: 210kW (282bhp)
0–96km/h (60mph): 8.1 secs
Top speed: 227km/h (141mph)
Production total: 1063

ASTON MARTIN DB6

1965–70

Engine: 3995cc (243 cu in), 6-cylinder
Power: 242kW (325bhp)
0–96km/h (60mph): 6.5 secs
Top speed: 239km/h (148mph)
Production total: 1755

Of all the six-cylinder Aston Martins, most enthusiasts agree that the DB6 is the best. Unlike the DB5, the car wasn't just an update of an existing design. It went much further than that, although the shape clearly belongs in the DB family.

The bodywork was constructed from aluminium alloy, just like its predecessors, but the labour-intensive Superleggera construction was dropped in favour of using folded metal for strengthening. This was simpler to produce, stronger and no heavier, because although more aluminium was used, it dispensed with the need for steel tubing.

Some think the upturned edge to the Kamm rear end looked a little clumsy but the DB6 was significantly more stable at high speed than the DB5 – partly due to revised rear spring and damper rates but also due to the aerodynamic advantages of that subtle rear spoiler.

The DB6 was launched in 1965 and was available with the usual Vantage engine option. A Mk II version appeared in 1969, with slightly flared wheelarches to accommodate wider wheels, as well as a fuel injection option.

The convertible version was named the Volante, although the first so-called DB6 Volantes were actually built on the DB5 chassis. These early convertibles are now known as 'short-chassis' Volantes to distinguish them from the real DB6 versions.

The DB6 is initially difficult to tell apart from the DB4 and 5. But look at the rear side windows which add strength to the rear roof pillars, and that distinctive rear end – a mostly aerodynamic feature.

ASTON MARTIN DBS

1967–73

Viewed from the side, the DBS looks like a progression of the DB shape. But in real life you realize just how wide it is. The finicky style of the alloy wheels were typical of the period; slender bumpers are refreshing for an era which gave us clumsy impact-resistant devices.

In 1967, Aston Martin unveiled a huge machine to the unsuspecting public. The DBS was fast, powerful and, above all, extremely large – a full 1.8 metres (6ft) wide. Its twin headlights and wide, squat snout gave it the appearance of an American muscle car. The overall styling, by William Towns, was deliberately aggressive and loved by some, loathed by others.

This model is still the cheapest way to own an Aston Martin. It wasn't a bad car, more misunderstood. It still used the basic chassis design of the previous Astons, but the back end was more sophisticated with a De Dion rear axle arrangement, which improved handling significantly. However, the huge weight of the DBS ensured that this was one Aston that could never corner quickly.

Initially, the DBS was powered by the old 4-litre (244 cu in) six-cylinder engine, but the company had always planned to use a new four-camshaft 5.3-litre (326 cu in) V8, designed in-house by Tadek Marek. The engine wasn't ready until 1970, when the DBS V8 appeared.

Problems with the Bosch fuel injection followed, giving the DBS a bad reputation it could never recover from. This wasn't helped by the car's very high fuel consumption of just 3.2km/l (9mpg).

Engine: 5340cc (326 cu in), V8-cylinder
Power: 279kW (375bhp)
0–96km/h (60mph): 6 secs
Top speed: 256km/h (159mph)
Production total: 962

ASTON MARTIN AMV8

1972–90

Engine: 5340cc (326 cu in), V8-cylinder
Power: 253kW (340bhp)
0–96km/h (60mph): 6 secs
Top speed: 261km/h (162mph)
Production total: 1600

The AMV8 was launched into the economic gloom of the 1970s and was a basic evolution of the DBS. The high fuel consumption was unaltered but the price had risen from £7000 to £9000. Otherwise the AMV8 was little different from the DBS V8, and it is now often known as a Series 2 V8. Single headlights replaced the twin units and the car also had a slightly longer body, a larger boot and a smaller front grille. Initially, it came fitted with the DBS V8's fuel injection, but this was still causing problems, so the company reverted to using four Weber carburettors and increased the size of the bonnet scoop for clearance. This version is known as the Series 3.

In 1978, a new version was introduced, known as the Series 4, or the Oscar. It had a tiny built-in rear spoiler and the bonnet scoop was replaced by a simple power bulge. Then fuel injection re-appeared, much more successfully thanks to a new Weber/Marelli system. The bonnet bulge disappeared and DBS alloy wheels were fitted, which distinguish the car as the so-called Series 5. This lasted right through to 1989.

Alongside, a V8 Volante convertible version was available, as well as (for a very short period) a very ugly stretched four-door Lagonda – not to be confused with the amazing William Towns Lagonda that followed.

DBS-style alloy wheels and the spoiler-less boot show that this is a Series 3 AMV8, complete with four snorting Weber carburettors.

ASTON MARTIN LAGONDA

1977–90

Still a shock beside other Astons, the William Towns Lagonda was nonetheless a big hit in Arab nations. Several were abandoned in the desert after breaking down.

The William Towns-designed Lagonda is legendary, but for the wrong reasons. It was conceived in the mid-1970s, just as the UK seemed to be leaving an economic gloom behind. A new confidence was apparent at Aston Martin, and the Lagonda typified this.

The idea was to build an attention-grabbing vehicle that no one could ignore. It would lead the way in style and technology, cost being no object. In retrospect, this was dangerous thinking for a company perpetually on the brink of financial disaster.

William Towns, who had also designed the DBS, had a fascination with wedge-shaped cars and was keen to showcase his new ideas – and Aston Martin were happy to let him do this. The AMV8 chassis was stretched by 0.3m (1ft) and,

within a year, the Lagonda prototype was on display at the 1976 London Motor Show.

It was long, angular and outrageous. The dashboard was a complicated affair, with touch-sensitive switches and digital displays – the first of its kind. All sorts of gadgets were featured,

including automatic locking.

But Aston's ambitions were well ahead of their budgets and the available technology. The launch was delayed and orders were left unfulfilled. Worse, the Lagonda was initially deeply unreliable, with dashboards failing, switches working only occasionally and the

automatic locking taking it upon itself to lock out the wealthy owner.

Engine: 5340cc (326 cu in), V8-cylinder
Power: 209kW (280bhp)
0–96km/h (60mph): 8.8 secs
Top speed: 231km/h (143mph)
Production total: 645

ASTON MARTIN V8 ZAGATO

1986–89

This was the 1980s when flush-fitting glass, disc-look alloy wheels and brutal styling were still *de rigueur*. The V8 Zagato, therefore, looks seriously dated now but future classic status is assured.

Aston Martin are well-known for producing some outrageous specials. Arguably the greatest of them all was the DB4GT Zagato of the 1960s, so using the Zagato company to design the bodywork again in the mid-1980s seemed perfectly logical.

Aston Martin were looking for a car that would remind the world of the company's roots, away from the ultra-luxurious, occasionally

vulgar machines in their 1980s line-up. The idea was to build a two-seater based around a lightened, shortened chassis and clothed in an exotic body. The company had seen how the market had reacted to such exotic specials as the Porsche 959 and Ferrari 288GTO, with investors buying them and storing them away, undriven. Aston Martin wanted to be in this exclusive club.

A V8 chassis was shortened by 40.6cm (15.9in) and shipped out to Milan for its new Zagato bodywork, then quickly returned in time for the 1985 Frankfurt Motor Show. The response to the new model was so good that the original plans to build just 50 were quickly scrapped.

The V8 engine was substantially updated, to give an incredible 315kW (423bhp). The fuel

injection had to be scrapped, though, which meant a return to Weber carburettors and an unwanted bonnet bulge to accommodate them. However, performance aims were met – the Zagato was a very fast machine.

Engine: 5340cc (326 cu in), V8-cylinders
Power: 315kW (423bhp)
0–96km/h (60mph): 5 secs
Top speed: 241km/h (150mph)
Production total: 83

ASTON MARTIN VIRAGE

Not the most elegant Aston Martin, but for sheer presence there's little to beat a Virage. The high flanks hint at the model's hefty weight, which had to be overcome by significantly boosting the V8 engine's output with help from an American tuning company.

For two decades, Aston Martin struggled on with the V8 model, producing basic evolutions of the DBS design. The car was looking ever more vulgar and dated and the company was in danger of not being taken seriously.

To remedy this, the Virage was introduced in 1988. If the V8 had been muscular, then this new car was even more aggressive, with a new hand-built aluminium alloy body designed by John Hefferman and Ken Greenley, tutors at the Royal College of Art in London.

The chassis, though, was virtually the same as the V8's, except for a new rear axle location system that actually gave the car

vague handling. The engine, too, was based around the old V8, but updated by US company Reeves Callaway Engineering to give four valves per cylinder and to run catalytic converters. The capacity remained at 5.3 litres (326 cu in) but power went up to 231kW (310bhp), despite more stringent emission controls. However, the

Virage was so heavy it actually needed more power than this extra boost gave.

The Vantage version was introduced to provide this, with even more power and an improved rear axle location system. A Volante convertible version also joined the line-up, and these models became the last Astons to

use the old chassis, before the 1994 DB7 appeared, by which time Aston Martin had been bought by Ford.

Engine: 5340cc (326 cu in), V8-cylinder
Power: 246kW (330bhp)
0–96km/h (60mph): 6.8 secs
Top speed: 253km/h (157mph)
Production total: n/a

AUBURN 851 SPEEDSTER

Engine: 4596cc (280 cu in), 8-cylinder
Power: 97kW (130bhp)
0–96km/h (60mph): n/a
Top speed: 170km/h (105mph)
Production total: 500

As makers of exclusive motor cars, the Eckhardt Carriage Company set up an independent operation in Auburn, Indiana, in 1903. It was from this factory that the spin-off brand called Auburn came into

existence, making luxury cars for the rich. The cars were big and handsome with powerful eight- or 12-cylinder engines.

Despite the Depression, Auburn survived under the careful leadership of Erret Cord – founder of Cord cars – who had joined the company in 1924. Yet debts spiralled out of control, and by the mid-1930s, Auburn was in financial trouble.

The 851 Speedster was its great hope for survival. Intended as an exclusive car for rich and famous owners, it was for a time the United States' most expensive car, while its beautiful boat-tail styling and sumptuous cabin meant it was

One of America's most famous cars in its heyday, the 851 Speedster was beloved by many Hollywood stars and gangsters alike.

a truly wonderful machine.

Power came from a 4.6-litre (280 cu in) supercharged side-valve straight eight and all cars were speed tested to at least 161km/h (100mph) before leaving the factory. But Auburn still couldn't cover its costs, and the company went into liquidation in 1937. Its rarity makes it one of the most collectable cars around and it has inspired a host of replicas.

AUDI 10/22

Modern Audis carry a badge featuring four intertwined rings to symbolize the union of four leading German car manufacturers in 1932. This was called Auto Union. Audi had been established in 1911 when August Horch left his original company, to which he had given his name, and formed Audi.

The first car to carry the Audi name was the 10/22, introduced in 1910. This relatively high-quality saloon car adopted many Horch practices: the four cylinders of the engine were cast in pairs and the engine used an overhead inlet valve (operated by small rocker arms) and a side exhaust valve, operated by a gear-driven camshaft.

In 1914, the 10/22 gained a new pointed grille, which came to symbolize the Audi. Ironically, one of the companies to join Audi under the new Auto Union banner was Horch. The others were DKW and Wanderer.

Engine: 2612cc (159 cu in), 4-cylinder
Power: 16kW (22bhp)
0–96km/h (60mph): n/a
Top speed: 75km/h (47mph)
Production total: n/a

AUDI 60

The Audi name had been lost in 1932 as Audi, Horch, DKW and Wanderer joined to become Auto Union. But in 1965, a new Audi emerged, based on the DKW F-102 but with a four-stroke engine instead of the DKW's trademark two-stroke.

The new Audi was named the D-B Heron (the engines used 'Heron' type combustion chambers within the engine). It signalled the beginning of the end for DKW's two-strokes and the start of a long line of front-wheel drive Audi saloons. The D-B Heron was updated to become the 75 which was then joined by the more affordable, smaller-engined 60. Keeping the engine capacity under 1.5-litres (91 cu in) kept the 60 in a cheap tax bracket in mainland Europe and ensured the model's success, even though it was hardly an exciting car to drive.

The 60 and 75 were available as two- or four-door saloons or three-door estates. Unusually for the period and the size of the cars, Audi fitted torsion bar independent suspension front and rear, so the ride was impressive. But with front-wheel drive and with so much of the cars' weight carried over the front wheels, they tended to understeer severely.

Although ultimately dull, the 60 and 75 range of Audis established the marque and allowed the car-buying masses to sample the company's solid, sensible design features.

Engine: 1496cc (91 cu in), 4-cylinder
Power: 41kW (55bhp)
0–96km/h (60mph): 18 secs
Top speed: 138km/h (86mph)
Production total: 416,852

With new simply styled bodies, these cars looked like Europeanized Vauxhall FB Victors from some angles. There's also a similarity with the Neue Klasse BMWs of the time. But underneath the Audis were quite different, with front-wheel-drive and torsion bar suspension.

AUDI 80

The way that the lower body tapers inwards and the front and rear valances rise sharply to the bumpers became typically Audi and VW styling cues during the 1970s. The VW Passat and Polo demonstrated this well, also keeping the 1980s large glass area, which made all these models easy to drive.

We now know Audi as a part of the massive VW-Audi Group, with common vehicle platforms shared between the two marques. Volkswagen's ownership started in the late 1960s and one of the first Audi models to share its design with a VW was the Audi 80.

The 80 looked similar to the larger 100 but was powered by a new Audi-designed overhead camshaft engine. The suspension was different too, with MacPherson struts all round; the geometry of the front struts were set deliberately for extra stability and safety, even in the event of a tyre blow-out. The later VW Passat was developed from the design of the 80, and the two models became crucial to the companies' fortunes. Just to underline how good the basic design was, the 80 won the coveted annual Car of the Year title in 1973, despite competition from the excellent Renault 5 and the Alfa Romeo Alfetta.

Engine: 1296cc (79 cu in), 4-cylinder
Power: 41kW (55bhp)
0–96km/h (60mph): 16.9 secs
Top speed: 145km/h (90mph)
Production total: 939,931

AUDI QUATTRO

As a road car, the Quattro was superb, but in rallying it was extraordinary, revolutionizing the sport with its four-wheel-drive layout.

In the 1970s, Audi developed a reputation for tough, no-nonsense saloons. But there were no exciting models to capture the imagination. To remedy this, Audi began rallying. Using basic elements from its range, Audi developed the four-wheel drive Quattro to compete in the World Rally Championship. The five-cylinder 2.1-litre (131 cu in) engine was a development of the unit from the 200 saloon, with a KKK turbocharger and Bosch fuel injection system, producing 149kW (200bhp).

The four-wheel drive idea had already been developed by Audi, though not for a rally car, but for a VW military vehicle called the Iltis. It was adapted for road use with a small differential between the gearbox and the driveshaft (to the rear axle) to avoid transmission wind-up (when the front wheels try to travel at a different speed to the rear wheels, usually during cornering). The floorpan and running gear were based around the Audi 80, with a new coupé bodystyle. However, the 80's beam rear axle was replaced by a more sophisticated independent rear suspension design.

The car that emerged had fantastic speed, thanks to its brilliant combination of performance and traction. In rallying, it quickly ended the decade-long domination of the rear-wheel drive Ford Escorts. Today, almost all successful rally cars are four-wheel drive.

Engine: 2144cc (131 cu in), 5-cylinder
Power: 149kW (200bhp)
0–96km/h (60mph): 6.5 secs
Top speed: 222km/h (138mph)
Production total: 11,560

AUSTIN SEVEN

The Seven transformed motoring in Britain, and was influential right across the globe. The subject of both admiration and derision for its malnourished size, it still attracts a fanatical following eight decades since the start of production.

The secret behind the Austin Seven's success was its price. Motoring had initially been the preserve of rich pioneers, but by the time World War I broke out the middle classes were experimenting with cars as well. Working-class families, though, were stuck with motorcycle and sidecar combinations and abominable cyclecars.

Herbert Austin, the founder of the Austin Motor Company, realized that there was a gap in the market for a small, basic machine that could transport a family at minimal cost. After all, more than one million of the larger Ford Model Ts had already been sold, mostly in the United States, and Herbert Austin aimed to make the Seven even more affordable.

Working at his home (because the Austin Motor Company had rejected the idea of the Seven) with a young draughtsman, Stanley Edge, Herbert Austin developed the car. It was to have a rudimentary chassis, with two main beams running the length of

Through clever design (and minimal seat padding), most Sevens really could seat a family of four. Controls are shockingly direct for anyone unused to Sevens, with just a couple of inches of movement on the clutch pedal and high-geared steering. Brakes tend to be unimpressive...

the car, and little else except for a basic suspension. Initially, the engine was a tiny four-cylinder side-valve unit of just 696cc (42 cu in), although this was enlarged to 747cc (46 cu in) shortly afterwards. The bodywork was a mixture of steel panels and aluminium-over-ash frame. It was very light and very simple.

The public's response to the new car was overwhelming when it was launched in 1922, advertised as the 'motor for the millions'. At just £225, it was the price of a well-equipped motorcycle and sidecar combination. Also, as more Sevens were sold, the price was reduced,

so that by 1926 it cost just £145.

By 1929, more than 100,000 Sevens had been sold, giving it a 37 per cent share of the British car market – and killing off sidecars and cyclecars for good. More variants were introduced – saloons, open-top tourers and even sports models, some with superchargers. Sevens were built for the army, to use as staff cars and wireless carriers, for tradesmen who used them as delivery vans, and there were even special versions for milk deliveries, with the back adapted to carry milk churns.

On the race track, the Seven collected speed records and irritated the drivers of larger, more powerful machinery. At Brooklands, the Seven became the first 161km/h (100mph) 750cc (46 cu in) car in England, and was even raced in the Le Mans 24-hour race, with some success.

Private owners began to compete in their Sevens, too. Trials (which involved trying to cajole a car up a muddy, slippery slope), rallies, hillclimbs and circuit racing were all deemed appropriate competitions for the little Austin. Remarkably, the car continues to be used in similar motor sports even now.

The Seven also prompted production from several overseas car manufacturers. In France, the

This Opal tourer version of the Seven is one of the later models, distinguished by the cowled radiator. Earlier Sevens were even more basic, with few (if any) curves and a much simpler radiator design with a plated surround.

rights to produce a French-built Seven were bought by Rosengart. In Germany, the car became the Dixi, and went on to form the basic BMW, and in the United States, it was bought by a new company, the American Austin Car Company. Bizarrely, a version of the US-built Seven went on to influence the original Jeep.

However, by 1939, and despite several facelifts, most notably the Austin Seven Ruby, with its larger, more sophisticated bodywork, the car looked dated against its rivals. The Seven was replaced by the Big Seven, which was more powerful, more comfortable and more expensive. It never sold like the original Seven and Austin had to wait until 1959 before it produced another truly revolutionary vehicle – the Mini.

Engine: 747cc (46 cu in), 4-cylinder
Power: 7.5kW (10bhp)
0–96km/h (60mph): n/a
Top speed: 84km/h (52mph)
Production total: 290,000

AUSTIN SHEERLINE

There was a time when the Austin name was prestigious enough to justify the company launching a series of upmarket models. The first of these was the A110 Sheerline. No one would deny that it looked impressive, though this was mainly because of its massive size. It was based on a box-section chassis, with large cross-bracing sections. The body was designed by Dick Burzi and was influenced by the razor-edge styling that some

Bentleys of the era also adopted (as did Triumphs, though less successfully).

To power this huge car, Austin resurrected a six-cylinder overhead valve engine that had previously powered pre-war trucks. It was initially 3.5 litres (214 cu in), producing 82kW (110bhp), which is how the first version of the Sheerline ended up being designated the A110. But within the first year of production, the

engine was bored out to 4 litres (244 cu in) and power went up to 93kW (125bhp) and the model then became the A125.

Alongside the Sheerline, Austin launched the more upmarket Princess, which had a more sweeping body style, produced in aluminium by Vanden Plas (newly acquired by Austin). The Princess was designated the A120, then the A135, both named after their power outputs.

The Sheerline and its posh brother the Princess really did resemble the various Bentleys of the period. Consequently they were often chosen by small-time dignitaries, such as town mayors, who aspired to a higher class of motor car.

Engine: 3993cc (243 cu in), 6-cylinder
Power: 93kW (125bhp)
0–96km/h (60mph): 19.4 secs
Top speed: 134km/h (83mph)
Production total: 8700

AUSTIN A70 HAMPSHIRE AND HEREFORD

The curvaceous Counties range of Austins started with the A40 Dorset and Devon, but the A70 Hampshire followed within a year. It had better styling and a six-cylinder engine, as opposed to the A40's four-cylinder unit (which went on to become the famous B-series, used in the MGB).

Bench seats front and rear were supposed to allow six adults to be seated in comfort. But, as the A70 was only 10cm (4in) longer than the dumpy A40, it was a squeeze. The more curvaceous, longer Hereford rectified that, replacing the Hampshire after two years.

Neither model handled well, but at least the brakes in the Hereford were fully hydraulic, instead of the part-hydraulic, part-mechanical system used in the Hampshire. Both models were also built as Countryman estates, with wood panelling down the sides, and

pick-ups, while the Hereford also came as a convertible.

Engine: 2191cc (134 cu in), 6-cylinder
Power: 50kW (67bhp)
0–96km/h (60mph): 21.5 secs
Top speed: 132km/h (82mph)
Production total: 85,882

AUSTIN A90 ATLANTIC

1948–52

Although based on the quintessentially British 'Counties' series of saloons, the Atlantic was glitzed up for America with styling features and plenty of chrome. Americans weren't impressed, but in the UK Atlantics now fetch high prices.

sweeping line from the top of the front wings right to the back of the car, rear wheel spats and even gold-faced gauges.

Initially, the A90 Atlantic was available only as a convertible, with power hood and electric windows (a first for a mass-produced car from Britain) as options. A saloon version emerged a year after the convertible.

But under all the ostentatious bodywork was nothing more than the underpinnings of the humble A70, although the four-cylinder engine had been bored out to 2660cc (162 cu in) and was later used to power the Austin-Healey 100. Perhaps not surprisingly, the Atlantic flopped, selling just 350 in the United States.

The glamour of the United States proved to be a great attraction for car designers working in the austerity of post-war Britain and the A90 Atlantic was supposed to reflect this.

The aim was to exploit the crucial export market, aiming for the United States in particular, as the model's name suggested. Austin's stylist Dick Burzi worked hard – perhaps a bit too hard – to

emulate the glitzy models being made in the US.

So, there were three headlights, the third in the middle of the grille, an excess of chrome (even three strips up and over the bonnet), a

Engine: 2660cc (162 cu in), 4-cylinder
Power: 66kW (88bhp)
0–96km/h (60mph): 16.6 secs
Top speed: 147km/h (91mph)
Production total: 7981

AUSTIN A40 SPORTS

1950–53

Austin's range in the early post-war years was reasonably varied but its attempts at producing cars with headline-catching glamour generally went awry. The Atlantic was one such attempt, as were the drop-top versions of the A70 Hereford, but none was good enough to really catch the public's attention. They were too clumsy, too obviously based around existing saloons.

So Austin approached the Jensen car company, who had been using Austin engines in their sports cars. Jensen produced a pretty aluminium sports body, which looked a little like the first Jensen Interceptor, albeit smaller. With a decent folding hood and four seats, this Jensen design still wasn't a real sports car but it was an attractive machine nevertheless.

Unfortunately, it had to be based on an unmodified A40 Devon chassis, with the only concession

Too tall to even look like a sports car, the A40 Sports had uncluttered lines all the same. The hood folded down neatly, unlike the hoods of many contemporaries. Few survive now, partly due to electrolytic corrosion between the aluminium body and the steel framework.

to performance being the twin carburettors fitted to the humble four-cylinder engine.

No more work was put into improving handling and power, so the A40 Sports proved to be another embarrassing flop for Austin. Most of the A40 Sports' production was sold in the United States.

Engine: 1200cc (73 cu in), 4-cylinder
Power: 34kW (46bhp)
0–96km/h (60mph): 25.6 secs
Top speed: 127km/h (79mph)
Production total: 4011

AUSTIN A30 AND A35

1951–68

With the A30 of 1951, the baby Austin finally made a reappearance, almost 30 years after the introduction of the best-selling Seven. In fact, Austin initially named the new car the Seven, a reminder of past glories.

The A30's rounded body and prominent grille hinted at US styling influences, but in size it was utterly European. Although it was extremely narrow, it was also tall and four adults could sit (very upright) in reasonable comfort. A four-door option was also offered. The tiny engine was the first incarnation of the A-series unit that would later go on to power the Mini, among others.

In 1956, the model was updated and became the A35. Its engine was enlarged to 948cc (58 cu in), the grille was changed from chrome to body colour and the rear window was made bigger. The gearshift was also changed, using remote linkage instead of the A30's long gearstick direct from the gearbox.

Against the larger and more modern-looking Morris Minor, the A30 and A35 did not look very impressive, but they still sold well and continue to have an enthusiastic following. They were made as vans, saloons, estates and even pick-ups; the vans were built until 1968.

Engine: 948cc (58 cu in), 4-cylinder
Power: 25kW (34bhp)
0–96km/h (60mph): n/a
Top speed: 102km/h (63mph)
Production total: 527,000

The odd proportions of the A30 (pictured) and A35 models did little to reduce their character and charm. Despite appearances, these cars were surprisingly roomy inside.

AUSTIN A40 SOMERSET

1952–54

The 1950s saw massive leaps forward in car design, headed by such notaries as the Morris Minor and later, the Mini and the Ford Anglia. But despite this brave new world, Austin and many other manufacturers could only afford to produce poor updates of existing, obsolete models.

The A40 Somerset was typical of this policy, although now it looks like a pleasant, characterful car. At the time, though, Austin simply took the running gear of the A40 Dorset and Devon – which was already antiquated – and gave it a body in the same style as the A70 Hereford and the A30.

The B-series engine was still a mere 1200cc (73 cu in) and, despite independent front suspension, the chassis didn't provide the car with great handling.

However, the prominent sweeping line down from the top of the front wing and the distinctive grille helped to ensure a place for the car in the British public's heart, so sales were reasonable.

The most interesting variant of the Somerset was the convertible, whose body was built by Carbodies of Coventry, as was the similarly styled convertible A70 Hereford.

There's no mistaking the curvy lines of one of the Austin Counties range of cars. The A40 Somerset is the most characterful looking of all and it is the best to drive too.

Engine: 1200cc (73 cu in), 4-cylinder
Power: 30kW (40bhp)
0–96km/h (60mph): 31.6 secs
Top speed: 111km/h (69mph)
Production total: 173,306

AUSTIN CHAMP

1952–55

The usefulness of the Willys Jeep during World War II was noted by Austin's designers and engineers and the company conceived plans to produce a Jeep-like machine. The result was the Champ, which emerged in 1952, four years after the similarly inspired Land Rover. Like the Land Rover, the Champ used four-wheel drive, clad in very basic bodywork.

It was available in two versions – military and civilian. Curiously, the military version was powered by a special version of the Rolls-Royce FB engine, with four cylinders and a capacity of 2.9 litres (177 cu in). But the Rolls-Royce engine was too sophisticated for army life. Partly because of this, as well as other problems, the Champ also proved to be unreliable and thus disliked by the military. However, the civilian variant used

The Champ could have been the champion of utility four-wheel-drive vehicles. Unfortunately, Austin released it too late.

a detuned version of the A90 Atlantic four-cylinder unit, but the Land Rover had already broken into that market.

Almost 13,000 were built, but just 1200 were civilian models and most of those were exported.

Perhaps if Austin had moved quicker after the war and not used the Rolls-Royce unit, the Champ might have been as successful as the Land Rover. Instead it became just another might-have-been.

Engine: 1971cc (120 cu in), 4-cylinder
Power: 78kW (105bhp)
0–96km/h (60mph): 11.4 secs
Top speed: 168km/h (104mph)
Production total: 83

AUSTIN A40/A50/A55 CAMBRIDGE

1954–71

Compare the Cambridge with its predecessor, the A40 Somerset, and you will soon see how far Austin moved the range on in appearance alone.

If there was anything that readily demonstrated that a manufacturer was failing to keep up with new technology during the 1950s, it was the production of models with a separate chassis. Austin's medium saloons, the Counties range, all had such a chassis.

So it was a very important step in the right direction for Austin when the Counties range was replaced by the Cambridge and the similarly styled Westminster. Gone was the separate chassis. In its place, a unitary construction body finally brought Austin into the modern world.

The A40 Cambridge continued to use the 1200cc (73 cu in) Somerset engine, while the A50 used a new version of the B-series engine, increased to 1489cc (91 cu in). Both models had independent

front suspension, hydraulic brakes and a four-speed column-change gearbox, typical of the era. In deluxe trim, the Cambridge came with extra chrome and a leather interior, again, a usual trim level for its time.

Both the A40 and A50 were replaced by the A55 in 1957. This model was basically the same as its predecessors but had a floor-mounted gearshift (in most cases), small fins on the rear wings, a longer boot and a larger rear window. In van and pick-up form, the A55 quite remarkably lasted until 1971.

Engine: 1489cc (91 cu in), 4-cylinder
Power: 37kW (50bhp)
0–96km/h (60mph): 28.8 secs
Top speed: 119km/h (74mph)
Production total: 299,500

AUSTIN A90/A95/A105 WESTMINSTER

1954–59

Engine: 2639cc (161 cu in), 6-cylinder
Power: 69kW (92bhp)
0–96km/h (60mph): 19.8 secs
Top speed: 145km/h (90mph)
Production total: 60,400

For years, mass-market British manufacturers had to have a semi-upmarket saloon powered by a straight-six engine. The Westminster was Austin's offering – long overdue and rather good.

The A90 Westminster followed on where the A70 Hereford had left off. And, where the A70 Hereford had looked very much like its lesser brother, the A40 Somerset, so the A90 Westminster closely resembled the A40 and A50 Cambridge.

However, only the doors were actually interchangeable between the models, as the Westminster was significantly bigger. Its engine was the C-series six-cylinder unit, which produced a modest 63kW (85bhp) with its small, single carburettor.

In 1956, the Westminster was updated to become the A95 and A105. Both had a larger rear

window, a squarer rear wing line and a new grille. The A95 gained a little extra power but the A105 was much improved, due to twin carburettors. The A105 also gained a lowered suspension, overdrive as standard and two-tone paint.

A little-known Vanden Plas version of the Westminster was also built, loaded down with lots of interior wood and leather which paved the way for the large amount of badge-engineering to come with the Farina range of saloons.

The Westminster is as sturdy as it looks. It was never deeply exciting to drive, but then it was never meant to be. All the same, it's not unknown to see a Westminster in historic rallies, often powered by an Austin-Healey specification engine.

AUSTIN GYPSY

1958–68

The Land Rover had shown just how useful a utility vehicle could be – and what an opportunity Austin had missed by being too slow to launch its overcomplicated four-wheel drive Champ.

To replace the Champ, Austin launched itself into the Land Rover market and produced a very similar looking vehicle called the Gypsy. Despite what you might assume, the Gypsy was actually a very good vehicle, arguably better than the Land Rover in many ways.

Its suspension was an all-independent Flexitor rubber design, while the Land Rover had a much less sophisticated leaf spring set-up. But the Land Rover had an alloy body while the Gypsy's was made of steel, which proved to be prone to corrosion.

After the problems with the Champ, the military unsurprisingly refused to buy the Gypsy. When Rover (and hence Land Rover) joined BLMC (British Leyland Motor Company) of which Austin was a part, the Gypsy was dropped.

Engine: 2199cc (134 cu in), 4-cylinder
Power: 46kW (62bhp)
0–96km/h (60mph): n/a
Top speed: 102km/h (63mph)
Production total: 21,208

The Gypsy may look near-identical to a Series One or Two Land Rover, but look at the small amount of suspension showing under the front wheelarch – a rubber-based design, which made for a good-quality ride.

AUSTIN FX4

The FX4 is more widely recognized as the London black cab. Introduced in 1958, it was another vehicle in a successful line of taxis produced by Austin since well before World War II.

What made the FX4 really special was its modern bodywork (for the period) as well as a series of minor luxuries that cab drivers really appreciated. An automatic gearbox made perhaps the biggest difference, but the independent front suspension and hydraulic brakes were important too; London taxicab designs had not been updated for many years.

Gradually, the FX4 evolved with a series of more powerful engines and a manual transmission option. Later, the Carbodies company took over the manufacture of the FX4, which is now called the Fairway and is powered by a Nissan engine.

The shape, though, has hardly changed at all.

Engine: 2199cc (134 cu in), 4-cylinder
Power: 42kW (56bhp)
0–96km/h (60mph): n/a
Top speed: 121km/h (75mph)
Production total: still made

AUSTIN A40 FARINA

Engine: 948cc (58 cu in), 4-cylinder
Power: 28kW (38bhp)
0–96km/h (60mph): 27.1 secs
Top speed: 121km/h (75mph)
Production total: 342,280

The humble A40 Farina is one of the most important cars ever made by Austin but it is also one of the most overlooked. It is noteworthy because it was the first post-war Austin to be designed without input from Dick Burzi, the company's design director. Instead, Italian company Pininfarina styled the car.

This was an important task because the A40 Farina was to take over from the A35. Pininfarina and Austin did a good job, introducing the two-box design that now defines all modern hatchbacks.

Under the bodywork, the same A-series engine that powered the A35 and all but the earliest Morris Minors was used. In fact, the A40 Farina's running gear was almost identical to the A35's, right down to the questionable hydro-mechanical brakes. Thankfully, the A40 Farina Mk II, introduced in 1961, gained all-hydraulic brakes, along with a slightly longer wheelbase and a new grille.

A year on, in 1962, the car was fitted with a 1098cc (67 cu in) version of the A-series engine, which gave it a little more, and much-needed, power. Nevertheless, the car remains generally unloved by enthusiasts.

The design of the A40 Farina, by Pininfarina, shows the features that would go on to shape the rest of the BLMC range: plenty of glass, sharp lines, tending towards sharp-edged fins at the rear, slab sides and those neat, upright rear lights.

A55 and A60 Cambridge

1959–69

Austin, glamorously, commissioned Pininfarina to update the Cambridge and Westminster range; the result hit the showrooms in 1959. The new 'Farina' range was certainly more modern than the outgoing models, with prominent rear fins which looked particularly good picked out in two-tone paint. However, the new car was slab-sided and extremely heavy.

Curiously, Peugeot had also commissioned a medium-sized saloon design from Pininfarina, so the French company's 404 model ended up looking almost identical to the Cambridge.

The A55 was the first version, a simple remodelling of the previous 'pre-Farina' Cambridge. The old 1489cc (91 cu in) B-series engine received an SU carburettor but was otherwise almost unchanged – but it was at least more powerful than the terrible diesel option that appeared with the Farina.

Many in the 1960s and early 1970s would have experienced the roomy, well-priced Farina saloons. The Austins were the most basic but most competitively priced. The full-width grille and restrained rear end shows this is an A60 pictured.

In 1961, the model was updated to become the A60. The engine was increased to 1622cc (99 cu in) – a worthwhile improvement – while the wheelbase was increased by 2.5cm (1in), the front grille was redesigned and, sadly, the rear fins were dropped.

A Countryman estate version of both the A55 and A60 was also offered. Both were popular, although few have survived today.

Engine: 1622cc (99 cu in), 4-cylinder
Power: 45kW (61bhp)
0–96km/h (60mph): 21.4 secs
Top speed: 131km/h (81mph)
Production total: 425,500

A99 and A110 Westminster

1959–68

Applying the Pininfarina styling of the A55 and A60 Cambridge to the Westminster worked well – it suited the Westminster's imposing look.

The previous pre-Farina Westminster had been a good car and the new A99 took the best bits from that model and improved them. The C-series engine was enlarged to 3 litres (178 cu in) and fitted with twin SU carburettors, the three-speed gearbox was given better synchromesh and the front brakes were changed from drum units to servo-assisted discs, a first for an Austin saloon.

In 1961, the Westminster was given a longer wheelbase to increase passenger room and give the car a more impressive presence. The following year, Austin added power steering and air-conditioning options. Later, in 1964, the A110 Westminster Mk II appeared with a four-speed gearbox, the finishing touch for a competent machine.

Engine: 2912cc (178 cu in), 6-cylinder
Power: 89kW (120bhp)
0–96km/h (60mph): 13.3 secs
Top speed: 165km/h (102mph)
Production total: 41,250

AUSTIN 1100 AND 1300

1963–75

In 1959, the Mini was launched, to great acclaim. Designed by Alec Issigonis, it was a masterpiece of automotive packaging and innovation. From the Mini, Issigonis turned his attention to a larger family car – the 1100 range.

His new design was technically brilliant: the 1100 was remarkably spacious inside, thanks to clever touches and the neat layout of its transversely-mounted front-wheel drive A-series engine and integral transmission.

The suspension was by an interconnected Hydrolastic unit, which used fluid within rubber spheres as the springing medium. The cooling system was sealed, which put an end to the need to constantly top up the system and there were disc brakes at the front.

The 1100 was joined by a 1300

version in 1967, as well as a bewildering variety of badge-engineered variants. The range became Britain's bestseller, although it didn't make BMC as much money as it should have because of the cost of developing and building such an innovative design – the Mini suffered from the same problem.

Engine: 1275cc (78 cu in), 4-cylinder
Power: 43kW (58bhp)
0–96km/h (60mph): 17.3 secs
Top speed: 142km/h (88mph)
Production total: 1,119,800

For the era, this was one of the most modern cars. But while the front-wheel-drive was advantageous, the front-to-rear linked Hydrolastic suspension wasn't so good as these cars undulated over bumpy surfaces.

AUSTIN 1800 AND 2200

1964–75

Engine: 1798cc (110 cu in), 4-cylinder
Power: 60kW (80bhp)
0–96km/h (60mph): 17.1 secs
Top speed: 145km/h (90mph)
Production total: 221,000

Alec Issigonis had created the Morris Minor, the Mini and the bestselling 1100 range. Next he designed another clever front-wheel drive model that looked like

an oversized 1100. It won Car of the Year when it was launched.

The first version, the 1800, used a detuned MGB engine mounted transversely and linked to a new

front-wheel drive transmission. The suspension was, like the 1100, by the Hydrolastic system.

It could have been a great success. The 1800 was strong and very spacious but it was let down by extremely heavy steering, a poor driving position and an terrible gearchange. The steering was improved in 1967 with the option of power-assistance but there was another problem that was typical of Issigonis-designed cars – the spartan interior. This was acceptable in the Mini but the 1800 was trying to compete in a much more luxurious market.

In 1972, the 2200 arrived. To improve performance and refinement it was fitted with a six-cylinder engine, also mounted transversely. The engine was actually based on the four-cylinder Maxi E-series overhead camshaft unit and was unimpressive. This was a sad ending for the range now known as the Landcrabs.

Look how far apart the occupants of this 1800 are sitting – but this is no 1950s mock-up in which people were always drawn way too small to exaggerate the size of the car. It's simply a fine demonstration of the excellent interior packaging that Issigonis gave the range. Shame about the driving dynamics though.

AUSTIN 3-LITRE

The Austin 3-litre (178 cu in) took over from the Westminster as the company's offering in the big, prestige saloon market.

Based around the body of the 1800 range of cars, the front was updated with twin headlights and a new grille but otherwise there was little outward justification for the 3-litre's much higher price tag.

Under the bodywork, the car was rear-wheel drive, with a big six-cylinder 3-litre (178 cu in) engine that found no other applications except in the MGC. The rear suspension was self-levelling, and power steering and a sumptuous interior were standard. Options included an automatic gearbox or a manual with overdrive. On paper, this was an appealing package, but it did not qualify as a prestige car.

Engine: 2912cc (178 cu in), 6-cylinder
Power: 92kW (124bhp)
0–96km/h (60mph): 15.7 secs
Top speed: 161km/h (100mph)
Production total: 9992

AUSTIN MAXI

Engine: 1748cc (107 cu in), 4-cylinder
Power: 63kW (84bhp)
0–96km/h (60mph): 15.8 secs
Top speed: 144km/h (89mph)
Production total: 472,098

The Austin Maxi is now regarded as an embarrassing joke, but in fact it was basically a good car, spoilt by minor details and atrocious quality control, just like so many British-built cars of the 1970s.

The central section of the Maxi was taken from the Austin 1800, which provided a well-designed and very spacious cabin. The front and rear were new, formed by a hatchback at the back and a wide, modern-looking grille at the front.

The Maxi was actually Britain's first hatchback. The seats were designed to fold into a perfectly flat double bed, a feature that received undue amounts of attention in company advertising and magazine road tests.

Unfortunately, the gearchange was terrible and the new E-series overhead camshaft engine was poor, especially when linked to the clumsy five-speed gearbox. The suspension was initially by the Hydrolastic system but was later changed to the much better Hydragas, so the ride was good.

The engine increased in size from 1500cc (92 cu in) to 1750cc (107 cu in), which improved the car, but by then it was too late.

During the 1970s you couldn't move without seeing a Maxi, because on paper they seemed to offer so much, once again thanks to excellent interior packaging and the unusual (for the period) option of a five-speed gearbox. Sadly, terrible quality control killed most off.

AUSTIN ALLEGRO

1973–82

Engine: 1275cc (78 cu in), 4-cylinder
Power: 44kW (59bhp)
0–96km/h (60mph): 18.4 secs
Top speed: 132km/h (82mph)
Production total: 642,350

Once the bestselling 1100 became outdated a successor was needed. The company had already introduced a hatchback model (the Maxi) and all the signs were that this format would be a great success.

So BMC launched the Allegro, a car perfectly shaped and sized to be a hatchback, but this was never incorporated into the design. Instead what it did have was awkward, dumpy looks, atrocious build quality and a square steering wheel dubbed 'Quartic' by BMC.

Under the bodywork, the Allegro used either the old A-series engine or the new 1500cc (92 cu in) and 1750cc (107 cu in) E-series units. The Hydragas suspension was a step forward from the 1100's Hydrolastic system, so the ride was good, but there were so many reliability problems with early Allegros that the car's ride became

The Austin Allegro is a prime example of what went wrong with the British car industry: missed opportunities and a fair measure of manufacturing mistakes. All the same, the Allegro demonstrated sufficient character to now attract a band of dedicated followers.

irrelevant. The structure was so poor that the rear window would sometimes pop out on bumpy roads and rust was also a problem.

As the years passed, the Allegro certainly improved but it never became good-looking or particularly enjoyable to drive. An estate was

launched which was so ugly that the saloon became desirable by comparison. Finally, a luxury Vanden Plas version was offered with a ridiculous pseudo-Rolls-Royce grille grafted onto the front. This terrible and much-derided car was finally dropped in 1982.

AUSTIN 18-22 SERIES

1975

This strange-looking, wedge-shaped car is better known as the Princess, but it started life as the Austin 18-22 Series, the replacement for the 1800/2200 'Landcrab' models.

It was styled by Harris Mann, the same man responsible for the much-derided looks of the Allegro.

The 18-22's suspension was Hydragas, just like the Allegro's, but the engines were borrowed straight from the Landcrab, providing a choice of either a four-cylinder B-series unit or a six-cylinder version of the Maxi and Allegro's E-series motor.

Although the shape of the 18-22

For all the quality control problems, British Leyland were brave enough to experiment with new styles, like the wedge shape of the 18-22 penned by Harris Mann. At the other end of the spectrum, William Town's radical design of the Aston Martin Lagonda demonstrated a similar shape.

lent itself to a hatchback, instead a conventional bootlid was fitted. However, the interior of the 18-22 was very spacious and comfortable. The advertising for the car claimed that this was 'not a car for Mr Average', and after six months it dropped the Austin name and became a separate Princess brand, taking the Morris and Wolseley names, also owned by the British Leyland group, with it.

The Series II, from 1978, was fitted with the new O-series engine, but the older six-cylinder 2200cc (134 cu in) unit was still available. The car was eventually reworked in 1981 to become the hatchback Austin Ambassador, but the reappearance of the Austin name tag indicated that the company's attempts to create a separate Princess brand had failed.

Engine: 1798cc (110 cu in), 4-cylinder
Power: 61kW (82bhp)
0–96km/h (60mph): 14.9 secs
Top speed: 155km/h (96mph)
Production total: 43,427

AUSTIN-HEALEY 100

The 'Big' Healeys were the archetypal British sports cars – unsophisticated and noisy, but effective and great fun. The first of the line was the 100. The Donald Healey Motor Company had been in business since 1946, producing low-volume sports tourers and sports cars like the Westland and the Silverstone. But Donald Healey spotted a gap in the market for a more affordable two-seater, to be sold between the offerings from MG and Jaguar. A small team started to work on a prototype, known as the Healey Hundred, in 1952.

Donald Healey's son, Geoffrey, designed the chassis in conjunction with Healey employee Barry Bilbie, while the body styling was provided by a relative newcomer to Healey, Gerry Coker. Donald Healey had the final say over the look of the car. Many of the defining features of the 100, such as the reclining windscreen, came about through offhand comments and instructions from Healey. For the windscreen, he said, 'Oh, by the way, make the windshield lay down.'

The prototype was built in aluminium by coachbuilders Tickford. The engine, a 2.6-litre (162 cu in) six-cylinder unit, and much of the running gear was borrowed from the Austin A90 (Healey had previously used running gear from Riley, Alvis and various other sources). The seats were a straight copy of those in Coker's own Austin Seven.

The prototype was taken to Belgium in October 1952, where it set a speed record of 179km/h (111mph) for its size of sports car. The car was then taken back to the UK in time for the 1952 Earls Court Motor Show in London. Legend has it that the prototype appeared on preview day as the Healey Hundred but an overnight meeting between Donald Healey and Leonard Lord of Austin resulted in a deal that saw the car rebadged for the first public day of the show as the Austin-Healey 100. However, it seems that Lord and Healey had already discussed such a deal. Austin needed a credible sports car to boost its profile, especially in the United States, while Healey needed a company that could build its new model at relatively high volumes.

While the Healey Motor

Company built a small batch of pre-production 100s, and Donald Healey toured the United States drumming up orders for the new car, Austin geared up its Longbridge plant for a planned production of 200 Austin-Healey 100s a month. At first there were problems, with some animosity between the Healey designers and those at Austin, who had been instructed not to meddle with the original plans for the car. The first 100 left the Longbridge production line in May 1953 but by July, only 100 had been made – a serious shortfall which left many orders unfulfilled.

After a few months, though, production settled down. The motoring press loved the 100 and orders continued to flood in, helped by the publicity gained by more record-breaking and racing in the

In typical Big Healey style, this car sits a little tail-down, leaving the exhaust ground-scrapingly low. But that was an accepted downside of owning and driving one of the best-looking and most exciting affordable sports cars of the time.

Mille Miglia, Le Mans and in the Carrera Pan Americana.

The Le Mans-specification racers were inspired by a factory upgrade kit for owners who wanted to put their cars on the track. The kit could be retro-fitted or included in the specification of new Austin-Healey 100s, which were then named 100Ms. By 1955, the 100M became a true production model; it was joined by another new model, the legendary 100S, which was a true competition car, with lightweight aluminium panels, no hood or bumpers, a high-output engine and disc brakes front and rear.

In the same year, the 100 was upgraded from its original BN1 specification to BN2, which featured a new four-speed overdrive gearbox (replacing the old three-speed one), improved front drum brakes and higher front wheelarch cut-outs. This model continued in production until mid-1956, by which time the Austin-Healey 100 was a best-seller, and well known for its track exploits.

Engine: 2660cc (162 cu in), 4-cylinder
Power: 67kW (90bhp)
0–96km/h (60mph): 10.3 secs
Top speed: 166km/h (103mph)
Production total: 14,634

AUSTIN-HEALEY 100-SIX

1956–59

Engine: 2639cc (161 cu in), 6-cylinder
Power: 76kW (102bhp)
0–96km/h (60mph): 12.9 secs
Top speed: 166km/h (103mph)
Production total: 14,436

The original four-cylinder Austin-Healey 100 was a fine sports car, but by the mid-1950s changes were needed. The crucial US market was looking for more luxury and Austin's big four-cylinder engine, which powered the 100, was going out of production.

So the 100 received a major update. A small number of prototypes, named 100-Six BN3s, were built using BMC's six-cylinder 2.6-litre (161 cu in) C-series engine, before going into full production in 1956, as the 100-Six BN4.

The 100-Six was given a 5cm (2in) longer wheelbase than the previous model to accommodate two small seats in the back, and the general specification was improved.

Unfortunately, the new engine added weight to the car and only produced 9kW (12bhp) more than the previous four-cylinder unit, resulting in blunted performance. In 1957, an improved version of the C-series engine was fitted with more power to remedy this problem.

Donald Healey experimented with a no-frills, low-cost version of the 100-Six, known as the BN5, but the project was dropped, so the next version of the 100-Six came in 1958, called the 100-Six BN6. This returned to the old two-seater format (built concurrently with the BN4) and was the car that initiated Healey's now-legendary rallying success across the world.

It's easy to assume the Big Healey was fitted with a six-cylinder engine to improve it. Actually, it was a measure to overcome the demise of the four-cylinder engine. All the same, the 100-Six continued the high levels of driver enjoyment set by the original 100.

AUSTIN-HEALEY SPRITE

1958–70

As the 1950s progressed, Donald Healey spotted another opportunity in the world motoring market – this time for a small, cheap sports car.

Once again, the Healey team set to work. Despite the tie-up with Austin, no design budget was made available, although Healey was free to use existing production parts. And so, a no-frills, open-top sports car, the Sprite, was engineered by Geoffrey Healey and styled by Gerry Coker.

The new car used the 948cc (58 cu in) BMC A-series engine from the Austin A35, along with the A35's gearbox, axle and front and rear suspension. The steering and brakes came from the Morris Minor. With its pod-mounted headlights, the Sprite soon gained the nickname 'Frogeye' (in the UK) and 'Bugeye' (in the United States). It wasn't particularly fast, but it felt nimble and the responsive handling ensured that it was great fun to drive. Competition success soon followed and sales soared.

The specification of the first Sprite was extremely basic – that front bumper was an optional extra and most came with steel disc wheels, not the wires that this example is shown with. But that didn't affect the fun factor at all, a characteristic which remained through several updates.

In 1961, the Sprite evolved into the Sprite Mk II, alongside the near-identical MG Midget Mk I. Over the years, the specification was improved, with disc brakes and 1098cc (67 cu in) and then 1275cc (78 cu in) engines. But the deal between Donald Healey and Austin terminated at the end of 1970, so in 1971 the model became the Austin Sprite, before being dropped six months later.

Engine: 948cc (58 cu in) 6-cylinder
Power: 32kW (43bhp)
0–96km/h (60mph): 20.5 secs
Top speed: 139km/h (86mph)
Production total: 129,350 approx

AUSTIN-HEALEY 3000

1959–68

Arguably the most famous of all Big Healeys was the 3000 series, which ran from 1959 to 1968. The 3000 started out as a simple upgrade to the previous 100-Six models, adding BMC's new 2.9-litre (178 cu in) version of the C-series six-cylinder engine, as well as front discs brakes.
Two versions were available, the two-seater BN7 and the 2+2 BT7 – the latter being by far the more

popular choice. With more power than the previous 2.6-litre (161 cu in) 100-Six models, the 3000's performance was impressive, with Autocar testing the car to 187km/h (116mph).
In 1961, the models were updated, to become the 3000 Mk II BN7 and BT7. The next model to appear was the 1962 3000 Mk II BJ7, with a proper fold-down hood and wind-down windows.

This new luxury continued with the 1963 3000 Mk III BJ8 Phase I, which incorporated a restyled fascia using walnut and a new centre console. But it wasn't until 1964, and the BJ8 Phase II, that one of the car's greatest failings – its lack of ground clearance – was finally addressed. The chassis was redesigned to remedy this problem – the last major change made to the Big Healey.

Engine: 2912cc (178 cu in), 6-cylinder
Power: 98kW (132bhp)
0–96km/h (60mph): 11.5 secs
Top speed: 180km/h (112mph)
Production total: 42,926

This Austin Healey 3000 has a proper folding hood, so it's a 1962-on model. It also has a luxurious interior and improved ground clearance, which mark it as the final, 1964-on BJ8 Phase II.

AUTOBIANCHI BIANCHINA

1957–68

Autobianchi is a car name you rarely hear, and yet the company has played a major part in the Italian car industry over the years. It started off with a different name though – simply Bianchi, taking its name from Edoardo Bianchi, who formed the company in 1899.
Bianchi produced cars and motorcycles, competing with the mighty Fiat in some markets. Its

car production was stopped after World War II, though, leading to severe financial problems. In 1955, an Italian industrialist arranged for Bianchi, Fiat and Pirelli to form a new company – Autobianchi.
This company built the Bianchina, a good-looking coupé rebody of the Fiat 500, which soon became available as a cabriolet as well. A Panoramica estate version

and the Berlina Quattroposti four-seater saloon were then offered. All were reasonably successful.
By 1963, Autobianchi was wholly owned by Fiat. Specific Autobianchi models continued into the 1980s, and included the Stellina sports car, the Primula saloon and the long-lasting A112, which was even modified by tuning specialists, Abarth.

In the 1990s, the Autobianchi name was used on the Lancia Y10 in certain markets but the division also served as a testing house for new Fiats.

Engine: 479cc (29 cu in), twin-cylinder
Power: 10kW (13bhp)
0–96km/h (60mph): n/a
Top speed: 100km/h (62mph)
Production total: 273,800

BEAN TWELVE

1919–27

Established in Dudley in the West Midlands, England in 1910, A Harper Sons and Bean started building cars in 1919. Originally, the company was a component supplier to other makers, but it acquired the rights to build the pre-war World War I Perry, sold in the US by Willys Overland, under licence.

The Bean Twelve was effectively this car, although as many as 90 per cent of the components were redesigned by Bean and produced in-house. The car offered superb value for money and was cheaper than rivals from Austin and Morris. But ultimately, it was just a bit too old-fashioned to appeal to those younger buyers.

It had a peerless reputation for reliability, however, and many remained in service for more than two decades thanks to their tough and reliable construction and mechanical simplicity.

Engine: 1796cc (110 cu in), 4-cylinder
Power: n/a
0–96km/h (60mph): n/a
Top speed: n/a
Production total: 10,000 approx

BEARDMORE 15.6

1928–30

Prior to World War I, most of Beardmore's income came from shipbuilding and armaments manufacture. However, its strong financial position – largely due to founder Sir William Beardmore's vast wealth – saw it gain many post-war contracts including the construction of cars and – more importantly – taxi cabs.

The first Beardmore taxis entered service in 1919 and were freighted to London by rail, and by the time the 15.6 appeared in 1928, over 6000 earlier models were already plying their trade in England's capital city.

The 15.9 added to this total considerably. Although no production records were kept, at least 4000 were licensed in London between 1928 and 1930, while others entered service in major cities across Britain. Beardmores were designed to be easy to own and maintain, so returned good fuel economy and needed minimal servicing. The driver sat alone at the front of the cab, with seating for four in the enclosed rear cabin.

Such was the demand for the Beardmore taxis in London that a separate factory was built there in 1930 to supply cabs to the city.

Engine: 1500cc (92 cu in), 4-cylinder
Power: n/a
0–96km/h (60mph): n/a
Top speed: n/a
Production total: n/a

BENTLEY 3-LITRE

1919–29

Engine: 2996cc (183 cu in), 4-cylinder
Power: n/a
0–96km/h (60mph): n/a
Top speed: 161km/h (100mph)
Production total: 1622

Not satisfied with any other cars on the market, London-based salesman WO Bentley decided to build his own expensive sports machine. The first Bentley 3-Litre was shown at the 1919 London Motor Show, although cars weren't available to the public until 1921.

Two lengths of chassis were available, while the colour of the radiator badge clarified the model's purpose. Red Label models were short-chassis, speed-orientated cars, Blue Label ones had a longer chassis and were designed to have formal coachwork added, while Green Label cars were those capable of at least 161km/h (100mph).

It was these Green Label cars that made Bentley famous, proving their reliability and performance at the Le Mans 24-hour race, winning outright in 1924 and 1927.

While the 3-litre was very fast for a four-cylinder model, with its unusually long stroke and four valves per cylinder, it was a difficult car to drive, with an awkward gear change, two-wheel brakes, a sharp clutch and little in the way of cabin comforts. The 3-Litre wasn't a huge commercial success, and were it not for the finances of millionaire racer Woolf Barnato, who funded Bentley from 1925 until it merged with Rolls-Royce in 1931, the company could easily have gone bankrupt.

A car of the highest order, the Bentley 3-Litre was developed to satisfy wealthy sports car fans who couldn't find anything else to suit.

BENTLEY 6.5-LITRE/SPEED SIX

1926–30

Engine: 6597cc (403 cu in), 6-cylinder
Power: 104kW (140bhp)
0–96km/h (60mph): n/a
Top speed: n/a
Production total: 545

Bentley did such a good job of creating a rival to Rolls-Royce that the two companies eventually merged, but not until a select group of owners had swapped their Rolls-Royces for one of WO Bentley's

more sports-orientated machines.

The 6.5-Litre appeared in 1926 and cost £1450 for the chassis alone, while coachbuilt bodywork was extra. It used an all-new 6597cc (403 cu in) overhead camshaft engine with 24 valves – years before such engine technology would become commonplace. The car was much easier to drive than the Bentley 3-Litre, with a single plate clutch and right-hand

gearchange. The 104kW (140bhp) 6.5-litre was joined by the awesome 134kW (180bhp) Speed Six in 1928 – and a distinctive Gurney Nutting-bodied example was bought and used as daily transport by Bentley financier Woolf Barnato.

Although most 6.5-Litres were sold as luxury touring cars, a few were stripped down and used for racing, with Bentley once again

taking the Le Mans crown in 1929 and 1930. Many cars had a sad demise, being stripped down and used as racing specials with replica Le Mans bodywork.

Unlike the 3-Litre, the Bentley 6.5-Litre was developed as a luxury car with all the trimmings. This is the Gurney Nutting-bodied example driven by Woolf Barnato.

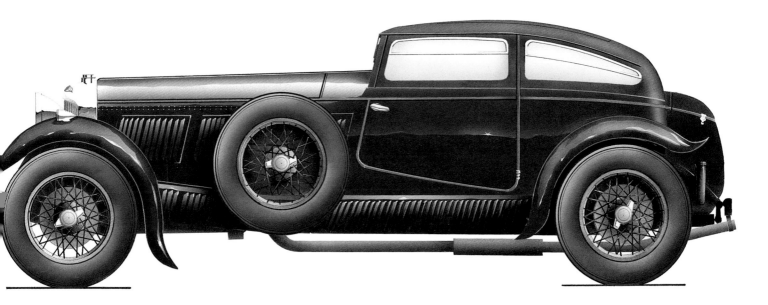

BENTLEY 4.5-LITRE

1927–31

Engine: 4398cc (268 cu in), 4-cylinder
Power: 77kW (104bhp)
0–96km/h (60mph): n/a
Top speed: 178km/h (110mph)
Production total: 720

The 4.5-Litre was the last four-cylinder Bentley, although its engine was really only a smaller version of the 6.5-Litre unit, sharing the same bore and stroke.

In most instances, the 4.5-Litre was quite a heavy car and didn't really feel as sporting as previous Bentley models, although sales were good enough to justify the appearance of a smaller model in the Bentley range.

Bentley team racing driver Sir Henry Birkin was disappointed with the 4.5-litre's performance and went to WO Bentley to discover if something could be done to improve it.

Bentley told Henry Birkin this was not necessary, as the 6.5-Litre was the vehicle that was intended for racing. In any case, the 4.5-Litre competed at Le Mans in 1928 and still managed to win.

But Birkin wasn't convinced by this and set about building a much more powerful version himself by fitting a supercharger. Fifty-five of the famous 'Blower Bentley' models were then built, all of which were constructed against WO Bentley's express wishes.

And although the Blower Bentleys' racing successes became legendary, WO Bentley never accepted any part in the project.

Thanks to racing driver Sir Henry Birkin, 55 Bentley 4.5-Litres were fitted with superchargers. The 'Blower Bentley' went on to become a racing legend.

BENTLEY MK VI

1946–52

Engine: 4257cc (260 cu in), 6-cylinder
Power: 102kW (137bhp)
0–96km/h (60mph): 16.3 secs
Top speed: 152km/h (94mph)
Production total: 5201

After a decade of being Rolls-Royce's sporting arm and using modified Rolls-Royce chassis, Bentley returned to an individual design for its first post-war model

launch. Rolls-Royce borrowed the MK VI's compact body styling for the Silver Dawn – an export-only model built to satisfy demand for compact luxury cars overseas.

The Mk VI was launched in 1946 and featured standard separate chassis construction. In other respects, it was very modern, with servo-assisted brakes, a four-speed gearbox and independent

front suspension.

The car was also another first for Bentley, as it offered a standard body style rather than just a chassis on which buyers could specify their own coachbuilt design.

Traditionalists could still have handcrafted bodies if they wanted – but at a price. Aluminium-bodied Park Ward, HJ Mulliner and James Young styles were very much a

The grille and rear wheelarch treatment are different, but the Bentley Mk VI is essentially the same as a Rolls-Royce Silver Dawn.

symbol of wealth, costing more than twice the price of a standard car. Reliable, comfortable, but not as exciting as Bentleys of old, the Mk VI was still an exquisitely well-made vehicle.

BENTLEY R-TYPE

1952–55

Criticisms of the MK VI's bulky bodywork were addressed in 1952 with the appearance of the R-Type. The new car again came with a standard body, but the chassis was longer and the bodywork more evenly proportioned, with a raked

rear end, sweeping wheelguards and streamlined front wings.

The bulky curves made access to the back seats difficult, however, while the car's small centre section meant accommodation in the cabin was cramped for such a large car.

The HJ Mulliner Continental Fastback (pictured) is widely regarded as one of the most beautiful and stylish cars ever made. Globally respected by collectors, it commands huge figures when offered at auction.

Power came from Rolls-Royce's acclaimed 4.5-litre (279 cu in) six-cylinder engine, with inlet-over-exhaust valves. This gave good performance and refined operation, which, married to excellent interior insulation, made the car a quiet cruiser.

Standard-bodied cars were mechanically tough, but rusted badly. A variety of coachbuilt bodies were also on offer, perhaps the most famous of which was the HJ Mulliner Continental R fastback, which is regarded as one of the most stunning car designs of all time. Most specials were aluminium and, therefore, did not rot.

Engine: 4566cc (279 cu in), 6-cylinder
Power: 112kW (150bhp)
0–96km/h (60mph): 14.4 secs
Top speed: 172km/h (106mph)
Production total: 2320

BENTLEY S-SERIES

Some said the S-Series was the end of Bentley's individuality, since the cars were just badge-engineered Rolls-Royce Silver Clouds. Although this was true, it did mean the cars were exceptionally well-built, refined and luxurious.

The S1, launched in 1955, used a 4.9-litre (298 cu in) six with inlet-over-exhaust valves and was the standard car in the range from 1959 to 1962. Also launched at the same time was the S1 Continental – a two-door grand tourer available as a hardtop or rare drophead coupé.

Major developments occurred in 1959 with the appearance of the S2, which was visually similar, but came with an all-new 6.2-litre (378 cu in) V8 developed for the Rolls-Royce Silver Cloud. Power steering and automatic transmission came as standard in all V8-engined cars.

A Continental version of the S2 appeared with the same mechanical changes and a few front end styling changes, while S3 versions of the saloon and Continental both appeared in 1962. The saloon had twin headlights and two-tone paintwork, while the Continental acquired highly unusual front end styling and angled headlights.

The unusual front end treatment of the Bentley S-Type S3 (above) earned it the nickname 'Chinese Eye' from the press. Earlier cars had conventional headlamps.

Engine: 4887cc (298 cu in), 6-cylinder
Power: 130kW (175bhp)
0–96km/h (60mph): 13.7 secs
Top speed: 170km/h (105mph)
Production total: approx 8000

BENTLEY T-SERIES

Launched concurrently with the Rolls-Royce Silver Shadow, the T1 was the first Bentley to have unitary construction bodywork. Like the Silver Shadow, it featured disc brakes all-round and Citroën-developed self-levelling suspension, although the Bentley had a firmer, more sports-like ride.

Other differences between the two included a different grille with no bonnet mascot on the Bentley, as well as restyled wheeltrims and no long-wheelbase option.

All cars came with air conditioning from 1969 onwards, while in 1970, the original 6230cc (380 cu in) engine, carried over from the S3, was increased in size to 6750cc (412 cu in). Since the unit was made by Rolls-Royce, the power output was a closely guarded secret (a standard Rolls-Royce practice), although most enthusiasts agree it is about 134kW (180bhp).

The T2 followed, though less than 600 were built between 1977 and 1980. Like the Silver Shadow 2 on which it was based, the T2 featured thick rubber impact bumpers and an entirely new fascia, as well as large side repeater lamps. New rack-and-pinion steering and suspension modifications made the T2 a better car to drive than the T1.

Engine: 6750cc (412 cu in), V8-cylinder
Power: n/a
0–96km/h (60mph): 10.1 secs
Top speed: 194km/h (120mph)
Production total: 2280

Only the grille and wheeltrims are externally different from the Rolls-Royce Silver Shadow. This is a rare two-door version.

BENTLEY CORNICHE

1971–84

Like the T-Series, the Corniche was simply a Rolls-Royce with different trim and badges. This is an American-spec car, identifiable by its large side reflectors.

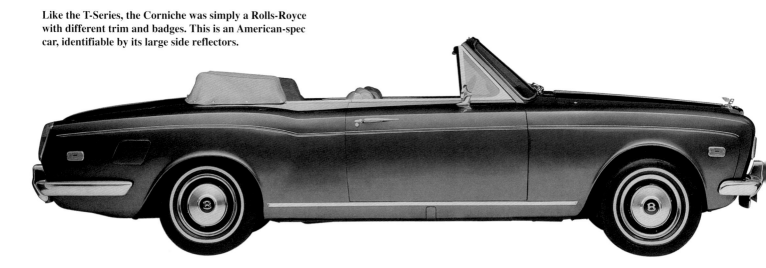

Engine: 6750cc (412 cu in), V8-cylinder
Power: n/a
0–96km/h (60mph): 9.9 secs
Top speed: 194km/h (120mph)
Production total: 149

Although a convertible version of the Bentley T1 was available from 1967, it wasn't until 1971 that it became a recognized model in the range, the Corniche.

Cars made between 1967 and 1971 were specially bodied by Mulliner Park Ward, and Rolls-Royce was so pleased with the results that by 1971 it had incorporated the Corniche versions of both the Bentley T1 and its own Silver Shadow into its standard model range.

Also available was a Corniche two-door saloon, launched in 1971, although very few were built with Bentley badges.

Production changes were similar to those of the saloon, with cruise control and ventilated disc brakes appearing from 1972 and split-level air conditioning from 1976. 1977 models onward came with

thicker bumpers and rubber front spoiler from the Bentley T2.

Although a Rolls-Royce Corniche stayed in the range right up until 1997, Bentley versions were dropped in 1984 and would remain absent until the Continental name made a welcome comeback in 1994, based on the platform of the Turbo R.

BENTLEY MULSANNE

1980–92

Badge engineering continued with the launch of the Mulsanne in 1980, but Rolls-Royce was starting to appreciate and celebrate Bentley's heritage. This proved to be a crucial factor in the firm's

survival towards the end of the 20th century, when the opulence suggested by the Rolls-Royce name became unfashionable.

The Mulsanne was named after the famous start-finish straight at

Le Mans – the scene of many a Bentley past glory – but in all other regards, the car was a reworked Rolls-Royce Silver Spirit.

Bentley versions differed by way of a matt black radiator insert,

alloy wheels with Bentley logos and sports-tailored seats, proving this was a car aimed at the owner-driver rather than one who liked to be chauffeured. Bentley's real revival occurred in 1982, with the Mulsanne Turbo.

The turbocharged engine was exclusive to Bentley and gave the Mulsanne a significant performance advantage over the Rolls Royce Silver Spirit, with a 0–96km/h (60mph) sprint time of less than seven seconds and a chassis that could cope with its power far better than its bulky looks suggested.

Engine: 6750cc (412 cu in), V8-cylinder
Power: n/a
0–96km/h (60mph): 6.8 secs
Top speed: 207km/h (128mph)
Production total: 2039

It looked like a Rolls-Royce Silver Spirit, but the Bentley Mulsanne Turbo had a completely different character. Although it was enormously fast, unfortunately the handling could be unpredictable.

BENTLEY EIGHT

Realizing the Rolls-Royce name was becoming unfashionable, bosses at the factory in Crewe, Cheshire, decided to promote the Bentley through the 1980s. The Eight was a very clever marketing exercise, aimed squarely at buyers who would otherwise have bought a Silver Spirit, and it was priced at a similar level.

It was instantly recognizable as a Bentley by its twin headlights, front spoiler and ornate mesh radiator grille, while levels of luxury and refinement remained unsurpassed. Slab-sided looks were compensated for by vibrant colours and sport-like alloy wheels, and while the Eight never enjoyed the same sales success as its Rolls-Royce cousin – accounting for about 10 per cent of sales orders from Crewe – it was popular enough to ensure Bentley's long-term revival and kept its sporting reputation intact.

Engine: 6750cc (412 cu in), V8-cylinders
Power: n/a
0–96km/h (60mph): 9.6 secs
Top speed: 207km/h (128mph)
Production total: 1734

BENTLEY TURBO R

Engine: 6750cc (412 cu in), V8-cylinder
Power: 238kW (320bhp)
0–96km/h (60mph): 6.6 secs
Top speed: 218km/h (135mph)
Production total: 4815

The 'Blower Bentley' made a celebrated return in the mid-1980s – and WO Bentley certainly wouldn't have approved. Not only did the car come equipped with a supercharger, which he famously despised, but once again it also shared its platform with a unitary construction Rolls-Royce.

Whether WO would have liked it or not, this was a Bentley in the sporting mould for which the company was famous. The press loved it, and that was enough to secure over 4000 sales in an 11-year career – for a hand-built car, these were significant figures.

To drivers, the Bentley had two distinctly different characters. In normal day-to-day use it was as refined, silent and easy to drive as its Rolls-Royce Silver Spirit sibling. Yet if you found a test track and pushed the accelerator, the Turbo R was a powerful car with alarming tendencies towards lift-off oversteer. Top speed was electronically limited to 218km/h (135mph), as Bentley couldn't find any tyres strong enough to cope

The Turbo R was based on the Rolls-Royce Silver Spirit and shared identical bodywork, but was a more sporting machine, with alloy wheels and a much more performance-oriented suspension set-up.

with the car's immense weight. Rumour has it unrestricted versions could top 270km/h (170mph). Production ceased in 1996 to make way for the Arnage.

BENZ VIKTORIA

1892–1900

Engine: 1724cc (105 cu in), single-cylinder
Power: 3kW (4bhp)
0–96km/h (60mph): n/a
Top speed: 20km/h (13mph)
Production total: n/a

Hailed by many as the father of the motor car, Karl Benz built his first 'cyclecar' in Mannheim, Germany, in 1885. The primitive three-wheeler was the first car to use an internal combustion engine and quickly became the blueprint from which other pioneers developed new and interesting ideas.

After initial sales of three-wheelers were slow, Benz introduced the four-wheeled Viktoria in 1892, although pneumatic tyres and suspension had still not been developed.

It was an important part of motoring history, however, as it was the first car to complete a documented 1000km (621-mile) journey. Czech businessman Theodore von Gondorf – a textiles millionaire – drove one in 1893 from Liberec to Koblenz without breaking down and that very car still survives today in the Czech Republic's national motor museum.

Karl Benz is credited as the inventor of the motor car as we know it – the Viktoria was his company's first four-wheeled example.

The Viktoria used a primitive single-cylinder engine. However, its replacement, the Parsifal, came with a choice of two-cylinder motors with varying power outputs which in top specification could reach speeds of up to 62km/h (40mph).

BERKELEY 322/328

1956–58

In the mid-1950s, a caravan manufacturer, the Berkeley Coachwork Company, commissioned small-time vehicle manufacturer Laurie Bond to design a new car – the Berkeley Sports 322.

Laurie Bond already had a reputation for clever, innovative design work, having produced the Bond Minicar (a Villiers-powered three-wheeler) and developed the Unicar for another manufacturer,

using glassfibre for the bodywork. The caravan company, meanwhile, had become expert in the use of glassfibre and this was, not altogether unsurprisingly, the material used for the new car.

The vehicle was a small but well-proportioned sports car, powered by a 322cc (20 cu in) Anzani two-cylinder two-stroke engine. This was later changed to a 328cc (20 cu in) Excelsior twin. Gearboxes had three speeds, except for late models which had four speeds, and all had a chain drive to the front wheels.

Because the cars were so small and light they were surprisingly fast and are still sought-after today.

Engine: 328cc (20 cu in), 2-cylinder
Power: 13kW (18bhp)
0–96km/h (60mph): n/a
Top speed: 105km/h (65mph)
Production total: 1418

The sleek, shrouded headlights and smooth curves along the front and rear wings have all the trademarks of a great-looking sports car. It's only when you see the height of the screen (or see someone sitting in the car) that you realize how small it is.

BERKELEY T60

Engine: 328cc (20 cu in), 2-cylinder
Power: 13kW (18bhp)
0–96km/h (60mph): n/a
Top speed: 97km/h (60mph)
Production total: 1830

The combination of Laurie Bond's designs and the backing and manufacturing expertise of the Berkeley Coachwork Company (a caravan manufacturer) was a successful formula for some time. The original four-wheeler baby sports cars, the 323 and 328, were updated to become the 492, and then the B95 and B105 (the numbers denote their respective top speeds).

But Laurie Bond liked three-wheelers, so it was almost inevitable that at least one of Berkeley's cars would be designed in this format. The car that emerged was the T60, a neat-looking sports car which tapered into a semi-point at the rear end.

Having just three wheels kept weight to an absolute minimum, so that the 328cc (20 cu in) Excelsior motorcycle engine that powered the T60 was still able to

provide good acceleration. In fact, the T60 was a fun car to drive, with decent handling despite the single rear wheel.

A handful of later T60s came

with a rear seat and more cars might have been made but for the collapse of the parent caravan company, which inevitably ended all car production.

Making the T60 a three-wheeler did not give it much of a disadvantage over other sports cars. The front wheels were driven in a Berkeley – the wheel deficit reduced weight.

BITTER CD

Engine: 5354cc (327 cu in), V8-cylinder
Power: 171kW (230bhp)
0–96km/h (60mph): 9.4 secs
Top speed: 208km/h (129mph)
Production total: 395

In the late 1960s, Opel developed a good-looking concept car called the Styling CD, based on a shortened Diplomat chassis, but decided that it wasn't practical for

the company to produce. In 1970, Italian styling house Frua took over the design and updated it a little, but still the car didn't make it into production.

But Erich Bitter, a racing driver and an agent for Abarth and Intermeccanica cars, had seen the Styling CD at the 1969 Frankfurt Motor Show and was determined to develop it. He had close links with Opel, having raced for the company, and decided to start his own company to produce the car.

He chose Baur of Stuttgart to build the car, using a modified Diplomat chassis, as originally intended. Opel helped him to develop the design, and Bitter chose to power the new car with a Chevrolet 327 V8 engine.

The first showing of the car was in 1973 at the Frankfurt Motor Show, where Bitter took 176 orders. Unfortunately, the then oil crisis resulted in a loss of business. But sales did pick up again, and the CD was produced until 1979.

Why isn't the Bitter CD as revered as, say, the De Tomaso Pantera? Perhaps it's because it's German-made and lacks the glamour of the truly Italian supercars.

BITTER SC

Engine: 3848cc (235 cu in), 6-cylinder
Power: 156kW (210bhp)
0–96km/h (60mph): 9 secs
Top speed: 210km/h (130mph)
Production total: 450

It is often said that the Bitter SC looks like a Ferrari 400. This is true, perhaps because the styling and much of the manufacture was undertaken in Italy, but under the skin there was the much more mundane running gear from the Opel Senator.

Erich Bitter developed the SC as a replacement for his previous car, the CD, with some help from Opel. But he also employed Italian stylists Michelotti for engineering detail and Pininfarina for aerodynamics, while the body itself had to be built in Italy because Baur (where the CD had been built) had no capacity to build the SC.

Firstly, the manufacture of the bodies went to OCRA in Turin, but when early cars exhibited chronic rust problems, Bitter found out that the company had been using recycled steel. So he turned to Maggiore, where Maserati and

Bristol bodies were also being produced at the time.

The SC sold reasonably well even though early versions with an Opel 3-litre (183 cu in) engine weren't particularly quick. A later 3.9-litre (235 cu in) unit was a

massive improvement, and Bitter even introduced long-wheelbase and cabriolet versions. However, profits margins were always tight, and production had to end in the mid-1980s, despite the fact that the SC was an excellent machine.

As exclusive cars go, the Bitter SC is one of the most useable, thanks to its Opel-sourced running gear. But it lacks glamour, despite Italian styling, while the performance isn't awe-inspiring. Those who own them swear by them, though.

BIZZARRINI GT STRADA 5300

The GT Strada 5300 was the product of Giotto Bizzarrini, one of Ferrari's best designers and creator of the superlative Ferrari 250GTO.

However, Bizzarrini later had an argument with Enzo Ferrari and left the company determined to

produce his own car, which he hoped would beat Ferrari's offerings. He set up an engineering and consultancy business and worked initially for Lamborghini and Renzo Rivolta, designing the Iso Grifo, as well as working for

Ferrari on the ASA 1000GT (arguments with Enzo Ferrari were quite common and usually swiftly forgotten by Ferrari, especially if it was convenient to do so).

In 1964, Bizzarrini raced a lightweight Iso Grifo at Le Mans,

winning the GT class. He then negotiated a deal to produce a lightweight version of the two-seater Grifo under his own name. This became the GT Strada 5300.

Like the Iso, the Strada was powered by a Chevrolet V8 engine. Its low-slung body was designed by Giugiaro and was available in aluminium or glassfibre. But the Strada faced tough competition, including Chevrolet's own Corvette, and few sold.

Engine: 5343cc (326 cu in), V8-cylinder
Power: 272kW (365bhp)
0–96km/h (60mph): n/a
Top speed: 258km/h (160mph)
Production total: 149

When the creator of the Ferrari 250GTO set out to build a competitor, the result was bound to be spectacular. The GT Strada always lost out to the 250GTO, though, although lately its more affordable price tag has added to its appeal over the GTO.

BIZZARRINI 1900 EUROPA

1967–69

Giotto Bizzarrini, having left Ferrari, decided to build his own cars. The first was the Chevrolet V8-engined Strada which was based on the Iso Grifo but with its own Giugiaro-styled body. The second car was intended to be more affordable.

This 'affordable' Bizzarrini was the Europa, which arrived by coincidence in the same year that Lotus launched its own Europa. The Bizzarrini version used a scaled-down version of the aggressively low, pointed Strada body around a steel platform chassis, with independent suspension and disc brakes all round.

But the Strada's V8 engine was replaced by Opel's four-cylinder overhead camshaft 1.9-litre (116 cu in) unit. In such a lightweight car, this wasn't as ineffective as it sounds but the car was almost as expensive as the Strada, which itself wasn't selling well. Not surprisingly, the Europa was unsuccessful and Bizzarrini's company closed down soon after.

You'd feel a million dollars turning up in this. A million dollars, that is, until any sharp-eyed car fanatic pointed out its 1.9-litre engine.

Engine: 1897cc (116 cu in), 4-cylinder
Power: 101kW (135bhp)
0–96km/h (60mph): n/a
Top speed: 206km/h (128mph)
Production total: 15

BMW DIXI 3/15

1927–31

Long before the BMW name appeared, cars were being built in a factory in Eisenach (later to become part of East Germany). In fact, car production started there in 1896 and, by 1904, the company had adopted the name Dixi. The firm struggled on into the late 1920s, often on the verge of bankruptcy.

Then Dixi licensed the production of the Austin Seven. Dixi's version, called the 3/15 DA-1, was introduced in 1927 and immediately became a bestseller. However, Dixi's founder had other business interests, so in 1928 he sold Dixi to a motorcycle and aircraft engine manufacturer, the Bayerische Motoren Werke – BMW.

The 3/15 DA-1 (3 stood for the number of gears, 15 for the horsepower and DA for German version) was built as a saloon, roadster, tourer and coupé. It was updated in 1929 to become the DA-2, with larger doors and four-wheel mechanical brakes, and this was followed by the DA-3, a tiny two-seater sportster. The final version was the DA-4, another basic but well-built saloon. By 1931, 25,000 3/15s had been produced and BMW was established as a carmaker.

An Austin Seven? No, a BMW-to-be, thanks to a deal by Austin that effectively launched BMW into the big time – and helped Austin raise funds into the bargain.

Engine: 747cc (46 cu in), 4-cylinder
Power: 11kW (15bhp)
0–96km/h (60mph): n/a
Top speed: 73km/h (45mph)
Production total: 25,000 approx

BMW 303

1933–36

BMW's car-building reputation might have been established by the motoring-for-all 3/15, but the company soon targeted the middle classes. The car that defined this shift in policy was the 303, introduced in 1933.

It brought with it the now-famous BMW kidney-shaped grille, which has been incorporated into every BMW since. It also used a new 1175cc (72 cu in) six-cylinder engine, an expansion of the four-cylinder unit used in an earlier model, the AM-4.

Although the engine now seems to be small, it was acclaimed as a powerful motor when the car was launched. The interior was unusually big too, which prompted BMW to advertise the 303 as the 'smallest big car in the world'.

It was certainly stylish as well, and was available in a choice of body styles, including a two-door saloon, a cabriolet and a two-seater sports car. Soon the 303 was also used as the basis for the cheaper four-cylinder 309, the more upmarket 1500cc (92 cu in) 315 and the more powerful 319.

Then came two cars that really made the motoring world take notice of BMW. These were the 315/1 and the 319/1 which were exclusive and rather expensive two-seater sports roadsters built in very low numbers.

Engine: 1175cc (72 cu in), 6-cylinder
Power: 22kW (30bhp)
0–96km/h (60mph): n/a
Top speed: 105km/h (65mph)
Production total: n/a

BMW 328

1936–39

Engine: 1971cc (120 cu in), 6-cylinder
Power: 60kW (80bhp)
0–96km/h (60mph): 8 secs
Top speed: 150km/h (93mph)
Production total: 461

Just eight years after BMW bought Dixi, along with its Austin Seven copy, it revealed a model that is still thought of as one of the finest sports cars ever built – the 328.

The first appearance of the 328 was in 1936, when it won the Eifelrennen race, one of the biggest races of the season. It looked incredible, with a curvy open-top two-seater body, much smaller running boards than was usual on cars of this era, and no side windows, just cut-down doors.

Under the beautiful bodywork was a completely redesigned 2-litre (120 cu in) version of the 303's six-cylinder engine, which produced an impressive 60kW (80bhp) – a lot for such a small, light car. The engine sat high in its bay, partly due to the size of the new aluminium cylinder head but mostly because of the three Solex downdraught carburettors. The body was mounted on a tubular frame and the brakes were hydraulic front and rear.

This was the ultimate evolution of the 315/1 and 319/1 sports cars, capable of 150km/h (93mph) in road trim. But it was the racing versions of the 328 that really made its reputation. Some produced 101kW (135bhp), which endowed them with a top speed of 200km/h (124mph). The 328 won race after race, and its finest hour came in the 1940 Mille Miglia, with special-bodied 328s finishing first, third, fifth and sixth.

To the layman the 328 might look little different from the usual open-top sportsters of the prewar era. But the 328 is a class above most, with great handling and performance for its age (it would catch a few modern hot hatches from a standstill).

BMW 501

Everything that BMW had achieved from 1928, when it bought out the Dixi car company, had been lost by the end of World War II. Everything, that is, except its reputation for building excellent cars for the middle and upper classes. So, after the war, it continued to pursue those same markets. The budget car market was too crowded anyway, so the company built a large, expensive saloon, in direct competition with Mercedes. The saloon in question was the 501, closely based on the prewar 326.

Its over-elaborate curves resulted in the 501 being dubbed the 'baroque angel', while under the bodywork there was the old six-cylinder engine and new all-independent suspension. It wasn't a bad car, but Mercedes had better cars at lower prices and a better distribution network too.

BMW worked hard to improve the 501, first with the 501A, then the 501/3. Finally, the model evolved into the V8-powered 502 – a much better machine.

Engine: 1971cc (120 cu in), 6-cylinder
Power: 48kW (65bhp)
0–96km/h (60mph): n/a
Top speed: 135km/h (84mph)
Production total: 6328

BMW 503

Engine: 3168cc (193 cu in), V8-cylinder
Power: 104kW (140bhp)
0–96km/h (60mph): n/a
Top speed: 190km/h (118mph)
Production total: 412

The BMW of the 1950s was a minor concern, struggling for survival, so it seems bizarre that it chose to build a handful of extremely upmarket cars, as well as the tiny Isetta microcar.

One of those upmarket models was the 503, designed by Count Albrecht Goertz, who years later styled the bestselling Datsun 240Z, among many others. It was sold alongside the 501 and 502 models, and used the same running gear as the 502 (including the V8 engine) but it looked very different.

First of all, it was a cabriolet.

Secondly, it had long, angular lines, with protruding headlights and a tall bulbous version of the BMW kidney grille; it was a good-looking car. It was much lighter than the 501 and 502, though, and the V8 engine had been uprated to produce 104kW (140bhp), so the 503 was fast and enjoyable to drive.

Unfortunately, it was also twice the price of the 501, which itself

This is the car that almost finished off BMW for good, because it was so expensive to build and so unlikely to sell in high numbers. But, that aside, the 503 is a good car to drive, if you can find one.

had a high price tag. So, despite its highly modern looks, the 503 was an expensive disaster which put BMW in financial trouble.

BMW 507

1956–59

At the 1955 Frankfurt Motor Show, BMW unveiled three stunning cars. One was a limousine, which never made it into production and the other two were sports cars designed by Albrecht Goertz – the 503 (see separate entry) and the 507.

The 507 was the better of the two. It was a lithe, low two-seater with a detachable hardtop and a folding hood that tucked out of sight behind the seats. The clean but muscular lines meant performance, which was amply provided by the running gear. Under the bonnet was the BMW V8 engine, which could propel the

507 to 193km/h (120mph).

Predictably, the 507 was extremely expensive and, in five years, just 253 were sold. But now it

is a legendary car and one of the most sought-after BMWs of all time, along with the prewar 328.

Engine: 3168cc (193 cu in), V8-cylinder
Power: 111kW (150bhp)
0–96km/h (60mph): 9.5 secs
Top speed: 193km/h (120mph)
Production total: 253

Enthusiasts believe this is the best-looking BMW ever built. It looks just as good with the detachable hardtop fitted. But don't expect to see one on the road, as few were built and even fewer emerge from their modern-day safe havens.

BMW 700

1959–65

Engine: 697cc (43 cu in), twin-cylinder
Power: 22kW (30bhp)
0–96km/h (60mph): 33.7 secs
Top speed: 113km/h (70mph)
Production total: 174,390

The 700 was the car that saved BMW from ruin in the early 1960s, despite the ultra-glamorous luxury saloons and high-performance sports cars in the range. But the 700 was a stopgap model that the BMW

management was ashamed of.

The car was built because BMW was desperate for a mid-range car to fill the massive gap between its Isetta microcar and its big saloons and sports cars. But there was no money available to develop such a car, so BMW simply used the mechanicals of the Isetta and put them under a saloon body.

The 700 was so-named because the engine of the Isetta had been

expanded to 697cc (43 cu in). There was even a 700 Sport model built (later called the 700CS), available as a coupé or a cabriolet. Then came the longer-wheelbase 700LS,

If you're struggling to grasp the relevance of the BMW 700 in the car market of the 1960s, think Triumph Herald and Ford Anglia – small, budget-priced saloons with more than a modicum of styling.

which took the 700 even further away from its microcar roots.

The car shouldn't have been a sales success as there were better cars in this market sector. But the 700 had two saving graces. The first was its looks – the body had been penned by none other than Michelotti of Turin and was good-looking. The second was that, for the market, the 700 was well equipped. BMW was saved.

BMW 1500

Engine: 1499cc (91 cu in), 4-cylinder
Power: 60kW (80bhp)
0–96km/h (60mph): 14 secs
Top speed: 148km/h (92mph)
Production total: 350,729

The 1500 single-handedly turned BMW's fortunes around and was the first of the company's Neue Klasse (New Class). Previous models had just broken even financially, but the 1500 began the transition of BMW from a slightly inept company, albeit one with high standards of engineering, to the world force in carmaking that it has become today.

The car was first exhibited in 1961 and immediately received glowing reviews in the motoring press. It looked right, with hints of the previous 700 in its styling, as well as an arrow-shaped nose that Albrecht Goertz had added to the fantastic 507 sports car. Somehow the new car conveyed quality and prestige, without resorting to distasteful excesses of chrome or self-conscious design features. In fact, the 1500 had been designed mostly in-house at BMW, although there had been some help from the Italian design house, Michelotti.

The four-cylinder, overhead camshaft engine was all-new but also trouble-free. The gearbox and axle weren't quite so successful initially, though, with failures which almost destroyed BMW's reputation for high quality. Luckily, the 1500 survived these early problems and BMW went on to introduce 1600, 1800 and 2000 versions using the same two- and four-door bodyshells. They were all a great success.

Few other models had achieved such clean lines as the Neue Klasse – look at the way the bonnet and boot curve round to the main swage line, simplifying the looks, especially with the indicators and door handles sat in the same swage line.

BMW 02-SERIES

BMW's best-loved model range quietly appeared in 1966 but went on to give rise to one of the greatest sports saloons ever, a truly ground-breaking design. The cars are now referred to as the 02-series, but the first was actually called the 1600-2, to distinguish it from the larger BMW 1600 (which itself was based on the 1500).

The 1600-2 was simply meant as a downmarket BMW, to introduce the masses to the company's cars, before (hopefully) graduating to the more glamorous models in the range. But the 1600-2 turned out to be surprisingly good to drive, with impressive levels of performance, handling and refinement.

With such a good base, a sports model was bound to be a success.

Firstly, BMW introduced a Ti version of the 1600-2. It was a good car, but couldn't meet the emissions regulations in the United States. So BMW slotted a 2-litre (121 cu in) engine into the 1600-2 body, and called it the 2002.

The 2002 was fantastic, and was followed by a Ti version, with twin carburettors, and a Tii with fuel injection. A Touring estate model was built too, as well as a cabriolet. But the most extreme was the 2002 Turbo, the first European turbocharged production car, and a very potent machine. It is now extremely sought-after.

Engine: 1990cc (121 cu in), 4-cylinder
Power: 97kW (130bhp)
0–96km/h (60mph): 8.3 secs
Top speed: 187km/h (116mph)
Production total: 698,943

Kidney grille, slanted nose, clamshell bonnet and boot shut lines – all these design cues went on to define BMW saloons for years.

BMW 3.0CS

1968–75

Two-door coupés have been a feature of the BMW range since 1965, when the Neue Klasse body was adapted to form a sleek coupé shape, and the car was fitted with a 2-litre (122 cu in) engine and named the 2000C or 2000CS, depending on specification. It wasn't long before larger engines appeared, matching performance to the looks.

The first was a 2.8-litre (171 cu in) six-cylinder unit to power the 2800CS, but when BMW introduced a 3-litre (182 cu in) six-cylinder engine in its big saloon range, it was inevitable that a coupé would follow. That coupé was the 3000CS. The CS was soon replaced by a fuel-injected version, the 3000CSi, which gave even greater performance with 149kW (200bhp) available. In fact, the CSi could match some Porsche 911s of the era in terms of acceleration and top speed.

Sales of the CS and CSi were helped by the increasing success on the racetrack of another version of the coupé – the 3.0CSL (L for lightweight).

The CSL was an incredible machine, a homologation special with aluminium body panels, a

Even without the adornment of the extra spoilers that the CSL version of this range was fitted with, these coupés are aggressively good-looking. They're fast but superbly smooth, thanks to their powerful six-cylinder engines, the most naturally balanced of all engine configurations.

front spoiler and 225km/h (140mph) performance. Initially, road-going versions of the CSL looked much the same as the standard CSi but that changed when BMW started experimenting with aerodynamics. The result was the outrageous 'Batmobile', a 3.0CSL with a roof spoiler, a massive boot spoiler and a larger front spoiler, as well as small bonnet-mounted aerodynamic aids. The car has since joined the 2002 Turbo as a BMW 'ultimate'.

Engine: 2985cc (182 cu in), 6-cylinder
Power: 149kW (200bhp)
0–96km/h (60mph): 7.5 secs
Top speed: 224km/h (139mph)
Production total: 20,301

BMW M1

1979–81

Engine: 3453cc (211 cu in), 6-cylinder
Power: 206kW (277bhp)
0–96km/h (60mph): 5.5 secs
Top speed: 260km/h (161mph)
Production total: 456

BMW had a long history of having a contradictory and confusing model line-up until the introduction of the Neue Klasse 1500 in 1961. In the late 1970s, however, the company returned to type by attempting to build a true supercar to compete with Ferrari and Lamborghini.

This new machine did not fit in with the existing saloons and coupés, although the car itself, the M1, was good. It was designed by Ital Design and engineered, curiously, by Lamborghini – not a name easily associated with precision German products.

The M1 was mid-engined, with a turbocharged 3.5-litre (211 cu in) unit producing 206kW (277bhp). The engine, with its 24-valve aluminium alloy cylinder head, went on to power other top-specification BMW road cars, including the M635Csi. In fact,

the 'M' of M1, which stood for Motorsport, was the first such badging for a BMW – now the M cars are legendary.

But BMW was no longer geared for low-volume production so some parts were made in Italy, and then assembled at Baur in Germany. There were quality problems and delays and ultimately the car didn't look as spectacular as its rivals. Also, the BMW name didn't have the prestige of Ferrari and Lamborghini in this market, and the planned entry into Group 5

racing went awry. In the end, the best that BMW could manage was a one-make racing series. This anti-climactic end to BMW's hopes for the M1s is sad, because the M1 was actually an excellent supercar; not as dramatic-looking inside or out as a Ferrari, perhaps, but just as competent and exciting to drive.

The red, light blue and mid-blue stripes are now synonymous with BMW's M-series cars and feature on steering wheels, instruments and exterior badging.

BMW M535i

Engine: 3453cc (211 cu in), 6-cylinder
Power: 162kW (218bhp)
0–96km/h (60mph): 7.1 secs
Top speed: 224km/h (139mph)
Production total: 1650

When BMW wanted to race its ill-fated supercar, the M1, it turned to its Motorsport division to develop the road cars needed to satisfy the competition homologation regulations. Despite the problems with the M1, the division proved its worth. When BMW decided to make a performance saloon car, the company knew which department to go to.

The M535i was the first true road car developed by BMW Motorsport division after the M1. It wasn't as spectacular in looks or performance as the M-cars that followed, but it was much quicker than it looked.

Into the standard 5-series bodyshell went the powerful six-cylinder engine from the 635CSi, along with a close-ratio gearbox, uprated brakes and special Bilstein suspension. From the outside, it was difficult to tell the car apart from a standard 535i. All that was different was the slightly deeper front spoiler and the wider alloy wheels – and the spoiler was optional anyway. Inside, Recaro seats and an M1 steering wheel were the only distinguishing features.

Perhaps you wouldn't give this BMW car a second glance if it passed you, but then it is one of the ultimate sheep-in-wolf's-clothing. The front spoiler on this model is a clue, but since the M535i's launch, spoilers like this have pretty well become run-of-the-mill.

The M535i paved the way for the wealth of M cars that have since appeared – it was the first of a new breed.

BMW M635CSi

Engine: 3453cc (211 cu in), 6-cylinder
Power: 213kW (286bhp)
0–96km/h (60mph): 6 secs
Top speed: 242km/h (150mph)
Production total: 5803

When the all-conquering 3.0CS family of coupés began to look dated, BMW introduced a worthy replacement, the 6-series. It was not quite as good-looking as the outgoing coupé range but dynamically it was a big improvement.

The running gear came from the new 7-series executive saloon, which meant customers got the usual six-cylinder engine, power steering and independent suspension. But for the top-of-the-range 6-series, BMW called upon the services of its Motorsport division.

The result was the fantastic M635CSi. It had BMW's excellent 3.5-litre (211 cu in) engine, tuned by Motorsport engineers to increase power from the usual 162kW (218bhp) to 213kW (286bhp). A close-ratio five-speed gearbox, alloy wheels, an M Technic bodykit, special seats and steering wheel were all standard.

Much of the appeal of the M635CSi was in its understated looks but, as similar cars were released by rival manufacturers, it became obvious that buyers didn't want their M-cars to look too understated. So the model was made a little more special with a full leather interior, electric front seats and new spoilers. It was still a fairly subtle car, designed to appeal to those in the know.

Not ones to leave their cars looking friendly or harmless, BMW styled cars to extremes of aggressiveness during the no-nonsense 1980s. With its exaggerated shark nose, the M635CSi typifies this approach.

BMW M3

1985–90

Inside the BMW M3 were sports seats, a tiny M logo found between the instruments, an 8000rpm revcounter and also an optional computer. All were left-hand drive.

If you see an early 3-series BMW with incongruously wide wheel-arches, a neat rear spoiler and left-hand drive, then you could be in the company of a legend – the E30 M3.

The E30 was the second generation of the 3-series saloon, the series which had succeeded the 02-series cars. The M3 was the Motorsport division's creation, based around the E30 with a four-

cylinder, 16-valve engine, roughly derived from the six-cylinder unit of the M1 supercar. In fact, during the M3's development, the engineers really did just chop off two cylinders and drop the result into the 3-series bodyshell.

There was actually room for the M1 six-cylinder engine in the 3-series but its extra weight would have spoilt the balance of the car, which was much smaller than both

the 5- or 6-series BMWs. And the M3 needed great handling as much as great straight line performance, because the plan was to race it.

Aerodynamics played a big part in the development of the M3 as well, with the Motorsport engineers even changing the rake of the rear window to improve the airflow. The intensive re-work was successful and the M3 joined the ranks of the original Ford Sierra

Cosworth, the Audi Quattro and other such saloon car greats.

Since the first E30 version, the M3 model has continued to the present day. But for enthusiasts, the original is still the best.

Engine: 2302cc (140 cu in), 4-cylinder
Power: 149kW (200bhp)
0–96km/h (60mph): 7.1 secs
Top speed: 226km/h (140mph)
Production total: 17,184

BMW Z1

1986–91

Engine: 2494cc (153 cu in), 4-cylinder
Power: 127kW (170bhp)
0–96km/h (60mph): 7.9 secs
Top speed: 226km/h (140mph)
Production total: 8000

The Z1 sports car was a happy accident. It was never planned as a production car but was simply intended as a test bed or 'mule' for the development of a new rear

suspension system for the 3-series of the 1990s.

At some point during the development work, BMW decided to clothe this mule with a neat sports

car body made from a steel and carbonfibre monocoque, with glassfibre outer panels and slide-down doors. However, it was still just an engineering experiment.

Eventually, the car was shown to the public and everybody wanted one of these intriguing little sports cars. The production version was fitted with BMW's 2.5-litre (153 cu in) straight-six engine, which was enough to give it a 226km/h (140mph) top speed.

The Z1 went on to sell 8000 units, an impressive figure considering it was never planned as a production car. In reality, it was very expensive for what it offered and it was never the great drive it was expected to be.

On the move, the BMW Z1 looks conventional. But, surprisingly, the doors don't hinge open but drop away instead. This was a hardcore sports car and a far cry from the unnecessarily soft-edged Z3 sports car that followed a decade later.

BOND EQUIPE

1963–70

In the immediate postwar years, Lawrie Bond made three-wheeled cars, similar to Reliant's models. Many were powered by Villiers two-stroke engines and all were poor machines.

However, Bond then added the Equipe GT4 to the line-up. This was a four-wheeler based on the Triumph Herald, using the Herald chassis, bulkhead and doors. The rest of the bodywork was glassfibre and the whole package was grandly advertised as 'the most beautiful car in the world'.

The GT4 wasn't a bad car, though, and was further improved in 1964 with the GT4S, which had

Looks familiar but unusual? That's because the doors are Triumph Herald/Vitesse, while the rest of the bodywork is Bond's own. This is the GT4S with sporty twin headlights, but under the skin is the four-cylinder Herald engine.

twin headlights, an opening boot and more headroom than the GT4. Then came the totally restyled Equipe 2-litre (122 cu in), based on the Herald's big brother, the Vitesse.

Along with this new six-cylinder engine, the car also inherited the Vitesse's unpredictable rear suspension. The MkII Equipe changed that and could also be bought as a convertible.

These Bonds were cheap and sporty and now enjoy quite a

following, even if the chassis and bulkheads are even more rust-prone than those of the Herald and Vitesse; legend has it that lack of storage space at the Bond factory meant that the bare structures used to get left outside in the rain.

Engine: 1998cc (122 cu in), 6-cylinder
Power: 71kW (95bhp)
0–96km/h (60mph): 10.7 secs
Top speed: 165km/h (102mph)
Production total: 4381

BOND BUG

1970–74

Depending on your point of view, the Bond Bug is either hilarious or horrific. But there's no doubt that it's fun to drive, especially with the sidescreens off (exposing you to more curious looks from other road users).

In the late 1960s, two of Britain's largest users of glassfibre were Reliant and Bond. Both companies had made a name for themselves with economy three-wheelers; both had then expanded into sports cars. But in 1969, Reliant took over Bond, and within a year the old Bond factory in Preston had been closed down and production moved to Reliant's Tamworth base.

For Reliant, this seemed the perfect opportunity to experiment without the chance of damaging the good name of Reliant. The company had already been working with designer Tom Karen of Ogle, who had come up with an idea for a new style of three-wheeler, with the emphasis on fun.

Reliant put Ogle's concept into

production under the Bond name, and called it the Bug. It had a fold-forward canopy, detachable sidescreens and came in bright orange; no other colours were available. The engine was one of Reliant's own four-cylinder units, initially with 701cc (43 cu in) but from 1973, with 748cc (46 cu in).

Considering the unusual nature of the car, the Bug was quite a success and typified the wacky nature of some products from the 1970s. Those who liked it, loved it; everyone else ignored it.

Engine: 748cc (46 cu in), 4-cylinder
Power: 24kW (32bhp)
0–96km/h (60mph): n/a
Top speed: 126km/h (78mph)
Production total: 2270

BONNET DJET

The Bonnet Djet (pronounced D-jet) was the first ever mid-engined road car. This was the brainchild of Frenchman René Bonnet, who had previously made sports and racing cars under the banner of CD, with Charles Duetz.

The Djet used Renault running gear, a backbone chassis, independent suspension front and rear and disc brakes all round. Its

Unconventional, the Djet beat even the Lamborghini Miura as the first mid-engined road car. It spawned Matra's car-building, resulting in the Bagheera and Murena.

glassfibre body was made by Matra, a giant in the aerospace industry, but who also made glassfibre and plastics.

Even in its early guise, with a

Gordini-tuned 1108cc (68 cu in) Renault engine, the Djet was fast. Later Djets (the II, the 5 and the 5S) were quicker still. But by 1964, the company was in financial trouble, owing Matra a large sum of money. To recoup its losses, Matra took over Bonnet and kept the Djet alive. This was Matra's first attempt at car manufacture, which continued right into the 1980s.

Soon Matra revamped the car with a larger 1255cc (77 cu in) engine and named it the Jet, before replacing it with the even more bizarre-looking M530.

Engine: 1108cc (68 cu in), 4-cylinder
Power: 48kW (65bhp)
0–96km/h (60mph): n/a
Top speed: 165km/h (102mph)
Production total: n/a

BORGWARD HANSA

The Borgward Hansa was the first all-new German car to be introduced after World War II. It was made by Carl Borgward, who had earlier produced Goliath and Hansa-Lloyd vehicles. After the war, Borgward decided the best way of increasing his allocation of raw materials was

to form three separate car companies – Lloyd, Goliath and Borgward.

The Borgward Hansa 1500 was released in 1949, making other German offerings outdated. It had full-width bodywork, inspired by the American Kaisers, and its specification was modern with an

all-synchromesh gearbox, overhead valve engine and independent front and rear suspension.

The 1500 was followed by a diesel and an 1800 petrol version before evolving into the Isabella. The Hansa name was still used, though, for a six-cylinder version

of the original car, called the Hansa 2400, which continued until 1958.

Engine: 1498cc (91 cu in), 4-cylinder
Power: 36kW (48bhp)
0–96km/h (60mph): n/a
Top speed: 105km/h (65mph)
Production total: 35,229

BORGWARD ISABELLA

1954–61

The Isabella was Borgward's most important and well-known model and kept the company going through the latter half of the 1950s. The standard car was offered as a saloon or estate and was a simple evolution of the earlier Hansa. The name came about when the Borgward engineers wanted to put a badge on a pre-production model to disguise the car's origins while they were testing it on public roads. Carl Borgward suggested Isabella – his wife's name – and it stuck.

Like the Hansa, the Isabella was advanced for its time, with the use of aluminium alloys and separate front and rear rubber-mounted subframes for improved noise insulation. It soon gained a reputation for longevity, and its success prompted two new models – the Coupé and Cabriolet.

These have since been referred to as the best-looking German cars of all time. They're superbly curvaceous and glamorous-looking, belying their 1498cc (91 cu in) engines. The Cabriolet, built by Deutsch of Cologne, was too expensive, though, and just 29 were sold.

Engine: 1498cc (91 cu in), 4-cylinder
Power: 56kW (75bhp)
0–96km/h (60mph): 17.4 secs
Top speed: 150km/h (93mph)
Production total: 202,862

The Isabella Coupé, shown here, is the thinking man's Volkswagen Karmann Ghia, a celebration of automotive curviness and a far cry from the staid Isabella saloons.

BORGWARD P100

1959–61

Engine: 2240cc (137 cu in), 6-cylinder
Power: 75kW (100bhp)
0–96km/h (60mph): 14.6 secs
Top speed: 161km/h (100mph)
Production total: 2587

It might seem surprising now, but Borgward became quite a force in German car manufacturing during the 1950s, and began to compete with Opel and Mercedes-Benz.

Its main weapon was the P100, a big US-style saloon with a 2.3-litre (137 cu in) six-cylinder engine and the option of air suspension – making it the first German car to use pneumatics. Borgward had invested a lot of money in the car, but it wasn't as good as it should have been, mostly because its engine did not provide enough power.

So Borgward's finances began to suffer, forcing its owner to approach the Bremen Senate for cash assistance – after all, BMW had been helped out only a year before. However, no money was forthcoming and Borgward went bankrupt in 1961. The P100 was then built in Mexico by another company, but Carl Borgward died broken-hearted in 1963.

BRICKLIN SV-1

1974–75

Engine: 5896cc (360 cu in), V8-cylinder
Power: 164kW (220bhp)
0–96km/h (60mph): n/a
Top speed: 197km/h (122mph)
Production total: 2897

Canada has never had any large car manufacturing aspirations, but in the 1970s, one man (and a government) attempted to change all that. The man was entrepreneur Malcolm Bricklin, who managed to persuade the Canadian government to fund the production of the SV-1 sports car by providing $23 million to pay for a new, high-tech factory.

The car itself was a good design, with a chunky, safety conscious but stylish body formed by a mix of acrylic and glassfibre. It even had gullwing doors. The car was originally fitted with an AMC 5.9-litre (360 cu in) V8 unit before the company switched to Ford V8 power. Most versions had automatic transmissions although a few manuals were also made.

But there were problems. It began to emerge that build quality was poor, especially as far as the gullwing doors were concerned. Within a year the project had totally collapsed, with plenty of recriminations at government level.

The impact bumpers and thick roof pillars look odd, but the SV-1 used similar styling to the Camaro. However, even that didn't ensure its longevity.

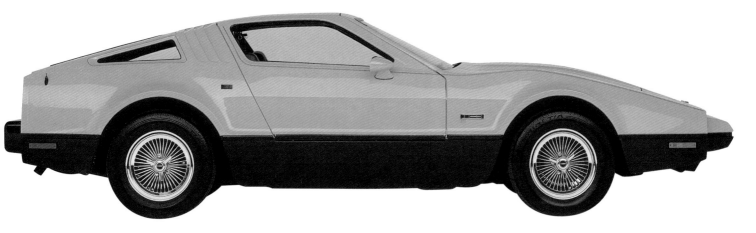

BRISTOL 400

1947–50

Developed with the help of a former BMW designer in the aftermath of World War II, aircraft manufacturer Bristol produced the 400 to an extremely high standard.

The Bristol Aeroplane Company turned to making cars after demand for its planes fell following the end of World War II.The company initially developed a prototype sports coupé, but destroyed it during testing on the company airfield. In fact, the car destroyed itself, due to highly dangerous handling problems.

So instead, the company started manufacturing existing designs and, thanks to war reparations, ended up with several from BMW. The company then secured the release from military detention of a former BMW designer and the Bristol 400 was born.

It had a BMW 326-type chassis and a body based on the BMW 327. The 400's engine was a

development of the BMW 328 six-cylinder unit. The steel-bodied, wood-framed 400 was built to high standards – aircraft industry standards, in fact – and soon the company developed a reputation for high quality products. Although the price tag was somewhat high, it did offer exclusivity.

Early examples of the 400 ran on a single carburettor and a low compression ratio to cope with the poor standard of fuel available in the UK after the war. Triple carburettors were introduced later, but performance was never really a key selling point. Instead, Bristol concentrated on good quality and

exclusivity, qualities that the company has continued to sell its cars on ever since.

Engine: 1971cc (120 cu in), 6-cylinder
Power: 60kW (80bhp)
0–96km/h (60mph): 14.7 secs
Top speed: 152km/h (94mph)
Production total: 700

BRISTOL 401

1948–53

Engine: 1971cc (120 cu in), 6-cylinder
Power: 63kW (85bhp)
0–96km/h (60mph): 15.1 secs
Top speed: 156km/h (97mph)
Production total: 650

The BMW-based 400 had established Bristol as a maker of high quality, exclusive machinery, but the car was essentially just an update of a prewar design. So

Bristol introduced the 401, a far more sophisticated car.

The 401 saw a change in direction as far as body construction went since it adopted the Superleggera

principle of using alloy body panels wrapped around a labyrinth of small diameter tubing. This was a technique pioneered by Italian coachbuilders Touring, whose designs also inspired the 401's teardrop shape.

But it was Bristol's aerodynamic work on the body that determined the shape. Using techniques from its aircraft manufacturing division, Bristol developed the shape of the 401 on the company's runway and emerged with a car that was ahead of its time in terms of aerodynamics and the subsequent reduction in wind noise. Even 20 years later, only four cars out of 100 made by other manufacturers were found to have a lower drag coefficient.

The 401 also spawned the convertible 402 and the more powerful 403 – Bristol's first 161km/h (100mph) car – both based on the same body shape.

Model by model, few other cars have ever looked like a Bristol. But, arguably, the 401, 402 and 403 were the most distinctive of all. Perhaps they weren't truly elegant but they were extremely efficient aerodynamically.

BRISTOL 404

1953–55

The 404 is the best of the pre-411 Bristols, thanks to an excellent combination of engine and chassis, along with less eccentric styling than that of previous models. The MPH 100 registration indicates that this was a Bristol press car.

Bristol enthusiasts generally regard the 404 as the best-looking car made by the company. An evolution of the previous models, it used a shortened version of the 403 chassis (which itself was almost the same as the 401 chassis but with an anti-roll bar at the front, improved steering and finned brake drums), the famous six-cylinder engine and an all-new body with a distinctive gaping front grille.

With the 404 came a few features that have since become Bristol hallmarks. The most obvious was the location of the spare wheel and the battery behind either front wheelarch, to provide extra luggage space elsewhere, and the shrouded instrument panel directly ahead of the steering wheel. Bristol referred to the 404 as 'The Businessman's Express' – a term that has been used since.

Because of its shortened chassis, the 404 had better, sports-like

handling than most Bristols. This improvement was complemented by a more powerful engine which increased output from 78kW (105bhp) to 93kW (125bhp).

A long wheelbase version of the 404, named the 405, was also offered and has since become the only Bristol ever made with four doors instead of two.

Engine: 2000cc (122 cu in), 6-cylinder
Power: 78kW (105bhp)
0–96km/h (60mph): 10.5 secs
Top speed: 170km/h (105mph)
Production total: 52

BRISTOL 411

1969–76

If ever there was a quintessentially British car then it was the Bristol. But early versions used engines developed from the BMW straight-six, while later models, epitomized by the 411, were powered by American V8s.

A new engine was eventually fitted to the 1961 Bristol 407. Made by Chrysler, the unit was big, strong and powerful enough to finally endow the Bristol saloons with the output they deserved. The 407 used the body styling of the previous 406 but, under the bodywork, its front suspension was upgraded from transverse-leaf spring to coils.

The 411 was little different in looks from the 410. But a few touches make it one of the best Bristols to drive – including a more powerful engine, limited-slip differential and improved suspension.

In 1963, the restyled 408 was launched, which still used the V8 engine but this time clothed in a less elaborate, more sporting body, which was carried over to the more powerful 409. This look was made made even sharper for the 410, which featured a new front grille. The 411 appeared in 1969, which earned its new designation by having a bigger 6.3-litre (383 cu in) version of the Chrysler V8.

The changes kept coming, so that by 1975, a Mk IV version of the 411 with a 6.6-litre (400 cu in) engine appeared. Now, the 411 is widely regarded as having the best mix of styling and performance to be found on any Bristol model.

Engine: 6277cc (383 cu in), V8-cylinder
Power: 250kW (335bhp)
0–96km/h (60mph): 7 secs
Top speed: 222km/h (138mph)
Production total: 600

BRISTOL 412

The 412 featured fantastic build quality, a powerful V8 and a prestige badge. However, it was not the best-looking car ever made and has been described as looking like a breeze block.

Surprisingly, the bodywork of the 412 was styled by Zagato, who had worked for Bristol before, and produced the wonderful curvaceous 406 Zagato, of which only seven were built. The 412 was certainly a long way from this.

However, the 412 was an important car for Bristol, since it was the first model from the company to be offered as a factory-built convertible. A saloon version was also offered and, from 1976, the convertible incorporated a

fixed roll bar and targa roof sections.

The 412's running gear and chassis was essentially the same as that used on the 411, although the 6.6-litre (400 cu in) engine was changed for a smaller 5.9-litre (360 cu in) version in 1977.

Engine: 6556cc (400 cu in), V8-cylinder
Power: n/a
0–96km/h (60mph): 7.4 secs
Top speed: 226km/h (140mph)
Production total: n/a

Today, the 412's styling seems shocking. But in the 1970s, when the model was launched, it was acceptable. As Bristol's first-ever factory-built convertible, it is a landmark car.

BRISTOL 603

'Evolution not revolution'. Many companies have used this saying to summarize their manufacturing philosophy, but none more so than Bristol. When the 603 was launched in the mid-1970s, it certainly looked like an all-new model, thanks to a controversial restyle. But under the bodywork, the chassis was almost the same as that used in the 1940s, married to a suspension and Chrysler V8 engine introduced in the early 1960s.

As ever, the body panels were alloy, with the trademark battery and spare wheel access panels in the lower trailing halves of the front wings. Opinion was divided on the styling – some loved it, some hated it – and it remains that way today.

There were two versions of the 603 available initially, the 5.2-litre (317 cu in) 603E and the 5.9-litre (360 cu in) 603S. Incredibly, the 'E' on the former model's name

apparently stood for economy, although how any large saloon with a massive V8 engine and a price tag of £20,000 in the mid-1970s

Not everyone was impressed by the general styling of the 603. The area around the headlights seemed unfinished and the Bristol grille sat awkwardly. Later, the grille was made all-black which had the effect of improving the looks no end, as did new, updated wheels.

could be considered an economy model is more than questionable.

Not surprisingly, the E version lasted just one year before the arrival of the 603 S2, which featured air-conditioning as standard.

Engine: 5900cc (360 cu in), V8-cylinder
Power: n/a
0–96km/h (60mph): 8.6 secs
Top speed: 213km/h (132mph)
Production total: n/a

BRISTOL BEAUFIGHTER

1980–92

Engine: 5900cc (360 cu in), V8-cylinder
Power: n/a
0–96km/h (60mph): 5.9 secs
Top speed: 242km/h (150mph)
Production total: n/a

The Zagato-designed 412 of the late 1970s received plenty of criticism for its box-like styling but Bristol still updated the shape in 1980 for a new model – the Beaufighter, whose name was taken from the legendary World War II aircraft made by the company.

All the usual Bristol features were present, including the archaic chassis, the excellent Chrysler V8 engine and the alloy-panelled body. But there were some new talking points as well.

The V8 engine was turbocharged, giving plenty more power, although no one is sure quite how much because Bristol had stopped releasing output figures (and production numbers) in the previous decade. Still, it was a brave move because turbocharging was then still relatively new – only BMW, Porsche, Saab and TVR had really tried it before. But the

turbocharging work wonderfully well, endowing the Beaufighter with tremendous performance for such a large machine.

Also new was the revised

styling, with a better-looking roll hoop than the 412's and a glassfibre lift-out roof panel. These changes enabled the Beaufighter to continue in production until 1992.

A few touches to the styling make the Beaufighter look better than the 412 that it was based on. The big difference is the quad-headlight front and the revised grille.

BRISTOL BRITANNIA

1982–83

There has never been unnecessary extravagance at Bristol, which is why the company has managed to continue making its very high-quality (if slightly eccentric) cars for so long. In the 1980s, with the car industry in turmoil, the company

sensibly chose to revamp its existing bodies to create new models.

So, like the Beaufighter, which came from the old 412, the Britannia appeared, modelled on the outgoing 603. Both names were inspired by planes previously made

by the aircraft division.

The Britannia featured the same fastback lines as the 603, but was distinguished by changes to the front and rear lights. Changes to the front were especially obvious, with large rectangular (almost

square) headlights in place of the old four-lamp design. The bonnet panel was flatter and the rear quarter lights extended further into the corner of the join between rear wing and roof pillar. Overall, the styling generally looked crisper and more modern.

There were few new mechanicals under the new bodywork – the Chrysler V8 was still powerful and reliable enough to remain unchanged.

Engine: 5900cc (360 cu in), V8-cylinder
Power: n/a
0–96km/h (60mph): 7.2 secs
Top speed: 226km/h (140mph)
Production total: n/a

Viewed from the side, you realize just how large these Bristols of the 1970s and 1980s were. It's this size that gives them great presence on the road, despite less-than-ideal styling. But the true cachet of owning a Bristol Britannia was in the exclusivity.

BRISTOL BRIGAND

Engine: 5900cc (360 cu in), V8-cylinder
Power: n/a
0–96km/h (60mph): 5.9 secs
Top speed: 242km/h (150mph)
Production total: n/a

The Brigand arrived a year after the Britannia and looked almost identical to it and the older 603. The big difference between the two cars was their performance. Bristol had taken the potent turbocharged V8 from the Beaufighter and transplanted it into the Britannia body to create the 'new' car.

The resulting machine combined Bristol's traditional high quality craftsmanship with near-supercar performance. The chassis was the same old design that had originated in the 1940s but it had been so well developed by the 1980s that it seemed capable of handling the extra power from the turbocharger. Wider 17.8cm (7in) alloy wheels were fitted to aid traction but, otherwise, there were few external signs of the Brigand's extra prowess over the Britannia.

The added appeal of the Brigand's performance added an extra cachet to Bristol's reputation and ensured that, despite very high prices, the marque remained highly desirable among connoisseurs.

Perhaps that desirability across the Bristol range wouldn't be immediately obvious to everyone, but buyers knew that they would get one-to-one service from none other than the company MD, Tony Crook, and that their cars were hand-built to extremely high standards.

None was as opulently fitted out as, say, a Bentley or Rolls, but to

There's little to indicate what's different about the Brigand compared to the Britannia. But the Brigand's performance is nothing short of astonishing for such a large, heavily built car.

someone with a six-figure sum to spend on a car, a Bentley or a Rolls could often be seen as too obvious. Anyway, the Brigand, like other Bristols, is exceptionally smooth, fast and quiet to drive, and arguably more enjoyable than most expensive luxury cars.

BSA TEN

Although it is a company that is now world-renowned for its motor-cycles, BSA was originally formed to make guns and ammunition. The name stood for Birmingham Small Arms, and in 1907 the company added cars to its manufacturing output, building them in a new

factory in the Sparkbrook area of Birmingham.

The 1921 Ten was BSA's most significant offering. A two-seater lightweight sports car, it featured a modest 1075cc (66 cu in) V-twin engine built on similar principles to the units used in its motorcycles

and had a surprising top speed of 84km/h (52mph). It was fun to drive, too, with light and direct steering, a reasonably easy-to-operate three-speed gearbox and effective brakes.

The BSA Ten earned a deserved reputation as a great trials car,

thanks to its eager engine and lightweight build.

Engine: 1075cc (66 cu in), V-twin cylinder
Power: 13kW (18bhp)
0–96km/h (60mph): n/a
Top speed: 84km/h (52mph)
Production total: 5000 approx

BUGATTI TYPE 13

1920–26

Italian Ettore Arco Isadoro Bugatti, born in 1881, was the son of an artist. Although his early intention was to study art himself, he instead became fascinated by the internal combustion engine. He made one of his own in 1909, and the Bugatti marque – and legend – was born.

The Type 13 was his first production model, a light car based on prototypes he had built at his villa. It was manufactured at Molsheim near Strasbourg, and was fitted with an advanced 1326cc (81 cu in) overhead camshaft engine, at a time when this configuration was still a novelty. The Type 13 also featured the genesis of Bugatti's trademark horseshoe grille, Ettore apparently having been told by his father that the most perfect shape in nature was the egg.

Production was halted during World War I, but restarted in the 1920s, using an enlarged single block 1496cc (91 cu in) engine. More significantly, it had a more powerful 16-valve head in place of the original eight-valve one.

The Type 13's trim, handling and performance brought it success in racing. As well as the standard model, longer-wheelbase Type 15s and 17s were also offered.

Engine: 1496cc (91 cu in), 4-cylinder
Power: 30kW (40bhp) approx
0–96km/h (60mph): n/a
Top speed: 140km/h (87mph)
Production total: 2500 (Types 13, 22 and 23) approx

Early versions of the Type 13 had a radiator surround with 'squared off' shoulders, as illustrated here. Later ones adopted a rounded, egg-shaped device which was part of Bugatti's gradual movement towards the definitive horseshoe shape which became the marque's cosmetic trademark.

BUGATTI TYPE 23/BRESCIA

1920–26

The Type 23 was a development of the Type 13. Like the Type 13, it featured a 1326cc (81 cu in) overhead camshaft eight-valve engine, later enlarged to a 16-valve 1496cc (91 cu in) unit when production restarted after the end of World War I.

The main difference between the two Types was the length of the wheelbase. The Type 13's version was 2m (6.5ft) long, while the Type 23's was stretched to 2.55m (8.3ft), which allowed different bodywork to be fitted. Suspension was by reversed quarter-elliptic springs, a system that eventually became a Bugatti standard.

An unusual feature of the engine was its elaborate lubrication system. The main pump took its oil from a reservoir under the dashboard, feeding it to an oil box at the end of the camshaft. Two other pumps then distributed it to the sump. This complicated but innovative system ensured that different amounts of oil could be distributed to different components, depending on their varying needs.

The Brescia name was adopted for the Type 13, Type 22 and Type 23 after great success in the 1921 Italian Grand Prix at Brescia, when Bugatti came first, second, third and fourth.

Engine: 1496cc (91 cu in), 4-cylinder
Power: 22kW (30bhp) approx
0–96km/h (60mph): n/a
Top speed: 105km/h (65mph)
Production total: 2500 (Types 13, 22 and 23) approx

The Type 23 had a simplistic appearance, and its success helped lay firm foundations for Bugatti's subsequent masterpieces.

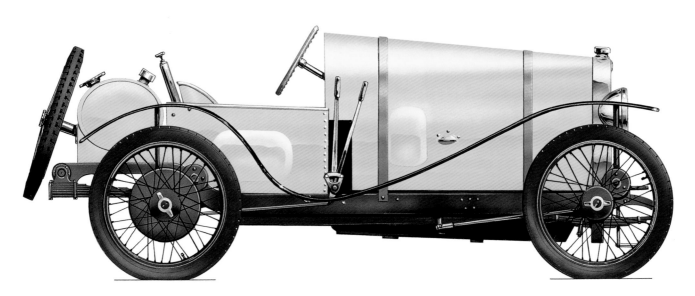

BUGATTI TYPE 22

1921–22

The Type 22 fitted in between the shorter Type 13 and the longer Type 23. This model, the 22nd car to be designed by Ettore Bugatti since 1898, had a 2.4m (7.9ft) chassis. Nevertheless, in most other ways it was the same car as the Type 13.

It first appeared before World War I, and was reintroduced after hostilities ended with a bigger 16-valve 1496cc (91 cu in) overhead camshaft four-cylinder engine replacing the original 1326cc (81 cu in) eight-valve unit. The handbrake worked on the rear wheels, while the footbrake acted on the drive.

Suspension was by reversed quarter-elliptic springs, which was known by the more complicated 'reversed demi-cantilever springs'.

This suspension gave the car excellent handling, while the 16-valve engine endowed it with good performance. Most Type 22s were fitted with touring bodies, leaving the smaller, open-bodied Type 13s to compete for racing glory.

Production of the Type 22 was carried out under licence in the United Kingdom by the Manchester firm of Crossley, using parts sent out from the Molsheim Bugatti factory. Diatto in Italy and Rabag in Germany also made the Type 22 under licence.

Engine: 1496cc (91 cu in), 4-cylinder
Power: 22kW (30bhp) approx
0–96km/h (60mph): n/a
Top speed: 113km/h (70mph)
Production total: 2500 (Types 13, 22 and 23) approx

BUGATTI TYPE 35

1924–31

Engine: 2262cc (138 cu in), 8-cylinder
Power: 97kW (130bhp)
0–96km/h (60mph): 7 secs
Top speed: 201km/h (125mph)
Production total: 340

The Type 35 was one Bugatti's greatest creations, and among the most beautiful racing cars ever built. Prior to the Type 35, little attention had been paid to the

bodywork of racing cars. But Bugatti's latest offering changed all that, looking like a luxury car in miniature, with long, lithe bodywork and polished aluminium spoked wheels.

The first Type 35s had 1990cc (121 cu in) engines, but variants soon followed. The 35C was supercharged, the 35T came with a larger 2262cc (138 cu in) engine

and the 35B combined both by coupling the bigger engine with the supercharger.

During its racing career, the car claimed over 2000 wins, a great record. It took a skilled driver to get the best out of a Type 35, but the ingenious chassis prompted tremendous handling. In the right hands, a Type 35 could beat any other car. It took a tough driver to

Distinctive features on the Type 35 were the bolt-on wheel rims, designed to overcome the potentially lethal problem of punctured tyres separating from their rims at speed.

master it as well, since there were few creature comforts within the cramped, open cockpit. But the Type 35 is still one of the most enchanting racers ever.

BUGATTI ROYALE

The Bugatti Royale was capable of dominating the roads and making other vehicles look inconsequential. Such automotive art was expensive though, and proved to be beyond even the deepest pockets.

The German Grand Prix of 15 July 1928 featured 17 Bugattis as well as an appearance by Ettore Bugatti to watch his cars in action. But neither the racing cars or 'Le Patron' himself caused as big a stir as what Bugatti unveiled at the race.

The event saw the debut of the prototype Type 41 Royale, a car on a truly epic scale. Designed to outshine a Rolls-Royce, the Royale was the culmination of Bugatti's aspirations to build the ultimate automobile. Fitted with striking bodywork, the Royale was powered by a monstrous 14,763cc (901 cu in) straight-eight engine producing 224kW (300bhp). Crowning the excessively long bonnet was an elephant mascot, in memory of Bugatti's dead brother Rembrandt, a talented sculptor who had specialized in animal models.

It was a curiously fitting figurehead for a vehicle that would turn out to be one of the biggest white elephants in motoring history. In six years, only six were made, and of those, just three were sold.

The visionary Ettore Bugatti had dreamed of building this fantasy car since 1913. Rolls-Royce was obviously his target. When an Englishman apparently told him

that 'if one desired to be fastest, one must choose a Bugatti, but it was evident that if one wanted the best, one must apply to Rolls-Royce', Bugatti is supposed to have replied that if this was true, it wouldn't be for much longer.

The prototype Royale featured a

Attention to detail extended to the eight-cylinder engine, which was beautifully built. The elephant radiator mascot was a tribute to Ettore Bugatti's late brother who had been a wildlife sculptor.

4.57m (15ft) wheelbase, but subsequent models had 4.27m (14ft) bases. The overall length was 6m (19.7ft), much of this given over to the extensive bonnet necessary to accommodate the huge engine (later reduced to 12,763cc (779 cu in)). Even the mechanicals were a work of art, the engine being perfectly rectangular with only a few extrusions to spoil the Cubist lines. The eight-cylinder unit was claimed to develop its 224kW (300bhp) at very low maximum revs of 1700rpm, but

modern estimates have put the output closer to 149kW (200bhp).

Whatever the true figure, there was no denying that the Royale was a powerful and thoroughly awe-inspiring machine. Such was the power of the car that a gearbox with only three-speeds was fitted, with first necessary for hill starts, and third serving as an overdrive for high-speed cruising. Second was all that was needed for all other driving.

Bugatti optimistically thought he could make and sell 25 cars, but less than a quarter of this total were produced. All Royales had different bodies, although some were rebodied more than once. After the prototype Torpedo (as driven by Bugatti to the German Grand Prix) came the Berline, Coupé Napoleon, Coach Weymann, Double Berline de Voyage, Cabriolet Weinberger, Coach Kellner, Roadster, Limousine Park Ward, Coupé de Ville and Coupé Binder. All were thoroughly imposing and very beautiful,

Few could argue that the Royale was the ultimate car but sadly even fewer could afford the huge Fr500,000 price tag – and that was for the basic chassis alone. The royal families of Spain, Bulgaria, Yugoslavia and Romania were all interested, but ended up buying Duesenbergs instead. This was a real blow to Bugatti's pride and he lost interest in the project, although he did keep four cars for his own personal use.

This wasn't quite the end of the Royale story though. The engine design went on to be a blueprint for the motors used in Bugatti trains on the French railways. The Royale car may have been a failure, but the Royale-engined railcars were built by the hundred, breaking several railway world records and staying in service until 1958.

Engine: 12,760cc (779 cu in), 8-cylinder
Power: 224kW (300bhp)
0–96km/h (60mph): n/a
Top speed: 200km/h (124mph)
Production total: 6

BUGATTI TYPE 57

1933–40

Engine: 3257cc (199 cu in), 8-cylinder
Power: 101kW (135bhp)
0–96km/h (60mph): n/a
Top speed: 153km/h (95mph)
Production total: 683

It was Ettore Bugatti's son, Jean, who was mostly responsible for this last great Bugatti. The Type 57 was an effort to build an exotic-looking, luxurious and fast grand tourer and is regarded as the marque's final flowering.

Power for the car came from a 3257cc (199 cu in) double-overhead camshaft eight-cylinder engine. As usual, it featured a one-piece cast-iron block with an integral cylinder head. Front suspension was by semi-elliptic springs, with reversed quarter elliptics at the rear.

The touring, saloon, coach, coupé and cabriolet bodies created by Jean Bugatti were exquisite, particularly the remarkable Atlantic coupé, a curvaceous, futuristic-looking design featuring a fin running down its centre. Other specialist coachbuilders produced their own bodies as well.

Variants of the Type 57 included the supercharged 119kW (160bhp) 57C and the modified sports-like 130kW (175bhp) 57S. A supercharger was added to the latter unit to produce the 149kW (200bhp) 57SC, capable of around 200km/h (124mph).

Jean Bugatti was killed while testing a 57C-based racing car in 1939, ironically for a race that never took place due to the outbreak of World War II on the very day it was due to be held.

The Type 57 was the last great car built by the Bugatti marque while under the control of Ettore and Jean Bugatti. Fitted with striking Atlantic coupé bodywork, with centre fin down the middle, the car looked very modern.

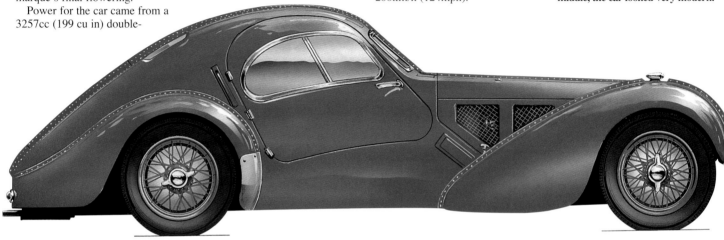

BUGATTI TYPE 101

1951–56

Engine: 3257cc (199 cu in), 8-cylinder
Power: 101kW (135bhp)
0–96km/h (60mph): n/a
Top speed: 169km/h (105mph)
Production total: 7

Following the death of the inspirational Ettore Bugatti, 'Le Patron', in 1947, keeping the Bugatti marque alive was always going to be a challenge.
The Type 101 tried to echo prewar glories, but failed to ignite the imagination of the wealthy buyers who bought the company's cars. As pretty as it was, only seven were built in five years.

The Type 101 was styled by the Gangloff coachbuilding firm, close to Bugatti's Molsheim plant. In looks, it resembled a larger version

The Type 101 introduced a new Bugatti style, but underneath was an antiquated and (by now) undynamic Type 57 chassis. That didn't impress potential customers who were expected to spend large amounts of money on buying one. Only a handful were sold.

of Jaguar XK120, especially around the front, where an effort was made to keep the traditional horseshoe grille. And in true Bugatti fashion, the car was very expensive.

The major disappointment was under the bodywork, where only a Type 57 chassis could be found, by now almost two decades out of date. With its rigid front and rear axles, it was far behind what other luxury sports car manufacturers were making. However, the Type

57 3.3-litre (199 cu in) engine did at least provide good performance, especially in supercharged form, with power boosted from 101kW (135bhp) to 140kW (188bhp). Only right-hand drive models were available.

BUICK 18/20

In 1916 Buick had sold an astounding 124,834 cars, but as material supplies became restricted because of World War I, sales fell back. However, the company pressed ahead with a new range in 1917. The old, large D-54 and D-55 were dropped while the new D-34 and D-35 were heavily promoted.

The new four-cylinder engine in these cars developed a competent 26kW (35bhp) from a displacement of 2786cc (170 cu in), although for taxation purposes the engine was rated at 18.2hp (13.6kW) – hence these models are commonly referred to as 18/20s. The engine also featured a detachable cylinder head as part of the design and the chassis used semi-elliptic springs rather than the usual cantilever units. Roadsters were available but the four-door touring cars sold in the largest numbers. Given new designations in 1918 as the E34, E35 and E37 a two-door saloon was added to the line-up.

In 1920, Buick switched to six-cylinder engines only and it seemed that the four-cylinder option was at a natural end.

However, in 1921, Buick reintroduced the four-cylinder unit for the 1922 model year. A development of the original engine, it was now rated at 13.6kW (18.23hp), although the displacement was no different.

Engine: 2786cc (170 cu in) 4-cylinder
Power: 26kW (35bhp)
0–96km/h (60mph): n/a
Top speed: 80km/h (50mph)
Production total: 88,500

BUICK STRAIGHT EIGHT

Engine: 3617cc (221 cu in) 8-cylinder
Power: 57kW (77bhp)
0–96km/h (60mph): 25 secs
Top speed: 119km/h (74mph)
Production total: 138,695

Introduced in July 1930, the Buick's new straight-eight engines were launched across the entire range. This was a brave move which set the company apart from the competition. As fitted to the 50 series, the smallest unit displaced just 3617cc (221 cu in) and would later be used in the 40 series. The 60 series of this year, which corresponded to the old 40 series, had a 4457cc (272 cu in) engine. The largest 5637 (344 cu in) unit was reserved for the Series 80 and 90 Buicks.

Sales of the straight-eights in the first year of production in 1931 were an outstanding 138,695 cars, although, as the Depression began to bite, this figure fell to 46,924 in 1933. Only when Buick restyled their range in 1936 did sales dramatically increase again.

The engines themselves were wonderfully smooth with a good turn of speed and could cruise comfortably at around 110km/h (70mph), which was remarkable for the time. The straight eights were also technically accomplished and featured an oil temperature gauge that cooled the oil at high engine revolutions and also warmed it in cold weather. The most desirable models from this era were the convertible coupé and phaeton, especially in the prestigious Series 90 format.

This is a Series 90 Model 96 coupé. Inside there was luxurious mohair upholstery, silk roller shades for the rear windows and carpeting.

BUICK SERIES 50

Engine: 3777cc (230 cu in) V8
Power: 64kW (86bhp)
0–96km/h (60mph): 19 secs
Top speed: 117km/h (72mph)
Production total: 690,500

Buick's decision to make only eight-cylinder cars could have hit sales hard. So to ensure profitable mass-market sales they introduced the Series 50. There were three new engines, but none had interchangeable parts and the smallest was rated at just 220 cu in.

Inside there was either mohair or cloth upholstery, carpeting for the rear seat floor area, dome lights and armrests. Midway through the model year a synchromesh transmission, previously a preserve of the upmarket Buicks, became standard. There was also a new look in 1932 with streamlined wings, tapered radiator and dual rear tail-lights. More body styles also became available, which were a two-door, five-passenger Victoria

coupé and a convertible phaeton model. A lack of chrome on the bodywork distinguished the Series 50 from the more expensive Buicks.

Here was a car that everyone could aspire to. If the smooth straight eight was not impressive enough the styling always turned

heads. A longer 302cm (119in) wheelbase for 1934 also meant a wider choice of bodies. In 1936, new art deco styling marked Buick's design revival as the lighter series 40 took over from the heavy 50. A semi-automatic transmission option offered in 1938 took the smallest

This convertible coupé series 50 was offered halfway through the model's first season in 1931 and proved to be a popular, stylish and profitable addition to the line-up.

Buick Special Series 40 to new levels of refinement.

BUICK ROADMASTER

A major redesign of the Buick range in 1936 saw the Roadmaster become the most prestigious model in the owner-driver class. Big and luxurious, with a 333cm (131in) wheelbase, it was cleanly styled and well engineered.

Initially, just two body styles

were offered – a four-door saloon and a convertible phaeton, but in 1937, a six-passenger formal saloon was added.

Big changes were made in 1938 as Buicks got coil springs for its rear suspension. Also, the chassis now had an X-member of channel

construction and the batteries were moved to the bonnet. Suddenly the Buick was much better to drive, with improved handling and lots more power. A new design of 'crowned' piston raised the straight-eight engine's compression ratio and boosted output to 105kW

(141bhp). Styling changes were minor as the grille became more upright to increase space under the bonnet.

In 1940, to make room for a new high specification Series 80 Limited, the Roadmaster Series 70 designation was introduced. It shared its bodyshell with the new Super line models with smoother styling and was available in four body styles. Sealed beam headlights and engine oil filters were important innovations. 1941 was the last year for the old body style and Roadmasters were now fitted with a revised 123kW (165bhp) engine. The legendary Roadmaster name had been established and would return triumphant in 1949.

Engine: 4070cc (248 cu in) 8-cylinder
Power: 80kW (107bhp)
0–96km/h (60mph): 16.4 secs
Top speed: 137km/h (85mph)
Production total: 70,000

This 1940 Roadmaster Model 76S sport coupé was nicely styled and solidly engineered. A smooth runner on the highway, it sold 28,000. No wonder 1940 marked the company's best production year to date.

BUICK ELECTRA

Engine: 6571cc (401 cu in) V8
Power: 242kW (325bhp)
0–96km/h (60mph): 9 secs
Top speed: 193km/h (120mph)
Production total: 1,220,340

The Electra was the spiritual successor to the old Roadmaster range, in that it was a big car with a sporty edge. As well as the standard model, Buick also produced the Electra 225 which, as its name suggests, was 225in (572cm) long (in the stretched body version). Power came from a 6571cc (401 cu in) V8, producing 242kW (325bhp).

In 1962, the standard Electra model was dropped, and the range revitalized by the styling influence of Bill Mitchell, GM's chief designer. The bodies were simpler

The 1959 Electra Series 4800 Buicks were regarded as the wildest models yet, with fins running from front to back. This 225 2-door convertible had a leather interior as standard and outsold the hardtops by 2 to 1.

and less bulky, especially the 'convertible look' two-door coupés.

For 1965, Buick's largest car, the Electra 225 got a major restyle and used the same 242kW (325bhp) V8 as the high-performance Buick Wildcat model. Lots of equipment came as standard, including power steering and power seats on the convertible. This was further improved in 1966 when a Custom series was introduced, featuring plush interior trim.

By 1967, the cars were getting bigger and bulkier again, but with more body contours and increased power output for the V8 engines, up to 268kW (360bhp). Two years later, the Electra 225 received another body rework and, although still a large car, looked graceful. However, as the excesses of the early 1970s grew, the 1971 range got longer and wider.

BUICK LE SABRE

Engine: 5965cc (300 cu in) V8
Power: 186kW (250bhp)
0–96km/h (60mph): 9.2 secs
Top speed: 170km/h (106mph)
Production total: 2,100,000

The Le Sabre name was first used in 1951 on a futuristic concept car that featured cast magnesium and aluminium body panels as well as a supercharged V8 engine. In 1959, the name was finally given to a production model. Buick customers

were treated to a radically restyled range with prominent fins that ran from the front to the rear of the body. Available as a saloon, a two-door hardtop, a convertible and an estate car, power came from a 5965cc (364 cu in) 186kW (250bhp) engine. As the entry level Buick, it proved an immediate success and 165,577 were sold.

Le Sabre styling became more subtle and, in 1962, was completely restyled with clean

square lines as the engine output went up to 209kW (280bhp). In 1965, a new body with wider and softer lines kept the Le Sabre as Buick's full-sized price leader. Another new body in 1967, as well as a Custom series, with enhanced levels of trim, saw the car increase in size, but the model range was trimmed back to the saloon and a hardtop coupé. In 1969 there was a new, lighter body style with a '400' option which included a 209kW

(280bhp) 5735cc (350 cu in) V8 with a new TurboHydramatic automatic transmission which briefly transformed the model. Sadly, it put on weight again in 1971 and mediocrity beckoned.

A new bodyshell for 1967 saw the introduction of the 45200 series and a good level of standard equipment. This Le Sabre was also available as a plusher Custom model with higher quality cloth and vinyl interior.

BUICK RIVIERA

Engine: 7459cc (455 cu in) V8
Power: 246kW (330bhp)
0–96km/h (60mph): 8.5 secs
Top speed: 200km/h (125mph)
Production total: 441,501

The Riviera represented one of the most successful attempts at capturing European styling and performance but on a much larger American scale. Positioned at the top of Buick's coupé line-up, the car was the company's best styling and performance package.

Known as model 4747, the Buick Riviera quickly became a huge success, selling around 40,000 in its first model year. It ushered in a new era of styling without all the chrome and fins that had characterized cars from Detroit. The leading edges of the front wings were actually grilles and the doors pioneered a new concept – frameless windows. The standard engine was a 6571cc (401 cu in) V8 with 242kW (325bhp), although for just $50 more, the buyer got a 6964cc (425 cu in) V8 with 253kW (340bhp).

In 1964 there was nothing to revise on the styling front, but there was always more room for more cubic inches. The 6964cc (425 cu in) engine could be ordered with a second four-barrel carburettor, which provided an extra 15kW (20bhp). Weighing 2000kg (4400lb), it needed all the power it could get and, unsurprisingly, handling was poor.

In 1965, a minor restyle introduced retractable headlights and expansive rear tail-lights but, more importantly, Buick became a competitor in the muscle car market by unveiling the Gran

Sport option. This included the 6964cc (425 cu in) 268kW (360bhp) engine along with a so-called Posi-Traction rear end. A major revamp in 1966 saw the retractable headlights moved back into the grille and the roofline adopted a more fastback style. The bonnet also became longer, the supposedly longest ever fitted to a production car. The 6964cc (425 cu in) 253kW (340bhp) unit became the only factory engine available.

For 1968, the Riviera lost some of its individuality because it now shared bodywork with both the Cadillac Eldorado and the Oldsmobile Toronado. However, the Buick remained rear-wheel drive. The grille was restyled again with large parking lights housed in

The 1971 Gran Sport was the most sporty of the remarkable boat-tail Rivieras. The 1971–1973 models did not just look good, they performed strongly too, and are now rightly regarded as design classics.

a new front bumper, although headlights still retracted above the grille. The Gran Sport option delivered real performance with a 209km/h (130mph) top speed, despite its huge 1915kg (4222lb) kerb weight. 1970 though was not a good year for the Riviera. A dreadful redesign added rear wheel skirts and deleted the retractable headlights. A new standard engine was introduced, a 7459cc (455 cu in) 276kW (370bhp) V8, but the extra weight blunted performance and buyers deserted the model.

The Riviera's saviour in 1971 was GM styling boss Bill Mitchell. Dubbed 'the boat-tail', the look was supposed to draw upon stylish cars of the 1930s. However, putting the design on a 554cm (218in) long, 1926kg (4247lb) car resulted in a look that was truly remarkable. The dramatic lines featured a more aggressive front end and curved hips as the bodywork rose over the rear wheels. The fastback roofline then narrowed down to a pointed boat-tail, which allowed for a sporty wraparound rear window,

The Riviera was progressively modified over the years. This is a 1969 Gran Sport model which has been stunningly customized. The body has been smoothed to remove as much chrome trim as possible, and 38-cm (15-inch) whitewall radials have been fitted.

reminiscent of the old Corvette Stingray. Sales and performance still suffered though because GM's engines had to be retuned to meet growing emission restrictions and run on unleaded petrol. Consequently the 455 engine was detuned, down to 235kW (315bhp) and when fitted in Gran Sport models, was rated at 246kW (330bhp).

Riviera sales actually picked up for the last year of the boat-tail look, but the model now went into decline. For 1974, an all-new model looked clumsy and weighed more than ever at 2074kg (4572lb) and the 455 V8 produced just 156kW (210bhp). Not surprisingly, sales dived and the model drifted into obscurity.

BUICK SKYLARK

1961–72

Buick revived the Skylark model name and created the all-new Skylark Sport in 1961. This cleanly styled model was originally launched as a coupé and was fitted with a standard 3523cc (215 cu in) V8 with a four-barrel carburettor, which was rated at 138kW (185bhp). The performance was highly impressive, and the general appeal of the model was enhanced when a convertible joined the range in 1962.

For 1964 there was a new body and more ostentatious trim for the Skylark range which got a performance boost with the addition of a new 4916cc (300 cu in) V8 with a four-barrel carburettor while the top of the line 'High Performance' V8 engine was rated at 156kW (210bhp).

1965 saw the introduction of the Gran Sport option, which eventually became its own model line as the Buick GS. A four-door

Sport Wagon was an interesting new estate model with a distinctive raised rear roof panel. The Skylark Custom range of 1968 became the plushiest models available. This was also the peak of the Skylark's performance, with the four-barrel engine gaining an extra 4kW (5bhp) to produce 212kW (285bhp). This then was a model range with sporting credibility, but the onset of 1970s emissions regulations put an end to them.

The 1961 Skylark with its all-aluminium V8 engine was the pioneer of the sports compact and closer in spirit and performance to the European offerings. Now a collector's item, the convertible is more highly prized than the coupé.

Engine: 6571cc (401 cu in) V8
Power: 242kW (325bhp)
0–96km/h (60mph): 7.4 secs
Top speed: 194km/h (121mph)
Production total: 1,462,316

CADILLAC TYPE 57

1915–23

Engine: 5146cc (314 cu in) V8
Power: 52kW (70bhp)
0–96km/h (60mph): n/a
Top speed: 88km/h (55mph)
Production total: 205,179

The new Cadillac V8 engine introduced in September 1914 was supremely sophisticated and would define what the marque was all about for generations to come.

Whatever coachwork surrounded the engine, it delivered a supreme driving experience that drivers were happy to pay dearly for.

The Type 51 was the model that cradled the innovative V8 engine and helped Cadillac become a world-renowned manufacturer. For 1915, the company offered four open and four closed body styles which ranged in price from $1975

to $3600, but those high prices did not stop more than 20,000 being sold that year. The Type 53 in 1916 saw Touring bodies offered on a special 335cm (132in) chassis. A year later, the Type 55 served with distinction during World War I as more than 2000 were sent to Europe as staff cars. The Type 57 in 1918 saw new Town limousine and Town Landaulet models, which

were 10cm (4in) narrower to cope with congested city streets.

By 1920 it was designated as the Type 59 with a restyled body, stiffer chassis and front wheels changed from 10 to 12 spoke items. The V8 was continually developed and that meant detachable cylinder heads for 1918 and further changes that would see the legendary unit endure until 1949.

CADILLAC 353

1930–32

Engine: 5786cc (353 cu in)
Power: 71kW (95bhp)
0–96km/h (60mph): 45 secs
Top speed: 96km/h (60mph)
Production total: 14,995

The 353 was rightly regarded as the high point of Cadillac luxury and design in the years before World War II, and was a more advanced development of the previous Series 341-B. The company offered seven Fisher Custom closed bodies, including a convertible coupé, and a Fleetwood Special Custom line with 11 basic bodywork combinations. The 5786cc (353 cu in) V8 was based on the previous (341 cu in) flathead unit introduced in 1928. This was truly a luxury car with power and style in abundance.

There was a long list of optional extras available to the well-heeled Cadillac customer to make the 353 even more exclusive. These included wire wheels, demountable wooden wheels, heater and a boot rack. A $175 radio was available and most 353 bodies came pre-wired with an aerial built into the roof. The old-fashioned Cadillac upright styling was gradually smoothed out from 1932 onwards and was even fashionably streamlined by 1934. Cadillac retained their technological edge firstly with syncromesh transmission, then with so-called 'no-draft' ventilation and vacuum assisted brakes in 1933, independent front suspension in 1934 and all steel bodies in 1935.

Sales in the first year were very strong at 14,995, but production dropped away dramatically after 1931 because of the Depression, falling to just 2906 in 1933.

CADILLAC 90

1938–40

Engine: V16 7064cc (430 cu in)
Power: 138kW (185bhp)
0–96km/h (60mph): 15 secs
Top speed: 145km/h (90mph)
Production total: 514

Cadillac was severely affected by the depression of the 1930s and had to cut costs to survive. Consequently their overhead valve V16 and V12 engines were replaced by a new flathead V16 which still managed to generate the same 138kW (185bhp) as before, while being lighter, easier and cheaper build, and more reliable. The advent of precision insert con rod bearings eliminated the knock and high wear that the earlier engines suffered. This engine was installed into the 90 which used the bodywork of the V8 Series 75. Room was not an issued because although the wheelbase was some 33cm (13 in) shorter than the old V16 powered limousines, the bodies were either equal in size or often larger. Most 90s were spacious Imperial limousines, only a few were coach built as open models.

However, Cadillac found it uneconomic to produce this V16 unit past 1940, even though it shared its wheelbase and several bodystyles with the V8 75 series. 1940 was the last model year for this car and also marked the last appearance of anything other than a V8 engine in a Cadillac. It was truly the end of an era for America's most prestigious carmaker.

The 1940 Sixteen Town Sedan could seat 5 passengers in fantastic levels of comfort. This model was one of the last built as Cadillac could not find enough customers to justify continued production.

CADILLAC ELDORADO

1953–70

From 1967 the Eldorado was reborn as a completely new front-wheel-drive six-passenger coupe. Indeed, this two-door hard top was described as a sport coupe, and was the only Cadillac with a disk-brake option.

Engine: V8 7021cc (429 cu in)
Power: 253kW (340bhp)
0–96km/h (60mph): 9.2 secs
Top speed: 193km/h (120mph)
Production total: 100,273

Eldorado means 'the gilded one' in Spanish. Cadillac's Eldorado was based on a 1952 concept car and featured a 'wraparound' windscreen, the first time this had ever been seen on a motor car. The cut-down doors were distinguished by a stylish dip, and a sparkling set of chromed wire wheels added a further touch of class. All conceivable luxuries came as standard with the exception of air conditioning. This was reflected in its price, a huge $7750.
A hardtop version of Eldorado, known initially as the Seville, was added in 1956 and an even more glamorous Eldorado Brougham joined the line the following year, but from 1961 to 1966, these were exclusively made as convertibles. The 1967 Cadillac Eldorado was a completely new front-wheel drive coupé. It was the first car to combine front-wheel drive with variable ratio power steering and automatic level control. Built on the Oldsmobile Toronado platform, the new Eldorado was shorter and lower than any other Cadillac but could still seat six in comfort because of the 'split driveline' layout. Cleverly styled by Bill Mitchell, it bore no physical relation to the Oldsmobile or Buick Rivera on which it was based. It was powered by Cadillac's own 429 unit modified for front-wheel drive, producing 253kW (340bhp). The car became a sales sensation.

CADILLAC COUPÉ DE VILLE

1953–70

Engine: V8 6384cc (390 cu in)
Power: 257kW (345bhp)
0–96km/h (60mph): 12 secs
Top speed: 185km/h (115mph)
Production total: 670,000

The Coupé de Ville was one of the most enduring and charismatic models in the Cadillac line-up, and coincided with the boom years for this marque. The 62 series in 1950 set the blueprint for this large and powerful V8 hardtop coupé with its prominent chrome grille, long bonnet and emerging rear fins.

By 1955, the distinctive torpedo front bumpers on the de Ville made the car look aggressive and unforgettable. However it was the 6200 series in 1959 that is regarded as the classic Cadillac Coupé de Ville style. Flamboyance and fins were fashionable, all propelled by a powerful 6384cc (390 cu in) V8 engine. The chromework was highly polished and the interiors were lavish colour-keyed arrangements with so-called 'juke box' style dashboards.

By 1960 the Coupé de Ville's wings had been clipped slightly and in 1962 the model became a sub-series, as the 6300. Four-door pillarless saloon models called Sedan de Villes appeared and within a few years a convertible was offered, too. By 1965 the model's famous fins had disappeared but the de Ville was still an imposing car. Redesigned in 1967, Cadillacs were getting fashionably squarer. In 1969, all Cadillacs were restyled in the image of the highly successful Eldorado and the de Ville lost its individuality.

Fins are to the fore with this 1959 Coupé de Ville which defined an era with its rocket inspired items. At 20ft long and 6ft wide and tipping the scales at two tonnes this pillarless two-door was an impressive sight.

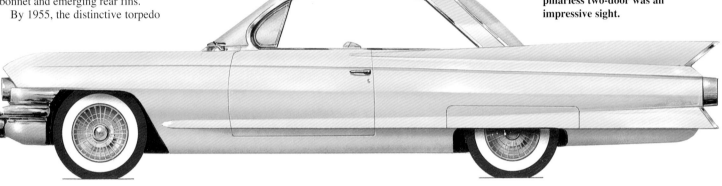

CATERHAM SUPER 7

1973–PRESENT

When Lotus decided to go up-market in 1973, Caterham Cars, a long serving dealer, snapped up the rights to the simple Lotus 7. Developed gradually over 15 years, Caterham soon dropped the fibreglass Series 4 and went back to basics with the Series 3 Super 7.

The car's tubular steel chassis, covered in aluminium panels with a plastic nose cone and wings could not have been simpler. Mechanically, too, the 7 was made from readily available parts with either Ford or Morris rear axles, although Caterham soon developed their own de Dion set up.

Power came from Lotus' own 1558cc (95 cu in) 94kW (126bhp) twin camshaft unit until stocks ran out. Caterham then switched to a 1298cc (79 cu in) Ford unit. Performance was always outstanding due to a high power to weight ratio, which meant the tiny Caterham always embarrassed more expensive machinery. The car always appealed to drivers who liked seat-of-the-pants motoring and in kit form, the buyer could get a real sense of satisfaction by building their own machine. The ultimate 7 was the JPE, the Jonathan Palmer Evolution, developed by the Formula One driver, which offered Ferrari-beating performance. Producing 186kW (250bhp), it could reach 96km/h (60mph) in just over three seconds.

Engine: V8 1598cc (98 cu in)
Power: 82kW (110bhp)
0–96km/h (60mph): 6 secs
Top speed: 177km/h (110mph)
Production total: 11,000

A sports car that has effortlessly spanned over half a century with same basic ingredients: four wheels and the bare minimum of bodywork. This '90s iteration has a Vauxhall two-litre unit producing 130kW (175bhp) and delivering supercar-beating performance.

CHAIKA GAZ-13

1958–65

Built by Gorky Motor Works, the GAZ M-13 was nicknamed the 'Seagull'. The styling was typically 1950s with lots of chrome, brightwork and fins. Indeed, like many other things in Soviet Russia it copied contemporary Western design. In this case, the GAZ-13 was a very close copy of the 1955 Packard Patrician.

A step below the Zil in prestige terms, it was only available to selected members of Soviet society. Only state officials and important professionals could enjoy the luxuries that included

The influence of mid-1950s American styling is clearly evident in this chrome-laden Chaika launched in 1959. Remaining in production for another 15 years unchanged, this V8-engined limousine proved to be perfect for the Russian elite who were too important to travel by Lada.

electrically operated windows, push button automatic transmission and a five-band radio. There were even two fully collapsible bucket seats for additional passengers. Power was provided by a US-inspired 5.5-litre (336 cu in) V8 engine. Although built as a four-door limousine, there was also a cabriolet version.

Chaika production was suspended in 1965, although

the model reappeared with the same engine, but with slightly more contemporary styling, in 1977. In 1978 it had the (dubious) honour of being named as President Brezhnev's favoured mode of transport.

Engine: 5500cc (336 cu in), V8-cylinder
Power: 145kW (195bhp)
0–96km/h (60mph): 15 secs
Top speed: 161km/h (100mph)
Production total: n/a

CHAMPION 250

1948–51

Engine: 250cc (15 cu in) 2-cylinder
Power: 11kW (15bhp)
0–96km/h (60mph): n/a
Top speed: 80km/h (50mph)
Production total: 8000

The Champion was essentially a cycle car right down to the spoked wire wheels. Designed in 1946, it

entered production in 1948. This two-seater roadster's design was owned by a cogwheel company based in Friedrichshafen who sold the rights to a former BMW engineer, Herman Holbein. Small, but perfectly formed, it resembled a Triumph TR2 but did not have the same power. Rear-mounted

250cc (15 cu in) motorcycle engines made by TWN provided the power, but performance was always poor. However, the coupé version in 1950 benefited from a larger 400cc (24 cu in) engine. But the cars, however, were expensive to build, with over 200 suppliers providing parts.

In 1955 the company was bought by two brothers, Otto and Wilhelm Maisch, who renamed the Champion the Maico. They even fitted a larger 500cc (31 cu in) engine to broaden the cars appeal. However, just 8000 models had been manufactured by the time the company went bankrupt in 1958.

CHECKER MODEL E

1925–26

Engine: 2000cc (122 cu in) 4-cylinder
Power: 17kW (22.5bhp)
0–96km/h (60mph): n/a
Top speed: 80km/h (50mph)
Production total: 930

One company had the confidence and ability to gamble its future on the production of just one type of vehicle, the humble taxicab, as epitomized by the Model E.

In 1921, an automobile body engineer named Lomberg asked Morris Markin, a Russian immigrant and self-made businessman, for a $15,000 loan to finance his car-body business. Markin eventually took the business over along with other car factories to form the Checker Cab Manufacturing Company. This would later become the Checker Motors Corporation.

Checker's Model E was typical of basic 1920s automobile design with a strong four-cylinder Buda engine and a spacious limousine body that could seat five in comfort. In addition, an open-backed Landau version was made available for the first year. Produced at the rate of around 75 per week, about 930 Model Es were built in just over a year, before the car was succeeded by the Model F.

CHECKER MARATHON

1959–82

The Marathon was a popular rugged car aimed squarely at the taxi trade with extra wide doors and lots of legroom. The vehicle was based on the Checker A-8, produced in 1956, and had the distinctive and now familiar quad-headlights of the 1958 A-9.

The first so-called civilian model Checker was the A-10 Superba, released in 1960, but it had limited appeal. In 1962 Checker used the Marathon name for the first time on the A-12, which was available as a four-door saloon and a station wagon.

Essentially, the styling stayed the same for the next 20 years and the

A classic shape that would be part of the New York Cityscape for over 30 years. The Marathon had wide doors and plenty of room inside. This is the 'civilian' version, a Town Custom limousine which could be bought by non-taxi drivers.

car became an essential part of New York City's backdrop. Five thousand Checker cabs roamed the city as late as the mid-1970s, but numbers quickly declined by the end of the decade. Luxury ranges such as the Town Custom Limousine and V8 engines were added to the line-up, which included the incredible Aerobus eight-door station wagon.

In the 1970s, oil prices doubled which became a problem for the Marathon since it only averaged 4km/l (11mpg). Cab drivers began buying smaller, more fuel-efficient vehicles, and on 12 July 1982, the Checker Motor Corporation of Kalamazoo, Michigan, made its last cab.

Engine: 3704cc (226 cu in) 6-cylinder
Power: 91kW (122bhp)
0–96km/h (60mph): 15 secs
Top speed: 177km/h (110mph)
Production total: 100,000

CHEVROLET 490

1920–22

Engine: 2803cc (171 cu in) 4-cylinder
Power: 19kW (26bhp)
0–96km/h (60mph): n/a
Top speed: 80km/h (50mph)
Production total: 356,406

Chevrolet made the decision to take on Ford at the lower end of the market, but not by matching them on price. The company positioned itself as a maker of premium-priced economy cars with more refinement and technical

merit. It believed that even at the budget end of the market, customers were still looking for something with style and quality. At the forefront of this theory was the Chevrolet 490, an entry-level four-cylinder range introduced in 1918. It proved to be very popular.

For 1920, Chevrolet surprised everyone by offering a restyled 490. Cars rarely changed their appearance at this time, but this was one of the first examples of a

manufacturer trying to stimulate sales through a redesign. The straight wings were replaced with curved ones and the headlights were mounted on steel brackets to eliminate the clumsy tie bar. Sales soared.

By 1922, Chevrolet had enhanced the practicality of the 490 by making the saloon a four-door model. The engines now had easy valve adjustment on the rocker arms, larger king pins on the

suspension and single pedal brakes. These cars were therefore easy and cheap to maintain and stole some sales from the more basic and less comfortable Ford Model T.

Chevrolet had an assembly plant in London in the early 1920s to get around import duties, which explains why this two-door hardtop 490 could be offered in the UK, often with unique coachwork to suit the buyer's tastes.

CHEVROLET AD UNIVERSAL

1930–31

Engine: 3180cc (194 cu in) 6-cylinder
Power: 37kW (50bhp)
0–96km/h (60mph): 40 secs
Top speed: 97km/h (60mph)
Production total: 864,243

Chevrolet called their model range the Universal in 1930. Power came from the legendary Chevrolet six-cylinder engine, which had arrived in 1929 in an effort to outperform

the Ford Model A, which had just four cylinders. Dubbed the 'Cast-Iron Wonder' the engine was a robust overhead valve unit that survived into the 1950s. It effectively offered motorists smooth six-cylinder motoring for the price of four.

The upright styling of Chevrolet's previous cars continued with the Universal, which now had a

slanting non-glare windscreen. The fuel gauge was moved to the dashboard while the other instruments were now circular with darker faces. Under the bonnet was a new manifold design to improve performance, while the chassis had new hydraulic shock absorbers.

There was a huge line-up featuring ten models. The AD Universal proved to be every bit as

responsible for motorizing the US as did the Ford Model A. Despite selling in huge numbers, some of the tremendously attractive and highly collectable roadster versions are now extremely difficult to find and have classic status among collectors. The model range was renamed the Independence for 1931 with some minor stylistic and mechanical changes.

CHEVROLET EC STANDARD 1935

Engine: 3409cc (208 cu in) 6-cylinder
Power: 55kW (74bhp)
0–96km/h (60mph): 25 secs
Top speed: 112km/h (70 mph)
Production total: 202,773

Chevrolet made the decision to give their mass-market models a technological edge over the competition. For example, in 1934, the company introduced independent 'Knee Action' front suspension, while Ford stuck to old-fashioned transverse-leaf springs. This gave buyers a reason to choose Chevrolet products, which helped the company become the best selling marque in the United States. The new model that spearheaded that technical edge was the EA Master Deluxe series. However, high technology was expensive, so the company offered the more basic transverse-leaf-sprung ED and EC Standard models as well.

Styling was similar to the DA of previous years, but the EC now had body-coloured headlight shells and, inside, the gauges were moved from the centre of the dashboard and grouped in front of the driver. Under the bonnet, the 'Blue Flame' six-cylinder engine had a new head and better lubrication.

Two-door sports roadsters, coupés and a phaeton were joined in the line-up by four-door saloons. The interior specification was spartan, but there were plenty of extras that could be ordered to suit. These goodies included bumper overriders, a radio, a heater, a cigar lighter, spot lamps, wire wheels and a rear-view mirror.

CHEVROLET MASTER GA 1937

Engine: 3548cc (217 cu in) 6-cylinder
Power: 63kW (85bhp)
0–96km/h (60mph): 20 secs
Top speed: 135km/h (84mph)
Production total: 519,024

Launched at the height of Chevrolet's battle with Ford to be the United States' favourite carmaker, this new range boosted the company's sales significantly. In 1937, Chevrolet reached the Number One spot ahead of Ford and two years later made its 15-millionth car.

The Master series was an all new model with a more compact and powerful 63kW (85bhp) version of the legendary 'Cast-Iron Wonder' six-cylinder engine, which now had a larger bore and shorter stroke and four main bearings. The car also used a stiffer box girder frame and hypoid rear axle across the whole range. The Unisteel body was completely new and had a fresh, so-called 'Diamond Crown' look, featuring safety glass in all the windows and straight wings. The grille was swept in on each side and the headlight shells were painted the same colour as the body.

This was a car that the ambitious working-class man could aspire to owning. The six-cylinder engines were very smooth and performance was impressive. Inside, the car had a high level of standard trim. This included a dashboard temperature gauge, front passenger armrest, twin tail lamps, double windscreen wipers, twin sun visors and more ornate bumpers with overriders. No wonder the 'Chevy' soon became the United States' people's car.

This Chevrolet Master sports sedan was among the most popular GA models, selling some 144,110 in 1937. This was the four-door family car that everyone aspired to, especially as it was well equipped.

CHEVROLET BEL AIR

Engine: 4639cc (283 cu in) 6-cylinder
Power: 212kW (285bhp)
0–96km/h (60mph): 8 secs
Top speed: 193km/h (120mph)
Production total: 3,293,543

The Chevrolet Bel Air evolved into one of the classic US cars of the era. Announced in 1950 as a sporty two-door hardtop, it had a six-cylinder engine and Powerglide automatic transmission. By 1953, the Bel Air name was extended to all four-door saloons and also appeared as a convertible. An estate version of the Bel Air was offered in 1954, which was badged as the Nomad. After a smart restyle in 1955 and mild facelift in 1956, Chevrolet arrived at the classic shape, with subtle fins and relatively clean lines. Every High School student now wanted to borrow their parents' Chevy.

The Bel Air became Chevrolet's top of the range model, available as a two- and four-door saloon and

a convertible with optional power hood. The three-door Nomad looked very different and is now highly sought-after on the classic car market.

Powered by six-cylinder and V8 engines, it was the installation of the 212kW (285bhp) fuel-injected unit that delivered real performance. However, the combination of great styling and performance only lasted for one model year; after that, the Bel Air became a more mainstream and anonymous car.

This 1955 Bel Air Hardtop Sport Coupé represented the top of the line for Chevrolet's budget-priced 'One Fifty' series. Gold Bel Air script and lots more chrome helped set this model apart. Although affordable, it was still desirable.

CHEVROLET CORVAIR

Engine: 2377cc (145 cu in) 6-cylinder
Power: 63kW (84bhp)
0–96km/h (60mph): 15 secs
Top speed: 144km/h (90mph)
Production total: 1,695,765

The Corvair became famous as the car that was killed by a book. Initially, the Corvair was General Motors' response to the increasing number of European economy cars, such as the Volkswagen Beetle, that were flooding the domestic market.

The car could not have been

more different from contemporary American designs with its rear-mounted, air-cooled, slat six-cylinder engine and independent suspension. This wasn't just a scaled-down car like those offered by Ford and Chrysler, but a genuinely new compact.

However, buyers remained cautious, preferring the conventional offerings from Detroit. Although the saloons struggled, it was the Monza coupés and convertible that eventually

found buyers, who appreciated their unique style and decent performance.

Unfortunately, Ralph Nader's book, *Unsafe at any Speed*, highlighted handling problems and high-profile accidents on the early models. Even though the handling only became unsafe if the differing front and rear tyre pressures were not properly maintained, the damage had been done.

Despite a new generation Corvair from 1964 with a pretty

restyle and revised rear suspension, time was running out for the innovative car, despite the later introduction of a turbocharged version that could produce up to 134kW (180bhp).

The Corvair Monza was the star of the line-up and the convertible Spyder was the most desirable model of all, identified by the cross flag badges on the rear deck. This 1962 model came with a turbo-charged engine.

CHEVROLET CORVETTE

1953–83

Engine: 5360cc (327 cu in) V8
Power: 268kW (360bhp)
0–96km/h (60mph): 6 secs
Top speed: 233km/h (145mph)
Production total: 684,652

The United States and General Motors finally took on the British sports car with a unique and innovative creation of their own, which has now become a legend. Just six months after the debut of a concept car at the GM Motorama, the first Corvette rolled off a makeshift assembly line in Flint Michigan on 30 June 1953. Only available as a two-seat convertible in Polo White with a red interior, each one was built by hand and had its pretty Harley Earl-designed body moulded from fibreglass. It sat on a shortened saloon car chassis, with a 259cm (102in) wheelbase and was powered by a so-called 'Blue Flame Special' engine, essentially an upgraded version of the standard Chevrolet 3851cc (235 cu in) six-cylinder producing 112kW (150bhp). A Powerglide two-speed automatic gearbox was the only transmission available. However, the cars were too expensive. Costing more than any Jaguar or Cadillac, just 183 were sold in 1953.

Changes needed to be made as sales had only increased to 700 units by 1955. It was Zora Arkus-Duntov, a Corvette engineer, who realized that the car needed V8 power and better handling. For 1956, the car was restyled featuring 'scooped out' sides, outside door handles, roll-up windows and an optional removable hardtop. The six-cylinder engine was dropped and a

4343cc (265 cu in) V8 was standardized, although it was rated at just 145kW (195bhp). However, in 1957 the revised styling gelled with the introduction of Chevrolet's most powerful engine to date, a four-barrel carburettor 4638cc (283 cu in) V8, which produced 164kW (220bhp). Sales took off as quickly as the Corvette accelerated (provided it was driven in a straight line).

Second-generation Corvettes arrived in 1963 with the unveiling of the classic Sting Ray body. A two-passenger coupé body style joined the convertible for the first time and featured a distinctive split rear-window design. The Corvette now had independent rear suspension, fuel injection and knock off wheels. Significantly, a track option, the Z-06, was also created by Arkus-Duntoz as a purpose-built racing car. It had a fuel-injected 5360cc (327 cu in) V8 and heavy-duty brakes and suspension. Luxury options such as power steering, air conditioning and leather seats were available for

the first time on Corvettes.

An all-new Corvette in 1968 marked a dramatic change in styling as it bore a striking resemblance to Chevrolet's Mako Shark II concept car. The new Corvette also introduced hidden windscreen wipers and removable T-tops on Coupé models. Under the bonnet, it gained several interesting engine options, including the 5360cc (327 cu in) V8 L79, rated at 261kW (350bhp), and the L89 aluminium head option for the L71. As Corvette production hit a record 28,566 units, in 1969 the car was officially listed as a 'Stingray'. The coupé outsold the convertible for the first time, and continued to do so in all subsequent years.

1973 saw a new-generation Corvette which was unique by combining a smooth body-coloured nose with the original 1968 cut off 'Kamm' tail. However, the engines were further detuned for cleaner emissions, which resulted in much lower power outputs. In 1974, the Corvette received a new, smooth body-colour rear end to match the

The 1963 Corvette was striking in coupé form with the sloping split rear window. Its headlights were hidden in an electrically operated panel. In these early models there was storage space under the seats.

front styling and accommodate the compulsory Federal 8km/h (5mph) bumpers. The car then began to change its character forever as engine outputs plunged. The top 5735cc (350 cu in) V8 was rated at just 153kW (205bhp). This was also the last year for the convertible, as falling sales and threatened safety legislation ended its production life.

However, as the Corvette celebrated its 25th anniversary in 1978, featuring a new fastback roofline and special two-tone paint jobs, a four-speed manual gearbox was reinstated as standard and a higher-output 5735cc (350 cu in) V8 was made available.

This 1959 Corvette has been mildly customized by removing some of the chrome and badging and fitting sports wheels with knock-off hubs. The fact that owners want to modify the Corvette confirms its status as an American cultural icon.

CHEVROLET IMPALA

1960–69

The Chevrolet Impala has been credited as the first true muscle car. Created as Chevrolet's top of the line model, the Impala became the symbol for performance in the early 1960s and introduced Chevrolet's Super Sport SS performance brand.

Saloons, estates, convertibles and two-door hardtops, powered by 5.4-litre V8s, made up the range. Less outrageous than their finned predecessors, the SS models were launched in 1961, powered by a big 6702cc (409 cu in) V8 engine.

The Impala was completely redesigned for 1965 losing its box-like shape and featuring a more streamlined look. The great 409 was phased out and replaced by the Mark IV 6489cc (396 cu in) V8, which would power Chevrolets for

the rest of the 1960s. The new 396 could be mated to a new automatic transmission, the Turbo Hydra-matic 350. 396s were available in all Impalas, but the SS continued as a separate model.

By 1966, the Caprice became the new top of the line Chevrolet, stealing the Impala's limelight, especially as the SS was now a performance car in name only. It also lost its six round tail-lights, the car's trademark since 1958. The Impala had been a big saloon with good performance, but by the end of the 1960s this image had been compromised.

Engine: 5359cc (327 cu in) V8
Power: 186kW (250bhp)
0–96km/h (60mph): 10 secs
Top speed: 172km/h (107mph)
Production total: 7,000,000

In 1962, the Impala's styling was more restrained and this 2-door hardtop Sport Coupé was by far the prettiest. It sat at the top of Chevrolet's range and this model had sports steering wheel, electric clock and rear seat radio speaker.

CHEVROLET CHEVELLE

1964–80

Engine: 6489cc (396 cu in) V8
Power: 279kW (375bhp)
0–96km/h (60mph): 7 secs
Top speed: 193km/h (120mph)
Production total: 3,282,066

Chevrolet's all-new Chevelle in 1964 was designed to fit between the compact Chevy II and the company's full-sized cars, becoming labelled as a 'senior compact'. Eleven models were available in two basic lines, called

the Chevelle 300 and the Malibu, as well as a convertible. The Supersport SS was Chevrolet's entry into the mid-size muscle car battle against the Pontiac GTO. With its own line of engines and performance equipment, the car started with a 5359cc (327 cu in) V8 and was later fitted with a powerful 6489cc (396 cu in) V8.

1968 saw a major redesign of the Chevelle and an estate car body

was made available. The front end looked rakish, the bonnet was stretched out and the bootline shortened, while the two-door got a new fastback look. The ultimate Chevelle SS soon had the most powerfullyrated engine in muscle car history, the LS6 454 in 1970. This was the Chevelle's high point. 1973 was the last year for the SS before the whole range was redesigned and the engines were

detuned. The new Colonnade hardtop styling meant inner and outer shells, and heavy roof pillars were used. Although undoubtedly safer, the four-door models in particular looked ungainly. The Chevelle had become just another big car.

A 1970 Chevelle in full Super Sports trim. Under the bonnet was a 260kW (350bhp) engine, and the SS-454 option with Z15 package uprated the suspension, brakes and wheels to keep pace with rival muscle cars.

CHEVROLET CAMARO

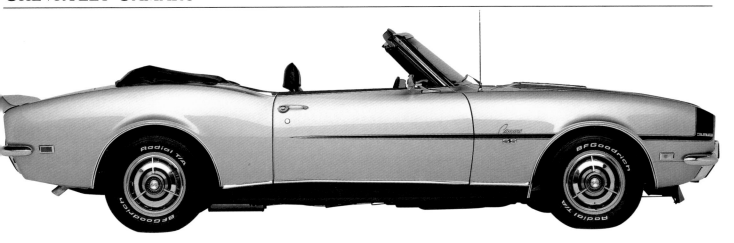

Stunned by Ford's success with the Mustang, General Motors began designing its response in 1964. By 1966 the car had a name, the Camaro, meaning 'friend'. 1967 was the first full production year and a hardtop coupé and convertible were launched with both V6 and V8 engines. The Camaro could be ordered with nearly 80 factory options and 40 dealer accessories arranged into three main option packages. The RS package included numerous cosmetic changes, including a blacked-out grill with hidden headlights and revised light clusters.

Better, though, was the SS package which included as standard a modified 5733cc (350 cu in) V8 engine. A 6489cc (396 cu in) big block version producing 242kW (325bhp) (L35), and a 279kW (375bhp) version raised the stakes even further complemented by simulated air-intakes on the bonnet, special bumble bee striping, and a blacked-out grille.

Even more exciting though was the Z-28, specifically designed to compete in the Club of America Trans Am racing series. This car had competition suspension and the engine could produce a staggering 298kW (400bhp). With a 225km/h (140mph) top speed, it dominated track racing for a while.

Dealers could effectively make their own high-performance models specifically for each customer from the General Motors parts bin. However, these were nothing compared to the factory Camaro ZL1 which was specially designed to compete in the NHRA Super Stock drag racing classes. At the heart of this model was an all-

aluminium engine producing almost 373kW (500bhp) – making it the most powerful engine Chevrolet ever offered to the public. The unit weighed just 227kg (500lb), the same as Chevy's 5359cc (327 cu in) small block engine, and came with a remarkable five-year/80,000km (50,000 mile) warranty and was fully street legal. The ZL1 pushed the cost of a standard car up to $7,200 and the company built 69 models to qualify for racing. The high price made them very difficult to sell and new ZL1s were still on offer in the early 1970s.

An all-new Camaro arrived in 1970 with a fabulous European-inspired restyle that would set the trend into the next decade. The new Camaro was 5cm (2in) longer, had 12.5cm (5in) longer doors and was more refined thanks to better noise insulation. For 1971, there were only detail cosmetic changes but the engines had to change. This was because General Motors had

stated that all its cars had to run on unleaded petrol, which meant lower compression ratios and power. So the high-output Z-28 saw its 5733cc (350 cu in) engine drop from a compression of 11:1 to 9:1 and horsepower fell from 268kW (360bhp) to 246kW (330bhp).

This was the shape of things to come as the 1970s were unkind to performance cars in general. A 174-day strike in 1972 at GM's Ohio plant did not help matters and even worse, 1100 unfinished Camaros had to be scrapped because they didn't meet 1972 US Federal bumper safety standards. There were even rumours that the Camaro name was to be dropped.

In 1973, the legendary SS option was discontinued. This meant that the only true performance Camaro was now the Z-28 although the model saw another decrease in power as hydraulic lifters replaced its solid ones. Another indicator that the character of the Camaro,

Chevrolet's answer to the Ford Mustang was this convertible in 1967 available with a variety of six-cylinder and V8 engines plus Super Sports and Rally Sports options. Chevrolet made ten times more coupés than convertibles.

and indeed, the profile of its buyers, was changing was that air conditioning became available on the Z-28 for the first time. This also explained the new Type LT option, effectively a luxury package which included a weak V8 and several trim items. As so often happened in this period, the neutering of such sports cars actually broadened their appeal and boosted sales. In 1979, Chevrolet had their best-ever year with the model when 282,571 were sold.

Engine: 5733cc (350 cu in) V8
Power: 224kW (300bhp)
0–96km/h (60mph): 8 secs
Top speed: 209km/h (130mph)
Production total: 2,636,007

CHRYSLER MODEL B

1924–25

Engine: 3294cc (201 cu in) 6-cylinder
Power: 51kW (68bhp)
0–96km/h (60mph): n/a
Top speed: 113km/h (70mph)
Production total: 32,000

Walter Percy Chrysler managed to start a motor company in the 1920s and make it survive into the 1930s. The date was January 1924 and the

location was the Commodore Hotel in New York where the first new Chrysler was presented. It was an attractively priced, innovative car which appealed to the mass-market. It was no wonder that by the end of the year around 32,000 examples had been sold, a first-year sales record in the highly competitive motor industry.

At the heart of the model was an L-head engine with a very high compression ratio. This meant it was powerful, producing 51kW (68bhp) at 3200rpm, providing great performance and a comfortable 113km/h (70mph) top speed. The engine featured aluminium pistons and full pressure lubrication and underneath, four-wheel hydraulic

brakes and a tubular front axle were fitted – both unique on a volume production car at the time. The Model B also excelled at motorsport, setting national records and winning many events. The Model B led the way for Chrysler to become the first American manufacturer to compete in the legendary Le Mans 24-hour race.

CHRYSLER C300

1955

Engine: 5425cc (331 cu in) V8
Power: 224kW (300bhp)
0–96km/h (60mph): 9 secs
Top speed: 206km/h (128mph)
Production total: 1725

The Chrysler C300 is generally regarded as the first muscle car. Underneath the bonnet was a 5425cc (331 cu in) Hemi V8 with two four-barrel carburettors, a full race specification camshaft, solid lifters, special manifolds and large

diameter dual exhausts which all helped boost power output to 224kW (300bhp). Not only was the engine special, but a modified PowerFlite automatic transmission guaranteed smooth gear changes, while the heavy-duty suspension set-up and Blue Streak racing tyres helped keep the C300 on the road. At the front was an imposing Imperial model-type grille.

The C300 was an exclusive car available in just three colours –

This most charismatic of Chryslers was powered by the most potent Hemi V8 and officially designated as the C300. This attractive model combined the egg-crate grille of the Imperial model with a New Yorker Newport two-door hardtop body with tremendous success.

black, red and white. Inside, leather upholstery was standard and the car was only ever available as a two-door hardtop. Part of its

muscle car image was the lack of a door mirror – the driver of a 300 was supposedly so focused on overtaking what was up ahead that nothing was ever going to sneak up behind. The C300 really was a fast car though, winning championship titles in both NASCAR Grand National and AAA stock car racing. The legend of the Chrysler 'letter' cars and indeed the great American muscle car had been born.

CHRYSLER IMPERIAL

1956–63

Engine: 6769cc (413 cu in) V8
Power: 257kW (345bhp)
0–96km/h (60mph): 9.8 secs
Top speed: 201km/h (125mph)
Production total: 171,000

Chrysler recreated their flagship model, the Imperial, in 1956 as an independent brand. The new Imperial was styled by Virgil Exner, the now famous designer credited with bringing a sense of style to the postwar Chrysler Corporation. The Imperial was now distinguished by the long bonnet, short boot proportions, bold grille work and tall free-standing tail-lights. Those who could afford an Imperial received what Chrysler claimed was 'The Finest Car America Has Yet Produced'.

In 1957 the styling, again by Virgil Exner, featured long, lean lines that contrasted sharply with the rotund, bloated designs produced by other car builders. The Imperial's majestic tail fins were subtle and graceful compared with contemporary rival products. Chrome-free body sides were

ahead of their time and the curved door glass was a real industry first. Bodies were offered as two-door hardtops, four-door hardtops, pillared saloons and a beautiful convertible. The Imperial had an industry-leading V8, delivering an impressive 242kW (325bhp) through a TorqueFlite push-button automatic gearbox.

Each model year brought a new look for the Imperial, but the 1961 design was dominated by large tail fins. Chrysler claimed that wind tunnel tests proved that these fins gave their cars high-speed stability. Despite their luxury and undoubted performance, these Imperials saw only limited production and just 12,249 cars were to be built before

Completely restyled for 1955 this 4-door sedan lasted for just one more year. The Imperial Eagle crest was located between the two sections of the front grille and the free-standing rear wing-mounted lights were unique to this model.

the model name was revived in the mid-1960s.

CHRYSLER 300F

1960–1961

Engine: 6769cc (413 cu in) V8
Power: 279kW (375bhp)
0–96km/h (60mph): 7.1 secs
Top speed: 233km/h (145mph)
Production total: 1212

On 15 January 1960, Chrysler announced the 'sixth in a famous

line', the 300F. These 'letter cars' were built for outright performance. The 6769cc (413 cu in) engine delivered 279kW (375bhp) in spectacular fashion. Using a clever ram induction intake manifold system, 76cm (30in) induction tubes placed over the carburettor fed each bank

of cylinders out beyond the rocker cover of the opposing cylinder head. The new induction set-up was 3.5kW (5bhp) less powerful than the previous year's model but added 61Nm (45 lb ft) of torque at 800rpm less. For drivers who wanted more outright power, an

engine tuned to produce 298kW (400bhp) was fitted with a four-speed Pont-à-Mousson manual transmission from France's big Facel-Vega models.

The body was structurally brand new with a welded monocoque construction. It was also visually striking with a trapezoidal grille and fabulous sloping tail fins as well as boomerang-like tail lights. Seating just four, the bucket seats were divided by a console that ran from front to back. The domed dashboard comprised a glass bubble in which the instruments seemed to float.

This was one of the most focused performance cars that the United States had ever produced. As usual, less attention was given to developing the car's handling – cornering was not its strong point.

The styling of the 300F was universally accepted in 1960, although unitary construction was a step forward. The rear spare wheel shape only lasted one year as from 1962 it was badged as the 300G.

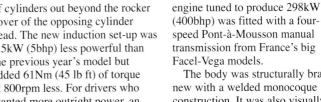
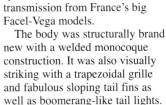

CHRYSLER NEW YORKER

1940–62

As part of the 1939 C-23 series, three distinct models were offered with the same engine/chassis platform – the Imperial, Saratoga and New Yorker. The New Yorker was marketed as the luxury model with distinctive two-tone upholstery and high quality trim. War interrupted production in 1942 and the prewar New Yorker was reintroduced after the conflict and not updated until 1949. By 1951, the wheelbase had been lengthened and a V8 engine became standard.

When Chrysler developed the Imperial as a stand-alone premium brand in 1955, the New Yorker became the top of the range model. Available as a saloon, two-door, convertible and station wagon, the next evolution came in 1957 when fins were added. Under the bonnet was the largest production engine of its kind, at 6425cc (392 cu in), producing 242kW (325bhp). The car was advertised as being 'the most glamorous car in a generation'. By 1959 that huge engine was no longer available as production costs were being slashed. A minor facelift in 1961 saw less garish trim being used. This was also the last year for the once-fashionable fins as Chrysler adjusted to the simpler styles of the 1960s.

Engine: 6425cc (392 cu in) V8
Power: 242kW (325bhp)
0–96km/h (60mph): 10 secs
Top speed: 193km/h (120mph)
Production total: 400,000

The New Yorker, here a convertible coupé, established the prominent rear wing look in 1957, especially as many customers ordered twin wing-mounted aerials to emphasize the sweep of those tail fins.

CHRYSLER LEBARON

1977–80

In 1977, Chrysler introduced the mid-size M-body LeBaron. The M-body series of cars were based on the Plymouth Volare and shared many parts. This was the company's attempt to gain a greater share of the profitable luxury market, intending to compete with the Cadillac Seville and Mercedes-Benz. Designed to be a light and lean range, the car weighed 1588kg (3500lb) and had a wheelbase of 286cm (112.7in). The LeBaron came in both two- and four-door models with either six-cylinder or V8 engines, the top model badged as the Medallion. From 1978, the LeBaron became more practical with the Town & Country estate,. This featured garish fake ash timber on the sides.

In fact, the model never really challenged the prestige marques it was competing against. A high specification LeBaron 5th Avenue edition in 1980 tried to offer more than the standard car but, again, had limited appeal. 1981 was the last year of the M-body wagon and the coupés. It was also the last year the LeBaron was offered as a rear-wheel drive car. For the 1980s a more compact, cheaper to produce layout meant that, like many other large American cars, the future was now front-wheel drive.

Engine: 3687cc (225 cu in) V8
Power: 97kW (130bhp)
0–96km/h (60mph): 12 secs
Top speed: 185km/h (115mph)
Production total: 360,000

The Town and Country wagon was an attempt to recreate Chrysler's wood-panelled glories from the 1940s. In 1982, however, plastic took the place of the real thing with disastrous aesthetic results.

CHRYSLER (UK/FRANCE) 180

1970–80

In 1970 Chrysler took over both the Rootes Group in the UK and Simca in France, its main aim was to try and centralize the two companies. It wanted to market models to challenge Ford of Europe and General Motors' Vauxhall and Opel badges. Its first effort was the Simca/Chrysler 180

in 1970. A rather odd medium-sized car, it was designed both in Coventry, England, and France. Originally intended as a new Humber, it also attempted to bring Simca back into the medium price bracket in the European market.

Built in France, the styling was that of an overgrown Hillman

Avenger with conventional MacPherson strut suspension. Although a 1.6-litre (98 cu in) version was available in France, the UK models had 1.8-litre (111 cu in) and, from 1972, 2-litre (122 cu in) engines with automatic gearboxes. Despite a ten-year production run, the car was a dull

and undistinguished model. When Talbot took over Chrysler, sales plummeted and the car was dropped.

Engine: 1812cc (111 cu in) 4-cylinder
Power: 72kW (97bhp)
0–96km/h (60mph): 13.6 secs
Top speed: 159km/h (99mph)
Production total: 60,000

CHRYSLER (UK/FRANCE) ALPINE

1975–86

In the 1970s, Simca wanted to move upmarket to a larger size class so launched the Alpine. Based on the 1967 Simca 1100, the car used the same floorpan (but with a longer 259cm (102in) wheelbase), the same independent suspension and 1294cc (79 cu in) and 1442cc (88 cu in) versions of the 1100 engine, wrapped up in a five-door hatchback body.

It was launched in late 1975 in Europe and early 1976 in the UK.

The first models were imported from the France Simca factory at Poissy but, from the end of 1976, the car was assembled in Coventry, England. The Alpine was an unusual machine because the

Beneath the hatchback body was an old Simca. But that did not stop this car being crowned European Car of the Year. It never capitalized on that success and was not developed into a real Cortina-beater.

hatchback configuration was still a novelty when all successful medium-sized cars, like the Ford Cortina, were saloons. It was even crowned European Car of the Year for 1976.

Although practical and comfortable, the engines could sound rough because they were underpowered for the size of the car. Front-wheel drive and no power steering also made it a heavy car to steer and park. Sales

of 30,000 units a year were not good enough, and despite the introduction of a saloon version and the new Talbot Solara in 1980, few customers were interested.

Engine: 1294cc (79 cu in) 4-cylinder
Power: 48.5kW (65bhp)
0–96km/h (60mph): 16.9secs
Top speed: 90mph/144km/h
Production total: 108,405 plus 77,422 Talbots

CHRYSLER (UK/FRANCE) SUNBEAM

1977–81

Engine: 928cc (57 cu in) 4-cylinder
Power: 31kW (42bhp)
0–96km/h (60mph): 25 secs
Top speed: 77mph/123km/h
Production total: 104,547 plus 116,000 Talbots

Launching the Chrysler Sunbeam took just two years from idea to production. Released for sale in late 1977, the new car had crisp, angular styling, with the familiar corporate front end, but with recessed headlights. At the rear, the car featured tail-lights similar to the Alpine and an unusual hatchback arrangement, effectively just the rear window glass hinged. Specification levels were high, with front disc brakes and electronic ignition across the range.

Engine: choices were 1295cc (79 cu in) and 1598cc (98 cu in) units from the Avenger, which delivered good performance, while the Hillman Imp's 928cc (57 cu in) all-alloy engine powered the entry-level model. Enthusiasts liked the Ti model with its alloy wheels, big spoilers and a twin-Webber carburettor 1.6-litre (98 cu in) engine.

However, the real performance car was the 1979 Sunbeam-Lotus. This had a 119kW (160bhp) version of the 2.2-litre (134 cu in) Lotus engine, alloy wheels, a five-speed ZF gearbox and a distinctive black-with-silver-stripe colour scheme. The Sunbeam was rebadged as a Talbot for 1980 and the car continued to be built until 1981 when the Linwood factory in Scotland, where it was made, closed.

A state of the art small car in the mid-1970s. A pity that only the rear glass lifted rather than a proper tailgate. Even so, it was well equipped and there were some serious performance models. But this is an entry level Sunbeam.

CHRYSLER (UK/FRANCE) HORIZON

1977–85

Although Chrysler Europe needed a replacement for the ageing Simca 1100, it nevertheless used it as a basis for a new car, the Horizon. Launched at the end of 1977, it incorporated many of the refinements already found on the Alpine. The original 1118cc (68 cu in) 1100 engine was used, along with the 1294cc (79 cu in) and 1442cc (88 cu in) versions from the Alpine, with a four-speed manual transmission as standard.

The car was wider and longer than the 1100, allowing more interior room in its comfortable cabin. The Horizon was marketed, like Alpine, as a brand new car and despite its roots, was actually voted European Car of the Year in 1978. It also became a 'world' car wearing Plymouth and Dodge badges offering efficient, inoffensive but somewhat dull urban transportation.

Engine: 1118/1294cc (cu in) 4-cylinder
Power: 44/51kW (59/68bhp)
0–96km/h (60mph): 15 secs
Top speed: 152km/h (95mph)
Production total: 50,000 plus 51,320 Talbots

CISITALIA 202

Italian entrepreneur Piero Dusio decided to concentrate his company's efforts on racing cars in the postwar era. His first Cisitalia single-seat racers were based on Fiats with 1100cc (66 cu in) engines tuned to produce more than 45kW (60bhp). 50 examples were built and they went on to dominate their class. In 1947, racing Cisitalias finished 2nd, 3rd and 4th at the Mille Miglia. The company believed it now had the image it needed to make and market

road-going versions of their racers.

The 202 is now more closely associated with the success of Pininfarina's design rather than the achievements of the car. Based on Fiat 1100 running gear, a multi-tubular chassis was designed by Fiat's own Dr Dante Giacosa. If the engines were ordinary, the bodywork was extraordinary and

the whole package very expensive, as the car was hand-built.

The Gran Sport coupé model is so beautiful that one is now enshrined at New York's Museum of Modern Art. This accolade came too late to save Cisitalia who could not afford to build the car. Dusio re-emerged in Argentina, but his cars were not the same. In all,

some 170 202s were built, including 60 cabriolets.

Engine: 1089cc (66 cu in) 4-cylinder
Power: 37kW (50bhp)
0–96km/h (60mph): 17 secs
Top speed: 129km/h (80mph)
Production total: 170

This striking and beautiful body could only be the work of Pinin Farina, who clothed the rather more ordinary running gear of a Fiat 1100. The coupé is arguably much prettier than the more rare cabriolet.

CISITALIA 750/850

Engine: 735cc (45 cu in) 4-cylinder
Power: 22kW (29bhp)
0–96km/h (60mph): 18 secs
Top speed: 140km/h (87mph)
Production total: n/a

The Cisitalia story is not a happy one. After the glorious 202 and Piero Dusio's failed attempt to form a Grand Prix team, his only option was to return to Italy from Argentina and start again. This he did, again using the Fiat 1100cc (66 cu in) unit as the basis for his cars. It was his ex-racing manager, Carlo Abarth, who showed the way forward.

After the advanced Porsche-designed Grand Prix car foundered through lack of funds, Abarth took over the team and made it successful. That gave Abarth the money to tune and develop his own Fiat-based cars.

Piero Dusio's son Carlo also decided that using Fiat running gear was probably the answer. An unsuccessful version of the Fiat 1900 and further experiments with the 1100 led to a break in production from 1958 to 1961.

However, Cisitalia returned for one last try with the Tourism Special. Essentially, this was a rebodied Fiat 600 with the choice of 735cc (45 cu in) or 847cc (52 cu in) engines. It was undeniably a pretty design, reminiscent of Pininfarina's

best. However, production was spasmodic and too many different designs were offered. Unlike Abarth, Cisitalia were not offering any great performance advantages or racing pedigree and consequently sales were few.

Cisitalia left the glory days behind with these less ambitious but still handsome Fiat specials. Powered by the smaller Fiat engines they handled sweetly enough, but the market was limited because a mass produced MG was cheaper.

CITROËN C4

1929–31

Andre Citroën launched his first car in 1919, and by the mid-1930s, his company had become Europe's biggest manufacturer. In 1926, the firm took the radical decision to replace all of its existing models with just a single car, although one for which 27 different body styles were available. It was known as the B14, and lasted three years before being replaced by the similar C4.

Considering Citroën's later reputation for technical innovation,

the C4 was unadventurous, although the cars did feature servo-assisted brakes. The model was available on two wheelbases and with 16 different passenger bodies as well

Customers could buy a variety of different bodies for the C4, but only the British could get a fabric one. Boss Andre Citroën didn't approve, but the firm's Slough factory in England built them specifically to cater for UK tastes.

as seven utility versions, most of which were influenced by American styling. The side-valve 1628cc (99 cu in) engine was all-new, designed by the ex-chief engineer of luxury French auto firm Delage.

Although nothing special, the C4, and its bigger six-cylinder sister the C6, were successful from the start. As well as France, the cars were also made at Citroën's plant in Slough, England. Models peculiar

to the UK were the fabric-bodied saloon and sportsman's coupé.

In 1932, the C4G arrived with more power, but (perversely) unassisted brakes. The C4 name has just been resurrected for Citroën's latest small car.

Engine: 1628cc (99 cu in), 4-cylinder
Power: 22kW (30bhp) at 3000rpm
0–96km/h (60mph): n/a
Top speed: 90km/h (56mph)
Production total: 243,068

CITROËN 10CV

1933–34

The 10CV was one of the last conventional Citroëns, a stop-gap effort while the finishing touches were put to the Traction Avant, the car which would transform the firm's image.

That was still a year away though and, in the meantime, the 10CV was entirely orthodox. It was based on the C4, with rear-wheel drive and a four-cylinder side-valve engine. The styling was still very

upright, although the sloping front grille became more rounded, and the design more aerodynamic. Perhaps the most noteworthy aspect was the one-piece bodies built using American equipment, as well as the first appearance of the double chevron decoration on the grilles.

A bewildering number of bodies were available. The range included the 8CV and the 15CV, and

between the three models, a staggering 69 different variants could be bought.

The two distinct versions of the 10CV were the Light 12, which used a shortened wheelbase, and the Big 12, which could easily accommodate seven passengers in some versions. Customers in the UK were provided with more practicality, with Slough-built cars featuring synchromesh four-speed

gearboxes and 12-volt electrical systems.

The 10CV was built for just two years, before Citroën unveiled its revolutionary front-wheel drive successor.

Engine: 1767cc (108 cu in), 4-cylinder
Power: 27kW (36bhp) at 3200rpm
0–96km/h (60mph): n/a
Top speed: 100km/h (62mph)
Production total: 49,249

CITROËN 2CV

1948–90

The Citroën 2CV remained remarkably unchanged throughout its long life – this is a late 1970s version. Apart from the square headlamps and other cosmetic nips and tucks, there was little changed from the early example below.

Engine: 602cc (37 cu in), twin-cylinder
Power: 21kW (28.5bhp) at 5750rpm
0–96km/h (60mph): 32.7 secs
Top speed: 114km/h (71mph)
Production total: 3,873,294

It should be able to carry two farmers, 50kg (110lb) of potatoes, a box of eggs and be capable of returning a fuel consumption of 30km/l (86mpg). It should be able to do all this over the most rutted roads in rural France. It should be simple to drive, and easy to maintain. 'If a box of eggs were placed in the car and it was driven over a ploughed field, not a single egg would be broken.' It should be 'four wheels under an umbrella'.

In these days of high spec, high tech cars, that recipe for the 2CV, as dictated by Citroën managing director Pierre Boulanger in 1936, seems childishly simple, and somewhat bizarre as well. But at the time, it was a tough challenge indeed to engineer all these features into one car, especially one intended to be sold at a budget price to the French masses. Its main rival wasn't any other automobile, it was the horse and cart.

It's doubtful whether Boulanger could have predicted how successful and famous his utilitarian people's car would become. The vehicle that would go on to become the 2CV was one of the greatest car designs of all time, deceptively

simple, yet rugged, practical and packed with personality.

Design work started immediately after Boulanger issued his verbal blueprint, with the vehicle taking shape in the utmost secrecy. Front-wheel drive, like that other great Citroën, the Traction Avant, was a prerequisite, but everything else was to be as simple as possible, with the body made out of corrugated aluminium. Launch was scheduled for late 1939, but World War II put the car on hold, and 2CV prototypes were hidden from the Germans when France was invaded.

After hostilities had ended, development work continued, and the 2CV was refined, with the aluminium body being dropped in

favour of steel. When the car did eventually appear, in 1948, it was almost universally derided. It earned the nicknames the Tin Snail or the Duck.

However, those who lambasted it didn't understand and were ultimately wrong. The masses it was intended to motorize took the eccentric car to their hearts and thousands of orders were placed within the first few days of its Paris Motor Show debut.

The formula was incredibly basic. The Deux Chevaux had a weak but tough 375cc (23 cu in) air-cooled flat twin engine driving the front wheels. The simple suspension, a single shock absorber on each wheel, was interconnected,

and would make the 2CV roll alarmingly on corners, yet always allow the driver to remain in full control. The roof was canvas, and could be rolled right back to the rear window.

Because the car was so primitive, improvements were natural. A 425cc (26 cu in) engine came in 1954, and a bigger rear window was installed in 1956. From 1958 to 1966, there was a bizarre 4x4 version (the 2CV Sahara) which used two engines and two transmissions to drive the four wheels. A facelift smoothed out the corrugated roof look in 1960, and a bit more luxury was added, but the car still retained its essential charm. A 602cc (37 cu in) engine was a welcome addition in 1963, and disc brakes were added in 1982, not that the slow 2CV needed them that badly.

The production 2CV lasted 42 years and sold millions and it was a sad day for many when the last one rolled off the production line on 27 July 1990. By that time it had become a legend, crossing all social boundaries and winning friends worldwide because of its quirky nature and sense of fun. Today, this unpretentious little French car still has a legion of followers.

It was labelled ugly during its early years, but millions eventually grew to love the distinctive and friendly 2CV shape. Citroën's current C3 small car mirrors the profile.

CITROËN TRACTION AVANT

1934–57

It's ironic that the model which made Citroën internationally renowned was also responsible for the firm's bankruptcy and, indirectly, the death of Andre Citroën. The Traction Avant was a revolutionary car for the mid-1930s, as it was the first mass-produced front-wheel drive car to be built by a major car manufacturer. However, the Traction Avant had cost so much to develop that Citroën was taken

over by tyre firm Michelin in 1934, and Andre Citroën died from cancer soon afterwards.

As well as front-wheel drive, the Traction Avant was also notable for its unitary construction and independent suspension. This mechanical combination resulted in a car which set unprecedented new standards for ride and handling.

As with anything so unfamiliar, there were initial teething problems. However, when the

long-lived 1911cc (117 cu in) engine appeared in 1935, the Traction Avant in its various guises started a long and successful career. The range included the practical Commerciale, with its hatchback door, and the Big 6, which could boast a six-cylinder 2866cc (175 cu in) engine. However, it was in Light 15 and longer wheelbase Big 15 forms that the Traction Avant achieved most of its sales.

Engine: 1911cc (117 cu in), 4-cylinder
Power: 42kW (56bhp) at 4250rpm
0–96km/h (60mph): 22.1 secs
Top speed: 122km/h (76mph)
Production total: 806,793

The Traction Avant was Citroën's first great car, a showcase for its front-wheel drive technology. It set the trend for most of the Citroëns that would follow: stylistically interesting, full of innovations and, above all, quirky and original.

CITROËN BIJOU

1959–64

Even for a traditionally innovative company like Citroën, the Bijou was strange. Built at the company's UK factory, the Bijou was a rebodied 2CV designed to seduce British customers wary of the original car.

The designer of the Bijou was Peter Kirwin-Taylor who had also

styled the Lotus Elite. Unfortunately, the glassfibre pseudo-French creation was nowhere near as pretty as the Lotus. In fact, the styling was awkward and gawky.

Because it was heavier than the 2CV as well, performance was very poor and the car could barely

reach 80km/h (50mph). To compound its problems, it was more expensive than the Mini, launched the same year. Its only two selling points were that it didn't rust and fuel economy was excellent.

In five years, only 207 Bijous

were sold, making it Citroën's biggest-ever flop.

Engine: 425cc (26 cu in), twin-cylinder
Power: 9kW (12bhp) at 4000rpm
0–96km/h (60mph): n/a
Top speed: 81km/h (51mph)
Production total: 207

CITROËN DS

Even today, the streamlined DS shape is beautiful. Back when it was launched in 1955, it must have seemed extraordinary. This post-1968 example features faired-in twin-headlamps. The inner set of lights turn with the steering to illuminate around corners.

It is not an exaggeration to say that the Citroën DS stunned the world. When it was launched at the 1955 Paris Motor Show, 749 orders were taken within 45 minutes. By the close of the first day, 12,000 people had put their name down for the startling new Deesse (French for 'Goddess').

Rarely had (or has) there been such an intense level of interest in a new car. But the advanced Citroën was extraordinary for its era. Remember, this was a Europe still suffering from the austerity of the postwar years. By contrast to what other manufacturers were offering, the space-age DS literally looked out of this world.

While other cars still used box-like, upright styling, the long sleek DS shark shape was years ahead of its time. Underneath lay complicated hydropneumatics for the clutch, power steering, brakes and self-levelling suspension, with the latter giving a supremely cushioned ride of unparalleled smoothness. The ride height was adjustable from inside the car, and there was no need to use a jack to change a wheel, the Citroën's suspension could cope with just three wheels fitted.

Everybody had been expecting something special from Citroën to replace the Traction Avant, but few were prepared for what eventually appeared. The DS came as a complete surprise, despite its lengthy genesis. The idea of a new big Citroën was first mooted in 1938, but World War II destroyed any prospects of a 1940 release. Italian stylist Flaminio Bertoni had designed the basic DS shape by 1945, and gradually refined it as work continued on developing the mechanicals.

Citroën had been working on hydropneumatic suspension since 1939. But it wasn't until the 1950s that it started working satisfactorily, at which point it made an appearance in the Traction Avant 15H which was more of a commercial testbed than a production model. During the development work, it became clear that a high pressure hydraulic pump driven by the engine could power much more than just the suspension.

When the DS went into production, the Traction Avant 1911cc (117 cu in) engine was the only old part of the car and was an anti-climax compared to the rest of the vehicle. An air-cooled flat six

engine had originally been planned, but development work stalled.

As with the Traction Avant, the first DSs suffered from teething troubles which threatened to overshadow the technical triumph. The hydraulics in particular proved initially somewhat unreliable. By 1957, however, most of the problems had been resolved.

For the budget conscious, or

technophobes, there was a cheaper and simpler version, the ID, from 1956. It shared the same looks, but was less gimmicky, with a sparser interior, detuned engine and conventional brakes and steering.

A sprawling Safari estate with a longer wheelbase and enormous carrying capacity was unveiled in 1958. For 1960, a Decapotable was launched, a DS with the roof cut off and made by France's last remaining traditional coachbuilder, Chapron, to create a chic convertible. More luxury was brought to the range by the Pallas saloon in 1965, and there were all manner of special-bodied types, including presidential versions.

Engines were enlarged in 1965 to 2175cc (133 cu in) for the DS21, and again in 1972, with a 2347cc (143 cu in) unit for the DS23. The cars themselves were subtly altered in 1968, when new front wings featuring faired-in headlights were fitted. Underneath the cowling, the inner set of light units now swivelled in the direction of the front wheels.

It was a testament to the original design that during its 20-year life, this minor styling change was all that was needed to keep the DS ahead of its contemporaries. Despite being pitched at the luxury marketplace, and costing more than many rivals thanks to its complicated nature, the DS still looked fresh and modern compared to its competitors when it was replaced in 1975.

Engine: 2175cc (133 cu in), 4-cylinder
Power: 81kW (109bhp) at 5500rpm
0–96km/h (60mph): 14.8 secs
Top speed: 171km/h (106mph)
Production total: 1,455,746

The interior was a masterpiece of French chic. The single-spoke steering wheel would become a Citroën trademark, while the neat dashboard design was years ahead of its time. Gears were controlled using the long lever on the left.

CITROËN AMI

When the world proved resistant to the 2CV, Citroën tried revamping it to boost sales. The Ami was the result. The later model here lacks the inward-sloping rear window of the original, superseded when the car was redesigned in 1968.

Considering the now iconic status of the 2CV, it may seem strange that during the 1950s and the 1960s, Citroën had trouble selling its economy car to anybody but the French. To remedy this, the company came up with a number of different 2CV-based formulas to boost sales, with varying degrees of success.

The Ami 6 was one of the stranger attempts. More powerful than the 2CV, thanks to its flat twin 602cc (37 cu in) engine, the Ami had very eccentric styling. It looked part 2CV, part DS and, at the rear, part Ford Anglia, thanks to its reverse rake rear window.

Sales in France were high, but

the unconventional looks failed to convince customers elsewhere, so Citroën redesigned it for 1969 with the rear window sloping the usual (boring) way, as well as adding a new grille and front disc brakes. It was renamed the Ami 8.

The conventional Ami was quick, but in 1972, Citroën put in a four-cylinder 1015cc (62 cu in) engine from the GS. The 45kW (61bhp) Ami Super had performance that was not only impressive, but scary as well. Not for the faint-hearted.

Engine: 602cc (37 cu in), 2-cylinder
Power: 16kW (22bhp) at 4500rpm
0–96km/h (60mph): 44 secs
Top speed: 112km/h (70mph)
Production total: 1,840,159

CITROËN DYANE

Engine: 602cc (37 cu in), 2-cylinder
Power: 23kW (31bhp) at 7000rpm
0–96km/h (60mph): 31.7 secs
Top speed: 126km/h (78mph)
Production total: 1,443,583

By 1967, the 2CV was approaching its 20th birthday, and Citroën felt the need to replace it. However, just as VW had tried to kill the Beetle, and British Leyland tried to replace the Mini, the 2CV proved a difficult car to drop, and in the end, it outlasted the vehicle meant to depose it: the Citroën Dyane.

The Dyane used the 2CV chassis as its basis, but had a new, more modern and more practical body on top. There was still a distinct resemblance to the 2CV, but the Dyane had a more angular shape. The headlights were incorporated into the wings, a hatchback was added, and the rear seats could be folded down for extra capacity. The full-length canvas roof from the 2CV was kept, effectively turning the Dyane into a type of convertible estate.

Two different models were available. The Dyane 4 had a 425cc (26 cu in) engine, while

the Dyane 6 boasted a 602cc (37 cu in) unit with almost twice the power, which gave it a useful top speed of 126km/h (78mph).

Sales reached almost one-and-a-half million, but the Dyane went out of production in 1985, five years before the 2CV.

The Dyane had a hatchback rear, as well as the full-length fabric roof of the earlier car. From 1968, front disc brakes were fitted.

CITROËN MEHARI

Another 2CV derivative, but this time Citroën's latest creation was not intended to be taken seriously. Very much in the style of the Mini Moke or Volkswagen Thing, the Mehari was a fun, recreational car.

Described as 'an all-road vehicle', the Mehari's box-like body was made of reinforced plastic, capable of withstanding minor impacts, although its resistance to fire was less effective. The soft top (and soft sides) could be taken off in minutes, making it very popular in warm climates but practically useless in cold ones.

Power came courtesy of the 2CV's 602cc (37 cu in) air-cooled engine and, as well as the standard model, there was a van and 4x4 version available. Only left-hand drive models were built.

Engine: 602cc (37 cu in), 2-cylinder
Power: 23kW (31bhp) at 7000rpm
0–96km/h (60mph): 40 secs
Top speed: 108km/h (67mph)
Production total: 143,747

CITROËN GS

Engine: 1220cc (74 cu in), 4-cylinder
Power: 45kW (60bhp) at 6500rpm
0–96km/h (60mph): 14.9 secs
Top speed: 154km/h (96mph)
Production total: 2,473,997

The GS was an attempt to bring new levels of refinement to the small car market. As expected from Citroën, the GS looked like nothing else, except, perhaps, for another Citroën. Head designer Robert Opron was responsible for the sleek, aerodynamic styling, which had echoes of both the DS and SM in miniature, but the car also exhibited its own distinctive nature. Available initially with a 1015cc (62 cu in) air-cooled flat four, the futuristic GS also featured wonderfully smooth self-levelling hydropneumatic suspension.

By 1972, an estate version had been introduced, as well as a 1222cc (75 cu in) engine, and from 1979, a 1299cc (79 cu in) engine was additionally available.

The range was updated the same year, when the GS became the GSA. The new car was longer, had plastic bumpers, reworked interiors and a practical hatchback.

By far the most intriguing GS was the Birotor, built from 1973 to 1975. It was powered by a Wankel rotary engine, but like other manufacturers, Citroën had trouble making the technology work effectively. Most of the 847

Small cars were traditionally regarded as poor relations when compared to larger, more expensive models. But Citroën tried to buck that view with the GS of 1970. The sleek styling was typical of the French firm, as was the complicated hydraulic system.

Birotors were eventually bought back by the company and destroyed, a rare case of a car that was too quirky even for Citroën.

CITROËN SM

1970–75

To create the SM, Citroën took one of the most technically advanced cars of all time, its own DS, reshaped it for a new decade, added a more luxurious interior and powered it with a specially designed 2.7-litre (163 cu in) V6

by Italian manufacturer Maserati. It was a spectacular car.

Citroën had bought Maserati in 1968, and immediately set about building a prestigious GT supercar. A complicated quad camshaft Maserati V8 with two cylinders

chopped off (almost literally) was used for power – driving the front wheels, as was Citroën tradition – while the DS provided much of the underpinnings, although with extra hydraulics installed to make the SM even more advanced. Stylist

Robert Opron was responsible for the brooding, angular looks, creating a sleek road prowler that looked like it would devour anything in its path.

Launched in 1970, the SM was regarded as a technical tour de force. But reliability problems soon began to spoil the image, and when the fuel crisis hit in 1973, the SM was in trouble. When Peugeot took over Citroën in 1975, the SM was one of the first cars to be dropped.

Engine: 2670cc (163 cu in), V6-cylinder
Power: 134kW (180bhp) at 6250rpm
0–96km/h (60mph): 9.3 secs
Top speed: 217km/h (135mph)
Production total: 12,920

One of the most glorious cars ever created, the SM was Citroën's vision of what a supercar should be. The wedge shape was futuristic for 1970 (and still looks advanced today), and the luxury cruiser bristled with mechanical originality.

CITROËN CX

1974–91

Engine: 2473cc (151 cu in) 4-cylinder turbo
Power: 125kW (168bhp) at 5000rpm
0–96km/h (60mph): 8.6 secs
Top speed: 206km/h (128mph)
Production total: 1,042,300

The CX was the last great traditional Citroën. A year after it came out, the company was bought by Peugeot, and Citroën's unique perspective on design and production was stifled.

It was difficult to replace the much-loved DS, but the CX managed to do it and confirmed Citroën's position as one of the world's most eccentric motor manufacturers. The beautifully crafted car used styling elements of the GS, but its larger size gave the shape greater impact. It was packed with innovation, including self-levelling hydropneumatic suspension, hydraulic brakes and 'Vari-Power' self-centring power steering. The concave rear window was kept clean simply by air flow, and the futuristic interior was like nothing that had been seen before.

Initially, the 1985cc (121 cu in) and 2175cc (133 cu in) engines were carried over from the DS,

but other units soon followed, including a diesel and a potent turbocharged 2500cc (151 cu in) fitted in the 1977 GTi. The huge estate versions were known as Safaris, while the long-wheelbase

Prestige models were the choice of French presidents.

Rust gave the CX a somewhat bad reputation which dented its image, although Series 2 cars from 1986 were better built.

The CX was pure Citroën. The shape was aerodynamic and gorgeous, and all the usual quirky features made an appearance, plus a few new ideas. Many see it as the last characterful car the firm built.

CLAN CRUSADER

Engine: 875cc (53 cu in) 4-cylinder
Power: 38kW (51bhp)
0–96km/h (60mph): 12.5 secs
Top speed: 161km/h (100mph)
Production total: 315

Paul Haussauer, an ex-Lotus employee, followed the principles of his former employer and set about building a glassfibre sports car. The mechanicals of the Crusader were based on the rear-engined Sunbeam Imp Sport. At the back of the car was a Coventry Climax 875cc (53 cu in) engine linked to a four speed all-synchromesh gearbox and final drive, all wrapped up in a light alloy case.

At the front was independent suspension also taken from the Imp while the rear comprised semi-trailing arms and coil springs. This combination produced a well-balanced and agile chassis. At only 381cm (12.5ft) long and weighing just 578kg (1275lb) it was quick too, as well as being comfortable,

refined and economical, returning 14km/l (40mpg).

Not only did the Crusader perform well, it looked good too. Well proportioned, this coupé was every inch a baby Lotus, but was

almost as costly. In its most basic form it cost £1118, but purchase tax pushed the price up to over £1400. In 1971, an MG Midget was under £1000. The high price signalled the end for this little car.

This looks just like a Lotus, not surprising as it was designed and built by ex-Lotus employees. That also explained the glassfibre bodywork and the use of lightweight Hillman Imp running gear.

CLYNO 10.8

Engine: 1368cc (83 cu in) 4-cylinder
Power: 10kW (14bhp)
0–96km/h (60mph): n/a
Top speed: 80km/h (50mph)
Production total: 35,000

Clyno was once the third largest car manufacturer in the UK after Austin and Morris. It proudly boasted that it offered a price level that was as low as any car of like rating in the world, and a value vastly higher. The company was formed by Frank and Ailwyn Smith in Northamptonshire, England, who designed and manufactured a pulley with a variable drive ratio for belt-driven machines. They called it the 'inclined pulley', which became abbreviated to 'clined' and finally became known as the Clyno. In 1909, they began to manufacture motorcycles, although the company had to be relaunched after a collapse in the motorcycle market bankrupted the firm.

The first car, designed by George Stanley and AG Booth, appeared in 1922. It had a 10kW (14bhp), 1368cc (83 cu in) four-cylinder Coventry Climax engine, a Clyno three-speed gearbox, electric

lighting, and sold for £250. It was designed to compete directly with the Morris Oxford. Orders were much higher than expected and, by 1923, all motorcycle production ceased and the car's price was

reduced to £238. Clyno continued to upgrade the specification and widen the product range as the 10.8 Family Model was developed. The company was liquidated again in 1929 and the 10.8 along with it.

Built to rival the Morris Oxford, the company's first car proved to be a runaway success. This spacious Family model was affordable and practical, establishing its own niche among 1920s car buyers.

CONNAUGHT L2

1948–54

Connaught was a firm in Surrey, England, which specialized in sports and high-performance cars. It was run by Rodney Clarke and Kenneth McAlpine, who were considered among the best of the Bugatti-driving amateur racers. Deciding to build their own competition car, the first Connaught, called the L-type, was a sports racing two-seater. It used many components from the 1767cc (108 cu in) Lea Francis. This engine, a four-cylinder unit with short pushrods and hemispherical combustion chambers, was very easy to tune. Also the chassis, with beam axle front and rear could be set up for track handling. Two cars were built and they dominated club racing. Although this success encouraged the company to divert into Formula Two and Grand Prix racing, they also set about building a road-going version of the L2.

Connaught's only street legal car was closely based on the racer with the Lea Francis engine tuned to produce 73kW (98bhp). With a magnificent forward tilting bonnet and swooping wings it looked like a real racer, too. From 1951, the stripped-down L3R model was offered, featuring cycle wings and torsion bar suspension, but this wasn't a sales success. In all, 27 road-going Connaughts were built – the company was bankrupt by 1959.

Engine: 1767cc (108 cu in) 4-cylinder
Power: 73kW (98bhp)
0–96km/h (60mph): 12 secs
Top speed: 161km/h (100mph)
Production total: 27

CORD L-29

1929–32

Engine: 5275cc (322 cu in) 8-cylinder
Power: 93kW (125bhp)
0–96km/h (60mph): 14 secs
Top speed: 129km/h (80mph)
Production total: 5000

Entrepreneur Errett Lobban Cord, who could already count Auburn and Duesenberg among his car companies, decided to create his very own marque. Already the owner of the Lycoming engine business, Cord commissioned racing car engineer Harry Miller to design a car, called the L-29.

The straight-eight Lycoming engine he used had to be modified because the L-29 was designed

On a front-wheel-drive car it is vital to save weight at the front, and so the front brake drums were mounted inboard next to the differential rather than being set outboard.

with front-wheel drive. The engine was turned around so that the clutch end faced forward and connected to a three-speed front-drive transaxle ahead of it.

This concept was almost unheard of in America and preceded the

Citroën Traction Avant in Europe by a full five years, to become the

The L29's innovative front-wheel-drive layout made it very attractive to coachbuilders because of its low-slung chassis which allowed them to create stunning designs. However, this convertible sedan built from 1930 was a standard production model but is nonetheless very beautiful.

first front-wheel-drive car built in the United States. Even more innovation appeared underneath because Miller had to use an advanced front suspension to cope with this complex new set-up.

A de Dion layout meant that a solid cross tube was suspended on four, forward-facing quarter-elliptic leaf springs. Although impressive technically, customers were not convinced as the sheer complexity of the whole package meant that breakdowns were frequent.

Performance was disappointing too, as the big 2087kg (4600lb) L-29 struggled to reach 129km/h (80mph). Shortly afterwards, the Wall Street Crash occurred, putting an end to production.

CORD 812

1936–37

Engine: 4729cc (289 cu in) , V8-cylinder
Power: 142kW (190bhp)
0–96km/h (60mph): n/a
Top speed: 177km/h (110mph)
Production total: 2320

Just three years after Cord had laid the L-29 to rest, the company decided to challenge orthodox production once again with the 810 and the supercharged 812. Gordon Buehrig was responsible for the sensational and distinctive styling with the headlights hidden under

flaps in the front wings. Smooth and futuristic it was a technical tour de force. Although the project was first conceived in 1933 as a Duesenberg, the decision was later made to substitute a Cord badge and create the 810.

The striking bodywork was a costly monocoque with a combined body/chassis unit. Beneath its so-called 'coffin-nose' bonnet was a new V8 engine and a complex front-wheel-drive arrangement retained from the ill-fated L-29.

The front suspension was modified though, with transverse-leaf springs and large trailing lower links. The transmission featured four forward gears, connected to an innovative selector system which used electro-vacuum operation.

This meant that only a small steering column stalk was necessary to change the gears. From 1936, a Schwitzer-Cummins supercharger boosted output to 142kW (190bhp) and produced the 812, with its highly elaborate

Here was the shape of things to come with a unitary construction body, electro-pneumatic gearbox and pop-up headlamps that were hidden in the front wings. The chrome-plated exhaust pipes means this open-topped version is a supercharged model.

chrome-plated external exhaust pipes. Commercially, though, the rather costly 810 and 812 were failures and production ceased after just two years.

CROSSLEY SPORTS 2-LITRE

1929–31

Engine: 1990cc (121 cu in) 6-cylinder
Power: 45kW (60bhp)
0–96km/h (60mph): 17.5 secs
Top speed: 124km/h (77mph)
Production total: 700

Crossley of Manchester, England originally made four-stroke gas

engines in the 19th century and progressed to motor manufacturing in 1904. After making staff cars and aircraft engines during World War I, they later developed a range of robust, quality cars in the 1920s and 1930s. Their first six-cylinder model arrived in 1925 and then in

1928, a lighter-engined model, the 1990cc (121 cu in) 11.7kW (15.7bhp) was launched.

A 2-litre (121 cu in) sports version was built on the same 15.7 chassis but the engine was modified. A revised camshaft and induction produced over 45kW

(60bhp) as opposed to the standard 34kW (45bhp). The radiator was rounded and Bentley-like and it had all the lines of a classic British sports car of that era. Capable of 7.5km/l (21mpg), it cost £625 for the open tourer model and £550 for the 15.7hp saloon version.

Deutsch-Bonnet HBR

1955–61

Engine: 851cc (52 cu in) 4-cylinder
Power: 41kW (55bhp)
0–96km/h (60mph): 21 secs
Top speed: 144km/h (90mph)
Production total: n/a

Charles Deutsch and Rene Bonnet were enthusiasts who decided to make their own Citroën-based sports and racing cars. At the 1952 Paris Motor Show, they started by offering road-going coupés but, by 1955, were able to offer a wider selection of models. The standard model was the HBR luxe, in two- or four-seat versions, powered by either a basic 750cc (46 cu in) two-cylinder engine, or supercharged 1100cc (67 cu in) or 1300cc (79 cu in) units. These cars were custombuilt to order on Dyna-Panhard chassis with fibreglass bodyshells. They looked fresh and modern with a downward sloping nose which hid the headlights. Aerodynamically, they were always efficient due to their low height, which was a maximum of 127cm (50in).

By 1957, there were just two engine options, a base 750cc (46 cu in) unit and an 851cc (52 cu in) unit, both twin-cylinder motors. Customers could specify how their cars were finished, until the partners went separate ways and the company was sold.

DAF 33

1967–75

Effectively the Dutch version of the 2CV, Beetle or Mini, the DAF range of small cars, culminating in the 33, was every bit as innovative and well-loved as all those other European icons. In 1959, seven years after the start of truck production, DAF started making passenger cars with a unique transmission system. The DAF 600 was fitted with an air-cooled, twincylinder, four-stroke engine which was steadily developed, so that by

A 1967 DAF 33 with optional sunroof and rear mudflaps. However, more important was its Variomatic transmission which meant that one gear suited all road conditions. The twin belt drive system and centrifugal clutch took the strain off the driver.

1963, the 600 was replaced by the model 31 and, in 1965, this was superseded by the model 32.

The ultimate incarnation was the DAF 33 in 1967. The lines of the bodywork of the original DAF 600 were still visible in the newer model, but had become tighter and more angular over the years. The 33 still had the 746cc (46 cu in) twin-cylinder, air-cooled boxer engine, but it now produced 24kW (32bhp). The tiny car weighed just 660kg (1455lb).

Its unique selling point was the so-called 'Variomatic' transmission. This was an automatic transmission that didn't have any actual gears. It was constructed out of a centrifugal clutch attached to a system of two belt-driven sets of conical metal wheels that were separately adjustable at the engine and at the rear wheel side.

Engine: 746cc (46 cu in) 2-cylinder
Power: 24kW (32bhp)
0–96km/h (60mph): 43 secs
Top speed: 113km/h (70mph)
Production total: 312,367

DAIHATSU COMPAGNO

1963–70

It may not look it, but here is the car that sparked off a revolution and spearheaded the Eastern invasion of Western car markets. A simple and well-proportioned small car, it featured an all-synchromesh gearbox and lively four-cylinder engine.

water-cooled 797cc (49 cu in) four-cylinder engine driving the rear wheels, with an all-synchromesh four-speed gearbox. The engine capacity rose to 958cc (58 cu in) in 1965 and power increased to 41kW (55bhp).

The range then expanded to include a four-door saloon and estate car based on the saloon body. More interesting was a convertible that had a more powerful engine thanks to a twin-barrel carburettor that boosted output to 48kW (65bhp) and produced a top speed of 145km/h (90mph). Worryingly, the owners' manual suggested that every 160km (100 miles) the wheel nuts should be checked, otherwise the wheels might fall off.

Daihatsu became part of the Toyota empire in 1967, effectively becoming its small car division.

Daihatsu was the first Japanese car company to export to many Western markets in the 1960s, and the Campagno was the model exported. This car was also the first four-wheeled Daihatsu to enter series production. The company turned to legendary Italian designer Vignale for the look, which was neat and stylish without much of the clutter and chrome that spoiled its Japanese contemporaries.

The layout of the Compagno when launched was relatively simple. This two-door car had a

Engine: 797cc (49 cu in) 4-cylinder
Power: 41kW (55bhp)
0–96km/h (60mph): 35 secs
Top speed: 113km/h (70mph)
Production total: 120,000

DAIMLER FOUR-WHEELER

1896

Engine: 2-cylinder (capacity not known)
Power: 3kW (4hp)
0–96km/h (60mph): n/a
Top speed: 32km/h (20mph)
Production total: n/a

The Daimler Motor Company was created in England by FR Simms principally to exploit the patents and designs of motoring pioneer Gottlieb Daimler. By 1896, the Coventry-based company had become part of Harry J Lawson's bicycle business empire. Lawson had seen the future in both France and Germany and knew it was motorized. The earliest catalogued Daimlers, though, were built either in Bad Canstatt, Germany, or in Paris as Panhards.

The key to its success had been

the development of the high-speed petrol engine made possible by the company's invention of the atomizing carburettor. Also heavily influenced by the Panhard models, the English Daimler had automatic inlet valves, tiller steering, tube ignition, four-speed and reverse gearboxes, chain drive and solid tyres.

Prices ranged from £398 for a phaeton, up to £418 for what was described as a 'private Omnibus'. This four-wheeler became the first car Daimler made in any significant numbers. At this time, Gottlieb Daimler himself was still a director of the English firm and he did not resign until 1898, by which time the company was making four-cylinder cars.

The first car to be built in Britain using the talents of pioneer Gottlieb Daimler. Described in the original advertisement as the twin-cylinder 6bhp Wagonette, it was first offered by the Great Horseless Carriage Company.

DAIMLER 45

1919–25

After World War I, Daimler got straight back to business by building the huge chassis and luxurious carriages they had become famous for. The 45 was sometimes known simply as the Special. It was powered by the 60kW (80bhp) 'Silent Knight' sleeve-valve engines which were very quiet.

The chassis alone cost between £850 and £1275. It featured semi-elliptic front and three-quarter elliptic rear suspension with an underslung worm axle. The large six-cylinder engines initially worked through a cone clutch, then, from 1920, used a disc system to control the four-speed gearbox, which had a right hand gearchange for the chauffeur.

Putting a limousine body on top meant that these Daimlers rarely left the works costing less than £2000. Both Daimler and outside coachbuilders produced their own bodies, which were built on subframes and then attached to the chassis with rubber fixings.

Always a favourite with the aristocracy, the 45 chassis was also used to build some replicas of George V's 1924 official car which had a massive 8500cc (519 cu in) 42kW (57bhp) engine. There were countless body and chassis combinations so there was no such thing as a standard 45, not least because all Daimler records were destroyed in World War II.

Engine: 4962cc (304 cu in) 8-cylinder
Power: 60kW (80bhp)
0–96km/h (60mph): n/a
Top speed: 104km/h (65mph)
Production total: n/a

Also known as the Special, the 45 was powered by the substantial 'Silent Knight' sleeve-valve engines. Coachwork was by Hooper, who built the Royal cars.

DAIMLER DOUBLE SIX

1926–30

Engine: 7136cc (435 cu in) 8-cylinder
Power: 112kW (150bhp)
0–96km/h (60mph): n/a
Top speed: 129km/h (80mph)
Production total: 500

Royalty, the wealthy and heads of state all demanded cars that were smooth and delivered their power silently. This led directly to the launch of the 7.1-litre (435 cu in) Daimler Double Six, which was Britain's first-ever V12 engine.

The credit goes to Laurence Pomeroy Snr, then Chief Engineer at Daimler. Derived from the existing 25/85 six, its cylinders were cast in four blocks of three, with detachable heads. Essentially then, it was two six-cylinder

Britain's first V12 engine, here shown installed into a 1929 Double Six, with the Phaeton coachwork by Weymann – although the version built in the largest numbers was the saloon. The Double Six was responsible for bringing the fluted grille to prominence.

engines joined together, hence the name, Double Six. Each bank of the 60-degree V had its own distributor, four-jet carburettor and eccentric shaft to drive its steel valve sleeves.

A smaller 3.7-litre (226 cu in) V12 based on the 16/55 cylinder blocks was introduced in 1928 and dubbed the Double-Six-30. After that, the 7.1-litre (435 cu in) version became known as the Double-Six-50 and both 12-cylinder models got a distinguishing strip of chrome running down the centre of their distinctive grilles.

The cars built on these chassis were enormous in size, dignified and largely silent. These features appealed directly to the wealthy customers who preferred them to contemporary Rolls-Royce products. A second generation Double Six followed in 1931 with monobloc engine casings, 5.3 litres (323 cu in) and 6.5 litres (397 cu in) in size.

DAIMLER DB 18

Here is a postwar DB18 Sports Special out on the road in drophead coupé form. A very heavy car, it was hardly sporty. Never mind, this was a very pleasant way to travel with good road manners.

Laurence Pomeroy Snr, Chief Engineer at Daimler was aware that the company's products were often too large, heavy and unwieldy to deliver real driving pleasure, or even take part in competition. The first sign of a change in direction was the appearance of the Light Straight Eight, which as a four-door saloon could touch 137km/h (85mph). However, it was the arrival of the smaller 'Fifteen' in 1935, featuring Daimler's first independent suspension set-up, that ushered in changes. When the engine grew from 2.1 litres (128 cu in) to 2.5 litres (154 cu in) in 1938, the car was renamed the DB 18.

In 1939, it proved competitive in national rally competitions. The 'Dolphin' was the sporting DB 18 which had wedge-shaped combustion chambers, twin carburettors, a raised compression ratio and modified exhaust to produce 67kW (90bhp) from an engine that previously managed just 48kW (64bhp).

The war interrupted further development, but the DB 18 appeared almost immediately after with a production Dolphin cylinder head. The standard four-door saloon and very pretty two-door convertible were joined in 1948 by a Special Sports, a focused performance model with drophead bodywork by coachbuilders Tickford. As the 1950s arrived, the DB 18 was developed into the much more sedate and rather staid Consort range.

Engine: 2522cc (154 cu in) 6-cylinder
Power: 67kW (90bhp)
0–96km/h (60mph): 28 secs
Top speed: 115km/h (72mph)
Production total: 3390

DAIMLER DE 27

Engine: 4095cc (250 cu in) 6-cylinder
Power: 82kW (110bhp)
0–96km/h (60mph): 29 secs
Top speed: 127km/h (79mph)
Production total: 255

New Daimler models were launched in 1946, one of them being the 4.1-litre (250 cu in) six-cylinder DE 27. This was regarded as the poor driver's alternative to the 4.6-litre (281 cu in) straight-eight DE 36 launched at the same time. There were significant advances over the old models, which had made do with worm drive. Now the chassis were equipped with Daimler's first hypoid differential.

Although the DE 27 was a large car, it was beautifully proportioned. Because the engine was set well back on the chassis, there was no ugly overhang at the front. At the time, Daimler had been buying other companies and had acquired two of the country's longest-established and most respected coachbuilders, including Barker and also Hooper. Those companies could then rework their magic on this impressive new chassis to create limousines and a 381cm (150in) wheelbase for Daimler's own hire service.

In fact, the DE 27 became one of the more versatile models.

By British standards in the postwar era this was a massive car, but beautifully proportioned. Daimler even made a limousine version with an even longer wheelbase for their Daimler Hire fleet which was given the nomenclature DH 27.

Hooper built an ambulance body onto a DE 27 chassis, but to ensure that there was a low, flat floor the whole drivetrain had to be offset. This meant that the propshaft ran down the side, rather than the centre, of the body.

DAIMLER CONQUEST

Daimler had established with the Consort that there was a demand for a compact model. The new Conquest was another indication that Daimler was trying to move away from its traditional staid image. The saloon was announced

in 1952 to coincide with Queen Elizabeth II's coronation. Although it was styled like a traditional Daimler, mounting the headlights on the wings and incorporating the wing line into the bodywork signalled some progression. A new

six-cylinder engine was rated at 56kW (75bhp), while the independent front suspension used laminated torsion bars, unlike other models, which used coil springs.

More adventurous was the Conquest Century roadster, the first

On the road, the Conquest was fun to drive, especially in high-powered Century specification. Inside it was still a traditional Daimler with plenty of wood and leather, although the body was rust prone.

real Daimler sports car since 1908. This alloy-bodied car had a wraparound windscreen, cutaway doors and tail fins, and although the whole package could hardly be called attractive, the later coupé was a little better.

If this car was too sporty, the company also offered the Drophead Conquest, a two-door model with a partly powered hood. Meanwhile, the most thrilling Conquest saloon was the Century with an alloy cylinder head and twin carburettors which produced a useful 75kW (100bhp). Incredibly, it made an impact in saloon car racing and did very well for a time.

Engine: 2433cc (148 cu in) 6-cylinder
Power: 56kW (75bhp)
0–96km/h (60mph): 24 secs
Top speed: 132km/h (82mph)
Production total: 9749

DAIMLER SPORTSMAN

Engine: 4617cc (282 cu in) 6-cylinder
Power: 104kW (140bhp)
0–96km/h (60mph): n/a
Top speed: 152km/h (95mph)
Production total: 75

The original Daimler Regency, a scaled-up Consort, was an attempt to build a new generation of limousines, but the idea never really went into major series production. Daimler decided to repeat these ingredients by launching a Regency II limousine that was essentially an overgrown Conquest. The standout model in this new range was the Sportsman saloon.

Sitting on a 290cm (114in) wheelbase, it shared the Regency limousine's front coil spring and

More elegant than the razor-edged Empress, what set the Sportsman apart was the wraparound rear window and also full hydraulic brakes instead of the hydromech items, plus an overdrive on top gear to make high-speed cruising even more comfortable.

rear semi-elliptic leaf springs. Significantly, it benefited from a 4.5 litre straight six engine, larger than that of the first Regency limousine. Top speed was around 152km/h (95mph) and braking was provided by a full hydraulic, rather than hydromech, system on the Regency limousine.

Stylistically, it was different from the standard limousine with four headlights, a wraparound rear window and even some prominent tail fins. Overdrive on top gear was offered on the Sportsman, but an automatic transmission finally became available for the first time in 1957. Even so, the familiar and

traditional pre-selector gearbox and fluid flywheel remained as the standard transmission system.

As interesting as the Sportsman was, the whole Regency II range was not produced in large numbers. At least Daimler had proved that large saloons could be sporty and this paved the way for the Majestic.

DAIMLER MAJESTIC

1958–62

This is the Majestic Major which was once described as a '120mph funeral taxi'. It was certainly quick and comfortable and, out of all the Majestic models, sold in the largest numbers, because between 1960 and 1968 some 1180 were made.

BSA (Birmingham Small Arms), the owners of Daimler, could see that Daimler was not keeping up with the times and that the marque desperately needed new models. Some odd proposals were made, including using a Vauxhall as the basis for a new Daimler model.

However, one model, the Majestic, signalled a change in direction. Daimler's existing six-cylinder engine was increased in size, with 7.5:1 compression and aluminium cylinder heads with revised porting which all meant 7.5kW (10bhp) more than its 3.5-litre (214 cu in) predecessors, at 110kW (147bhp). For Daimler, the styling, a variation on the 104 limousine, was almost daring, with flush-sided bodywork and a gently sloping bonnet. It was the 161km/h (100mph) top speed and good acceleration that impressed all, along with the disc brakes.

In 1960, the Majestic was stretched by 15cm (6in) and a larger 4.5-litre (278 cu in) V8 producing 164kW (220bhp) was

installed, providing excellent performance. An automatic gearbox and power steering on all but the earliest examples meant that it was easy to drive, with good

handling. The Majestic Major was available up until 1968 and was the last real Daimler, replaced by the more sedate and largely Jaguar-based DS 420.

Engine: 4561cc (278 cu in) V8
Power: 164kW (220bhp)
0–96km/h (60mph): 10secs
Top speed: 193km/h (120mph)
Production total: 2120

DAIMLER SP 250 'DART'

1959–64

Engine: 2548cc (155 cu in) V8
Power: 104kW (140bhp)
0–96km/h (60mph): 10.2 secs
Top speed: 194km/h (121mph)
Production total: 2650

The SP 250 was a big departure from the limousines, saloons and special-bodied roadsters that had been the company's mainstay. With this particular model, Daimler were aiming directly at the sports car market. The new management, specifically ex-Triumph motor designer Edward Turner, was

This SP 250 is the later C specification model with the stiffer chassis and body of the B series plus more chrome trim. The pictured model also has an optional glassfibre hardtop roof, although it would look even better with wire wheels.

responsible for the change.

Originally called the Dart, until American manufacturer Dodge lodged a complaint, the SP 250 could not have been more different

from existing Daimlers. The chassis and suspension were heavily influenced by the Triumph TR3A. The engine was all-new, a light alloy 2.5 litre (155 cu in) V8

which owed much to prevailing motorcycle engineering principles. Stopping the car were disc brakes, a rarity at the time. It was economical, powerful and competitively priced, but it was also controversial. Not everyone liked the ornate styling, which featured pronounced rear wings and headlights. Even more radical for a Daimler was the glassfibre bodywork.

This body was not initially suited to a high-performance car and modifications were soon made. 'B' models from 1961 had a stiffer chassis and stiffer bodywork and 'C' versions from 1963 had better trim. However, since Jaguar had taken over the company, it did not want any competition for its own E-type, so production was discontinued from 1964.

DAIMLER V8 250

Once Jaguar had taken over Daimler it was essential for the company to develop a hybrid model that would both make a profit and enhance the old marque's image. The result was the 2.5-litre (155 cu in) saloon, which was rebadged in 1968 as the V8 250.

Jaguar took the best elements from each product line and combined them. Jaguar's Mark 2 was the basis for the new car, a curvaceous and compact-looking saloon, although it was long at 457cm (15ft). Usually powered by Jaguar's legendary XK twin-camshaft powerplants, transplanting Daimler's own small V8 was a masterstroke. Previously used to power the SP 250 sports car, it perfectly suited the lithe Jaguar

The Daimler V8 engine was designed by Edward Turner, and Sir William Lyons provided the Mark II Jaguar body. Together they made the perfect combination of style and speed. Most of these models had automatic transmission.

chassis. More interestingly, it was a significantly quicker car than Jaguar's existing Mark 2 2.4, accelerating enthusiastically up to 177km/h (110mph).

Jaguar were able to charge more for the V8 250 because the Daimler brand still appealed to a group of

wealthy buyers more interested in refinement, luxury and prestige. Thus the Daimler came with standard automatic transmission, more chrome trim and a distinctive fluted bonnet grille. The result was the best-selling postwar Daimler to date. When rebadged as the V8

250, the bumpers became slimmer, but this was the only change.

Engine: 2548cc (155 cu in), V8
Power: 104kW (140bhp)
0–96km/h (60mph): 13.8 secs
Top speed: 177km/h (110mph)
Production total: 17,620

DAIMLER SOVEREIGN

If there was any indication of what lay in store for the Daimler marque, it was what happened when the new Jaguar 420 was 'Daimlerized' to create the Sovereign. In 1967 the Sovereign/420 retained the Jaguar

S-Type's rear and sections, and had the larger Jaguar 420G's front end grafted on.

The Sovereign name was used and it marked the beginning of badge-engineered Jaguars and the

end of the technical and design independence of Daimler. The differences between the 420 and Sovereign were only cosmetic. On the front was the famous fluted grille, with its pattern repeated on

the boot handle. The scripted letter 'D' adorned the plain chrome hubcaps, and inside there was just a bit more trim.

Nevertheless, the Sovereign was a good car. The quad headlights gave a clue as to the appearance of the next-generation Jaguar XJ saloons, and under the bonnet was Jaguar's 4.2-litre (258 cu in) XK unit, but with Daimler inscribed on the rocker covers. This made it a fast car, while the limited slip differential and dual-circuit brakes provided good handling and stopping power. The Sovereign name then became associated with Daimler saloons for decades.

Engine: 4235cc (258 cu in), 6-cylinder
Power: 182kW (245bhp)
0–96km/h (60mph): 9.9 secs
Top speed: 197km/h (123mph)
Production total: 5700

This was a Jaguar 420 with luxury Daimler touches. The fluted grille and boot handle, the D script on badges and hub cap centres, plus inside some uprated trim, were all that separated the two models.

DAIMLER DS420

1968–92

Engine: 4235cc (258 cu in), 6-cylinder
Power: 183kW (245bhp)
0–96km/h (60mph): 15 secs
Top speed: 169km/h (105mph)
Production total: 3,717 limousines and 802 chassis

The DS420 was built as a rival to the Rolls-Royce Phantom V limousine and was similar in width, length and interior dimensions.

Powered by a Jaguar 4235cc (258 cu in) engine, with twin carburettors and an automatic transmission, it weighed 2087kg (4600lb).

Seating in the rear compartment consisted of a standard bench seat with foldout centre armrest, two side armrests and two occasional foldout seats, which stored away against the central divider. The chauffeur's compartment consisted

of a bench seat from 1968 until 1983, then dual bucket seats until 1992. The standard central division was a sliding glass window.

In 1972, a change was made to the window configuration. The two rearmost windows were combined to form one pop-out window which stopped water leaks and rust. In 1979, the front end had square air grills and indicators. Four years

The limousine of choice in the United Kingdom for over 30 years. Based on the Jaguar 420G floorpan with independent suspension, the bodywork could only be the elegant work of Hooper. Production moved to Vanden Plas in the early 1980s.

after production officially ended in 1988, both the Queen and Queen Mother acquired new DS 420s.

DAIMLER DOUBLE SIX

1972–92

Although a Jaguar by any other name, the Double Six still appealed to a hard core of traditional Daimler buyers who did not want something as racy as a 'Jag'. The magnificent V12 engine was

thoroughly Jaguar, but it also provided a wonderful opportunity to revive the famous prewar name.

Not only that, the Daimler badge finally gave Jaguar the opportunity to challenge Rolls-Royce, still

regarded as the world's best car manufacturer. In 1973, *Motor* magazine in the UK made a direct comparison between the top of the range Daimler Double Six Vanden Plas and a Rolls-Royce Silver

Shadow, which cost twice as much. It concluded that the cars were evenly matched. Although the Rolls had a better finish and more comfortable interior, the Double Six had much better performance, more assured handling and was actually quieter on rough roads.

A Series II appeared in 1973 followed by a Series III in 1979. To improve the car's high fuel consumption, an HE (High Efficiency) engine was fitted from 1981. The prettier Double Six continued in production until 1992 because the V12 would not fit in the new Jaguar XJ40.

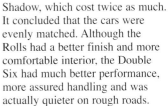

Engine: 5343cc (326 cu in), V12
Power: 188kW (253bhp)
0–96km/h (60mph): 8 secs
Top speed: 222km/h (138mph)
Production total: 14,500

Daimler revived a famous name when the V12 engine became available. This is a Series 1 example made between 1972 and 1973. This is the longer-wheelbase Vanden Plas version. Just 342 were made.

DARRACQ 4-LITRE

1936–39

Engine: 3996cc (244 cu in), 6-cylinder
Power: 104kW (140bhp)
0–96km/h (60mph): 15 secs
Top speed: 161km/h (100mph)
Production total: n/a

In 1920 Darracq became part of the English Sunbeam and Talbot group of companies known as STD. The models produced by this group gradually went into decline until the Rootes Group took them over. In 1935, Antonio Lago, who was already an employee, was put in charge of Darracq and transformed their products and image.

A 4-litre (244 cu in) straight-six engine designed by Walter Becchia with a hemispherical cylinder head and a higher compression ratio was at the heart of Lago's masterpiece. Producing upwards of 104kW (140bhp), the overhead valve unit was mounted on a short 294cm (115in) chassis. The car had independent front suspension and the chassis frame was cross-braced.

On the road, the two-door saloons and drophead coupés looked great, especially when dressed by coach-builders such as Figoni and Falaschi.

A sporty car, it was inevitably modified for the track. Using a short 264cm (104in) chassis it impressed in the French Grand Prix, where the cars finished first, second and third, and Tourist Trophy races. These cars were badged as Darracq's or Talbot Darracqs in the UK, but as Talbots in France.

DATSUN FAIRLADY

1962–69

Engine: 1982cc (121 cu in), 4-cylinder
Power: 101kW (135bhp)
0–96km/h (60mph): 10.3 secs
Top speed: 173km/h (108mph)
Production total: 40,000

The Fairlady was Nissan's first serious attempt at building a sports car. Although similar in layout and style to the MGB it did in fact appear two years before the British roadster, and was launched at the 1960 Tokyo Motor Show. Unlike the MG it had a separate chassis with front coil-spring suspension and double wishbones. At the rear was a live axle, which was hung on semi-elliptic springs.

Initially, power was provided by a 1499cc (91 cu in) engine which produced only 53kW (71bhp) and getting to 96km/h (60mph) took over 15 seconds, way behind contemporary UK cars. So the engine was uprated in 1963 to produce a more usable 63kW (85bhp), but the brakes were still only all-round drums and could not really cope with the extra pressure put on them to stop.

Everyone took the Fairlady more seriously in 1964 when a 1596cc (97 cu in) engine producing 72kW (96bhp) appeared, along with synchromesh on first gear and front disc brakes. However, the ultimate model was the 2000 in 1967. This featured a brand new overhead camshaft 1982cc (121 cu in) engine producing 101kW (135bhp).

The smart styling matched the performance and suddenly MG had

Early versions of the Fairlady were tame, but after 1967 the Fairlady Sports 2000 like this one had a more serious 2-litre overhead cam engine which delivered real power. Still popular, this example has non-standard alloy wheels.

something to worry about, especially as a series of 2+2 Silvia coupés were offered to rival the MGB GT. Although the Fairlady was built in small numbers, this was the shape of things to come.

Datsun 240Z

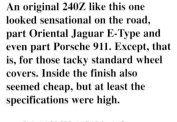

An original 240Z like this one looked sensational on the road, part Oriental Jaguar E-Type and even part Porsche 911. Except, that is, for those tacky standard wheel covers. Inside the finish also seemed cheap, but at least the specifications were high.

Engine: 2392cc (146 cu in), 6-cylinder
Power: 112kW (151bhp)
0–96km/h (60mph): 9 secs
Top speed: 201km/h (125mph)
Production total: 150,076

Almost without anybody noticing, the Japanese had become the third largest producer of cars in the world behind the US and Germany, but had a reputation for building unexciting cars. Although British-built sports cars had been the benchmark, especially in the lucrative American market, things were starting to change. Nissan had built a good reputation for relia-bility and performance with their Fairlady, although the styling was dull. As the Jaguar E-type aged, the Austin Healey disappeared and the MGC struggled, the market was ready for something new – something like the Datsun 240Z.

The astounding success of this car was built on the fact that it looked great, drove brilliantly and

The 240Z was powered by a straight-six engine from the large Cedric saloon which resulted in eager yet smooth performance. Not only that, the Zed's handling was equally impressive with an all-independent suspension set-up making it sharper than many contemporary rivals.

was fantastic value for money. Getting the styling right was absolutely crucial to the car's appeal. Regarded as an Oriental E-type, with its impressively long bonnet and chopped off tail, the design attracted controversy – not because it was ugly, but because of who actually deserved the credit.

Albrecht Goertz, who had also designed the beautiful BMW 507 in the 1950s, was hired as a design consultant by Nissan in the early 60s. However, he left Nissan in the late 60s and the company continued development of the car. According to Nissan records, the

team that really produced the Z Car that we know today was: Chief Designer: Yoshihiko Matsuo; Interior Design: Sue Chiba; Exterior Design: Akio Yoshoda; Engineering: Mr. Hidemi Kamahara and Tsuneo Benitani.

The engine was designed for the 240Z by adding two more cylinders to the overhead camshaft engine from the Datsun 1600, which itself had been a copy of the early 1960s Mercedes 220 six-cylinder engine with two cylinders removed and suitably stroked and bored. The result was a smooth and punchy unit that delivered a

useful 112kW (151bhp) from 2392cc (146 cu in). That power was fed via a five-speed gearbox to a very well-designed strut and wishbone rear suspension set-up. With struts at the front end as well and precise rack-and-pinion steering, the handling was a revelation at the time. Although the engine also powered the humble Nissan Cedric saloon, the straight-six could growl like a grown-up sports car, and even the company's decision to offer a three-speed automatic gearbox did little to lessen the appeal of this lithe and macho sports car. It is hardly surprising then that there was a ten-year domination of the SCCA (Sports Car Club of America) C class production category. There were annual wins from 1970 to 1979 and the Z also had many notable wins in the IMSA (International Motor Sports Association) series.

The 240Z was the best-selling sports car of the 1970s, notching up 150,076 sales due in no small part to a list price in the United States of only $3526. Incredibly, the insatiable demand of the sports car-buying public actually pushed used values up to $4000 in 1970. On the Japanese market, the 240Z was known as the Fairlady Z and had a 2-litre (122 cu in) 97kW (130bhp) engine.

Much more exciting was the Fairlady Z432 with a unique twin overhead camshaft 119kW (160bhp) engine, which also stayed in Japan. That, however, was the standard road car; for racing applications, output was nearer 149kW (200bhp). Just 419 of these very special Zs were built.

Undoubtedly the Datsun 240Z is the model that changed the sports car landscape forever as well as everyone's previously prejudiced attitude to Japanese cars. In fact, the 240Z is such an icon that in the late 1990s Nissan comprehensively rebuilt and resold 'as new' 240Zs through their US dealerships.

DATSUN 260Z

Engine: 2565cc (157 cu in), 6-cylinder
Power: 104kW (139bhp)
0–96km/h (60mph): 9.9 secs
Top speed: 193km/h (120mph)
Production total: 472,573

Stricter emissions requirements in the US led to the introduction of the 260Z. It had a bigger engine at 2.6 litres (157 cu in) although power dropped down to 104kW (139bhp). For many, this marked the beginning of the end for the

true Z car, but Nissan were just being realistic. Not only that, their customers liked the new models even more. In 1975, a single-year Z car sales record was set when 63,963 examples were sold. This may be because Nissan broadened its appeal by introducing a 2+2 body style, which featured fold-down rear seats as the rear section of the car was stretched out to accommodate extra passengers. Externally, the 260Z was identical

to the 240Z except for new emblems. Only the bumper was changed to a larger crash bumper late in 1974 to meet new safety regulations.

In 1975, still wrestling with emission requirements, Nissan replaced the carburettors on the Z cars with Bosch L-Jetronic fuel injectors and increased the engine displacement to 2.8 litres (168 cu in) and power increased to 111kW (149bhp). In 1977, a five-speed

The 260Z looked like the old 240Z. But, as this profile confirms, it sat on a longer wheelbase with a revised rear window. Yet again an owner unhappy with the standard wheel trims has fitted aftermarket items.

overdrive transmission was added and power again climbed, to 127kW (170bhp). Once more, the Z set sales records as 1977 saw 67,331 models sold, making sure it stayed the world's favourite sports car.

DATSUN 280ZX

Engine: 2753cc (168 cu in), 6-cylinder
Power: 104kW (140bhp)
0–96km/h (60mph): 11 secs
Top speed: 180km/h (112mph)
Production total: 414,358

The 280ZX was essentially a major re-design of the 280Z. It was longer, wider and slightly heavier. Although the ZX had the same engine as the earlier 280Z, the car had a new semi-trailing independent rear suspension and disc brakes all round. Clearly this machine was designed to be a luxury GT rather than a compact sports car. Because of this added luxury, the name was given the letter X to make it the 280ZX.

For many Z fans, XL for extra large might have been more appropriate, as the Z changed character. Nevertheless, this was clearly what the buying public

wanted and in 1979, the 280ZX set another sales record for the Z line, with 86,007 sold.

As a new T-bar roof option was introduced and proved particularly popular, Nissan started to notice that performance was suffering. In a decade, the Z had become 16km/h (10mph) slower and took two seconds longer to reach 96km/h (60mph). To remedy this, in 1981 US specification cars were offered with a turbocharged engine, but this was a crude fix. Weight went up again as a 2+2 was introduced and the Z car finally lost all its original charm and character.

Bigger, heavier and less exciting. European specification cars like this still had a normally aspirated engine, while in other markets, like the US, there was turbo power.

DE DION BOUTON 6HP POPULAIRE

1904

Engine: Single-cylinder
Power: 6kW (8bhp)
0–96km/h (60mph): n/a
Top speed: 64km/h (40mph)
Production total: n/a

De Dion Bouton can be traced back to 1880 when Comte de Dion produced a variety of steam vehicles ranging from a powered bicycle to an Omnibus. At the end of the century, the Comte entered into partnership with Monsieur Bouton who designed an extremely efficient 2.6kW (3.5bhp) single-cylinder petrol engine.

This engine was so popular that, by 1903, 40,000 had been made and it was increased in size. The 6kW (8bhp) arrived in 1902 and, fitted into the model K, combined a front-mounted engine with a 'coal-scuttle' bonnet, which was fairly similar in style to a contemporary Renault.

An unusual feature of the control of these early cars, and one which lasted up until World War I, was the decelerator pedal which progressively reduced the engine speed. The driver would then apply

the transmission brake. The model was also known for its outstanding reliability which made it very appealing to doctors who found them invaluable in rural districts.

Another feature of the car was

that the single cylinder engine ran very smoothly and developed its full power at 1600rpm. The range of models available then started to grow as the company built twin-cylinder engines.

When advertising this car, the company was keen to stress that driving these models was such a joy that prospective buyers would sack the chauffeur and pictured him sitting idle in the passenger seat!

DELAGE D6

1946–54

Engine: 2988cc (182 cu in)
Power: 97kW (130bhp)
0–96km/h (60mph): 14 secs
Top speed: 137km/h (85 mph)
Production total: 250

The D6 can be traced back to the prewar D6-70 and D6-75 models. These tourers, saloons and specials were essentially Delahaye designs mated with Delage short stroke 2729cc (167 cu in) and 2800cc (171 cu in) engines. In fact, Delahaye had owned Delage since 1935. Relaunched in 1946 as the plain D6, the car had a 3-litre (182 cu in) engine with a Cotal electric gearbox with four forward speeds and one reverse. It was stopped by hydraulic brakes.

A carry-over from the prewar model, the chassis of the D6 still proved popular with specialist builders. Not all interpretations were successful, however. Here is a fussy and undistinguished 1947 D6 drophead coupé with coachwork by Vesters and Neirinch.

The majority of cars were supplied as chassis only with the buyer then selecting their favoured coachbuilder. Interestingly, the D6, like many prewar European cars, was only available in right-hand drive since it was apparently felt that this cockpit layout was safer

when negotiating Alpine passes. Despite the D6 being regarded as overweight and underpowered in racing trim, it won the 1938 TT and took second place in the Le Mans 24-hour race in 1939 and 1949.

Although Delage could have continued producing reworked

versions of Delahayes, the French government effectively wiped out its indigenous bespoke car industry. It did this by favouring mass production and penalizing small manufacturers. This forced a merger with Hotchkiss in 1954 and meant the end of the marque a year later.

Delahaye 135M

1936–52

Engine: 3227cc (197 cu in), 6-cylinder
Power: 89kW (120bhp)
0–96km/h (60mph): 14 secs
Top speed: 161km/h (100mph)
Production total: 2000

Delahaye seemed to be just another small manufacturer making fairly ordinary, albeit well-built and finished, touring cars. In 1935, all that changed when engineers took a truck engine from one of the company's commercial vehicles and installed it in one of their car's

chassis. This combination created the 135, available as a two-door saloon, a cabriolet and countless specials. The four-bearing six-cylinder engine was available in various states of tune from a 71kW (95bhp) single carburettor version to a triple Solex carburettor unit that produced 82kW (110bhp). The Coupé des Alpes model had transverse-leaf independent front suspension, Bendix brakes, centre-lock wire wheels and a choice of conventional non-synchromesh

four-speed, or electric Cortal, transmissions.

The bigger-engined 3557cc (217 cu in) 135MS produced 97kW (130bhp) and more and spearheaded the company's competition effort in two-seater form. Winning the 1937 and 1939 Monte Carlo rallies and winning at Le Mans in 1938 were just some of the model's achievements. The MS returned after the war, but these were difficult times for small French manufacturers as their

labour intensive work methods were heavily penalized by the French government. Some pretty coupés and dropheads were built on the chassis, but this sort of car had gone out of favour.

Developed from the road-going Type 135, this competition version produced an impressive 119kW (160bhp) and proved to be effective on the track. This car is a 1936 model and belonged to the famous British racing legend Rob Walker.

Delahaye 148

1937–52

Engine: 3557cc (217 cu in), 6-cylinder
Power: 67kW (90bhp)
0–96km/h (60mph): 21 secs
Top speed: 129km/h (80mph)
Production total: n/a

The 148 was essentially the same car both mechanically and structurally as the 135. However, the 148 was a much less sporting and consequently less powerful

derivative. Sitting on a longer 335cm (132in) wheelbase, it was powered by the 3557cc (217 cu in) straight-six engine. The main difference from the 135 was that its engine had a low compression ratio and single carburettor, which produced only 67kW (90bhp). Consequently the 148 was mainly built with formal saloon and limousine bodywork rather than the

extravagant sporting styles of the 135. An interesting though ugly variation on the 148 theme was the 168 of 1939, which used a Renault Viva Grand Sport body mounted on the 148 chassis. It was only ever available in France.

Production of the 148 resumed after the war. Rather than the dull limousine body styles of the pre-war days, the company now

offered more interesting designs. There were some fabulous art deco creations, particularly those penned by Henri Chapron, whose convertibles featured voluptuous rounded wings and long bonnets patterned with louvres. However, there were not enough customers for the dated chassis and production of all but one Delahaye model was discontinued by 1951.

DELAHAYE 175

1946–52

Engine: 4455cc (272 cu in), 6-cylinder
Power: 93–104kW (125–140bhp)
0–96km/h (60mph): 12 secs
Top speed: 177km/h (110mph)
Production total: 150

Delahaye launched their first new postwar model at the Paris Motor Show in 1946. While most manufacturers were content to bring back their prewar cars or present austerity models, the 175 caused a sensation by being unashamedly glamorous and expensive. But then Delahaye were aiming the 175 at the lucrative export markets and made the car available in both left- and right-hand drive. There was even a choice of wheelbase lengths.

The engine was a development of the old 135 six-cylinder unit. This seven-bearing motor had now been bored out and displaced 4.5 litres (272 cu in) and, depending on the state of tune (with up to three carburettors), produced from 93kW (125bhp) to 104kW (140bhp). The unit was linked to a Cotal

Here is a Type 175S that has bodywork by Figoni and which was built in 1949. Under that long, stylish bonnet is a triple-carburettor engine. There was to have been a Delage-badged version of this car, but it never went on sale.

electromagnetic gearbox and, altogether, the 175 was a very fast car. The axle tube passed through the side members of the chassis and hydraulic brakes were fitted.

However, the chassis design was an unsatisfactory combination of Dubonnet independent suspension and a rear de Dion set-up. On top was a variety of body styles, some of which were more successful than others, but all were dramatic and dynamic. As a car, however, the 175 and the companion Type 180 proved to be commercial and dynamic failures.

DELAHAYE 235

1951–54

Engine: 4455cc (272 cu in), 6-cylinder
Power: 113kW (152bhp)
0–96km/h (60mph): 10 secs
Top speed: 193km/h (120mph)
Production total: 400

In what must have seemed like a final roll of the dice, Delahaye released the Type 235 in 1951. The company looked as though it was finally going to replace the old 135 but, in fact, the chassis was exactly the same. That meant it retained the original mechanically operated drum brakes which by the early 1950s were proving inadequate, especially on what turned out to be a high-performance car.

At least the styling was all-new with a standard and supremely handsome body that was built by coachbuilders Antem and also Letoumeur. A large, US-influenced grille, long bonnet and two-door coupé body were contemporary and striking. The engine had been upgraded as well and now produced 113kW (152bhp). This helped make the 235 a very fast car indeed. In a straight line, top speed was an impressive 193km/h (120mph).

So it was no surprise when the Delahaye 235 had its moment of competition glory in 1953 when it set a record for crossing Africa from Cape Town to Algiers. However, no one was fooled by the old 135 underpinnings, or convinced enough to pay the high asking price, so less than 400 235s were made before Delahaye finally went out of business.

During the company's final years, Delahaye concentrated on chassis and engine development, preferring to leave the coachwork to others. This 1953 253M model has particularly elegant coupé bodywork by Chapron and has been a successful entrant in *concours* competitions.

DE LOREAN DMC-2

1981–82

The engine is in the rear because DeLorean believed his car should be compared with the Porsche 911. However, the DeLorean was not a serious rival to any contemporary sports car.

Engine: 2849cc (174 cu in), V6
Power: 98kW (132bhp)
0–96km/h (60mph): 10.2 secs
Top speed: 194km/h (121mph)
Production total: 8583

Ex-General Motors star John Z DeLorean challenged the automotive industry when he rolled out his so-called 'ethical' sports car from a state-of-the-art factory in Dunmurry, Northern Ireland. However, no other car company has been dogged by such controversy and scandal, which didn't help the DMC-2's prospects in the least.

Powered by a rear-mounted Peugeot-Renault-Volvo fuel-injected, aluminium 2849cc (174 cu in) V6 engine with a Bosch K Jetronic fuel-injection system, it was conventional enough. More ambitious was the Lotus-designed, double-Y, backbone-frame chassis and independent four-wheel suspension.

It had a wide 157cm (62in) track, and its front wheels were 2.5cm (1in) smaller in diameter than the rear ones to minimize oversteer and offer better overall handling. This was the theory anyway, because the heavy V6 in the back made handling very suspect and badly compromised its performance.

Giorgetto Giugiaro's design was realized in glass-reinforced plastic with a high-quality grade-304 brushed stainless steel skin, which looked good, especially on its distinctive gullwing doors, but was easily marked. DeLorean's vision of the ethical sports car wasn't put into practice except on pre-production prototypes.

In fact, the DeLorean Motor Company could not have been run on more unethical lines and collapsed amid accusations that £60 million of taxpayers' money had been misappropriated.

DESOTO MODEL K

1928–30

Engine: 2867cc (175 cu in)
Power: 41kW (55bhp)
0–96km/h (60mph): n/a
Top speed: 97km/h (60mph)
Production total: 100,000

The Chrysler Corporation launched the DeSoto marque in 1928 and it set a first-year sales record of 81,065 cars sold which stood for three decades until the Ford Falcon exceeded this landmark figure. The car was named after the Spanish explorer, Hernando DeSoto, who discovered the Mississippi River in 1541, and offered an alternative to contemporary machines from rivals Pontiac and Oldsmobile.

The Model K had a straight-six engine and was available in a wide variety of body styles including roadsters and saloons. It was a good value package, the L-head engine delivering a useful 41kW (55bhp), along with high-quality branded Lockheed hydraulic brakes, Lovejoy shock absorbers and Hotchkiss driveshafts. Buyers certainly thought that at $845 they were getting a very good deal.

DeSoto had begun life during boom years, but these ended with the Depression of the 1930s. These were difficult times for carmakers, but Chrysler actually fared better than most during the Depression and DeSoto certainly helped out.

In the short term, though, sales of the Model K held up and De-Soto felt confident enough to add a bargain-priced eight-cylinder car to the fledgling range. Thanks to the Model K, DeSoto were here to stay.

A DeSoto Six, Series K roadster did not change very much during its production run. From its hydraulic brakes to the chromium-plated ribbon radiator and rear-mounted spare wheel this was a very modern car offered at a bargain price.

DeSoto Airflow

Engine: 3958cc (242 cu in), 6-cylinder
Power: 75kW (100bhp)
0–96km/h (60mph): 20 secs
Top speed: 121km/h (75mph)
Production total: 31,797

DeSoto struggled in the 1930s and there were two reasons for this. Firstly, Chrysler decided it was not wise to have two of its marques, Dodge and DeSoto, competing in the same price class. Consequently the DeSoto was pushed up into a higher price bracket but below Chrysler. Secondly, from 1934, all DeSotos got Chrysler's controversial streamlined Airflow styling.

The radical design saw the wings fared into the bodywork and the headlights also become part of the car. The bonnet extended down to the front axle and had horizontal louvres. This monocoque, rather than separate chassis, range was truly striking, indeed it proved rather too striking for the buying public. Nevertheless, DeSoto actually managed to sell more Airflows than Chrysler, some 15,000 units compared to the parent company's 11,000, but then

DeSoto's were exclusively Airflow model cars.

During 1935 and 1936 only 11,797 cars were sold by DeSoto, which prompted the introduction of the more conventional Airstream range in 1935. A new front end for the Airflow that year saw the radiator become more V-shaped. The Airflow III of 1936 saw more changes to the styling including new bumpers, tail-lights and a revised interior, but it was too late to shore up already slow sales.

A 1934 DeSoto Airflow SE Coupé, which was sold in the United Kingdom as the Chrysler Croydon. Racing driver Harry Hartz set some 32 speed records in an SE and drove from New York to San Francisco spending just $33 on fuel.

DeSoto Fireflite

Engine: 6277cc (383 cu in), V8
Power: 190kW (255bhp)
0–96km/h (60mph): 9 secs
Top speed: 193km/h (120mph)
Production total: 95,000

In 1955, DeSoto sales rebounded strongly with the introduction of the Chrysler Corporation's 'Forward Look', penned by stylist Virgil Exner. The 'Forward Look' cars took the tail fin fashion to its aesthetic conclusion and were arguably the most beautiful of all the big tail fin machines of the 1950s. DeSoto was no longer dull and the Fireflite was the most

charismatic model in the line-up with a strong 190kW (255bhp) engine. Indeed sales leapt again with another redesign in 1957 which saw the Fireflite's fins get even bigger.

Under the bonnet was a 5588cc (341 cu in) V8 that had a massive power output of 220kW (295bhp) due to its four-barrel carburettors. Available as a saloon, two-door coupé and station wagon, the

six-seater wagon was called the Shopper while the nine-seater version was labelled the Explorer.

The 1959 DeSoto was the last of the chassis-based Chrysler cars. The 1960 model run began with DeSoto's first monocoque design, but by this time, sales had slowed and the marque was doomed. The once top of the range Fireflite was downgraded and eventually cancelled in November 1960.

Since then, though, the DeSoto and Fireflite in particular have emerged as an icon of the 1950s simply because *Happy Days'* Richie Cunningham drove one.

This is a 1955 DeSoto Fireflite 2 door Sportsman hardtop coupé. Note the special side colour sweep 'beauty panels' which were standard on both these and the convertible models. Inside was full leather upholstery, but an electric driver's seat was $70 extra.

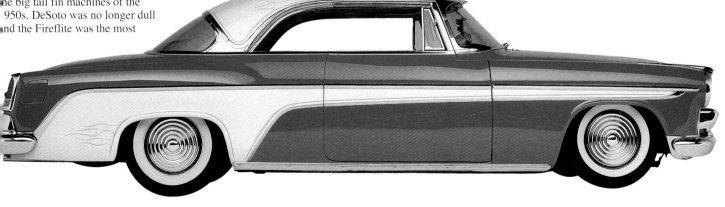

DE TOMASO VALLELUNGA

1965–67

Engine: 1498cc (91 cu in), 4-cylinder
Power: 75kW (100bhp)
0–96km/h (60mph): 10 secs
Top speed: 176km/h (110mph)
Production total: 50

Alejandro de Tomaso was born in Argentina, but escaped the harsh political climate by moving to Italy in 1955. There, he indulged his passion for racing cars and began to drive OSCA machines for the Maserati brothers. However, De Tomaso was ambitious and wanted to build his own cars. From 1959, he concentrated on Formula One racing and, as early as 1962, began working on a production car. This was an open two-seater with a pressed steel backbone chassis, tubular subframes and an independent coil-spring and wishbone suspension system. In the middle of the car was a

Named after an Italian race course, the Vallelunga looked good. But the decision to make the engine part of the chassis meant that the rear suspension was supported by the gearbox. This situation did not promote good handling.

humble four-cylinder engine from a Ford Cortina, tuned to produce 75kW (100bhp).

The theory was that de Tomaso expected a major manufacturer to buy the design and put it into production. This did not happen. So in 1965 Giorgetto Giugiaro, then working at Ghia, was asked to clothe the two-seater in prettier coupé bodywork. The result was the Vallelunga. It certainly looked

good but when it was driven hard, the chassis flexed. This occurred near the drivetrain and caused a myriad of problems that proved difficult to cure. This flawed car was quickly replaced.

DE TOMASO MANGUSTA

1966–72

De Tomaso had been developing a Ford V8-powered car, called the 70P, for the legendary racer and engineer, Carroll Shelby. Intended as a mid-engined sports racing car, the project foundered. However, de Tomaso was now the owner of coachbuilders Ghia. Its chief designer, Giorgetto Giugiaro, had produced a stunning coupé for Italian company Iso, who had rejected it. De Tomaso put the two abandoned projects together to

create the Mangusta (the Mongoose).

First seen as a prototype in 1966 with a glassfibre body, this was soon replaced by a Ghia-built steel version with some aluminium panels. Effectively a racing car mildly tamed for the road, the cockpit was cramped, hot and uncompromising. The speed and handling too were uncompromising

and unforgiving, especially as most of the weight was over the rear wheels. The styling was sensational as the rear bodywork split into, and lifted up, in two sections for access to the huge V8 engine.

As impressive as it was to look at and drive in a straight line, the handling was very suspect. It was only sold for four years.

Engine: 4727cc (288 cu in), V8
Power: 227kW (305bhp)
0–96km/h (60mph): 7 secs
Top speed: 249km/h (155mph)
Production total: 400

Lamborghini's first production car was named after the mongoose. It was aggressively styled, with four exhaust pipes and large cast-alloy eight-spoke wheels. But it had virtually no visibility out of the rear windows.

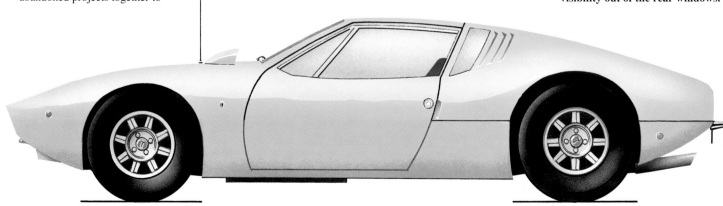

DE TOMASO PANTERA

Engine: 5769cc (352 cu in), V8
Power: 246kW (330bhp)
0–96km/h (60mph): 5.5 secs
Top speed: 256km/h (159mph)
Production total: 9500

Legend has it that Elvis Presley actually shot his Pantera in a fit of pique and many owners have shared his frustrations over the years. However, the Pantera has been one of the most consistent and endearing supercars ever made, and has been manufactured for more than 20 years.

De Tomaso replaced the Mangusta with an equally brutish and uncompromising car, the Pantera, or 'Panther'. First unveiled at the New York Motor Show in 1970 it put right what was wrong with the Mangusta. In engineering terms, the Pantera had a thoroughly reworked chassis designed principally by Giampaolo Dallara. The weight distribution was still biased towards the rear, but now 'only' 57 per cent was directly over the rear wheels. Handling was therefore much improved and far less traumatic than on the Mangusta.

The Pantera was also a more comfortable car to drive. Both driver and passenger had more elbow room and there was even some space for their luggage. Most important of all, air conditioning was standard in the hot cabin. The car was offered in three states of tune – 209, 231 or 246kW (280, 310 and 330bhp).

De Tomaso knew that an Italian supercar should look good. Styling was now by Tom Tjaarda at Ghia, who had reinterpreted the uniquely Italian mid-engine layout in brilliantly uncompromising fashion. Yet technically, the Pantera was a simple car with a unit construction steel body and chassis monocoque. That meant it was relatively easy to build. Also, de Tomaso had secured an amazing production and marketing deal with the mighty Ford organization.

In a highly complex deal that also involved taking control of Ghia, Ford also agreed to take on the Pantera and sell it through their Lincoln Mercury dealers in America. This also ensured that Ford would supply a larger capacity version of their V8 engine, but in a lower state of tune

than had been the case in the Mangusta. The increase in capacity would ensure performance was not unduly affected and the detuned engine would ensure that reliability would not be an issue. Well, that was the theory anyway.

Things started well enough for this historic link up between a small Italian supercar maker and one of the world's largest automotive corporations. In 1972, 2506 Panteras were built and sold although this dropped to 1604 the following year. Clearly, there were some problems. One of them was the looming oil crisis, which meant that expensive and thirsty V8 supercars were losing their appeal. New emission control regulations reduced power outputs to 212kW (285bhp) and 198kW (266bhp). Finally, in 1974, just the smaller

A Pantera II, which had a more powerful Ford V8 and substantial new bumpers which added weight and length to the car. The brakes were uprated with ventilated discs at the front and larger-diameter items at the rear.

output version was available. These problems were compounded by the fact that Pantera build quality was poor. Owners complained about rust, overheating, noise and the general lack of quality of the product. Unsurprisingly, Ford withdrew their support and the imports stopped. However, this did not stop the Pantera.

Although production dropped to an average of 50 cars a year, the Pantera lived on. In Europe, the standard car had 224kW (300bhp), although a GTS version had 246kW (330bhp). A limited production GTS with flared wheel arches delivered 261kW (350bhp) but even rarer still was the GT4, with an outrageous 373kW (500bhp). Essentially, the Pantera remained stuck in 1970 with only varying power output options and the occasional tasteless piece of body kit to keep it looking contemporary. In many ways, this was a credit to the original concept, which only received its first major overhaul in 1990. Even then, the styling was only slightly softened and, underneath, the original structure and V8 engine of the brilliantly brutal and simple original Pantera were kept.

DE TOMASO DEAUVILLE

1971–88

Engine: 5763cc (351 cu in), V8
Power: 246kW (330bhp)
0–96km/h (60mph): 8.6 secs
Top speed: 241km/h (150mph)
Production total: 355

Alejandro de Tomaso could be one of the greatest automotive

opportunists, and the Deauville is cited as one of the best examples of his ability to exploit an idea.

Back in the late 1960s, it was the Jaguar XJ6 that set the benchmark as the ultimate luxury sports saloon. De Tomaso liked what he saw so much that he essentially

copied the design. Although the wheelbase of the Deauville was shorter and it was claimed it was around 159kg (350lb) lighter than the Jaguar, the track was wider. De Tomaso's ambition was to build a car that was more comfortable, more glamorous but much less

Still available in the 1980s, this large and luxurious saloon was built in tiny numbers. The company even managed to develop another four-door from this model, called the Quattroporte III, with the same suspension and longer wheelbase.

complicated than the sophisticated Coventry product. Using the standard Pantera V8 engine under the bonnet, there was a choice of manual or American Ford automatic gearboxes. Ghia's bodywork was good and the independent suspension was competent with double wishbones front and rear.

It was a good try, but not good enough in a market that did actually demand some sophistication. A rumbling Ford V8 engine was not what was wanted. This, combined with a poor dealer network, conspired against the Deauville. Also, the fact that the car was never sold in America meant that production numbers were tiny.

DE TOMASO LONGCHAMP

1972–90

Engine: 5763cc (352 cu in), V8
Power: 224kW (330bhp)
0–96km/h (60mph): 6.7 secs
Top speed: 241km/h (150mph)
Production total: 410

The Longchamp was the product of de Tomaso looking for another successful model to emulate, in this case, the Mercedes-Benz 450SLC. The new car was intended as a grand-tourer 2+2 coupé that could carry its passengers in comfort and luxury. To achieve this, de Tomaso shrank the Deauville to smaller proportions and ensured that the styling was suitably Germanic.

Ghia built the structure of the car and it was then delivered to de Tomaso in Modena for completion. Sitting on a shorter Deauville floorpan it also shared the same V8 engine and suspension set-up. Indeed, de Tomaso liked the Longchamp so much that he produced a replica of it at Maserati, which he bought in a recuse package. The car he commissioned there, the Kyalami, was a reworked Longchamp but fitted with a quad-camshaft Maserati V8 engine.

As for the Longchamp, a GTS version with a five-speed manual gearbox was briefly available along with five factory-produced convertibles, badged as spiders.

The Longchamp ultimately failed because it never really had the build quality, driving dynamics or good enough image to compete with the main prestige players.

A 1989 Longchamp with wider wheelarches and body-coloured detailing. Unfortunately, this model never became fashionable or popular and was never replaced.

DKW MEISTERKLASSE

1950–54

This vehicle was to be the first DKW passenger car of the post-Second World War era. This model emerged from the production line of their brand new factory in Düsseldorf in mid-1950.

Featuring the modern-looking, aerodynamic steel body of the prewar F 9, it was at first unclear whether the car would ever be manufactured since the blueprints for its design were stranded on the wrong side of the Iron Curtain.

In the event, it actually took a great deal of clever espionage, subterfuge and skulduggery to get these blueprints to the West.

Underneath, some fairly old technology was used to create the Meisterklasse. This included a modified chassis supplied by Auto Union, and a twin-cylinder, two-stroke engine that came from the prewar F 8. Given the model designation F 89 P, it was initially offered for sale as a saloon and

helped to get the German people and economy moving again.

As German buyers started to become more prosperous and economically confident again, a four-seat convertible with Karmann coachwork and a Hebmuller-supplied convertible and coupé version were offered.

A 'Universal' estate car featured a combination of timber and steel, resulting in woody-looking bodywork. Later, however, an all-

steel version became standard.

This modern, aerodynamic and harmonious body design was to characterize the DKW look until the early 1960s. But, underneath, the cars still used noisy, polluting and slow two-stroke engines.

Engine: 684cc (42 cu in), 2-cylinder
Power: 17kW (23bhp)
0–96km/h (60mph): 45 secs
Top speed: 100km/h (62mph)
Production total: 59,475

DKW (AUTO UNION) 1000 S COUPÉ

1958–63

A famous car marque was to reappear in the world of motoring at the end of 1957 when Auto Union launched the Auto Union 1000 Coupé de Luxe.

Stylistically and technically somewhat similar to the DKW 3=6, this model was an upmarket version of that car. The engine, which had been increased in size from 900cc (55 cu in) to 981cc (60 cu in), initially developed a power output of 33kW (44bhp).

However, this particular car wasn't really that inspiring either to look at or, indeed, to drive. The 1000 S was a distinct move in the right direction, though, as it was powered by a more powerful 37cu in (50bhp) engine. Also, it now sported a particularly eye-catching and sophisticated-looking wraparound windscreen.

However, the 1000 model quickly looked dated as it was still closely related to the prewar F 9.

That was not the only factor that made it appear out of date in the car market, however. The two-stroke engines were now antiquated and unreliable. In particular, cars used for short journeys suffered crankshaft damage from corrosion and the engine would seize. Fuel consumption was additionally unimpressive at 8.5km/l (24mpg).

Regarded by many enthusiasts as perhaps the last of the true

DKW-based vehicles, the 1000 was discontinued in 1961. A new era arrived with the modern F102 in 1963, which set the style of future Audis. However, this car was still defiantly powered by a two-stroke engine.

Engine: 981cc (60 cu in), 3-cylinder
Power: 33kW (44bhp)
0–96km/h (60mph): 25 secs
Top speed: 135km/h (84mph)
Production total: 6640

DKW 3=6 MONZA COUPÉ

1956–69

Following a series of outstanding victories by the DKW 3=6 in European touring car racing, two racing drivers decided to develop a sports body for this successful model.

Together, Günther Ahrens and AW Mantzel designed a record-breaking car based on the DKW 3=6 which had a lightweight plastic body. This body had been specially manufactured by

Dannenhauer & Stauss.

The 980cc (60 cu in) engine in their car was tuned to deliver well over 37kW (50bhp) for racing purposes, although some enterprising engineers managed to deliver 75kW (100bhp).

A number of well-earned long-distance speed records were subsequently set at Monza in Italy in December 1956. A limited edition of approximately 230 of

these powerful models were then made available. These cars were named, appropriately enough, the 'Monza'.

Heidelberg DKW dealer Fritz Wenk arranged for them to be built by the local engineering concern Massholder, and later by Schenk in Stuttgart. These engineers used a 41kW (55bhp) 980cc (60 cu in) engine which could reach 161km/h (100mph).

This powerhouse was matched by some excellent handling characteristics. A few prototype open-topped Spyder versions were also made, but were never to be sold commercially.

Engine: 980cc (60 cu in), 3-cylinder
Power: 37kW (50bhp)
0–96km/h (60mph): 25 secs
Top speed: 135km/h (84mph)
Production total: 230

DKW MUNGA

1956–68

In 1954, Auto Union was fortunate enough to secure the German Federal Army's lucrative contract for an all-purpose vehicle which had good off-road capability. In securing this contract, Auto Union had managed to overcome some intense competition from both Porsche and Borgward.

This all-purpose vehicle, called the Munga, quickly went into production the following year.

It was manufactured some 13 years until 1968, when the Federal Army's contact expired.

The Munga was characterized by unfussy, utilitarian styling with flat-ribbed panels and a flat, upright front screen. Most were open models with canvas hoods.

Although the Munga was given the model designation F91/4, from 1962 it was officially to be described as a 'Multi-Purpose

Universal Off-Road Vehicle with All-Wheel Drive'. Perhaps not unsurprisingly, most people simply referred to it by its German acronym, Munga.

The Munga was originally fitted with the familiar three-cylinder 896cc (55 cu in) two-stroke engine. This, however, meant that its power output of 30kW (40bhp) wasn't anywhere near sufficient. Therefore, from 1958, a 980cc

(60 cu in) 41kW (55bhp) unit helped the vehicle to cope better with tough conditions. Some prototypes were built with V6 engines but these never reached production.

Engine: 896cc (55 cu in), 3-cylinder
Power: 30 kW (40bhp)
0–96km/h (60mph): n/a
Top speed: 97km/h (60mph)
Production total: n/a

DKW (Auto Union) 1000 Sp Roadster

1958–65

The Auto Union 1000 Sp Roadster was, it could be argued, one of the most visually and dynamically successful European models of the postwar era.

Despite a somewhat limited production run, approximately 6640 coupés and roadsters were made. The 1000 Sp Roadster's styling was directly inspired by American automobile design. In particular, a number of stylistic features were rather successfully borrowed from the contemporary Ford Thunderbird.

However, the 1000 Sp Roadster also looked good because the design was generally in proportion to the size of the car and it fitted in perfectly with smaller-scale European motoring. This was unlike the clumsy, fashionably winged models offered by other manufacturers at the time.

The 1000 Sp was first presented as a coupé in 1957, followed by the roadster in 1961. The pretty roadster was built in relatively small numbers – only around 1640 were sold. Using a DKW 1000 chassis, it also shared the DKW's transverse-leaf and lower wishbone all-independent suspension and front-wheel drive layout. From 1963, it also featured front disc brakes. The 980cc (60 cu in)

three-cylinder two-stroke engine, which was also used by Saab, was tuned to produce a useful 41kW (55bhp). The bodies were manufactured by the coachbuilder Baur, based in Stuttgart.

Engine: 980cc (60 cu in), 3-cylinder
Power: 41kW (55bhp)
0–96km/h (60mph): 25 secs
Top speed: 140km/h (87mph)
Production total: 6640

DKW Junior

1959–63

Launched in 1959, the DKW Junior could be said to be a typical DKW offering – in particular, the front-wheel drive and a three-cylinder two-stroke engine.

However, the torsion-bar front and rear suspension was a new feature for DKW vehicles. The Junior's design used some rather obvious American-influenced stylistic elements. These included the slight suggestion of dramatic American tail fins and the 'shark' radiator grille. The Junior even had a fashionable wraparound rear window.

In 1961, a new Junior evolved from the old one, with a slightly larger 796cc (49 cu in) unit which was still rated at 29kW (39bhp).

There was no longer any need to pre-mix the oil and petrol because an automatic system injected the oil at the carburettor. The styling changed only marginally with round sidelights at either end of the front grille.

This Junior proved to be the company's first substantial seller in the market, so a brand new plant

was set up in Ingolstadt to make the car. This became Auto Union's headquarters in 1962 and is now the headquarters of Audi.

Engine: 741cc (45 cu in), 3-cylinder
Power: 25kW (34bhp)
0–96km/h (60mph): 27 secs
Top speed: 113km/h (70mph)
Production total: 237,605

Dodge Type A

1924–26

Sales of Dodge cars had been falling rather alarmingly, and its model range was badly in need of updating and revitalization to pull the company out of the trough it found itself languishing in.

The Dodge brothers' major innovation was the introduction of one of the first all-steel bodies in the Type A. This Dodge model was made available as a two-door roadster or as a four-door saloon.

Constant innovation was an important key feature. In particular, the wheelbase was lengthened for more interior room. Additionally, a slightly lower overall height stopped the vehicle from looking too bulky. Dodge also replaced the quarter-elliptic springs with semi-elliptics.

Inside, lowering the seats and moving the gear lever and foot pedals forward meant even more legroom. Customers could also order a deluxe model which had

nickel-plated radiators, bumpers, windscreen wipers and bright metal step plates on the running board.

In 1924, the Type A helped Dodge to regain its former position as the number three vehicle manufacturer in the United States. This was also a time when the company expanded its production capacity and the Type A was built in Walkerville, Ontario.

For 1925, further technical

changes were made as the engine was upgraded and 51cm (20in) wheels and a one-piece windscreen were fitted. Along with Chevrolet and Ford, Dodge was now a recognized maker of cheap mass-market cars.

Engine: 3480cc (212 cu in), 4-cylinder
Power: 26kW (35bhp)
0–96km/h (60mph): n/a
Top speed: 88km/h (55mph)
Production total: 810,861

Dodge Victory Six

1928–29

Dramatically unveiled at the New York Motor Show in 1927 to a rapt public, the new Dodge Victory Six was soon to become a sought-after vehicle among car buyers. This phenomenon occurred because of the Victory Six's outstanding performance, highly attractive styling and, perhaps most importantly, because of the sheer value for money it offered.

The Victory Six bodies were built by Budd Manufacturing with a distinctive moulding that went around the upper bodywork like a belt. Two models were offered, the 130 and 13, the latter with larger wheels to provide more ground clearance. This made the 13 ideal for use in difficult climatic conditions and on rough roads.

Standard equipment on all Victory Six models included internal hydraulic brakes, chassis lubrication and aluminium pistons. Deluxe and sport options featured bumpers, wire wheels and a side-mounted spare.

The Victory Six remained available during 1929 with relatively few changes. This was because the production run of cars that were built in 1928 had yet to be sold.

Because of the difficult, if not calamitous, economic conditions that were produced by the Wall Street crash, prices were judiciously lowered by Dodge in an attempt to stimulate sales. Additionally, some new body styles were added featuring lower,

longer bodies with 7.5cm (3in) wider doors and smaller rear quarter windows on the saloons.

This was an important period of change for the company as Chrysler took over and the Dodge brothers name was simply changed to 'Dodge'.

Engine: 3410cc (208 cu in), 6-cylinder
Power: 43kW (58bhp)
0–96km/h (60mph): n/a
Top speed: 103km/h (64mph)
Production total: 58,500

DODGE D-8
1938

Dodge's 'Beauty Winner' six-cylinder range, as the engines were called, entered production in 1935 and initiated an era of six-cylinder only Dodge models. At this time, the company was one of the top five US manufacturers. Badged as the D-8 for 1938, the car was only mildly redesigned for that model year. A new radiator grille had narrower stripes down the centre with narrower horizontal bars on either side. The headlights were moved to the top of the wings and for the very last time, a Dodge brothers emblem was used on the grille.

An all-steel 'silent-safety' body was now used with insulated roofs, rear quarters and door panels, while the front seats were now adjustable. Standard equipment included Autolite ignition, hydraulic brakes, single windscreen wipers and dual rear lights. Better engine mounts also made the D-8 quieter, a self-lubricating clutch reduced service times and a 73-litre (16-gal) petrol tank improved the driving range. Dodge offered ten distinct body styles which included a seven-seat limousine with a longer wheelbase and a divider window between passenger and driver. Reliable, sophisticated and comfortable, this was a car that was also affordable and sold in large numbers.

Engine: 3568cc (218 cu in), 6-cylinder
Power: 65kW (87bhp)
0–96km/h (60mph): 26 secs
Top speed: 124km/h (77mph)
Production total: 109,747

DODGE CHARGER
1967–69

Engine: 7211cc (440 cu in), V8
Power: 279kW (375bhp)
0–96km/h (60mph): 7.2 secs
Top speed: 217km/h (135mph)
Production total: 201,088

The 1967 Charger was an MPV. This multi-purpose vehicle was intended to be used as a track car, as a basis for dragsters, and also be the place where you could find two of the most potent Dodge engines, the 440 Magnum and 428 Hemi. However, the distinctive fastback styling made it unstable on the track so NASCAR officials allowed a small rear spoiler to be fitted. A new Charger R/T (Road and Track) model in 1968 emphasized even more the dual purpose of the model with a less square and more voluptuous design which famously pursued Steve McQueen's Mustang in the film *Bullitt*.

Given a slight facelift in 1969, the standard Charger R/T was becoming just another model in the ever-increasing range of performance cars offered by Dodge. However, it still used a 7211cc (440 cu in) 279kW (375bhp) Magnum engine as standard. Joining the line-up was the Dodge Charger 500 which had aerodynamic enhancements such as a flush grille to help the car on the racetrack.

It wasn't quite as extreme, though, as the Dodge Charger Daytona. Featuring a fibreglass nose cone and a massive two-foot-high rear wing, this model was

In 1967, the rebodied Charger was effectively transformed from a clumsy-looking coupé into a much more purposeful machine in what was then described as the 'semi-fastback' style. The aggressive looks were matched by an equally outstanding performance fully deserving its legendary status.

built in a run of 500 cars for homologation purposes. On the track, it could reach an outrageous 322km/h (200mph).

DODGE CHALLENGER

1970–74

Engine: 7202cc (439 cu in), V8
Power: 279kW (375bhp)
0–96km/h (60mph): 6 secs
Top speed: 209km/h (130mph)
Production total: 188,606

It took the Chrysler Corporation some time to respond to the incredible success of the Ford Mustang, Chevrolet Camaro and Pontiac Firebird models. Although the Dodge Charger series did well, the cars were too large and did not

have the same mass-market appeal. The Challenger and its sister model, the Plymouth Barracuda, were supposed to change all that.

The Challenger was a thinly disguised reinterpretation of the Mustang. A good-looking car, it could be bought both as a coupé and convertible. Available in standard or R/T (Road and Track) specification, the company offered something for the real enthusiast as well as the ordinary car buyer who

just wanted some style.

Over the four-year life span of the model there was a confusing mixture of engine options. At entry-level was a six-cylinder engine, while the V8s ranged from a 5.2-litre (317 cu in) 112kW (150bhp) unit to the legendary 7-litre (427 cu in) 317kW (425bhp) 'Hemi' although the 'standard' engine was the 7.2-litre 375bhp unit. Unlike the Mustang in the Swinging Sixties, the Challenger

Dodge responded to the popularity of the Trans American racing series to introduce the Challenger T/A in 1970 with a 340 cubic inch V8, four-speed manual transmission, bonnet bulge, rear spoiler and decals. Only 1000 of these were built.

did not catch on and had poor fuel consumption and build quality. The 1970s were all about the energy crisis and new emission regulations and the model had to be dropped.

DODGE DART

1960–76

Engine: 5572cc (340 cu in), V8
Power: 205kW (275bhp)
0–96km/h (60mph): 6.3 secs
Top speed: 196km/h (122mph)
Production total: 5,000,000 approx

The Dart was essentially Dodge's entry into the compact market, but when first introduced in 1960, it

was just a Plymouth Valiant with more extreme styling. However, the car established itself as a useful performance machine, available as three models, the Seneca, Pioneer and Phoenix. Engine choices included a 5211cc (318 cu in) V8 with either a two- or four-barrel carburettor, or a 5916cc (361 cu in)

V8 with 231kW (310bhp). All three models were available with Dodge's D500 performance option using the 5916cc (361 cu in) V8.

When relaunched in 1963, the Dart became a true compact, using a shorter wheelbase, but the bodywork was unattractive and there was no V8 engine option for

the hardtop or convertible. In 1964, the Dodge Dart GT got a performance boost with the addition of Chrysler's 4474cc (273 cu in) V8 delivering 134kW (180bhp). In 1968, Dodge introduced a new GTS trim. The car was available with either a standard 5572cc (340 cu in) V8 with 205kW (275bhp) or an optional 6276cc (383 cu in) V8 with 224kW (300bhp).

For 1971, an all-new Dodge Demon, based on the Plymouth Duster, was offered as a two-door fastback but performance-minded buyers opted for the Demon 340, the spiritual successor to the Dodge Dart GTS. Subsequent Darts were neutered by emissions legislation.

The restyled 1963 Dodge Dart 2-door sedan may have been a compact car, but it was still larger than the Lancer model it replaced. 51,000 were built in that first year, and all them had six-cylinder engines. The 170 series shown here was the basic entry-level model.

DODGE CORONET

1949–73

Engine: 7210cc (440 cu in), V8
Power: 279kW (375bhp)
0–96km/h (60mph): 6.6 secs
Top speed: 197km/h (123mph)
Production total: 2,500,000 approx

The Dodge Coronet always had strong performance and began life as a top of the range luxury model. Completely restyled for 1953 with a downsized chassis available in two sizes, it was available as a four-door saloon, a two-door hardtop, an estate and a convertible as well as a so-called 'Red Ram V8', which produced 104kW (140bhp). In 1956, the Dodge Coronet D500 was the company's qualification car for NASCAR racing and used a 5162cc (315 cu in) V8 producing 194kW (260bhp), but looked totally standard on the outside. The 253kW (340bhp) D501 a year later was just as good but the Coronet range was discontinued after 1959.

However, the name was revived in 1965, when it became Dodge's midsize car. It was available with a full race 426 Hemi engine rated at

317kW (425bhp) but which actually produced around 447kW (600bhp). Saloons, two-doors, convertibles and station wagons were all offered for sale. In 1967, the car was facelifted front and rear with simulated air vents and racing stripes. Another variant, the

Coronet R/T (Road/Track) was an important addition to the line-up. Changes again in 1968 saw the introduction of fashionable 'Coke bottle' curvy lines.

Another new look in 1970, including a smooth split grille, coincided with slumping muscle

Shown here is a standard and very purposeful-looking 1969 Coronet R/T hardtop coupé.

car sales and Dodge became more concerned with promoting its saloons and the Charger. The Coronet faded away.

DUAL GHIA

1956–58

Engine: 5162cc (315 cu in), V8
Power: 172kW (230bhp)
0–96km/h (60mph): 9 secs
Top speed: 193km/h (120mph)
Production total: 117

Haulage contractor Eugene Casaroll formed Dual Motors in Detroit to build a car based on Virgil Exner's Dodge Firebomb/Firearrow concept car from the early 1950s. So when Chrysler decided not to put the design into production, Casaroll

simply bought the Firebomb and made it himself. Re-engineering the car, the company installed a 5162cc (315 cu in) Dodge D500 engine. Designer Paul Farago added extra passenger and luggage space to make the concept more practical.

Building it, however, was far from practical as chassis were shipped to Turin, Italy, where the Ghia coachworks hand-produced the bodies. The interior was exquisite, covered in Connolly

hide. Attention to detail on the exterior included using chrome-plated brass clips to hold trim in place. After work had been completed in Italy, the drivetrain and interior trim were then fitted.

All this expense, transcontinental assembly and commitment to quality was not reflected in the price. At $7646, the Dual Ghia cost less than contemporary Cadillacs. Not surprisingly, Hollywood stars, including Frank Sinatra, wanted

one, since it was fast and stylish. However, Casaroll could not sustain the losses accumulating on every car and just 117 were built. However, that didn't stop Dual Ghia trying a comeback in 1961.

All but two of these models were convertibles, but underneath that show-car body was an ordinary, if slightly modified, Dodge chassis. Incredibly for such a luxury car, power steering was a $95 option.

DUESENBERG MODEL J

No two Duesenbergs are exactly alike and this coachbuilt Rollston Sport sedan was built some time between 1933 and 1936 for its inevitably wealthy owner. Earlier Model J's were more distinctive, but by this time the marque was close to extinction.

Engine: 6882cc (420 cu in), V8
Power: 149kW (200bhp)
0–96km/h (60mph): 10 secs
Top speed: 193km/h (120mph)
Production total: 470

Founded by Fred and August Duesenberg in 1920, the company was best known for its racing exploits. EL Cord then bought it when it hit financial trouble. Cord provided the finance for the brothers to build the ultimate Duesenberg, the Model J, which he christened the 'King of the Classics' when announced in 1928. Powered by a twin-camshaft, nickel-plated crankshaft 32-valve Lycoming straight-eight, it produced at least 149kW (200bhp). Despite its size and weight at 2540kg (5600lb) the Model J was agile and pleasant to drive and customers could specify whatever body style they liked.

Top of the range was the supercharged SJ for 1928 which marshalled 238kW (320bhp), but with the so-called 'rams horn' manifolds, the output exceeded 298kW (400bhp). This incredible power translated into a top speed of 225km/h (140mph), which was remarkable at the time.

Even so, the SJ could be driven sedately like a limousine. Wealthy and famous owners included Gary Cooper and Clark Gable who ordered the only two short chassis roadsters, designated SSJs. A less exciting and pared down JN model appeared in 1935. But this car, along with the innovative Cord 800 series, fell victim to EL Cord's shaky industrial empire. There were, unfortunately, no more of these 'Kings' after 1937.

EDSEL

Engine: 3655cc (224 cu in), V8
Power: 110kW (147bhp)
0–96km/h (60mph): 12 secs
Top speed: 174km/h (108mph)
Production total: 111,000

One of the great automotive disasters, losing Ford some $300 million, the Edsel was born out of a need for Ford to have a mid-market car that owners of more basic models could aspire to. Creating a new brand name after Henry Ford II's father, Edsel, it effectively plugged the gap between the Lincoln and Mercury ranges.

In theory, the good-value Edsel Rangers and Pacers were slightly more expensive than Fords while the Edsel Corsair and Citation were more costly than a Mercury. The models looked identical, although the more expensive versions had larger V8 engines. Despite lots of marketing hype, sales proved to be slow and incautious dealers who over-ordered went bankrupt.

These were good cars, but launched at a time when buyers had started to 'downsize'. Also the Edsel had a 'horse collar' grille that some customers found distasteful. The expensive models were dropped in 1959 and the Villager station wagon was introduced, but it was too late.

Even a redesign in 1960 and a line-up that consisted of just two models, the Ranger and the Villager, with either 108kW (145bhp) six-cylinder or 224kW (300bhp) V8 engines, could not save the marque.

This 1958 Edsel Citation convertible was based on a Mercury chassis and had much better trim than the Edsel Corsair versions. A year later, the Citation had been dropped from the line-up and the Edsel range quickly restyled.

ELVA COURIER

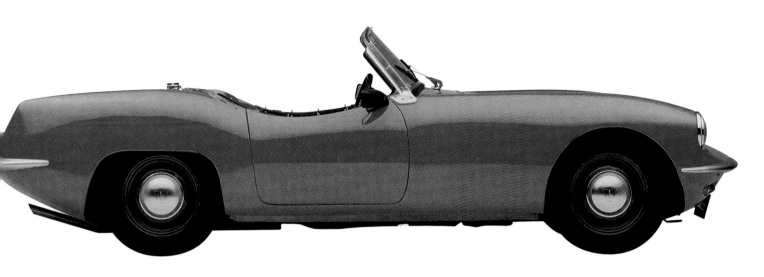

Engine: 1489cc (91 cu in), 4-cylinder
Power: 49kW (66bhp)
0–96km/h (60mph): 9 secs
Top speed: 121-209km/h (75-130mph)
Production total: 500

The successful garage proprietor Frank Nichols had motor racing ambitions and aimed to produce a low-cost racing car. This concept proved successful in the United Kingdom and was particularly appealing in the United States to amateur drivers in the SCCA

racing series. The car's name was derived from the French for 'she goes' (*elle va*), and it was the first road-legal Courier in 1958 that firmly established the company internationally.

The Mk I Courier had a tubular ladder frame, a 1.5-litre (92 cu in) Riley engine and gearbox (later changed to MGA units) as well as a rigid rear axle with coils at the back. On top was a pretty roadster or coupé body. The Mk II was exported to the United States

exclusively until 1960 and could be bought in the United Kingdom only in kit form.

In 1962, the Courier was taken over by Trojan who fitted a square tube frame and moved the engine further forward for the Mark III, which made it cramped and ruined the handling.

A Mark IV returned the engine to its original position and added independent rear suspension. Several styles of coupé were offered and even a Ford GT engine

With the minimal amount of modifications this 1959 model would be eligible for race track competition. An MGA engine under the bonnet provided the power and also the whole four-speed transmission system. Inside this sparse car were leather bucket seats.

became an option over the MGB unit, but production slowed and eventually stopped in 1965 due to lack of sales.

EMW 327

After World War II, it was the East Germans who set about building the first BMWs with what was left of the main manufacturing plant on the Soviet side of the Iron Curtain. The first postwar cars built there were three Type 321s hand-assembled from left-over parts and, by Christmas 1945, an additional

68 cars had been completed.

The following year Autovelo, the state-owned car company, began the process of reorganizing all the car and motorcycle operations in the Eastern sector. These fundamental changes were designed to give the impression that the old BMW concern was

back in business.

Around 2000 cars came off the production line in 1947, and another 4600 by mid-1948 when the company reintroduced the prewar 327 coupé and convertible. Later on it was modified with big, rather clumsy-looking grilles and upright lights. The company was

eventually forced to modify its badge to read EMW Eisenach Motoren Werke.

Engine: 1971cc (120 cu in), 6-cylinder
Power: 41kW (55bhp)
0–96km/h (60mph): 30 secs
Top speed: 125km/h (78mph)
Production total: n/a

EMW 340

The introduction of the EMW 340 coincided with the company being forced to change its name. The state car company, Autovelo, was obviously infringing trademarks by continuing to badge their models as BMWs.

Consequently, after some legal pressure, the Eisenach branch of BMW AG was dissolved on

28 September 1949. It was then that the Munich-based company could become the sole owner of the BMW trademark.

This was important because at least half of the Eisenach's factory car manufacturing output was exported to the West. Without modifying the cars, Autovelo simply renamed them EMWs.

This acronym (EMW) stood for Eisenach Motoren Werke. Autovelo took the precaution of additionally changing the blue sectors in the propeller badge to a much more appropriate Bolshevik red.

Like the EMW 327, the power unit was the prewar 1971cc (120 cu in) six-cylinder engine and the saloon was based on the equally

prewar 326. Rather than being elegant and stylish, they had terrible US-influenced grilles that did not suit the car at all.

Engine: 1971cc (120 cu in), 6-cylinder
Power: 37kW (50bhp)
0–96km/h (60mph): 32 secs
Top speed: 124km/h (71mph)
Production total: n/a

ENZMANN 506

Engine: 1192cc (73 cu in), 4-cylinder
Power: 42kW (56bhp)
0–96km/h (60mph): 20 secs
Top speed: 121km/h (75mph)
Production total: 100

Designed and marketed by Garage Enzmann in Schupfheim, Switzerland, this was one of the earliest examples of a component car based entirely on the running gear of the Volkswagen Beetle. Curiously, Enzmann did not sell this as a self-assembly kit. The company actually bought brand new Beetles and removed what they needed, particularly the floorpan and engine. They then commissioned a boatyard called Staempfi to put a glassfibre body on top.

The result was very attractive, if unorthodox and boat-like. There were no doors and the rear-mounted engine meant there was no need for a radiator grille. In effect, there was a nautical 'bow' which had a

type of boat guard rail bumper. A removable hardtop was made available that resembled an aircraft canopy which cantilevered backwards onto the rear engine deck. Very little modification took place over the years and the standard 1192cc (73 cu in) proved adequate enough. However, modified by an Okrasa tuner unit, more impressive performance was provided and speed was increased to 161km/h (100mph).

This was an expensive car to build and sales were tiny over the decade it was available. Production only just topped 100 units.

Enzmann proved what could be done with the floorpan and running gear of a Volkswagen Beetle, yet this was no cheap kit car, but a production-built sports car. Unfortunately the factory-built Beetle-based Karmann Ghia was prettier and cheaper.

EXCALIBUR

Engine: 4738cc (289 cu in), V8
Power: 215kW (289bhp)
0–96km/h (60mph): 7 secs
Top speed: 201km/h (125mph)
Production total: 1848

The Excalibur was arguably the first and most successful make of nostalgia cars. Brooks Stevens was a leading industrial designer with a passion for racing and a love of European styling. Although content to build racing cars based on

Kaiser chassis and using a variety of engines from Willys to Jaguar, in 1964 he conceived a road car which he called the Studebaker SS. Essentially a high-quality contemporary replica of a Mercedes SSK, it was based on a Lark Daytona convertible chassis with a glassfibre body.

Studebaker withdrew their endorsement of the project, but so stunning was the reaction to the car at the 1964 New York Auto Show that Stevens put it into production

himself. In 1966, the Excalibur was powered by the Chevrolet Corvette's V8 engine and a four-door body was offered for sale.

By 1970, production was in the hands of Stevens' sons, David and William, and the Excalibur II now had a purpose-built chassis and a bigger 350 Chevrolet V8 engine. Cleverly, the brothers restricted production to no more than five cars a week to maintain demand and profitability. The Excalibur

Series III from 1975 was the last car to be directly descended from the original SS and had a big block 454 V8 powerplant. Perfect for those who dared to be different.

A 1965 Excalibur SSK roadster Series 1 is the most sought-after for several reasons. Not only did it have pure 1930s styling, it also offered real sports car performance, was one of the fastest cars available and just 265 examples were built.

FACEL VEGA FV

1954–58

Engine: 5801cc (354 cu in), V8
Power: 262kW (325bhp)
0–96km/h (60mph): 8.5 secs
Top speed: 209km/h (130mph)
Production total: 357

Jean Daninos' company, Forges et Ateliers de Construction d'Eure et Loire, better known as Facel, manufactured high-quality metal products. After the war, it became

better known for building complete car bodies for Panhard, Simca and Ford France. Daninos had a dream of building his own GT cars, hence the creation of the Facel Vega.

The Vega established the template for subsequent models. Under the bonnet was a 4.5-litre (274 cu in) DeSoto V8 engine which produced 134kW (180bhp), fed through a two-speed automatic

gearbox, although a costly four-speed manual transmission option was available. It was attached to a tubular chassis frame with coil-spring and double wishbone front suspension and a live rear axle on semi-elliptic springs. Most striking of all was the finely crafted bodywork which accommodated four in relative comfort. It was also speedy, reaching 209km/h (130mph)

with a real sense of urgency.

Over the years more engine options were offered, starting at 4.5-litre (274 cu in) and moving to 5.8-litre (354 cu in) Chrysler V8s. In 1957, a revised three-speed automatic gearbox and brake servo brought the car up to date and disc brakes later became optional. A good first try but Facel needed to do better to survive.

FACEL VEGA HK500

1958–61

Engine: 6286cc (384 cu in), V8
Power: 268kW (360bhp)
0–96km/h (60mph): 8.5 secs
Top speed: 225km/h (140mph)
Production total: 4554

Effectively, the HK500 was an uprated Vega FVS, immediately distinguishable by its stacked quad headlights, but used the same 267cm (105in) wheelbase. The bodywork was less rounded than before and the front grille had a raked forward appearance that made the car look

like it was alive. Under the skin, the most notable feature was the massive 268kW (360bhp) 6.3-litre (384 cu in) engine.

This was a truly awesome machine, especially when options like power steering and disc brakes had been standardized. Often compared with the big-engined Italian coupés, the HK500 may have matched them for performance, but the handling of this heavy car was not very good. Even so, this model established the company as

There was never a proper explanation for the new model name, HK500, but here was a much more powerful car with high, yet comfortable cruising speeds. It was no surprise that this fabulous-looking vehicle sold in large numbers over three years.

a maker of high quality performance cars with a style and layout that many more established makers would emulate. In particular, both Bristol and Jensen in the UK began installing similar- or identical-sized Chrysler V8 engines to power their own coupés.

Facel Vega cars were always

more expensive than their European rivals and it was easy to see why – the detailing on the interior and exterior was exquisite. There was a stylish amount of chrome, and the cockpit, decked in leather and walnut, was the match of anything that a UK trim shop could produce.

FACEL VEGA EXCELLENCE

1958–64

The original hardtop Facel Vega was joined by an innovative four-door limousine with the back doors hinged at the rear. Inside was leather upholstery and a high level of finish on fixtures and fittings.

Obviously the car had to be long, heavy and reinforced, but that was not enough. The Excellence would literally, when fully loaded, sag in the middle. This meant that doors could not be opened or closed, which was very embarrassing for their rich owners. At least the Excellence had a suitably large engine and surprising turn of speed, but this was not enough to convince the world's high rollers that this was the limousine to be seen in. The last eight models built were restyled and lost their fins and wraparound windscreen.

Engine: 5801cc (355 cu in), V8
Power: 264kW (355bhp)
0–96km/h (60mph): 8.8 secs
Top speed: 209km/h (130mph)
Production total: 230

It was always Jean Daninos' intention to extend and enhance the Facel Vega range. With this in mind, he showed a prototype four-door car at the Paris Motor Shows of 1956 and 1957. Sales eventually began in 1958. Called the Excellence, Daninos expected the car to appeal to heads of state and tycoons worldwide.

The Excellence predated the similar Lincoln Continental, which was the favoured transport of American presidents, and shared one very obvious design detail – both had a pillarless door layout.

The front doors hinged conventionally at the front while the rear doors were hinged at the rear in a 'clap hands' arrangement as they closed towards each other.

FACEL VEGA FACELLIA

1959–63

Engine: 1647cc (101 cu in), 4-cylinder
Power: 85kW (114bhp)
0–96km/h (60mph): 13.7 secs
Top speed: 183km/h (114mph)
Production total: 1258

The Facellia was an attempt by the company to reach a wider and more profitable market. By building a smaller four-cylinder convertible they hoped to attract sports car enthusiasts who bought British cars made by Austin Healey, Triumph and MG. It was equally important that the price was competitive too. Although based on the V8 Facel Vegas, the Facellia was much lower and the wheelbase shorter.

Styling was certainly similar to the larger cars, with single round headlights above the fog lights in the same housing protected by a Mercedes-like cover. Indeed, that aerodynamic touch was credited with boosting top speed by 8km/h (5mph). The convertibles came first with an optional hardtop, followed by the coupé in 1961.

Overall, the Facellia was an impressive package with good performance, pretty styling and tidy handling. What let it down was the engine. Designed by UK firm Westlake but built by Pont-á-Mousson in France, who also supplied the manual gearboxes, the engine proved very unreliable.

Curing the problems, which included burnt valves, took some time and by then sales had been badly affected. In the end, this was the model that helped propel Facel into receivership in the mid-1960s.

The 'affordable' Facel Vega had distinctive front end treatment that set it apart from the V8 models with a more square centre grille and lower side grilles. Inside the finish was high and leather-lined.

FACEL VEGA FACEL II

Engine: 6286cc (384 cu in) V8
Power: 291kW (390bhp) (manual) 261kW (350bhp) (automatic)
0–96km/h (60mph): 8.3 secs
Top speed: 240km/h (149mph)
Production total: 184

Yet again, the company restyled one of its models, in this case the HK500, to produce a new car. Using the same 264cm (104in)

wheelbase, power output from the Chrysler V8 engine rose to 291kW (390bhp). Visually, the Facel II was similar to the old car and the same two-door, four-seat coupé only layout was continued, but with sharper lines.

Effectively Facel retained the original bodywork, but restyled the cabin and doors and replaced the swept back 'dog-leg' front

windscreen pillars. There was more glass area than before with more angular pillars, a flatter roof and a considerably larger rear window. There was a smaller front end than before with a narrower, squarer grille. Quad Marchal headlights were stacked vertically in oval housings with amber lights between each pair, which gave the car a Mercedes SL look.

Most customers opted for the automatic TorqueFlite gearbox in their Facel II, which no longer had distinctive push button operation, and a reduced power engine rated at 261kW (350bhp). Dunlop disc brakes, which were essential on such a powerful car, were standard. Optional items included Borrani wire wheels, which looked very attractive.

FAIRTHORPE ATOM

Engine: 646cc (39 cu in), 2-cylinder
Power: 26kW (35bhp)
0–96km/h (60mph): 25 secs
Top speed: 120km/h (75mph)
Production total: 44

Fairthorpe was founded by Air Vice-Marshal Don 'Pathfinder' Bennett. Not surprisingly, the company was initially involved with the aircraft industry, but later became a pioneer manufacturer of glassfibre bodies. Its first car was

called the Atom, and Fairthorpe described the car in its literature as having 'a very low total weight for what is in effect a reasonably spacious car'.

The problem was that the Atom was a strange contraption that resembled the economy bubble cars that flourished in Europe at the time. It was harder to argue with their next statement that 'the economy of running and of first cost is a unique achievement and

the features of independent four wheel suspension and of the plastic bodies are additional attractions'.

The body was certainly more attractive than the range of chain-driven motorcycle engines that provided the power. Anzani's 322cc (20 cu in) unit and BSA's 250cc (15 cu in) and 350cc (21 cu in) motors were the main engines, powering the car up to a scary 121km/h (75mph) top speed. The follow-up model, the Atomota,

This is the bizarrely styled Atom in its original Mark 1 guise with the headlamps mounted on top of the front wings. At the rear, power is provided by either single or twin cylinder BSA motorcycle engines.

was a more conventional machine with a live rear axle and a proper car-like four-speed synchromesh gearbox. It was also marketed as a kit car, which pointed the way forward for the marque.

FAIRTHORPE ELECTRON

Here is an Electron Minor with a twin carburettor Triumph engine rather than the Coventry Climax unit of the more expensive Electron. On the options list to make the Minor more exciting was a super-charger and a hardtop.

After the questionable styling of the Atom, Fairthorpe got it right with the attractive glassfibre-bodied Electron. A Microplas Mistral-designed body, available at the time to specialist builders, was fitted on a Fairthorpe ladder frame while a Coventry Climax FWA engine provided the power. It was quick, with 67kW (90bhp) available to propel just 508kg (1120lb), handled nicely and, considering it had a sophisticated Climax engine, was very good value for money. However, the buying public thought it was just another special based on a Ford Ten that would struggle on the racetrack. Front disc brakes were fitted from 1957, but sales were still sluggish.

The Electron Minor from 1957 was unfairly described as the poor owner's Electron. Built to a price, it soon proved very popular despite the fact that the styling was ugly. The Minor shared the ladder chassis with the grown-up Electron and had Triumph front suspension and engine, and a twin-carburettor 948cc (58 cu in) 37kW (50bhp) unit. However, a 1147cc (70 cu in) Spitfire engine in 1963 and a 1.3-litre (79 cu in) version in 1969 boosted performance, and front disc brakes from 1966 along with an optional supercharger also helped transform the model. Indeed, the mildly restyled Minor, to everyone's surprise, remained available until 1973.

Engine: 1098cc (67 cu in), 4-cylinder
Power: 67kW (90bhp)
0–96km/h (60mph): 10 secs
Top speed: 177km/h (110mph)
Production total: 30

FERRARI 166

Engine: 1995cc (122 cu in), V12
Power: 104kW (140bhp)
0–96km/h (60mph): 10 secs
Top speed: 201km/h (125mph)
Production total: 75

The Type 166 road car evolved from the first three Ferraris built in 1947. Those cars, designed by Gioacchino Colombo, were Type 125s with 1.5-litre (92 cu in) V12s. Enlarged to 1900cc (116 cu in) as the Type 159 in late 1947, the 1995cc (122 cu in) Type 166 went on to win the Grand Prix of Turin.

Producing around 104kW (140bhp), what made this car seem so advanced was that it had a five-speed gearbox. However, the construction was very basic, consisting of a tubular chassis with coil-spring and double wishbone front suspension with a live rear axle on semi-elliptic springs.

This didn't stop the 166 emerging as the dominant force in racing because in 1949 alone the car notched up victories at Le Mans and the Mille Miglia, which explains why the tuned 120kW (160bhp) 166 from this date onward has an MM suffix. Indeed, those 166 models intended for competition were designated Sport and all other road-going 166s as simply Inter.

By the end of 1950, 40 Type 166 road cars had been built with bodywork by a wide variety of coachbuilders including Ghia, Vignale and Bertone. Just three Sport, but 32 MMs, were also delivered by 1953. The 166 was the car that established Ferrari as a marque and prompted Enzo to establish a factory in Maranello.

The first true production Ferrari mostly recognized as a roaster, it is pictured here as a berlinetta coupé built by Touring with Borrani wire wheels. Essentially, it is the third version of the 166 Inter with a crosshatch grille with small round parking lights at the front.

FERRARI 195

Engine: 2341cc (143 cu in), V12
Power: 97kW (130bhp)
0–96km/h (60mph): 11 secs
Top speed: 177km/h (110mph)
Production total: 25

The first of the 195s were essentially 166s modified by the factory specifically for racing. Ferrari's attention was now focused strongly on Grand Prix competition with the sole intention of beating Alfa Romeo. Unfortunately, the 195 was not a very successful racing car.

The engine was enlarged to 2.3 litres (143 cu in), which was achieved by increasing the bore by 5mm (0.2in). The Inter, or road version, produced around 97kW (130bhp) using a single Weber carburettor, while the competition Sport engine could produce 119kW (160bhp) or more by using triple Webers. This made the top speed around 177km/h (110mph). The 195 Inter also had a longer 250cm (98in) wheelbase to improve high-speed stability.

As was usual practice at the time, the 195 chassis provided the basis for a number of coachbuilders to create their own designs. Two-seat touring, sports-racer berlinetta coupés and convertibles were the most numerous bodies. The majority of the work was carried out by either Pininfarina or Vignale, although production of the 195 was very small at around 25 units. Significantly, the cars seen at the 1952 Paris Motor Show were among the very first Ferraris to be built as left-hand drive models.

This 195 Inter was built by Carrozzeria Ghia and was regarded as less flamboyant than the Vignale bodies, but they made up for it by having more opulent interiors. Under the bonnet, the majority of 195s made do with a single Weber carburettor.

FERRARI 340 AMERICA

Engine: 4101cc (250 cu in), V12
Power: 164kW (220bhp)
0–96km/h (60mph): 8 secs
Top speed: 193km/h (120mph)
Production total: 22

Just a minimal number of 340 Americas were built, but it started a whole succession of Ferraris that were developed from the original 166/195/212 chassis and aimed at the North American market. The 340, though, was powered by a larger, long-block V12 engine, 107cm (42.1in) long.

Designed by Aurelio Lampredi, the 4101cc (250 cu in) engine had first been used in racing, initially as a 3.3-litre (201 cu in) unit. It was later enlarged to 4.1 and then 4.5 litres (275 cu in).

Like the original Colombo-designed V12, it had two inclined valves per cylinder and hairpin type springs, but with the bore centres further apart, a much larger displacement was possible. Other innovations in the 340 included roller camshaft followers and separate valve ports which all helped to take the output to 164kW (220bhp). The single disc clutch marshalled the power to the five-speed gearbox.

Coachbuilt coupé bodies, often designed by Vignale, had long bonnets and short tails, although there were some open Barchetta versions made by Touring. An all-out racing version known as the Mexico also appeared, so-called because it was designed for the Carrera Panamericana race.

This model had a coupé body styled by Michelotti with a longer 260cm (102.4in) wheelbase and an engine that produced around 209kW (280bhp).

FERRARI 212

1951–53

Engine: 2562cc (156 cu in), V12
Power: 97kW (130bhp)
0–96km/h (60mph): 11 secs
Top speed: 177km/h (110mph)
Production total: 80

The 212 was another variation on the 166/195 theme with an even larger engine. The V12 engine was bored to 68mm (2.7in) to create a displacement of 2562cc (156 cu in). It retained the same stroke as the final version of the 166, which precluded any need to change the

crankshaft, so although the horsepower rating never increased, the top speed certainly did. A single Weber carburettor on the road-going Inter version produced 97kW (130bhp), but in racing tune, triple Webers produced at least 112kW (150bhp).

The 212 Export model had a chassis that was shortened to a mere 223cm (87.6in), remarkable considering that the 166 itself was only 241cm (95in) long. The Export's engine was rated at

127kW (170bhp), which pushed the top speed up to 242km/h (150mph).

There was no such thing as a standard 212, because customers could specify exactly what they wanted. The 212 Inter potentially had three different suffixes after the chassis numbers – E, EL and EU – which designated a long or short chassis length. In addition, Export engines could be fitted to Inter cars. Bodywork could also be quite different as customers commissioned both Ghia and

Touring companies. However, with the 212, it was now clear that Pininfarina was Ferrari's favoured coachbuilder.

Here is the Touring Barchetta which used a tubular steel framework to support a non-structural lightweight alloy body. With power from an enlarged version of the original V12, it made a large impact in the United States and firmly established the Ferrari marque there.

FERRARI 250 EUROPA

1953–55

Engine: 2963cc (181 cu in), V12
Power: 149kW (200bhp)
0–96km/h (60mph): 9 secs
Top speed: 217km/h (135mph)
Production total: 21

First shown at the Paris Motor show in 1953, the Europa was effectively the replacement for the 212. Instead of just being an adapted racing car, the Europa was

specifically designed for the road and pointed the way to a profitable future for the marque. Even though it was the final version of the 166, the Europa was closely related to the America models with similar coachwork, smaller engines and lower prices. The long wheelbase chassis came from the Type 375 to make it more comfortable and refined for road use. This also made

the 250, along with the 375, the largest Ferraris of the time.

The car was powered by a smaller 2963cc (181 cu in) version of the Lampredi V12 and was exclusive to this model, producing 149kW (200bhp). This power was marshalled through a four-speed, all-synchromesh gearbox.

Italian coachbuilders all offered their own interpretations of the

Europa, and all produced coupés, except for Vignale, who made a cabriolet. The 'standard' body style was similar to the America and mostly built by Pininfarina as an elegant 2+2. Europas were largely exported to America though, strangely, Ferrari customers were not yet ready for a refined and civilized everyday sports car, which explains why sales were so low.

FERRARI 250 GT

1954–62

Engine: 2953cc (180 cu in), V12
Power: 179kW (240bhp)
0–96km/h (60mph): 7 secs
Top speed: 202km/h (126mph)
Production total: 1811

The 250 range was significant for a number of reasons: it was the first Ferrari built in large numbers; it included in its numerous variants the first production Ferrari with disc brakes; it was the first four-seat Ferrari; and it was the first commercially available mid-engined Ferrari, as well as being a proven race winner.

The 250 GT Europa had a 2953cc (180 cu in) V12 engine producing 179kW (240bhp) and was followed in 1956 by the 250 GT Boano & Ellena. The first of these 75 Pininfarina-styled cars were built by Boano in Turin and the remaining 49 were made by Ellena from 1957. A revised 2953cc (180 cu in) V12 produced 164kW (220bhp) and disc brakes

later became standard. 1958 saw the introduction of the Pininfarina 250 GT coupé on the same wheelbase. Around 343 were built and power went up to 175kW (235bhp).

Ferrari's first production four-seater arrived in 1960, the Pininfarina-designed 2+2 / GTE.

The 179kW (240bhp) engine was moved forwards to create more space for passengers. It became the most numerous Ferrari of the time as some 950 cars were built. The last 250 GT in 1962 was the Lusso, which had a shorter 240cm (94in) wheelbase but more luxurious trim. Built by Scaglietti, the familiar

This is a special coupé model based on the 250 GT and a real one-off by Pininfarina. The rear end was similar to the 375MM, with aerodynamic fins and a tailgate that even raised the rear window.

2953cc (180 cu in) unit produced 186kW (250bhp).

FERRARI 250 GT BERLINETTA 'TOUR DE FRANCE'

1955–59

Engine: 2953cc (180 cu in), V12
Power: 194kW (260bhp)
0–96km/h (60mph): 7 secs
Top speed: 202km/h (126mph)
Production total: 84

Ferrari achieved what they set out to with this version of the 250 GT and that was to win races. 250 GT Berlinetta 'Tour de France' was unofficially named after the victories in the road race of that

name in 1957, 58 and 59. This model was created specifically as a result of Ferrari's experiences with the 250 Mille Miglia and the 250 Europa. The first official car was originally a 250 GT Europa built for competition with an aluminium body by Pininfarina in 1955, but not released until a year later. Then between April and July 1955, Pininfarina built three more 250 GTs that were 250 MM lookalikes.

In 1956 specialist builder Scaglietti unveiled their own prototype with distinctive 14-louvre panels at the bottom of the front wings. Production of these competition-orientated 250 GTs was now the responsibility of Scaglietti in Modena. However, Zagato also built special-bodied coupé versions of this car for their customers to use on the road.

Power came from the Colombo-

designed 3-litre V12 which increased its power output over the years from 179kW (240bhp) to194kW (260bhp) at the height of the model's success on the track.

A 250 GT Berlinetta with distinct fastback styling, although the louvres were not common on all models. Later models had a higher roofline called Ellena. This example is in competition trim.

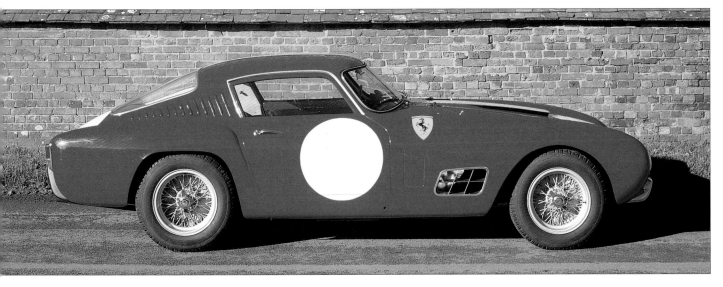

FERRARI 410 SUPERAMERICA

1956–59

Engine: 4963cc (303 cu in), V12
Power: 253kW (340bhp)
0–96km/h (60mph): 8 secs
Top speed: 257km/h (160mph)
Production total: 38

Taking over from where the 375 had left off, this new Ferrari was

aimed squarely at the US market and was designed to be the fastest and the best of its kind. With that in mind, Ferrari installed the largest and most powerful engine they could design, a 4963cc (303 cu in) V12 producing 253kW (340bhp). Previously seen in a racing 375

where it had stormed to victory at Le Mans, the V12 was mounted in a brand new chassis with coil-spring independent front suspension, which was also used on the 250 GT cars. Series II models arrived in 1957 with a shorter 250 GT wheelbase, 259cm (102in) rather

With an engine larger than in any previous Ferrari, this is a 1959 model by Pininfarina. The louvres on the rear side panels are a particular feature in that year.

than 279cm (110in). Just eight Series II examples were built, including a 283kW (380bhp) 'Superfast' version.

Ferrari had to concentrate on the successful and profitable 250 GT range so the Superamerica had a brief sabbatical before returning in 1959 as a Series III model. Now with a 4963cc (303 cu in) 298kW (400bhp) engine, just 14 were made. Although a Ferrari, it was still outrageously expensive and this resulted in poor sales. The luxury sports car market also demanded reliability, but this was a highly-strung thoroughbred and few owners forgave the regular breakdowns.

FERRARI 250 GT SWB

1959–63

Engine: 2953cc (180 cu in), V12
Power: 209kW (280bhp)
0–96km/h (60mph): 6 secs
Top speed: 241km/h (150mph)
Production total: 250

At the 1959 Paris Motor Show, the 250 GT Berlinetta was introduced with a shorter 240cm (94in) wheelbase, hence the model name, SWB. This was the first Ferrari to feature disc brakes and had a

reworked V12 engine. The spark plugs were repositioned and coil valve springs helped boost the power output to 209kW (280bhp). The first 21 cars were competition models, which meant that the bodywork was all alloy rather than steel, saving at least 91kg (200lb) in weight. The car was soon recording strong competition performances with fourth and fifth places in the 1960 Le Mans 24-

hour race and Sebring 12-hour event. The shorter and stiffer chassis made a great difference as drivers reported a superbly balanced car with exceptional road holding and great stopping power.

Lusso type road cars did not emerge until 1960 and although the body was steel, there were lightweight alloy bonnets, bootlids and doors. And what beautiful, purposeful bodies they were – the

shorter wheelbase must have suited Pininfarina. During 1959, a Spyder California with a Scaglietti body was made available, another very handsome interpretation of what is now a classic design.

The SWB's body was a combination of alloy and steel panels. The shorter wheelbase gave more muscular proportions and the air intakes and exits were essential.

FERRARI 400 SUPERAMERICA

1959–64

Engine: 3967cc (242 cu in), V12
Power: 253kW (340bhp)
0–96km/h (60mph): 8 secs
Top speed: 257km/h (160mph)
Production total: 48

The new 400 Superamerica made its debut at the Brussels Motor Show in 1960. Replacing the 410, the new car used a shortened 250 GT chassis and a larger, 3967cc (242 cu in) version of the shorter Colombo-designed V12 in its most developed form. This engine unit was lighter than the V12 used in the 410 and contributed to the lower overall weight of the 400 model. Using cylinder heads also derived from the 250 GT, and triple Weber carburettors, it produced 253kW (340bhp). This was advertised as turning the car into a 257km/h (160mph) missile so the chassis had to be right. The suspension set-up comprised wishbones and coil springs at the front, while the conventional live axle was retained at the rear. The four-speed transmission also featured overdrive while braking was by discs on all four wheels.

Less than 50 examples were built, mostly with bodywork by Pininfarina in various styles, including coupés and cabriolets. From 1962, approximately half the production run had a lengthened wheelbase. In theory, the car was good, but the Superamerica proved to be another Ferrari misjudgement of the US market.

The 400 Superamerica was an expensive and indulgent machine – most were sold in America.

It was too expensive and not much more attractive or faster than the 250 GT.

FERRARI 330 GT

1963–67

Engine: 3967cc (242 cu in), V12
Power: 224kW (300bhp)
0–96km/h (60mph): 7 secs
Top speed: 230km/h (143mph)
Production total: 950

At the end of 1963, Ferrari started to deliver 250 GTE 2+2s equipped with the new 330 engine and the 50 or so cars converted were soon dubbed the 330 America. An all-new car, the 330 GT was formally announced in January 1964 featuring more interior space, thanks to a wheelbase which was 5cm (2in) longer, and uprated disc brakes with two separate front and rear systems. The styling had changed, too. Not regarded as one of Pininfarina's best, the quad headlamp installation looked garish and clumsy, so 18 months later, those four headlights were replaced by one on either wing.

The 330 signalled Ferrari's intention to please the customer as much as possible. So as well as restyling the front end, power steering and air conditioning were soon added to the options list. One thing they did not do was install an automatic transmission, but the American importer Luigi Chinetti certainly did. He acquired a General Motors Hydromatic transmission, as used in the Chevrolet Corvette, and even got unofficial assistance from the American company. Although the conversion worked very smoothly, Maranello resisted the temptation to build their first official automatic model.

Not everyone was impressed by the styling of this four-passenger coupé. But from 1965, examples like this one had two rather than four headlamps and a new front end.

FERRARI 250 GTO

Engine: V12 2953cc (180 cu in)
Power: 224kW (300bhp)
0–96km/h (60mph): 6 secs
Top speed: 274km/h (170mph)
Production total: 39

Undoubtedly, the Ferrari 250 GTO has become one of the most desirable, collectable and revered cars of any era. Only 39 GTOs were made between 1962 and 1964, and even fewer survive after countless epic race track performances. Of course, rarity is one reason for its classic status but, more importantly, the GTO has an enviable racing history and reputation.

Ferrari's reasons for developing the GTO were obvious. The name, Gran Turismo Omologato, was supposed to mean that this model was the homologated racing version of the 250 GT SWB. What is truly surprising is that Ferrari managed to convince the racing authorities that the GTO was simply an evolution of the existing SWB, when in fact it seemed to be an all-new design.

Another surprise is that the GTO must have been technically illegal, as Ferrari never made the required 100 models to qualify for racing. So although Ferrari kept the 250 GT's short wheelbase, it set about changing much of the tubular steel frame's bracing and mounting

joints for extra rigidity. A live axle was retained, but it was well located with parallel trailing arms and the addition of a Watts linkage. As a result, this set-up provided exceptional poise and balance on the racetrack. Providing the power was the Colombo-designed V12 used in the 250 TR, with just a few modifications, such as bigger valves and dry-sump lubrication, so that it would fit under the lower bonnet. The aim was to exceed a target of 74.5kW (100bhp) per litre, and it is said that any engine which did not develop between 221 and 225kW (296 and 302bhp) when bench tested had to be rebuilt.

Ferrari had realized that, although the SWB had been a fast car, its aerodynamics let it down. So using the same short chassis, the body-work was designed from scratch by Giotto Bizzarrini with the extensive use of a wind tunnel. Thus a distinctive shape emerged, rather than being deliberately styled. Step by step, the GTO's bodywork gradually and scientifically evolved into a slippery shape that is now renowned as one of the most beautiful automotive designs ever. With its low nose and high tail, it was certainly eye-catching and featured a body-integrated rear spoiler, which was the first time

this innovation had ever been seen on a road car. However, Ferrari never really intended the 250 GTO to stray too far from the track, even though all the model needed to be legal on the road was the installation of a speedometer.

That great V12 engine and superb aerodynamic body both combined to give the GTO a phenomenal top speed in excess of 274km/h (170mph). Soon, the GTO was racking up impressive results and overall victories. There were class wins in the Sebring 12-hour, Targa Florio, Spa 1000km and Le Mans, where it also finished second overall in 1962 and 1963. Ferrari also won

the GT World Championship in 1962, 1963 and 1964.

Just three 4-litre GTOs were built with 3967cc (242 cu in) engines producing 291kW (390bhp) at 7500rpm. They needed a large and rather ugly bulge on the bonnet to accommodate the units. Another development occurred in 1964 when three 'second series' GTO/64 cars were built. Needing wider wheels and tyres to remain competitive required an all-new 'notchback' body like the contemporary 250 LM (four first-series cars were also converted). The power in these later models went up to 224kW (300bhp) at 7700rpm.

Bizzarrini and Piero Drogo also made some lightweight racers based on 250 SWB components with distinctly odd, though very aerodynamic, van-type styling. However, the GTO's competitive racing days were over. Still, its place in history was assured, and this explains why collectors now pay six-figure sums for these cars.

The three air vents in the nose of this 1962 250 GTO help to cool the V12 engine and feed the six hungry downdraught Weber carburettors. The white roundels suggest that this example is still regularly used as Enzo Ferrari intended, on the track.

FERRARI 275 GTB

Engine: V12 3286cc (201 cu in)
Power: 209kW (280bhp)
0–96km/h (60mph): 7 secs
Top speed: 246km/h (153mph)
Production total: 735

Ferrari had to replace the 250 GT eventually and, when it did, it did it in magnificent style. The 275 GTB was a Ferrari road car with state-of-the-art racing car underpinnings featuring a chassis that had independent rear suspension and a gearbox transaxle. On top of this was a beautiful Pininfarina body, which seemed to combine all the best elements of the previous GT and a GTO, such as the cut-off tail. The cowled headlights formed part of what was called the 'short-nose' body and, from 1965, a 'long-nose' style was also offered.

The chassis of the 275 GTB may have been new, but the tubular frame was directly linked to the earliest Ferraris. The engine was a development of the V12 with a larger cylinder bore and dry-sump lubrication that delivered a lot more mid-range torque. Three twin-choke Weber carburettors pushed the output to 209kW

(280bhp), although there was also the option of a six-carburettor 238kW (320bhp) version.

The really interesting feature was the transaxle, where the five-speed gearbox was mounted at the rear of the 275 GTB adjacent to the axle. This had the effect of

giving even weight distribution and allowing more interior space.

By 1966, a 275 GTB/4 was offered which had a twin camshaft version of the 3.3-litre (201 cu in) engine. This particular Ferrari was just as sensational to look at as it was to drive.

This is a later long-nose GTB with a smaller radiator air intake. This improved aerodynamic efficiency for what was already a fast car with perfect 50/50 weight distribution thanks to the rear-mounted gearbox. A total of 206 of these long-nose models was built.

FERRARI 500 SUPERFAST

Much less dramatic than the 400 Superamerica, here is a Series 2 car which has distinctive louvres on the front wings. What you cannot see is the all-synchromesh five-speed gearbox. It was the last of the limited-production closed Ferraris.

Engine: V12 4962cc (303 cu in)
Power: 298kW (400bhp)
0–96km/h (60mph): 6 secs
Top speed: 280km/h (174mph)
Production total: 37

The 500 Superfast, which replaced the 400 Superamerica, was to appear for the first time at the 1964

Geneva Motor Show. It used a new 4962cc (303 cu in) engine, which was an interesting development of both the Colombo and Lampredi V12s, and generated 298kW (400bhp). As befitted the name 500 Superfast, it was capable of speeds of more than 274km/h (170mph) and reportedly could exceed

161km/h (100mph) in second gear. The body was a development of the Pininfarina 'Coupé Aerodynamico' seen on the 400 Superamerica, but it was not one of the most successful or coherent designs.

The chassis was similar to the 330 GT and after the first 25,500 Superfast cars had been built using

the four-speed gearbox from the 400 Superamerica, the five-speed gearbox from that car was made available. Indeed, some 12 second-series cars, identifiable only by louvres on the front wings, had the five-speed gearbox. These were built during 1966, after which production suddenly stopped.

In total, just 37 cars were made, which indicated that this attempt to break into the North American market had not really worked. Ferrari had offered lots of luxury options and features fit for wealthy, high-profile customers such as actor Peter Sellers, but there were not enough multimillionaires in the world to buy them.

FERRARI 365 GT 2+2

1967–71

Ferrari replaced the 330 2+2 with the largest and most luxurious Ferrari ever in the shape of the 365. The wheelbase remained at 264cm (104in), but the overall length of this car was a not inconsiderable 488cm (192in). This meant that the

365 was a full four-seater with a good-sized boot, reflecting the requirements of the less sport-orientated, more practically minded Ferrari owner. Standard equipment included air conditioning, electric windows and, for the first time on

a Ferrari, power-assisted steering.

These extras made the car large and heavy at 1588kg (3500lb), so handling was diminished, although the performance was still very respectable. The single overhead camshaft 4.4-litre (268 cu in) V12

produced 238kW (320bhp), could exceed 241km/h (150mph) and was able to reach 96km/h (60mph) in just seven seconds, making it the most powerful Ferrari listed at the time. Unlike the 275 GTB, the five-speed gearbox was mounted up front with the engine, and there was a new axle at the back.

The 365 GT was a remarkable package that ultimately managed to satisfy every kind of Ferrari owner, proving to be both a comfortable grand tourer and a sports car. It is no surprise that, during its production run, the car accounted for more than 50 per cent of the company's sales.

Engine: V12 4390cc (268 cu in)
Power: 238kW (320bhp)
0–96km/h (60mph): 7 secs
Top speed: 245km/h (152mph)
Production total: 801

FERRARI DINO

1967–74

Engine: V6 2418cc (148 cu in)
Power: 145kW (195bhp)
0–96km/h (60mph): 8 secs
Top speed: 227km/h (141mph)
Production total: 4064

A combination of Enzo Ferrari's unwillingness to build a V6 car and his desire to build a tribute his late son Alfredino led to this small-engined car being badged as a Dino until the mid-1970s. From 1967, the Dino 206 GT had a transversely mounted 1987cc (121 cu in) V6 producing 134kW (180bhp), and it was built by Fiat.

The pretty design, comprising an alloy body over a steel frame, was by Pininfarina, with construction of the bodies undertaken by Scaglietti and final assembly completed at Maranello. With its small size, low weight and fine balance, the Dino was lauded as a pure driver's car.

In 1969, the 246 GT arrived with a larger 2418cc (148 cu in) unit, now with a cast-iron block producing 145kW (195bhp). This increased power, however, could

not compensate for the increased weight of the cast-iron block, stretched wheelbase and steel body, which dented performance.

Other modifications included a larger fuel tank, five-stud wheel fittings and even electric windows. The 246 GTS in 1972 had a

removable targa roof panel which meant that the rear side windows were deleted and three-slat vents became part of the revised styling.

Production of both models continued until 1973, by which time 2732 GTs and 1180 GTSs had been built.

This 246 is distinguished from the earlier 206 because of the cover over the filler cap and the bolt-on cast alloy wheels which were replaced by the more traditional knock-off items. In addition, the entire body was reinforced for better rigidity and handling.

FERRARI 365 DAYTONA

1968–74

Engine: V12 4390cc (268 cu in)
Power: 262kW (352bhp)
0–96km/h (60mph): 5.4 secs
Top speed: 278km/h (174mph)
Production total: 1423

As serious Italian supercar rivals such as Lamborghini were starting to build mid-engined machines, Ferrari remained content with its established front V12 engine and rear-wheel drive layout. It had no reason to change, especially when the range-topping model that replaced the 275 GTB and GTB/4 was as sensational as the 365 GTB/4. It was nicknamed the 'Daytona', in honour of Ferrari's incredible 1–2–3 line abreast finish in the Daytona 24-hour race in 1967. The name Daytona was a familiar one in the United States, where Ferrari hoped the car would appeal most, but this was always an unofficial name and never appeared on the car or in any brochures.

The Daytona was a heavy car, weighing more than 1600kg (3527lb), but it had more than enough power to cope. The 4.4-litre (268 cu in) direct overhead camshaft V12 was not new and was derived from the familiar Colombo-designed unit that could be traced back to the earliest models. However, the engineers at Maranello managed to stretch the engine, enlarging it from 3.3 litres (201 cu in), as used in the 275

There may be sports leather seats, air conditioning and comprehensive instrumentation inside the Daytona, but there was no radio fitted as standard.

GTB/4, to 4.4 litres (268 cu in). First used in the 500 Superfast, it was the biggest engine Maranello had ever developed, with an output of 262kW (352bhp) and producing about 429Nm (318 lb ft) of torque. As a unit, it was it was smooth and flexible, and those who could afford a Daytona were not concerned about the car's heavy 5km/l (14mpg) fuel consumption.

Arguably the greatest front-engined GT of all time, its beautiful, aerodynamic body was styled by Leonardo Fioravanti at the Pininfarina studio. His achievement was to design a car with a massive engine in the nose that still looked sleek. The solution was to lengthen the bonnet and install the engine as far back as possible, which produced the distinctive shark-like styling. At first, for the European market, the headlights were

hidden behind glazed panels, but cars sold in North America and other territories had pop-up items instead. To offset the extra length at the front, Fioravanti restricted the rear overhang to the bare minimum.

The basis of the Daytona was the 275 GTB/4 chassis with wishbone independent front and rear suspension. Also, to balance the whole package, a rear axle-mounted gearbox transaxle was adopted, with a rigid torque tube connecting it to the engine. While this meant that gear changes would not be so slick, that minor detail did not get in the way of the very high performance. The 365 GTB/4 could achieve a 278km/h (174 mph) top speed and took just 5.4 seconds to get to 96km/h (60mph), which crucially made it faster than its greatest rival, the Lamborghini Miura. Bringing it

The Daytona caused a sensation when it was launched in 1968, being bigger, better, faster and prettier than the 275 GTB4 it replaced. Endowed with awesome performance, it also remained docile in traffic, rode well and had unflappable race-bred handling.

all to a halt were new ventilated disc brakes. These were positioned behind new-style, five-spoke cast alloy wheels every bit as distinctive as the Muira's.

Just 122 open-top Spyder versions were built between 1969 and 1973, badged as 365 GTS/4s. The specification was the same as for the coupé, although the majority of cars came with wire spoke wheels. However, a large and unspecified number of coupés were given the Spyder look during the classic car boom of the 1980s to boost their value. Another special model was the racing Berlinetta coupé with an aluminium body and an engine tuned to produce up to 302kW (405bhp).

All the design and engineering elements came together to make a car that offered pin-sharp handling, yet was well balanced and always enjoyable, with plenty of feel. Certainly the ride was firm at lower speeds, and the unassisted steering felt very heavy; however, all that changed when the Daytona was driven at speed, as Ferrari had always intended. Obviously the Daytona was very well developed because, during its brief six-year production run, no significant modifications had to be made. As the saying goes, you cannot improve on perfection.

FERRARI 365 GTC/4

1971–72

Engine: 4390cc (268 cu in)
Power: 253kW (340bhp)
0–96km/h (60mph): 7 secs
Top speed: 241km/h (150mph)
Production total: 500

The 365 GTC/4 was a short-lived although certainly very popular model, which replaced the 365 GT 2+2 and the 365 GTC. It soon accounted for half of Ferrari's front-engined production. It was a combination of contemporary Ferrari parts, using a Daytona chassis together with an independent suspension. However, a front-mounted gearbox was used with a revised 4390cc (268 cu in) V12 with the six Weber carburettors mounted outside the V on the sides of the cylinder heads to reduce the overall height of the unit. Wet-sump lubrication was part of the revised unit, and it achieved a power output of 253kW (340bhp). The ventilated discs of the Daytona were also used, while the 365 GT 2+2 contributed the air conditioning unit, power steering and self-levelling rear suspension.

The design, by Pininfarina, was a two-door coupé with 2+2 seating which shared some styling elements with the Daytona, but had a stubbier nose. Pop-up headlights were a distinctive feature, as were the Cromodora five-spoke alloy wheels. A total of 500 examples was produced before production ceased in 1972, and it represented the last of the big 2+2 road cars. The 365 GTC/4 was the end of an era: future Ferraris would either be two-seaters or full four-seaters.

Essentially a more civilized Daytona, it had more room, but the styling was criticized for having too many sharp edges. It looks much better today and that long, low bonnet line was possible because of the six sidedraught Weber carburettors.

FERRARI 308 GT4

1973–80

The GT4 was the first Ferrari to use the new 2927cc (179 cu in) V8 engine. This lent the car its designation, the 308, which indicated that it was a 3-litre machine with a V8 engine.

The Dino 308 GT4 was first presented at the Paris Motor Show in 1973, initially bearing no Ferrari badges. It was a two-door, 2+2 coupé with a body designed not by Pininfarina, Ferrari's favourite since 1953, but by Bertone. It was the first Ferrari ever styled by the company. The new engine, with timing belts rather than chains, was mounted transversely directly behind the seats. The tubular chassis was effectively a stretched version of the one which was used for the 246 GT.

Most enthusiasts were critical of the box-like styling, which seemed plain and unremarkable compared with previously classic shapes. That did not harm sales (2826 were sold), however, and nor did it detract from the handling, which was balanced and pin-sharp.

The V8 engine had four Weber carburettors which in European tune produced 186kW (250bhp), could power the car to 96km/h (60mph) in just over six seconds and could produce a top speed of 241km/h (150mph).

From 1977, the Ferrari badge was used, and the Dino name was dropped, although the script still appeared on the boot.

Engine: V8 2927cc (179 cu in)
Power: 186kW (250bhp)
0–96km/h (60mph): 6.4 secs
Top speed: 241km/h (150mph)
Production total: 2826

With the 308 GT4, Bertone styled a Ferrari for the first time, even though the first models only had Dino badges, while the elongated cabin meant that there was just room for four. A transitional model for Ferrari, it would form the basis for some real 1970s and 1980s Ferrari classics.

FERRARI 308 GTB/S

Pininfarina's first V8 Ferraris marked the debut of the air intakes that would become a distinctive feature of future Ferraris. American market examples had larger bumpers.

If the GT4 had disappointed Ferrari enthusiasts, fortunately they did not have long to wait for the true successor to the voluptuous 246 GT. Ferrari unveiled its latest two-seater at the 1975 Paris Motor Show, which was based on the mechanicals of the 308 GT4, and called it the 308 GTB. Using a shortened 308 GT4 chassis, it had the same wheelbase as the original 246 GT, but with a wider track. For Europe, the engine also adopted dry-sump lubrication. The bodywork, designed by Pininfarina, was uniquely made from fibreglass, except for the aluminium bonnet.

It was the body that received all the attention at first, and the genius behind it was Leonardo Fioravanti at Pininfarina. With Fioravanti having styled the Dino, it was no surprise that the 308 GTB should look similar. Certainly the dimensions and the focused sports car buyer market it was aimed at were more or less identical. Both cars had extremely low waistlines, slim noses, a sleek overall shape and a large and steeply raked windscreen. Also, the flat engine cover and flying buttresses only served to emphasize the mid-

Inside the Ferrari 308 GTB/S, apart from the traditional metal gear lever gate, the instrument binnacle was rectangular and quite plain in its design.

engined layout. The 308's pop-up headlights helped to produce a more aerodynamic front end, beefed up with bonnet grilles and side air ducts. Its side windows were large and gave the cabin a light and airy environment.

Best of all, the 308 GTB was not merely good to look at, it delivered a pure driving experience as well. Its transverse V8 had more than enough power and torque, and the car had a wonderfully smooth and direct gear change. The maximum European power output, 190kW (255bhp), was enough to push the car to 248km/h (154mph) and could produce a 96km/h (0–60mph)

time of just over six seconds. This was a great achievement from a normally aspirated 2926cc (179 cu in) V8, one which was aided by the car's lightness and agility.

Many road testers thought that the 308 GTB's handling was adequate, rather than outstanding and, unsurprisingly, the ride was firm. Like all the great Ferraris, it was unhappy at unfamiliar low speeds and only really came into its own when driven hard, as it was designed to do.

In 1976, after 712 cars had been built, the bodywork was changed to steel construction and, in the following year, the GTS was added to the range. Unveiled at the Frankfurt Motor Show in 1977, this model, with a removable roof, had some additional strengthening to compensate. The roof panel could be stored behind the seats, and the black louvred panels which replaced the rear quarter windows were another identifying feature. At the same time, the European-only dry-sump lubrication was deleted and replaced with a wet-sump system. The last few cars also lost some power due to modifications for more stringent emission controls. Production of the original GTB ceased in 1979, by which time a total of 2897 examples had been built.

For 1980, the engines in both the GTB and GTS received a Bosch K-Jetronic fuel injection system and a Marelli Digiplex electronic ignition, and the models became known as the GTBi and GTSi. The power of these emission-friendly engines dropped to 159kW (214bhp) for the European market and to 155kW (208bhp) for sales to the United States. Strictly for the tax-sensitive Italian market, there was also a 2-litre (122 cu in) version producing 127kW (170bhp). Later, in 1982, a fuel-injected turbo-charged version offered 164kW (220bhp) and remained available after the production of the earlier European and US models had ended the same year. By then, 494 GTBis and 1749 GTSis had been built.

Those who thought that Ferrari was concentrating too heavily on Formula One and not producing race-bred road cars were reminded that the 308 did find some success but, surprisingly, not on the race track. Jean Claude Andruet scored some notable rally victories in a 308, winning the Tour de France in both 1981 and 1982.

Engine: V8 2926cc (179 cu in)
Power: 190kW (255bhp)
0–96km/h (60mph): 6 secs
Top speed: 248km/h (154mph)
Production total: 5140

FERRARI 400 GT

Engine: V12 4823cc (294 cu in)
Power: 253kW (340bhp)
0–96km/h (60mph): 7 secs
Top speed: 241km/h (150mph)
Production total: 502

At the Paris Motor Show of 1976, Ferrari revealed its first car to be fitted with an automatic transmission, the 400A. This was essentially a revised 365 GT4 2+2 using the same chassis and suspension. As big as a Jaguar XJ6, the mildly revised Pininfarina styling helped to create a more compact shape. Retaining the pop-up headlights, it looked like an updated Daytona (which was no bad thing), and under the long bonnet was a larger 4823cc (294 cu in) development of the V12 engine.

The transmission itself was a three-speed General Motors GM 400 Hydramatic unit as used in contemporary Cadillacs and also the same one chosen by Rolls-Royce and Jaguar.

Oddly enough, a car that was perfect for the North American market was never actually exported there because of the high costs of meeting the prevailing legislation.

A manual model, the 400 GT, was launched at the same time, and it looked identical to the automatic version, with its new front spoiler and revised tail lamps. Even more importantly for Ferrari's credibility, it offered strong performance, with a top speed of 241km/h (150mph).

One of its poorer aspects, however, was the vehicle's fuel consumption, which in the GT rarely bettered figures of 3.5km/l (10mpg). Still, at least the GT could be considered a practical car and was also a proper four-seater, even if the rear legroom was tight.

FERRARI 512 BB

Engine: V12 4942cc (302 cu in)
Power: 253kW (340bhp)
0–96km/h (60mph): 7 secs
Top speed: 282km/h (175mph)
Production total: 1936

Ferrari was being left behind. In the 1970s, as its Modena neighbours Maserati and Lamborghini were offering sophisticated mid-engined supercars, at the top of the Ferrari range was the old-fashioned front-engined Daytona. The car Ferrari created to remedy this was the 365 GT4 BB. BB stands for 'Berlinetta Boxer', in which Boxer indicates a horizontally opposed engine, just like the layout used in contemporary Formula One cars.

The 4.4-litre (268 cu in) engine used in the 365 was losing power because of emission controls, so Ferrari enlarged it to a full 5 litres (302 cu in), losing 20bhp in the process, but increasing its torque by 39Nm (29lb ft). The maximum revs dropped from 7750rpm to 6500rpm. This dry-sump design now had responsive acceleration, but a slightly lower top speed. Ferrari called this car the 512 BB: the '5' designated 5 litres, and the '12' stood for 12 cylinders.

Featuring prominent air ducts behind the doors to cool the brakes and a two-tone paint scheme with a black finish at the bottom, it was more aggressively styled than the 365, making do with four rear lights rather than six.

The 512BB was to remain in production until the 1980s and received fuel injection in 1981. Although it was not one of the greatest Ferraris, its boxer engine was developed and later became the heart of the new Testarossa.

The 512 BB was Ferrari's successor to the front-engined Daytona. The styling was by Pininfarina and there were 12 cylinders, but it was still a huge departure for the company. Fibreglass lower body panels in black and a flat Boxer engine set it apart.

FERRARI 400I/412I

Engine: V12 4942cc (302 cu in)
Power: 253kW (340bhp)
0–96km/h (60mph): 6.7 secs
Top speed: 249km/h (155mph)
Production total: 2558

In 1979, the engines on the 400 range gained a Bosch K-Jetronic fuel injection system and were designated as the 400i. This addition actually reduced power to 231kW (310bhp). The self-levelling rear suspension was revised, and improved gas shock absorbers made this the softest-sprung Ferrari for years. The emphasis was on comfort and luxury, indicated by the option of split air conditioning systems for front- and rear-seat passengers. In production until 1985, some 884 automatic and 424 manual versions were produced.

The 412 was a further evolution of the original 365 car. The styling

Getting the 400GT into the United States was the idea behind fitting Bosch K-Jetronic fuel injection. The later 412 looked remarkably similar, but had a larger boot.

was essentially the same as the 400i; however, the boot was larger and the interior was revised with touch-sensitive switches and electrically controlled seats. The engine now displaced 4942cc (302 cu in), and power output went back up to the pre-injection level of the 400, at 253kW (340bhp). Later, a 242kW (325bhp) version with a catalysed exhaust system briefly became available. The GM automatic gearbox was now the standard transmission, although a five-speed manual still remained an option.

The most important technical innovation on this car was the standard installation of ABS brakes, which was a first for Ferrari and, indeed, for any Italian-built car. Otherwise, the 400 range was a largely uninspiring one and faded away in 1989.

FERRARI 328 GTB/GTS

Engine: V8 3195cc (195 cu in)
Power: 201kW (270bhp)
0–96km/h (60mph): 6.4 secs
Top speed: 262km/h (163mph)
Production total: 7412

Almost a decade after Ferrari launched its best-selling 308 model range, it was only logical that the company should further develop this successful package. Launched at the Frankfurt Motor Show in 1985, the classic 308 had been only mildly restyled. The most obvious change was the new, more prominent colour-matched bumpers front and rear, which seemed to make the 328 look more bulky because of the front spoiler and a more prominent air intake. Indeed, the 328 was actually slightly longer than the old car, as the chassis had been stretched by 1cm (0.4in).

Also stretched was the engine, bored and stroked to a capacity of 3195cc (195cc) and producing 201kW (270bhp). It was still transversely located behind the two seats. The QV Quattrovalve head was retained from the previous V8 and with a healthy 301Nm (223lb ft) of torque, Ferrari could claim that its bestseller could now exceed 257km/h (160mph).

This compact sports car looked sensational and delivered a superb driving experience. During the production lifetime of the car there were only minor changes, such as revised interior door handles. More significant was the availability of ABS brakes as an option in 1988.

Sales of the GTS model were to comfortably outstrip those of the GTB: a total of 6068 GTSs was sold compared to 1344 GTBs.

On the surface, there is not a huge amount of difference between the 308 and its successor, the 328, except for body-coloured bumpers and a front spoiler which was now a standard feature. The car pictured here is the GTS with a pop-out roof panel.

FERRARI 288 GTO

Engine: V8 2855cc (174 cu in)
Power: 298kW (400bhp)
0–96km/h (60mph): 4 secs
Top speed: 306km/h (190mph)
Production total: 273

Loosely based on the 308, the 288 GTO was in fact marked by many significant differences and was designed purely as a homologation special for the new Group B racing regulations. The fuel-injected engine had a reduced capacity of 2855cc (174 cu in) to meet the maximum capacity of 3 litres (183 cu in), and it also had twin IHI turbochargers and Behr intercoolers, producing a massive 298kW (400bhp) and a top speed of 306km/h (190mph).

The positioning of the vehicle's engine was different to that of the 308, as the 288 GTO's engine was mounted longitudinally, and the tubular chassis was stretched by 11cm (4.3in). The chassis also

When the GTO was launched at the Geneva Motor Show in 1984, it was the fastest roadgoing car in the world, and was Ferrari's most radical model.

featured increased track widths front and rear, as well as other modifications which were designed to reduce weight and boost stiffness. There is independent double wishbone suspension front and rear, with coil springs, coaxial Koni dampers and anti-roll bars.

The body was basically that of a 308 with numerous extra vents and ducts, and it was made from a variety of light materials including Nomex, Kevlar, aluminium and fibreglass to keep the car's weight

As a limited production car homologated for racing, the 288 GTO will always be remembered as one of Ferrari's all-time greats. The GTO can be instantly recognized by its high-mounted door mirrors, engine-cooling slats behind the rear wheels and flowing Pininfarina lines.

down to the absolute minimum. Other distinguishing features on the 288 were the additional driving lights in the front grille, the unique wing mirrors and the slatted vents behind the rear wheels.

Two hundred units were required to be produced to comply with the homologation regulations, and

ultimately 273 288 GTOs were built during 1984 and 1985 to qualify the car for Group B racing. The proposed racing formula never materialized, however, so the 288 GTO remained a very special road car with sensational performance and handling, enjoyed only by a privileged few.

FERRARI TESTAROSSA

Engine: V12 4942cc (302 cu in)
Power: 291kW (390bhp)
0–96km/h (60mph): 5.8 secs
Top speed: 291km/h (181mph)
Production total: 7177

As the designated replacement for the 512 BB, the Testarossa made a huge impact at the Paris Motor Show in 1984. Pininfarina's huge and hugely influential design was dominated by the massive side intakes that directed air to the rear-mounted radiators.

The chassis was a stretched and much modified development of the BB's, still with the same basic double wishbone suspension, but now featuring twin coil-over units at the rear to cope with the increased weight. Wider track and substantial 240/45 and 280/45 section front and rear tyres helped to keep the Testarossa on the road.

The 4942cc (302 cu in) engine from the 512 BB now had four valves per cylinder, Bosch K-Jetronic fuel injection and Marelli electronic ignition, and it produced 291kW (390bhp). This set-up

succeeded in moving this massive supercar at a furious rate, topping speeds of 290km/h (180mph) and being able to reach 96km/h (60mph) in less than six seconds.

The brash bodywork was remarkable, much copied and admired by those who bought a Testarossa because they wanted to be noticed. Apart from the large air intakes, the rear lights were covered by a black slatted grille, while a black band covered the lower part of the sills and front air dam.

The drag coefficient of 0.36 seemed disappointingly high, but was justified because the shape was primarily designed for maximum downforce. This big, loud Ferrari seemed to sum up the attitude of the 1980s.

The mid-mounted engine is kept cool by two radiators, one on each side with air fed into them through two huge and distinctive side strakes. The whole of the rear end above the wings can be lifted up for engine access.

The front air intake of the Testarossa feeds air to the front brakes and the air conditioning system. The Testarossa looks huge from the front: at 197cm (77.8 inches), it was the widest production car of its day.

FERRARI F40

Engine: V8 2936cc (179 cu in)
Power: 356kW (478bhp)
0–96km/h (60mph): 3.9secs
Top speed: 323km/h (201mph)
Production total: 1315

The F40 not only was created to celebrate Ferrari's 40th birthday, but was intended to upstage Porsche's 959 as the world's fastest production car as well. The F40 was duly revealed to the world in the summer of 1987, designed and engineered to be the nearest thing to a racing car for the road – although Ferrari never intended to put it on the track.

The engine and chassis were loosely based on the 288 GTO. The engine was a 2936cc (179 cu in) development of the V8, still with four valves per cylinder, twin IHI turbos and Behr intercoolers which increased efficiency and helped to generate a huge 356kW (478bhp). The compression ratio was on paper a modest 7.8:1; however, the turbo boost pressure used was an exceptional 16psi.

This V8 was an exotic creation made from the composite material Silumin, with shrink-fitted alloy liners in the block itself. On top

were twin belt-driven camshafts for each bank of cylinders. Best of all, this work of art was clearly visible through the louvred plastic engine cover in the middle of the F40. If all that power were not enough for some buyers, however, there was a factory upgrade kit available with larger turbochargers and revised camshafts that could add another 149kW (200bhp).

The F40 chassis retained the wheelbase and basic suspension arrangement of the GTO, but featured wider tracks front and rear. The wheels were huge 43cm (17in) diameter Cromodora items, 33cm (13in) wide at the rear and fitted with 335/35 Pirelli P-Zero tyres. At the front, the wheels were 'only' 20cm (8in) wide, with 245/40 tyres. Due to the low ground clearance, some cars featured suspension height control.

The bodywork, which clothed the tubular steel frame, was a completely new design by Pininfarina. Using carbon fibre, Kevlar, aluminium and honeycomb parts, it was perfect, being aerodynamic, functional and, above all, light. The F40 weighed just 1089kg (2400lb), which translated into a

remarkable power to weight ratio of less than 3kg per kilowatt (5lb per bhp).

This ratio was further aided by the use of plastic for all the windows except the windscreen. Indeed, many early F40s had fixed side windows, but owners who used them more regularly preferred to have manually wound ones.

The bodywork was peppered in ducts and vents to cool the brakes and engine, and feed the turbos. These aerodynamic tricks also kept the F40 glued to the road, especially the massive hand-finished rear wing. However, that distinctive tail would have been illegal under racing regulations if the F40 had ever been officially entered in motor sport events.

As extravagant and eye-catching as the F40 was on the outside, inside there were no luxurious touches. Lots of Kevlar was visible, but no carpet – this was a stripped-out racer. There was one concession to cockpit comfort, however, which was the standard installation of air conditioning. What Ferrari had created was its fastest ever model, capable of reaching 96km/h (60mph) in under

Initiated by Enzo Ferrari himself to celebrate his company's 40th anniversary, the F40 was certainly a landmark car – a barely tamed racer for the road. Under the louvred, clear plastic engine cover was a twin turbocharged, four-cam, 32-valve V8 engine.

four seconds. It also reached its goal of breaking the 322km/h (200mph) barrier, recording a top speed of 323km/h (201mph). For a time, this made the F40 indisputably the fastest production car in the world, which in turn initiated a mini supercar war that hastened the production of the Lamborghini Diablo and Jaguar XJ220. Indeed, the F40 was reckoned by some industry pundits and engineers to be a fairly crude exercise in performance. At least one other Formula One manufacturer thought that it could do better, and the Le Mans-winning McLaren F1 was the ultimate hi-tech response.

To the eternal disappointment of speculators, but not the real enthusiasts, Ferrari's initial plans to build just 450 F40s were modified several times, and a total of 1315 cars was eventually built.

FERRARI MONDIAL T

Mid-engined, despite that long and louvred bonnet, yet the Mondial still managed to be a full four-seater. Pictured here is a later Quattrovalvole, with four valves per cylinder and also available as a full open-topped cabriolet.

The Mondial T, introduced in 1989, effectively combined the old Mondial, based on the 308GT4, with the new 348. From the outside, however, the changes did not look that extensive. A redesign of the rear saw air intakes become smaller, neater, rectangular shapes, while the bumpers and door handles became body-coloured, and inside there were folding rear seats to boost luggage space.

Like the 348TB, the Mondial T had its engine mounted longitudinally and significantly lower in the chassis than before. Also, the transmission was now mounted behind the final drive, and the long-wheelbase tubular chassis was modified to support the relocated engine and transmission.

There were several technical upgrades that made the Mondial T safer and easier to live with than the old Mondial. ABS brakes were now part of the standard specification, as were driver-controlled damper settings, and the rack-and-pinion steering now had power assistance.

Often derided by purists, the Mondial was still a true Ferrari, with a 3405cc (208 cu in) engine taken from the 348. It had four valves per cylinder, but was now able to run on unleaded fuel and had an increased power output of 224kW (300bhp).

The car was never simply a cynical compromise, but a proper four-seater supercar.

Engine: V8 3405cc (208 cu in)
Power: 224kW (300bhp)
0–96km/h (60mph): 6.3 secs
Top speed: 254km/h (158mph)
Production total: n/a

FIAT 514

Engine: 4 cylinder 1438cc (88 cu in)
Power: 26kW (34.5bhp)
0–96km/h (60mph): n/a
Top speed: 88km/h (55mph)
Production total: 36,970

The 514 was introduced with a new 1.4-litre (88 cu in) engine, but was built on a similar wheelbase to the previous 509. Regarded as a dull but reliable family car, it had six-volt ignition, a four-speed gearbox and mechanical brakes with a four-wheel handbrake. During its production life, the 514 was gradually uprated with hydraulic dampers to replace the original friction units, as well as other small improvements. Body styles included Berlina, Coupé, Cabriolet Royal, Torpedo and Spider, as well as a longer wheelbase variant, the 514L, which was designed to be used as a taxi and also fitted with a van body. Coachbuilders Mulliner in the United Kingdom also offered a fabric-bodied saloon. A 515 derivative with an X-braced frame

and hydraulic brakes was made available as well.

Not all 514s were boring family transport. Three sport versions were built and could reach 113km/h (70mph). The 514S used a slightly tuned engine in the

Always regarded as a stodgy but reliable family car and often used as a taxi, here is a slightly more interesting model of the 514, a four-door open tourer. This is an early example because wire wheels would have been fitted after 1931.

standard chassis, while the 514MM (Mille Miglia) used a more highly tuned engine in a longer van chassis. The 514CA (Coppa delle Alpi) used the more highly tuned engine in the standard chassis. Wire wheels were usually standard.

FIAT 508

1937–48

Engine: 4 cylinder 1089cc (66 cu in)
Power: 24kW (32bhp)
0–96km/h (60mph): 40 secs
Top speed: 116km/h (72mph)
Production total: 11,947

The Balilla range, also known as the 1100 or 508C, got a new 1089cc (66 cu in) engine producing 24kW (32bhp), while the body resembled an enlarged Topolino (see next entry). Indeed, it closely resembled the larger 1500 with the same recessed door handles and pillarless doors. A longer wheelbase 508L and a cabriolet was also added to the range to broaden the appeal while, for the Mille Miglia race of 1938, Fiat even developed the MM in coupé form with an engine tuned to give 31kW (42bhp). The MM won its class.

The 508C served throughout the war, being produced from 1939 to 1945 in 'Militare' form as a sort of Jeep-like vehicle. A 'Coloniale' model, a much larger, heavier duty staff car, was also offered and produced until 1943. Both models were powered by the 22kW (30bhp) 1089cc (66 cu in) engine with the four-speed transmission.

After the war, the 508C and 508L were reintroduced, using almost the same specification. Closely related to the 1100, the 508 continued to provide dependable family transportation, while the 1100 became the more glamorous, sporty model. Production came to an end in 1948, and the car's place was taken by the 1100, until the all-new 1100-103 was introduced in the early 1950s.

One of the most successful of Fiat' prewar models, the 508 was also produced in France, Germany, Czechoslovakia and Poland under licence. Most were saloons, but a few pretty cabriolets such as this were also produced.

FIAT TOPOLINO

1936–48

Engine: 4 cylinder 569cc (35 cu in)
Power: 10kW (13bhp)
0–96km/h (60mph): n/a
Top speed: 84km/h (52mph)
Production total: 131,000

This 'baby' Fiat, the 500, best known as the 'Topolino', was easily the smallest mass-produced car of its time. With just two seats, a 10kW (13bhp) 569cc (35 cu in) engine and a 200cm (79in) wheelbase, it was conceived to bring motoring to the Italian masses. Not surprisingly, it proved to be an incredible success.

The car remained in production until 1948 in its original form, when more than 110,000 had been sold. During that long run, relatively few changes were made, and the only notable modification was the change from transverse-leaf independent suspension to a quarter elliptic set-up from the middle of 1938.

Production was restarted after World War II, and the new 500B looked identical to the old model; however, changes were made under the skin. The engine received an extra 2.5kW (3.5bhp), and the brakes, suspension and electrical equipment were all improved. An estate version, the 500 Giardiniera-Belvedere, was launched in 1948, which made the small car much more practical because it was finally able to carry four people in its longer body made from steel, wood and plastic.

In 1949, there were to be more changes, as the 500C model arrive with both a new front end and an engine with aluminium cylinder heads. These models were also the first of the Fiats to have interior heating systems.

FIAT 1100

Engine: 4 cylinder 1089cc (66 cu in)
Power: 24kW (32bhp)
0–96km/h (60mph): 40 secs
Top speed: 116km/h (72mph)
Production total: 327,496

The 1100 was essentially a 508C with a new grille, and it became the quintessential Italian family car, providing spacious, practical and reliable transport. Various versions were produced, including a Berlina, a Berlina with canvas opening roof, a cabriolet, a long-wheelbase and a taxi version. In 1947, a touch of glamour was added with the 1100S, a two-seat coupé with a 38kW (51bhp) version of the 1089cc (66 cu in) engine. The 1100 proved to be a good basis for coachbuilders, including Cisitalia, with its beautiful GS. A coupé designed by Pininfarina, the 1100ES, was equally striking and used the mechanicals of the 1947 1100S to great effect.

The 1100 was brought up to date and badged as the 1100E or the long-wheelbase EL, both launched in 1949. Visually, one major change was made. The spare wheel was moved from the bootlid to inside the luggage compartment. The gear lever was moved to the steering column from its previous position on the floor, and the transmission was uprated with synchromesh now available on second, third and fourth gears. The Balilla/508/1100 family of models' legacy lived on in subsequent mid-sized Fiats.

FIAT 8V

Engine: V8 1996cc (122 cu in)
Power: 78kW (105bhp)
0–96km/h (60mph): 12.6 secs
Top speed: 193km/h (120mph)
Production total: 114 (chassis)

When Fiat first decided to go against its utilitarian car roots and build a flagship V8, everyone was surprised and ultimately disappointed, not least because the prototype proved slow and cumbersome; the project was ultimately cancelled. This left Fiat with a 2-litre (122 cu in) V8 engine, but no car to put it in. The solution was to put it in a sports car and so the 8V, or Otto Vu, arrived at the Geneva Motor Show in 1952.

The car looked fantastic, and the Pininfarina-inspired lines were all designed in-house by Fiat design boss Dante Giacosa. The car was aerodynamically efficient which helped Fiat's chief test driver, Carlo Salomano, to record a stunning average speed of more than 193km/h (120mph).

Siata was contracted to build the cars, while the bodies were built at

As seen at the 1952 Paris Motor Show, here was a futuristic coupé that wowed the crowds even if few could ever have afforded it.

Lingotto by Fiat's experimental workshop. Underneath the body was standard 1100 independent suspension, giving it unusually crisp handling.

FIAT 1100 MK II

The 1100-103 may have had similar running gear to the old 1100, but the monocoque bodyshell was all new. The familiar 1089cc (66 cu in) engine provided power to the rear wheels through a four-speed gearbox with a column-mounted shift. More interesting was the 103 TV ('Turismo Veloce'), producing 37kW (50bhp). An estate version, the Familiare, followed in 1954, and a distinctive 103 TV 'Trasformabile' roadster was offered from 1955. Yet again, this model became the standard Italian family form of transport across two decades.

Second-generation models from 1956 had more power at 39kW (53bhp), followed by the 103D in 1957 with a longer boot, revised grille and better brakes. At the same time, a 103H Lusso version with 37kW (50bhp) was offered. The new 1100D in 1963 came as a saloon and an estate with cleaner styling. Although badged as an 1100, a 1221cc (75 cu in) engine was now fitted, generating 41kW (55bhp).

The last 1100 in 1968 was the 1100R, which saw a return to the 1089cc (66 cu in) powerplant and the installation of front disc brakes. Soon replaced by the front wheel 128, the 1100 lived on in India as the Premier Padmini.

The 1100 had a prewar look simply because it was a prewar design. Fiat claimed that it had 'new aerodynamic lines' and was a 'brilliant, economical car with smart acceleration'.

Engine: 4 cylinder 1089cc (66 cu in)
Power: 30kW (40bhp)
0–96km/h (60mph): 30 secs
Top speed: 124km/h (77mph)
Production total: 1,019,378

FIAT 600

Engine: 4 cylinder 633cc (39 cu in)
Power: 22kW (29bhp)
0–96km/h (60mph): 40 secs
Top speed: 106km/h (66mph)
Production total: 2,695,197

Another genuine people's car, the 600 had a monocoque body with two B pillar hinged 'suicide' doors which opened backwards and seated four. It was powered by a 633cc (39 cu in) 16kW (21.5bhp) water-cooled four-cylinder engine located behind the rear seats, which drove the rear wheels. It also featured independent suspension.

A year after the saloon, a full-length canvas sunroof became an option. More significantly, a new type of vehicle was also launched – the Multipla. This was arguably the first people carrier, albeit a very small one. With three rows of seats, it could accommodate six people. In addition, the two rear pairs of seats could be folded into the floor, leaving a large, flat loading area. To cope with the expected extra weight, the brakes, suspension and steering were all uprated.

Revised in 1960, the car was now badged as the 600D. This model had a bigger engine, a 767cc (47 cu in) unit producing 22kW (29bhp). For 1964, the 600D finally got front-hinged doors, while the last changes in 1965 saw new headlights and a larger fuel tank.

Incredibly it was possible to get four bodies into the 600, which was smaller than a Topolino.

FIAT 1800

1959–68

Engine: 4 cylinder 1795cc (110 cu in)
Power: 56kW (75bhp)
0–96km/h (60mph): 19 secs
Top speed: 145km/h (90mph)
Production total: 30,000

New range-topping six-cylinder models, the 1800 and 2100, headed up the Fiat list in 1959. Powered by either a 1795cc (110 cu in) unit with 56kW (75bhp) or a 2054cc (125 cu in) with 61kW (82bhp), these cars were the first Fiats to use torsion bar suspension at the front and the first postwar Fiats to feature straight-six engines.

Alongside the pretty Pininfarina Berlina saloon was a Familiare estate. From 1960, the 1800 could be ordered with many luxury car features, including a sunroof, radio, electric radio aerial, whitewall tyres and a heated rear window. Fiat, though, could convince few buyers outside Italy that it had made a 'proper' prestige car, as the model had only average refinement and patchy build quality.

From 1962 onwards, the engine from the 1500 was now offered in the 1800's body; however, this did not mean that the model was taken any more seriously by the car-buying public.

The 1800 was the first in a long line of big car embarrassments for Fiat, and tempting buyers away from the reliable Mercedes marque was always going to be a difficult, if not impossible, proposition.

FIAT 850

1964–72

Engine: 4 cylinder 843cc (51 cu in)
Power: 28kW (37bhp)
0–96km/h (60mph): 27 secs
Top speed: 125km/h (78mph)
Production total: 2,670,913

From the Fiat 600 was born the new Fiat 850. The 850 was still a two-door, rear-engined car and it retained many of the mechanicals seen on the 600; however, apart from the new, more spacious bodywork, there was also a new 843cc (51 cu in) four-cylinder water-cooled engine. Two versions of the saloon were built, the Normale, which produced 25kW (34bhp), and the Super, which produced 28kW (37bhp).

In 1965, better-looking and sweeter-handling models of the Fiat 850 followed with the launch of the Coupé and the Spider. The Coupé was designed by Centro Stile Fiat and built by Fiat, while the Spider model was designed and built by Bertone.

The Coupé's tuned engine produced 35kW (47bhp) and the Spider's engine 37kW (49bhp), while front disc brakes replaced the former drum items. In 1966, a semiautomatic transmission was made available which did without the clutch pedal.

A Familiare model was also offered in the range, replacing the old 600 Multipla, but again using three rows of seats. This particular variant remained in production until 1976, using a 903cc (55 cu in) engine from 1970 onwards.

Revised for 1968, an 850 Special went on sale, and this was a saloon which had the Coupé's engine and

Despite the engine being rear-mounted, the 850 handled very sweetly, plus it offered much more room than the cramped 600 on which it was based. This is a very early UK-registered example with optional whitewall tyres.

disc brakes. The distinctive Sport Spider variant now had two upright headlights, and the Sport Coupé featured four round headlights; both models were equipped with the new 903cc (55 cu in) engine, producing 39kW (52bhp).

FIAT NUOVA 500

1957–75

Engine: 4 cylinder 499cc (30 cu in)
Power: 13kW (18bhp)
0–96km/h (60mph): 45 secs
Top speed: 98km/h (61mph)
Production total: 3,678,000

The successor to the legendary 'Topolino', this was Fiat's most famous baby people's car. Probably the biggest part of the model's appeal was its ability to cruise easily at 98km/h (61mph), yet deliver an astounding 19km/l (53mpg). The handling was good, too, with wonderfully direct steering.

This 'nuova 500' adopted a similar layout to the 600. A rear-mounted engine drove the rear wheels, and the car featured all-round independent suspension and rear-hinged 'suicide' doors. A first for Fiat was the air-cooled engine, which was a two-cylinder 479cc (29 cu in) unit producing 10kW (13bhp). This was attached to a four-speed manual gearbox with a floor-mounted gear lever. Initially, however, the car was not the great success that Fiat had expected. This prompted the company to launch two distinctive versions: the 11kW (15bhp) 'Economica' and the 'Normale'. Essentially, the Economica was the original 'nuova 500', but with a more powerful engine and lower price tag. The Normale also had the uprated engine, plus various other upgrades. These improvements

included opening door windows and a more usable rear seat.

By 1958, Fiat was able to introduce a 'Sport' model, having been inspired by some epic performances on the track, notably a first, second, third and fourth in class at the Hockenheim 12-hour race. This model was fitted with an uprated version of the standard engine, enlarged to 499cc (30 cu in), with a revised camshaft, valves, cylinder head and fuelling. As a result, it now produced a very creditable 16kW (21.5bhp). With a distinctive red stripe down each side, the Sport was difficult to miss. Another feature was its solid

roof, in contrast to the canvas roll-back roof found on standard production cars. The Sport was offered with an open-air option from 1959.

A 'Giardiniera' estate version was introduced for 1960 which rode on a stretched wheelbase and differed from the saloon by having a horizontally mounted engine. Later that year, the 500D was to arrive, with a 499cc (30 cu in) engine from the discontinued Sport, but reduced power output of 13kW (18bhp).

The 500D was replaced by the 500F in 1965, where the most noticeable changes were the over-due adoption of front-hinged doors and a revised transmission. In 1968, the 500F was joined in production by the 'Lusso', which offered several touches of big-car luxury including reclining seats and even carpet. As well as the uprated interior trim, there were external differences, too, most notably the thin, miniature bull-bars adorning the front and rear bumpers.

One of the most interesting things about the 500 was the number of spin-off models that

Inside the 500, the seats consisted of little more than fabric pads on rubber strips. The rear quarter windows were fixed, although the doors did have quarterlights that aided ventilation.

Transportation at its most basic, the 500 was available in a wide range of variants. This original two-door design accounted for the most sales.

were created on its tiny platform. As well as the famous sporting Abarth-tuned models, the 500 was transformed by some of Italy's most famous coachbuilders. Vignale's Fiat Gamine was a smart little roadster, while the Ghia Jolly had the roof removed and basket-weave seats. Siata built a miniature open-topped classic car. The 500 was also a genuine world car, built by SEAT in Spain and by Motor Holdings in New Zealand, while the NSU-Fiat Weinsburg 500 from Germany offered typically straight-edged mini-limousine styling.

The final version of this car emerged in 1972 as the 500R, which used a new 594cc (36 cu in) engine from the 126, with a reduced output of 13kW (18bhp). The R also had the floorpan from its successor and adopted the new Fiat logo, with different wheels and a few other changes. However, the basic drum brakes were never updated, while the 'crash' non-synchromesh gearbox provided lots of noisy entertainment.

Sales started to fall and the arrival of the Fiat Panda heralded the end of the 500, the production of which was transferred to Sicily.

FIAT 124 SPIDER

Engine: 1438cc (88 cu in)
Power: 67kW (90bhp)
0–96km/h (60mph): 12 secs
Top speed: 170km/h (106 mph)
Production total: 198,000

The most successful Italian sports car ever was made by Fiat. The 124 Sport Spider sold in Europe and the United States in huge numbers over a 20-year period. Based on a shortened Berlina chassis, the Spider body was designed and built by Pininfarina, with final assembly carried out by Fiat. The original AS series was fitted with a 67kW (90bhp) 1438cc (88 cu in) double overhead camshaft engine and a five-speed transmission.

The revised BS models from 1969 soon received a 1608cc (98 cu in) engine with twin Weber 40 carburettors producing 82kW (110bhp), and the car needed twin bonnet humps to accommodate them. Pretty styling, a character-filled engine, good handling and competitive pricing were the major reasons why people chose to buy the Fiat Spider.

The fastest version of the car, the Abarth Rally with twin 44IDF carburettors, produced 95kW

(128bhp) and also had a limited slip differential, revised independent rear suspension, composite bonnet and boot, and aluminium alloy doors. Slightly more than 1000 of these vehicles were built.

If the Spider was exciting, the standard car became less so, as Spider sales were concentrated solely on the United States from 1974 onwards. Spider Americas were detuned to comply with emissions regulations and by 1976 only produced 65kW (87bhp). Fitting a larger 1995cc (122 cu in) engine and fuel injection meant the Spider bowed out with a barely adequate 76kW (102bhp).

Pininfarina's perfectly proportioned small sports car, the 124 Spider, is a short-wheelbased relative of the 124 coupé. Never available in right-hand drive or seriously marketed in the United Kingdom, this is a rust-free import from the United States that has been restored.

FIAT DINO

At the 1966 Turin Motor Show, the press and public stared open-mouthed at the Fiat Dino Spider. As well as a beautiful body designed and built by Pininfarina, the other surprise was that Fiat were going to fit a reworked Ferrari competition engine under the bonnet. This 1997cc (122 cu in) quad camshaft V6 fitted with three Weber twin 40DCNF carburettors produced 119kW (160bhp) working through a five-speed gearbox and limited slip differential.

The Dino was no accident because Ferrari needed an engine derived from a homologated production run of 500 cars within 12 months to compete in Formula

The convertible Fiat Dino is very differently styled from the coupé. Here is the extremely curvaceous Pininfarina-bodied Spider, the first version on the market. The coupé had a longer wheelbase, allowing for two-plus-two seating.

Two. In 1967, the Dino Coupé appeared, designed and produced by Bertone using the same mechanicals as the Spider, on a stretched wheelbase.

Second-generation Dinos in 1969 benefited from a new engine which featured a cast-iron block, rather than the alloy block of the 1997cc (122 cu in) version. This larger unit now displaced 2418cc (148 cu in) and produced 134kW (180bhp). In addition, the rear suspension was also changed to a sophisticated strut and trailing arm system derived from the 130. The close cooperation needed for this project led to Fiat taking over Ferrari. The Fiat badge did not have the feel-good Ferrari factor, however, and sales were slow.

Engine: V6 2418cc (148 cu in)
Power: 134kW (180bhp)
0–96km/h (60mph): 8 secs
Top speed: 208km/h (130mph)
Production total: 7577

FIAT 130

1969–77

Engine: V6 3235cc (197 cu in)
Power: 123kW (165bhp)
0–96km/h (60mph): 10 secs
Top speed: 189km/h (118mph)
Production total: 19,385

Fiat's new flagship in 1969 to replace the old 2300 was the 130.

Powered by a completely new 2866cc (175 cu in) 60-degree V6 with 104kW (140bhp), it had a Ferrari Dino-type bottom end and used a cogged drive belt rather than chains to cope with half the number of camshafts. With a conventional front-engine, rear-wheel drive layout, the 130 was fitted with an automatic transmission as standard, although a manual five-speed ZF transmission was an option. It sat on independent suspension all round using torsion bars at the front and coil springs at the rear. Spacious but heavy, and not that fast, this was an expensive car which failed to tempt many prestige buyers away from Mercedes.

In 1970, the engine was boosted by 15kW (20bhp); however, just a year later, a new engine, this time with a capacity of 3235cc (197 cu in) producing 123kW (165bhp), was accompanied by a stronger automatic transmission. The only visual clue to any changes was the replacement of the four round headlights with two large, rectangular items.

Also making its debut was a new Coupé, designed and built by Pininfarina. Using the same engine, mechanicals and floorpan as the saloon, the car's angular styling could not be ignored and was much more distinguished than the unloved saloon.

Pininfarina was responsible for the 130's styling, which may look bland now, but was very contemporary in the early 1970s and much better than the dull saloon on which it was based. The Ferrari V6 engine undoubtedly helped, too.

FIAT 127

1971–83

Engine: 4 cylinder 903cc (55 cu in)
Power: 35kW (47bhp)
0–96km/h (60mph): 17 secs
Top speed: 137km/h (85mph)
Production total: 3,779,086

Voted Car of the Year in 1971, this was the model that brought Fiat into the modern era, adopting the front-wheel drive layout from its bigger sister, the 128. Most of the mechanicals were based on the 128, although the 903cc (55 cu in) engine was a derivative of the 850 Sport unit. Performance was perky, and the handling was very sharp. Initially launched in two-door form, it only really made sense as a three-door hatchback.

Series II cars from 1977 had a redesigned front end and a new 1049cc (64 cu in) engine, produced in Brazil, which was still sold alongside the smaller unit. Three levels of trim became available, the 'L', 'C' and 'CL'. The 127 Sport joined the range in 1978, with the 1049cc (64 cu in) engine tuned to give 52kW (70bhp) and with improved brakes, a larger anti-roll bar and suitably sporty interior and exterior trim. A five-door 127, the 'C', arrived in 1980, powered by the 903cc (55 cu in) engine. This was followed by the Panorama estate and the option of a 1301cc (79 cu in) diesel engine.

The final version, the Series III of 1981, saw another facelift, as the Sport received a new 1301cc (79 cu in) unit producing 56kW (75bhp), and Fiat was more than pleased with the huge sales figures that followed.

Arguably the world's first supermini, the 127 was very cleverly packaged and proved hugely popular in Europe and later South America. This later example with a full-width grille and matt black bumpers dates from 1980.

FIAT 126

The Fiat 126 was first seen at the 1972 Turin Motor Show and proved to be a logical, if not so endearing, successor to the legendary 500. Using an enlarged 594cc (36 cu in) engine, it retained the familiar running gear of its predecessor, housed in an all-new bodyshell. Styled with fashionable straight-edges, rather than the 500's rounded curves, it at least soon became available with a canvas rollback roof. Performance was poor, as was the level of refinement. In 1977, a new 652cc (40cu in) 18kW (24bhp) engine was introduced.

In 1987, the 126 underwent a significant transformation when a water-cooled flat-twin 704cc (43 cu in) engine producing 19kW (26bhp) was installed and the model was launched as the 126bis. Now capable of just reaching 113km/h (70mph), the engine was mounted horizontally instead of vertically. This new arrangement created significantly more rear luggage space and allowed the bodywork to be styled as a three-door hatchback with a folding rear seat. The 126bis lived on in Poland, built by the FSM company until September 2000, where it prospered as the most basic and cheapest car available in Europe.

Engine: 4 cylinder 594cc (36 cu in)
Power: 17kW (23bhp)
0–96km/h (60mph): 62 secs
Top speed: 104km/h (65mph)
Production total: 1,970,000

The 500 was reborn in a rather more squared-off body. It was the same size as the Mini, but with less room and certainly less fun to drive.

FIAT X1/9

Engine: 4 cylinder 1498cc (91 cu in)
Power: 63kW (85bhp)
0–96km/h (60mph): 10 secs
Top speed: 180km/h (112mph)
Production total: 180,000

Having developed the front-wheel drive package for its new small cars, Fiat thought it only logical to replace the 850 Spider with a 128-based derivative. Bertone, however, had other ideas, namely putting the engine in the middle, rather than at the front.

Certainly, the Fiat X1/9 was a radical departure from conventional small sports car layouts. Launched in 1972, it was an all-new car, utilizing the 1290cc (79 cu in) unit modified to produce 56kW (75bhp) (49kW [66bhp] for the North American market). The engine was positioned behind the two seats and drove the rear wheels. MacPherson struts were chosen as the suspension set-up, and there were disc brakes all round. The low seating position, mid-engined layout, pop-up headlights and clever removable Targa top made the X1/9 both look and drive like a half-size Ferrari.

In 1978, a 1498cc (91 cu in) 63kW (85bhp) engine was borrowed from the Ritmo range, and this, mated to a five-speed gearbox, improved performance. The front and rear bumpers were also changed to comply with US safety regulations, which spoilt the clean lines. In 1983, the production of the X1/9 became the sole responsibility of Bertone and the car was now badged as Bertone X1/9. It continued to be sold through Fiat dealers, however, until production stopped in 1988, when small sports cars went out of fashion.

A mid-engined sports car that did not cost Ferrari-type money. This is the later model X1/9 with its more prominent Federal bumpers to comply with US safety regulations – although in 1981 the Fiat rather than the Bertone badges were to the fore.

FIAT STRADA 130TC

1984–87

The biggest clue to the performance potential of this hatchback could be found in the scorpion badge of Abarth on the tailgate and front grille. Launched in June 1983, the Abarth 130TC, which replaced the 125TC, was regarded as the ultimate sporting Ritmo, or Strada, as it was known in some European markets. Under the bonnet was an Abarth-bred 1995cc (122 cu in) double overhead camshaft engine with twin 40 DCOE carburettors producing 97kW (130bhp). This charismatic engine had more than enough power to humble all the contemporary hot hatch rivals, from Ford's XR3i to Volkswagen's legendary Golf GTi.

The close ratio ZF gearbox was a delight to use, getting the car to 96km/h (60mph) in under eight seconds. The uprated brakes and firmer suspension ensured that handling was always precise and superbly balanced. Inside, the extra instrumentation, closely fitting Recaro seats and adjustable three-spoke steering wheel all helped to remind drivers that they were not piloting a humble 105TC.

Not much was changed on the 130TC during its short production life. For 1985, a slight facelift added a new, deeper front bumper, closely fitting grille and deeper side rubbing strips, but these were the only visible changes. The massively underrated 130TC was discontinued along with the rest of the Ritmo/Strada range in 1987.

Engine: 4 cylinder 1995cc (122 cu in)
Power: 97kW (130bhp)
0–96km/h (60mph): 7.9 secs
Top speed: 188km/h (117mph)
Production total: n/a

This 1984 130TC was as good as it got for Fiat, as this hottest of hatchbacks delivered a rock-hard ride and no refinement whatsoever. But that was actually not the point because here was a focused performance car.

FORD AG TAUNUS

1948–71

Engine: 4 cylinder 1698cc (104 cu in)
Power: 56kW (75bhp)
0–96km/h (60mph): 15 secs
Top speed: 161km/h (100mph)
Production total: 2,500,000

Ford AG was established in Germany in 1925 to import vehicles and build them under licence. After World War II, production restarted in 1948 with the 1930s line of models, including the Taunus Standard, Special and De Luxe. It was the Taunus which provided the basic family transportation.

From 1952, there was a new generation of no-frills cars, all badged Taunus with the M designation which stood, modestly, for 'Masterpiece'. The new 12M had a more contemporary body with a 1.2-litre (73 cu in) engine producing 28kW (38bhp). Revamped in 1955, the 15M was added to the range with a 1.5 litre (92 cu in) 41kW (55bhp) engine and shared some of the running gear and structure with the UK-built Consul. Facelifted again in 1957, a 17M with a 1.7-litre (104 cu in) engine now topped the range. A pretty new body was introduced for 1960 and, by 1962, the 12M benefited from a powerful, compact V4 engine, maintaining the car as one of Germany's bestsellers.

In 1966, the final bodywork changes were made to the Taunus range, and 2.3-litre (140 cu in) and 2.6-litre (159 cu in) V6 engines were offered. The UK-built Cortina, related to the Taunus, took over from the smaller four-cylinder engined models in 1970, while the bigger V-engined versions became Consuls and Granadas from 1972.

Pictured below is a Taunus 12M from 1963. This car has the distinction of being the first production Ford to utilize front-wheel drive, a full 16 years before it was seen on the Fiesta. This was also the first model to use the V4 engine.

FORD OSI 20M

1967–68

Engine: 4 cylinder 1998cc (122 cu in)
Power: 67kW (90bhp)
0–96km/h (60mph): 10 secs
Top speed: 172km/h (107mph)
Production total: n/a

The Italian OSI company (Officine Stampaggi Industriali) in Turin had gained a reputation for designing its own cars, predominantly based on those of Alfa Romeo and Fiat.

OSI presented an interesting sports coupé at the 1966 Geneva Motor Show, however, which was based on the running gear of the Ford Taunus 20M. The reaction to this pretty car, which could easily have been a wholly Latin sports machine, was so strong that both Ford in Cologne and Italy's OSI decided to launch the 20M TS into limited production.

This OSI was entirely based on the Ford P5 20M TS, taking the engine, transmission, axle, brakes and steering set-up. Both of the V6 engines used in the Taunus were available, either a 2-litre (122 cu in) 67kW (90bhp) version or the 2.3-litre (140 cu in) 80kW (108bhp) version. Performance was good and the car's handling was reassuring, if not overtly sporting.

The underlying problem was that the combination of the OSI and Taunus did not create the right image for what was always going to be a relatively expensive hand-built car. The market simply was not there and the car proved difficult to sell through the existing Ford network. In 1968, rival coach-builder Ghia acquired OSI, and production of the coupé stopped.

FORD UK MODEL T

1911–27

Engine: 4 cylinder 2890cc (176 cu in)
Power: 15kW (20bhp)
0–96km/h (60mph): n/a
Top speed: 68km/h (42mph)
Production total: 300,000

The legendary Model T made sense in Britain because it was tough, reliable and affordable. Assembled in the United Kingdom from 1911 onwards at Trafford Park in Manchester, parts were imported direct from the United States.

Indeed, Trafford Park had a key role in Ford production before the advent of the moving production line. A moving line was introduced first for the assembly of the Model T's flywheel generator in 1913 at the main Ford plant in Detroit and line assembly began in Manchester within a year.

The Model T was a reassuring, basic car with a strong four-cylinder side-valve engine. The 3-litre (176 cu in) engine produced 15kW (20bhp) and had pedal-operated epicyclic gears, making it easy to drive. The gears, two forward and one reverse, were simple enough, as was the transverse semi-elliptic suspension front and rear. There were brakes on only two wheels, although these proved adequate.

A number of bodystyles were available, including a Roadster, Tourer, Tudor, Fordor and Town Car. Many companies took advantage of the chassis to build their own coupés and convertibles based on the straightforward running gear. No wonder that, in 1919, 41 per cent of all vehicles registered in the United Kingdom were Fords.

A British-registered four-door Tourer which could have been assembled at Trafford Park in Manchester from 1913 onwards, but before 1916, because from then on the brass radiator was replaced by a black-painted item.

FORD UK MODEL A

1928–31

This is an American Model A Tourer with a large four-cylinder engine that proved too expensive to own in Britain. Despite being modified for use in the United Kingdom and the company offering predominately hardtops, it never emulated the T's success.

The Model T could not go on forever, even though old Henry Ford took some convincing of this fact. Although the Model A became a sales sensation in the United States, it was not a car that translated easily to Europe. This was because the A came equipped with a large four-cylinder side-valve 3285cc (200 cu in) engine. While good for the open spaces of the United States, such a large engine could never survive in the United Kingdom, where cars were taxed on the size of their engines.

To counter this drawback, a small 2043cc (125 cu in) unit was fitted to what was known as the Model AF. It cost £5 more than the 3-litre, but it did not really solve the problem of high fuel consumption. Nevertheless, with proven transverse springs, plenty of ground clearance and a smooth three-speed gearbox, this car proved durable and unstoppable. Available as a roadster, two-door touring, four-door touring, fixed coupé and cabriolet, and various saloons, there was a model for

everyone whatever their particular needs and tastes.

However, this was still the wrong sort of car to be selling in Europe, and the newly opened Dagenham

factory in Essex, England, apparently built just five Model A cars in its first three months of operation in 1931 because demand for the vehicle was so low.

Engine: 4 cylinder 2043cc (125 cu in)
Power: 30kW (40bhp)
0–96km/h (60mph): n/a
Top speed: 105km/h (65mph)
Production total: 14,516

FORD UK MODEL Y

1932–39

Engine: 4 cylinder 933cc (57 cu in)
Power: 17kW (23.4bhp)
0–96km/h (60mph): n/a
Top speed: 96km/h (60mph)
Production total: 157,668

Ford had to move fast to cope with the demise of the Model A, so the Y was developed in record time and made it from drawing board to production line in the United Kingdom within a year. Without the arrival of the Y, the Dagenham factory could have been shut down, such was the crisis. Seemingly almost overnight, though, the Y had given Ford almost half of the crucial 8hp market. Part of its appeal was the bargain price – the Model Y Popular retailed for just £100, seriously undercutting the

An early Model Y, up to 1933, distinguished by its straight front bumper and in conventional two-door saloon format. Four-door versions of this vehicle were offered, and English coachbuilder Jensen even offered some tourers which were not factory approved.

cost of vehicles from major rival manufacturers such as Morris.

The models that left Dagenham were two- and four-door saloons with a so-called 'short radiator look' and straight bumpers. By 1933, though, the radiator shell was much longer and the bumpers dipped attractively in the middle. Instruments were now moved from the middle to where the driver could actually see them behind the steering wheel. A foot-operated dipswitch and central opening windscreen were other improvements. Capable of almost 96km/h (60mph), it was a fast enough car for its time. Not surprisingly, the Y is credited with giving many people in the United Kingdom their first taste of motoring.

FORD UK ANGLIA/PREFECT/POPULAR

Engine: 4 cylinder 933cc (57 cu in)
Power: 22kW (30bhp)
0–96km/h (60mph): n/a
Top speed: 97km/h (60mph)
Production total: 701,553

The Anglia name made its debut in 1939, a restyled version of the old 7Y. War interrupted production at the Dagenham factory until 1945, when production of cars began again. Although there were no high-specification De Luxe models, bigger brakes were a feature of the car. In 1948, Ford took the unusual step of effectively reintroducing the pre-war 7Y, with a new grille and a more pronounced boot. Overnight, the Anglia became the cheapest car on sale, even though buyers did not receive any frills for their money.

The more luxurious four-door Prefect, the first Ford with a name rather than a model number, arrived in 1938, and it was based on the 7W. It had been given a facelift to include a more modern streamlined grille and a so-called 'crocodile' bonnet. Like the Anglia, it was reintroduced after the war and updated in 1948 with big front wings, integral headlights and an upright grille.

From 1953, the Ford Popular, or the 'Pop', took over from the Anglia and the Prefect as the most basic car in Ford's vehicle range.

Essentially, the Popular was a 1949 Anglia with a 1172cc (72 cu in) engine and no other specification to speak of, not even indicators. Even so, motorists on a budget kept on buying it right up to 1959.

The prewar Anglia E04A above left is distinguished by its running board. On the right is a E93A model launched in 1949. Below, a postwar E93A Prefect, available as a four-door from the late 1940s on.

FORD UK V8 PILOT

The V8 Pilot E71A at left was Dagenham's first new model to be built after World War II. Below is a V8-40. Although this is an American example, the V8-40 proved to be the first to be built in Europe – in Cologne and Cork.

Rod-operated Girling brakes were something of a throwback to earlier times, and the column gearshift was the most obvious indication of influence from the United States. Interestingly, the Pilot had built-in hydraulic jacks, which were never featured on any other UK Ford.

The V8 Pilot proved to be very popular as a saloon and a police car, and its chassis lent itself to other commercial applications. A rare pick-up was built by Reynolds in Dagenham and wood-panelled shooting brakes and all-steel estate models were also made. V8 engines, though, never had a long-term future in the United Kingdom.

Ford UK's first model launch into an expectant market after the war was the Pilot. Taking the body of a pre-war V8-62, it featured a new high-front bonnet and radiator. However, if the body was not really new, the 2.5-litre (152 cu in) engine certainly was. Unfortunately, the unit was slow and Ford was forced to quickly switch to the classic 221 flathead 22kW (30hp) V8 that had been built in huge numbers for military vehicles. Although not a frugal car, despite being launched in an era of petrol rationing, for those who were guaranteed regular supplies, such as doctors, it was a refined, robust and reliable choice.

Engine: V8 3622cc (221 cu in)
Power: 63kW (85bhp)
0–96km/h (60mph): n/a
Top speed: 133km/h (83mph)
Production total: 35,618

FORD UK 100E

1953–62

The Anglia/Prefect range was to represent Ford's departure from dated construction methods, as this was their first small car with a one-piece body and chassis. The entry-level Anglia was a two-door only model, while the higher specification Prefect had four doors. Under the bonnet was old technology in the form of a 1172cc (72 cu in) side-valve engine, which had actually been built from scratch and featured adjustable tappets. MacPherson strut suspension first seen on the Consul/Zephyr range meant that handling was assured and turned the little car into a competitive racer.

Both Anglia and Prefect models received a facelift in 1957 with larger rear windows, redesigned tail lights and new grilles. An unexpected touch of sophistication came with the availability of a

With the arrival of the 105E Anglia, the old 100E became the new Popular, with simpler, round rear headlights. This is a De Luxe version, which had a parcel shelf, overriders on the bumpers, opening quarterlights and additional chrome trim.

semi-automatic transmission, which was so unexpected that few were actually sold.

The appeal of both the Popular and the Prefect was as basic, no-nonsense transportation. The three-door commercial Escort van and Esquire estate car widened the model's appeal even further, while wooden strips on the Esquire were an interesting stylistic touch.

Prefects available in De Luxe trim with extra chrome, two-tone interiors and lockable glove compartment proved to be all the growing 1950s family needed to get around. With a new Anglia on the way, the 100E was renamed the Popular in 1960.

Engine: 4 cylinder 1172cc (72 cu in)
Power: 27kW (36bhp)
0–96km/h (60mph): 29 secs
Top speed: 112km/h (70mph)
Production total: 626,453

FORD UK CONSUL/ZEPHYR/ZODIAC

1950–66

When the Consul/Zephyr range was launched at the Olympia Motor Show in 1950, Ford had unveiled one of the most advanced designs of the era. The cars featured a combined monocoque bodyshell,

Ford's first overhead valve engine and innovative MacPherson independent suspension, which is still in use today. Ford also switched from six-volt to 12-volt electrics, still the industry standard. The

The Mark 1 Zephyr saloon differed from the Consul mainly in the front-end treatment. The higher specification Zephyr Zodiac's two-tone paint and gold-plated trim set it apart from other models.

main differences between the Consul and the Zephyr were the differing front-end design and the Zephyr's 10.2cm (4in) longer wheelbase, which helped to accommodate its larger six-cylinder engine. A higher specification Zephyr Zodiac variant was introduced in 1953.

Rebodied in 1956 with a more spacious and Americanized design, the engines were also uprated. Convertible models were available immediately, and a substantial facelift in 1959 saw lower roof lines and revised interiors. In 1966, the whole range moved upmarket when the Mk II models were badged as just Zephyr and Zodiac. A rival to the cheaper Jaguar saloons, the Zephyr 4 replaced the Consul, while the six-cylinder models became Ford's first cars to officially do the 'ton' – 161km/h (100mph). Extra rear-seat legroom in 1962 involved major structural changes. In 1965, a top of the range Zodiac Executive indicated exactly how eager Ford was to compete in the luxury market.

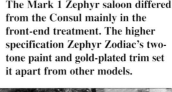

Engine: 6 cylinder 2553cc (156 cu in)
Power: 81kW (109bhp)
0–96km/h (60mph): 13.4 secs
Top speed: 166km/h (103mph)
Production total: 942,217

FORD UK ANGLIA

1959–67

In the mid-1950s, Ford opened a research and development centre in the heart of the British motor industry in Birmingham. Only one production model emerged from this creative 'hothouse', however, the 105E Anglia. It proved to be

something of a departure for Ford. Most obvious was the American-type styling, which was not too surprising as a visiting designer from Ford USA, Elwood Engel, was credited with many features and responsible for extensive

wind-tunnel testing. Rear wings, reverse rake windscreen and hooded headlights made the car stand out. Despite the vague recirculating ball suspension, the handling was certainly impressive, as was the car's performance.

Here is an Anglia Super with full chrome wheel trims and twin bodyside chrome strips. Under the bonnet from 1963 was a 1200cc (73 cu in) engine which was soon to be offered in the all-new Cortina.

One of the best features of the new Anglia was the engine, which was an over-square, high-revving overhead valve unit which was attached to Ford's first four-speed transmission. It was no surprise to discover that this drivetrain soon became a favourite in racing circles, where it was installed in single-seat Formula Juniors. Estate cars were added to the range in 1962 and proved very popular. A more luxurious Super model had a longer stroke 1200cc (73 cu in) engine and an all-synchromesh gearbox. This made the Anglia a great all-round vehicle which sold in huge numbers to first-time motorists.

Engine: 997cc (61 cu in)
Power: 29kW (39bhp)
0–96km/h (60mph): 21 secs
Top speed: 128km/h (80mph)
Production total: 1,083,960

FORD UK CONSUL CLASSIC/CAPRI

1961–64

They looked all-American, but the two- and four-door saloon Consul Classic and fastback Capri were actually designed and built in Dagenham, England. The intention with the Classic range was to offer a model between the existing Anglia and higher specification Consuls. Indeed, the powerplant and gearbox were the same 1340cc (82 cu in) unit as used in the Anglia, but reworked for a larger car. The biggest thing about the Classic was its boot, with a massive 0.6 cubic metres (21 cu ft) of space. The Classic was a good effort, especially when a 1500cc (91 cu in) engine was fitted in 1962 to give better performance. Its production life was cut short by the arrival of the all-conquering Cortina.

The pretty Capri was essentially a Classic with a sloping roof. Again, the Capri had a large boot and

subtle fins. The most significant model was the GT variant in 1963 with twin-choke carburettors, four-branch exhaust, bigger exhaust valves and performance camshaft,

features which transformed the 1500cc (91 cu in) engine. Despite this, the Capri never really sold well, and production figures were poor by Ford standards.

The Classic and Capri were the pioneers of the quad-headlight look. In profile, the Classic featured a reverse rake rear windscreen first seen on the 105E Anglia.

Engine: 4 cylinder 1340cc (82 cu in)
Power: 43kW (57bhp)
0–96km/h (60mph): 13.7 secs
Top speed: 153km/h (95mph)
Production total: 24,531/6868

FORD UK CORTINA

1962–82

The ultimate Cortina was the virtually race-prepared Mark 1 Lotus model. This example is fitted with lightweight alloy wheels.

Engine: 4 cylinder 1198cc (73 cu in)
Power: 37kW (49bhp)
0–96km/h (60mph): 15 secs
Top speed: 153km/h (95mph)
Production total: 4,299,669

The Cortina changed the face of motoring in the United Kingdom forever. The creation of a true medium-sized family car also helped generations of company car drivers to reach their pressing appointments on time. Credited with bridging the gap between small and large cars, the Cortina was born out of rivalry between Ford UK and Germany. When the UK chairman, Sir Patrick Hennessy, discovered

that a front-wheel drive model, codenamed Cardinal, was being developed in Germany with Ford US assistance, he initiated project Archbishop. As it was already a year behind its rivals, a conventional rear-drive platform was used, while the innovative use of aircraft stress calculations saved precious weight in the bodywork without losing structural integrity. The crisp styling was the work of American Roy Brown, who had previously designed the ill-fated Edsel.

Launched in 1962 with a name inspired by the venue of the 1960 Winter Olympics, the Cortina also carried Consul badging on the

bonnet for the first two years. When lined up against the opposition, principally the British Motor Corporation's 1100/1300 range, there was only one winner. The Cortina was bigger and cheaper, with better performance. The BMC car remained the nation's favourite for a while, but the Cortina also proved to be an export winner and, within a year, more than 250,000 had been sold – a record at the time. The 'Dagenham Dustbin', as it was affectionately dubbed, had arrived. Initially only available as a 1200cc (73 cu in) two-door, a four-door model soon followed and a 1500cc (92 cu in) engine became available.

To brighten Ford's dull but worthy, cheap yet cheerful image, the company linked up with sports car company Lotus. Cortina bodyshells were sent to the Lotus works in Cheshunt, where they were fitted with twin camshaft engines, racing suspensions and light alloy doors, bonnets and bootlids. This model became a force to be reckoned with on the racing track.

In 1966, the Cortina got a new, square-cut body, ran on a wider track and at the entry level received a new five-bearing 1300cc (79 cu in) engine. As before, there was a variety of trim levels for the Mark II, called Base, De Luxe Super and GT, with the Lotus Cortina at the top of the list (although this was now a more conventional package with no light alloy panels, and it was built at Dagenham, rather than

First-, second- and third-generation Cortinas such as these dominated the sales charts.

at Lotus). In 1967, a new 1600cc (98 cu in) engine was fitted to one of the most significant models, the 1600E. The E stood for Executive, and it was what every ambitious company car driver dreamed of. With its GT engine, Lotus suspension, wide-rim Rostyle sports wheel and wooden veneer dashboard, it was no surprise that, at the end of 1967, the Cortina was crowned as Britain's bestselling car.

The Cortina evolved again in 1970, and the Mark III had an unashamedly American style, penned by Harley Copp. Like contemporary US models, there was a so-called 'Coke bottle' curve to the bodywork. Now the Cortina model range was becoming as complex as the company car buyer hierarchy it served. Base, X, XL, GT and GXL models with new overhead camshaft 1600cc (98 cu in) and 2000cc (122 cu in) Pinto units were offered.

The last Cortina in 1976 was another clever redesign, this time by Uwe Bahnsen, who also styled its more radical jellymould successor, the Sierra. The Cortina Mark IV could not have been squarer, but there was more glass area, which created a feeling of space in the cabin. The GT model was replaced by an S and the engine options were 1300cc (79 cu in), 1600cc (98 cu in) and 2000cc (122 cu in), although a 2.3-litre (140 cu in) V6 was added in 1977. A minor facelift in 1980 freshened up the style and meant even larger windows, but a new design was just around the corner. Even so, underneath the new Sierra was a lot of reliable old Cortina parts.

FORD UK CORSAIR

1963–70

Ford worked hard on the Corsair, or the 'Buccaneer' as it was known internally. After a two-year market survey, the company came up with a car that was very conventional yet looked slightly strange. Its distinctive wedge nose was clearly influenced by other Fords, notably the Taunus in Germany and the Thunderbird in the United States. Intended to fill the gap between the Cortina and the Zephyr, it never really caught on. Buyers did not like the impractical two-door layout, and the sum total of the innovations the car could boast was a printed circuit board inside the instrument panel – an industry first.

Replacing the existing 1498cc (91 cu in) engines with the new V4s at 1663cc (101 cu in) and 1996cc (122 cu in) actually slowed the car and made it less economical than before because these were less efficient engines. A lot of the car's weight was positioned over the front wheels, which did not inspire confident handling. However, Ford released GT and 2000E versions with reworked engines and high levels of standard trim to tempt buyers. Sales improved, but most customers still preferred the better-value Cortina. Specialists such as Abbott converted the Corsair into estate cars, and Crayford built convertibles, but sales remained poor until the car's demise in 1970.

Engine: 4 cylinder 1498cc (91 cu in)
Power: 45kW (60bhp)
0–96km/h (60mph): 14 secs
Top speed: 158km/h (98mph)
Production total: 331,095

A top-of-the-range Corsair 2000E with a standard vinyl roof replaced the outgoing GT model.

FORD UK GRANADA

1972–85

Engine: V6 2495cc (152 cu in)
Power: 61kW (82bhp)
0–96km/h (60mph): 9 secs
Top speed: 193km/h (120mph)
Production total: 1,486,049

When Ford decided to replace the dated Mark IV Zephyr/Zodiac range in the early 1970s, the idea was to bring the large car down to a more compact size. Entry-level models were badged as Consuls, with 2-litre (122 cu in) V4 or 3-litre (183 cu in) V6 engines. At the top of the range, though, were the 2.5-litre (152 cu in) and 3-litre (183 cu in) Granadas, available as a base car or a GXL with automatic transmission and a distinctive vinyl roof. Estate models added practicality and, with a coupé version in 1974, provided some real four-seat, fastback style. However, it was the high-specification Ghia to which most middle-managers aspired.

A very clever redesign of the Granada by designer Uwe Bahnsen instantly updated the model for the right-angled late 1970s. Built exclusively in Germany, there were now 2.3-litre (140 cu in) and 2.8-litre (171 cu in) V6 engines with optional fuel injection for the larger engine. Even a diesel engine was now offered. The estate version was especially successful, with a large load bay and clean purposeful lines. The Granada in Ghia trim grew in popularity as an executive car and was often chauffeur-driven. Few other manufacturers could offer the same levels of equipment, refinement, space and low running costs. A slight facelift in 1981 only served to enhance the model's appeal and popularity.

A 1984 Granada 2.8 Ghia X with a colour-keyed louvred front grille finished in a bright metallic silver that was popular at the time. The specification was impressive, with air conditioning, trip computer, central locking, halogen foglights, headlight washers and a sunroof.

FORD GT40

Engine: V8 4737cc (289 cu in)
Power: 250kW (335bhp)
0–96km/h (60mph): 6 secs
Top speed: 274km/h (170mph)
Production total: 133

At the beginning of 1963, the company approached Ferrari with a view to buying the marque. Ford came very close, but the deal fell through at the last minute, much to the fury of its directors, who took rejection very badly. At that point, Ford decided to create its own racing team and build a sports car that would beat Ferrari in the legendary Le Mans 24-hour race. The United Kingdom was chosen as the country the car would be built in because of its reputation as a centre of excellence for the motorsport industry.

Although styled at the Ford headquarters in Dearborn, the fibreglass body was moulded in England and the cars assembled at Ford's Advanced Vehicle Factory in Slough. The heart of the car was a Lola-based V8-engined prototype designed by Eric Broadley. John Wyler from Aston Martin was appointed to coordinate the whole construction and racing programme. The car was named the GT40 because its height was less than 40in (102cm). Beneath its beautiful plastic skin was a heavy steel monocoque with a Ford 4.2-litre (256 cu in) V8 positioned in the

middle, operating through a Colotti transmission. However, all the production cars used a 4.7-litre (289 cu in) V8 and ZF transmission boxes. An independent coil spring double wishbone suspension was used at the front, while, at the rear, a coil spring upper plus lower trailing arms with upper link and lower wishbone set-up was used. Four-wheel disc brakes brought the car to a halt from its top racing speed of around 322km/h (200mph).

Some road cars were made specifically for wealthy customers and became available from 1965. These had fully trimmed interiors and even luggage boxes in the engine compartment. The later Mark IIIs were only built as road cars and had quad headlights and a conventional central gear change, instead of a racing right-hand set-up. These cars cost what in the 1960s was a substantial £6450.

The first GT40s ran at Le Mans in 1964, and, although none of the cars finished, driver Phil Hill managed to establish the fastest lap. Next-generation GT40s now had 4.7 litre (289 cu in) engines, although the most important change was that Carroll Shelby was employed to run the racing programme. In 1965, the Mark II GT40 boasted a 7-litre (427 cu in) V8 engine and, by 1966, production began in the United States of the so-called 'J' models, which used a bonded honeycomb chassis. Significantly, none of these cars was actually ready to compete in the target event: Le Mans. In the 1966 event, a mixed group of Mark I and II GT40s was entered with spectacular results. Three Mk IIs crossed the line together in an historic first win.

In 1967, Ford's Slough facility was taken over by JW Automotive

These photos show a 1967 Mark III, only available prepared for road use, rather than as a racer. The interior was fully trimmed, with luggage boxes in the engine compartment, and the car had quad headlights and a central rather than a racing right-hand gear lever.

Engineering, which was partly run by John Wyler. It concentrated on supplying road-going GT40s, while Ford took its Mark IV 'J' cars to Le Mans and won again in 1967.

Ford decided to retire from endurance racing while at the top; however, one of JW Automotive's high-profile customers was Grady Davis, the vice-president of Gulf Oil. Davis saw the public relations value in taking GT40s racing again, and he commissioned the company to build a team of three cars. These were lightweight 5-litre (305 cu in) GT40s known as 'Mirages', painted in the distinctive light blue colour scheme of Gulf Oil. These cars, GT40 P/1075s, won the 1968 Le Mans race. The same GT40s went on to win yet again in 1969.

Incredibly, the GT40 proved difficult to sell, as it effectively became an obsolete racing car and, as a road car, it was not particularly easy to live with. Since then, it has been widely copied by kit-car manufacturers and 'real' GT40s are now almost priceless.

FORD UK ESCORT

Engine: 4-cylinder 1993cc (122 cu in)
Power: 82kW (110bhp)
0–96km/h (60mph): 8.6 secs
Top speed: 175km/h (109mph)
Production total: 2,906,144

During the Swinging Sixties, it became clear that the ageing Anglia would have to be replaced. Ford had first started to think about a new model in 1964, and the intention was to build a car that could be sold and built in Europe. Indeed, the creation of Ford of Europe in 1967 made this an imperative. So, although styled in the United Kingdom, the all-synchromesh gearbox was designed in Germany and the designated production plants were Halewood in England and Saarlouis in Germany. The car they would build was called the Escort.

A spacious, good-value and reliable newcomer, it was only available as a two-door model at first. A new but unfamiliar front suspension set-up was replaced in less than a year by the proven MacPherson strut system, while the Escort became the first Ford to have rack-and-pinion steering. The engines were reworked versions of the existing units, but now with five bearing cranks and crossflow cylinders. A new 1098cc (67 cu in) unit provided entry-level power in the Basic, De Luxe and Super models. The 1298cc (79 cu in) powered the Super, but the GT had a new cylinder head, high-lift camshaft, revised manifold and a dual-choke Weber carburettor producing 54kW (72bhp).

Clearly Ford was serious about making performance versions of this exciting small car and introduced the Twin Cam. This had the running gear of the Lotus Cortina, but in an Escort shell that was 136kg (300lb) lighter. Eventually built at Halewood, the uprated mechanicals were installed into a specially strengthened bodyshell with generously flared wheelarches. It is no wonder that the Escort went on to totally dominate the world of international rallying and that these models are still competitive in amateur events today.

It was the more mundane Escorts, though, that made Ford millions of pounds. Estate versions appeared in 1969 when the long overdue four-door became available. Nevertheless, the sporting Escorts continued to grab attention and generate sales. Ford now set up an Advanced Vehicles Operation in

Aveley to hand-build its specials. Its first project was the RS1600 with a new 16-valve twin-camshaft Cosworth unit. Inspired by victory in the 1970 World Cup Rally, it then launched the Mexico with a larger 1558cc (95 cu in) engine for reliability, while the RS2000 had the 2-litre (122 cu in) Pinto engine and bold side graphics. This model had less performance, however, and was built in Germany.

The Escort Mark II had been called 'Project Brenda' during development, which had begun in 1972 and was mostly a Ford of Europe effort. The new bodywork was down to the architect of a whole new generation of Fords, Uwe Bahnsen, and was a fashionably square, spacious and airy design with much more glass area. Just as complicated as before was the huge model line-up powered by 1100cc (67 cu in),

In 1979, Ford's team scored in nin
events and won five times, includin
the Lombard RAC Rally. Althoug
Hannu Mikkola won more times,
was Bjorn Waldegaard's consistenc
in this RS1800 which led to him
being crowned the first official
world rally champion.

1300cc (79 cu in) and 1600cc (95 cu in) engines. L, GL and Ghia plus Sport and GT models were o offer, and Ford was still committe to its motorsport programme.

The RS1800 with a double overhead camshaft BDA unit was another homologation special. In fully modified form, it had a 2-lit (122 cu in) engine, uprated suspension, ZF close-ratio gearbo disc brakes all round and a bigger axle. This was the car which went on to win the World Rally Championship in 1979. Less specialized were Mark II Mexicos and RS2000s. The Mexico had a 1.6-litre (95 cu in) engine producing 71kW (95bhp), but it was not a big seller. The RS2000 had a distinctive plastic front end, with four headlights and a prominent spoiler.

However, it was the standard Escorts that were the most important. The three-door estate was always a popular choice, and Ford reintroduced the Popular name for its base, no-frills model which was later joined by the Popular Plus. After a slight restyle in 1978, the range was augmented by regular special edition models which prevented the car looking tired and dated.

Ford UK Fiesta

1976–83

Engine: 957cc (58 cu in)
Power: 35kW (47bhp)
0–96km/h (60mph): 19 secs
Top speed: 127km/h (79mph)
Production total: 1,750,000

This car was a real milestone for the previously cautious European arm of Ford. The Fiesta was its first supermini and its first transverse-engined front-wheel drive model. The designer of the Fiesta's neat three-door bodyshell was Tom Tjaarda, who worked at Ford's Ghia studio in Italy. Luckily for Ford, the development of this new small car, codenamed 'Bobcat', coincided with the world oil crisis, so it seemed even more sensible to design a small car with one of the smallest engines the company had ever produced.

The Fiesta was launched in 1976 with a 957cc (58 cu in) engine (in low or high compression tune) or a 1117cc (68 cu in) unit. A 1298cc (79 cu in) was added to the range, producing a highly successful line-up of small cars. The trim levels

ranged from base (later named Popular) to L, LS and the high-specification Ghia. In 1979, the Fiesta Million celebrated the building of the millionth model.

Ford was also well aware of the value of putting a sporting option in the Fiesta range. The 1600cc (98 cu in) Fiesta XR2 duly arrived in 1982, and it effectively created the 'pocket rocket' version of the 'hot hatch'. The XR2 offered style and performance coupled with Ford's trademark low running costs and reliability. In Europe, the Fiesta really did become a people's car.

The 1981 Ford Fiesta Ghia represented the pinnacle of the small hatchback range. It meant bright window surrounds, tinted windscreen, alloy wheels, wood fascia and a multifunctional clock. The specification was available across most of the engine range.

Ford UK Cosworth Sierra

1986–90

Engine: 4-cylinder 1993cc (122 cu in)
Power: 152kW (204bhp)
0–96km/h (60mph): 8 secs
Top speed: 233km/h (145mph)
Production total: 5000

The humble, family-friendly Ford Sierra did not seem like a good basis for a racing car, but that is exactly what Ford produced and, as a result, dominated saloon car racing during the 1980s. Group A

regulations specified a production run of 5000 cars to qualify, and Ford selected the three-door bodyshell for the Cosworth.

It certainly did not look like the standard car, with a large front air dam, 'whale-tail' rear spoiler and bonnet vents. It was also revamped under that aggressive skin. The engine was a 2-litre (122 cu in) turbocharged unit reworked by Cosworth Engineering to produce

over 149kW (200bhp). However, there was potential to tune the engine in racing trim to well over 224kW (300bhp). In 1987, 500 very special versions were built by Aston Martin Tickford with 167kW (224bhp) which could be tuned to produce some 410kW (550bhp) in competition.

The Cosworth became a legend on the track and won so many races that the authorities had to

change the rules to give others a chance. From 1988, Ford used the four-door shell and, from 1990, fitted a four-wheel drive system. This changed the Cosworth into a four-door supercar that rivalled the best of the German saloons, such as the BMW M5.

Finished in black, the RS500 was a more powerful and race-prepared limited edition variant of the Cosworth using the hatchback Sierra bodyshell. As the name suggests, just 500 of this model were built, specifically for Group A racing qualification.

FORD UK CAPRI

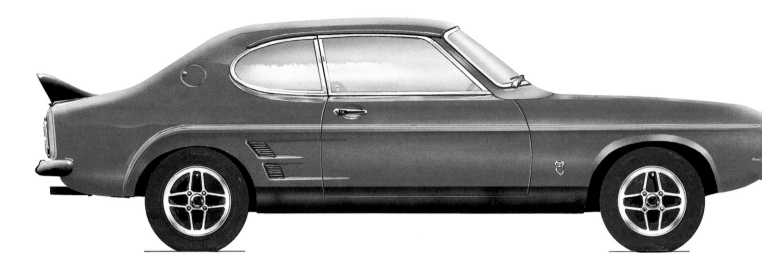

Engine: V6 1297cc (79 cu in)
Power: 42kW (57bhp)
0–96km/h (60mph): 7 secs
Top speed: 204km/h (127mph)
Production total: 1,497,445

Back in 1969, 'the car you always promised yourself' was, according to Ford, the Capri. In many ways, this was the European version of the phenomenally successful Ford Mustang. This meant that the car looked great, was fun to drive and yet was still very affordable. Designed at Ford's research centre in Dunton, Essex and codenamed 'Colt', this (cramped) four-seater coupé with its long bonnet replicated the success of its American cousin.

A large range of engines was offered, from the barely adequate 1.3-litre (79 cu in) unit, to the competent 1.6-litre (98 cu in) and 2-litre (122 cu in) units, to the brutish but fast 3-litre (183 cu in) powerplant. More important was the way the car looked, and a large range of equipment packages and options set each car apart in X, XL, XLR or E formats. It has been calculated that there were more than 900 derivatives offered in the United Kingdom alone between 1968 and 1987. This was the central appeal of the car – customers were expected to aspire to more expensive and better-equipped versions.

The 3000GT in 1969 put a modified Zodiac V6 under the bonnet, which needed a bulge to accommodate it. There were even

limited production, high-speed RS versions – the RS2600 (which was sold only in Germany) and the RS3100. Not surprisingly, the Capri excelled at motorsport and twice won the European Touring Car Championships.

'Project Diana' was the codename for the new-generation Capri launched in 1974. Sales had been falling away in Europe, and the Capri II was meant to be a more practical car with a more convenient hatchback boot. It was larger, heavier and much less exciting than the old car. However, customers did not mind, and 183,000 were sold in its first year. Sales in Europe, though, fell again; surprisingly, production in the United Kingdom, the Capri's biggest market, stopped

and was transferred to Cologne in Germany. The United States also stopped imports of the Capri, which had not really managed to emulate the Mustang.

'Carla' was the next project name for the final-generation Capri. In many ways, the car looked better than it had done since the 1960s. Four round headlights, a reprofiled bonnet, larger tail-lights, black wraparound bumpers and a revised interior all helped to give the car a more purposeful look.

The only really sporting model was the S, and this was essentially a cosmetic package. It was distinguished by a sidewinder stripe, alloy wheels, rear spoiler and overriders. Inside was a smaller 36cm (14in) steering wheel

This Capri 3100 is finished in Sebring Red with the distinctive side stripes, a large rear spoiler which greatly aided motorway stability, cast alloy wheels and matt black front quarter bumpers. Underneath the bonnet, the enlarged V6 engine gave the model sports car performance.

and optional Recaro seats. A sunroof, a five-speed gearbox and sports seats were fitted in 1983.

Although there was no return to the glorious RS models, arguably the best version of the standard Capri was the 2.8i, which was launched in 1981. The fuel-injected 2.8-litre (170 cu in) V6 produced 119kW (160bhp) and came with a sunroof, pepper cylinder alloy wheels, sports steering wheel and Recaro seats although a five-speed gearbox only came as standard in 1983. A year later, the car was rebadged as the 'Special' with spoke alloy wheels, a colour-coded grille and, from 1985, limited slip differential.

The most exclusive Capri was a 153kW (205bhp) turbocharged Tickford model, transformed by Aston Martin in 1983 and 1984. Finished in white with a bodykit and colour-coded alloy wheels, inside there was leather trim, walnut fascia and velour carpets. The final run of 1038 Capris in 1987 was called the Capri 280. Finished in Brooklands green with 38cm (15in) RS alloys and 'Raven' leather trim with burgundy piping, it was a fitting end to a great car.

FORD UK RS200

Engine: 4-cylinder 1802cc (110 cu in)
Power: 186kW (250bhp)
0–96km/h (60mph): 6 secs
Top speed: 225km/h (140mph)
Production total: 200

A new set of regulations for the World Rally Championship was to create a new category, Group B. In the early 1980s, car manufacturers set about designing the ultimate off-road rally weapons, and the two-seater Ford RS200 was one of them. To qualify for Group B, only 200 examples of the vehicle had to be built for the road, hence the name of Ford's entry.

Ford Motorsport effectively designed the new car from scratch, with valuable input from racing car specialist, Tony Southgate.

What the team came up with was a two-seater coupé with a mid-mounted engine. The engine was called the BDT, a development of the BDA unit which had powered many Escorts to rally success, but with a turbo attached. The engine was based the RS1700T, with modifications.

The four-wheel drive chassis was designed by FF developments and featured three viscous coupling differentials. The chassis itself comprised a carbon-fibre, Kevlar and steel tub. The suspension set-up was all-independent and was also height-adjustable. The RS200 was produced in both left- and right-hand drive.

Conceived in 1983 and finally ready in 1985, it was too late to enter the Group B fray. High-profile fatalities and accidents convinced the authorities that they were just too dangerous. The result was 200 unsold mini-supercars, the bargain racers of the decade.

FORD MODEL T

Engine: 4-cylinder 2896cc (177 cu in)
Power: 15kW (20bhp)
0–96km/h (60mph): n/a
Top speed: 72km/h (45mph)
Production total: 15,000,000

'You can have any colour you like, so long as it is black,' said Henry Ford to explain why the T was so cheap. The first production Model T Ford was assembled at the Piquette Avenue Plant in Detroit on 1 October 1908. Over the next 19 years, Ford built 15,000,000 cars with the Model T engine, the longest run of any single model apart from the Volkswagen Beetle. From 1908 to 1927, the Model T hardly changed. Henry Ford had succeeded in his quest to build a car for the masses.

'I will build a motorcar for the great multitude,' said Ford. The car that finally emerged from Ford's secret design section at his factory changed motoring forever. For $825, a Model T customer could take home a car that was light, at about 544kg (1200lb); was quite powerful, with a four-cylinder, 15kW (20hp) engine; and was fairly easy to drive, with a two-speed, foot-controlled 'planetary' transmission. In its first year, more than 10,000 'Tin Lizzies' were sold, which was a record.

This is not surprising because the T was a very good car. The simple ladder-frame chassis was particularly robust and the development of light but tough vanadium-steel alloys was crucial. As there were hardly any significant changes during the T's long production run, components were interchangeable, and cars could keep on running. The transverse-leaf spring suspension allowed the chassis and wheels to easily negotiate the unmade roads that made up most of the US road network at the time. And a wide variety of body styles meant that there was a Model T for every

A Ford Model T Touring from around 1914. This was when Ford managed to slash the chassis build time from 12.5 hours down to 1.5 hours, and mass production was born. That year, more than 300,000 Model Ts were built.

This is a Tourabout body, which had two roadster-type front seats, but no doors. The standard wheels used on the Model T were wooden spoke with demountable rims, although wire wheels did become an option in 1925.

buyer. Whether it was a sporty speedster or a hard-working pick-up or van, Henry Ford had the market to himself.

Growing demand for the new Ford meant production methods had to change. A new factory in Highland Park, which opened in 1910, was designed by the nation's leading industrial architect, Albert Kahn. The four-storey factory was organized from top to bottom into a production line, as assembly wound downwards, starting from the fourth floor. Production was to increase by 100 per cent in each of the first three years, from 19,000 in 1910, to 34,500 in 1911 and on to 78,440 in 1912.

Ford was determined to reduce the T's price continually. When it sold for $575 in 1912, the Model T cost less than the average annual wage in the United States. Although profit margins fell as he slashed prices to $99 in 1914, sales rose to an astounding 248,000 in 1913. In 1921, the Model T Ford held 60 per cent of the American new-car market. Plants around the world turned out Model Ts at a furious rate, and Henry Ford's only problem 'was figuring out how to make enough of them'. However, this attitude was going to lead to problems, not least because the company was too reliant on one model. Customers appreciated the cheapness of the T, but increasingly wanted something that was more sophisticated. The Chevrolet company, in particular, targeted the same customers with better designed and styled cars featuring important innovations such as smooth three-speed gearboxes.

Chevrolet continued to take sales from the Model T. By 1926, sales of the T had plummeted. On 25 May 1927, Ford abruptly announced the end of production for the Model T; soon after, the Highland Park factory closed for six months. Ford did this because, incredibly, he had no replacement lined up and needed time to design one.

FORD MODEL A

1927–31

Engine: 4-cylinder 2043cc (125 cu in)
Power: 30kW (40bhp)
0–96km/h (60mph): n/a
Top speed: 105km/h (65mph)
Production total: 3,562,610

How do you follow the Model T? Only Henry Ford could do it, and he created another legend in a matter of months. Although it had the transverse-leaf suspension essentially borrowed from the T, the Model A was a much more sophisticated car. The four-cylinder 2-litre (125 cu in) engine produced a top speed of 105km/h (65mph), and the car had a modern electrical system, vacuum windscreen wipers, a three-speed gearbox and excellent brakes on all four wheels. It was easy to drive, fairly refined and comfortable, while buyers certainly appreciated the well-proven, tough and reliable mechanicals.

More important for Ford was the fact that the Model A represented excellent value for money and could consistently outsell Chevrolet. From 1930, the Model A got even better, with a nickel-plated radiator and headlight shells, lower, wider wings, a higher bonnet line and smaller diameter wheels with bigger tyres. There were new body styles, including a very handsome Victoria Coupé.

The Model A was not just good value throughout its production life, during which it sold more than three million units, but it was also very well built. This meant plenty were still in use across the United States well into the 1950s.

A Ford Model A roadster with its carrying capacity boosted by a very interesting trailer. A class apart from the Model T it replaced, the styling was clearly influenced by the contemporary Lincoln. These early models featured contrasting body colours.

FORD 40 SERIES

1933–34

Engine: V8 3622cc (221 cu in)
Power: 56kW (75bhp)
0–96km/h (60mph): 18 secs
Top speed: 140km/h (87mph)
Production total: 485,700

Henry Ford made history in 1932 when he announced the Ford V8. The engine was not unique, but when combined with typical Ford value pricing it was a truly remarkable product. For 1933, Ford combined that great engine with the new Model 40 which was available in a huge range of body styles.

This model had a longer 284.5cm (112in) wheelbase and an X-member double drop chassis. It was a very stylish car with sweeping front and rear wings, and a new radiator design with vertical bars slanted back to match the inclined windscreen, as well as acorn-shaped headlight shells. Most striking were the one-piece bumpers with a centre 'V' dip. You really could have any colour you wanted; however, the wings were always painted black over 43cm (17in) wire spoke wheels.

Inside the car there was a new dashboard with an attractive machine-turned panel that put all the instruments directly in front of the driver. That V8 engine was running better than ever with a new ignition system and improved cooling, as well as a higher compression ratio and aluminium cylinder head, producing a healthy 56kW (75bhp).

For those customers who could not afford the V8 version, a straight four was also offered.

FORD FAIRLANE SKYLINER

1956–59

Engine: V8 4453cc (271 cu in)
Power: 142kW (190bhp)
0–96km/h (60mph): 12 secs
Top speed: 177km/h (110mph)
Production total: 48,394

The Fairlane, which was named after Henry Ford's Fair Lane mansion in Dearborn, was introduced in 1955 as the new top-of-the-line, full-size Ford. The Fairlane was originally offered in six different body styles, including the usual saloons, plus a plastic-topped Crown Victoria, a steel-roofed Victoria and the convertible Sunliner. The most distinctive version of the Fairlane, though, was launched for the 1957 model year, in the shape of the Ford Fairlane 500 Skyliner.

Unlike the gaudy and contrived excesses of some late-1950s cars, the Ford Fairlane 500 Skyliner was quite simple and understated. Small fins and single rear lights contribute to this example's uncluttered look.

This had the world's first production retractable hardtop. Although a stunning idea in theory, it proved to be very complicated and somewhat troublesome in practice. Not only that, but it was expensive at $400 more than the convertible Sunliner as well. Ford stylists designed the roof to be shorter than on other models, and its front section was hinged to fold for more compact storage into the larger boot. Despite this, the Skyliner still ended up with a higher and longer rear deck.

It also differed from other Fairlanes with its standard V8 engine and the relocated petrol tank, now found behind the back seat. On top of this, there was little luggage space when the top was down. The Skyliner briefly became the Galaxie in 1958; however, the troublesome roof simply had to go. The 500 is now a sought-after design classic.

One of the most novel models in the whole Ford line-up was the Fairlane 500 Skyliner. The Skyliner's clever trick was that its steel roof was able to be folded into the car's boot. The Skyliner name and concept were continued when Ford launched the Galaxie in 1959.

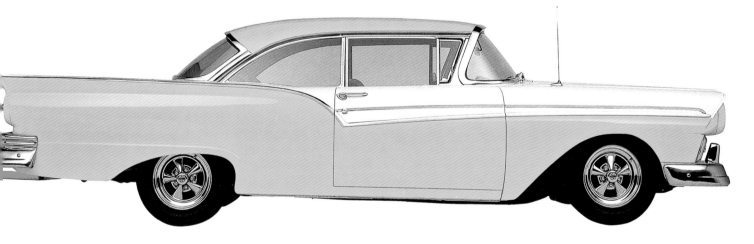

FORD THUNDERBIRD

1955–63

Engine: V8 5113cc (312 cu in)
Power: 168kW (225bhp)
0–96km/h (60mph): 9 secs
Top speed: 182km/h (113mph)
Production total: 447,660

The Thunderbird was effectively Ford's answer to the Chevrolet Corvette, although it was also a response to the British invasion led by the Jaguar XK120. Ford even held a contest to name the car and chose Thunderbird, which was a magical totem of the Pueblo Indians. Introduced in 1955, the car had style, refinement and V8 power. Only available as a convertible, a distinctive removable hardtop with circular porthole windows was available as an option. Underneath what was arguably the first sporting Ford were conventional parts from the Mainline and Fairlane models.

In 1956, a larger V8 option with 5113cc (312 cu in) and 168kW (225bhp) was offered, indicating that the company was becoming serious about performance. However, it was the following year, when new versions of the Y-block V8s were announced, that power was to become a real issue. The E-code 312 V8 featured two four-barrel carburettors and was rated at 201kW (270bhp). The F-code 312 V8 featured a single four-barrel carburettor boosted by a McCulloch centrifugal supercharger. The F-code engine was rated at 224kW (300bhp), or at 253kW (340bhp) with the optional NASCAR 'racing kit'. A minor facelift that year created what, for enthusiasts, will always be the classic Thunderbird.

The year 1958 ushered in a new-generation Thunderbird with four seats and a hardtop coupé, as well as the convertible body style. The styling was now more box-like, with a wide-pillar roof, which lead to the new car's nickname, the 'Squarebird'. The new model Thunderbirds also had monocoque construction bodies and pioneered the use of bucket seats. A retractable hardtop version was planned, but this was abandoned after the difficulties that were experienced with the Fairlane Skyliner.

Engine choices were all new, with the addition of a larger 5768cc (352 cu in) V8, and, in 1959, a Lincoln 7046cc (430 cu in) V8 rated at 261kW (350bhp) helped to boost sales. As 1960 was the last year of the second-generation Thunderbirds, the only change was the introduction of a special 'Golden Edition' hardtop, as well

as America's first postwar sliding steel sunroof.

Third-generation Thunderbirds arrived in 1961, and their new look soon saw them dubbed 'Projectile Birds'. They had a severely pointed front end with quad headlights, modest fins above huge round tail-lights and softer roof contours on hardtops. The chassis was reworked for a smoother ride and better handling. The interior featured a dash which curved at each end to blend in with the door panels, and the first 'Swing Away' steering wheel, which would pivot to the side when the car was parked. Just one engine was available, a 6391cc (390 cu in) V8, rated at 224kW (300bhp).

In 1962, the two-seat Thunderbird made a return. A Sports Roadster package, which featured a fibre-glass tonneau cover, designed by Bud Kaufman, covered the rear

Above is a 1962 Thunderbird. This is the sports roadster with streamlined headrests which was intended to bring back the sexiness of the original two-seater models. Pictured below is a 1957 Ford Thunderbird with less prominent rocket-shaped bumpers.

seat and effectively transformed the four-seat Thunderbird into a two-seat roadster. The tonneau cover even featured twin headrests, which flowed back to the rear, but the convertible top could still operate even with the cover in place. The package also included a dash-mounted grab bar for the passenger, and wire wheels. The rear wings even had extra clearance to allow for the wheels' knock-off centres.

Ford catered to the enthusiasts by offering a special 'M-code' 6391cc (390 cu in) FE V8 rated at 253kW (340bhp). This featured three Holley two-barrel carburettors and an aluminium manifold, which kept the carburettors level and at the same height. Only 145 Thunderbirds were built with the 'M-code' option, including 120 Sports Roadsters.

The Thunderbird remained in production for the 1963 model year, with the Sports Roadster and M-code 390 engine still being available. A new option was a Landau hardtop with simulated hood irons on its rear roof panels. This featured on the Thunderbird range for many years after as, gradually, the car became more conventional, less sporting and lost its iconic status. The car that had symbolized rock 'n' roll for a generation was dead.

FORD FALCON

This 1964 Sprint model with V8 engine, bucket seats and wire wheel covers, has been modified with spoilers front and rear, a bonnet scoop, rev counter mounted on the bonnet and alloy wheels.

ngine: V8 4261cc (260 cu in)
ower: 194kW (260bhp)
–96km/h (60mph): 9 secs
op speed: 197km/h (123mph)
roduction total: 2,700,697

he Falcon marked Ford's entry into he compact car market, a simple nd handsomely styled car that had vide appeal. Although it was almost m (3ft) shorter than the full-sized models, there was still plenty of room inside both the two- and four-door models. Power was provided by a smooth six-cylinder engine and, in 1963, the car was able to reach a broader and more sporty market with the introduction of a convertible and two-door hardtop.

Another significant addition was the availability of V8 engines. The Ford Falcon Futura Sprint was an important part of Ford's Total Performance programme and was available with high-power V8s. However, it was the Mustang's success which saw the Sprint discontinued. In 1964, the Falcon gained weight, and an even bulkier restyle in 1966 saw the convertible and two-door hardtop dropped.

The top trim level for the Falcon was the Futura, which was still offered as a sports coupé, even though it was not as attractive as the earlier model.

By 1969, the range was being badged as either Falcon or Torino, but the Falcon name was dropped for the 1970s – a sad end for what had once been a popular model.

Pictured below is a 1964 Falcon Sprint in competition colours.

FORD GALAXIE

Ford's contribution to the horsepower war was the Galaxie. Although it initially had more power than the similar Chevrolet Impala, it never sold as well because of its dull styling, poor aerodynamics and sheer weight. The Galaxie did, however, help to usher in the muscle car era at the full-size end of the model spectrum.

Despite disappointments, Ford kept trying and continued to install larger and larger engines, reaching a pinnacle with the most powerful

engine Detroit ever made – the Cammer 427. Producing 489kW (657bhp), this engine was fitted in only a few examples, and in fact it was eventually banned by the NASCAR authorities.

The Galaxies were revamped for 1965, with sharper styling and stacked headlights, as well as a redesigned and tougher front suspension. Ford soon understood that buyers who wanted pure performance would choose more compact models so, from 1967, the

company put the emphasis on luxury, which meant more size and weight, rather than muscle.

In 1968, The GT package separated performance Galaxies from the XL series, which no longer came with standard bucket seats and V8 power. Despite the introduction of a sleek Sports Roof fastback body style which came with a recessed rear window and concealed headlights, the Galaxie still became just another big, dull Ford in the 1970s.

A 1968 Ford Galaxie hardtop sports coupé which has been extensively customized with alloy wheels and a 'flame' paint work. Below is an earlier 1963 model two door convertible, most likely an XL series with a V8 engine, which has been completely restyled.

Engine: V8 6386cc (390 cu in)
Power: 224kW (300bhp)
0–96km/h (60mph): 9.5 secs
Top speed: 196km/h (122mph)
Production total: 4,726,105

FORD MUSTANG

Engine: V8 4727cc (288 cu in)
Power: 202kW (271bhp)
0–96km/h (60mph): 8.3 secs
Top speed: 120mph (193km/h)
Production total: 2,385,039

Lee Iacocca, Ford's General Manager, had always believed that a smaller American sports car could succeed, and so the 'pony car' was born. It was originally designed as a European-style two-seater, but Iacocca knew that volume sales were crucial. So the Mustang was based on the compact Falcon to keep production costs down and was powered by either a six-cylinder or V8 engine. Originally named after the P51 Mustang fighter plane, it came with a rear seat and lots of options to enable buyers to customize their cars.

In mid-1964, Ford introduced a sporty 2+2 fastback body style to go along with the hardtop coupé and convertible. Enthusiasts loved the new 202kW (271bhp) V8 that finally delivered the performance to match its sensational looks. However, for those who wanted more, Carroll Shelby and Ford collaborated to produce the Shelby GT-350, a Ford Mustang fastback. The 4736cc (289 cu in) V8 produced 228kW (306bhp) in standard tune and this rose to 268kW (360bhp) in GT-350R race tune. These Shelbys were stripped out for racing and were only available in white.

In 1967, there was a considerable revision of the Mustang, as the styling became more aggressive with more sheet metal, a new grille, a concave tail panel and a full

fastback roofline for the coupé. There was now more room for a big block 6391cc (390 cu in) unit to replace the 4727cc (288 cu in) engine. Shelby-tuned Mustangs became more outrageous, as the new GT500 was powered by a reworked 7014cc (428 cu in) V8; however, these were the last Shelby Mustangs that were actually built by Shelby-American.

The Mustang was completely restyled for the 1969 model year and the character of the once lithe, lean and mean car had begun to change. It was now 9.5cm (3.8in) longer and around 64kg (140lb). heavier. The Mach 1 model came with a 5752cc (351 cu in) V8, but could also be bought with the 7014cc (428 cu in) Cobra Jet unit in three states of tune. The ultimate version was the Super Cobra Jet with a shaker hood scoop, a

modified crankshaft and stronger connecting rods. So-called 'Drag Pack' models also came with limited-slip 3.91:1 or 4.30:1 rear axles and no air conditioning.

The 'Boss' series Mustangs were named after stylist Larry Shinoda's nickname for Ford president Semon Knudson. Boss Mustangs were built to qualify for the the NASCAR series, and they came with a race-ready 7030cc (429 cu in) V8 with ram air induction, header type exhaust manifolds running through a four-speed manual gearbox and a 3.91:1 Traction-Lok axle. Also included were an oil cooler, boot-mounted battery and full race suspension.

The year 1971 was to be a watershed one for the Mustang, as it became 5cm (2.1in) longer, 7cm (2.8in) wider and about 45kg (100lb) heavier. Just as damaging to

Above is a hardtop sports coupé model with GT specifications. This meant a V8 engine, quick ratio steering, front disc brakes, foglights built into the front grille and more comprehensive instrumentation. Pictured below is a 1968 two-door convertible.

the Mustang image was the disappearance of the Shelby and some Boss models. Engines were detuned, and only the Mach 1 Mustang continued the performance tradition. Matters reached a nadir for the 1974 model year. Emission legislation severely reduced engine outputs, and the 351 V8 produced just 116kW (156bhp). New US federal guidelines also meant the appearance of 8km/h (5mph) impact bumpers.

The restyled Mustang II in 1974 abandoned any pretence of offering performance. Top speed from the six-cylinder 2.8-litre (171 cu in) engine was a paltry 164km/h (102mph), and 96km/h (60mph) could only be achieved in 13 seconds. Unbelievably, the Mach 1-badged V6 was even slower and could not reach 161km/h (100mph). The fact that the 5-litre (305 cu in) V8 produced only 99kW (133bhp) tells its own story. The car did not even look good. A gaudy grille, huge federal-regulation bumpers, wide-eyed headlights and emaciated bodywork were evident. The only people celebrating were Ford, as sales of the Mustang II hit 338,129 in 1974 – a record. Over five years, the car achieved sales of 1,107,718. The Mustang was now little more than a brand.

FORD TORINO

1962–76

Engine: V8 7022cc (428 cu in)
Power: 250kW (335bhp)
0–96km/h (60mph): 8 secs
Top speed: 217km/h (135mph)
Production total: 2,024,189

The Fairlane range was repackaged and relaunched in 1962 as Ford's entry into the competitive muscle car market. With less weight than the full-size Galaxie, but the same powerful engine, the Fairlane, and its spin-off, the Torino, had soon established themselves as street and drag-strip legends.

In 1968, the exciting new Torino series appeared. Torino GTs had a standard 4949cc (302 cu in) V8 engine, bucket seats, centre dashboard console, decals, side stripes and distinctive trim, and deluxe wheelcovers. Muscle car options included a 6391cc (390 cu in) V8 and the 7022cc (428 cu in) V8 291kW (390bhp) engine. Available as fastback, hardtop and convertibles,

entry-level Cobra models were added a year later with a standard 7022cc (428 cu in) Cobra Jet V8, rated at 250kW (335bhp).

Also new for 1969 was the introduction of the Torino Talladega. Specifically aimed at NASCAR racing, it was based on the two-door hardtop and had an extended sloped nose, flush grille and revised rear bumper. These features improved aerodynamics, but made the car 15cm (6in)

A 1971 Ford Torino Cobra Sports Roof coupé with four-speed manual transmission, competition suspension, a black bonnet with locking devices and Cobra badging

longer. Restyled again for 1970, the Torino became even bigger, a trend that continued in 1972 as the car became more luxury orientated. Cobra and convertible versions were discontinued, and the GT became just a badge.

FORD PINTO

1971–80

Ford was determined to produce a car to rival imported sub-compact cars and smaller US-made machines such as the AMC Gremlin and Chevrolet Vega. Its answer was the Pinto, which proved to be one of the most successful economy cars of the fuel-starved 1970s. Launched first as a two-door, it was followed by the hatchback Runabout. Power came from a British-built 1600cc (98 cu in) or a much more popular German 2-litre (122 cu in) unit, available with a Cruise-O-Matic three-speed automatic transmission.

A three-door estate was added in 1973 and, in 1974, massive federal-regulation bumpers seemed to almost overwhelm the small car.

Although the Pinto was an economy car, there was an optional 2.8-litre (171 cu in) V6; however, this was only available with an

A two-door sedan from 1971. In this first year, some 352,402 were made. The Runabout arrived midseason and, as well as a rear door, had a fold-down rear seat and more extensive carpeting.

automatic gearbox and only on the station wagon model. The 2.3-litre (140 cu in) US-built four-cylinder proved more popular as the standard unit. A Stallion model in 1976 looked sporty, while the entry-level variant was called the Pony MPG, featuring minimal trim. New front ends in 1979 and a new range of option packages, including the Pinto Cruising Wagon and sporty ESS, signalled that the era of the pure economy car was over. The Pinto was replaced by the Escort.

Engine: 4-cylinder 1599cc (98 cu in)
Power: 56kW (75bhp)
0–96km/h (60mph): 18 secs
Top speed: 131km/h (82mph)
Production total: 3,150,943

FORD VEDETTE

1947–54

Engine: 2158cc (132 cu in)
Power: 49kW (66bhp)
0–96km/h (60mph): n/a
Top speed: 144km/h (90mph)
Production total: 100,000

A purpose-built factory in Poissy resumed Ford production in France in 1947 with a car designed in the United States three years previously. With its US-influenced full-width

grille, two-piece windscreen and fastback styling, it was quite unlike any contemporary European model. Being a US car, it was no surprise to find that there was a 2158 cc (132 cu in) V8 engine under the bonnet. Unfortunately, this side-valve engine proved very unreliable.

Vedettes were initially four-door saloons, but coupés and convertibles appeared during 1949. Facel even

built a sporting coupé based on the car and called it the Comte.

For 1953, the Vedette acquired a modern one-piece windscreen and the rounded rear end disappeared to make space for a proper boot. The engine size went up in 1953 to 2355cc (144 cu in), as did the compression ratio, which helped power to climb from 49 to 60kW (66 to 80bhp). Later in the year, a

This is one of the earliest Vedettes with contemporary American styling, the streamlined fastback being designed by Bob Gregorie.

4-litre (244 cu in) 71kW (95bhp) version was offered, but the car was now slow, thirsty and dated. Ford had a replacement ready, but that monocoque-based car never went into production.

FRAZER NASH SUPER SPORTS

1928–30

Archie Frazer Nash left cyclecar manufacturers GN to set up his own car-making enterprise in 1924, building on what he had learnt at GN. He added a proper chassis and used conventional water-cooled four-cylinder engines in his cars. The result was a basic but technically very effective racer which won many fans.

While providing little in the way of comfort, the so-called 'Chain Gang' Frazer Nash models with their unique transmission (separate exposed chain and sprockets, dog clutches for each gear) and solid rear axle were prized for their sharp handling, slick gearchange and superb traction. Due to its light-weight construction, the Super

Sports enjoyed an excellent power–weight ratio and, despite developing only 35kW (47bhp), it performed surprisingly well in competition. Because the solid rear axle dictated that the track remained narrow (just 107cm [42in] at the back), the car's ride was extremely hard, but owners particularly loved the sensitive steering and lively

handling which were a result of this. Later cars adopted the HE (high efficiency) engine which developed 39kW (52bhp).

Engine: 1496cc (91 cu in), 4-cylinder
Power: 35kW (47bhp)
0–96km/h (60mph): n/a
Top speed: 109km/h (68mph)
Production total: n/a

FRAZER NASH TT REPLICA

1932–38

The Frazer Nash TT Replica drew its name from its repeated successes in the British Tourist Trophy races of the early 1930s, and it became one of the most popular of all the Nashes.

One of the most popular of all Nash cars, the TT Replica was so-called because of its success during the Tourist Trophy of the early 1930s. It was a true thoroughbred in every sense, with stark lines, set-back radiator, cycle wings and squared-off rear fuel tank. Like other 'Chain Gang' Nashes, it had the famed unique transmission with separate and exposed chain and sprockets for each gear.

As well as being good to look at, TT Replica also handled well with its solid rear axle and high-geared rack-and-pinion steering. These allowed on-the-limit 'power on' cornering and controlled four-wheel drift.

Many of the car's model designations were taken from race circuits such as Shelsey, Boulogne, Exeter, Colmore and Nurburg, and no two cars were the same, with owners able to specify engines, state of tune and body trim.

The majority of cars had the four-cylinder Meadows engine with two overhead valves per cylinder; however, a few did have the superb twin-camshaft Blackburn engine, which could produce an impressive 112kW (150bhp) when it was supercharged.

Engine: 1496cc (91 cu in), 4-cylinder
Power: 46kW (62bhp)
0–96km/h (60mph): 8.8 secs
Top speed: 130km/h (80mph)
Production total: 85

FRAZER NASH LE MANS REPLICA

1948–53

Chosen to accompany their successful chain-driven models, a Bristol-BMW-powered lightweight racing car was developed by Frazer Nash that would be suitable for fast road use, as well as being competitive on the racetrack.

Featuring rack-and-pinion steering, with 89kW (120bhp) from its three-carburettor engine in a car that weighed just 690kg (1520lb), it very much lived up to its original 'High Speed' name.

When a privateer took his car to Le Mans in 1949 and finished a spectacular third place overall, the model name was changed to 'Le Mans Replica'. Thanks to transverse-leaf independent front suspension, handling was taut, light and highly predictable, and the car stormed to victories on racetracks all over the United Kingdom and abroad.

While postwar Nashes adopted a somewhat less aggressive appearance than predecessors, their sporting prowess remained undiminished – the Le Mans Replica was uncompromisingly quick, with awesome performance, pin-sharp handling and impressive race reliability.

As usual with Frazer Nash, as its cars were completely hand-built, no two machines produced at the Isleworth factory in Middlesex, England, were the same, with buyers being able to dictate the precise set-up of both engine and suspension, along with the colour and body details.

In 1952, an even lighter, slimmer Le Mans Replica Mk II appeared, and in 1953, its last year of production, it was further improved by the fitting of a De Dion-type rear axle.

Engine: 1971cc (120 cu in), 6-cylinder
Power: 89kW (120bhp)
0–96km/h (60mph): 8.9 secs
Top speed: 185km/h (115mph)
Production total: 34

GHIA L.6.4

1960–62

ased on the Virgil Exner–styled Dart, the L.6.4 was Ghia's second attempt at selling a car under its own brand name, the first being the Italo-American Dual-Ghia Firebomb, which did exactly what its name suggested and was dogged by poor reliability.

Built by Casaroll and Company, the L.6.4 was a coupé on a grand scale, with a huge panoramic windscreen, lots of chrome and an imposing grille, all of which drew heavily on US-style cars. Indeed, the car was marketed at US buyers, and singer Frank Sinatra became one of the first owners.

Chrysler underpinnings and a powerful Chrysler V8 powerplant sat under the hand-crafted Ghia body (which was manufactured in Turin), which meant that the Ghia L.6.4 was easily capable of reaching 224km/h (140mph).

Only 26 examples of the L.6.4. were built between 1960 and 1962, which was hardly surprising given the car's high price. It was very expensive to produce because of high overheads. Today, few examples survive, so they remain even more of a rarity, commanding strong prices in the unusual event of one coming up for sale.

Engine: 6279cc (383 cu in), 8-cylinder
Power: 250kW (335bhp)
0–96km/h (60mph): 8 secs
Top speed: 224km/h (140mph)
Production total: 26

GHIA 450SS

1965–68

Italian coachbuilders Ghia used the Plymouth Barracuda as the basis for its 450SS model, made in very limited numbers from 1965. The 450SS was available as an attractive drop-top or a two-door coupé, and it shared the Plymouth's V8 powerplant.

The Ghia 450SS was the inspiration of Californian Bert Sugarman, who spotted a Ghia-bodied Fiat 2300S on a magazine cover and was so impressed that he chose Ghia to build a sports cars for him. The company agreed, and production started in 1965.

Fundamentally, the 450SS was little more than a rebodied Plymouth Barracuda with the same huge Chrysler Commander V8 under the bonnet; however, Ghia design transformed the vehicle into an exceptionally beautiful car with clean lines.

Ghia was to make both coupé and convertible versions – the convertible was particularly appealing with its almost flat-folding hood making it a true classic. The only thing to spoil the 450SS's looks were the ugly twin headlights and the prolific use of chrome on the bumpers. Inevitably, Ghia was selling the car to the American market.

Only a very few cars were made, perhaps because its price at the time was four times that of the Barracuda. Unfortunately, only a handful of these cars survive today, and most form a rare and desirable part of private collections.

Engine: 4490cc (274 cu in), 8-cylinder
Power: 175kW (235bhp)
0–96km/h (60mph): 8.9 secs
Top speed: 200km/h (125mph)
Production total: 12

GHIA 1500GT

1962–67

Convinced that there was a market for a two-seater coupé based on simple Fiat 1500 running gear, Ghia started making the 1500GT from 1962.

The car's styling was beautifully simple, with a long, flat bonnet, sharp sweeping lines and rakish rear windscreen. In fact, the Ghia 1500GT is seen by many as perhaps one of the most underrated (and indeed understated) classic coupés of its time.

Performance, unfortunately, did not match the looks, and top speed was just over 160km/h (100mph). Road-holding capabilities were not very good, either, with plenty of body roll and underwhelming cornering ability. Despite this, the 1500GT was a very practical car to own and enjoy. Being of such humble origins, it has also become reasonably affordable.

Carrozzeria Ghia's production of the 1500GT at a rate of around five cars per day was impressive, as each of them was built by hand. However, the ravages of corrosion and owners with artificially high expectations of its driving ability has meant that only a small proportion of the 925 cars made still exist today.

Engine: 1481cc (90 cu in), 4-cylinder
Power: 63kW (84bhp)
0–96km/h (60mph): 12 secs
Top speed: 168km/h (105mph)
Production total: 925

GILBERN GT

1959–67

Originating from Pontypridd in South Wales, the GT was originally available either made up or as a kit, the latter providing a loophole for potential owners to save money on purchase tax. Either way, it provided an affordable entry into the sports car market for many people.

Wales's only long-standing car manufacturer, Gilbern, produced the Gilbern GT in kit form, using power from a variety of sources – including the MGB from 1963. Using a glassfibre body, it was a good-quality car and provided excellent value.

Underneath the fibreglass body was a tubular chassis and running gear taken from the Austin A35, BMC and MG. Despite its diminutive engine size, the Gilbern GT's performance was reasonably impressive thanks to the addition of an optional Shorrock supercharger to the standard Austin A-Series engine, which pushed power up from 31kW (42bhp) in the standard car to 51kW (68bhp).

Successive cars were sold with either the 1098cc (67 cu in) Coventry Climax unit or the 1588cc (97 cu in) or 1622cc (99 cu in) engine from the MGA. After 1963, the company was to offer the 1798cc (110 cu in) engine taken from the MGB.

The Gilbern GT's body styling was neat and unpretentious, and the two wide-opening doors provided good access to a utilitarian bench seat in the back, enabling the claim that the GT could seat four.

Engine: 948cc (58 cu in), 4-cylinder
Power: 31kW (42bhp)
0–96km/h (60mph): 17.4 secs
Top speed: 147km/h (91mph)
Production total: 166

GILBERN GENIE

1966–69

The Gilbern Genie was a more angular version of the GT with a stronger chassis, making it a grand tourer that could compete against cars such as the Jensen, but at a fraction of the price.

Engines were uprated V6 units from Ford in either 2.5- (152 cu in) or 3-litre (183 cu in) guises. Some even had fuel injection, which boosted power output to 123kW (165bhp), giving the Genie a top speed of approaching 192km/h (120mph).

Sadly, the Gilbern Genie's failing was its chassis, which had an unfortunate tendency to flex when pushed hard. However, once again, Gilbern had produced a car that was not only affordable to buy, but was also straightforward enough for most owners to maintain themselves on only a modest budget.

Engine: 2495cc (152 cu in), 6-cylinder
Power: 83kW (112bhp)
0–96km/h (60mph): 10.7 secs
Top speed: 176km/h (110mph)
Production total: 174

GILBERN INVADER

1969–74

With a stiffened chassis and improved suspension, the Gilbern Invader became the natural successor to the Genie, sharing its sharp lines and sporting pretensions. The Invader was more refined than the Genie in many ways – it was better finished and provided its occupants with a much more comfortable ride.

The Invader only used the Ford 3-litre (183 cu in) V6 engine offered on the Genie, with overdrive on third and fourth gears as standard, as well as the option of automatic transmission. Performance was brisk, with good acceleration and top speed.

The Mk II had a few detail changes, such as flush door handles, while the Mk III was heavily modified with a lower overall ride height, flared wheelarches, revised rear end and wider front grille. It also gained Ford Cortina front suspension and

Engine: 2994cc (183 cu in), 6-cylinder
Power: 107kW (144bhp)
0–96km/h (60mph): 10.7 secs
Top speed: 192km/h (120mph)
Production total: 561

Ford Taunus live rear axle, which improved both the car's ride quality and its handling.

The company also offered an unusual estate version of the Invader, which was based on the Mk II, but only 105 of these were made between 1971 and 1972.

The Invader was the last car to be manufactured by Gilbern, and the Welsh factory ceased production in 1974.

The Gilbern Invader was the company's most refined car yet, with lusty Ford V6 power and the availability of an automatic gearbox. Based on the MkII, just 105 estate versions were made between 1971 and 1972.

GINETTA G4

1961–69

Engine: 997cc (61 cu in), 4-cylinder
Power: 29kW (39bhp)
0–96km/h (60mph): n/a
Top speed: 144km/h (90mph)
Production total: 500

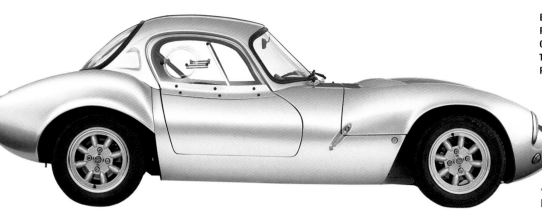

Ginetta established its sports car kudos by creating cars based on basic but exceptionally well-sorted chassis clad in good-looking glassfibre bodies.

Brothers Bob, Trevor, Ivor and Douglas Walklett started making Ginetta cars in Woodbridge, England, before moving to Witham in Essex in 1958. Here, they launched the G2 as their first production vehicle. However, the G4 was their first volume-selling car and, like most Ginettas, was also sold in kit form to allow prospective owners to build the car themselves to avoid the necessity of paying purchase tax.

Underneath a sporty-looking glassfibre body was a tubular space frame, initially with coil springs at the front, a live rear axle and optional front disc brakes. Power

was derived from the humble Ford Anglia 105E 997cc (61 cu in) unit and subsequently from the 1498cc (91 cu in) Ford Cortina. A reasonable power-to-weight ratio allowed the G4 to be highly competitive, particularly at club racing events.

A short-tail Series II appeared in 1963, and a BMC rear axle replaced the Ford item. The Series III was very different again, with an improved chassis, Triumph Herald front wishbones and stylish pop-up headlights. The model was reintroduced in 1981, albeit in a much revised form, and enjoyed its more recent success as the G27.

The G4 was Ginetta's first volume-selling model, and a version of the car is still being made to this day.

GINETTA G15

1967–73

Launched at the Earls Court Show in London in 1967, the beautiful little G15 became the company's bestselling model. It used the aluminium engine from the Hillman Imp (mounted ahead of the back axle) married to the excellent Imp gearbox, with Triumph Spitfire front suspension, steering and disc brakes. The independent rear suspension was again borrowed from the Imp.

These features were mounted on a lightweight tubular frame, onto which a pretty fibreglass two-seater body was bolted. A few G15S models were produced with an uprated 998cc (61 cu in) engine, offering an impressive 184km/h (115mph) top speed.

The attractive G15 was to become Ginetta's most popular model. Triumph Spitfire-derived front suspension provided precise steering and nimble handling.

Being so lightweight, the tiny G15 performed well, but was also very economical on fuel. Over its six-year production lifetime, small refinements were offered with such luxuries as a sunroof (or a heater) appearing on the options list.

These cars cost just £799 in kit form new, and good examples are still sought-after today. Sadly, changes to taxation and the introduction of VAT in 1973 killed off kit cars in general, and Ginetta suffered as a consequence.

Engine: 875cc (53 cu in), 4-cylinder
Power: 41kW (55bhp)
0–96km/h (60mph): 12.9 secs
Top speed: 152km/h (95mph)
Production total: 796

GINETTA G21

Gradual evolution in design was apparent in the G21, which drew much on the Michelotti-inspired Triumph GT6 for its front end and sweeping back.

The car used a new backbone/tubular steel chassis with coil-spring and wishbone suspension at the front and a subframe for the suspension and final drive at the rear. Like all previous Ginetta's, the G21 had a well-constructed fibreglass body, which proved to be both rigid and lightweight. Power was provided either by the Ford 3-litre (183 cu in) V6 unit or, more

often, by the Rootes Sunbeam Rapier 1725cc (105 cu in) engine which, when uprated by the tuning company, Holbay, produced 71kW (95bhp).

As the Ginetta G21 was only available as a two-seater, fixed-head coupé, it failed to compete successfully with its main rival, the MGB, which also had the added convenience of an opening rear tailgate. Due to the introduction of VAT in 1973, which had the effect of virtually killing off the kit-car market, most of the 170 cars were supplied already built.

Despite attractive styling, lack of an opening rear hatch meant that the Ginetta G21 lost out to more practical rivals such as the MGB GT. Most G21s were sold as complete cars, not kits.

Engine: 1725cc (105 cu in), 4-cylinder
Power: 59kW (79bhp)
0–96km/h (60mph): 10.8 secs
Top speed: 180km/h (112mph)
Production total: 170

The G21 had Ford V6, Rootes Rapier or Rapier H120 engines, gearboxes and overdrives. The bonnet and wings formed the front nose section and hinged together, there was a child's bench seat and the back end sloped sharply in true fastback tradition.

GINETTA G32

Still based on the same principles of a box section steel chassis and fibreglass body, the G32 was the last of the company's cars to be produced before financial problems forced the Walklett family to sell to new owners, based in Scunthorpe, England, in 1989.

Double wishbone and coil springs at the front and struts at the back, taken from the Ford Fiesta, gave tenacious handling, and Ford's 1597cc (97 cu in) XR2i engine and gearbox, mid-mounted and turned round to drive the rear wheels, provided the G32 with plenty of power and impressive acceleration.

Styling of this pretty two-door coupé was very much of the time, with a wedge-like profile, pop-up

headlights and a short, stubby rear end. As always, the finish of the Ginetta body was of a high quality. An open-top version of the G32 appeared in 1990, and production ceased in 1992. The Ginetta company still makes cars today at its factory in Sheffield.

Double wishbone and coil-spring front suspension and struts taken from the Ford XR2 at the rear along with its mid-engine configuration gave the G32 terrific handling to match its exotic looks.

Engine: 1597cc (97 cu in), 4-cylinder
Power: 82kW (110bhp)
0–96km/h (60mph): 8.2 secs
Top speed: 192km/h (120mph)
Production total: n/a

GLAS GOGGOMOBIL

The brainchild of Hans Glas, and his first attempt at vehicle manufacture, the Goggomobil was a clever two-cylinder four-seater that became very popular in Europe, significantly undercutting the price of the Volkswagen Beetle.

A two-cylinder two-stroke 250cc (15 cu in) engine mounted in the rear provided the diminutive car with its power, but this gave poor performance, especially when the car was fully loaded. Later, bigger-engined T300 and T400 versions improved matters.

The car underwent various minor changes throughout its long lifespan and in 1964 the original suicide-type forward opening doors were changed to front hinges.

There was also a two-seater TS Coupé available from 1956, with a cute dummy grille and stylish wraparound rear window. Less practical than the saloon, it could still seat 2+2 in an overall length of just 305cm (10ft). There was even a TS300 Cabriolet built between 1957 and 1958, though only seven such cars were made.

The name came from Glas's grandson, who was nicknamed 'Goggo', and there is currently a cult following for the marque.

Engine: 247cc (15 cu in), 2-cylinder
Power: 10kW (14bhp)
0–96km/h (60mph): n/a
Top speed: 75km/h (47mph)
Production total: 280,709

Named after Glas's grandson, who was nicknamed 'Goggo', the twin-cylinder two-stroke Goggomobil was capable of seating four adults. The last ones were badged as BMW following a 1966 takeover by the company.

GLAS 2600 V8

An interesting configuration of two 1300GT four-cylinder engines joined together to make up a V8 sharing a single crank formed the basis of what was to be Glas's most ambitious car.

It was based on the same floorpan as the company's 1700 model, with a De Dion rear end suspended by semi-elliptic springs and Boge automatic self-levelling suspension.

Styling was by Italian design house Frua, and it took on a semi-fastback form which earnt it the nickname 'Glaserati'. Adorned with plenty of chromework, the car was specifically aimed at the prestige German market, and it carried a suitably expensive price tag to match.

BMW took over production after 1966 with a stroked V8 and a new name, BMW-Glas 3000. Production of this luxury model was to continue under BMW stewardship until BMW brought out its own 2800CS model in the late 1960s.

Sadly, Glas had become the instigator of its own end by mistakenly moving away from making more humble 'people cars', at which it had become relatively successful.

The last Glas-built car had either a 2580cc (157 cu in) or a 2982cc (182 cu in) V8 engine, sporting bodywork by Frua and De Dion rear axles.

Engine: 2580cc (157 cu in), 8-cylinder
Power: 104kW (140bhp)
0–96km/h (60mph): 8.7 secs
Top speed: 195km/h (121mph)
Production total: 300

GOLIATH GP 700

1950–57

Goliath was one of German car-maker Borgward's cheaper lines, and underneath a modern-looking body was prewar machinery in the form of a two-stroke twin, mounted transversely and driving the front wheels, a dated tubular chassis and an antiquated power chain. The car was successful, however, providing useful everyday transport for ordinary people in Europe in the postwar years.

Early examples of the GP 700 were very underpowered, but standard carburation was replaced on later cars with a fuel injection system which improved both performance and reliability – the use of such technology on a car of this type was quite an innovation at the time.

From 1955, the capacity was increased to 886cc (54 cu in), providing the Goliath with a good turn of speed. Having to mix oil with petrol to power the two-stroke engine was still a chore for most owners, though.

There were three body styles to choose from: a two-door saloon, an estate and a convertible, the last of which was only made in very small numbers and is a rarity today.

Goliath's modern-looking rounded bodywork on the GP 700 disguised predominantly prewar technology. The two-door convertible version was particularly rare.

Engine: 688cc (42 cu in), 2-cylinder
Power: 18kW (24bhp)
0–96km/h (60mph): n/a
Top speed: 94km/h (59mph)
Production total: 36,270

GOLIATH 1100

1957–61

The boxy 1100 marked a turning point for Goliath, featuring a water-cooled four-stroke flat-four engine, fully synchromesh gearbox and all-new coil-spring suspension. This attractive early Goliath 1100 coupé was displayed at the 1958 Geneva Show.

abandoned, and standard carburation was used instead.

After 1958, the model was renamed Hansa, and delicate fins were added to the rear wings. There were four body styles to choose from in the range, which were a saloon, estate, coupé and a cute-looking convertible. The coupé was nothing more than a saloon with a slightly shorter roof, but it was introduced to compete with the more expensive Volkswagen Karmann Ghia.

More than 40,000 examples of the 1100 in its various guises were sold during its four-year lifespan.

In common with other vehicle manufacturers at the time, Goliath was keen to advance technically and move away from the continued reliance on dated, prewar mechanicals on its cars.

The 1100 spearheaded this move with a number of company firsts. It employed an all-new water-cooled four-stroke flat-four engine, and the column-change four-speed gearbox was replaced with a floor-mounted all-synchromesh unit. In addition, the leaf-sprung front suspension was dropped in favour of coils to improve ride and stability. Interestingly, however, the novelty of fuel injection was

Engine: 1094cc (67 cu in), 4-cylinder
Power: 30kW (40bhp)
0–96km/h (60mph): 19 secs
Top speed: 125km/h (78mph)
Production total: 42,695

GORDON KEEBLE GK1/1T

Styled by Bertone, the Gordon Keeble was one of the fastest four-seaters of its time, with a top speed of 217km/h (135mph) and devastatingly quick acceleration. Production problems led to its eventual demise in 1966.

'The car that was built to aircraft standards' was how the company from Eastleigh, England, marketed its glassfibre-bodied, Bertone-styled four-seater coupé. The brainchild of John Gordon and Jim Keeble, a steel-bodied prototype nicknamed 'The Growler' was first seen at the 1960 London Motor Show. However, it was not until 1964 that the car, renamed GK1, but also known as the International Tourer, finally went into production.

The beautifully understated styling was the work of 21-year-old Giugiaro, then chief stylist at Bertone, who later moved to Ghia before setting up his own studio.

The car utilized cheap American V8 power and had blistering performance. Handling was very good, too, thanks to De Dion rear suspension and a complex square section space-frame chassis.

After a year, the company had produced just 80 cars. Component supply problems and underinvestment meant that Gordon Keeble never realized its true potential. An additional 19 cars were built in 1966 under new management, but the company ceased trading later that year. Being fibreglass and therefore rustproof, about 90 still exist.

Just 99 Gordon Keebles were built at Eastleigh near Southampton, but use of glassfibre means that they do not suffer from corrosion, so survival rate is high.

Engine: 5395cc (329 cu in), 8-cylinder
Power: 224kW (300bhp)
0–96km/h (60mph): 7.5 secs
Top speed: 217km/h (135mph)
Production total: 99

GRAHAM 97

A producer of cars for the American middle classes in the late 1920s, the Paige-Detroit firm went into decline during the Depression years, only to be saved from extinction by the intervention of the charismatic Graham brothers, Robert, Joseph and Ray, in 1927. The cars were then called Graham Paige for three years until 1930,

when the name was shortened to simply Graham.

The 1938 'Sharknose' range was ugly and was seen as a publicity stunt, despite being good to drive and entirely reliable. Today these cars have a strong following, especially in the United States, where they have become the favourite subject of customizing.

Sadly, despite the earlier introduction of the innovative 'twin top' four-speed gearbox, the trend-setting Blue-Streak of 1932 and the blown straight-eights of 1934, the Sharknose did nothing to halt the company's eventual demise. Following World War II, the car-making side of Graham Paige was absorbed by the Kaiser car

company, while the brothers themselves moved on to making farm machinery before becoming involved in real estate.

Engine: 3560cc (217 cu in), 6-cylinder
Power: 19kW (25bhp)
0–96km/h (60mph): 19 secs
Top speed: 139km/h (87mph)
Production total: n/a

GSM DELTA

1958–64

GSM used a stiff ladder chassis, light body and Ford engines to make their two-seater Delta into a feisty competition car that would have more appeal for club racers than the less competitive road-going public.

Originating in Cape Town, South Africa, production of this Ford-based two-seater sports car also took place in the United Kingdom (at West Malling, Kent) for one year in 1960, before the Kent plant eventually closed due to under-

capitalization. Production was then moved once again to South Africa until 1964.

GSM (Glass Sports Motor) was created by Bob van Niekirk and Vester de Witt, and the Delta featured a steel tube ladder chassis

with power coming from a tuned Ford Anglia engine. There was also the option of a more powerful Coventry-Climax unit for racing purposes. The car's underpinnings took the form of transverse-leaf springs at the front and a Ford 100E rear axle and further coil springs at the rear.

Body options were either open-top or coupé, the latter of which had a Ford Anglia-style reverse-rake rear windscreen. Both versions shared the same sharp-finned rear wing tops, similar to the Daimler Dart, a car which Niekirk had also become involved in developing.

The Delta proved successful at club competition level throughout the 1960s and, during the latter part of its production lifespan in South Africa, an improved version was sold, called the Flamingo.

Engine: 997cc (61 cu in), 4-cylinder
Power: 42kW (57bhp)
0–96km/h (60mph): n/a
Top speed: 161km/h (100mph)
Production total: 35 in UK

GUTBROD SUPERIOR

1950–54

The Gutbrod Superior was advanced for having double wishbone front suspension, but antiquated in its use of two-stroke engines. As with many cars from the postwar era, modern styling was used to disguise largely pre-war mechanicals.

Agricultural machinery manufacturers Gutbrod founded the Standard motorcycle factory in 1926 and started making the rear-engined Standard Superior in 1933, before introducing the Gutbrod Superior from 1950.

Like many cars of the postwar era, it featured an antiquated two-stroke two-cylinder engine which powered the front wheels. Elsewhere, the technology was more up to date, with a double wishbone coil combination front suspension and a more traditional swing axle suspension at the back, all of which was bolted to a platform chassis.

The Superior was essentially a two-door coupé with bulbous front wings, a virtually flat front

windscreen and oval-shaped headlights which sat each side of an unconventional-looking slatted chrome grille. The coupé also featured a roll-back fabric roof. However, the company also offered a saloon, an estate and a convertible,

as well as a very rare Wendler-built sports roadster version.

A larger 663cc (40 cu in) engine option became available after 1951 which provided the Superior, which was always very well made, with a more respectable performance.

Engine: 593cc (36 cu in), 2-cylinder
Power: 15kW (20bhp)
0–96km/h (60mph): n/a
Top speed: 96km/h (60mph)
Production total: 7726

HANSA 3500 PRIVAT

1936–39

The Hansa company was founded in 1913 by two men, August Sparkhorst and Dr Robert Allmers, who set up their workshop in the Westphalian town of Bielefeld. The following year, they merged with Lloyd of Bremen to become Hansa-Lloyd, although the Hansa name lived on independently.

The early Hansa cars were influenced strongly by the French models of the time, including the Alcyon voiturette. Also, before World War I, Hansa even built vehicles under licence for the British Royal Air Force.

In the 1920s, Hansa, along with a number of other car making ventures, created a new consortium of companies known as GDA (Gemeinschaft Deutscher Automobilfabriken), and between the two world wars Hansa offered a variety of four-, six- and eight-cylinder engined cars for buyers to choose from.

The Privat featured an overhead valve six-cylinder engine with a capacity of 3485cc (213 cu in), with a four-bearing crankshaft and twin SU carburettors, mounted on a pressed steel platform chassis with cruciform side members and independent all-round suspension.

An interesting feature was the Vogal system of centralized chassis lubrication, as well as the innovative hydraulic brakes which served all four wheels.

The last of the Hansa cars, which were manufactured in 1939, were called Borgward.

Engine: 3485cc (213 cu in), 6-cylinder
Power: 67kW (90bhp)
0–96km/h (60mph): 24 secs
Top speed: 120km/h (75mph)
Production total: n/a

HEALEY 2.4 WESTLAND

1946–50

The all alloy-bodied Westland roadster was one of the most potent postwar four-seaters available.

Rare and highly sought-after in any form, the Warwick-built Healey was one of the fastest British four-seaters of the postwar era. Its appeal came from its alloy-over-wood body which weighed around 1000kg (1 ton), combined with a stiff box-section chassis and an accomplished high-camshaft Riley engine. Handling was predictable, too, thanks to coil springs all round, with trailing arms at the front. The car also featured hydraulic brakes – a rarity for British cars in the 1940s.

The Westland was the roadster version and the most desirable of the models, but there was also an Elliot saloon (which was one of the fastest closed cars produced in Britain at the time) and a slab-sided drophead coupé known as the Sportsmobile which, despite its 77kW (104bhp), proved unpopular with British car buyers.

There were also some special-bodied cars made by Duncan and even Italian stylists Bertone, but these are rare and fetch high premiums on the classic car market.

Engine: 2443cc (149 cu in), 4-cylinder
Power: 67kW (90bhp)
0–96km/h (60mph): 12.3 secs
Top speed: 168km/h (105mph)
Production total: 64

HEALEY SILVERSTONE

1949–51

The Healey Silverstone featured twin headlights positioned behind the grille, retractable windscreen and a horizontally stowed spare wheel that protruded at the back to act as a rear bumper.

Unveiled in the summer of 1949, the no-nonsense Healey Silverstone sported cycle wings and a number of unusual design features that included a windscreen that retracted into the scuttle, albeit for a section of the top which remained proud to act as a wind deflector, twin headlights within the deep, sloped grille and a spare tyre that stowed horizontally at the back and also acted as a rear bumper.

The stressed skin alloy body (which was manufactured by Abbey Panels) meant that the car actually weighed very little, and the 77kW (104bhp) engine gave it an impressive top speed of 180km/h (112mph).

In early 1950, the first version of the Silverstone, the D series, was superseded by the E series, which possessed a slightly wider body, a larger cockpit and better luggage stowing capacity. The E series could be distinguished from the D by its front bumper and bonnet-top air intake.

Despite the car's relatively low production volume, the stunning-looking Silverstone in fact gained many competition successes throughout the 1950s, and it was finally replaced by the Nash-Healey in 1951. Today, examples of the Silverstone fetch high prices and, in what could be seen as an indication of its desirability among collectors, several fakes have been uncovered.

Engine: 2443cc (149 cu in), 4-cylinder
Power: 77kW (104bhp)
0–96km/h (60mph): 11 secs
Top speed: 180km/h (112mph)
Production total: 105

HEALEY G-TYPE

1951–54

Healey's own version of the Nash-Healey, which was aimed directly at the American market, was officially known as the 3-litre (183 cu in) Sports Convertible and more commonly referred to as the Alvis-Healey, or G-Type.

A more conservative and slightly austere styling policy meant that the Healey's front grille was smaller and neater than the Nash,

as were the front and rear bumpers, and there was less use of chrome throughout. Meanwhile, the walnut dash and leather upholstery appealed more to British buyers.

Using the Alvis TB21 engine meant that there was no need for bonnet bulges like those seen on the Nash. However, the wide and heavy body resulted in the G-Type feeling very underpowered, and

competition from the likes of Jaguar, with its cheaper, faster and much prettier XK120 ended any pretensions of success.

In total, only 25 examples were produced, making the Healey G-Type a particularly rare sight today. For this reason alone, it has become very desirable among those wanting the ultimate in 1950s British sports car exclusivity.

The Healey G-Type never really stood a chance against competition from the faster Jaguar XK120. It sported a neater grille than its close relation, the Nash-Healey.

Engine: 2993cc (183 cu in), 6-cylinder
Power: 79kW (106bhp)
0–96km/h (60mph): 11.4 secs
Top speed: 160km/h (99mph)
Production total: 25

HEINKEL

1956–65

Fondly known as the bubble car, Professor Ernst Heinkel's rounded three- and four-wheeler was launched a year after BMW's Isetta in order to satisfy the bubble-car boom of the mid-1950s. While both cars were very similar, Heinkel, an aircraft-manufacturing company based in Stuttgart, had developed a number of improvements over the BMW. Heinkel's car was lighter, had provision for at least four people and was arguably better looking.

Unitary construction was used, with hydraulic front brakes and a single door at the front, but without

the BMW's swing-away steering. As well as the conventional three-wheel configuration with a single wheel at the back and two at the front, a number of narrow track four-wheelers were also produced.

When German production finally ceased in 1958, the design was sold to Dundalk Engineering in the Irish Republic, and from 1961 Trojan also manufactured the car in England. Additionally, 2000 or so were subsequently built in Argentina. Many examples still survive today because of their excellent build quality.

Popular in its time, the Heinkel was exceptionally well engineered. Production took place in Germany, England, the Republic of Ireland and Argentina.

Engine: 197cc (12 cu in), 1-cylinder
Power: 7kW (9bhp)
0–96km/h (60mph): n/a
Top speed: 83km/h (52mph)
Production total: 29,000

HILLMAN 11HP

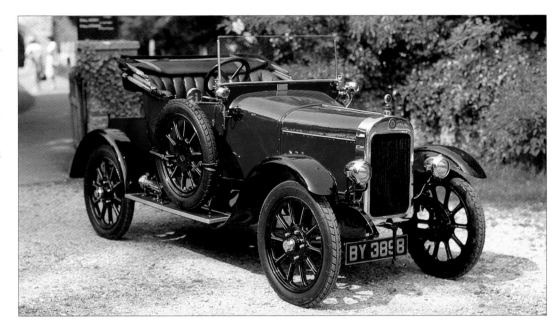

Cycle manufacturer William Hillman founded the Hillman Motor Car Company in 1907 and in his first year commissioned Louis Coatalen to design his first car for the Tourist Trophy race. After the 18kW (24bhp) four-cylinder Hillman was eliminated early in the race due to a crash, Coatalen left to join the Sunbeam company, and Hillman started making models that included a 9.7-litre (592 cu in) six-cylinder unit, a 6.4-litre (391 cu in) four and the 1357cc (83 cu in) monobloc (cast from a single block of metal) four-cylinder which grew to 1593cc (97 cu in) and 8kW (11bhp), before being reduced to 1496cc (91 cu in). This last version developed 13kW (18bhp), or 19kW (25bhp) in its more sporting guise.

A similar version of the car's side-valve engine was used in the speed model of 1921, which featured diecast light alloy pistons and a lighter crankshaft and flywheel. Using the company's three-speed gearbox, ratios were changed to enable the car to reach speeds in excess of 96km/h

(60mph). Production was dropped to make way for the growing demand for the 8kW (11bhp). These small Hillmans, made in Coventry, proved very successful, before finally being discontinued in 1925.

The Coventry-built Hillman 11hp, featuring traditional wooden 'wagon' wheels and an open two-seater body, proved very popular with the public. Production lasted until 1925.

Engine: 1593cc (97 cu in), 4-cylinder
Power: 8kW (11bhp)
0–96km/h (60mph): n/a
Top speed: n/a
Production total: n/a

HILLMAN 20 STRAIGHT EIGHT

Between 1926 and 1928, Hillman concentrated its production efforts on just one model – the roomy Fourteen, with its side-valve engine and four-speed gearbox. By 1929, and now owned by Rootes, the

company decided to introduce a larger model with an uncharacteristically big engine called the 20 Straight Eight which, as its name suggests, had a 2.6-litre (158 cu in) straight eight-cylinder engine.

Perhaps better known as the Vortic, this roomy four-door saloon was famed for its smoothness and impressive flexibility at low speeds. The Straight Eight was described in a contemporary *The Autocar* road

Sometimes known as the Vortic, the Hillman Straight Eight, with its 2.6-litre (158 cu in) straight-eight cylinder engine and four-speed gearbox, was known for being particularly smooth and flexible at low speeds, and it could carry four people in comfort.

test as being, 'An interesting car with a good engine and comprehensive equipment…and comparing most favourably in performance with transatlantic machines possessing much bigger engines.' It also reported on the car's good road-holding, suggesting that it exhibited virtually no body roll, thanks possibly to its having adjustable shock absorbers.

The car also featured vacuum servo-assisted brakes, bolt-on wire wheels and the traditional Hillman three-piece bonnet.

Engine: 2597cc (158 cu in), 8-cylinder
Power: 15kW (20bhp)
0–96km/h (60mph): n/a
Top speed: 112km/h (70mph)
Production total: n/a

HILLMAN MINX PHASE 1

1939–47

The Minx Phase I was was commonly used for military service, as its production coincided with the start of World War II, and it also features in many old war movies. At the time, its half-unitary construction was a novelty, and the car-buying public wanted it once the war had ended.

Interestingly, the Minx was one of the first British cars to utilize an 'alligator' bonnet, that is, one where the sides lifted at the same time as the grille.

As with all cars designed immediately prior to the conflict, the running gear was dated by the time the car actually went into production, with a side-valve engine, semi-elliptic springs and Bendix brakes. Only the floor gearchange felt modern.

As well as the four-door saloon with its front suicide doors, there was an elegant two-door coupé from 1946, as well as an estate car (based on the Commer van) and a convertible version.

The Phase II that replaced it had integral headlights and hydraulic brakes, and went back to a column change. It remained as austere-looking as its predecessor.

The half-unitary construction of the Phase 1 was quite revolutionary at its launch in 1939 – a number of these vehicles were built for military service.

Engine: 1185cc (72 cu in), 4-cylinder
Power: 26kW (35bhp)
0–96km/h (60mph): n/a
Top speed: 104km/h (65mph)
Production total: n/a

HILLMAN MINX SERIES I

1956–57

The thoroughly modern Series I Minx lasted only a year before it was superseded by the better looking Series II in 1957, with its shallower grille and cleaner lines. Production of its final incarnation, the Series IIIC, ended in 1963.

seats, as opposed to the usual bench seat, while the De Luxe version had column change and bench seats as standard.

An estate version was launched in 1957, just prior to the arrival of the Series II, which can be distinguished by its shallower grille. The Series III from 1958–59 had a 1494cc (91 cu in) engine, while the Series IIIA had fins added, another grille, better brakes and the option of automatic transmission. The Series IIIB of 1960 received a Hypoid rear axle, and the Series IIIC received a more powerful 1592cc (97 cu in), 42kW (57bhp) engine.

Launched in 1956, the all-new Hillman Minx was really only a four-door version of the Sunbeam Rapier, which had been announced the previous year.

The Series I was bigger than the previous Minx, with lots more space inside, and it was heavier, too. However, it did gain an extra 7kW (9bhp), which meant that the

car could still achieve a top speed of 128km/h (80mph).

There were several trim options, including the Special, which had floor gearchange and separate front

Engine: 1390cc (85 cu in), 4-cylinder
Power: 38kW (51bhp)
0–96km/h (60mph): 27.7 secs
Top speed: 128km/h (80mph)
Production total: 500,000

HILLMAN SUPER MINX

Heralding the start of an exciting new decade, the Super Minx burst into the scene with hooded headlights, chiselled tail fins and American-influenced wraparound front and rear screens. Underneath, however, all the previous Minx running gear was used, with the addition of a central gear lever, optional Smiths Easidrive automatic transmission and a 5in (12cm) longer wheelbase. As well as the two-door saloon, there was an estate version, along with a very attractive drop-top, although this only ran from 1962 to 1964.

The Series II from 1962 had front discs, the option of a Borg Warner automatic gearbox and individual, rather than bench, front seats. The Series III from 1964 had larger front and rear windscreens, a sharper roofline and veneer-effect fascia. The Series IV from 1965 had the new 1725cc (105 cu in) powerplant and optional overdrive.

The Series IIIA proved to be the most popular model of all, with its combination of classic looks and performance. Good convertible

IIIA's are rare and very sought-after today, and the saloon itself, with its quirky pillarless windows, is quickly becoming a desirable classic among collectors.

Engine: 1592cc (97 cu in), 4-cylinder
Power: 58kW (78bhp)
0–96km/h (60mph): 22.5 secs
Top speed: 128km/h (80mph)
Production total: 135,000

American influences are obvious on Super Minx, with its whitewall tyres, hooded headlights, tail fins and wraparound screens. Series III had more glass, a sharper roofline and wood-finish veneer fascia.

HILLMAN IMP

Despite its design originating in the mid-1950s to counter rivals such as Ford's 105E and the Mini, problems over planning permission for a new factory meant that production of the Imp at Linwood, near Glasgow, Scotland, did not begin until 1963.

Built hurriedly by mostly local ex-shipbuilders, early Imps were plagued with reliability problems which lost it ground against the competition – a shame because in many ways the Imp was a very accomplished little car. Following

the European carmaker's trend of positioning the engine in the rear, the Imp's alloy Coventry Climax engine weighed very little and was surprisingly lively. The Imp was also technically advanced, with independent suspension all-round

The Imp, with its many technical innovations, should have become more than a match for the Mini. It had a rear-engine format, fully independent suspension, hinged rear window and fold-down rear seats but, sadly, it never really caught on with the British car-buying public.

and a clever hinging rear window giving access to folding rear seats to simulate a hatchback.

The Super Imp from 1965 gained a few luxuries, while the trendy Californian from 1967 had a coupé roofline and no hatch. Particularly sought-after are the other two coupé options, the Chamois (1967–70) and the Sunbeam Stiletto (1967–72), which boasted the fast 38kW (51bhp) sports engine, a tauter suspension, servo-assisted brakes and spectacular quad headlights.

Engine: 875cc (53 cu in), 4-cylinder
Power: 28kW (37bhp)
0–96km/h (60mph): 25.4 secs
Top speed: 130km/h (81mph)
Production total: 440,032

HILLMAN MINX/HUNTER

1966–67

Engine: 1496cc (91 cu in), 4-cylinder
Power: 45kW (60bhp)
0–96km/h (60mph): 17.8 secs
Top speed: 138km/h (86mph)
Production total: 470,000

Despite input from British styling guru William Towns, the Hillman Minx was worthy but devastatingly dull in all respects. Later versions were renamed Hunter, and an estate version accompanied the four-door saloon.

It is difficult to imagine looking at the slab-sided Hunter today that, back at its launch in 1966, this vehicle represented a revolution in car design – even Aston Martin seat designer William Towns became involved in the styling.

It was the first born of a new family of 'Arrow'-designated cars, and was to be joined by a Singer Vogue version and estate cars Minx and Singer Gazelle. An obvious take on Ford's Cortina, it cost less to produce and was lighter than any previous Hillman.

However, MacPherson strut suspension, front discs, overdrive and even the option of automatic transmission did nothing to add appeal to what was fundamentally a very dull car. The standard powerplant of this four-door saloon, and its estate variant was the reasonably proficient 45kW (61bhp) 1725cc (105 cu in) Rootes engine; however, from early 1967, there was also the option of a 1496cc (91 cu in) engine.

The Mk II of 1967 received a mild cosmetic makeover, while much-needed servo-assisted brake became standard on the Hunter from 1968. The Minx name eventually died in 1970, when it became known as the Hillman Hunter. Of these, the 1972 GLS with 69kW (93bhp) and sporty chrome-finished Rostyle wheels was one of the most successful variants.

HILLMAN AVENGER

1970–81

The Avenger was another worthy but dull offering from Hillman, which, by this time, had fallen under Chrysler ownership. An entirely new range of engines matched with MacPherson struts at the front and beam axle at the rear did not do much to improve matters.

In an attempt to woo buyers, a number of sporty options was made available, including the GT which had twin-carburettors, front discs, more elaborate instrumentation and a stiffened suspension set-up to aid handling.

In 1972, the GLS was launched; it borrowed the GT's engine and gained Rostyle wheels, servo-assisted brakes and fashionable vinyl roof. The two-door version of the GT also gained a part-vinyl roof to add appeal.

In 1973, with tighter emissions testing restricting engine performance, the 1250 and 1500 engines were upped to 1300 and 1600 respectively.

The car was badged as a Chrysler from 1976 and Talbot from 1979

following a buy-out by Peugeot that year. It was also known by various other names around the globe, being marketed as a Dodge and a Plymouth in some countries.

Engine: 1248cc (76 cu in), 4-cylinder
Power: 39kW (53bhp)
0–96km/h (60mph): 19.8 secs
Top speed: 134km/h (84mph)
Production total: 826,353

The technically inspiring but very dreary-looking Avenger did nothing to stir the emotions, and it was marketed under various names in different countries.

HINO CONTESSA

The sharp-looking Hino Contessa was made in Japan, but followed the European trend of positioning the engine in the rear. This is the Contessa I, which lasted until 1964.

Engine: 893cc (54 cu in), 4-cylinder
Power: 26kW (35bhp)
0–96km/h (60mph): n/a
Top speed: 115km/h (72mph)
Production total: n/a

Hino could have been a household name like Nissan, Honda and Toyota, but its carmaking operation was bought by Toyota in 1966 and killed off completely just four years later.

Having been involved initially in assembling Renault 4CVs, the company began making the Contessa from 1961, basing much of its mechanicals on the little French car with which its engineers had become so familiar.

The styling of the four-door saloon, with its boxy looks and small glass area, appeared to have almost Eastern European utilitarian influences; in fact, it is actually a nice design. Better still was the design for the Michelotti-styled

two-door coupé version, which was introduced in 1962; however, the coupé was unfortunately shelved very soon after production of it had begun.

The same Italian styling house was responsible for a redesign of the Contessa range in 1964, when the engine capacity was increased to 1251cc (76 cu in).

Very few cars were ever made and even fewer examples exist today outside of Japan.

HISPANO-SUIZA TYPE 15T

Few people would consider the Spanish to be prolific carmakers; however, Swiss engineer Marc Birkigt, who had gone to Spain to work for an engineering company, was experienced in European road conditions, and he set about adapting a successful racing design for road use.

The resulting car pioneered the 'big flexible four' sports car

cylinder type well before the likes of Vauxhall and Bentley, and it is seen today as one of the very first 'production' sports cars. The frail-looking Hispano-Suiza Type 15T also featured other innovative items, including a three-speed gearbox that was in unit with the engine, propeller shaft final drive instead of chain drive, and the use of semi-elliptic suspension.

The Type 15T was given the nickname 'Alfonso', as motoring enthusiast King Alfonso XIII was one of the first to experience the 15T's high top gear flexibility and precise steering.

Several body styles were available, the most popular being a short, open two-seater with large-diameter centre-lock wire wheels. In late 1911, Hispano-Suiza moved

its production from Barcelona in Spain to Paris, France, where production of the T15 was to continue until the outbreak of World War I.

Engine: 3620cc (221 cu in), 4-cylinder
Power: 45kW (60bhp)
0–96km/h (60mph): n/a
Top speed: 128km/h (80mph)
Production total: n/a

HISPANO-SUIZA H6

The Hispano-Suiza H6 featured Swiss engineer Marc Birkigt's innovative mechanically operated four-wheel servo-assisted braking system later copied by Rolls-Royce.

Having seen the company switch to manufacture of aero engines during World War I, the motoring public waited for the first of Marc Birkigt's postwar Hispano-Suiza cars. The H6, as it was known, did not disappoint when it was revealed at the 1919 Paris Show, being one of the most technically advanced cars of its time.

Birkigt himself designed the mechanically operated servo-assisted four-wheel braking system – technology that was later copied by Rolls-Royce for its own vehicles. Elsewhere, the H6 represented the pinnacle of

technical endeavour, with beautifully finished engine componentry, a superb pressed steel chassis and virtually peerless coachwork. Indeed, such was the quality of build throughout that only the privileged few could afford the sporting four-seater's high asking

price. Made at its factory in Paris under what was effectively a 'one model' policy, the H6 was developed through experience both on and off the racetrack.

In 1924, Birkigt launched the H6C Sport and Boulogne models with engine capacity enlarged to

almost 8 litres (488 cu in), and both models later went on to enjoy various competition successes.

Engine: 6597cc (403 cu in), 6-cylinder
Power: 101kW (135bhp)
0–96km/h (60mph): n/a
Top speed: 139km/h (87mph)
Production total: n/a

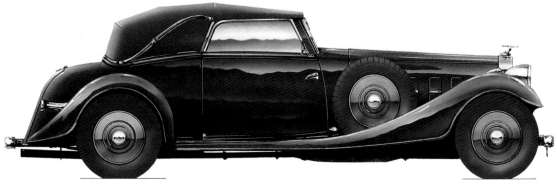

HISPANO-SUIZA J12

The massive 9424cc (575 cu in) V12 powerplant at the heart of the J12 was really a refined Birkigt wartime aero engine, but that makes it no less impressive. Indeed, it made the J2 one of the most powerful and most technically advanced saloons of its time, easily capable of cruising at 161km/h (100mph). It also made it into one of the most expensive and opulent French cars ever made, a 'white elephant' that even rivals the Bugatti Royale in terms of prestige and sheer inefficiency.

Despite the Hispano-Suiza J12's size and the availability of a 4.01m (13.3ft) wheelbase, the size of the engine and gearbox meant that there was little room for more than two people in the car, and the three-speed gearbox was insufficient for driving over hilly terrain where frequent gearchanges were necessary.

A number of European coachbuilders adopted the car and so a variety of body styles exist, the most elegant of which must be the sweeping lines of the Saoutchick two-seater touring. The company later developed the Type 68-Bis, which had a 11.3-litre (690 cu in) V12 engine producing more than 186kW (250bhp).

Engine: 9424cc (575 cu in), 12-cylinder
Power: 142kW (190bhp)
0–96km/h (60mph): n/a
Top speed: 161km/h (100mph)
Production total: n/a

HONDA S800

Engine: 791cc (48 cu in), 4-cylinder
Power: 52kW (70bhp)
0–96km/h (60mph): 13.4 secs
Top speed: 152km/h (95mph)
Production total: 11,400

Motorcycle technology was the basis of much of the workings behind Honda's first attempt at car production, which began with the S500 in 1963, with chain final drive to the rear wheels and peak power at a screaming 8000rpm. Elsewhere, the diminutive Japanese sports car – it was just 3m (10ft) long – featured a separate chassis, which was dated even for the time, disc brakes at the front and independent suspension.

Later in its production, the car was fitted with conventional drive to the rear wheels and a live rear axle located by trailing arms and a Panhard rod.

The car represented good value at the time, undercutting the price of the Mini Cooper, and was commended for its precise gearchange and impressive economy. Considering its tiny engine, the S800 produced 52kW (70bhp) and had good acceleration with firm suspension and confident handling.

Body styles included a neatlooking convertible with a flat folding fabric roof and a coupé

The S800's engine employed twin overhead camshafts, twin exhausts for each cylinder pair and four sidedraught Kei-Hin carbs. Most of the engine's power kicked in at 8000rpm, but it is capable of reaching a staggering 11,000rpm.

version with an opening rear hatch adding to practicality. There is a strong, dedicated following of the car today, especially in Japan.

HONDA N600

The Honda N600 originated from the N360, which was top of the company's 'K' class of microcars at its launch in 1966 with its innovative front-mounted 345cc (21 cu in) air-cooled twin-cylinder engine.

Like its sister car, the N600 was seen as technically radical at the time, with its wonderfully free-revving all-alloy 599cc (37 cu in) engine. However, it never really succeeded against European competition from the likes of the Mini or Volkswagen's Beetle.

Handling was surprisingly good with a firm ride and assured steering, and engines could rev to almost 10,000rpm, giving drivers fabulous flexibility on the road. The price of such a wide rev range was that it soon became very 'buzzy' while trying to keep up with other traffic and was therefore unsuitable for journeys beyond the usual city limits where it was undoubtedly best suited. Again, like its sister, the N600 featured an air-cooled twin-cylinder engine which was front-mounted and drove the front wheels.

Only a saloon version of the

N600 was made, and very few examples of these exist today outside Japan or specialist Japanese car collections.

Based on the N360 of 1966, the N600 was a spectacularly interesting miniature four-seater. It exhibited fine handling and a reasonable level of performance from its buzzy twin-cylinder engine, albeit with little in the way of refinement.

Engine: 599cc (37 cu in), 2-cylinder
Power: 31kW (42bhp)
0–96km/h (60mph): 29.3 secs
Top speed: 136km/h (85mph)
Production total: n/a

HONDA Z600

Honda's cute-looking Z600 was known as the Z Coupé in Japan and featured lots of interesting gizmos at its launch in 1970.

Moreover, all were a bright shade of orange, and some even sported optional 'go-faster' black stripes along the sides.

For the Japanese market only, there was the Hard Top model (from 1972) which had stylish pillarless doors, but most other markets throughout the world only had the four-seater two-door coupé model. Despite being officially described as a four-seater, back-seat passengers would have been rather cramped.

The car was famous among those who were interested in economy for holding *Motor* magazine's fuel consumption record.

This quirky-looking micro-coupé started out in Japan as the 345cc (21 cu in) engined Z Coupé, but European markets only received the

bigger-engined Z600 with a detuned N600 engine fitted.

A number of idiosyncratic features set the Z600 apart from

other cars on the road at the time, including aircraft-style overhead consoles and an unheard-of high level of trim for a car of this type.

Engine: 599cc (37 cu in), 2-cylinder
Power: 24kW (32bhp)
0–96km/h (60mph): 32.6 secs
Top speed: 120km/h (75mph)
Production total: n/a

HORCH TYPE 853

1936–39

Prestige vehicle manufacturer August Horch became a pioneer of Germany's motor industry, first working for Benz before selling his own cars from as early as 1900. However, it was not until the 1920s that he gained his reputation as a quality carmaker before having an argument with fellow directors and leaving to found the Audi marque in 1932.

In 1923, Paul Daimler was employed, and his first designs were the straight-eight twin camshaft engines of 1926 which were developed throughout the 1930s, later having just a single camshaft which formed the basis of the 853.

In reality, the car was really only a second-division Mercedes and was sold in large numbers to the Nazi hierarchy for use as staff cars. Some had rigid axles, others had independent front suspension, while later 950 and 951 models had De Dion rear suspension fitted.

Both the V8 and straight-eight models continued to the outbreak

of World War II, but production could not continue after 1945 because the factory had fallen into Russian hands and was now part of what was then East Germany.

German manufacturers Horch made supremely elegant and highly luxurious cars during the 1930s, including the 853. The exotic roadster was particularly desirable.

Engine: 4946cc (302 cu in), 8-cylinder
Power: 75kW (100bhp)
0–96km/h (60mph): n/a
Top speed: 160km/h (100mph)
Production total: n/a

HOTCHKISS 2050

1950–54

French luxury carmaker Hotchkiss made its name before World War II, but by the 1950s it was almost bankrupt due to dwindling markets and lack of new product development.

The straight-six cylinder powerplant for the elegant 2050 was effectively a prewar design, used initially in the 686 (from 1946) and later as the 686 S49. The

car, with coil-sprung independent front suspension and twin Zenith carburettors, was renamed the 2050 in 1950, or the 1350 if a four-cylinder engine was fitted instead.

There were four body styles to choose from: the Anjou four-door saloon, the limousine, the Chapron bodied Antheor convertible and a magnificent two-door 97kW (130bhp) Grand Sport. The latter is much sought-after today and commands the highest prices. The later facelifted model featured a 'V' screen and recessed headlights.

The Hotchkiss company then went on to waste a lot of money on developing a flat-four part aluminium-chassied car called the Grégoire (of which just 180 were made) before merging with Delahaye and venturing into the manufacture of trucks.

Despite being built just north of Paris, the elegant six-cylinder Grand Tourer made by Hotchkiss after the war actually resembled limited-production quality British cars in character.

Engine: 3485cc (213 cu in), 6-cylinder
Power: 75kW (100bhp)
0–96km/h (60mph): n/a
Top speed: 141km/h (88mph)
Production total: n/a

HRG 1.5-LITRE

The HRG company was named after its three founders, E.A. Halford, G.H. Robins and H.R. Godfrey, and it produced cars that, although crude mechanically, were well liked by enthusiasts and successful in competition.

The 1.5 two-seater sports cars were produced at the Tolworth works in Surrey, England, and they were very purposeful in their design with little in the way of styling, with running boards and cutaway doors. The upright chromed radiator was set back in true classic style, revealing the

With its cycle wings, cutaway doors and exposed driving position, the HRG offered little in the way of creature comforts. However, it was well liked by enthusiasts because of its flexibility, performance and nimble handling.

tubular front axle, reversed quarter-elliptical front springs and huge cable-operated drum brakes. At the rear, suspension was by semi-elliptic leaves sliding in trunnions.

A Meadows four-cylinder engine was fitted to the HRG 1.5-Litre, usually equipped with twin SU carburettors and a Scintilla magneto. The gearbox was a Moss unit that did not have the luxury of synchromesh.

Best of all the car's attributes was its flexibility, and it soon proved a popular choice among club racers for its terrific driving ability, whether it be on fast roads, hillclimbs, trials or rallying.

Engine: 1497cc (91 cu in), 4-cylinder
Power: 43kW (58bhp)
0–96km/h (60mph): 18.4 secs
Top speed: 145km/h (90mph)
Production total: 26

HRG 1500

Although the HRG 1500 looked fundamentally the same as the 1.5, a switch was made under the bonnet from the ageing Meadows engine to a more refined three-bearing Singer unit with synchromesh gearbox. A smaller 1.1-litre (67 cu in) version shared the same body style, but had a slightly shorter wheelbase.

Like many cars of this era, specification and levels of tune were determined by the owner, so no two cars ever left the factory the same. The last dozen or so 1500s were given the suffix WS and were fitted with Singer SM engines.

After World War II, the company experimented with a modern, low-drag closed body design called the Aerodynamic, with a full-width body supported by outriggers and driven by a 48kW (65bhp). The car was far from successful, however, and only 35 were made between 1946 and 1947.

The company moved away from making motor vehicles after 1956 and became involved in general engineering works. Today, HRG is

a very desirable marque that is particularly liked by purists, and virtually any example will command a high asking price.

Looking little different to the prewar car, the HRG 1.5-Litre, and sharing its incredible versatility, the HRG 1500 was more refined and a fair bit quicker than its predecessor – a factor which made it an instant success when it came to competition.

Engine: 1496cc (91 cu in), 4-cylinder
Power: 45kW (61bhp)
0–96km/h (60mph): n/a
Top speed: 152km/h (95mph)
Production total: 173

HRG Twin Camshaft

1955–56

Tired of being renowned for making 'yesterday's car today', HRG broke away from tradition and embarked on the development of a brand new sports car, the Twin Camshaft. This had a modern-looking lightweight alloy racing body, bolted to a twin-tube chassis and featured independent suspension all-round, four-wheel disc brakes and novel magnesium alloy wheels.

As its name suggests, power for the car came from a modified 1497cc (91 cu in) HRG twin-camshaft engine on a Singer SM block. Being so light, the little open-top racer was very fast from a standstill and was easily capable of reaching 184km/h (115mph).

Despite the company pinning their hopes for future success on the new car, demand for the HRG Twin Camshaft was low, and it was generally ignored by existing HRG enthusiasts. It was no surprise then that only four examples ever left the Surrey factory before the company finally gave up making cars altogether.

Consequently, the fiery little two-seater is very rare indeed today and highly sought-after by classic car enthusiasts.

Engine: 1497cc (91 cu in), 4-cylinder
Power: 80kW (108bhp)
0–96km/h (60mph): n/a
Top speed: 184km/h (115mph)
Production total: 4

Hudson Eight

1935–39

Detroit department store magnate Joseph J. Hudson, founder of the Hudson company, first offered cars for sale in 1909, in the shape of the underpowered 15kW (20bhp) Model 20. This had a 2534cc (154 cu in) engine, and the car became an immediate bestseller.

Hudson himself died in 1912, but the company lived on, the same year launching its first six-cylinder car, the Model 6-54, which produced 40kW (54bhp) and was available in a number of different body styles. By 1914, the Hudson company was proclaiming itself to be the world's largest manufacturer of six-cylinder cars.

In 1916, the four-cylinder engines were dropped altogether, and Hudson adopted a one-model policy with the 4739cc (289 cu in) Super Six, which remained almost unchanged until the 1930s when it was superseded by the straight-eight engined cars.

Stylewise, the car could be easily identified by its exaggerated 'waterfall' chrome grille. Also peculiar to the car was the 'Electric Hand' electric gear shift, which became optional in 1935, and the 'safety engineered chassis' with hydraulic brakes and a secondary mechanical system for emergencies which was introduced in 1936.

Prior to World War II, Hudson was one of America's most important motor manufacturers – its cars from the mid- to late 1930s being distinguishable by their ornate 'waterfall' chrome grilles.

Engine: 4162cc (254 cu in), 8-cylinder
Power: 84kW (113bhp)
0–96km/h (60mph): n/a
Top speed: 128km/h (80mph)
Production total: n/a

HUDSON HORNET

Engine: 5047cc (308 cu in), 6-cylinder
Power: 119kW (160bhp)
0–96km/h (60mph): 12 secs
Top speed: 177km/h (110mph)
Production total: n/a

Emerging from World War II, Hudson developed an all-new unitary construction process for their cars called the 'Step Down', as you literally stepped down over the structural body sills into the car. The Hornet emerged from this range in 1951, and it featured smooth flanks, bright new fabrics and one-piece windscreen.

Power for the Hornet came from the company's old 5047cc (308 cu in) L-head six-cylinder engine, and the car became famous for being almost invincible when it came to stock car racing.

While everyone else was using V8 power, Hudson steadfastly refused to shift from its traditional six-cylinder arrangement, although there was the choice in 1954 of a Twin-H power option with a 'hot' camshaft and an alloy head and increased compression ratio that

pushed the car's power up to 127kW (170bhp).

In fact, Hudson sales had peaked in 1950 and, lacking funds to re-tool, a compact model, the Jet, was abandoned in 1953 before Hudson was forced to merge with Nash to form American Motors in 1954. The Hudson name disappeared completely in 1957.

The conventionally booted two-door Hornet (as pictured here) had a less sloping back than the four-door. Fins were added to the rear wings after 1954.

HUMBER 16/50

Thomas Humber, one of the oldest motor manufacturers in Britain, had been in business since 1898, with factories at both Coventry and Beeston in Warwickshire until 1908. During the 1920s, the company successfully established a reputation for producing good quality, no-nonsense cars. In 1926, it expanded into the commercial vehicle market by taking over the Luton-based Commer Cars.

In 1928, garage owner, motor trade distributor and businessman Billy Rootes planned to merge Humber with the Hillman company to create a more efficient operation at the factory in Humber Road, Coventry. By the time the shareholders had agreed the merger, the 1930 models were already on sale – including the stately 16/50. The 16/50, termed the 'medium' six, officially superseded the 14/40 and was available in what was described as a 'dual purpose' body style with lever wind-down sidescreens.

Production of the car with its inlet over exhaust engine lasted

just two years before further investment by Rootes resulted in the all-new 1.7-litre (104 cu in) 9kW (12bhp) model and the side-valve–engined 16/60.

The 16/50 sported a number of modern features. Its traditional looks, high-quality fittings and finish, and competitive pricing was aimed firmly at the middle classes.

Engine: 2110cc (128 cu in), 6-cylinder
Power: 37kW (50bhp)
0–96km/h (60mph): n/a
Top speed: n/a
Production total: 8183

HUMBER SUPER SNIPE I

Badge engineering is nothing new, and, in fact, the postwar Humber Super Snipe I was nothing more than a prewar 1938-style Snipe which itself was simply a luxury version of the prewar Hillman 14.

Visually, the Super Snipe had an upright stance, with a chrome grille, individual chromed front headlights, a long bonnet, flat screen and 'suicide' forward-opening front doors.

All of the postwar Humber models, however, featured hydraulic brakes as opposed to cable-operated technology, modern independent front suspension, luggage compartments that

extended beyond the rear body line and the additional luxury of a sliding metal sunroof.

Despite its impressive engine size of just over four litres (249 cu in) and six cylinders, the Humber Super Snipe was never very fast due mainly to its excessive body weight. Indeed, top speed was a mere 130km/h (81mph).

There was also a Pullman version with a 30cm (12in) longer wheelbase than the Super Snipe. Only around 500 of these limousines were made throughout the production years of 1945 to 1948.

The luxurious Super Snipe was Humber's first postwar offering. Despite offering 75kW (100bhp), the car's heavy body resulted in an unimpressive performance.

Engine: 4086cc (249 cu in), 6-cylinder
Power: 75kW (100bhp)
0–96km/h (60mph): 24.5 secs
Top speed: 130km/h (81mph)
Production total: 3909

HUMBER IMPERIAL II

Taking a number of styling cues from the company's prewar designs, the big new Humbers of the late 1940s and early 1950s married old-fashioned 'alligator' style bonnets, pillbox windscreens and narrow running boards with modern features such as a full-width body and integral headlights.

Mechanically, too, this car was dated, with column gearchange and

a side-valve engine. The only concessions to modernity came in the form of 'Evenkeel' transverse-leaf independent front suspension.

The Imperial was based on the Pullman limousine version which rested on a massive 330cm (131in) wheelbase, and was identical apart from the lack of division in the passenger compartment. Production continued until 1954, by which

time it had gained a more modern overhead-valve engine, improved ride and more effective braking.

The model shared much of its running gear with its earlier cousins, the Super Snipe II and III, which ran from 1948 to 1952. Imperial models included a Touring limousine and, from 1949, an elegant but heavy-looking Tickford two-door convertible.

The stately Humber Imperial lived up to its name with its impressive 330cm (131in) wheelbase, and remained in production, with improvements, until 1954.

Engine: 4138cc (252 cu in), 6-cylinder
Power: 84kW (113bhp)
0–96km/h (60mph): 26.2 secs
Top speed: 131km/h (82mph)
Production total: 4140

HUMBER HAWK III

1948–50

Gone were the traditional running boards, and in came modern full-width bodywork on the Humber Hawk. Underneath that exterior, however, it was woefully archaic with its side-valve engine and column gearchange.

Refreshingly, however, the car did feature a new coil-spring independent suspension instead of the old transverse-leaf type, which helped to provide an altogether much more refined ride to suit the car's modern looks.

The Hawk was priced at £799 when new, and it became a steady seller throughout its evolution, which spanned the next nine years. Its immediate successor, the Hawk Mk IV was launched in 1950 and had a much-needed 2267cc (138 cu in) engine, higher gearing and wider tyres.

aymond Loewy, the man who was sponsible for the design of the ll-new Hawk, was almost certainly nfluenced by manufacturers from e United States, creating obvious S styling in the form of flush-ounted headlights in the front wings, a deep screen and a bulbous front nose.

However, apart from the new, shorter chassis – which meant less bulk, weighing 1250kg (2758lb) – the Humber Hawk remained quaintly antiquated underneath, with old-fashioned channel section side members and the same old side-valve four-cylinder engine under the bonnet that had originated in the early 1930s. The Hawk also retained the archaic column gearchange.

Engine: 1944cc (119 cu in), 4-cylinder
Power: 42kW (56bhp)
0–96km/h (60mph): 30.7 secs
Top speed: 110 km/h (69mph)
Production total: 10,040

HUMBER SUPER SNIPE/IMPERIAL

1958–67

he new generation Super Snipe as really nothing more than an pmarket monocoque Hawk aunched 18 months earlier), but ith a 2.6-litre (162 cu in) six-ylinder engine, which itself was developed in collaboration with Armstrong Siddeley and featured spherical combustion chambers, opposed valves and modern cross-flow breathing. All that was different, visually, between the Super Snipe and the Hawk was a bonnet mascot, fluted chrome grilles surrounding the sidelights and the availability of US-inspired two-tone colour schemes. A three-speed came as standard, with optional overdrive, automatic transmission and power steering.

The Series II in 1959 gained a 3-litre (183 cu in) engine and front discs, while the Series III from 1960 had twin headlights arranged horizontally in each front wing. In 1963, the Series IV pushed power up to 99kW (133bhp) and gained more chrome, while the 1964 SV had the Hawk's sharper roofline, twin carburettors and power-assisted steering. The Imperial model was simply an SV with a black roof and automatic transmission fitted as standard.

The six-cylinder Humber Super Snipe borrowed the Hawk's bodyshell, but with the added glitz of a bonnet mascot, a full-width chrome grille that incorporated the side lights and the option of special duotone paintwork.

Engine: 2651cc (162 cu in), 6-cylinder
Power: 83kW (112bhp)
0–96km/h (60mph): 19 secs
Top speed: 144km/h (90mph)
Production total: 30,031

HUMBER SCEPTRE I/II

1963–67

Humber was being slowly swallowed into the Rootes' empire, and the Super Snipe was the last model specifically designed as a Humber. In fact, the Humber Sceptre was really just a restyled Hillman Super Minx or Singer Vogue with a slightly modified roofline and wraparound front screen. No surprise either that there is a similarity between the front end styling of the Sceptre with its quad headlights, chrome grille and rounded chrome trim around the sidelights with that of the Sunbeam Rapier, as it had actually been developed as a Rapier until a late stage in production. It even had the Rapier's 60kW (80bhp) twin carburettor engine at the outset.

New, however, was a modern dashboard and servo front disc brakes, self-cancelling dual overdrive and a quality interior which made it one of the most upmarket cars of the Super Minx family at that time.

The Mk II from 1965 was fitted with the Rootes Group five-bearing crankshaft 1725cc (105 cu in) engine, with automatic transmission as an option. It, too, borrowed from the Hillman Super Minx by copying its frontal styling

Engine: 1592cc (97 cu in), 4-cylinder
Power: 60kW (80bhp)
0–96km/h (60mph): 17.1 secs
Top speed: 141km/h (88mph)
Production total: 28,996

HUMBER SCEPTRE

1967–76

In the period prior to launch, the newly formed Rootes-Chrysler group decided to make a clean sweep of its range, dropping its two old families of 'medium' cars and the 'big' Hawk/Super Snipe/Imperial models and replacing them with the smooth but slightly anonymous Arrow cars.

With it came the new Sceptre in 1967, with its MacPherson strut suspension, twin carburettors, 1725cc (105 cu in) engine, Sunbeam Rapier driveline, four-headlight nose and modern-looking wheel trims.

Inside, plush new reclinable front seats were augmented by an impressive wooden fascia, while the luxury models in the range had a black vinyl roof and twin reversing headlamps.

The car proved popular with businessmen in particular. Overdrive was standard on all cars, with automatic transmission being offered as an optional extra. The last Sceptre was made in 1976 and with it, the Humber name was finally allowed to die.

Engine: 1725cc (105 cu in), 4-cylinder
Power: 61kW (82bhp)
0–96km/h (60mph): 13.1 secs
Top speed: 161km/h (100mph)
Production total: 43,951

The last model designed specifically as a Humber, the Sceptre gained wraparound side grilles and four headlamps. It was available with a 1592cc (97 cu in) engine initially, then a 1725cc (105 cu in) unit after 1965.

HUPMOBILE CENTURY

1929–32

The Hupmobile company was formed by Bobby Hupp and E.A. Nelson in 1908, and their first car, a 2.8-litre (171 cu in) Detroit-built runabout with two-speed transmission, was an instance success.

This car continued in production until 1925, when it was joined by America's first budget-priced straight-eight cylinder car. A year later that was replaced by a 3.2-litre (195 cu in) six-cylinder side-valve unit with three forward gears. In 1929, Hupmobile bought out another manufacturer, Chandler, and began to build its low-priced models in Chandler's Cleveland factory as well as in its factory at Detroit.

The Century was an elegant car with upright grille, wooden spoken wheels, large inset headlights and four doors, and it could easily seat five passengers in comfort. Known as the 'top gear' car, it could easily accelerate in top gear from walking pace, and the car was renowned for its silent, smooth running.

Hupmobile's last automotive venture was a rear-wheel drive version of the Cord 810/812. This did absolutely nothing to revive its fortunes, which had been been waning because of slow sales. The company finally decided to end car production altogether and moved instead into car spare parts, electronics and kitchen products.

Engine: 3505cc (214 cu in), 6-cylinder
Power: 19kW (25bhp)
0–96km/h (60mph): 37 secs
Top speed: 107km/h (67mph)
Production total: 47,253

INNOCENTI SPIDER

1960–66

Ghia's Tom Tjaarda was responsible for the styling of Innocenti's pretty Spider with its wide grille and uncluttered lines. Production ceased in 1966 with the introduction of the Coupé, which used the same running gear.

When Innocenti, maker of the famous Lambretta scooter, ventured into motor car manufacture in 1960, making Austin A40s under licence in Milan, it seemed only natural that it would eventually want to make a sports car. The result was the diminutive Spider, a rebodied Austin-Healey Sprite with bodywork designed by Tom Tjaarda, an employee of the Ghia styling house in Turin.

From late 1961, a removable hardtop was offered and, in 1963, the Spider was fitted with the larger Austin 1098cc (67 cu in) engine, producing 43kW (58bhp) at 5500rpm, along with front disc brakes as standard.

The Spider went out of production in 1966 when it was replaced by the new C (or Coupé) model, which was manufactured by Ghia's neighbour OSI. Production of this car, which used the same running gear as the Spider, was to last until 1968.

Today, the Spider can still be seen on the roads of Italy, but in ever decreasing numbers. However, it undoubtedly made an interesting variation on the popular MG Midget/Sprite theme.

Engine: 948cc (58 cu in), 4-cylinder
Power: 32kW (43bhp)
0–96km/h (60mph): 12 secs
Top speed: 136km/h (85mph)
Production total: 6857

INNOCENTI MINI

1965–76

Production of the Milan-built Mini began in late 1965 when Innocenti gained the licence to build the 850.

The big difference between the Italian and British models was the upmarket specification which included opening rear quarterlights, lever pull doorhandles and more exciting trim.

On the outside of the car, the Innocenti models received a unique grille which incorporated the Innocenti logo and slightly different rear lights.

The Cooper version of the Mini arrived in 1966, and the Mk II Mini from 1968 had a high-compression engine.

The Mk II Cooper was faster than Longbridge's version, and it also gained a full-width fascia with five dials instead of the British version's three. The Mk III was launched in 1970 with winding windows, and there was a 1300cc (79 cu in) version which was available from 1972.

The Export 1300 was perhaps one of the most exhilarating of them all, and it was made between 1973 and 1976, the later models gaining extra instrumentation. This was against a backdrop of rationalization at British Leyland that saw the demise of the British-built Cooper in 1971 although, as a marque, the Mini was to be voted 'Car of the Century'.

Engine: 1275cc (78 cu in), 4-cylinder
Power: 57kW (76bhp)
0–96km/h (60mph): 10.9 secs
Top speed: 152km/h (95mph)
Production total: 450,000

INNOCENTI MINI 90/120

1974–82

Way ahead of its time in many ways with its opening rear hatch and folding rear seats setting the trend for later hatchback styling, the Innocenti Mini 90/120 was an interesting proposition. The 90 had the 998cc (61 cu in) engine and the 120 the 1275cc (78 cu in) unit – a detuned version of the engine used in the Mini Cooper.

Its development was partly financed by British Leyland, using a traditional Mini floorpan; however, this time the company turned to Italian design house Bertone for the bodywork. Underneath, the remainder of the running gear was all Mini, with the exception of the exhaust, the 12in (30cm) wheels and the front-mounted radiator.

Although ideal for city centre use, the little hatch proved somewhat cramped for passengers.

There were also reports of build problems and lack of rigidity. However, it did have a lifting tailgate that gave access to the boot and the rear seat could be folded down to provide a larger flat area for storage.

The Italian company De Tomaso bought Innocenti in 1976 when British Leyland went bankrupt, and a Japanese Daihatsu engine was fitted to the car from 1982.

Innocenti's Mini 90/120 helped satisfy the Italians' insatiable desire for small cars. However, its crisp, boxy styling represented a distinct break with tradition and a marked contrast to the much-loved Fiat 500

Engine: 998cc (61 cu in), 4-cylinder
Power: 37kW (49bhp)
0–96km/h (60mph): 13.4 secs
Top speed: 140km/h (87mph)
Production total: 220,000

INTERMECCANICA ITALIA

The Intermeccanica Italia grew from the remains of the aborted TVR-based Griffith Omega, a stylish coupé designed by ex-Bertone stylist Franco Scaglione. Frank Reisner, a Hungarian living in the United States and the man behind the Omega project, was left with about 150 Italian-made body-chassis units, and it was these that were to form the basis of the Italia. American-Italian influences are evident in both the styling (especially of the roofline and aggressive haunched rear wings) and the choice of powerplants, with Reisner choosing the V8 engine from the Ford Mustang to power his new creation. There was even, strangely, an automatic transmission option, which was obviously aimed at the US market.

A convertible version of the coupé appeared in 1967, called the Torino. The last examples adopted a glassfibre construction and were labelled IMX coupés.

The cars were nicely styled, with some delicate touches such as the narrow chrome bumpers front and rear, but suspect build quality proved to be the failing of the Italia, and only around 1000 cars were ever made.

Engine: 4949cc (302 cu in), 8-cylinder
Power: 149kW (200bhp)
0–96km/h (60mph): 8.8 secs
Top speed: 200km/h (125mph)
Production total: 1000

INTERMECCANICA INDRA

The German representative for the Intermeccanica company, Eric Bitter, suggested that owner Reisner should switch to Opel drivetrains instead of the American units used in the past, which Bitter promptly did with the Indra.

The Opel Admiral/Diplomat was the model upon which the car was based, with a shortened floorpan and bodywork again styled by the Italian designer Scaglione. This time steel was the preferred material for the Indra's bodyshell, and it had De Dion rear suspension and power steering. The Opel engines included a 2.8-litre (171 cu in) six-cylinder unit or the 5.4-litre (327 cu in) V8.

The Intermeccanica Indra was available in both coupé and convertible body styles, the latter of which was particularly exotic. In total, 127 cars were completed.

The level of equipment and overall styling of the Indra met with universal approval, although poor build quality again spoiled the car, forcing Reisner to leave carmaking and relocate to California once production of the Indra had drawn to a close in 1975. Bitter himself later set up his own sports car manufacturing business under the Bitter name.

Engine: 2784cc (170 cu in), 6-cylinder
Power: 142kW (190bhp)
0–96km/h (60mph): 8.2 secs
Top speed: 203km/h (127mph)
Production total: n/a

INVICTA 4.5-LITRE

In 1924, Noel Macklin and Oliver Lyle of the British sugar-making company formed Invicta to produce luxury vehicles combining British build standards with American performance and engine flexibility. The Invicta factory was set up in the three-car garage of Macklin's family home in Chobham, England.

The 4.5-Litre (273 cu in) 'flat iron' was one of the most famous Invictas, with its trademark riveted bonnet and fierce performance, though the chassis was supplied in two forms, 'high' and the lowered S-type, usually with lightweight competition bodywork. Donald Healey, who helped to develop the car, won first place in the Monte Carlo rally of 1931 in this car.

Although colloquially known as the '100mph' Invicta, the standard production car was really only capable of 144km/h (90mph). However, late on in production, power was increased to 104kW (140bhp), and this car would have undoubtedly been able to reach the magic 161km/h (100mph) mark.

Sadly, the Depression affected Invicta badly, and production ceased after only 77 4.5s were made. Macklin then sold out to Earl Fitzwilliam, who revived the Invicta name again in 1946.

The lightweight, low-slung S-type, with its hard ride, was not the most comfortable car, but it exhibited tremendous cornering ability – making it a devastatingly talented competition car.

Engine: 4467cc (273 cu in), 6-cylinder
Power: 86kW (115bhp)
0–96km/h (60mph): n/a
Top speed: 161km/h (100mph)
Production total: 77

INVICTA BLACK PRINCE

1946–50

The Invicta company lasted just four years after World War II, when another company, AFN Ltd, took over its assets. Part of the reason for the company's failure was the highly unsuccessful Black Prince, with its Meadows-based double overhead camshaft, straight six 3-litre (183 cu in) engine, novel semi-automatic transmission and the novelty of built-in hydraulic jacks. As there was no gearbox as such, power was transmitted via a Brockhouse hydraulic torque converter. The car's suspension was fully independent with torsion bars at the front.

The car was designed by W.G. Watson, who had been responsible for the original Invicta of the 1920s, and was offered at the very high price of £3000 although, by the time production had finally drawn to a close in 1950, the price had increased to nearly £4000. Needless to say, despite the financial investment and the brave use of previously untried technology, very few examples were sold.

As a goodwill gesture, rather than for commercial gain, the remaining cars and all the spare parts were bought by AFN Ltd, makers of the Frazer Nash.

The lugubrious Black Prince proved a disastrously bad seller for Invicta, despite featuring a variety of complex technical innovations such as all-independent suspension.

Engine: 2997cc (183 cu in), 6-cylinder
Power: 18kW (24bhp)
0–96km/h (60mph): n/a
Top speed: n/a
Production total: n/a

ISO RIVOLTA

1962–70

Italian company Iso, known for making refrigerators and motor scooters, started making cars in the 1950s. Its first model was a bubble car, later built by BMW under licence. The Rivolta was its first

venture in the GT market, and the car's credentials were impeccable. The bodywork was designed by a young Giugiaro, with a chassis created by former Ferrari engineer, Giotto Bizzarrini.

In many ways, the Iso Rivolta was similar to the British Gordon Keeble, having a similar box-section frame with De Dion rear suspension and an elegant Bertone-built steel body.

The elegant four-seater Iso Rivolta was the Italian company's first venture into the GT market, being cheaper than the equivalent Ferrari and just as quick, with tenacious handling courtesy of De Dion suspension at the rear.

The Rivolta, too, had an American V8 under the bonnet, which gave the Rivolta a very impressive turn of speed. In fact, it was easily capable of more than 224km/h (140mph).

At less than two-thirds the price of the cheapest Ferrari at the time, commercially the Rivolta was a success, being fast as well as practical with its four-seat capacity. Only a few good examples of this exotic sports car exist today; as with much Italian exotica from the 1960s, the car's thin, unprotected steel construction fell victim to severe corrosion.

Engine: 5357cc (327 cu in), V8-cylinder
Power: 224kW (300bhp)
0–96km/h (60mph): 8 secs
Top speed: 224km/h (140mph)
Production total: 797

ISO GRIFO

The Iso Grifo, launched a year after the Rivolta, featured a shortened Rivolta chassis and a truly beautiful Bertone coupé body with a long bonnet, a steeply sloping rear back with a wraparound rear screen and four headlights set into a shallow front grille.

Again, power came from a Corvette V8 which was available in two states of tune, either 224 or 272kW (300 or 365bhp), with the latter propelling the car to an impressive top speed of 256km/h (160mph). Controversially for a supercar of this type, and unlike any of its competitors, automatic transmission was listed alongside the conventional four- or five-speed manual gearboxes.

From 1970, Series 2 Grifos, designed by Gandini, had a more chiselled front end with pop-up headlights. The rakish-looking Coupé model generally proved more popular than the Spider.

In 1968, in order to provide credible opposition to the likes of the Ferrari Daytona and Maserati Ghibli, power was increased by fitting a 7-litre (427 cu in) 290kW (390bhp) engine which, Iso claimed, could achieve a staggering 273km/h (170mph). Acceleration on this flagship coupé was also breathtaking, reaching 112km/h (70mph) in first gear alone. A hump in the bonnet distinguished these formidable 7-litre (427 cu in) cars from their smaller-engined counterparts.

Towards the end of production, in 1970, the Grifo received a facelift with a more chiselled nose and pop-up headlights, enhancing its already stylish good looks.

Engine: 5359cc (327 cu in), 8-cylinder
Power: 224kW (300bhp)
0–96km/h (60mph): 7.4 secs
Top speed: 241km/h (150mph)
Production total: 504

The macho Iso Grifo combined American muscle-car power with pretty Italian GT styling. Platform chassis, four-wheel discs and De Dion rear suspension underpinned glamorous Bertone bodywork. The power came from a General Motors V8 engine.

ISO FIDIA

The Iso Fidia was a restyled replacement for the Rivolta, but it was not nearly as elegant.

As its range began to grow, Iso decided it needed a four-seater, four-door grand tourer in its stable to rival the likes of the Maserati Quattroporte. The result was the unimpressive-looking Fidia, which used a stretched Chevrolet-engined chassis taken from the Rivolta, this time featuring bodywork by Ghia.

Despite its bulk and high equipment levels, the Fidia was quick, managing a credible 221km/h (138mph) top speed in its final 242kW (325bhp) Ford 5.8-litre (351 cu in) form (the Corvette engine was swapped for a Ford V8 unit in 1973).

Unfortunately, the Fidia's poor construction quality and high price – it was as expensive as a Rolls-Royce Silver Shadow – made the car unsuccessful.

Just fewer than 200 cars were produced before the Iso company went bankrupt during the oil crisis of 1974. However, a few more examples continued to be made until 1979 under the Ennezeta brand name.

Engine: 5359cc (327 cu in), 8-cylinder
Power: 224kW (300bhp)
0–96km/h (60mph): 8.1 secs
Top speed: 205km/h (128mph)
Production total: 192

ISO LELE

Using the same Corvette-based chassis as all the other Iso cars, the four-seater Lele was an angular-looking replacement for the Rivolta, but went out of production shortly after its launch in 1969. Coachwork was by Marcello Gandini from Bertone, but lacked much in the way of style or innovation, although it did at least offer the practicality of being able to seat four passengers.

A Chevrolet V8 engine was fitted under the bonnet, providing it with more power than the Rivolta although, like the Fidia, the Lele switched to a Ford 5.8-litre (351 cu in) 242kW (325bhp) powerplant in 1973. As with all Isos, there was the peculiar option

Using the same basic running gear as other Isos at the time, the Lele featured Bertone styling and American V8 powerplants sourced from Chevrolet and Ford.

of an automatic transmission to accompany the four- or five-speed manual standard gearbox.

In 1973, Iso launched a special 'Marlboro' edition of the car in an attempt to boost sales; however, it was short-lived and did nothing to help the struggling company sell the expensive Lele, especially at a time when sales of big supercars were falling anyway.

Only 317 examples of the Fidia left the Iso factory, its demise coinciding with the decline of the company itself in 1974.

Engine: 5359cc (327 cu in), 8-cylinder
Power: 224kW (300bhp)
0–96km/h (60mph): 7.3 secs
Top speed: 224km/h (140mph)
Production total: 317

SUZU 117 COUPÉ

Most will associate the Isuzu company with farmers, being the manufacturer of strong off-roaders which score high on ability but low in luxury and image. However, the Japanese firm did have a brief foray into the sports car market, employing the services of top Italian stylist Giugiaro (then working at Ghia of Turin) to design what turned out to be a very attractive little coupé. In fact, fans of Italian cars in particular could be forgiven for mistaking it for a scaled down version of the Fiat Dino with its rakish lines, narrow chrome bumpers and four-headlight grille.

Mechanically, it shared its running gear with the Florian saloon, made initially with a 1.6-litre (97 cu in) engine, then upgraded to a 1.8-litre (111 cu in) twin-camshaft unit in 1970. The XE version even had fuel injection, pushing power up to a credible 104kW (140bhp).

Despite the fact that production continued into the early 1980s, few were officially imported to Europe.

Isuzu's cute 117 Coupé had a twin-cam, twin-carburettor 1800cc (111 cu in) engine.

Engine: 1584cc (97 cu in), 4-cylinder
Power: 67kW (90bhp)
0–96km/h (60mph): 8 secs
Top speed: 161km/h (100mph)
Production total: n/a

JAGUAR 1.5-LITRE

When Bill Lyons started making motorcycle sidecars in the early 1920s at his Swallow factory in a backstreet in Blackpool, England, who could have imagined that he would be responsible for creating one of the most evocative names in British motor manufacturing history.

Production of Jaguar cars soon followed in 1931, when Lyons moved his works to Coventry, beginning with the sensational-looking SS sports cars and accompanying SS saloons.

The Jaguar 1.5-Litre was launched four years before the start of World War II, first with a side-valve four-cylinder, then with a four-cylinder engine with overhead valves, which was considered to be advanced at the time. Less modern was the retention of the fixed front axle and the rod-operated drum brakes.

Contrary to its name, the capacity of the engine was in fact 1776cc (108 cu in); however, with the car's huge bulk, even the performance of this bigger engine was abysmal. When combined with poor aerodynamics, this meant that the car's top speed was just 112km/h (70mph).

Despite this, the Jaguar 1.5-Litre was a devastatingly attractive and elegant car. It was available as a four-door saloon and, later, a drophead coupé, both of which seated five. Most were exported to the United States, especially the exotic drophead coupés made between 1947 and 1948.

Jaguar's 1.5-Litre featured a novel Salisbury back axle which lowered the height of the transmission tunnel, thus allowing more room inside the car.

Engine: 1776cc (108 cu in), 4-cylinder
Power: 49kW (66bhp)
0–96km/h (60mph): 25.1 secs
Top speed: 112km/h (70mph)
Production total: 13,046

JAGUAR 3.5-LITRE 'SS100'

1938–41

Advertised originally as the 'The Car with the £1,000 Look', despite only costing £325, the charismatic SS Jaguars were poorly received among enthusiasts who thought of them as cheap and shoddy. It was not until the company had attained respectability later on that the astonishing virtues of these cars were truly realized. These included ravishingly good looks and sensational performance.

The first SS100 was born in 1935 and used a shortened version of the chassis developed for the new SS generation of saloon cars and a side-valve 2663cc (162 cu in) Standard six-cylinder engine. Later, it was fitted with the all-new, very powerful 3485cc (213 cu in) engine, allowing the car to reach the magical 161km/h (100mph) figure, something exceedingly rare for a car of that era.

Few concessions, however, were made to comfort. Instead, the 100 concentrated on style and performance, with sweeping front wings and hugely charismatic twin

headlights being the vehicle's most memorable features.

The 3.5-Litre SS100 did much for Jaguar's reputation leading up to World War II and, because just 118 were made, original cars command high prices today.

The SS was hallowed for its impressive flexibility and vigorous top-gear acceleration. It was one of the fastest cars of its era, with a generally accepted top speed of 161km/h (100mph). It was this that gave it its 'SS100' name.

Engine: 3485cc (213 cu in), 6-cylinder
Power: 93kW (125bhp)
0–96km/h (60mph) 10.4 secs
Top speed: 161km/h (100mph)
Production total: 118

JAGUAR MK V

1948–51

Launched shortly after the war, the Mk V was a stopgap model destined to be replaced just two years later by the Mk VII. It did, however, provide a creditable link between the post- and prewar models with its strange mix of styling, incorporating both old and modern design elements. New were the integrated headlights, set into the inner edge of the front wings so that they looked as if they were standalone, the curvy roofline and the modern-looking rear wheel spats, while the narrow screen and old-fashioned running boards were retained. Perhaps Jaguar's approach was meant to test public opinion, while not offending the traditionalists.

The Mk V's all-new chassis formed the platform of all Jaguar's big saloons throughout the 1950s. Other innovations for this car were hydraulic brakes and independent front suspension which Jaguar engineer William Heynes based on the low-stress torsion-bar technique pioneered by Citroën. It was fitted with either a 2664cc (163 cu in) or 3485cc (213 cu in) engine, both of which were six cylinders.

In terms of refinement, Jaguar had reached new heights with the Mk V, even offering an exotic drophead model, of which just 1001 were made.

Engine: 2664cc (163 cu in), 6-cylinder
Power: 77kW (104bhp)
0–96km/h (60mph): 17 secs
Top speed: 139km/h (87mph)
Production total: 10,466

The Mk V was a mix of old and new styling with its sweeping front wings and big bumpers, and the all new independent front suspension designed by William Heynes.

AGUAR Mk VII

espite the fact that the six-
linder, twin overhead camshaft
gine had already been used in the
K120 and the chassis was nothing
ore than a modified version of the

Mk V, which the Mk VII replaced
(there was no Mk VI, as Bentley
had already used the name), the
overall effect of the Jaguar Mk VII
was spectacular.

Here, at last, was a car that was
not only spacious, plush and
supremely elegant but one that was
also easily capable of travelling at
over 161km/h (100mph) as well.

Even more attractive was its
price – just £1276 which, at the
time, was exceedingly good value
for such a luxurious, fast car.

Gone were all those prewar
styling features, and in came a
totally new rounded shape with a
full-width body, spats to cover the
rear wheels and headlights that
were now fully integrated into the
front wings. The poor two-speed
automatic option from 1953 was
replaced in 1954 by an improved
overdrive option, while the Mk
VIIM from 1954 had more power
and wraparound chrome bumpers.

The Mk VIII in 1956 had a
facelifted grille, duotone paint, cutaway rear wheel spats, chrome side
trim and a one-piece windscreen.

Engine: 3442cc (210 cu in) 6-cylinder
Power: 121kW (162bhp)
0–96km/h (60mph): 14.3 secs
Top speed: 61km/h (100mph)
Production total: 37,181

**The Jaguar Mk VII handled and
performed well for such a colossal
car and incorporated all-important
servo-assisted brakes.**

AGUAR Mk IX

osmetically, there was very little
ifference between the Mk IX
aguar and the last of the Mk VIII
ersions, as most of the changes
ook place under the four-door's
legant skin. New to the car was a
ored-out twin carburettor version
f Jaguar's 3.8-litre (231 cu in) XK
ngine, which itself was a detuned
ersion of the unit already used in
he D-type racing car. This gave the
1k IX a much better high-speed
ruising ability.

Other mechanical improvements
ncluded the fitting of power
ssisted steering as standard and
ll-round disc brakes. Most cars
ame with automatic transmission
s standard, but there was also the
ption of a four-speed manual with
verdrive, and the majority were
ffered with modern duotone
aintwork, the two colours being
eparated by a delicate chrome
trip along the side.

A total of around 10,000 cars
ere produced at Jaguar's
oventry, England, plant during
he car's three-year production

lifespan and, despite the rust
problems inherent in big Jaguars
of this era, there are still plenty of
examples of this generously
proportioned and technically
advanced car around today.

**The Mk IX was the first Jaguar
to have disc brakes and power-
assisted steering fitted as standard.
It was also the first to use the
fabled 3.8-litre (231 cu in) six-
cylinder powerplant.**

Engine: 3781cc (231 cu in), 6-cylinder
Power: 166kW (223bhp)
0–96km/h (60mph): 11.6 secs
Top speed: 184km/h (115mph)
Production total: 10,009

JAGUAR XK120

The darling of the 1948 Earls Court Motor Show in London, the stunning Jaguar XK120 was the stuff of dreams after the hardships of World War II. Beautifully purposeful and very quick, the XK120 heralded new hope amid all that postwar austerity.

In terms of design, the two-seater roadster, with its classically simple flowing lines, slender tail and deliciously exotic flush-sided body, was unparalleled at the time, while it also set new standards in terms of performance.

At its heart was an all-new twin overhead camshaft straight-six with twin SU carburettors. This powerful 3.4-litre (210 cu in) unit was used in numerous subsequent Jaguars and survived right up until the 1990s. This engine came at a time when no other company was making mass-produced twin-camshaft engines. Producing a silky smooth power delivery, its 120 name tag was nothing of an exaggeration, as the car was easily capable of reaching 120mph (192km/h), although later SE (Special Equipment) versions with high-lift camshafts, twin exhausts and 134kW (180bhp) were even faster than this.

To demonstrate the car's awesome abilities, Jaguar took an XK120 to Belgium's Jabbeke straight test road, fitted an undershield and a racing-type windscreen, and achieved a spectacular 213.32km/h (132.56mph) over a flying mile, and 203km/h (126mph) with the standard windscreen, hood and sidescreens fitted. Thus it was rightly lauded as being one of the fastest production cars in the world. Even the usually restrained

The Autocar did nothing at all to disguise its enthusiasm in a contemporary report on the car.

'In trying to convey in a word-picture the supreme position which the XK120 two-seater occupies, there is a temptation to draw from the motoring vocabulary every adjective in the superlative concerning the performance, and to call upon the devices of italics and even the capital letter!'

The XK120 was further commended for being so flexible – the car almost had 'dual character', as it had the ability to speed along a quiet country road at high speed one minute, while behaving impeccably amid traffic on city streets the next. Its tenacious grip and perfect handling was accompanied by light steering and taut

A snug two-seater fixed-head version of the Jaguar XK120 appeared in 1951 with its bulbous roofline reminiscent of 1930s Bugattis. The SE (pictured here) featured wire wheels and extra lights at the front.

yet comfortable suspension, allowing the car to be hurled around bends with extreme confidence.

Not as impressive, however, were the drum brakes, which were prone to fade (unless special linings were fitted) due to poor cooling – the car's modern, enclosed bodywork contributed to this. Despite its diminutive size, the Jaguar XK120 was also a practical car with a useful luggage compartment, obstructed only by the spare wheel.

Lyons saw the Jaguar XK120 as a limited edition machine, originally envisaging a production

run of just 200 cars, which is perhaps why the first examples used a wooden ash body frame and aluminium skin panels. However, he was unprepared for the huge impact that the car would make and, as demand accelerated, he switched to steel mass production in 1950, by which time only 240 cars had left the Coventry factory.

An elegant fixed-head version of the car appeared in 1951, with a bulbous roofline (no doubt inspired by the Bugatti coupés of the 1930s), deeper windscreen and wind-up windows. A delightful drophead coupé was offered in 1953 with a more luxurious interior and walnut veneer dashboard. Plans to build an XK100, with a weak but perhaps more universally popular 71kW (95bhp) 2-litre (122 cu in) XK engine were never to reach fruition.

The early alloy-bodied roadsters now command twice the value of the steel-bodied cars. Interestingly however, the steel-bodied cars are actually lighter.

Engine: 3442cc (210 cu in), 6-cylinder
Power: 119kW (160bhp)
0–96km/h (60mph): 12 secs
Top speed: 196km/h (122mph)
Production total: 12,055

AGUAR C-TYPE

therwise known as the Jaguar K120C, the sleek two-seater with ero screens and all-aluminium odywork was developed with just ne thing in mind – winning Le Mans, which it achieved in 1951.

The car's underpinnings ncluded a new tubular steel hassis, rack-and-pinion steering, rengthened front suspension and transverse torsion bar at the rear nd. The twin-camshaft engine eatured an uprated cylinder head, new camshaft and a higher ompression ratio of 9:1, capable f producing 152kW (204bhp). lsewhere, its mechanical omponentry was taken directly om the XK120.

After its Le Mans win, the C-ype's abilities as a competition car ere further enhanced by a umber of improvements which ncluded adding twin carburettors the engine and a Panhard rod to he suspension to aid stability. It lso gained more powerful servo-ssisted braking on all four wheels.

Despite the fact that only 54 cars ere ever produced, some did fall

into the hands of private owners, who relished the C-type as the ultimate road car. Today, few original examples survive, although it has become a favourite among replica manufacturers.

Jaguar's C-Type was one of the most illustrious road cars of all time with its lightweight body, exceptional performance and fabulous chassis. Even racing driver supremo Fangio owned one.

Engine: 3442cc (210 cu in), 6-cylinder
Power: 152kW (204bhp)
0–96km/h (60mph): 8.1 secs
Top speed: 230km/h (144mph)
Production total: 54

AGUAR XK140

he Jaguar XK140 was the result f a good car made even better. eplacing the fabled XK120, the 40 featured more powerful ersions of the twin-camshaft ngine, rack-and-pinion steering, n optional overdrive and better

equipped interiors. There was also a very rare automatic transmission option offered.

Cosmetically, there was little difference between the XK140 and its predecessor, apart from a slightly modified radiator grille (it

had a couple of extra chrome spokes) and more sturdy front and rear chrome bumpers. It was also slightly wider, giving improved cabin space – especially on the fixed and drophead coupés – although this did increase the

weight of the car and necessitated an increase in power to 142kW (190bhp) to compensate for this. What had not changed, however, were the mediocre brakes and the heavy steering.

Again, like the XK120, there was a more powerful SE version, which used the cylinder head from the C-type, developing 156kW (210bhp), but these are very rare.

There were three body styles available for the XK140 – a roadster, a coupé and a drophead coupé. The coupés, however, only had a very small bench rear seat.

The XK140 lost much of the clarity of its predecessor. A clumsy chrome strip appeared along the length of the bonnet and bootlid, while big ugly bumpers replaced the delicate ones fitted to the XK120. However, moving the engine forwards in the frame improved the car's balance.

Engine: 3442cc (210 cu in), 6-cylinder
Power: 142kW (190bhp)
0–96km/h (60mph): 8.4 secs
Top speed: 200km/h (125mph)
Production total: 9051

JAGUAR XK150

Heavier than its predecessors, and looking just a little overweight after the slender lines of the original XK120, the Jaguar XK150 gained a less distinctive higher waistline and a modern one-piece wraparound front screen. At the same time, the car became much more refined, being more comfortable and more civilized to drive.

The continuation of the rear bench seat from the XK140 and the increased availability of the Borg Warner automatic transmission underlined the fact that Jaguar wanted the car to be seen more as a grand tourer than a true sports car. Dunlop disc brakes were fitted to all four wheels, and handling was more assured than that of the earlier XKs.

The drophead coupé, with its beautifully lined and trimmed hood, was heavier still, and despite efforts to keep weight down by making the XK150 bonnet and boot lid from aluminium, this version weighed in at a ponderous 1498.6kg (3304lb). Jaguar obviously needed more powerful engines.

The 156kW (210bhp) Blue Top engine was used alongside the 142kW (190bhp) unit, although top speed fell to 200km/h (125mph). In 1958, however, to counter accusations that the XK150 had become 'middle-aged', Jaguar launched the S version with 186kW (250bhp), and, from 1959, all cars were fitted with the 3.8-litre (232 cu in) engine, increasing power to 164kW (220bhp) (197kW [265bhp] on the S versions).

Despite sharing the same twin-cam engine and stout chassis, the third and final member of the Jaguar XK family was more of a grand tourer than an out-and-out sports car, although it was the first production Jaguar to feature disc brakes.

Engine: 3442cc (210 cu in), 6-cylinder
Power: 142kW (190bhp)
0–96km/h (60mph): 8.4 secs
Top speed: 198km/h (125mph)
Production total: 9398

AGUAR D-TYPE

1957

gine: 3442cc (210 cu in), 6-cylinder
wer: 183kW (245bhp)
96km/h (60mph): 7 secs
p speed: 288km/h (180mph)
oduction total: 45

nnounced in 1954, the Jaguar D-
pe became the spiritual successor
the earlier C-type, and it is today
en as one of the most evocative
orts cars of its generation.
lthough it used the six-cylinder

engine from the production cars of
the time, the rest of the D bore little
resemblance to its predecessor,
being smaller, lighter and more
modern in conception.

Specifically, the D-type featured
an all-new magnesium-alloy
monocoque, with the engine and
suspension held in a tubular frame.
During its lifetime, the traditional
wire wheels were replaced by alloy
disc wheels, and a new Jaguar

four-speed gearbox was specially
developed for the car.

Visually, the D-type was
distinguished by its sleek lines and
curious stabilizing fin running
directly behind the driver. Its low
bonnet height (and superb
aerodynamic qualities) were the
product of Malcolm Sayer, who
devised a way of reducing frontal
area by including a dry sump and
separate radiator header tank.

The D-type was to enjoy many
spectacular race successes,
including outright wins at Le Mans
in 1953, 1955, 1956 and 1957.

**Aerodynamicist Malcolm Sayer
was responsible for the glorious
streamlined shape of the D-type –
he specified using a dry sump and
canting the engine by eight degrees
to lower the car's bonnet height.**

AGUAR XKSS

1957

ynics would say that the XKSS
as only produced because Jaguar
anted to shift unsold D-types (the
tter being purely a limited-market
cing car). Others might say that
e company was interested in
eating the superlative road car by
utting a door in the centre of the
-type's centre section, dropping
e fin, adding a full-width screen
nd offering a primitive hood.

Whatever the case may be, the
resulting Jaguar XKSS was
something of a sensation – a
240km/h (150mph) two-seater
which provided little in the way of
creature comforts.

Sadly, hopes for long-term
success with the model were
dashed when Jaguar's Coventry
factory suffered a major fire, in
which several of the cars were

destroyed, along with much of the
assembly fixtures.

Moreover, there was a policy
change within the company, which
meant attention was switched from
sports cars to the development of
the saloon car range. Luckily for
Jaguar racing fans, however, the
theme of the XKSS was reborn
with the launch of the E-type
several years later.

Only 16 examples of the Jaguar
XKSS were made, making it
extremely rare and, like the C-type,
the market is flooded with modern
replicas of this car.

Engine: 3442cc (210 cu in), 6-cylinder
Power: 186kW (250bhp)
0–96km/h (60mph): 5.2 secs
Top speed: 238km/h (149mph)
Production total: 16

AGUAR MK I

1955–59

enerally overshadowed by the
ter Mk II, the 2.4-litre (146 cu in)
k I of 1955 actually spearheaded
guar's entry into the lucrative
nall luxury car market. The first
the company's cars to feature
nitary construction, early Mk Is
ere heavy-looking and could be
asily identified by their thick door
osts, rear wheel spats, deep side
anels and wide wraparound
hrome bumpers.

Underneath the bonnet was a
short-stroke version of Jaguar's
twin-camshaft six-cylinder engine,
which was available as an
automatic with overdrive or a poor-
quality standard automatic from
1957. Suspension was by
independent coils and springs.

The 2.4-litre (146 cu in) car was
joined by the 3.4-litre (207 cu in)
in 1957, which substantially
increased power to 156kW

(210bhp) and gave the Mk I a
much more respectable 192km/h
(120mph) top speed. These later,
more powerful cars could be
distinguished from their predecessors by a slightly wider grille,
cutaway rear spats and wire
wheels. At the same time, all-round
disc brakes were introduced on all
models and, soon after, the 2.4-litre
version also gained the wider grille
seen on the 3.4-litre.

Of the 37,397 cars produced,
19,992 had the 2.4-litre (146 cu in)
unit and 17,405 had the 3.4-litre
(207 cu in) one. The Mk I was
replaced by the Mk II, announced
towards the end of 1959.

Engine: 2483cc (152 cu in), 6-cylinder
Power: 83kW (112bhp)
0–96km/h (60mph): 14.1 secs
Top speed: 162km/h (101mph)
Production total: 37,397

JAGUAR MK II

The preferred car of bank robbers and gangsters throughout the 1960s, the Mk II won many admirers for its performance and handling.

It was a big improvement on the Mk I, with a bigger glass area (including a much bigger rear window), a better interior, a slightly wider rear track (to improve road-holding), a different grille and all-round disc brakes as standard. It also had a much wider range of engines, including the fabulous 3.8-litre (232 cu in) twin-camshaft from the XK, making it one of the fastest production saloons of its era. Inevitably, these higher powered cars are more highly sought-after today than the smaller capacity ones.

An all-synchromesh gearbox for the Mark II arrived in 1965 and, from 1966, there was a reduced specification which included Ambla plastic on the seats, instead of leather, and no fog lamps. From 1967, the Mark II was available with optional power-assisted steering, which helped what was otherwise a heavy car to drive.

A loyal band of enthusiasts has ensured that the elegant Mk II remains as desirable today as it was when new.

The Mk II became the most successful Jaguar until the arrival of the XJ6 in 1968. Its classic sport saloon styling was replicated by Jaguar in the late 1990s with its 'new' S-type model.

Engine: 3781cc (231 cu in), 6-cylinder
Power: 164kW (220bhp)
0–96km/h (60mph): 8.5 secs
Top speed: 200km/h (125mph)
Production total: 83,980

JAGUAR 240/340

The 240/340 replaced the Mk II Jaguar in 1967, and they were cheaper and slightly less opulent than their predecessor, with plastic Ambla trim instead of leather, different hubcaps and chrome grilles where the foglights would have been.

Purists at the time scowled at such rationalization, and even today the 240/340 range remains unfavoured by Jaguar aficionados. However, controversially perhaps, they are nicer-looking than the model they replaced, with their slender chrome bumpers replacing the overelaborate examples found on the Mk II. More importantly, they were also faster, with power raised from 89 to 99kW (120 to 133bhp).

Sadly, however, the fast 3.8-litre (232 cu in) option was discontinued, although a handful of cars did leave the factory with the

splendid twin-camshaft unit fitted under the bonnet. Some owners fit their own foglights to look like a Mk II, and there are also cars with leather; however, it is not possible to fit Mk II bumpers.

The 240 and 340 were poverty spec 'run-out' versions of the Mk II with plastic Ambla upholstery instead of leather. The steering in both cars was heavy and low geared, and there was no power assistance.

Engine: 2483cc (152 cu in), 6-cylinder
Power: 99kW (133bhp)
0–96km/h (60mph): 12.5 secs
Top speed: 170km/h (106mph)
Production total: 856,428

JAGUAR E-TYPE

If asked to name the most evocative, most sensuous sports car of all time, there is no doubt that the Jaguar E-type would be high up on most people's list. Craved after by pop stars, royalty and racing drivers alike, the E-type captured the spirit of the Swinging Sixties and was reaching legendary status by the time its performance and looks were compromised by American safety standards at the end of its production in 1975.

The E-type's beautifully sleek profile was no accident, but more a masterpiece of function, having been conceived by aerodynamicist Malcolm Sayer, who was also responsible for the earlier racing D-types.

The origins of the car can be traced back to a lightweight prototype, raced at Le Mans in 1960, but it was at the Geneva Show in March 1961 that the E-type first met the public's gaze, and both open roadster and fastback coupé versions became available in July of that year.

Not only was the E-type ravishingly beautiful to look at, but it was also devastatingly fast, achieving an impressive 240km/h (150mph) in contemporary road tests. The reason for this performance was that under its

In its early, purest form, Jaguar's E-type was devastatingly beautiful.

One of the greatest cars ever? Possibly, but the later Series III E-type was not particularly pretty nor was its handling up to scratch. The V12 engine proved thirsty and worryingly unreliable.

sleek bonnet was that famous 3.8-litre (232 cu in) XK twin-camshaft engine. At the same time, road-holding was impressive, with good grip from its new wishbone and coil-sprung independent suspension while at the same providing a relaxed and comfortable ride.

The 3.8-litre (232 cu in) that ran from 1961 to 1964 had cleaner lines and ultimately better performance than the later 4.2-litre (258 cu in) version. It was available as a stunning open-top or slightly less revered but more practical coupé hatch.

The Series I, which was introduced in 1964, came with a new 4.2-litre (258 cu in) XK engine with more torque, and it came with a much better gearbox and brakes, along with improved electrics and more opulent trim. Arguably, this was the best E of all, being technically advanced while retaining virtually all of its purity.

In 1966, a third model, the 2+2, arrived, with an extra 23cm (9in) wheelbase, a reshaped, slightly higher roofline and 110kg (243lb) more weight. Despite pleasing some with its extra room, it never received the critical acclaim of other E-types.

Two years later, American safety legislation resulted in the Series II, with its uncowled headlights, bigger raised bumpers and bigger front and rear light clusters mounted below bumper level. The bonnet also lost its characteristic streamlined shape. At the same time, several technical changes were made, including twin electric fans for improved cooling, improved brakes, power-assisted steering, an automatic option on the 2+2 and even the option of air conditioning.

In the final transformation of Jaguar's super car, the Series III, which was introduced in 1971, the company also introduced its new alloy 203kW (272bhp) V12 engine with its massive torque and incredible acceleration. By this time, only two models options were offered, the roadster and the 2+2, both of which were hung on the longer 2+2 chassis.

Sadly, alongside all the added refinement that came with it, including power steering as standard, ventilated disc braking and an automatic transmission option on both models, came a style problem. Sporting flared arches, overelaborate quadruple tailpipes, a horrendous egg-crate grille and dripping with chrome, the E-type lost its svelte charm of old. The 1960s icon, tarnished by ever more stringent safety regulations, had lost its looks and become a pale imitation of its former self. They even painted some of the last cars pink! Around 80 per cent of these final models were exported to the United States.

Engine: 4235cc (258 cu in), 6-cylinder
Power: 197kW (265bhp)
0–96km/h (60mph): 7.1 secs
Top speed: 218km/h (136mph)
Production total: 72,507

JAGUAR MK X

1961–66

The barge-like Mk X was the widest car on the road in Britain for a time, but more power was needed to improve the performance of this gargantuan luxury cruiser.

At 193cm (6.3ft) wide, the X-type held the dubious distinction of being the widest British car ever made until the Jaguar XJ220 arrived in 1992 – and it was heavy,

too. Its cigar-like shape helped to disguise its bulk; however, despite being 5.2m (17ft) long, it was not particularly easy to get in or out of because its sill was awkwardly

high. Still, it was roomy inside and supremely comfortable, and it definitely fell into the category of luxury cruiser.

Surprisingly for a car of this size, it handled reasonably well, albeit with a fair amount of body roll. Part of the reason for this was that the Mk X borrowed its all-round independent suspension from other cars in the Jaguar range – notably the Mk II for the front and the E-type for the rear. Refinements included Kelsey Hayes power-assisted all-round disc brakes and power steering as standard.

Originally fitted with the 3.8-litre (232 cu in) engine from the XK150, the X-type gained the company's new 4.2-litre (258 cu in) unit with its superb mid-range torque from 1964. At the same time, an all-synchromesh gearbox was fitted to the car.

The car was given a new name,

Engine: 3781cc (231 cu in), 6-cylinder
Power: 197kW (265bhp)
0–96km/h (60mph): 12.1 secs
Top speed: 192km/h (120mph)
Production total: 25,212

JAGUAR S-TYPE

1963–68

Arguably, the S-type was a better car than the Mk II. Not only did it handle better, thanks to independent rear suspension and extremely powerful in-board (inset rather than at the wheels) all-round disc brakes, but it was also sleeker, having adopted the flatter rear end from the Mk X. In fact, the S-type was a clever bit of marketing, being almost halfway between the two cars.

Of the two engines on offer, the 3.8-litre (232 cu in) was favourite, with good acceleration and the ability to cruise at well in excess of 192km/h (120mph). Of the 25,171 cars made, 10,036 were fitted with the 3.4-litre (210 cu in) engine, and 15,135 with the 3.8-litre (232 cu in) unit. An all-synchromesh gearbox was made standard in 1965, as well as the popular Borg Warner automatic transmission and, like the Mk 2, later versions were rationalized with Ambla plastic trim instead of leather.

Strangely, the S-type never received the recognition it deserved

and has been largely overlooked by enthusiasts. As a result, prices are cheaper than those of the more sought-after Mk II, despite the S-type arguably handling better.

The S-type was based on the Mk II, but had an extended rear end similar to the Mk X. It also gained the X's hooded headlights and had independent rear suspension.

Engine: 3781cc (231 cu in), 6-cylinder
Power: 156kW (210bhp)
0–96km/h (60mph): 10.2 secs
Top speed: 195km/h (122mph)
Production total: 25,171

JAGUAR 420

With sales faltering, the 420 was introduced in 1966 to fill a gap between the Mk II and the flagship Mk X. Based to some extent on the S-type, it featured the Mk X's four headlight arrangement and backward-sloping grille.

Nevertheless, the 420 unit still had 183kW (245bhp) available, which could easily power the car to 200km/h (125mph) and was available with Jaguar's four-speed manual gearbox or the Borg Warner three-speed automatic option. Elsewhere, the car gained components from its other Jaguar stablemates – the 420's interior came largely from the S-type, while its dual-circuit Girling all-round disc brakes were derived from the X-type.

Although the 420 may have seemed in some respects like a stopgap car, it is actually an underrated vehicle and a far more practical proposition than the whale-like 420G.

The final incarnation of the Mk II was the Jaguar 420, which was nothing more than a slightly more luxurious version of the S-type fitted with a 4.2-litre (258 cu in) engine. From the windscreen back, the styling was pure S-type, but the squared up grille and the four-headlamp configuration was a throwback to the Mk X.

The 4.2-litre (258 cu in) engine was taken from the Mk X; however, it was detuned and only had twin SU carburettors, not the triple set-up of the Mk X.

Engine: 4235cc (258 cu in), 6-cylinder
Power: 183kW (245bhp)
0–96km/h (60mph): 9.9 secs
Top speed: 200km/h (125mph)
Production total: 9801

JAGUAR XJ6/12

The XJ6 enjoyed a lifespan that was to last an astonishing 23 years and pioneered the approach of rationalizing the use of different chassis types to reduce production costs. It represented excellent value and high levels of refinement.

The XJ6 was a car that could do all that Jaguar's previous saloon cars could, but with more pace and far more grace. Inspired by William Lyons himself, the shape was timeless. The Series 1 was available initially in short-wheelbase form, with a longer wheelbase version appearing in 1972. It was at this time that the fabulous V12 engine was introduced, offering peerless refinement, but much higher fuel consumption.

The Series 2 came in 1973 with its higher front bumpers, smaller grille and US-safety standards compliant lighting, and the engine range was expanded to include a 3.4-litre (210 cu in) option in 1975. Sleek new pillarless coupé versions, called the XJ6C and XJ5.3C, appeared on the market in 1975, based on the short-wheelbase floorpan. All cars had black vinyl roofs as standard and suffered from poor weather sealing.

Four years later, Pininfarina helped to bring Lyons's original design up to date by making the windows bigger, flattening the roof and adding a more subtle front nose. While still mostly using Series 2 engines, build quality and general refinement were significantly improved. The XJ6 range was replaced by the XJ40 in 1986 and 1987, but the V12 version carried on until 1991.

Engine: 5343cc (326 cu in), 12-cylinder
Power: 212kW (285bhp)
0–96km/h (60mph): 8.8 secs
Top speed: 237km/h (148mph)
Production total: 328,800

JAGUAR XJS

1975–93

Using the platform from the short-wheelbase XJ12, the XJS was the spiritual successor to the hallowed E-type. Its controversial styling, however, was never to gain universal acclaim.

Everyone hoped the XJS would become the spiritual successor to the much loved E-type but, despite being fabulous to drive, the XJS was rejected for its slab-sided looks, odd flying buttresses and cramped interior. Its plastic bumpers and lack of grille did nothing to attract admirers either. Inheriting the suspension, brakes and wonderful fuel-injected V12 from the XJ6, all on the short wheelbase platform, the XJS was a supreme grand tourer, capable of a 245km/h (153mph) top speed.

A six-cylinder, twin overhead camshaft, 24-valve, 3.6-litre (219 cu in) version was produced in 1983 and, with a manual gearbox fitted, was actually quicker from a standstill than the V12, reaching 96km/h (60mph) in just 7.1

seconds. The range of engines was further increased in 1991 with the introduction of a 4-litre (244 cu in) unit with a catalytic converter, and, in 1993, the 5.3-litre (326 cu in)

engine was replaced by the 6-litre (366 cu in). As well as the coupé, there was also an attractive cabriolet and a highly modified XJR-S producing 248kW (333bhp).

Engine: 5343cc (326 cu in), 12-cylinder
Power: 212kW (285bhp)
0–96km/h (60mph): 5.5 secs
Top speed: 245km/h (153mph)
Production total: 145,490

JEEP CJ-7

1978–86

The 'general purpose' vehicle produced by the US defence department for use in World War II became known by its initials – GP – and so it was that the name 'Jeep' came into existence.

The CJ-7 was little changed from the 250kg (0.25 ton) vehicle upon which it was based, and it featured a rugged steel chassis with live axles front and rear suspended on semi-elliptical springs.

The body styling also owed much to tradition, with the re-emergence of the familiar headlights set inwards of the wings, each side of a vertical slatted grille. Unlike its wartime

cousin, however, and in keeping with the glitzy 1970s into which it emerged, the CJ-7 came dripping with chrome, vinyl and flared wheelarches. Drive was usually to the rear wheels, although it could be added to the front wheels as well when on slippery ground, transforming it into a true 4x4.

American Motors acquired the Jeep Corporation in 1980, which then sold out to Chrysler in 1987. Today, the same company produces a similar-looking vehicle to the original CJ-7 which has gained increasing popularity among those wanting a retro off-roader.

The late 1970s Jeep differed little in appearance to the 1940s original, and it used the same tough chassis with live axles on semi-elliptic springs at the front and rear. The vehicle's engines were either 4.2-litre (258 cu in) or 5-litre (304 cu in) V8 units.

Engine: 4235cc (258 cu in), V8-cylinder
Power: 82kW (110bhp)
0–96km/h (60mph): 14.1 secs
Top speed: 149km/h (93mph)
Production total: n/a

JENSEN PW

Allan and Richard Jensen were coachbuilders who set up their own company in 1934, launching the first car to carry their name, a 3.6-litre (220 cu in) Ford V8-engined tourer, a year later. Jensen survived the war and, despite a financially turbulent postwar period, produced its elegant PW model (which stood, appropriately, for 'Post-War'). This was available in two body styles – a four-door saloon and then, from 1948, a drophead coupé.

The expansive and expensive body was mounted on a tubular-braced chassis from the prewar HC model, and it featured a number of technical innovations at the time, including independent coil-sprung suspension at the front and the luxury of all-round hydraulic brakes.

Power for the opulent PW came from a straight-eight Meadows engine, but vibration problems hastened a switch to a prewar 4.2-litre (256 cu in) Nash unit after just 15 cars had been made. From 1949, Austin A135 engines were offered instead.

Only a few of these hand-built cars were ever made at Jensen's

West Bromwich factory despite a production lifespan of six years. In fact, only about nineteen examples were made and, unfortunately, only one convertible survives today.

The plutocratic Jensen PW was made as a sports saloon and a convertible, and the car featured a tubular braced chassis and independent suspension.

Engine: 3993cc (244 cu in), 6-cylinder
Power: 97kW (130bhp)
0–96km/h (60mph): n/a
Top speed: 152km/h (95mph)
Production total: 19

JENSEN INTERCEPTOR

Jensen's first Interceptor, launched in 1949, started life as a two-door convertible based on a modified Austin chassis.

proportions, the Jensen was well known for passenger comfort, with its bench front seat, folding front seat backs to provide good access for rear-seat passengers, and a generous amount of rear legroom.

As with the PW, power came from Austin's straight-six 3993cc (242 cu in) A135 engine, enabling the streamlined but somewhat slab-sided Interceptor to reach speeds of 161km/h (100mph).

A hardtop version made its appearance in 1951, with a full fabric-covered roof. Overdrive became standard from 1952, and the bonnet was lowered after 1953.

Not to be disheartened by the lack of success of its PW model, Jensen launched the first of its Interceptor range. The car started production as a two-door drophead mounted on a

modified Austin chassis, but later became available as a four-door saloon. Its main purpose was as a grand tourer. Its looks were not to everyone's taste and, indeed, its

frontal aspect was rather peculiar, with an oval-shaped grille, bug-eye headlights perched above it and an air intake in the front of the bonnet.

Thanks to its immense external

Engine: 3993cc (242 cu in), 6-cylinder
Power: 97kW (130bhp)
0–96km/h (60mph): 13.7 secs
Top speed: 161km/h (100mph)
Production total: 88

JENSEN 541

1955–63

Jensen's 541 was a revelation at its launch in 1953, with its evocative streamlined styling (by Eric Neale) and panoramic windscreen. However, it would be another two years before the car was to go into production, by which time the company had chosen glassfibre instead of steel for the construction of the body.

Underneath was a new type of chassis featuring longeron tubing braced by box sections and flat floor platforms, along with Austin-type wishbone front suspension. Austin also provided much of the drivetrain with its 4-litre (244 cu in) engine and gearbox. A moving flap where the grille would normally be controlled air intake to the radiator and could be shut off completely in cold weather.

From 1956, there was an uprated 112kW (150bhp) version of the 541 which had wire wheels, and it was one of the first British production cars to feature all-round disc brakes.

In 1957, the Jensen 541R appeared with the same 112kW (150bhp) engine, along with rack-and-pinion steering and an opening bootlid. The 541S of 1960 was made slightly wider and longer, and it had a limited slip differential fitted as standard.

The 541's streamlined body was designed by Jensen's own stylist Eric Neale, and the car has a drag coefficient of just 0.39cd. The Jensen 541R from 1958 was one of the fastest cars of its time.

Engine: 3993cc (244 cu in), 6-cylinder
Power: 97kW (130bhp)
0–96km/h (60mph): 12.4 secs
Top speed: 174km/h (109mph)
Production total: 546

JENSEN CV8

1962–66

Sporting a controversially-styled glassfibre body, the Jensen CV8 used American V8 muscle. It was offered with Ferguson four-wheel drive from 1965 and had four-wheel disc brakes by 1966.

The Jensen CV8 effectively replaced the 541S, and it utilized the same PW chassis and glassfibre body configuration. New was the somewhat controversial styling, with its slanting quad headlights and redesigned front and rear end.

New to the car, too, was the addition of a huge Chrysler V8 unit under the bonnet, which was coupled to a Torqueflite automatic transmission which propelled the sleek-looking CV8 to more than 208km/h (130mph) and up to nearer 224km/h (140mph) after the 6.3-litre (383 cu in) V8 was installed in 1964.

The Mk II, which appeared in 1963, had adjustable Selectaride shock absorbers, while the Mk III of 1965 had equal-sized front headlights, better brakes and reclining front seats, along with a number of other refinements to the car's interior.

The CV8 was heavy to drive and had very high fuel consumption. It was expensive at £3861 at launch, so very few cars were sold. Nevertheless, it has a strong following today, and many original examples still survive, aided by the fact that they are made of corrosion-proof fibreglass and have bulletproof American engines.

Engine: 5916cc (361 cu in), V8-cylinder
Power: 227kW (305bhp)
0–96km/h (60mph): 8.4 secs
Top speed: 206km/h (129mph)
Production total: 499

ENSEN INTERCEPTOR

he Interceptor of 1966 had a triking profile with its long, flat onnet and rounded boat-tail rear nd. It was also exceptionally fast, apable of accelerating to 96km/h 60mph) in less than seven seconds.

he Interceptor's sleek grand-tourer ody was designed by Italian tylists Touring. Early examples ere actually made in Italy, while ooling was installed at Jensen's West Bromwich factory. Distinctive eatures included its huge curvy lass rear screen, macho V8 engine nd exclusive price tag. New, the nterceptor was considerably dearer han many Ferraris.

The FF (Ferguson Formula) ersion, which ran from 1966 to 971, was famed for being the orld's first four-wheel drive roduction car, using a transmis-ion developed by Harry Ferguson f tractor fame. Combined with Junlop's Maxeret aircraft-inspired nti-lock braking system, the car as known as being one of the astest yet safest cars on the road. he FF can be identified from

other Interceptors by its twin air intakes behind the front wheels and its slightly longer wheelbase.

The Interceptor was available as a hatchback coupé, a rare convertible (only 267 were made) and a rather odd-looking notchback coupé, while

the FF only came with a glass opening hatch. The Mk II from 1969 had a revised front, while the Mk III from 1971 gained cast alloy wheels. The SP, from 1971 to 1973 had a massive 7.2-litre (440 cu in) engine and louvres in the bonnet.

Engine: 7212cc (440 cu in), V8-cylinder
Power: 287kW (385bhp)
0–96km/h (60mph): 6.9 secs
Top speed: 240km/h (150mph)
Production total: 6727

ENSEN-HEALEY

ensen's sports convertible was the rainchild of new American owner Kjell Qvale, who appointed Donald Healey and his son Geoffrey onto he management board.

It was the Healey family who tyled the car which, in reality, orrowed most of its components rom other manufacturers. Lotus upplied the 16-valve engines and auxhall supplied the suspension nd steering (derived from its

Viva), while the gearbox was provided by Rootes.

Exciting prototype models were dumbed down to produce what is essentially a very bland-looking car with few redeeming features. Meanwhile, the Lotus engine was to prove unreliable and the body rusted very quickly.

A Getrag five-speed gearbox was fitted to the Jensen-Healey after 1974, which improved matters

slightly, and these later cars were the best. However, the car was an acquired taste, and it was never really what Qvale had envisaged for his 'dash for growth'.

In the end, the Jensen-Healey's anonymity, its lack of charisma and the global oil crisis led to the car's demise – and the company's. The Jensen name has since been revived, however, and is still making sports cars today.

The bland-looking Jensen-Healey was made even less attractive by bigger rubber bumpers fitted to comply with US safety regulations. The car was improved in later years by the fitting of a Getrag five-speed gearbox.

Engine: 1973cc (120 cu in), 4-cylinder
Power: 104kW (140bhp)
0–96km/h (60mph): 8.8 secs
Top speed: 200km/h (125mph)
Production total: 10,926

JENSEN GT

Engine: 1973cc (120 cu in), 4-cylinder
Power: 104kW (140bhp)
0–96km/h (60mph): 9 secs
Top speed: 192km/h (120mph)
Production total: 473

The Jensen GT followed the latest fad for touring cars with an opening hatch – such as the Volvo P1800 and the Reliant Scimitar. Despite the car's aspirations towards practicality, the interior was horribly cramped.

The mid-1970s saw an ever-increasing interest in sports cars which could also be practical for family use, hence the arrival of the Scimitar GTE and the Volvo 1800ES. Jensen's GT was a similar idea, being based on the bland Jensen-Healey, but with the addition of a rear opening hatch and a slightly higher roofline. Donald Healey had also decided to end his association with the Jensen company at this point, so the new car was known simply as the Jensen GT.

Despite an attempt at practicality, the 2+2 interior was cramped, and the back seat remained more of a bench than a serious attempt at accommodating children. To compensate, Jensen gave the car luxury fittings with burr walnut dashboard, electrically operated windows and optional leather seat facings and air conditioning.

The early problems with the Jensen-Healey had been mostly resolved by the time the Jensen GT went on sale, so in many respects the GT was a better car, and all models had the Getrag five-speed gearboxes fitted. However, the GT never really lived up to its promise, and it looked a very expensive proposition in comparison to its more mass-produced rivals.

JOWETT 8HP

Benjamin and William Jowett's company started producing cars in Bradford, England, in 1906, and one of its early offerings was a light two-seater, powered by a 816cc (50 cu in) flat-twin engine. Somewhat remarkably, the basic layout of this 1910 car was to remain in production until 1954.

The Jowett's engine capacity was increased to 907cc (55 cu in) after World War I, and the hard-working twin-cylinder engine gained a reputation for performing well and offering enviable reliability. It also proved to be extremely economical, returning very good fuel consumption figures.

The 1920s saw an electric starter fitted to the car and the arrival of a four-seater model, culminating in the launch of a saloon version in 1929.

Jowetts of the early 1930s also used the proven twin-cylinder

The austere-looking Jowett 8hp produced between 1937 and 1940 was identifiable by the rounded '8' symbol at the base of its chrome radiator. Top speed was a paltry 80km/h (50mph).

configuration and were often named after various forms of wildlife – including the sporty Kestrel of 1934 and the twin-carburettor Weasel – and, from 1935, the cars gained a four-speed transmission and centrifugal clutch mechanism.

Four-cylinder cars appeared in 1936, but the run of twin-cylinder cars continued with an increase in capacity to 946cc (58 cu in), producing 13kW (17bhp).

Engine: 946cc (58 cu in), 2-cylinder
Power: 13kW (17bhp)
0–96km/h (60mph): n/a
Top speed: 80km/h (50mph)
Production total: n/a

JOWETT BRADFORD

1946–54

Despite being built just after World War II, much of the technology behind Jowett's Bradford, such as its flat-twin engine, cart springs and cable brakes, dated back to the early part of the century, as did the use of an alloy over ash body and an agricultural three-speed gearbox.

It was available in a number of guises, including four- and six-light (window) forms (seating four and six people, respectively), but its most common use was as a commercial lightweight van. In this role, it was ideal and gained an excellent reputation as a worktool.

Performance was unsurprisingly poor, and the ride was very hard, but that did nothing to dent the car's appeal. Part of the Bradford's charm was its invincibility – it just never wore out, no matter what it was used for. A rugged, practical and reliable car, demand continued right up until the end of its production in the mid-1950s.

Even today, the Bradford has a strong following among vintage commercial enthusiasts, and a large proportion of the vehicles still exist.

Engine: 1005cc (61 cu in), 2-cylinder
Power: 19kW (25bhp)
0–96km/h (60mph): n/a
Top speed: 85km/h (53mph)
Production total: 40,995

JOWETT JAVELIN

1947–53

The Javelin represented an exciting new car in an otherwise gloomy postwar period. It had an all-new aerodynamic profile designed by Gerald Palmer, a flat-four engine and an advanced torsion-bar independent front suspension and rack-and-pinion steering. Its modern unitary construction was by local firm, Briggs Motor Bodies of Doncaster, England.

The end result was a car that not only looked very different, but also could carry a family of six (thanks to the unusual engine configuration which meant that it sat well forward of the cabin), handled and drove well, and could cruise at 128km/h (80mph).

Ultimately, the Jowett Javelin was never the success it should have been, partly because of its high price (being far more

expensive to run than more ordinary 9kW [12hp] Austins) and partly because of early problems with engine reliability and, later, with supply of bodies.

Plans to build a bulky two-door drophead with three abreast seating and a dickey seat (an extra row of seating extending from the boot), never went into production, despite a prototype appearing in 1948.

The Javelin was inspired by the curvy Lincoln Zephyr. Its flat four-cylinder engine gave it a low centre of gravity, providing the car with excellent road-holding.

Engine: 1485cc (91 cu in), 4-cylinder
Power: 37kW (50bhp)
0–96km/h (60mph): 22.2 secs
Top speed: 133km/h (83mph)
Production total: 22,799

JOWETT JUPITER

1950–54

The technologically advanced Jupiter, with its tubular framework construction, gained notoriety through its instant competition successes, which included first place in the 1950 under 1.5 litre class at Le Mans.

Having developed an advanced tubular chassis, Jowett decided to build an open roadster with wind-up windows and split front windscreen called the Jupiter.

While the running gear for the Jupiter was taken from the Jowett Javelin, the body was made from aluminium pressings on a tubular framework and was almost completely hand-built.

A key feature of the Jowett Jupiter was its huge one-piece lift-up nose section, a feature used

eight years later on the Austin-Healey 'Frogeye' Sprite. Like the Jowett, the Sprite also dropped the separate opening bootlid, with the luggage compartment only accessible by folding the seats in the cabin.

Jowett obviously had some reservations about the practicality of this idea, however, and, by 1952, the Jupiter MK IA had a proper bootlid, along with reshaped wings and more power.

The Jupiter gained successes at Le Mans between 1950 and 1952, and also had rally successes at the Monte Carlo International Rally, among others. By late 1953, despite the company experiencing financial problems, a prototype competition Jupiter, the R4, was shown with a shortened wheelbase, new chassis and stubby two-seater body. Three prototypes were built but, unfortunately, plans to produce the car died with the company a year later.

Engine: 1485cc (91 cu in), 4-cylinder
Power: 45kW (60bhp)
0–96km/h (60mph): 16.8 secs
Top speed: 134km/h (84mph)
Production total: 899

KAISER MANHATTAN

1950–55

Henry J. Kaiser was an American multimillionaire who had made his fortune mass-producing ships and houses before turning his hand to making cars, hoping to use his entrepreneurial skills to make even more money. The plan never became reality and none of his projects was successful.

The Manhattan was the first of a new series of cars which celebrated Kaiser's collaboration with the Dutch car designer Howard 'Dutch' Darrin, and it featured a striking body style with a low waistline and the use of vivid colour schemes. Technically it was quite advanced, with a number of safety features built in and good, sharp steering compared to other American cars of the time.

Exotic trim for the car included plastic that was made to look like alligator skin in the Manhattan 'Dragon' model, and the 1953 Manhattan even had a bamboo effect painted onto the roof.

Despite being successfully individual, the lack of a powerful V8 engine option was the main reason for the Manhattan's demise in 1955, despite the final examples being fitted with a supercharger.

The Kaiser Manhattan drove and handled well for a car of its size, but reliance on six-cylinder engines rather than the then industry norm of using eight meant that it was not popular with the American public.

Engine: 3707cc (226 cu in), 6-cylinder
Power: 86kW (115bhp)
0–96km/h (60mph): n/a
Top speed: 138km/h (86mph)
Production total: 202,856

KAISER-DARRIN

eputedly as a result of an rgument between the ill-tempered aiser and the creative Darrin, arrin spent his own money esigning the sleek, glassfibre- odied two-seater sports car at his alifornia studio. The result was the aiser-Darrin, with its pursed- pped front end and unusual doors at slid forwards into the front ings.The first Darrins had no turn gnals and a boot-lid that slid open istead of being hinged. Interest- gly, too, it was one of the first cars feature seat belts as standard.

All cars were mounted on a modified chassis made by Kaiser and used Kaiser steering and front suspension components. Power came from a weak single- carburettor six-cylinder Willys engine that produced just 67kW (90bhp), although at the end of production the remaining unsold stock (around 100 cars) was fitted with supercharged Cadillac V8s which were capable propelling the car to 224km/h (140mph).

The Kaiser-Darrin's folding Landau hood, which had an

unusual intermediate half-up position, could be replaced by a hardtop, giving the car a reasonable-looking profile.

Despite its wacky styling and sunny disposition, the car was a flop, and only 435 were made, of which many remained unsold. The gimmicky doors rattled and became stuck, and the vehicle's performance, initially, was unremarkable. Even worse was that the Kaiser-Darrin was more expensive than the faster, more glamorous Chevrolet Corvette.

The imaginatively styled Darrin bodies were made by boat builders Glasspar – the Kaiser-Darrin featured controversial sliding doors which had an unfortunate tendency to stick. The convertible version was less cramped inside than the steeply sloped hardtop.

Engine: 2638cc (161 cu in), 6-cylinder
Power: 67kW (90bhp)
0–96km/h (60mph): 15.1 secs
Top speed: 157km/h (98mph)
Production total: 435

LADA 2100 SERIES

1966, Italian car manufacturer iat collaborated with the then oviet government to provide the ecessary know-how and expertise produce cars, and the first roduct to leave the Russian Togli- ttigrad factory was the VAZ 2101, hich was basically a Fiat 124 with

a 1.2-litre (73 cu in) overhead camshaft engine.

Quickly becoming Russia's best- selling car, its export to western Europe started soon after, where it was renamed the Lada and badged simply as the 1200. Also available were 1300, 1500 and 1600 models.

Prices were cheap, but poor build quality and lack of product development meant that the Lada never received the same acclaim as it did in its home market.

Until recently, the same classic boxy shape from the 1960s could still be bought, known as the Riva,

although imports mostly came to an end in 1997.

Engine: 1198cc (73 cu in), 4-cylinder
Power: 46kW (62bhp)
0–96km/h (60mph): 16.6 secs
Top speed: 139km/h (87mph)
Production total: n/a

LAGONDA 11

The quintessentially British car company actually owed its existence to an American would-be opera singer. Wilbur Gunn came to England at the end of the 19th century hoping to find success on the stage, but instead ventured into motor transport. Even the company's name was slightly misleading, as it was actually taken from the town in Ohio from which Gunn originated,

Lagonda Creek, rather than having any continental overtones.

Starting in 1905, Gunn began manufacturing motorcyles before moving on to tricycle cars, then four-wheeled vehicles in 1907. Prior to World War I, his factory in Staines, Middlesex, was a specialist in the field of high-performance, big-engined cars which sold very well to imperial Russia.

Soon after, the company revised its policy and began making lightweight cars, one of which was a two-seater 8kW (11hp) roadster model, although an integral chassis and body construction actually served to make this a heavy car.

With its simple but effective longitudinal valve rockers operating the inlet valves, side exhaust valves and plunger type oil pump, the car

appeared many times in racing form at Brooklands; however, it was never officially categorized a a sports car despite being very successful in competition.

Engine: 1100cc (67 cu in), 4-cylinder
Power: 8kW (11hp)
0–96km/h (60mph): n/a
Top speed: n/a
Production total: n/a

LAGONDA 3-LITRE

Following World War I, Lagonda reworked its 1099cc (67 cu in) '11', and a 1420cc (87 cu in) engine was installed by 1921. In 1926, the company completely changed direction with its new 14/60, which featured a twin overhead camshaft, 2-litre (122 cu in) engine and powerful Rubery brakes – a car which was undoubtedly aimed at the lucrative Morris market. It was expensive, however, and sales suffered as a result.

Making the decision to venture into the sports car field instead, by the end of the 1920s, Lagonda had launched a 3-litre (183 cu in) six-cylinder car.

The 3-Litre featured traditional cycle mudguards and huge twin headlights which were set either side of the rounded grille and running boards. Lagonda wanted to produce a large car without the undue complication of complex mechanicals and so employed a

pushrod overhead-valve Meadows engine with a massive seven-bearing crankshaft and twin SU carburettors. Suspension was provided by half-elliptic springs, while the car's brakes were activated by rods at the front and cables at the rear.

Both well equipped and easy to maintain, the Lagonda 3-Litre was a worthy forerunner to the great pre-war 4.5-litre (275 cu in) Rapide and V12 Lagondas.

The conservative-looking 3-litre (183 cu in) had the traditional Lagonda right-hand gearchange, with top and third gear nearest th driver. A special low chassis sport version of this car was to appear in late 1929.

Engine: 2931cc (179 cu in), 6-cylinder
Power: 15kW (20bhp)
0–96km/h (60mph): 40 secs
Top speed: 125km/h (78mph)
Production total: 570

LAGONDA 2.6-LITRE

1946–53

The 2.6-Litre appeared just prior to the buy-out by Aston Martin in 1947 and utilized an engine and chassis designed by W.O. Bentley, along with rack-and-pinion steering and all-independent suspension.

Having been miraculously rescued from receivership in 1935 by Alan Good (who paid just £67,000 for the company), Lagonda's fate continued to look uncertain until David Brown's Aston Martin company bought it out in 1947. By this time, the new 2.6-litre (157 cu in) saloon had been introduced, designed by none other than the company's technical director at the time, W.O. Bentley.

Much smaller than the previous 1930s Lagondas, it featured a sturdy channel-section cruciform chassis with an all-independent suspension, with swing axles and torsion bars at the rear, rack-and-pinion steering and rear wheel inboard brakes.

There were two body types available, a two-door saloon and a sleek-looking four-seater convertible, each having semi-fared headlights, curving rearward chrome grille and sweeping front wings. The 1952 Mk II version had a variety of minor changes both inside and out, most of which were cosmetic. Only 550 of these luxurious cars were made during its seven-year production lifespan.

Engine: 2580cc (157 cu in), 6-cylinder
Power: 78kW (105bhp)
0–96km/h (60mph): 17.6 secs
Top speed: 144km/h (90mph)
Production total: 550

LAGONDA RAPIDE

1961–64

An excellent engine, sophisticated suspension and a handcrafted aluminium body should have been the perfect recipe for success. Sadly not – the Lagonda Rapide was a flop due to its diminutive cabin area in relation to the rest of the body and peculiar front end styling.

Lagonda's impressive new four-door saloon was like nothing that had gone before, but an eager public despaired at Touring's hideous treatment of the front end styling. Not only that, but the tiny cabin was completely out of proportion with the rest the car as well, with its vast bonnet and huge slab sides.

The Lagonda Rapide's platform chassis was a longer version of that used on the Aston Martin DB4, but with the exception that it had De Dion and torsion bar rear suspension, instead of the DB4's coil-sprung set-up. It also had the new Tadek Marek 4-litre (244 cu in) engine, inherited by the DB5 three years later. Borg Warner's automatic transmission was fitted as standard, with a manual all-synchromesh version offered as an optional extra.

What promised to be a beautiful car with its handcrafted aluminium body, wonderfully responsive engine and dual circuit servo-assisted all-round disc brakes proved a disappointment instead. Indeed, the Lagonda Rapide is still an unpopular car today.

Engine: 3995cc (244 cu in), 6-cylinder
Power: 176kW (236bhp)
0–96km/h (60mph): n/a
Top speed: 224km/h (140mph)
Production total: 54

LAMBORGHINI 350GT

The production version of the 350GT featured slim window pillars for extra visibility and unusual oval headlights atop the front-hinging bonnet section. While the overall design of the car was neat, the tail area of Touring's body was aesthetically disappointing.

Giotto Bizzarrini was responsible for the chassis and superb V12 engine, while Touring of Milan styled the lightweight aluminium body. Another star engineer, Giampaolo Dallara, introduced a number of other technical innovations such as the Girling disc brakes, ZF steering box, five-speed transmission and Salisbury differential at the back.

Despite being very fast, flexible and exhibiting superb handling, the Lamborghini 350GT lacked finesse – its odd gear ratios were partly to blame. It is certainly true however, that the 350 paved the way to future successes.

Ferruccio Lamborghini made his living making air conditioning equipment and air-cooled diesel tractors at the same time as harbouring a life-long obsession with motor cars, even competing in the 1948 Mille Miglia. He went on to buy a Ferrari; however, having received a dismissive response from the famous Maranello factory when it went wrong, he began a personal feud that was to result in him starting up his own sports car manufacturing company, poaching some of Ferrari's top engineers in the process.

The 350GT was the company's first production car. Ex-Ferrari man

Engine: 3463cc (211 cu in), 12-cylinder
Power: 201kW (270bhp)
0–96km/h (60mph): 6.8 secs
Top speed: 243km/h (152mph)
Production total: 120

LAMBORGHINI 400GT

The all-steel 400GT looked similar to its predecessor, the 350GT, but no two body panels were the same. The big difference was its extra two seats, making it into a 2+2. Headroom requirements meant that it was 6cm (2.5in) taller than the earlier car.

Stylists Touring of Milan altered the design of the 350GT to make it into a 2+2 with two extra seats in the back, albeit very small ones with restricted headroom.

For reasons of cost and to start something resembling mass production at its Sant'Agata Bolognese works, Lamborghini decided to use steel instead of alloy for the construction of the body (although the bootlid and bonnet were still aluminium). Ultimately, the car looked virtually the same as the 350GT, but with quad headlights and a suitably chopped fastback roofline.

To cope with the extra weight of the steel body, which was an extra

150kg (330lb) heavier than the 350GT, the 400GT was given extra engine capacity, more torque and more power. The V12, with its six twin-choke Weber carburettors, was very smooth, and top speed remained an impressive (but very noisy) 248km/h (155mph). There was also a two-seater convertible offered, although these were sold in low numbers.

With Touring in trouble, the last cars were produced by a company called Marazzi.

Engine: 3929cc (240 cu in), 12-cylinder
Power: 238kW (320bhp)
0–96km/h (60mph): 7.5 secs
Top speed: 248km/h (155mph)
Production total: 273

LAMBORGHINI MIURA

1966–72

It is almost impossible to describe in words the sensuous nature of the Lamborghini Miura. Breathtaking in its simplicity, it epitomized the glamour and the sheer exuberance of the 1960s. The Miura truly was a beautiful car, very much designed for beautiful people.

The company's engineers Giampaolo Dallara and Paolo Stanzani were both racing enthusiasts and, impressed with the recent successes of the mid-engined Ford GT40 and Ferrari 250LM, put forward plans for a road car based on similar racing car technology. Lamborghini approved and gave the go-ahead for development of the Miura (named after a breed of fighting bull, as Lamborghini himself was born under the Taurus astrological sign – the charging bull emblem was to appear on all Lamborghinis), but insisted that the car never be aimed at competition use.

With the Touring company rapidly going bankrupt, rival stylists Bertone enlisted its new young designer Marcello Gandini to design a suitable aluminium body to fit the Miura's chassis, and the result was pure beauty.

The chassis, complete with a transverse-mounted V12 engine positioned just behind the driver, was first shown at the 1965 Turin Motor Show, and it featured a steel monocoque chassis, along with double wishbones and coil springs front and rear, with an anti-roll bar at each end.

Low and wide, the Miura featured a slender rear-hinged tail and a front-hinging nose section that included the radiator and headlight units. Weight distribution was near perfect at 45:55, thanks to the careful positioning of the spare wheel and fuel tank at the front of the car.

Distinguishing features included retractable headlights that aligned with the bodywork and, on early cars, little strakes or 'eyelids' above and below the lights, a sharply raked windscreen (which served to roast the car's occupants in direct sunlight), small windows, large doors, and scoops in the rear wings to cool the rear brakes.

As if the styling itself were not enough, many cars were painted in gaudy orange and green, choices typical of flamboyant late 1960s colour schemes.

The Miura's cockpit was functional and cramped, and some of the controls – the gearchange in particular – were heavy. Driver comfort was further hindered by the position of the engine directly behind him or her, which produced immense heat and deafening noise. Not that there would have been many owners, exhilarated by the sound of that finely tuned V12, who would have complained much.

As you might expect, storage space in the Miura was limited – just a tiny shelf ahead of the passenger – although later cars gained generous door bins which helped the situation.

New Zealander Bob Wallace, a former racing mechanic, was put in charge of the car's development, and the Miura was greeted by universal applause from motoring pundits at the time, who raved about its handling, ride and braking ability. At the same time, a number of build problems, and the fact that

The Miura received beefed-up suspension and wider tyres later in life to combat the tendency towards front-end lift at high speed.

the steering was perhaps too light, the chassis flexed when driven hard and the nose section tended to lift at speed, went almost unreported.

Lamborghini claimed a top speed of 272km/h (170mph); in reality, however, only the 1969 S version with its 276kW (370bhp) and revised rear suspension could realistically come close to this figure. At this time, conditions for the driver were improved with a proper cockpit and the availability of air conditioning in the car for the first time.

In 1971, having received progressive strengthening of the chassis, the more aggressive-looking SV was born, with its wider wheelarches accommodating

The Miura's purity of form was the essence of its lasting beauty. Its mid-engine configuration was pioneering at the time.

wider wheels, which improved stability. To compensate for the extra drag, the V12's power was increased by 11kW (15bhp).

Today, the Miura is the ultimate in desirability and, while not without fault, its credentials as one of the most stunning sports cars of all time remains undented.

Engine: 3929cc (240 cu in), 12-cylinder
Power: 261kW (350bhp)
0–96km/h (60mph): 6.7 secs
Top speed: 272km/h (170mph)
Production total: 775

LAMBORGHINI ISLERO

1968–70

Engine: 3929cc (240 cu in), 12-cylinder
Power: 242kW (325bhp)
0–96km/h (60mph): 6.3 secs
Top speed: 260km/h (162mph)
Production total: 225

The Islero's subdued styling was intended to suit its role as a 'businessman's express', although later S models had flared arches, wider wheels and more power.

The Islero took over where the 400GT left off, and Ferruccio Lamborghini himself had one as his personal car. He also played a part in its rather subdued styling, making it more of an 'executive express' than a thoroughbred racer.

More of a 2+2 than a four-seater, the car took its name from the bull that killed a famous matador in the late 1940s. It was based on the same square-tube chassis as the earlier 350GT and 400, but was wider and slightly shorter.

Styling was by Marazzi, a company made up from the remnants of the Touring design house, and featured retractable headlights (with covers) and delicate chrome bumpers to give the car a clean, understated look.

Underneath the shallow bonnet line was the company's famed V12 powerplant, providing fantastic performance.
The S version was announced to answer criticism that the car was just a bit too subtle, and the addition of wider wheels and flared arches, foglights, sporty vents behind the front wheels and increased power – to 261kW (350bhp) – went some way toward achieving this.

LAMBORGHINI ESPADA

1968–78

The sleek-looking Espada, with its V12 engine at the front, was a true four-seater G, but its steeply sloping roofline limited rear headroom.

Marcello Gandini's four-seater concept car for the 1967 Geneva Show, the Marzal, provided the foundations for Bertone's magnificent Espada with its front-mounted V12 engine, steel platform chassis and integral bodywork..
The Lamborghini Espada (which means 'matador's sword') was a wide and bulky car, but Gandini's clever design made it look sleek from any angle, with its low bonnet and gently raked rear end. Wide-

opening conventional doors replaced the Marzal's whacky gullwing items, and the clever use of glass in the tail section meant reversing was easier than in any other supercar.
Inside, the Espada provided its occupants with every luxury, including leather and walnut trim. Despite having four seats (and four headrests), back-seat passengers had limited legroom.
A major irritation with the car was its poor driving position, and it seemed that little thought had been given to the location of instruments and other controls. Some drivers even reported that they could not reach the handbrake with their

seatbelt on. More headroom was added in 1969, and a special edition with a glass roof (harking back to the Marzal) was offered.

Despite its weight and road-hogging proportions, the Lamborghini Espada was easily capable of 248km/h (155mph).

Engine: 3929cc (240 cu in), 12-cylinder
Power: 261kW (350bhp)
0–96km/h (60mph): 6.9 secs
Top speed: 248km/h (155mph)
Production total: 1217

LAMBORGHINI JARAMA

Not a pretty sight from this angle, the Lamborghini Jarama featured unusual half-hooded headlights and a steeply sloping angular rear end. Unfortunately, weight and poor build quality let it down.

The Jarama was launched as a successor to the Islero and, being a 2+2, was meant to complement the Espada – sharing many of its components, but with a shorter chassis. It also attracted similar criticisms for its poor driving position and heavy steering.

Styling by Gandini gave the Jarama an aggressive look with its half-hooded headlights and large air intakes for the engine encroaching on an otherwise completely flat bonnet. Again, the name was associated with bullfighting, Jarama being a region of Spain famous for the activity.

Marazzi assembled the bodies, while Bertone made the steel panels and, being a bulky car, the Jarama weighed in at a heavy 1630kg (3590lb). To make up for this extra weight, power was increased to 261kW (350bhp).

The Jarama S (sometimes known as the 400GTS) was announced at the Geneva Show in 1972, and it had a much improved cockpit with even more power – 272kW (365bhp). Power steering and the Espada's Torqueflite automatic transmission were listed as options.

Never particularly popular, the Lamborghini Jarama, which was to be the last of the front-engined Lamborghinis, remains something of a hidden gem.

Engine: 3929cc (240 cu in), 12-cylinder
Power: 261kW (350bhp)
0–96km/h (60mph): 6 secs
Top speed: 260km/h (162mph)
Production total: 327

LAMBORGHINI URRACO

For some time, Lamborghini had wanted a 'small' entry level car in their range, but it was not until the arrival of the Urraco (meaning 'young bull') in 1970 that these plans reached fruition. However, in reality, the car was not particularly small or particularly successful.

Paolo Stanzani's engineering in many respects followed that of the Miura with its transverse mid-mounted engine, but the Urraco was otherwise all new, with a cheaper V8 powerplant and more simplistic mechanicals. Design by Bertone was clean-looking with

The well-proportioned Urraco (which means 'young bull') had a centrally mounted V8 engine. This vehicle was Lamborghini's attempt at making a 'small' car, and the Urraco appeared as a rival to Ferrari's 308 Dino.

retractable headlights, fastback rear and a long cabin area. Aspirations towards practicality were evident in the generous rear luggage compartment although, strangely, owners had to lift the engine cover to gain access to the filler cap. The driving position was again criticized, with drivers needing short arms and very long legs to operate the controls comfortably.

Production did not get properly under way until 1972, and a year later sales were still slow. This ushered in the P300 version in 1974 with an enlarged V8 and improved suspension and interior which continued until a tax-dodging 2.5-litre (153 cu in) car arrived in 1976.

Engine: 2463cc (150 cu in), 8-cylinder
Power: 164kW (220bhp)
0–96km/h (60mph): 7.2 secs
Top speed: 232km/h (145mph)
Production total: 776

LAMBORGHINI COUNTACH

The concept for what was to become the supercar icon of the 1970s appeared at the 1971 Geneva Motor Show; however, it took until 1974 before the fantasies of the Bertone designers were translated into a production car.

The Lamborghini Countach carried on where the stunningly beautiful Miura left off, continuing with the mid-engined configuration while seeking to avoid some of the shortcomings by using an altogether different approach. The 4-litre (240 cu in) V12 engine, instead of being mounted transversely, was positioned in line behind the driver and in front of the rear wheels. Hence its designation, the LP400, meant 4-litre (240 cu in) Longitudinale Posteriore. Legend has it that the car inherited its name when an engineer working at the Sant'Agata Bolognese factory saw the car for the first time. He is said to have exclaimed 'Countach!' (a Piedmontese expression for astonishment), a word he apparently often used when he saw a beautiful woman.

Paolo Stanzani, who had worked with Dallara on the Miura, had now become chief designer and engineer following Dallara's departure, and he enlisted the talented Massimo Parenti to help

Some of the purity of the earlier cars was lost in later years with the addition of flared wheelarches, and front and rear spoilers which did nothing to improve the already impeccable road-holding. Still, the Countach remained imposing.

him. Early examples had a semi-monocoque chassis, but this was soon replaced by a complex tubular spaceframe construction, over which was placed the unstressed aluminium bodywork. Most of the other running gear such as the suspension, steering, wheels and brakes were carried over from the Miura. Needless to say, the Countach's handling and performance were out of this world. Not only was it the world's fastest production car on paper, but also, thanks to its mid-engined configuration and leech-like grip, it was one of the most explosively thrilling cars if you were lucky enough to be behind the wheel.

Bertone's stylist, Marcello Gandini, based much of the Countach's explosive styling on racing cars of the late 1960s and,

rather than being beautiful like the Miura, the car was more brutal in appearance. Features included a short, stubby nose section, pop-up headlights, a steeply raked rectangular screen and quirky upwards-opening doors that hinged at the front. Later cars also had a huge rear spoiler. However, the low-slung bodywork created virtually no lift, so the spoiler was merely cosmetic and, in practice, only added to weight and drag.

The shape of the side windows ruled out any kind of winding mechanism, so they were divided horizontally, with the top half opening. Concerned commentators at the time could only assume that passengers would kick out the windscreen to escape in the unlikely event of a roll.

The cabin of the earliest cars mirrored the futuristic exterior, with a single spoke steering wheel and a variety of warning lights in front of the driver. However, as production went on, the interior became more conventional, with much use of black plastic and a huge central tunnel.

Indeed, this was how the Countach developed. From its early pure, uncluttered wedge-like shape, it became adulterated with mirrors, spoilers, additional air intakes and wheelarch extensions. US Federal law even imposed the fitting of ugly low-speed impact bumpers on later examples.

Production had reached just 23 cars by the time the LP400S arrived in 1978, the main

The Countach became the supercar of the 1970s. With suspension, steering and brakes carried over from the Miura, it featured an unstressed aluminium body and a V12 engine positioned longitudinally behind the driver.

difference being an improvement in the chassis and suspension, as wider, low-profile Pirelli P7 tyres were fitted to give more grip than the earlier Michelins. As a sacrifice to looks, wheelarch extensions had to be fitted to accommodate the new tyres. While being slightly lighter, the S had extra drag and was actually less powerful.

Following a change of ownership at Lamborghini, with the Mimran brothers taking control, the larger 4754cc (290 cu in) V12 appeared in the LP500S which restored power output to 279kW (375bhp). Later, engine capacity was again increased to 5167cc (315 cu in) and a new four-valve cylinder head was introduced. Called the Countach Quattrovalvole, this new engine produced 339kW (455bhp) and had a top speed of 295km/h (183mph). In 1990, the last cars, called the Anniversary (celebrating the 25th year of its conception), left the factory, and a legend went out of production.

Engine: 3929cc (240 cu in), 12-cylinder
Power: 287kW (385bhp)
0–96km/h (60mph): 5.2 secs
Top speed: 288km/h (180mph)
Production total: n/a

LAMBORGHINI SILHOUETTE

The two-seater Silhouette appeared at the Geneva Motor Show in 1976 and featured a targa-top removable roof section. Meant as a 'baby Countach' and based on the Urraco, it was never particularly liked.

Lamborghini built the targa-bodied Silhouette in an attempt to break into the 'open' car market, and indeed the Silhouette was the first open-top Lamborghini.

Its Bertone-styled body bore an uncanny resemblance to the Countach with its various angular features and familiar 'telephone dial' wheels. It was even named

the 'baby Countach' by some commentators at the time. In reality, however, the Silhouette was really nothing more than a restyled Urraco P300 with just two seats instead of four and a strengthened chassis to cope with the removable targa-type roof panel.

Despite looking good and being more refined than the Urraco, the

Silhouette was let down by a lack of development and poor build quality and reliability.

Perhaps worse still, in order to save money, the company made absolutely no effort to alter the car so that it would comply with US safety regulations, thus thwarting sales in a market that may have made the car a success.

After just one year, production of the Lamborghini Silhouette was stopped after a total of only 52 cars had been made.

Engine: 2996cc (182 cu in), 8-cylinder
Power: 197kW (265bhp)
0–96km/h (60mph): 5.6 secs
Top speed: 250km/h (156mph)
Production total: 52

LAMBORGHINI JALPA

The name 'Jalpa' harked back to earlier Lamborghini times and was the name of another fighting bull. Derived from the Urraco, and closely resembling the Silhouette, the car became the most successful

V8 in Lamborghini's stable, selling up to 200 units annually in its decade-long production lifespan.

Visually, it looked like a tamed Countach with its long nose section, air intakes mounted high

on top of the rear wings and its blunt rear end. The only big change was the wheels, with a switch being made to the more attractive Campagnolo alloys. The car, sanctioned after the takeover by the

Mimran brothers, was given little financial backing; however, any money available was devoted to mechanical upgrading under the control of ex-Maserati engineer Giulio Alfieri. A gifted man, Alfieri increased the stroke of the existing V8, making it very free-revving and much more refined than the earlier unit.

Meanwhile, there was still no power assistance for the rack-and-pinion steering, but this was not a problem because of the light front end caused by the Jalpa's 43.57 weight distribution.

The Jalpa carried on the Silhouette theme, but mechanical changes and a much-improved interior made it one of Lamborghini's bestselling V8 models. Top speed was a creditable 233km/h (145mph).

Engine: 3485cc (213 cu in), 8-cylinder
Power: 190kW (255bhp)
0–96km/h (60mph): 6.5 secs
Top speed: 233km/h (145mph)
Production total: n/a

LANCHESTER TWIN-CYLINDER

1900

The Lanchester company was formed by brothers George and Frederick, who made their name during Edwardian times with a number of technical innovations. Employing no one, the brothers were responsible for all their own engineering – even their complex and highly effective two-speed and reverse epicyclic gearbox, low-tension magneto ignition and worm-drive axle.

Lanchester's first car first appeared in 1895 with a single-cylinder 3.5kW (5hp) engine but, by 1900, it had developed this into a horizontally opposed two-cylinder 6kW (8hp) unit.

The engine itself featured two superimposed crankshafts, each with its own flywheel, rotating in opposite directions. These were subsequently geared together and linked to two pistons by six connecting rods. As the engine was operating in complete reverse rotation, it remained perfectly balanced and vibration-free at all times – a ground-breaking achievement. The engine was used in other Lanchester cars until 1905. By this time, the company had developed cantilever suspension and pre-selector three-speed epicyclic gears

Engine: 4035cc (246 cu in), 2-cylinder
Power: 6kW (8bhp)
0–96km/h (60mph): n/a
Top speed: n/a
Production total: n/a

LANCHESTER 40

1919–31

The Lanchester 40 sold in small numbers to the gentry and rivalled Rolls-Royce as being the finest car in the world in its era. It was a favourite of the then Duke of York, later King George VI.

The 40 was a stately machine, with a long wheelbase and limousine-type coachwork. Top speed was a mere 104km/h (65mph) because of its size and weight, but that did not worry those who wanted to travel with dignity in a high level of refinement.

The Lanchester brothers themselves were responsible for much of the car's mechanical integrity, manufacturing most of

the complex mechanical items themselves, even producing all-round brakes in 1924. Although not entirely hydraulic, the brakes relied on servo-assisted mechanical linkages fed via the gearbox.

A number of different body styles were available, even a highly modified racer built in 1921 which raced successfully at Brooklands, including winning a number of long-distance awards. The 40 was available until 1931, when it was replaced by the Straight Eight.

The Lanchester 40 appeared as a rival to Rolls-Royce, noted for its build quality, technical excellence and outstanding refinement.

Engine: 6178cc (377 cu in), 6-cylinder
Power: 75kW (100bhp)
0–96km/h (60mph): n/a
Top speed: 104km/h (65mph)
Production total: n/a

LANCHESTER 21

1923–31

The '21', as it became known, had an overhead camshaft, six-cylinder 2982cc (182 cu in) engine and was sold alongside the Sporting 40 which lasted until 1929. Nicknamed the 'pup', it was sold as a direct rival to the 'baby' Rolls-Royce Twenty, which was £50 more expensive at the time. Little more than a scaled down version of the 40, the 21 featured a four-speed sliding pinion gearbox, while the Rolls-Royce Twenty only had a three-speed transmission. It also had front brakes, with large-diameter aluminium drums lined with cast iron and deeply ribbed for circumferential strength and heat dispersion.

By 1931, financial troubles forced the Lanchester company to merge with Daimler to provide access to a cheaper market, and the factory was moved to Coventry. Lanchesters after that time were really nothing more than Daimlers with a Lanchester badge, and even this was to finally disappear altogether in 1956.

Frederick Lanchester went on to design electrical and mechanical inventions right up until his death in 1946. His brother George left the company to join Alvis, and he died in 1970.

Engine: 2982cc (182 cu in), 6-cylinder
Power: 16kW (21bhp)
0–96km/h (60mph): n/a
Top speed: 104km/h (65mph)
Production total: n/a

The Lanchester 21 was a scaled-down 40, with four-wheel servo brakes an option on later cars. It was priced to undercut the Rolls-Royce Twenty and was good for 104km/h (65mph).

LANCHESTER 14/LEDA

1950–54

Following BSA's buy-out of Daimler in 1910, BSA decided to add Lanchester to its portfolio in 1931. Thus the Lanchester 14 was mostly a precursor to what would become the Daimler Conquest (which followed in 1953), but with a Lanchester grille and new four-cylinder 45kW (60bhp) engine instead of the Conquest's six-cylinder unit. Made from pressed steel, the body was mostly hand-built. Cars for the UK market had a wooden frame, while those for the export market (called the Leda) used steel.

Underneath was a box-section chassis with torsion bar and wishbone independent front suspension, fluid flywheel, hydromechanical brakes, and Bijur automated lubrication to the central parts of the chassis.

There were three body types available – a saloon, drophead and coupé – and there were also plans to introduce two other body styles, the Dauphin and Sprite, but these were never put into production.

The 14 was an unremarkable car, and relatively uninspiring to look at. The Lanchester name, though not used on a car since the cancelled Sprite project of 1955, was purchased by Jaguar in 1960.

Engine: 1968cc (120 cu in), 4-cylinder
Power: 45kW (60bhp)
0–96km/h (60mph): n/a
Top speed: 120km/h (75mph)
Production total: 2100

LANCIA LAMBDA

1928–31

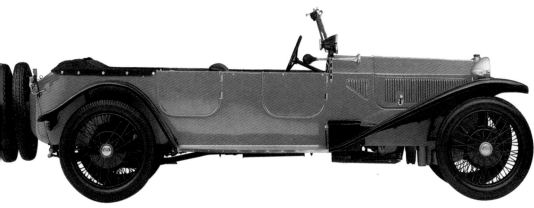

Vincenzo Lancia, the creator of the marque that bore his name, was on a sea trip when he became interested in the way the ship was built. The hull was far more rigid than could ever be achieved with the conventional separate chassis of a car, and Lancia started to think about applying the principles of hull construction to motor engineering. In 1919, he patented his idea, which later became universally known as unitary construction.

The first car to use the principle was the Lancia Lambda of 1923. Although the cars looked quite conventional on the surface, the all-in-one chassis and body structure was revolutionary. It made the Lambda very strong and gave it superb road-holding, unlike anything else available at the time. Its compact V4 engine gave the car performance to match.

The Lambda pioneered the use of monocoque engineering during the 1920s, but customers and coachbuilders objected to how difficult it was to put different bodies on the cars, so the Lambda went back to a conventional chassis in 1928.

Series 8 and 9 Lambdas, built from 1928 to 1931, dispensed with the monocoque design, however, in order to make it easier for coachbuilders to fit their own bodies. Yet the car's engine capacity and performance were increased, as if to make up for this technologically backwards move.

Engine: 2569cc (157 cu in), V4-cylinder
Power: 51kW (69bhp)
0–96km/h (60mph): n/a
Top speed: 120km/h (75mph)
Production total: 4403

LANCIA APRILIA

1936–49

Compared to the standard vehicles mass-produced by other European firms, the Aprilia was years ahead of its time. Its specification sheet read like that of a car built in the late 1950s, not the 1930s, and it became one of Lancia's most significant models ever.

The Lancia Aprilia boasted monocoque construction, all-round independent suspension, hydraulic brakes and neat, pillarless styling. A wind tunnel was used to develop the modern design, making the shape very aerodynamic for its era. Power came from a small V4 overhead camshaft engine, which was small, at 1352cc (83 cu in), but lively. In fact, an Aprilia could outperform many supposedly superior sports cars. Three different wheelbase lengths were available, and two could be supplied in conventional chassis format for those customers who wanted to fit their own coachbuilt special bodies.

At the end of World War II, production of the Aprilia restarted, with a 1486cc (91 cu in) V4 being used in place of the previous engine. The last example was built in October 1949 and, when it came out of the factory, a handwritten note by an unknown employee was found in the boot, paying tribute to one of Italy's most innovative cars.

Engine: 1352cc (83 cu in), V4-cylinder
Power: 36kW (48bhp) at 4300rpm
0–96km/h (60mph): 22.8 secs
Top speed: 132km/h (82mph)
Production total: 27,642

Italy's coachbuilders put some wonderful-looking bodies on the Aprilia chassis. However, owners who went for the standard Lancia bodies did not lose out by much. They benefited from getting a car with monocoque construction and could also choose three different lengths.

LANCIA AURELIA

The Aprilia was a tough car to follow, but the Lancia which superseded it was just as dynamic, both in terms of mechanical specification and looks. The main innovation was the all-alloy V6 engine, designed during World War II. The cylinder banks were mounted at a 60-degree angle to each other, giving the smooth engine impeccable balance. The Aurelia perpetuated the unitary construction and all-independent suspension of its predecessor, but had its sleeker body designed with assistance from Pininfarina. Despite the bigger engine, it was a slower car than the Aprilia because it was heavier.

The saloon was known as the B10, and there was also the B15 model (a limousine). Most attention, however, was reserved for the coupé B20 GT version, which had a twin-carburettor 2-litre (121 cu in) V6, and elegant styling by Pininfarina.

Pininfarina also designed the handsome B24 Spider convertible in 1955, which used a new 2451cc (150 cu in) V6. The Spider name was to be short-lived, however. After a year, the design was altered slightly (losing the original wraparound windshield) and the vehicle renamed the GT 2500 Convertible.

Engine: 1991cc (121 cu in), V6-cylinder
Power: 52kW (70bhp) at 4500rpm
0–96km/h (60mph): 18 secs
Top speed: 148km/h (92mph)
Production total: 16,897

One of Lancia's most memorable designs ever was the B20 Aurelia Gran Turismo (right), with its impressive aerodynamic flowing lines and performance engine. However, Pininfarina also turned in memorable styling for the B24 Spider convertible (below), which was launched in 1955.

LANCIA APPIA

The Appia was Lancia's budget model for the 1950s and early 1960s, built to replace the Ardea. Despite being smaller and cheaper than the Aurelia, the Appia (named after a Roman road) shared many styling similarities with its bigger sister; however, it was more basic both mechanically and in terms of interior trim.

The Appia featured a brand-new, small-capacity V4 engine, with the V angle a very sharp 10 degrees. The engine was not very powerful; however, the car's performance was surprisingly good, thanks to the aluminium doors, boot, bonnet and rear wings, which made the Appia a very light vehicle.

In 1956, a Series 2 model appeared, with a more pronounced notchback rear end, which provided more luggage space as well as updating the general look of the car. The car's individual

front seats were also replaced with a single bench seat.

Power output increased as well, which improved the car's top speed. In 1959, power climbed again to 39kW (53bhp) for the Series 3, and a new horizontal grille was also adopted.

As well as van, ambulance and pick-up versions, coachbuilt models appeared, styled by carrozzeria such as Vignale, Farina, Lombardi, Viotti and Scioneri. Most notable of these special Appias was the Zagato GT coupé, which was unusually shaped, but immensely stylish and also extremely rare – only 721 of these vehicles were built. Production of the Appia finished in 1963.

It was small and it was cheap, but the Appia was still a stylish machine. The earliest cars had a vertical grille but, by 1959, this had been changed for a wider item to update the look for the 1960s.

Engine: 1090cc (67cu in), V4-cylinder
Power: 32kW (43.5bhp) at 4800rpm
0–96km/h (60mph): 23 secs
Top speed: 132km/h (82mph)
Production total: 107,245

LANCIA FLAMINIA

1956–70

Although intended to replace the Aurelia, Lancia's aristocratic Flaminia (another Roman road name) appeared two years before its predecessor was dropped. In look, it was very different to the rotund Aurelia, as Pininfarina chose to style the car with more angular lines. At the rear, there were even small fins, giving the Italian saloon something of an American look. With the Aurelia engine unable to be developed any further, Lancia put a new 2458cc (150 cu in) V6 unit in the Flaminia, as well as new wishbone and coil-spring front suspension.

There were no major changes until 1959, when a range of new Flaminias appeared, all with sporting pretensions. A very elegant coupé based on the Pininfarina Floride II show car) was joined by the more striking Flaminia GT coupé and convertible, with a substantially shortened wheelbase and very effective use of quad headlights to give a purposeful front aspect. Zagato also came up with pretty

and fast two-seater coupés, named the Sport and Supersport.

From 1963, all Flaminias were uprated with a 2775cc (169 cu in) V6 engine – the coupés and convertibles were tuned to produce more power than the saloon.

There were several different variants of Flaminia, but one of the best-looking ones was the Flaminia convertible, with design by Touring of Milan. Four limousine versions of the Flaminia were also built for use by the Italian government.

Engine: 2458cc (150 cu in), V6-cylinder
Power: 82kW (110bhp) at 5200rpm
0–96km/h (60mph): 14.5 secs
Top speed: 169km/h (105mph)
Production total: 12,685

LANCIA FLAVIA

1960–74

It was no surprise that the new mid-sized Lancia of 1960 perpetuated Lancia's tradition of using Roman road names. What was more surprising was its mechanical design. The Flavia was the first front-wheel drive Lancia, and it turned away from the usual V-shaped engine by using an alloy flat-four 'boxer' unit.

It did not stop there. The Flavia had disc brakes on all wheels, with vacuum assistance and a dual hydraulic system for extra safety. However, the styling was ordinary. Lancia did the work itself, and the overall look was angular and conventional, although the quad headlights did add a little flair. Pininfarina did better with the coupé version in 1961, and Vignale built an attractive convertible from 1962. As usual, though, it was Zagato who stole the limelight with the Flavia Sport of 1963. The uniquely styled Sport was highly individual yet strangely appealing.

The Flavia saloon remained in production for 14 years, during which time engine size went up to 1.8 litres (110 cu in) and then to 1991cc (121 cu in). The saloon was also restyled in 1967, and again in 1969, when the coupé version was updated as well.

With the spread of front-wheel drive cars during the 1960s, Lancia got in on the act with the Flavia. Another feature of the car was mountings for front seatbelts. At the time, only a few car companies offered this safety option.

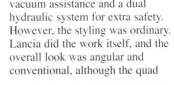

Engine: 1.5-litre (92 cu in), 4-cylinder
Power: 58kW (78bhp) at 5200rpm
0–96km/h (60mph): 18.7 secs
Top speed: 154km/h (96mph)
Production total: 106,476

LANCIA FULVIA

1963–73

The replacement for the small Appia in 1963 was the Fulvia, featuring a completely new V4 engine, but with the same front-wheel drive layout as the Flavia. The Fulvia also shared the same suspension and disc brakes as its mid-sized sibling and similar box-like styling, although the Flavia looked the better of the two.

Once the saloon had established itself, Lancia started to introduce different variants. First came the Fulvia coupé in 1962, which cosmetically shared no similarities with the saloon at all. Built on a shortened floorpan, the compact coupé was an attractive design. A year later came an HF (High Fidelity) coupé version with no bumpers, more power, aluminium panels and Plexiglass windows. This car was intended more for competition than for road use.

Zagato received its chance to produce a Fulvia offshoot in 1967. Its effort was another coupé but, as usual for Zagato, its Sport model was radically different to the

mainstream efforts, especially at the front, which had a strange headlight layout.

Changes to the Fulvia up until 1973 included revised styling, larger and more powerful engines, and new five-speed gearboxes.

Standard Fulvia coupés such as this had a purposeful front aspect, thanks to their quad headlights. The Zagato Sport was even more dramatic, with fastback rear styling, bizarre rectangular front lights and lightweight aluminium body.

Engine: 1298cc (79 cu in), V4-cylinder
Power: 65kW (87bhp) at 6000rpm
0–96km/h (60mph): 15.6 secs
Top speed: 164km/h (102mph)
Production total: 339,653

LANCIA STRATOS

1973–75

The Fulvia distinguished itself in rallying, but there was no obvious competition successor in the Lancia line-up. Then, in 1970, competition director Cesare Fiorio saw a Bertone concept car at the Turin

Motor Show. The wedge-shaped, low-slung futuristic design impressed and inspired him. When he saw a restyled version in 1971, fitted with a mid-mounted Ferrari Dino V6 engine, Fiorio knew he

had his new rally car. The use of the Dino engine was made possible by Fiat's 1970 takeover of Lancia, shortly after it had also gained control of Ferrari. The rest of the car was a steel monocoque, with all

the panels constructed from glassfibre. First and foremost, the Stratos was built solely to win the World Rally Championship; however, 500 road cars had to be built for homologation purposes.

Throughout the 1970s, the Stratos utterly dominated rallying, winning the World Championship three years in a row. It needed a skilled driver to get the best from the car, but it could beat any competitor in the right hands.

The Lancia Stratos was built from 1973 to 1975, but some of the road cars could still be bought 'new' up until 1980.

One of Lancia's most extreme models and most outrageous cars ever, the Stratos had a dramatic wedge profile which underlined its performance, and the combination of the fibreglass shape and Ferrari engine made it a rally legend.

Engine: 2481cc (151 cu in), V6-cylinder
Power: 142kW (190bhp) at 7000rpm
0–96km/h (60mph): 7 secs
Top speed: 225km/h (140mph)
Production total: 492

LANCIA BETA

robably the most interesting ancia Beta variant was the HPE, high-speed load-lugging estate. he ribbed black trim on the rear anel lined up with slats covering he hatchback's rear window.

With Fiat in charge, Lancia's eputation started to crumble – or, ather, rust. With the Beta, Lancia's orrosion problems became well nown, and buyers began to focus n the cars' appalling ability to dissolve, rather than the fact that the range was quite an impressive entry in the Lancia catalogue.

The Beta was the first design to appear since the Fiat takeover, and it used Fiat's new twin-camshaft engine for power, fitted transversely and driving the front wheels. Over the course of its Beta career, it was available in 1297cc (79 cu in), 1438cc (90 cu in), 1592cc (97 cu in), 1585cc (97 cu in), 1756cc (107 cu in) and 1995cc (122 cu in) sizes.

Launched first was the fastback saloon, with its neat styling making it look like it should actually have been a hatchback. The shortened coupé introduced in 1973 was designed by Zagato and, although less individual than previous Lancia efforts, it was still a very attractive car.

The Lancia Beta Spider, which was launched in 1975, was based on the coupé; however, the Spider had a convertible targa roof. In the same year, the Lancia Beta HPE (High Performance Executive) appeared, which was a very stylish sporting estate.

Supercharged Volumex versions of both the coupé and HPE were available by the mid-1980s.

Engine: 1756cc (107 cu in), 4-cylinder
Power: 82kW (110bhp) at 6000rpm
0–96km/h (60mph): 10.7 secs
Top speed: 175km/h (109mph)
Production total: 387,365

LANCIA BETA MONTECARLO

he Montecarlo name referred to ancia's victory in the 1975 Monte arlo Rally and, although named s a Beta model, it was really a istinct model in its own right. It ay have used parts from the eta, but they were put together in very different way.

The Montecarlo was conceived s a Fiat, a bigger sister for the 1/9 sports car. Pininfarina esigned the entire car, and there ere initial plans to fit a 3-litre 183 cu in) V6 engine. However, he fuel crisis put an end to this dea so, when the Montecarlo ppeared with a Lancia badge, it as fitted with a mid-mounted ersion of the Beta 2-litre (122 cu n) engine. For the US-market corpion versions, 1756cc (107 cu n) engines were installed, but a ow 60kW (80bhp) power output

The Beta Montecarlo had very little in common with other Beta models. It was intended as a Fiat, then mooted as an Abarth model, before receiving a Lancia badge by default.

resulted in poor performance.

Serious handling and braking problems caused the Montecarlo to be withdrawn in 1978. Modified versions returned in 1980, with a revised grille and new alloy wheels externally signalling the relaunched series, but the new version was unavailable in the United States.

Engine: 1995cc (122 cu in), 4-cylinder
Power: 89kW (120bhp) at 6000rpm
0–96km/h (60mph): 9.8 secs
Top speed: 193km/h (120mph)
Production total: 7595

LANCIA GAMMA

1976–84

The Gamma's birth was a difficult one, and its production life was not easy either. The coupé was an interesting though angular effort by Pininfarina, but its mechanical failings are what most people now remember the Gamma for.

The first Lancia Gamma was made in 1910, then, in the 1970s, Lancia joined with Citroën to start work on its second range of cars to be named after the third letter of the Greek alphabet.

The Gamma was not one of Lancia's better products. The 'technical information sharing' agreement between Italy and France ended in 1972 when French President Charles de Gaulle became nervous about the amount of information being passed to the Italians. So Lancia developed the car alone, raiding the Beta parts bin and coming up with new flat-four engines of 1999cc (122 cu in), for the Italian market only, and 2484cc (152 cu in), for export, to drive the front wheels.

Pininfarina styled the bodies, a saloon and a coupé. Aimed at the executive market, the saloon was a rather awkward-looking car, but the coupé was very stylish.

Neither was reliable or well built, though. A design flaw in the engine meant that camshaft belts would slip, with calamitous and expensive consequences. Overheating was a problem as well. Even if the Gamma survived both these faults, however, rust was still a major issue. Despite fuel-injection appearing in 1981, sales of the Lancia Gamma never came close to expectations.

Engine: 2484cc (152 cu in), 4-cylinder
Power: 104kW (140bhp) at 5400rpm
0–96km/h (60mph): 9.7 secs
Top speed: 195km/h (121mph)
Production total: 22,085

LANCIA DELTA HF TURBO

1986

Lancia's return to rallying resulted in an impressive new breed of potent Lancias. Work started on the Lancia Delta in the mid-1970s, with the 1301cc (79 cu in) and 1498cc (91 cu in) engines designed by Fiat's Lampredi and the hatchback body designed by Giorgio Giugiaro, fresh from his success with the Volkswagen Golf.

The car was launched in September 1979 and, once the standard version had established itself, Lancia started to release more interesting offshoots. By far the most fascinating – at least until the arrival of the Integrale – was the Delta HF Turbo. The HF Turbo featured not only four-wheel drive, but also a turbocharged 1995cc (122 cu in) twin overhead camshaft engine with electronic fuel injection – a very 'hot hatch'.

Visually, there was little to distinguish the HF Turbo from the less high-specification Delta versions, which probably added to the fun. Apart from alloy wheels, air intakes on the bonnet, round twin headlights on each side and supplementary lights under the bumper, the HF Turbo could easily be mistaken for an 'ordinary' Delta – at least until the driver pressed the accelerator pedal. The HF Turbo lasted just a year, before it was replaced by an even more extreme Delta special model.

The Lancia Delta HF Turbo's styling was far removed from the Stratos, being based on a humble hatchback. But the four-wheel drive and turbocharger made it almost as exciting.

Engine: 1995cc (122 cu in), 4-cylinder turbo
Power: 123kW (165bhp) at 5250rpm
0–96km/h (60mph): 6.6 secs
Top speed: 209km/h (130mph)
Production total: n/a

LANCIA DELTA INTEGRALE

1987–94

Lancia built the Delta Integrale for the public because it had to build 5000 road examples; however, underneath lay pure rally car. The Delta's 'house brick' styling was enhanced by bodywork extrusions on the Integrale.

The Delta was chosen as the basis for Lancia's revived rally campaign, and an HF 4x4 managed to win the World Championship in 1987. That was not enough for Lancia, though. In October 1987 came the Delta Integrale, the word *integrale* meaning 'complete' in Italian. It was an apt description because the Integrale was a complete performer. Developed from the four-wheel drive HF turbo, 5000 road cars had to be built for homologation purposes.

Despite the car's angular, aerodynamic appearance, the Integrale had electrifying handling, and a top speed approaching 240km/h (150mph). And all this despite still looking like a humble

hatchback, albeit a muscular version with a body kit and big wheelarches.

For 1990, there was a 16-valve version, and in 1991 came the Integrale Evoluzione, with more power, a better suspension set-up and a tailgate spoiler to improve

stability. An Evoluzione 2 appeared in 1992. In competition, the Integrale won the World Rally Championship for Makes every year from 1987 to 1992, providing great publicity for Lancia. The Integrale was dropped in 1994, with nothing to replace it.

Engine: 1995cc (122 cu in), 4-cylinder turbo
Power: 138kW (185bhp) at 5300rpm
0–96km/h (60mph): 6.4 secs
Top speed: 209km/h (130mph)
Production total: n/a

LANCIA THEMA 8.32

1986–92

Lancia teamed up with other European manufacturers to build the Thema. Its mid-1980s executive saloon was a collaboration with Saab, Fiat and Alfa Romeo, with the other versions of the car

eventually appearing as the Saab 9000, the Fiat Chroma and the Alfa Romeo 164.

Lancia launched its variant in November 1986. Although visually similar to the others, the Lancia

Is it a Lancia, a Saab, a Fiat or an Alfa Romeo? Actually, it's all four. The Thema was the result of a collaboration between all of these companies, with the 8.32 a high-performance luxury range-topper.

Thema had different engines and suspension. And, in 1986, a radical high-performance version, the 8.32, appeared as well.

The Lancia Thema 8.32 was so-called because it had a V8 engine (which was closely related to the Ferrari 308 unit) and 32 valves. Fuel injection was fitted as standard, and a novel feature was a rear wing which could be manually operated by the driver.

Although the 8.32 looked like other models in the Thema range, it had a more luxurious wood and leather interior, as well as extra hand-built touches to further justify its expensive price tag.

Some minor styling changes were carried out on the Thema 8.32 in 1988, in common with the rest of the Thema range. The angle of the car's grille was changed, and the lights were redesigned, while side skirts were added which made the car look sleeker.

Engine: 2927cc (178 cu in), V8-cylinder
Power: 160kW (215bhp) at 6750rpm
0–96km/h (60mph): 7.2 secs
Top speed: 225km/h (140mph)
Production total: 2370

LA SALLE V8

1937–39

The La Salle, part of the General Motors stable, was initially a lower-priced running mate for Cadillac, and later bodyshells were shared with American car manufacturers Buick and Oldsmobile.

Californian designer Harley J. Earl set up La Salle under the wing of General Motors in an attempt to produce a budget-priced range of cars designed to run side-by-side with Cadillac. With its big V8, the car was prized for its supreme flexibility in top gear, its acceleration and its excellent column-mounted three-speed transmission, which offered synchromesh on second and top gear.

Despite its size, the car was noted for its manoeuvrability and handling. Although there were big, externally mounted independent coil springs at the front, the ride was soft with lots of body roll; however, the car's roadholding ability was surprisingly good.

Also commented on at the time were the car's excellent brakes, which were operated hydraulically and had self-servo shoes that worked progressively according to the amount of pressure put on the pedal by the driver. Two spare wheels were placed alongside the bonnet, and the car was equipped with a generous amount of space for luggage in the boot.

Towards the end of its lifespan, the La Salle's bodyshell was shared with both Buick and Oldsmobile. Production of this car finally ceased in 1939.

Engine: 5277cc (322 cu in), 8-cylinder
Power: 28kW (37bhp)
0–96km/h (60mph): n/a
Top speed: 149km/h (93mph)
Production total: n/a

LEA-FRANCIS 1.5-LITRE TYPE S

1928–3

Having made a name for itself by producing quality motorcycles, Lea-Francis, based in Coventry, England, began making cars. Its first efforts were small sporting cars with light chassis. The Meadows-engined 11/22 model was one of Lea-Francis's first complete cars.

When the company later adopted a 1.5-litre (91 cu in) Meadows unit, it began producing some creditable sports cars, such as the Cozette-supercharged Hyper model with its fabric or metal two-seater body.

Due to its light weight, and despite its narrow width and tall height of its two-seater body, the 1.5-Litre Supercharged Type S proved to be a very quick car and gained honours by winning the very first Ulster TT race with driver Kaye Don at the wheel.

As well as the two-seater, the company also offered a four-seater and a saloon, as well as a more slender Brooklands sports version.

The Hyper, with its distinctive backward-sloping grille, was one of the first British production cars to feature supercharging, and it was capable of an impressive 136km/h (85mph).

Engine: 1496cc (91 cu in), 4-cylinder
Power: 9kW (12bhp)
0–96km/h (60mph): n/a
Top speed: 136km/h (85mph)
Production total: n/a

LEA-FRANCIS 12HP

1938–40

Having closed temporarily in 1935, Lea-Francis went back into business in 1937, only to have to deal with a high purchase tax and shortage of raw materials due to the onset of World War II.

Their elegant 12hp model was available in three body styles – a four-light (seater) saloon, a six-light saloon in which the rear quarter-lights hinged open vertically, and an attractive two-door drophead coupé with forward-opening suicide doors. All used the same metal-over-ash frame construction.

The four-cylinder engine was a twin-camshaft unit, but differed by having both camshafts located close to the top of the cylinder block, as opposed to the head itself, which was the conventional overhead arrangement to aid cooling. There was a single-plate clutch, a four-speed gearbox and a divided propshaft and spinal bevel rear axle.

By the 1950s, the company was in financial trouble again and closed, although a third appearance was made in 1960 with the odd and entirely unsuccessful Ford Zephyr-engined Leaf-Lynx. This was the end of the firm until the 1980s, when a brief alliance with Jaguar resulted in the production of an unsuccessful roadster.

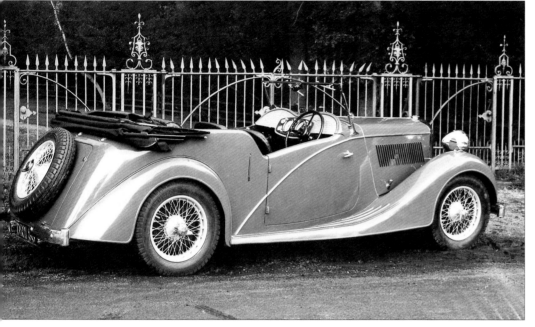

The open-top two-door coupé version of the Lea-Francis 12hp model was particularly alluring, and it featured 'suicide' forward-opening doors and a metal-over-ash frame construction.

Engine: 1489cc (91 cu in), 4-cylinder
Power: 38kW (50bhp)
0–96km/h (60mph): n/a
Top speed: n/a
Production total: n/a

LEYLAND EIGHT

1920–23

The magnificent Leyland Eight, designed by J.G. Parry Thomas during World War I, was built with aspirations to becoming the best car in the world, and nothing was spared in terms of cost, with only Rolls-Royce being seen as a competitor. The dream could have become reality if the Leyland company had given Thomas the backing he deserved instead of concentrating on the manufacture of trucks. Indeed, the car was rudely dropped after postwar financial problems took their hold.

The Leyland company's first attempt at producing a luxury car where money was no object was to be the Leyland Eight. Launched at the 1920 Olympia Show, only 18 left the production line.

Visually, the car was robust-looking with an upright rectangular grille, a flat hinged windscreen and peculiar steel disc wheels with conical centre caps. The Eight was a masterpiece of technical detail, with leaf-spring control of the valves and an unusual camshaft drive. It even featured an early form of vacuum servo-assisted rear drum brakes, although there were no brakes at all at the front.

Some examples were given an increased stroke which increased capacity of the straight-eight cylinder engine to 7266cc (443 cu in). Only one example of the Eight exists today – a short-chassis sports car which was built in 1927 from parts held at Brooklands.

Engine: 6987cc (426 cu in), 8-cylinder
Power: 149kW (200bhp)
0–96km/h (60mph): n/a
Top speed: n/a
Production total: 18

LEYLAND P76

1973–74

Engine: 2622cc (160 cu in), 6-cylinder
Power: 97kW (130bhp)
0–96km/h (60mph): n/a
Top speed: 168km/h (105mph)
Production total: 22,000

Big cars are popular in Australia, and the Australian-built P76 was supposed to compete directly against the likes of Holden, Ford and Chrysler. Running gear consisted of MacPherson strut suspension, front disc brakes and a choice of either a three- or four-speed automatic Borg Warner transmission.

Despite styling by Michelotti and the choice of either an overhead camshaft six-cylinder Leyland-derived unit or Rover V8 engine, the Leyland P76 proved to be a disaster. Indeed, it was cruelly described as the 'Australian Edsel'. Its conventional styling did not help, nor did production problems

and reports of poor build quality.

A short-wheelbase 'Force 7' coupé version was built in an attempt to rescue sales, but only a handful of cars was ever made. Finally, the oil crisis and its general lack of appeal killed the car off in

1974, at the same time Leyland was being nationalized by the British government and was about to become British Leyland. A total of around 22,000 cars was made, but very few were exported outside of Australia.

Leyland's Michelotti-styled P76 was powered by a conventional six cylinder engine, although there was also the option of Rover's all-alloy V8 unit. A coupé version of the car was added to the range, but it, too, failed to catch popular appeal.

LIGIER JS2

1970–7

The French-built JS2 coupé was the brainchild of former international rugby player, racing driver and multi-millionnaire Guy Ligier. J.S. were the initials of a racing driver, Jo Schlesser, a friend of Ligier, who was killed while competing on the track in 1968.

The constituents of the Ligier JS2 were a pressed-steel platform

chassis dressed in a glassfibre two-door coupé body, and the car was powered by a mid-mounted Citroën SM V6 engine which was turned through 180 degrees (Ligier was also responsible for building the SM engine).

Servo-assisted all-round disc brakes and fully independent suspension completed the car.

Styling of the JS2 mirrored the era, with Perspex-enshrouded headlights, large screen, squat rear end and alloy wheels. There was even an air intake resembling that of the Lamborghini Countach on top of the rear wing to blow air onto the engine.

The car never sold particularly well, although it does have a strong

following in its native France. Guy Ligier himself later achieved motor racing fame by making Formula One cars.

Engine: 2965cc (181 cu in), V6-cylinder
Power: 142kW (190bhp)
0–96km/h (60mph): n/a
Top speed: 245km/h (153mph)
Production total: 150

LINCOLN KB

1932–3

This attractive 1932 12-cylinder sports two-seater with bodywork by Brunn was based on the Lincoln KB chassis.

Henry M. Leland was responsible for setting up first Cadillac, then the Lincoln Motor Company, which started trading in 1917. During World War I, Lincoln supplied the US military with powerplants for Liberty aeroplanes. In 1922, the company was bought by Ford.

The huge KB range of cars was seen by many as the archetypal American car of the 1930s, and it became a firm favourite of the White House, conveying presidents from state to state in complete luxury. The body was a four-door convertible design with a lengthy hood that folded at the back by two substantial chrome hinges. A covered spare wheel was positioned in front of the driver's door.

Braking was mechanical (but vacuum-assisted), and Lincolns were renowned for their lack of independent suspension. However Leland's longitudinal semi-elliptic suspension design, which actually dated back to the 1920s, worked well enough.

The KB series was to run until 1940 in various forms; however, it never sold in large numbers and certainly not when compared to cars manufactured by the likes of Chevrolet and Ford.

Engine: 7340cc (448 cu in), V12-cylinder
Power: 112kW (150bhp)
0–96km/h (60mph): n/a
Top speed: 150km/h (90mph)
Production total: 2000

LINCOLN ZEPHYR

The new ultra-streamlined Lincoln-Zephyr, styled by Tom Tjaarda, made its debut in 1936. It was to become one of Lincoln's bestsellers. Of 18,994 Lincolns sold that year, 17,715 were Zephyrs, and it was later to form the basis of Edsel Ford's classic Lincoln Continental.

The prewar Zephyr was introduced in late 1935 and became available to buy in early 1936 as a lower-priced member of the Lincoln family. The Zephyr was seen as the first successfully designed streamlined car in the United States, reflecting the 1930s preoccupation with streamlining which showed up in designs for everything from toasters and other electrical goods to office and apartment buildings. It was a combination of both style and solid performance.

Built on a 317.5cm (125in) wheelbase, the Zephyr was powered by a water-cooled 4784cc (292 cu in) 75-degree V12 engine. Vacuum-assisted brakes were fitted as standard. Other components, which would later become associated with the Lincoln name, were the three-speed gearbox with steering column gearchange and the Columbia two-speed rear axle. The car also used Ford's transverse-leaf suspension.

A number of standard body options was offered by the company, along with a variety of custom designs from the likes of Le Baron, Brunn (who, in 1939, made a town car used by the wife of none other than Edsel Ford, the man behind the later Lincoln Continental), Judkin, Dietrich and Willoughby.

The Zephyrs made after this period carried over many design elements of the prewar cars. They were monolithic in proportion and remained long, tall and boxy until a facelift took place in 1942.

Later Zephyrs carried over many of the prewar car's styling elements, being tall, long and boxy. The use of spats to partially cover the rear wheels was popular during this period.

Engine: 4784cc (292 cu in), V12-cylinder
Power: 82kW (110bhp)
0–96km/h (60mph): n/a
Top speed: n/a
Production total: n/a

LINCOLN CONTINENTAL

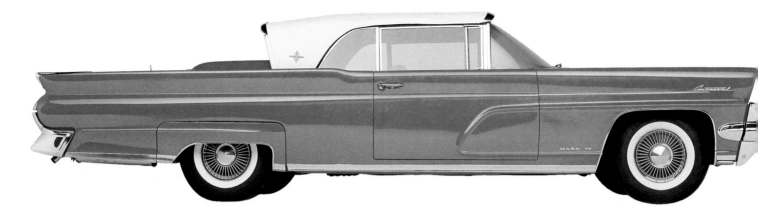

If the Zephyr's size was impressive, the motoring public was left gasping by the elephantine Continental when it burst on to the motoring scene in 1941. With its huge, bull-nosed bonnet, a wheelbase that would challenge that of a Winnebago motorhome and generous dousing of chrome, the Continental was aimed exclusively at the rich and famous. The name itself became synonymous with Lincoln and was carried over onto various subsequent models up until the late 1960s.

The first car was the responsibility of Edsel Ford who, feeling guilty about Ford's shoddy treatment of Lincoln since its takeover in the early 1920s, decided to build a car that would restore the Lincoln name to its former glory.

Due to financial restraints, virtually all of Edsel's investment was put into the body (setting up one of the first in-house design studios in Detroit) at the expense of the mechanicals, which were mostly carried over from the earlier Zephyr. The car sold well, but was dropped in 1942 due to the war. Postwar, it was revised, until production ended in 1948.

In 1956, the Continental name was reborn in Mk II coupé form, designed by John M. Reinhardt, and sold well for a car that was almost hand-built and many times the price of offerings from its competitors, although its high price meant that

Later Continentals were more restrained, this 1965 model looking considerably more sober than its more glitzy predecessors. However, the ride, refinement and sheer kudos of owning a Continental remained undiminished.

very few were actually made. An attractive convertible prototype version was made in 1957; however, it never went into commercial production.

The Mk III of 1957 continued the Continental trademark of being enormous (it was 572cm (18.8ft) long), covered with chrome and highly visible. However, it represented a slight re-think by Ford, who dropped the price in order to compete with other cars of its type. At this time, the car was offered in a confusing range of body styles, including saloon, hardtop saloon, coupé, convertible and limousine.

The Mk IV from 1958 and 1959 had small design changes, while the Mk V from 1959 and 1960 incorporated style changes to make it look less portly.

In its final incarnation, which ran from 1961 to 1969, the scalloped wings and hideous diagonal quad headlights were dropped. In their place came a significantly smaller model, available as a saloon, four-

The Mk IV Lincoln Continental which ran from 1958–59 was monstrous in the extreme, being 572cm (18ft 9in) long and weighing in at more than two and a quarter tons. It was significantly downsized after 1961.

door convertible (with electric hood and rear-hinged 'clap-doors') and coupé.

Infamously, John F. Kennedy was assassinated in a 1961 Continental in November 1963. Despite being fitted with two-way radio and thick bulletproof steel plating along the side, the car could do nothing to protect its hapless rear-seat passengers. This car was later fitted with a permanent steel roof and now resides in the Henry Ford Museum in Dearborn.

Inside, the Mk VI Continental was the height of 1960s tasteless-ness with quilted leather seats, power-assistance on every control and lots of fake wood veneer trim. Air conditioning was obligatory, as were power steering, electric windows and locks that operated as soon as the car began to move.

From 1964, the Continental got an extended wheelbase, while the

two-door coupé and the bigger 7565cc (462 cu in) engine, produc-ing 272kW (365bhp), appeared in 1966. The car rapidly became a bestseller, praised for its almost 'European' looks and its straight-line 200km/h (125mph) perfor-mance. Needless to say, it was less impressive when cornering.

The Continental name continued into the 1970s, with the TV detective, Frank Cannon, making the 1972 Continental famous, with its Rolls-Royce inspired grille, shuttered headlights and 'opera' oval rear side windows. Indeed, the Lincoln Continental continues to evoke the image of glitz, luxury and outstanding opulence.

Engine: 7045cc (430 cu in), 8-cylinder
Power: 224kW (300bhp)
0–96km/h (60mph): 11 secs
Top speed: 192km/h (120mph)
Production total: 384,230

LLOYD 600

1955–62

Unrelated to the UK-based company of the same name, the West German Lloyd company was owned by Borgward.

In the 1950s, due to postwar shortages of metal, Lloyd cars were made from fabric body panels stretched over a wooden frame, which not only kept prices low, but also made the cars very economical to own. They also featured twin-cylinder air-cooled engines.

The LP600 was a bigger-engined version, introduced in 1955, with an all-new four-stroke overhead camshaft, two-cylinder engine. After 1957, it was renamed the

The German Lloyd 600 featured a four-stroke two-cylinder engine. It was capable of a respectable 99km/h (62mph), and it was capable of out-accelerating its arch rival, the Volkswagen Beetle.

Alexander, and it was fitted with fully independent suspension and a four-speed gearbox, with the added option of Saxomat automatic transmission.

With its lightweight configuration, the Lloyd 600 was quicker off the mark than its main rival, the popular Volkswagen Beetle; however, it was slightly higher in price, which led to its rapid decline in the last part of the decade.

There was also a van-like version called the LT600, which had an additional row of seats. There was even a convertible model; however, only a handful of these was ever made.

Engine: 596cc (36 cu in), 2-cylinder
Power: 14kW (19bhp)
0–96km/h (60mph): n/a
Top speed: 99km/h (62mph)
Production total: 176,524

LMX 2300 HCS

1969–74

From the plethora of sports car concepts being developed in Italian design studios in the late 1960s, the Italian-built LMX actually made it into production, becoming available as a coupé or convertible.

Strangely, much of the under-pinnings were Ford-derived. Suspension and disc brake set-up came from the old Zodiac Mk IV,

while the Ford Taunus donated its 2.3-litre (140 cu in) V6 powerplant. Being a sports car, the engine was available in several states of tune, including a supercharged 156kW (210bhp) version which accelerated well and showed an impressive turn of speed.

The stylish fibreglass body was designed by a company called

Eurostyle, based in Turin, and featured slightly strange rectangular headlights, an American-style power bulge in the long bonnet, flared arches and an aggressive-looking rear end. Despite this, the overall result was a car with clean lines and one which looked good among its more exotic Italian sports car rivals.

Very few examples of the 43 2300s made are still in existence, but those that are are very much sought-after.

Engine: 2293cc (140 cu in), V6-cylinder
Power: 80kW (108bhp)
0–96km/h (60mph): n/a
Top speed: 197km/h (123mph)
Production total: 43

LOTUS MK VI

1952–56

Lotus Engineering was conceived by Colin Chapman and his wife-to-be, Hazel Williams, in 1952, with Chapman first working on a variety of Austin-based trials cars before moving on to sports car production at Hornsey, North London, and later at Cheshunt in Hertfordshire.

The Mk VI was seen as the first true Lotus, having little in common with anything that went before, and it had a tubular space frame steel chassis (which was both light and strong), with stressed aluminium body panels forming the floor, scuttle and sides.

All were sold in kit form, using components taken mostly from the Ford Ten/Popular range of cars, including Ford's renowned rigid axle at the rear. Soft suspension

combined with a rigid chassis gave the MK VI great road-holding ability, making it a popular choice among club racers.

The car's power came via Ford, too, either from the 1172cc (72 cu in) side-valve unit or the Consul engine, reduced in capacity to qualify for the 1500cc (92 cu in) competition category.

The Mk VI was still victorious in competition throughout the 1950s, long after production of the car had ceased.

Engine: 1099–1500cc (67–92 cu in), 4-cylinder
Power: 30kW (40bhp)
0–96km/h (60mph): n/a
Top speed: 120km/h (75mph)
Production total: 110

The primitive-looking Lotus Mk VI, featuring a space frame and aluminium body, went into production after winning numerous racing accolades with amateur mechanic/racer Colin Chapman at the wheel.

LOTUS SEVEN

Later Lotus Sevens differed little in concept to the original 1950s car, although this S4 which appeared in 1970 was criticized for its ugly squared-off nose section and angular styling.

Who could have imagined that the Lotus Seven, with its skinny tyres, minimal body and uncomfortable ride, would become one of Britain's best-loved sports cars, enjoying a production lifespan of 16 years. During this time, there were four series models before production rights passed to Caterham Cars in 1973, who still make what is essentially the same car, with the same character as the original.

The first car was based on the chassis from the Mk VI, which was modified and progressively strengthened as the Seven gained more power and increased performance. Suspension took the form of wishbones and coil-spring/damper units at the front, and a live axle, initially from the Standard Ten or Austin Metropolitan, then later from the Ford Escort.

Early cars used the same 40bhp 1172cc (72 cu in) Ford side-valve unit as the Mk VI, while the Super Seven, which could be identified by its wire wheels, had a 55kW (75bhp) 1097cc (67 cu in) Coventry Climax engine married to a four-speed BMC gearbox. This was replaced by the 71kW (95bhp) Cosworth 109E engine after 1961. By the time the S2 had been introduced in 1960, with its flared GRP (glass reinforced plastic) front wings, most cars were using Ford power and Ford all-synchromesh gearboxes. The ultimate Seven, the S3, had either a 1.6-litre (98 cu in) Holbay-tuned

Ford engine or Lotus's own fiery twin-camshaft unit taken from the Elan. The latter, however, is rare, as only 15 Sevens were fitted with this particular engine.

There were no driver comforts, and early cars did not even have opening doors. The cockpit itself was narrow and cramped, and did not accommodate taller drivers. Even those that did fit had to adopt the notorious 'elbows-out' driving position. Two cushions – one on the floor, the other on the back panel – were all the driver and passenger had in terms of seating. On entry models, the canvas hood and windscreen wipers were listed

as extras – there was not even a fuel gauge as standard until the S3 arrived in 1968.

The S2 Seven America did, however, have carpets, as did the S3. At the same time, the Super Seven could have a heater fitted. The S2 was equipped with more comprehensive instrumentation, soft top and side screens, and its long, sweeping front wings were often retro-fitted to earlier S1 cars.

Bootspace on the Seven was severely limited, being only just big enough to store the fabric hood and side screens. Like traditional 1930s sports cars, the spare wheel was mounted externally on the boot lid.

The S4, introduced by Lotus in 1970, was a complete departure from previous models and looked ugly in comparison, with its squared-off nose cone and angular wings and rear end. The body, styled by Alan Barrett, was made from fibreglass instead of aluminium, and it was bonded to a new chassis featuring suspension from the Europa at the front and Watt linkage at the rear.

Despite the car selling well, Graham Nearn at new owners Caterham, obviously agreed that the S4 did not hold the same allure as the timeless earlier models, and it was shelved in October 1972.

Thus ended a long and successful lifespan of a little car that was light, fast and incredible to drive. Still, the legend lives on, made by Caterham and based on the old S3 shape. It was not until the arrival of the Elise in 1995 that Lotus regained its former glory as a truly great sports car manufacturer. Sadly, its founder, Colin Chapman, suffered an untimely death in 1982.

With a good power-to-weight ratio, low ride height and staggering road-holding abilities, Lotus Sevens offered drivers true seat-of-the-pants motoring.

Engine: 1599cc (98 cu in), 4-cylinder
Power: 86kW (115bhp)
0–96km/h (60mph): 7.7 secs
Top speed: 163km/h (102mph)
Production total: 2477

LOTUS ELEVEN

The Eleven, seen here at the 1958 Geneva Motor Show with special Ghia-Suisse coachwork, was primarily a racing machine with its complex spaceframe construction.

The Eleven was really just a track car converted to everyday road use by the addition of headlights and a basic fabric roof. It featured a clever spaceframe chassis and wonderfully aerodynamic and imaginative bodywork – the nose section was hinged at the front to expose the entire engine, and the rear-hinged tail section provided space for the battery, spare wheel and minimal luggage.

The perspex wraparound screen was so shallow that even drivers of moderate height could look over it. None of this mattered, as the Eleven was really a competition car and dominated the racing scene in the 1950s, with considerable success at Le Mans in 1956 and 1957.

Three versions of the Eleven were available: the Le Mans (with a Coventry Climax engine and a De Dion rear end), the Club (again with a Coventry Climax unit and live axle/coil springs) and the Sport (with a Ford side-valve engine and live rear axle). Series 2 cars were to arrive in 1957 and were fitted with wishbone and coil-spring independent front suspension and strengthened rear axles.

Several 'specials' were made, based on the Eleven, including a practical open two-seater by Ghia and a gullwing made by Frank Costin, who was responsible for the original Eleven's bodywork.

Engine: 1098cc (67 cu in), 4-cylinder
Power: 56kW (75bhp)
0–96km/h (60mph): 10 secs
Top speed: 200km/h (125mph)
Production total: 426

LOTUS ELITE

The Elite, or Lotus 14, appeared at the same time as the Eleven, but was in complete contrast to the track car. Indeed, it was Chapman's first attempt at a true road car.

The world's first glassfibre monocoque construction car, the Elite was a technical success, if not a particularly good seller. The ride was harsh – and it was noisy – but exceptional road-holding rewarded sporting drivers.

Technically, it was a marvel, featuring the world's first glassfibre monocoque, made by Bristol Aircraft in England. The sleek little GT looked like being a success at its launch at the London Motor Show in 1957.

Using independent wishbone/coils at the front and Chapman struts at the rear, the mechanical components were bolted through the glassfibre, with metal inserts at mounting points. The ride was firm, but fabulously nimble, and disc brakes were fitted to all four wheels.

Coventry Climax engines were used, and S2 cars had optional twin carburettors. The SE version of 1962 had 63kW (85bhp), while the Super 95, Super 100 and Super 105 Elites were named according to their power outputs.

The Elite was praised for its low drag (0.26cd), attributable to its stylist, Peter Kirwan Taylor. However, it also had a reputation for being noisy and harsh, with plenty of vibration from the poorly ventilated monocoque shell. Technically good in many respects, the Lotus Elite nonetheless lost Lotus a lot of money.

Engine: 1216cc (74 cu in), 4-cylinder
Power: 56kW (75bhp)
0–96km/h (60mph): 11.4 secs
Top speed: 183km/h (114mph)
Production total: 1078

LOTUS ELAN

It was the Elan that, for the first time, made other international sports car manufacturers take notice of Lotus, and from its factory in Hethel, Norfolk, emerged a car of truly world-class status.

What made it so good was its superb handling. A steel back-boned chassis with forked sections front and rear provided the Elan with the rigidity so lacking in the Elite, while independent wishbone and coil suspension at the front (derived from the Triumph Herald) with Chapman struts with lower wishbones at the back made the car both agile and responsive. The ride itself was excellent – soft, but sure-footed and predictable. Steering came courtesy of Triumph, and Girling provided the all-round disc braking system.

Power came from Lotus's own twin-camshaft unit, the block and bottom end coming from a Ford Cortina, with an aluminium twin-camshaft head designed by Harry Mundy placed on top. The powerplant was then mated to a Ford four-speed gearbox.

Early Elans had a 1498cc (91 cu in) 75kW (100bhp) unit, but this was soon replaced by the high-revving and extremely flexible 1558cc (95 cu in) version, rated at 79kW (106bhp). This engine is easily identifiable by its 'blue' painted camshaft cover. Being so light and compact, with a kerb weight of just 668kg (1473lb), the

Elan's power-to-weight ratio was superb, giving it exhilarating performance and cornering.

Although hardly luxurious (the dashboard resembled that of a Triumph Herald), cabin space was better than Lotus cars of the past, with ample luggage space for a weekend's excursion. Lotus's own design and development engineer, Ron Hickman, designed the body, and it was made by Lotus. At launch, there was only an open-top car, but a hardtop followed in 1963, and a coupé was introduced with the S3 Elan in 1965.

The S2 of 1964 had better brakes and more impressive instrumentation, while the S3 of 1965, now also available as a coupé, gained a higher final drive. A year later, the SE was also introduced, with a

86kW (115bhp) rated engine, servo-assisted brakes, centre-lock wheels and the luxury of fitted carpets. The S4 of 1968 also got the more powerful brakes plus flared wheelarches to accommodate lower-profile tyres.

The final incarnation of the Elan came in 1971 with the introduction of the Sprint. Tuned by engine specialist Tony Rudd, giving it 25 per cent more power, the Sprint was very quick, accelerating faster than almost any other car on the road, including the powerful exotic sport cars of the time. These 'big-valve' Sprints used twin Weber carburettors (instead of the 'suffocating' Strombergs fitted to conform to US emissions regulations) and were more oil-tight and less raucous than the other engines. This time a

The Lotus Elan was one of the most outstanding small sports cars of the 1960s. The Series 4 from 1968 (pictured) was recognizable by its slightly flared arches.

sporty red paint replaced the blue on the camshaft covers. Offering a higher top speed – 193km/h (120mph) – they would often be married to five-speed Austin Maxi gearboxes to provide more relaxed high-speed driving.

Sprints were distinguishable by their two-tone 'Gold Leaf' paintwork, slightly extended wheelarches and knock off centre wheel nuts, and remain the most sought-after model in the Elan range.

In 1973, the last Lotus Elan left the factory in Norfolk. Lotus wanted to lose its 'kit car' image (all of the Elans were sold in kit form) and was determined to build more up-market machinery, such as the Elite and the Esprit.

Lotus design and development engineer Ron Hickman styled the Elan. Hickman later went on to invent the folding workbench, selling the concept to Black & Decker, who marketed it worldwide as the Workmate.

Engine: 1558cc (95 cu in), 4-cylinder
Power: 79kW (106bhp)
0–96km/h (60mph): 8.7 secs
Top speed: 185km/h (115mph)
Production total: 9150

LOTUS ELAN + 2

1967–74

The Lotus Elan + 2 from 1967 satisfied the growing demand for a four-seater. It was longer and wider than the original Elan and weighed more, but was nevertheless still an exhilarating car to drive.

Amid pressure to build a four-seater and with an eye on Italian coachbuilders Frua, which built its own 2+2 fastback body onto an Elan in 1964, the Elan + 2 was born. Two tiny rear seats qualified for the new description; however, they were too small for adults and were usually only used to stow and luggage.

Although 580mm (23in) longer and 190mm (7.5in) wider than the S4, the + 2 was more than just a stretched Elan. Its combined sidelights and indicators in the front wings, outboard of the pop-up headlights, better equipped cockpit and improved cabin ventilation were all improvements on the original car.

Despite its added weight and firmer ride, the + 2 was still an exhilarating car to drive, and better aerodynamics served to reduce wind noise at high speed. This improvement was at the expense of only slightly slower acceleration.

Overall, the finish of the + 2 was much better than its predecessor and, indeed, this was the first Lotus to be offered as a complete car, as well as being available in kit form.

Engine: 1558cc (95 cu in), 4-cylinder
Power: 88kW (118bhp)
0–96km/h (60mph): 8.2 secs
Top speed: 185km/h (115mph)
Production total: 3300

LOTUS EUROPA

1966–75

Lotus's 'car for Europe' (hence its name) was in many respects the spiritual successor to the outmoded Seven, and it was intended to be a cheaper alternative to the popular Lotus Elan.

Interesting technically, with its mid-engined configuration and distinctive high-sided rear end (designed by John Frayling), the Elan won both praise and criticism from commentators at the time.

They liked the way that the car handled, with its lower ride height and responsive Renault 16 engine (turned through 180 degrees, before being slightly tuned by Lotus itself), but hated the cramped cockpit, poor rear visibility and fixed single-pane door windows, which suffocated the driver in hot conditions. The S2 from 1968 did much to remedy the latter criticism by having electrically operated windows and a better interior.

Criticism that the Europa was underpowered was answered in 1971 with the arrival of the twin-camshaft-engined car, which also received a more spacious interior with better leg and elbow room. The 1972 Special, which often appeared in the black and gold JPS colours worn by Team Lotus cars, was given the 94kW (126bhp) 'big valve' engine.

The 'Lotus for Europe', hence Europa, was a pretty mid-engined GT that used a Renault engine and gearbox turned through 180 degrees. Triumph components were used for the front suspension.

Engine: 1470cc (90 cu in), 4-cylinder
Power: 58kW (78bhp)
0–96km/h (60mph): 10.7 secs
Top speed: 179km/h (112mph)
Production total: 9230

LOTUS ELITE

1974–80

Seen as an entry into the lucrative GT market by Colin Chapman, the Elite represented a move upmarket by the Norfolk-based company. The backbone chassis remained; however, the sleek Elite body, with its steeply raked screen, hatch opening rear and angular wedge-like profile, was met with mixed reaction at the time.

The Elite's saving grace was its diminutive 1973cc (120 cu in) all-alloy 16-valve '907' twin-camshaft engine, which made its timely debut during the height of the oil crisis, and it was later used in the

ill-fated Jensen-Healey. Despite a few teething problems, it provided the Elite with stunning performance, especially once power was increased to 119kW (160bhp).

There were three basic models: the entry-level 501, the 502 (with

The name Elite was inherited from a pioneering earlier model dating from 1957, one of the company's first true road cars.

air conditioning fitted as standard), the 503 (with power-assisted steering) and the 504 (which was offered with Borg Warner automatic transmission from 1976).

The 2.2-litre (134 cu in) version arrived in the spring of 1980 and was designated the 912. The power remained the same at 119kW (160bhp); however, it had much improved torque and a better Getrag five-speed gearbox.

Lotus owner Colin Chapman saw the Lotus Elite as an entry into the GT sector, becoming a direct competitor to the likes of Aston Martin. It used a 1973cc (120 cu in) Lotus twin-cam engine.

Engine: 1973cc (120 cu in), 4-cylinder
Power: 115kW (155bhp)
0–96km/h (60mph): 7.8 secs
Top speed: 200km/h (124mph)
Production total: 2535

LOTUS ECLAT

1975–80

Sometimes referred to as the 'Elite coupé', the Eclat shared the same mechanicals as the Elite, but with a fastback body. Surprisingly, it was also lighter, weighing just over 1100kg (2420lb) – 100kg (220lb)

less than the Elite. Being more of a 2+2 than a true four-seater (headroom was severely limited in the back), the Eclat became the cheapest car in the Lotus range in the second half of the 1970s.

There were five models: the entry-level 520, the 521 (with a five-speed gearbox, wider alloy wheels and a radio), the 522 (with air conditioning and other accessories), the 523 (with power

steering) and the 524 (the automatic transmission version).

As with the Elite, the 2.2-litre (134 cu in) engine became available in spring 1976, and at this time the car was offered as a 'Riviera' special edition, with a lift-out roof panel, special alloy wheels and a shallow chin spoiler below the front bumper and a subtle boot spoiler on the rear hatch.

The Eclat ended production in the summer of 1982, with sales in its last two years growing due to reductions in price.

The 2+2 Eclat was really nothing more than an Elite coupé. The Riviera special edition had an adventurous lift-out roof panel.

Engine: 1973cc (120 cu in), 4-cylinder
Power: 119kW (160bhp)
0–96km/h (60mph): 7.9 secs
Top speed: 208km/h (129mph)
Production total: 1519

LOTUS ESPRIT

erhaps predictably, Lotus returned to the mid-engine configuration once more with its stunning-looking Esprit, designed by Giugiaro, who was then working for ItalDesign. The classic ackbone chassis was used again, nd the 907 engine was positioned entrally and mounted to a Citroën M transaxle and gearbox.

The S1 was renowned for its ooling problems; however, this vas remedied in 1979 with the aunch of the S2, with its wider vheels, better interior and integrated front spoiler. As well as ne 1973cc (120 cu in) engine, a .2-litre (133 cu in) unit was also vailable from 1980. Needless to ay, all of the cars exhibited enacious handling and grip.

The Turbo version also arrived n 1980, using the 2174cc (133 cu n) engine with a Garrett T3 turbo dded. At the same time, the sus-ension was stiffened, improving urther the Esprit's already rodigious handling capabilities. he S3, which included nodifications to the Turbo, ran rom 1981–87.

Undoubtedly a supercar to challenge the best, its sales were hurt by poor reliability and finish. Like the early Lamborghini Countach, the S1 in its purest, unadulterated form is the most beautiful.

Based on a striking design by Italian stylist Giugiaro, the wedge-shaped Esprit was a mid-engined successor to the Europa. A 158kW (210bhp) Turbo version was introduced in 1980.

Engine: 1973cc (120 cu in), 4-cylinder
Power: 119kW (160bhp)
0–96km/h (60mph): 8.4 secs
Top speed: 200km/h (124mph)
Production total: 2062

LOTUS ESPRIT SE

Vith the original Giugiaro design eginning to look a little dated, eter Stevens made subtle in-house esign changes that were to give ne 1987 SE and Turbo versions a nuch more rounded look. The esult was a heavier car, but one that was much more aerodynamic than the original Esprit.

In an attempt to improve build quality, Lotus also changed the manufacturing process to give greater uniformity and save time and labour costs as well.

Peter Stevens's in-house facelift of the then 12-year-old Esprit design resulted in the Esprit SE, production of which ran from 1987–1990. Heavier, but more aerodynamic and well finished, the car was an immediate success.

Meanwhile, the cockpit, although looking broadly similar in appearance to the earlier Esprits, was brought up to date by stylist Brian Cox.

Engine options were either the 2174cc (133 cu in) normally aspirated unit or the Turbo. The Turbo was then replaced in 1989 by the Turbo SE, fitted with a high-boost pressure-charged engine rated at 197kW (264bhp) and capable of a blistering 262km/h (164mph). A Renault GTA transaxle replaced the earlier Citroën unit, and the rear brakes were relocated in-board.

The Esprit was to go through numerous other changes throughout the 1990s, with the emergence of the S4 and, in 1996, it even gained a V8 powerplant, aggressive body styling and spoilers.

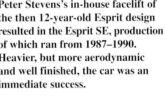

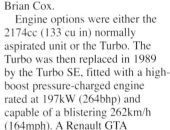

Engine: 2174cc (133 cu in), 4-cylinder
Power: 128kW (172bhp)
0–96km/h (60mph): 6.5 secs
Top speed: 221km/h (138mph)
Production total: 385

LOTUS EXCEL

1982–92

The Lotus Excel was originally badged as the Eclat 3 and subsequently the Eclat Excel to avoid the expense and time-consuming process of Lotus having to apply for new Type Approval in order to be allowed to manufacture it.

Sharing the same suspension and chassis as the Lotus Eclat, the Excel featured a number of body styling changes designed to make it look sleeker and more aerodynamic than its stablemate. It also featured an upgraded gearbox and final

drive, and had ventilated disc brakes — all of which were supplied by Toyota.

In response to customer demands for more aggressive styling, Lotus designer Peter Stevens reworked the Excel's body, making subtle

changes to the top half, while keeping the bottom half mostly the same, which allowed the company to reuse the moulding for the lower section of the car.

The cabin of the Excel was also given a makeover, with a new fascia installed and the use of German VDO gauges. Rear-seat passengers gained extra headroom; however, they still had to cope with awkward access.

The SE of 1986 put power up to 134kW (180bhp), and the SA (Sport Automatic) was introduced year later. It became the last of the front-engined Lotus cars when production ceased in 1992.

Toyota components were used for the Lotus Excel, also known as the Eclat 3 and the Eclat Excel. Sold in relatively low numbers, the car had an uprated interior and softer lines than its namesake predecessors.

Engine: 2174cc (133 cu in), 4-cylinder
Power: 119kW (160bhp)
0–96km/h (60mph): 6.8 secs
Top speed: 211km/h (131mph)
Production total: 1327

LOTUS ELAN (FWD)

1989–94

The new Elan should have been a fitting successor to its 1960s namesake. Instead, however, the economic recession of the early 1990s meant that the Isuzu-engined two-seater was to be shelved after just two years.

Again, Peter Stevens was involved with the design of the all-new body, with ex-racing driver John Miles responsible for the novel interactive wishbone front suspension. Being front-wheel drive caused quite a stir at the time,

but the little Elan's stunning chassis and fabulous handling soon won it admirers. As well as being great to drive, it was also comfortable to sit in, with a spacious cabin, plenty of storage space and well laid-out instrumentation.

However, the car was expensive and sales of the vehicle were slow as a result, forcing Lotus to drop the model in 1991. However, Bugatti bought Group Lotus from General Motors in 1993, and this offered a temporary reprieve for the Elan.

Indeed, a further 800 cars were built (known as the S2) with larger diameter wheels and changes to the suspension and hood.

All of these cars were sold in time for the unveiling of the Lotus Elise in 1995.

The 2+2 Elan was the result of a continuing collaboration with Toyota. It used the company's dohc 16-valve engines and running gear, but the front-wheel drive Elan's 'stubby' styling was not to everyone's taste.

Engine: 1588cc (97 cu in), 4-cylinder
Power: 123kW (165bhp)
0–96km/h (60mph): 6.6 secs
Top speed: 220km/h (137mph)
Production total: 4657

MARCOS GT

The peculiar Marcos GT, which first appeared in 1960, was given the nickname 'wooden wonder' as a result of its crude wooden monocoque construction. Later restyles increased the use of glassfibre.

Formed by Jem Marsh and Frank Costin in the 1950s, Marcos began making specials based on marine-ply wooden chassis. The odd-looking GT, with its long nose and pod-like cabin, was one of its first products. Nicknamed the 'Wooden Wonder', the gullwing coupé featured a wooden monocoque construction and a glassfibre nose-cone. The rest of the body was shaped exclusively from specially formed ply.

The front suspension was borrowed from the Triumph Herald. At the back, there was a Ford live axle, located by a Panhard rod. Power came from Ford's 105E engines, and these were available in a variety of forms.

While proving very successful on the track in the hands of drivers such as Jackie Stewart, the GT's ugly-bug looks were never likely to prove commercially successful.

Indeed, in its four-year production, and despite a makeover by Dennis Adams to make it look less unattractive and increase the use of fibreglass instead of wood, only 39 cars were ever sold. The story of the GT ends well, however, because today, due to its rarity, existing examples command very high prices.

Engine: 997cc (61 cu in), 4-cylinder
Power: 31-48kW (41-64bhp)
0-96km/h (60mph): 9.1 secs
Top speed: 152km/h (95mph)
Production total: 39

MARCOS 1800

A much sleeker, Volvo-engined Marcos with glassfibre bodywork (designed by Dennis Adams) and the trusted laminated plywood chassis arrived in 1964. With its enclosed sloping headlights, hinging front nose section, wide doors and aggressive Ford GT40-influenced rear end, it created a trademark Marcos look that became a classic and was to last the lifetime of the company.

Dennis Adams created the 'classic' Marcos design of the 1800 – and you still can buy a similar-looking car from the company today. The glassfibre body was mounted on a laminated plywood chassis.

The 1800's engine was Volvo's P1800 unit, while Triumph again provided the front wishbones, with a semi-De Dion and coil-sprung set-up at the rear. Sold mostly in kit form, at a fairly high price for the time, the car held the road well and gained a strong reputation and a certain amount of respect among sports car enthusiasts.

The cabin of the 1800, however, was very cramped. Its fixed semi-reclining seats offered little in the way of choice for the driver, and adjustment of the pedal assembly was the only concession to taller-than-average drivers.

The shape of the Marcos 1800 still looks modern today, although existing examples from this early period suffer from rotted wooden chassis, which can prove rather costly to repair.

Engine: 1780cc (108 cu in), 4-cylinder
Power: 85kW (114bhp)
0-96km/h (60mph): 9.1 secs
Top speed: 184km/h (115mph)
Production total: 99

MARCOS 3-LITRE

Having been applauded for its 1800 coupé, Marcos was called on by the critics for just one major improvement to make the car even better – more power. Thankfully, their calls were answered in 1968, when Jem Marsh decided to fit the powerful Ford 3-litre (183 cu in) V6 unit. Transmission was a four-speed manual with overdrive.

The extra weight at the front actually helped the car's handling by reducing the tendency of the nose to lift, and top speed went up to around 200km/h (125mph).

A year after production started, a coil-sprung live axle took the place of the De Dion unit at the rear. Then, after about 100 cars had been built, a switch was made from the wooden ply chassis to a conventional steel tube construction; in 1970, Volvo's 164 3-litre (183 cu in) powerplant replaced the Ford engine.

The range was complemented by a 2.5-litre (153 cu in) unit taken from the Triumph TR6 in 1971.

This was followed by a 2-litre (122 cu in) Ford V4 unit, which continued in production until the company finally collapsed due to a combination of production, relocation and export problems.

Engine: 2978cc (182 cu in), 6-cylinder
Power: 105kW (140bhp)
0–96km/h (60mph): 7.8 secs
Top speed: 200km/h (125mph)
Production total: 350

Using the same basic design from the 1800, Marcos upped the power to 2978cc (182 cu in) by fitting a Ford V6 engine. Top speed rose to 200km/h (125mph). Early cars had the same wooden chassis, but later models switched to steel.

MINI-MARCOS

Based on a prototype called the DART, the Mini-Marcos was of glassfibre construction, with complete Mini front and rear subframes bolted through metal plates. Sold in kit form very cheaply, the Mini-Marcos had almost no driver comforts and owners saw the car mainly as a cheap competition tool as opposed to an everyday road car. Indeed, it finished in an impressive 15th place at Le Mans in 1966 and was the only British car to finish in 1971 – quite an accomplishment for a kit car that was nothing more than an uprated Mini.

The car was improved over the years, gaining more in the way of refinements, until the Marcos company went bankrupt in 1971. At that time, the company was bought out by the Rob Walker Group, which modified the rear end of the Mini-Marcos to include an opening rear hatch (to improve practicality) and offered wind-up windows instead of the fixed items.

From 1975 to 1981, it acted as a blueprint for Harold Dermott, who built the similar-looking Midas Bronze, which was also Mini-based. The Mini-Marcos has recently been relaunched in Mk V form.

As its name would suggest, Mini-Marcos used the complete front and rear subframes from the Mini. Crudely made and rather hideous looking, incredibly it was the only British finisher at Le Mans in 1971

Engine: 1275cc (78 cu in), 4-cylinder
Power: 57kW (76bhp)
0–96km/h (60mph): n/a
Top speed: 168km/h (105mph)
Production total: 1200

MARCOS MANTIS

The Mantis was the archetypal eccentric British kit car, featuring odd styling, a plastic body and the lure of a good six-cylinder engine. Needless to say, very few were produced, and those that were were universally criticized. In fact, some unfairly blame it for the company's demise, which coincided with the end of the car's production in 1971.

Broadly, much of the condemnation was directed at the Mantis's styling. which was distinguished by its odd mix of sharp edges and curves; the end result was not particularly pleasing to the eye.

Underneath was an all-new semi-spaceframe chassis, engines from the Triumph TR6, independent front suspension (from the Triumph GT6) and a coil-sprung live rear axle. Combined, the ride and road-holding were surprisingly good.

Being Marcos's first attempt at producing a four-seater car, the Mantis had an interior that was luxurious and well equipped, although rear headroom was somewhat restricted by the steeply raked rear windscreen.

Expensive, despite being sold in kit form, the Mantis attracted few buyers – only 32 vehicles were made. Nevertheless, the car's rarity makes it highly valued today.

Despite being styled originally by design guru Dennis Adams, the Mantis was absurd-looking and a sales disaster. Powered by a Triumph TR5 engine, it played a big part in the company's downfall.

Engine: 2498cc (152 cu in), 6-cylinder
Power: 112kW (150bhp)
0–96km/h (60mph): n/a
Top speed: 200km/h (125mph)
Production total: 32

MARCOS MANTULA

When Jem Marsh bought back the rights to the original Marcos company, production of cars looking not dissimilar to Dennis Adam's first GT designs in 1964 began again in 1981. The 3-litre (183 cu in) version still retained the same square-section steel tube chassis, wishbone front suspension and live rear axle.

This offering was followed in 1984 by the Mantula, which was fitted with the lightweight Rover V8 engine, which provided

Featuring a new nose section with a deeper air dam to prevent the front end of the car lifting at speed, the Marcos Mantula still exhibited a strong resemblance to Dennis Adam's original GT concept from the 1960s.

astonishing performance. In order to cope with the extra power (and the tendency for the front end to lift at high speed), the Mantula was fitted with a new nose, featuring a deep integral air dam, and side skirts along the sides of the car.

The Mantula was available as a two-door, two-seater sports coupé or an attractive convertible with flush-folding fabric hood. In 1989, the bigger 3.9-litre (241 cu in) V8 with fuel injection was fitted, along with independent rear suspension in place of the radius arms and Panhard rod, and more effective disc brakes. It was this version, sold in kit form, that continued in production until 2000.

Engine: 3528cc (215 cu in), 8-cylinder
Power: 138kW (185bhp)
0–96km/h (60mph): 5.4 secs
Top speed: 240km/h (150mph)
Production total: n/a

MARENDAZ 1.5-LITRE

1926–30

Cars bearing the Marendaz name were constructed by Captain Marendaz, first in Brixton, London, and later at Maidenhead in the county of Berkshire.

Early examples of the marque were mainly derived from a light car made by Marseal, another company in which Marendaz had an involvement. Unlike Marseal, however, which built a number of uninspiring sports cars from the early 1920s, the Marendaz badged-cars looked like attractive, scaled-down vintage Bentleys, utilizing a side-valve Anzani engine.

Later machines had a 6-litre (366 cu in) engine of American origin, with distinctive flexible side exhaust pipes emerging from the side of the bonnet, while still retaining the Bentley-shaped radiator. Only the Anzani-engined four-cylinder cars, however, sold in any numbers.

Marendaz cars did particularly well in competition, with the mother of racing driver Stirling

Moss being among the successful drivers, along with another lady, Miss Summers, who was employed as a secretary at Marendaz's Maidenhead works.

The Marendaz name was killed off by World War II, leaving a legacy of handsome and much-acclaimed sports cars which today are highly sought-after.

Engine: 1496cc (91 cu in), 4-cylinder
Power: 9kW (11.8bhp)
0–96km/h (60mph): n/a
Top speed: 128km/h (80mph)
Production total: n/a

Cars built by Marendaz were particularly good at competition – Captain Marendaz is pictured here after beating the world 24-hour record. The 1.5-Litre, frequently supercharged, featured shock absorbers on all four wheels, something of a rarity at the time

MASERATI A6

1947–51

The Maserati brothers – Carlo, Bindo, Alfieri, Ettore and Ernesto – started building racing cars in 1926. After the end of World War II, new owner Omar Orsi realized that, for the company to survive, it had to diversify, so the move to road cars was made with the A6 of 1947.

The new 'Maser' for the road made its debut at the 1947 Turin Motor Show, with production starting the following year.

Maserati supplied the tubular steel frame chassis, fitted with wishbone front suspension and a live rear axle, and customers were left to put individual bodies on. Most chose Pininfarina or Zagato to supply them, but Vignale, Frua, Guglielmo and Allemano also produced their own, while Scaglietti came up with some attractive racing styles. Most A6s were coupés. The engine was an all-aluminium 1488cc (91 cu in)

six-cylinder unit based on a pre-war Maserati racer. One carburettor was standard, but three carburettors could be supplied as an option, for extra power.

With an enviable reputation forged on the world's race tracks, Maserati's first road car was the A6. Some of Italy's most prominent styling houses provided designs on the chassis.

A competition version, the A6G of 1951, had a bigger cast-iron 1954cc (119 cu in) engine, and it was followed in 1956 by the A6G/2000, which used a twin-camshaft Formula 2 engine.

Engine: 1488cc (91 cu in), 6-cylinder
Power: 48kW (65bhp) at 4700rpm
0–96km/h (60mph): n/a
Top speed: 145km/h (90mph)
Production total: 61

MASERATI 3500GT

1957–64

Maserati's trademark trident motif was prominent on the front grille of the Maserati 3500GT. Although special coachbuilt bodies were available, most went for the 'standard' Touring coupé or the Vignale Spyder.

The 3500GT signalled Maserati's move into the premier league of Italian car manufacturers, allowing it to take its place alongside Ferrari as a builder of some of the world's most desirable cars.

Introduced in 1957, the 3500GT was a successor to the A6G/2000; however, it was more than just a replacement. It represented the transformation of Maserati from racing car manufacturer to fully fledged road car builder. The new, immensely stylish car ushered in unprecedented levels of production. Although only 2223 examples of the 3500GT coupé and convertible Spyder version were built in seven years – a fraction of what a mainstream company such as Ford or Austin could turn out in a day – in specialist car manufacturing terms, this could be considered almost assembly line numbers.

Although much of the 3500GT was completely new, elements were carried over from Maserati's previous models. The substantial tubular steel chassis was based on the A6G, with coil-spring independent front suspension and a live rear axle on semi-elliptic springs. The straight-six engine, substantially more powerful than the A6G's, could trace its roots to the 250F Grand Prix cars and the 300S and 350S sports racers. Chief engineer Giulio Alfieri reworked the twin overhead camshaft unit to make it suitable for the road, with three Weber carburettors and two spark plugs per cylinder. To the untrained eye, it looked like a straight 12-cylinder engine. Displacement was 3485cc (213 cu in), producing 164kW (220bhp).

Just as the engines were special, so were the bodies. The majority of the attractive coupé bodies were built by Touring using aluminium panels and Superleggera (extra light) principles; however, Bertone, Allemano and Frua also contributed their own styles, while Moretti and Boneschi built one-offs.

While Ferrari seemed purely interested in sheer performance, Maserati was more concerned that its 3500GT was a practical and consummate grand-tourer. Owners were treated to more luxury and equipment than could be found in the nearest Ferrari equivalent. Maserati drivers had almost an overdose of gauges and switches.

The company continuously developed the 3500GT during its life, and 1959 was a particularly significant year. Front disc brakes were introduced, but the most noteworthy issue was the appearance of the Spyder convertible. Responsible for the beautiful body design was Giovanni Michelotti, who worked for Vignale. Most of the mechanics were the same as the fixed head models, but the Vignale-built bodies were substantially different to the Touring coupés and were made out of steel. And, as if the lack of a roof were not enough to distinguish them, all the Spyders had odd serial numbers as well.

The year 1961 saw the next major changes to the 3500GT formula. In response to the Jaguar E-type – which worried the Italian supercar manufacturers – Maserati fitted Lucas fuel injection to create the 3500GTI, thus creating the first Italian production car to feature an injection system. Ironically enough, it was the same unit as used by many Jaguar racing cars. It proved troublesome but, when working properly, power was boosted by 11kW (15bhp) and top speed was also raised significantly. Other changes around this time included the introduction of a five-speed manual transmission, disc brakes all round, a re-routed exhaust system, deletion of the front fog lights and revised indicators and rear lights. By the end of production in 1964, even automatic transmission had been introduced, reinforcing the GT status of the car.

The 3500GT was in fact a major triumph for Maserati. It was to form the basis for several later models, enhanced the company's reputation and gave it the confidence and financial ability to start building some real supercars to take on Ferrari.

The 3500GT was a well-equipped car. Maserati did not just place the emphasis on speed, but sold its cars on opulence as well. This was a more inviting environment than you would find in an equivalent Ferrari of the era.

Engine: 3485cc (213 cu in), 6-cylinder
Power: 164kW (220bhp) at 5500rpm
0–96km/h (60mph): 8.1 secs
Top speed: 204km/h (127mph)
Production total: 2223

MASERATI 5000GT

Maserati's illustrious racing career came to a dramatic end in 1957 at the World Sports Car Race in Venezuela when its entire team of 450S racing cars was written off. This proved financially crippling, and the company withdrew from racing to concentrate on building road cars. The 5000GT was a direct result of the Venezuela disaster. Maserati was left with a number of 450S V8 quad-camshaft racing engines, of 4935cc (301 cu in) capacity. Supposedly at the suggestion of the Shah of Iran, the engines were fitted into the 3500GT chassis, giving birth to the new Maserati 5000GT model.

The 1959 Italian Motor Show at Turin saw the launch of the stunningly powerful car. It featured disc brakes on the front brakes, a four-speed gearbox, and the same suspension as the 3500GT. Originally, the cars came with Weber carburettors; however, from 1961, Lucas fuel injection was fitted. All-round disc brakes and

ZF five-speed transmission were later fitted. Of the 32 cars produced, 21 had bodies built by Allemano, with Touring responsible for another four. Pininfarina, Bertone, Frua, Michelotti, Vignale and Monterosa constructed the others.

The awesome 5000GT effectively used a racing engine tamed for the road, although, with 276kW (370bhp) on tap, it was hardly subdued by very much. A top speed of 282 km/h (175mph) in 1959 was an astounding figure.

Engine: 4941cc (302 cu in), V8-cylinder
Power: 276kW (370bhp) at 6000rpm
0–96km/h (60mph): n/a
Top speed: 282km/h (175mph)
Production total: 32

MASERATI SEBRING

Engine: 3485cc (213 cu in), 6-cylinder
Power: 175kW (235bhp) at 5500rpm
0–96km/h (60mph): 8.4 secs
Top speed: 222km/h (138mph)
Production total: 444

The Maserati Sebring was another offshoot from the 3500GT and was first seen in 1962. The graceful yet purposeful styling was created by Vignale and mounted on the short wheelbase 3500GTI convertible chassis. Although most of the body was made out of steel, an alloy bootlid and bonnet were fitted.

Originally, the car was called the 3500GTI, but almost instantly it became the Sebring instead, the name reviving Maserati's past glories on the racetrack. It was publicized as a 2+2, but rear seat accommodation was very small.

As the United States was seen as its main marketplace, the options list for the Sebring was long. Air conditioning, a radio, a limited slip differential and a three-speed automatic transmission could all be

specified. Fitted as standard on all cars were disc brakes on all four wheels, fuel injection and a five-speed manual transmission.

Series II cars were introduced in 1965 and came with bigger 3694cc (225 cu in) or 4014cc (245 cu in) engines and more power. Externally, cosmetic changes were less noticeable. The quad headlights received hoods, the rear lights were redesigned and the bonnet air intake was made less prominent.

The Sebring, designed by Vignale used the 3500GT engine and chassis, albeit shortened. It was a well-specified car, coming with a five-speed gearbox, disc brakes and fuel injection. The latter invariably proved troublesome, though, and many cars were converted to carburettors.

MASERATI MISTRAL

Maserati again used a revised 3500GT chassis to produce another new model. The Mistral coupé appeared in prototype form at the 1963 Turin Motor Show, using the same engine as the Sebring; however, the chassis was even shorter, and it was stiffened and strengthened with square section tubing designed to enhance the car's handling.

A year after the coupé was launched, the convertible Spyder appeared. The design for both versions was by Frua, with the bodies being built by Maggiora using aluminium for the panels, except the rear wings of the Spyder, which were made of steel.

The coupé was notable for its large glass hatchback, while the Spyder had a hardtop which included a sloping rear window and small buttresses.

Mechanically, the Mistral had a similar suspension layout to the Maserati 3500GT, with disc brakes on all four wheels. The coupé had the 3694cc (225 cu in) engine from new, while the Spyder used the older 3485cc (213 cu in) unit. From 1967, the Mistral's 4014cc (245 cu in) unit became available. All versions were fitted with Lucas fuel injection.

The Mistral's individuality was somewhat compromised by Pietro Frua using almost the same design

By the mid-1960s virtually all European high-performance cars used disc brakes, and the Mistral was no exception, with Girling discs front and rear.

for the British AC 428, even recycling some Maserati panels for it. Despite this, it is still considered a classic and indeed beautiful design by many.

Its production began in 1964 and was continued until 1969.

Engine: 3692cc (225 cu in), 6-cylinder
Power: 183kW (245bhp) at 5500rpm
0–96km/h (60mph): 7.5 secs
Top speed: 233km/h (145mph)
Production total: 948

Frua was behind the design of the Mistral, both the coupé and convertible versions. He was also responsible for the British AC 428 car, which bore an uncanny resemblance to the Mistral when it appeared two years later.

MASERATI QUATTROPORTE

1963–70

Maserati started a new trend in Italian exotica with its Quattroporte of 1963. The saloon supercar concept, combining luxury comfort with superb performance, was a theme that would be adopted by Lamborghini with its Espada and Ferrari with the 365 GT4 2+2.

The Quattroporte was introduced at the Turin Motor Show in 1963 and was the fastest four-door car in the world when launched. Frua designed the coachwork, but it was built by Vignale.

Power came from a 4.2-litre (252 cu in) quad-camshaft V8, derived from one of Maserati's racing engines. The chassis was all new,

with the engine mounted on a subframe to cut down on noise an vibration. The front suspension followed established double wishbone practice, but at the rear was a De Dion axle. It proved troublesome in operation and, by 1966, it had been replaced by a conventional live axle with semi-elliptic springs

In 1969, the Type 107A Quattroporte superseded the original. There were few noticeab cosmetic changes (the headlights had been revised in 1967), but more power was added by a 4.7-litre (287 cu in) engine with an extra 22kW (30bhp).

Although it could easily seat four in relative comfort, Maserati's luxury Quattroporte cruiser did not scrimp on performance. It wa a solid-looking yet elegant design.

Engine: 4136cc (252 cu in), V8-cylinder
Power: 194kW (260bhp) at 5200rpm
0–96km/h (60mph): 8.3 secs
Top speed: 222km/h (138mph)
Production total: 759

MASERATI MEXICO

1965–72

The Mexico was intended to replace the 5000GT, but lacked th performance, power and much of the style of its illustrious predecessor. Vignale's square-cut styling did not have the originalit and flair of the 5000GT.

Engine: 4136cc (252 cu in), V8-cylinder
Power: 194kW (260bhp) at 5200rpm
0–96km/h (60mph): 7.5 secs
Top speed: 230km/h (143mph)
Production total: 250

A shortened Quattroporte chassis and styling by Michelotti and Vignale were used to create the Mexico, a replacement for the Maserati 5000GT, which had gone out of production the year before the Mexico was unveiled in 1965.

Apart from the shortened chassis, mechanically the new Mexico was much the same as the Quattroporte, with an identical 4.1-litre (252 cu in) V8 quad-camshaft engine. However, a live rear axle and leaf springs were fitted from the beginning, along with ventilated disc brakes – a first for Maserati.

The body was all steel and directly welded onto the oval tube frame.

Although it had only two doors, the Mexico was a full (if cramped) four-seater aimed at the luxury market. It came with full leather trim, a wooden dashboard, electric windows and other gimmicks. From 1969, air conditioning became standard, too, while power-assisted steering was optional (as was an automatic gearbox).

However, even the availability of a 4.7-litre (287 cu in) engine in 1969 could not boost sales, and just 250 were built in seven years.

MASERATI INDY

Quad headlights operated by twin electric motors were concealed underneath the Indy's tapering bonnet, which helped to aid the aerodynamics. By contrast to its predecessor, the Sebring, the Indy was a far more distinctive creation, a fact reflected in good sales.

After the Sebring went out of production, Maserati introduced a much sleeker 2+2 coupé to replace it. The Indy of 1968 first appeared as a motor show design concept by Vignale at the Turin Motor Show, but one year later the company put it into production after first displaying the car on its own stand at the Geneva show.

It shared similar looks to the Ghibli, but, while that had been designed by Giorgetto Giugiaro, Vignale was responsible for both designing and building the Indy. Like the Ghibli the Indy featured pop-up headlights to improve its aerodynamic qualities, but had a higher fastback roof line at the rear designed to accommodate back-seat passengers.

Underneath, the Indy used the Quattroporte chassis, although the body was welded to the frame in a form of semi-unitary construction. This manufacturing process was a first for Maserati, but its lack of experience in monocoque engineering meant that the car later developed a reputation for rust. The Quattroporte's quad-camshaft 4136cc (252 cu in) V8 engine, fed through four Weber carburettors, featured on the first cars; however, by 1970, capacity had grown to 4930cc (301 cu in). That was not to be the end of the engine changes, though. In 1973, a 4930cc (301 cu in) V8 engine heralded a big leap in power and performance.

Part of the Indy's success was down to the luxurious options available from Maserati. An automatic gearbox and limited-slip differential could all be specified, while electric windows were standard.

Engine: 4719cc (288 cu in), V8-cylinder
Power: 216kW (290bhp) at 5500rpm
0–96km/h (60mph): 7.5 secs
Top speed: 253km/h (157mph)
Production total: 1136

In Maserati terms, the Indy was a good seller, with sales of 1136 cars in six years almost counting as mass production for a specialist maker.

MASERATI GHIBLI

Of all the cars to bear the illustrious trident motif, the Ghibli is regarded as being the most charismatic and stylish. Although at the time it was overshadowed by the Ferrari Daytona and Lamborghini Miura (even though it managed to outsell both of them), the gorgeous looks of the Ghibli have since earned it a well-justified place in the supercar hall of fame.

The Ghibli, like many Maseratis, took its name from a type of wind. This was a good metaphor for the aerodynamic supercar, which was capable of breezing along at great speeds. The design was based mechanically on the previous Mexico model; however, it used a shortened version of the tubular frame chassis and a more powerful 4719cc (288 cu in) quad-camshaft V8 engine. This was mounted at the front of the car, despite moves by other manufacturers such as Lamborghini towards mid-mounted units. The V8 engine was the most powerful Maserati had built. It was all-alloy, with four camshafts and four Weber carburettors to feed fuel at the rate of around a gallon every 18km (11 miles).

The Ghibli also used the Mexico's live rear axle and leaf springs, a very basic configuration for a car that was capable of extreme levels of performance. Although the car handled very well, at high speed the rear end could prove difficult to control.

So, mechanically, there was little to get excited about. Cosmetically, however, the Ghibli was fantastic, and designer Giorgetto Giugiaro's bodywork was breathtaking. By having a dry sump for the engine, Giugiaro (at the time, the chief designer for Ghia) was able to lower the profile of the bonnet, keeping the front end long, low and shark-nosed. Retractable headlights helped to keep the lithe looks during daylight hours, and the lengthy, gently tapering rear end completed the distinctive Ghibli look. The Ghibli helped to establish Giugiaro's reputation as a top-flight designer, and the car was – and still is – generally acknowledged to be the most beautiful Maserati ever.

The Ghibli was introduced at the 1966 Turin Motor Show and was actually displayed on the Ghia stand. It stole the show and went

into production a year later. One year after that, a convertible was launched, bearing the Spyder name. It, too, was designed by Ghia and was intended to appeal to the US market, although only a small fraction of total Ghibli production was open-topped. The Ghibli Spyder looked good with its soft top up or down, or even with the optional removable hardtop in place, something few supercars are capable of. The Spyder kept more or less the same lines as its fixed-head sister, as extra strengthening was not necessary for the rugged coupé chassis.

Automatic transmission became optional on both versions in 1968. In 1970, the Ghibli SS was launched. Although nothing was changed cosmetically, the SS used the 4930cc (301 cu in) V8 engine. It was not much more powerful than the previous unit, but had enormous reserves of torque which made the car even more flexible on the road.

Sales of the Ghibli were good, with more orders coming in than could possibly be fulfilled, and fellow manufacturers Ferrari and Lamborghini must have been envious of how the car managed to

Maserati's crowning glory was the Ghibli, a car to rival the best that competitors such as Ferrari and Lamborghini could offer. From an angle, it was a beautiful car and one of the favourite designs of its creator, Giorgetto Giugiaro.

outsell both the Daytona and the Miura, despite being mechanically less competent.

The Ghibli's production life was comparatively short, however. Maserati put its first mid-engined road car into production in 1971, leaving the earlier front-engined car to retire gracefully in 1973.

The Ghibli legend remains undiminished. It was the peak of Maserati's road car production, a steel sculpture of power and speed No other Maserati – and certainly not the Biturbo pretender named after it in 1992 – would ever be as sublime again.

What lay underneath the Ghibli's bonnet was not for the faint-hearted or for those with delicate wallets. The V8 used in various forms throughout the Maserati range was a complicated piece of kit, constructed out of alloy with four camshafts and carburettors.

Engine: 4719cc (288 cu in), V8-cylinder
Power: 253kW (340bhp) at 5500rpm
0–96km/h (60mph): 9.5 secs
Top speed: 248km/h (154mph)
Production total: 1372

MASERATI BORA

Engine: 4719cc (288 cu in), V8-cylinder
Power: 231kW (310bhp) at 6000rpm
0–96km/h (60mph): 6.5 secs
Top speed: 261km/h (162mph)
Production total: 571

The 1970s proved to be a difficult decade for Maserati. However, there was little sign of the trouble ahead when Maserati, under new owner Citroën (which had bought the Italian concern in 1968), unveiled its stunning Bora at the 1971 Geneva Motor Show.

The Bora was Maserati's attempt to catch up with rivals Lamborghini and Ferrari. The mid-engine configuration had already been demonstrated as the way forward for sports car design with the Miura and (later) the Dino. The Bora was Maserati's first attempt at mimicking this layout.

The 4719cc (288 cu in) alloy V8 was mid-mounted longitudinally on a subframe, attached to a ZF five-speed transaxle. Suspension was independent by double wishbones all around. Citroën's influence was apparent with the sharp pneumatic brakes and hydraulically adjustable seats, pedals and pop-up headlights.

As he had been so successful with the Ghibli, Giugiaro (by now working for Italdesign) was invited back to design the body, and he produced another excellent piece of styling. Construction was unitary and, although most cars appeared with steel bodies, some were built with aluminium panels.

The US market got a 4930cc (301 cu in) Bora in 1975, but Europe had to wait until 1977 for this model.

Maserati's styling became more angular and wedge-shaped during the 1970s. Having the considerable resources of Citroën behind it meant that – initially at least – Maserati could afford to experiment, and thus the exciting and modern Bora was the company's first mid-engined car.

Although the Bora was not designed using a wind tunnel, Giugaro's sleek lines give it a drag coefficient of just 0.30.

MASERATI MERAK

If the Bora was Maserati's answer to the Lamborghini Miura, then the smaller-engined V6 Merak, which was launched a year after the Bora, was Maserati's response to the Ferrari Dino.

The Maserati Merak was effectively a re-engined, slightly

In profile, the Bora and the Merak are difficult to tell apart. The chief difference is that the idiosyncratic flying buttresses on the Bora are enclosed by glass while, on the Merak, they are open. The front is also slightly different.

lighter Bora, with only a few, token styling modifications to mark it out as a different model. In sales terms, however, the Merak was more successful than its more powerful sister, and it was to remain in production longer.

Citroën's impact was even more noticeable on the Merak. The V6 engine came from the Citroën SM, and the instruments and steering wheel were borrowed from the same car. The five-speed gearbox, pneumatic brakes and hydraulic clutch were also French items.

Cosmetically, the front was altered from the Bora, and the flying rear buttresses were open, instead of enclosed. Otherwise, there was little to distinguish the two cars externally.

As well as the standard 3-litre (181 cu in) engine, a Merak 2000 was made for the Italian market only. More exciting was the Merak SS from 1975, with a highly tuned engine producing 295bhp (220kW). It also used the ZF gearbox from the Bora, and dropped the Citroën instruments and brakes, too.

The Maserati Merak used the same Giugiaro bodyshell as the Bora; however, it featured a V6 engine which was basically the long-lived V8 engine with two cylinders lopped off the end, as also utilized in the Citroën SM. Sales of the Merak were almost double that of the Bora.

Engine: 2965cc (181 cu in), V6-cylinder
Power: 135kW (182bhp) at 6000rpm
0–96km/h (60mph): 9.5 secs
Top speed: 214km/h (133mph)
Production total: 1140

MASERATI KHAMSIN

1973–82

The Khamsin was the 2+2 coupé replacement for the Indy, but was a more satisfactory design thanks to the influence of stylist Marcello Gandini, whose major triumph had been the Lamborghini Miura seven years earlier.

Mechanically, though, the Khamsin was something of a step backwards. Because of the 2+2 configuration, there was no room for a mid-mounted engine, so the Khamsin reverted to a conventional front engine/rear-wheel drive layout, although with all-independent double wishbone suspension throughout. Power for the car came from the familiar 4930cc (301 cu in) quad-camshaft V8. In order to make the long bonnet as low as possible, the engine was dry sumped. Citroën supplied the hydraulics for seat adjustment, pop-up headlights, power steering, clutch and brakes.

As Gandini was working for Bertone by this time, the unitary construction body was built by the Italian Carrozzeria. There was less headroom for rear-seat passengers than with the previous Indy. This

time, few compromises were made for the occupants, with the rear bodywork sloping back steeply to the Kamm-type tail.

Although not a spectacular sales success, the Khamsin did remain in production until 1982.

Despite having Marcello Gandini, creator of the Lamborghini Miura, as its designer, the Khamsin was not one of the most attractive Maserati models and reverted to the tradition of front engine and rear-wheel drive.

Engine: 4930cc (301 cu in), V8-cylinder
Power: 238kW (320bhp) at 5500rpm
0–96km/h (60mph): 6.5 secs
Top speed: 257km/h (160mph)
Production total: 421

MASERATI KYALAMI

1977–83

Citroën was taken over by Peugeot in 1974, who quickly put Maserati into liquidation. The Argentinian forming racing driver Alejandro de Tomaso mounted a rescue mission and, in 1975, Maserati became independent again.

A piece of Maserati's soul had disappeared, though, and with

tough financial constraints imposed on it, the company became less of a supercar manufacturer and more of a mainstream producer. The Kyalami was the first indication of what was to come.

If the Kyalami looked familiar to buyers, that was because it was effectively little more than a De

Tomaso Longchamp with the front restyled by Ghia to include quad headlights and Maserati's traditional trident motif.

There were changes to the interior, and the major difference was the Longchamp's Ford V8 engine being replaced by one of Maserati's own 4136cc (252 cu in)

V8s, and was slightly faster than the Longchamp as a result – although, from 1977, the 4930cc (301 cu in) engine was available as an option.

The Kyalami was less of a Ferrari or Lamborghini competitor, and more of a Mercedes, BMW or Jaguar rival. This meant that Maserati's traditional customers stayed away in droves, and the badge-engineered Maserati was unsuccessful and plagued by reliability problems. Production of the Kyalami ceased in 1983.

A De Tomaso by any other name… The Kyalami was a badge-engineered version of the De Tomaso Longchamp, introduced after the Argentinian bought Maserati in 1975. The Kyalami used a Maserati V8 for power.

Engine: 4136cc (252 cu in), V8-cylinder
Power: 201kW (270bhp) at 6000rpm
0–96km/h (60mph): 7.6 secs
Top speed: 237km/h (147mph)
Production total: 150

MASERATI QUATTROPORTE III

1977–90

The imposing Quattroporte had two big engines to match its appearance, the 4930cc (301 cu in) V8 being the most popular.

Citroën revived the Quattroporte name for a big, front-wheel drive V6 saloon just before it quit its interest in Maserati in 1975. This new luxury cruiser used the engine, transmission and suspension of the SM, but only six of the Bertone-styled vehicles were built before the project was abandoned – seven more were later assembled from parts.

When De Tomaso took over Maserati, he decided to have another go. Giugiaro was brought in to style the Quattroporte III, designing a huge but restrained-looking monster.

As with the Kyalami, de Tomaso turned to his 'other' company to provide a basis for the new Maserati. The underpinnings for the Quattroporte III were borrowed from the De Tomaso Deauville, and the original Citroën plans for front-wheel drive were dropped, to be replaced by traditional rear-wheel drive.

The car could be ordered with either the Maserati 4.1-litre (252 cu in) V8 or with the 4.9-litre (301 cu in) version. Most customers chose the latter option and, by 1985, it was the only engine available.

For those wanting more luxury than even a standard Quattroporte could supply, the SD coachbuilding firm offered a stretched limousine version. In 1987, the Quattroporte was renamed the Royale, but was dropped from the range in 1990.

Engine: 4930cc (301 cu in), V8-cylinder
Power: 215kW (288bhp) at 5600rpm
0–96km/h (60mph): 9.3 secs
Top speed: 198km/h (123mph)
Production total: n/a

MASERATI BITURBO

1981–PRESENT

If proof were needed that Maserati had become a mere shadow of its former self by the end of 1970s, then the Biturbo range was it. Maserati's new direction was far removed from its supercar heyday. The Biturbo was styled in-house and looked nondescript and unexciting. In fact, it looked much like any other 1980s saloon, not the product of one of Italy's most evocative marques.

Power was provided by an 18-valve twin-camshaft 2-litre (122 cu in) V6 fitted with two turbochargers, hence the name. A confusing number of model and engine variations which included 2.5-litre (152 cu in) and 2.8-litre (171 cu in) units with intercoolers, fuel injection, catalytic converters and so on were gradually introduced.

The original two-door saloon was joined by the four-door 420 in 1982, and the Zagato-built Spyder convertible appeared in 1984. Facelifts came in 1987 and 1992.

The Shamal of 1989 was a two-door Biturbo with a more aggressive body, while 1992's Ghibli was an undeserving recipient of the once great name. The Quattroporte name was also brought out of retirement in 1996 to denote the four-door Biturbo. The Ghibli was replaced by the far more exciting 3200GT in 1998, but the Quattroporte still remains in production today.

To those used to Maseratis being special, the Biturbo range must have been a major disappointment. Gone were the V8 engines, and the styling was blandly anonymous. It would take until the 1990s – and ownership by Ferrari – to revitalize the marque.

Engine: 2491cc (152 cu in), V6-cylinder
Power: 138kW (185bhp) at 5500rpm
0–96km/h (60mph): 7.2 secs
Top speed: 201km/h (125mph)
Production total: n/a

MATRA DJET

The French Matra company was much better known for its missiles than its cars when it decided to buy out the financially ailing Bonnet company, whichwas based in Champigny-sur-Marne, and make the mid-engined Djet, which was based on René Bonnet's existing Renault-engined car.

The Matra-Bonnet Djet 5, to give its full name, featured a narrow, plastic body with a sleek nose (much like the later Opel GT), pencil-thin chrome inserts in the front and rear bumpers, large-diameter steel wheels and a typical GT-style rear end with a reasonable-sized boot for luggage.

The Renault 8 powerplant was tuned to produce 52kW (70bhp), while the 5S version gained the Gordini engine, producing 71kW (95bhp). This engine was uprated in 1966 to 1255cc (77 cu in) and 77kW (103bhp), and it was renamed the Jet 6.

All the cars were made in left-hand drive form only, and all were two-seater coupés. Once the Matra company had learnt the basics of making frames and bodywork, it produced a more ambitious plan to build a larger machine.

Engine: 1108cc (68 cu in), 4-cylinder
Power: 52–71kW (70–95bhp)
0–96km/h (60mph): 9.8 secs
Top speed: 174km/h (109mph)
Production total: 1681

MATRA 530

The Matra company moved to larger premises at Romarantin to build a larger, more refined version of the Djet, called the M530, which was first shown at the Geneva Motor Show in 1967. Power came from a German Ford V4 which fitted well into the new platform, made from pressed steel. The car's chassis was built waist-high at the scuttle and around the engine just like the monocoque construction of the racing Matras.

The body was plastic, and the car had a number of quirky features which aroused much curiosity at the time. These included concealed headlights which were worked by a strong spring with its own heavy

The Gallic-looking Matra 530 featured glassfibre 2+2 bodywork and Ford V4 power mounted midships. Early cars had pop-up headlights and a lift-out targa roof panel – models after 1971 had four free-standing headlights.

pedal in the footwell operated by the driver. Another interesting feature was the gearchange, which was meant for front-wheel drive so that all the gear selections were the wrong way round, with first gear at the top right and top gear bottom left. The removable targa top and upwards-hinging rear window (which looked more like a front windscreen) were further oddities.

Road-holding ability was good, although, with just 56kW (75bhp) available, the car was very under-powered. It was noisy, too, thanks to its mid-engine configuration.

Engine: 1699cc (104 cu in), 4-cylinder
Power: 56kW (75bhp)
0–96km/h (60mph): 15.6 secs
Top speed: 161km/h (100mph)
Production total: 9609

MATRA SIMCA BAGHEERA

In 1969, Matra switched allegiance from Renault to fellow French company, Simca, to develop the Bagheera. This car was unique in exploiting its width and lack of transmission tunnel to allow three-breast seating. A further unusual feature at the time was the car's opening glass rear window, which effectively made the Bagheera a sporty hatchback.

The chassis was of spaceframe construction using tubes and sheet steel, and the plastic body was created by French stylist Philippe Guedon. Underneath the coupé body was torsion-bar independent suspension, all-round disc brakes and, mounted transversely in the middle of the car, a Simca 1.3-litre (79 cu in) engine. Again, this unit lacked power, which ended any true sports car pretensions, though the post-1975 Bagheera S, with its

Continuing the mid-engined, fibreglass body theme, the sleek-looking Matra Bagheera was unique for having three-abreast seating at the front. Power came from the Simca 1100 initially.

1442cc (88 cu in) engine, was better, allowing the car to reach a respectable 184km/h (115mph).

The car remained in production, selling well, until the PSA takeover of Chrysler-Simca in 1980, by which time it was known as Talbot-Matra. That year, the Bagheera was replaced by the Talbot-Matra Murena (see over). All cars were made in left-hand drive form only.

Engine: 1294cc (79 cu in), 4-cylinder
Power: 63kW (84bhp)
0–96km/h (60mph): 9.2 secs
Top speed: 163km/h (102mph)
Production total: 47,802

MATRA RANCHO

1978–84

Ahead of its time in concept, the glassfibre Rancho featured chunky off-road styling, despite its lack of four-wheel drive making it far better suited to the tarmac. The running gear was workaday Simca 1100/Alpine.

rear seat to provide a usefully large, flat rear loading space.

Its 1442cc (88 cu in) engine came from the Bagheera, and it had a (rust-prone) steel floorpan and mainly glassfibre body, with a high roof section which was designed specifically to make the interior seem more spacious.

The suspension was by independent wishbone/torsion bar at the front and independent trailing arms/transverse torsion bar at the back.

In 1979, the car's name was changed to Talbot-Matra, in line with other Matra products.

With hindsight, the Matra Rancho, with its chunky go-anywhere looks, never received the acclaim it deserved. Poor build quality, weak Simca mechanicals and phoney off-road pretensions made it a

target for criticism; however, in concept, the Matra Rancho was years ahead of its time, creating the entirely new genre of 'soft' off-roaders and multi-purpose vehicles that are so popular today.

Front-wheel drive only, not 4x4, the Rancho was one of the most practical vehicles of its time, with a split tailgate, child-proof interior trim and high ride height. There was also the bonus of a folding

Engine: 1442cc (88 cu in), 4-cylinder
Power: 58kW (78bhp)
0–96km/h (60mph): 12 secs
Top speed: 144km/h (90mph)
Production total: 56,700

MATRA MURENA

1980–84

The Murena was mostly just an uprated Bagheera. However, styling changes did give the car a sharper front end, which lowered the drag coefficient to just 0.32cd, which was an impressive figure at the time. The big difference was that the body was now made from steel instead of glassfibre, and coil springs replaced the old, outdated torsion-bar front suspension.

The original engine was the 1.6-litre (98 cu in) unit from the Renault Alpine; however, more impressive was a 2.2-litre (132 cu in) Chrysler unit, which produced 88kW (118bhp) and a useful amount of torque. The trademark Matra three-abreast seating arrangement continued, and the majority of cars were left-hand drive, with just five being converted to right-hand drive.

The car was marketed under the Talbot name, as Matra had now become part of the giant PSA organization. However, Matra left PSA in 1983 and became part of Renault, where it was involved in

the development of the trend-setting Espace MPV – no doubt drawing on the company's previous experience gained during the construction of its equally forward-thinking Rancho.

Using the same basic build as the earlier Bagheera, but with better coil-spring suspension in place of torsion bars, the sleek Murena boasted a cd factor of just 0.32 which was exceptional in its day.

Engine: 1592cc (97 cu in), 4-cylinder
Power: 88kW (118bhp)
0–96km/h (60mph): 9.3 secs
Top speed: 194km/h (121mph)
Production total: 10,613

MAYBACH ZEPPELIN

1931–40

Having developed engines for airships prior to World War I, the Maybach company named its 1931 8-litre V12-engined Mayback D58 touring car the 'Zeppelin'. All Zeppelins had seven-speed gearboxes.

At the turn of the 19th century, Wilhelm Maybach was always associated with famous engineers and products. These included Gottlieb Daimler, Emil Jellinek (founder of Mercedes cars) and later the famous Zeppelin airships, having developed the huge 21-litre (1282 cu in) powerplants that propelled them. When Wilhelm died of pneumonia in 1929, his son, Karl, established the Maybach automotive company.

Maybach cars were not for the masses, but instead were very expensive luxury limousines for the rich. The W5 of 1927 was one of Maybach's first creations. It had a six-cylinder, 7-litre (488 cu in) engine with bodywork by German coachbuilders Spohn and weighed a staggering 3500kg (7700lb). The Zeppelin followed in 1931 and was equally huge, but was powered by a more suitable V12 engine.

Due to the size of the cars and the big engines required to power them, it was inevitable that the company would venture into commercial vehicles, and it is in this form that Maybach exists today (known as Motoren Turbinen Union), making heavy diesel engines and teaming up with its old ally, Mercedes.

Engine: 7995cc (488 cu in), V12-cylinder
Power: 149kW (200bhp)
0–96km/h (60mph): n/a
Top speed: n/a
Production total: n/a

MAZDA COSMO

1967–72

Mazda's attractive Cosmo 110S became the world's first mass-produced rotary-engined car, beating the NSU Ro80 by just a few months. It was also the company's first sports car, securing much publicity for the fledgling company that had yet to make its name in Europe.

The company's interest in rotary engine technology came in the early 1960s, when it acquired a licence from NSU to build Wankel engines, although it had produced its own prototypes much earlier.

The Cosmo featured De Dion rear suspension with leaf springs, and coils and wishbones at the front. It also had front-wheel drive and front disc brakes.

Despite being quite powerful, the reliability of the twin-rotor engine was suspect. However, important lessons were learnt which would serve the company well during further developments of the rotary engine in its later models.

Mazda took an early interest in developing the Wankel engine, producing the twin-rotor engined Cosmo in 1967. It was technically interesting but plagued by chronic reliability problems.

The L10B version which was available from 1968 gained a longer wheelbase and a more prominent under-bumper grille and, from 1969, the Cosmo received more power and a five-speed transmission.

Engine: 491cc (30 cu in), twin rotor Wankel
Power: 82kW (110bhp)
0–96km/h (60mph): 10.2 secs
Top speed: 185km/h (115mph)
Production total: 1176

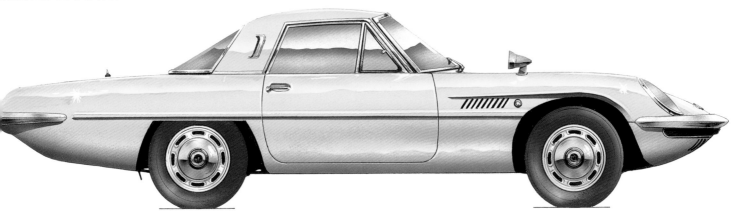

MAZDA LUCE

1966–72

Although Mazda's first car was only built in 1960, by the mid-1960s, the company had become Japan's third-largest motor manufacturer, and the Luce model was developed to further consolidate this growth, particularly in respect to its export business. This factor accounted for the conventional European appearance of the Luce saloon and estate car range – a range which was developed by styling house Bertone and originally intended for use by the Italian manufacturer Alfa Romeo.

Unremarkable in many respects, the car featured a shallow chrome grille, twin headlights, servo-assisted disc brakes at the front and a high level of specification inside the passenger compartment. Engines were overhead camshaft units, in either 1500cc (92 cu in) or 1800cc (110 cu in) guise, and both provided unremarkable but adequate performance.

The coupé version of the Luce, known as the R130, was launched in 1969. This was a different car altogether, and it featured a twin-rotor 655cc (40 cu in) Wankel engine producing 94kW (126bhp), front-wheel drive and a hardtop.

Reliability was a problem, however, as Mazda had still to overcome a number of teething problems with its rotary engine technology. Both the saloon and coupé versions were revised in 1972.

When Alfa Romeo rejected Bertone's design, it was sold to Mazda and used for its Luce model. Conventional overhead camshaft engines were joined by rotary units on the R130 coupé version.

Engine: 1490cc (91 cu in), 4-cylinder or 655cc (40 cu in), twin-rotor Wankel
Power: 69kW (92bhp)
0–96km/h (60mph): 19.3 secs
Top speed: 161km/h (100mph)
Production total: 160,845

MAZDA RX4

1970–7

The third and largest of the Mazda's rotary-engined saloons, the RX4 was underwhelming in every respect, as was the conventionally engined 1.8-litre (110 cu in) saloon version of the car,

badged the 929. All the versions were bland, and little attempt was made to endow them with any kind of lasting appeal.

Very successful in terms of sales, the car featured front disc brakes

and a choice of saloon, estate and coupé body styles. Otherwise, the RX4's mechanicals were to remain entirely conventional and totally uninspiring.

Its rotary engine originated from the RX2, which also arrived in 1970, and it was later increased in capacity in 1974 when it became the equivalent of 2.6 litres (159 cu

in). At this time, the RX4 also gained a five-speed gearbox.

The only moderately interesting car in the range was the pillarless coupé with its obvious American-influenced styling, which made it look like a scaled-down version of a Ford Mustang.

Very few examples exist today, despite more than 200,000 having been made between 1970 and 1977, as many of these cars succumbed to severe rust problem

The RX4 was the rotary version of Mazda's conventional 929 saloon. It sold well, but failed to stir the emotions – although it should be said that the coupé version was vaguely more interesting.

Engine: 1796cc (110 cu in), 4-cylinder or 573cc (35 cu in) twin-rotor Wankel
Power: 89kW (120bhp)
0–96km/h (60mph): n/a
Top speed: 189km/h (118mph)
Production total: 213,988

MAZDA RX7

Having doggedly continued with the rotary concept, Mazda managed to solve most of its reliability problems by the time it launched the RX7 in the late 1970s. The company's determination paid off, as the pretty 2+2 coupé's engine was smooth and powerful, and the resulting agile car was fun to drive, with excellent cornering abilities.

The early 78kW (105bhp) engine was increased to 86kW (115bhp) in 1981, which added further performance. A fuel-injected and turbocharged version appeared in 1983, its 123kW (165bhp) engine giving a top speed of 220km/h (137mph). The car looked good, too, with pop-up headlights creating a sleek profile and a neat rear end. Despite its unconventional engine, however, the RX7 was really rather ordinary underneath, with strut front suspension and a live rear axle at the rear.

Almost 500,000 cars were built before the RX7 was given a makeover in 1989, when it

received the new 13B engine, producing 110kW (148bhp), and a new chassis featuring complex independent rear suspension.

A turbocharged convertible version of the RX7 arrived in 1988 and ran until 1992.

Engine: 573cc (35 cu in), twin-rotor Wankel
Power: 78kW (105bhp)
0–96km/h (60mph): 8.4 secs
Top speed: 181km/h (113mph)
Production total: 474,565

The incredibly agile RX7 was the legacy of Mazda's love affair with the Wankel engine – its shape and powerplants evolving throughout the 1980 and 1990s. The light-weight twin-rotor sports car won the 24-Hour Le Mans in 1991.

The RX7 became more rounded and less wedge-shaped with time. As the car was so low to the ground, Mazda had no choice but to use pop-up headlights to meet required height regulations.

MAZDA MX5

1989–PRESENT

The MX5 is what the Lotus Elan from the 1960s should have been – fun to drive, reliable and, above all, affordable. No wonder the little Mazda has rapidly gained a place in the hearts of sports car fans right around the globe.

Its simple design works well, and the typical Japanese levels of build quality and reliability are far above 1960s sports cars such as the Lotus and Frogeye Sprite it mimics so well.

Another difference is the comfort in the cabin. None of the shakes and rattles of old sports cars – the MX5 is refined and well equipped, with many even affording passengers the luxury of air conditioning. There is even the option of a decent hardtop.

A front end facelift in order to comply with safety regulations in April 1998 did away with the Mazda's characteristic pop-up headlamps, the body was made more rigid and glass was used instead of plastic for the rear window. The rear end also went through a mild redesign.

Performance from the overhead camshaft engine is impressive, and the handling is superb thanks to all-round independent wishbone/coil suspension.

The only criticism is that the 1.6-litre (98 cu in) engine is a little weak, making the 1.8-litre (112 cu in) version the car to have.

Engine: 1839cc (112 cu in), 4-cylinder
Power: 104kW (140bhp)
0–96km/h (60mph): 8 secs
Top speed: 203km/h (127mph)
Production total: n/a

Mazda's cute two-seater has all the charisma of the traditional British sports car from the 1960s; however it is also highly civilized, great to drive and ultra-reliable. The Mazda MX5 is known as the Euno Roadster in Japan.

Gottlieb Daimler partnered Wilhelm Maybach in producing the first petrol-powered internal combustion engine in 1883, and by 1886 they had created the first Daimler car, with production starting in 1890.

Rich diplomat and motoring enthusiast Emil Jellinek joined Daimler in 1900 with the intention of persuading the company to manufacture a high-performance car. The resulting car, which

appeared in 1901, featured many technical innovations.

Mercedes was the name of Jellinek's daughter and was first used for Daimlers sold in France to avoid licensing infringements; however, it was adopted for all Daimler cars built at Cannstatt from 1902.

Based on the earlier Mercedes-Simplex cars, the 60 featured open two-seat or four-seat bodywork, a separate pressed-steel chassis frame with semi-elliptic leaf spring suspension and wooden 'artillery'-style wheels.

The car famously competed in the Gordon Bennett races in Ireland

The Mercedes 60, with its low chassis and cast-alloy engine, used technology from which the majority of modern cars evolved. A Mercedes 60 triumphed in the Gordon Bennett race in 1903.

and, following a fire at the factory which destroyed all five of the competition cars, owners were asked to 'donate' their vehicles to the company for the event. One such car, loaned by an American, won a memorable victory at the hands of Camille Jenatzy at an average speed of 79.1km/h (49.2mph).

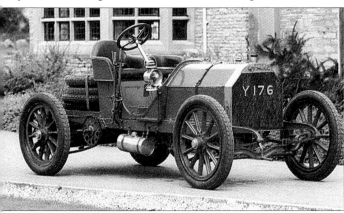

A beautifully preserved 1903 Mercedes 60 open two-seater. Note the plentiful spare tyres at the rear.

Engine: 9293cc (567 cu in), 4-cylinder
Power: 48kW (65bhp)
0–96km/h (60mph): n/a
Top speed: 106km/h (66mph)
Production total: n/a

MERCEDES-BENZ SSK

World War I saw Daimler making aero engines and, from 1921, Ferdinand Porsche became the traditionally conservative company's chief engineer. Up to that time, Daimler had a reputation for producing reliable but dull vehicles. Then the postwar recession forced Daimler into a cooperative arrangement with car manufacturer Karl Benz in 1924, and the two companies merged to become Mercedes-Benz in 1926.

The legendary SSK was derived from the supercharged Model K

touring car, and it worked on the principle of using a big, under-stressed engine and a long, open touring body. However, the car had very poor brakes, perhaps as a result of all the emphasis on power.

There were four basic stages in the car's evolution, beginning with the S (Sport) with its 6.8-litre (414 cu in) engine and four-seater body, followed by the SS (Super Sport) which had a bigger bore 7.1-litre (433 cu in) engine and lower ride height, then followed by the SSK (the K denoting 'kurz' or 'short')

with its lighter, shorter wheelbase and 168kW (225bhp) powerplant.

This brilliant engine was both powerful and agile, and it powered Mercedes to countless victories, including various European hillclimb events such as the Mille Miglia, the 1930 Irish GP and the 1931 Belgian 24-hour event.

The SSK was superseded by the rare SSKL (the L in the name standing for 'leicht' or 'light'), which had a drilled chassis and larger blower (supercharger), giving 197kW (265bhp).

Engine: 6789cc (414 cu in), 6-cylinder
Power: 168kW (225bhp)
0–96km/h (60mph): n/a
Top speed: 200km/h (125mph)
Production total: n/a

The Mercedes-Benz SSK evolved at the hands of Ferdinand Porsche and the resulting car had a lighter, shorter-wheelbase chassis than its predecessors and a 168kW (225bhp) engine. Agile and very responsive, the SSK went on to win numerous European hillclimb events during the 1930s.

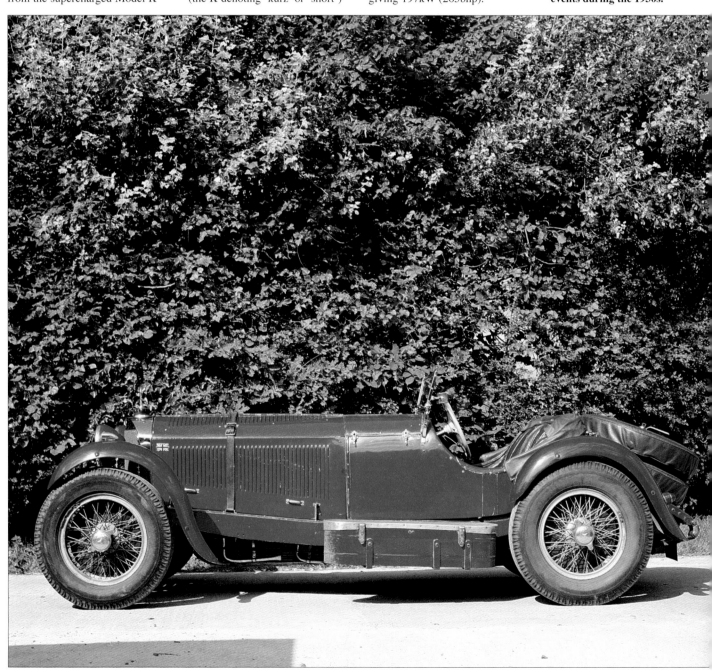

MERCEDES-BENZ 260D

1936–39

[Th]e 260D, codenamed the W138, [w]as the world's first diesel [p]roduction car and gained notoriety [a]s being the car of choice for the [d]readed Gestapo during World War [I]. It was also used by the German [n]aval and air forces. While most [w]ere used in their civilian form, [m]any specialized bodies with no [d]oors and fabric hoods were [a]dopted. Some were even modified [f]or use as commercial vehicles, [a]ppearing as ambulances and light [a]rtillery tractors.

Borrowing the chassis and all[r]ound independent suspension of [th]e 230 model, the 260 provided a [c]omfortable ride and, because of [i]s cheap running costs, was partic[u]larly favoured by taxi drivers.

The innovative 260's engine [c]ould rev up to 3000rpm, which [w]as rare for a diesel, and

The 260D was the world's first production diesel car and a favourite of the German Gestapo during World War II. According to contemporary road tests, it performed well for a diesel.

contemporary testers suggested that the acceleration was comparable to 3-litre (183 cu in) petrol-engined cars of the time. The gearbox was a three-speed manual and, after 1937, a fourth gear was added.

Like the 230, the 260 was available for general sale with tourer, saloon or folding hood laundaulette body options.

Engine: 2545cc (155 cu in), 4-cylinder
Power: 34kW (45bhp)
0–96km/h (60mph): n/a
Top speed: 109km/h (68mph)
Production total: 1967

MERCEDES-BENZ 540K

1936–39

[H]ans Nibel was to take over from [F]erdinand Porsche as chief [e]ngineer in 1928, and with his

appointment came an entirely revised range of more refined sporting machines, starting with the

supercharged 380 in 1933, then the magnificent 500 of 1934 and, finally, the elegant, supercharged

540K (K for 'kompressor', or 'supercharger') of 1936.

The 540K is considered by many to be the epitome of the classic car shape – where at least half its length is hood – and for that reason it has been replicated by modern kit car manufacturers ever since.

Key features were its pram-like folding hood, sweeping front wings, front-opening suicide doors, twin spare wheels stowed forward of the A-post on each side of the car and an upright chrome grille sporting the now-famous Mercedes-Benz three-pointed star emblem.

The formidable 540K featured a straight-eight engine set well back from the front of the car, followed by cabin space for two with room behind the seats and further boot space at the car's rear for luggage. It was a truly extravagant way to transport just two passengers.

Mercedes 540K was a formidable car, with its supercharged straight-eight-cylinder engine, long bonnet and graceful sweeping front wings. Despite its prodigious proportions, it only seated two people.

Engine: 5401cc (330 cu in), 8-cylinder
Power: 134kW (180bhp)
0–96km/h (60mph): n/a
Top speed: 161km/h (100mph)
Production total: 444

MERCEDES-BENZ 220

1951–55

The Mercedes factory had suffered terrible devastation during World War II bombing campaigns, so the first cars to leave it after the war were based on the antiquated 170 model. The 220 was one such 'new' vehicle, but had six cylinders and an overhead camshaft engine.

In terms of style, the 170 and 220 cars were virtually identical, apart from the headlights, which had now been integrated into the front wings, and fixed bonnet sides. In addition to four-door saloons, the 220 range was offered with cabriolet and two-door closed-coupé body styles (after 1954), the latter of which being the rarest, as only around 85 were made. The chassis was also made available separately for coach-builders wishing to convert the cars into light commercials.

Despite looking somewhat dated at the time with its flat, letterbox screen, the 220 was to play an

important part in the company's revival during the early part of the 1950s, and it offered buyers reasonable performance and economy from its six-cylinder, 60kW (80bhp) engine, as well as solid build quality.

Reasonable performance and economy from its overhead camshaft six-cylinder engine made the dated-looking 220 a popular choice among postwar Germans. The 220 range included a saloon, coupé and convertible (pictured).

Engine: 2195cc (134 cu in), 6-cylinder
Power: 60kW (80bhp)
0–96km/h (60mph): 19.5 secs
Top speed: 147km/h (92mph)
Production total: 18,514

MERCEDES-BENZ 220 PONTON

1954–59

Given the name Ponton (meaning 'pontoon' in German) because of its unitary construction (first used by Mercedes on its predecessor, the slightly smaller four-cylinder 180 of 1953), the Mercedes-Benz 220

Ponton featured full-width body, integrated headlights, a six-cylinder engine and longer alligator bonnet, as well as opening rear quarterlight windows and a wraparound front windscreen.

The brakes became servo-assisted a year after production started, and the 220S Ponton, introduced in 1956, had twin carburettors and more power. The same year, the shorter wheelbase 219 also

appeared. The cars sold well and helped to establish Mercedes' reputation for engineering excellence, fabulous build quality and first-class dealer back-up and customer service.

The 220 Ponton coupé and convertible body styles were to make their debut at the 1955 Frankfurt Motor Show, and they entered production with the twin-carburettor 'S' engine in 1956, and with the 'SE' fuel-injected engine in 1958. These are undoubtedly the most sought-after cars of the 220 Ponton range, and because of their rarity – only 7345 coupés and convertibles were made – they command high prices today.

Inheriting its name from its unitary method of construction, the Ponton featured a variety of modern styling cues such as a full-width bodywork and alligator bonnet. Less adventurous was its prewar side-valve engine which was taken from the 170 model.

Engine: 2195cc (134 cu in), 6-cylinder
Power: 63kW (85bhp)
0–96km/h (60mph): 15.2 secs
Top speed: 162km/h (101mph)
Production total: 116,406

MERCEDES-BENZ 300

The cabriolet version of the 300 was an elegant four-seater made between 1952 and 1956. The more sober but equally well-proportioned four-door saloons often found favour among heads of state.

The 300 was aimed directly at competition from the likes of BMW's 501 and became one of the most opulent prestige cars of the decade, with its smooth, alloy overhead camshaft straight-six engine, all-synchromesh four-speed gearbox and cosseting independent rear suspension. Mercedes was also among the first exponents of the hypoid type of bevel gear and a tubular chassis that was separate from the body.

The 300B of 1954 had a tuned engine and servo-assisted brakes, while the 300C of 1955 had an automatic transmission option. There was also an elegant four-door cabriolet made between 1952 and 1956. The fabulous two-door 300S of 1951 featured a shortened chassis and three body styles – a fixed head coupé, a convertible and a roadster. The SC version of 1955 had direct fuel injection and dry-sump lubrication.

Completing the range, the 300D from 1957 had a longer wheelbase and a restyled body with a more upright stance, wraparound rear screen and fully wind-down windows, making the sides completely pillarless.

The car was only made in limited numbers – just 3008 were built. Rarer still, however, were the cabriolets. Only 65 of these were ever produced.

Engine: 2996cc (183 cu in), 6-cylinder
Power: 86kW (115bhp)
0–96km/h (60mph): n/a
Top speed: 161km/h (100mph)
Production total: 12,221

MERCEDES-BENZ 190SL

With its blistered wheelarches and purposeful grille, the Mercedes-Benz 190SL could easily be described as a smaller version of the 300SL; however, underneath the two cars could not have been more different.

Instead of the 300SL's powerful six-cylinder engine, the 190 had the twin-carburettor version of the standard 1.9-litre (116 cu in) overhead camshaft unit, producing a weak 78kW (105bhp), and instead of the column gearchange

Looking a lot like a scaled-down 300SL, the 190 shared none of the appeal of its more sporty relation, with its feeble 78kW (105bhp) four-cylinder 1897cc (116 cu in) engine. Not a great handler, it was also criminally overpriced when new.

there was a more conventional floor-mounted gearlever. The 190 was based on a shortened version of the 180 chassis and, considered overall, the car's specification was much more conventional.

Aimed squarely at the North American market, the diluted 190SL was an expensive option for what it was, and it was not particularly good to drive either, despite offering a firm ride from its all-round independent suspension. Needless to say, it did not figure in competition events.

The car received a slight facelift in 1955, and it was fitted with servo-assisted brakes a year later. Mercedes also offered a coupé version (with conventional doors, not the gullwing type as on the 300SL), as well as a roadster with the option of a removable hardtop.

Engine: 1897cc (116 cu in), 4-cylinder
Power: 78kW (105bhp)
0–96km/h (60mph): 13.3 secs
Top speed: 168km/h (105mph)
Production total: 25,881

MERCEDES-BENZ 300SL

The 300SL's charismatic gullwing doors were integral to the car's complex spaceframe construction. Swing-axle independent rear suspension resulted in severe oversteer at times, requiring the lightning-fast reactions of a racing driver to correct it.

The 300SL (Sport Leicht, with 'leicht' meaning 'light') must be considered as one of the most breathtaking cars of the 1950s, with its classic 'gullwing' doors and sensational performance.

It all began with a prototype racing car, the W194, which appeared two years earlier using the 300S's impressive fuel-injected six-cylinder engine coupled with a complex multi-tube spaceframe chassis. The car, of which only 10 had been made, placed first and second at Le Mans and, even more significantly, gained success at the Carrera Panamericana. As a result, and despite lack of money at the time, Mercedes decided to develop a production version, which followed in 1954.

The unusual centre-hinged doors, comprising windows and part of the roof, were less of a style feature than a device to preserve the structural integrity of the car and were combined with a thick sill section. A low bonnet, to maintain the car's aerodynamic qualities, was only made possible by canting the dry-sump engine at 45 degrees.

The W198 production car was launched in New York in early 1954 and refined in appearance with restrained use of chrome and a Bosch fuel-injected 179kW

(240bhp) powerplant. Much of the suspension and the gearbox, as well as the engine, was derived from the previous 300, and the car featured larger gullwing doors than the prototype to aid practicality.

At the time, the car was roughly twice the price of a Jaguar XK140, making it the preserve of the rich and famous and, despite its race pedigree, the car suffered from tremendous oversteer, thanks largely to its lively swing-axle rear suspension. To drive a 300SL to its limit required enormous driver skill and very fast reflexes. In addition,

the car's complex spaceframe construction meant that it was expensive to repair.

Finally, after just 1400 cars had been produced, it was replaced in 1957 by a roadster version which featured a more predictable low-pivot rear swing-axle suspension, conventional doors, a modified spaceframe and a slightly more powerful fuel-injected engine. Not only was this car cheaper to make, but it was also far easier for owners to live with.

The hood folded flush with the body behind the sports bucket

seats, and was neatly hidden by a steel sliding cover. A removable hardtop became available in 1958. Like the gullwing it replaced, the body was of steel construction, with the use of alloy for the doors, bonnet and boot lid. There were 29 all-alloy-bodied cars made, and these gained much competition success, including fifth in the 1955 Mille Miglia event.

The 300SL's top speed varied according to the rear axle ratio; however, claims that the car could reach 264km/h (165mph) were largely rejected. It seems likely that a more accurate figure would be 248km/h (155mph).

Despite the roadster version being less claustrophobic inside, easier to get in and out of, and far less challenging to drive, much of the 300SL's original purity had been lost. However, the roadster did prove a success with buyers, and 1858 cars were made before production finally ceased in 1962, when the 300SL made way for the less auspicious 230SL range.

The engine itself, in a less highly tuned form, became the backbone for Mercedes' production car range until the end of the 1960s, when it was replaced by a new 3.5- (214 cu in) and 4.5-litre (275 cu in) V8 unit. The use of gullwing opening doors, however, remained a design feature peculiar to the 300SL, although it was later echoed to some extent by the awesome Lamborghini Countach with its quirky front-hinged lifting doors.

Engine: 2996cc (183 cu in), 6-cylinder
Power: 179kW (240bhp)
0–96km/h (60mph): 8.8 secs
Top speed: 224km/h (140mph)
Production total: 3258

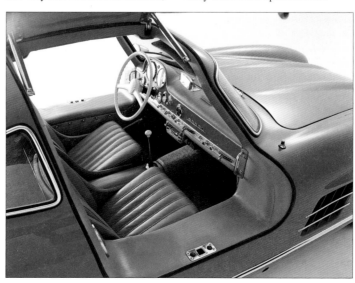

Spaceframe structure had obvious implications for gullwing passengers – the high sill height meant you literally had to climb inside. After 1957, the roadster made life easier, but much of the original character was lost.

MERCEDES-BENZ 300 FINTAIL

1961–65

The angular 'fintail' range, as it became known, started with the 1959 220, which was designed by Karl Wilfert and featured wraparound front and rear windscreens, along with the famous mark's fin pointed rear wing tips.

The 300SE, which was introduced in 1961, was undoubtedly the finest of all the fintails, and it could be easily distinguished from the 220 by its opulent extra chromework. The most significant differences, however, were underneath. The car's long, flat bonnet hid a powerful 3-litre (183 cu in) fuel-injected engine (indirect, this time), and the all-round brake discs were power-assisted. Mercedes also added its own brand of air suspension, which was self-levelling at the rear.

The car also introduced an all-new four-speed automatic transmission, pioneering technology that would be used later on various other models. Indeed, this was one of the most luxurious Mercedes yet and also one of the most expensive, being almost double the price of the lesser 220. Nevertheless, the 300 definitely set the standard for other manufacturers to follow.

In 1963, the SEL was introduced with a slightly longer wheelbase, providing owners with an even more impressive 'magic carpet' ride.

Engine: 2996cc (183 cu in), 6-cylinder
Power: 119kW (160bhp)
0–96km/h (60mph): 10.9 secs
Top speed: 171km/h (107mph)
Production total: 6750

Elegant 'fintail' rear wings made their first appearance on the 220 in 1959; however, they better suited the stately 300 with its extra chromework, self-levelling air suspension and high price tag.

MERCEDES-BENZ W108/109 S-CLASS

1965–72

The long-wheelbase W109 had more legroom in the back than the shorter W108, but neither were as interesting or salubrious as the model they replaced – gone were the fins, and coils replaced the air suspension.

Big changes were planned in Mercedes' home in Stuttgart and, while some of the fintail models continued, the new W108 S-class, with its wider, flatter, more rounded body, was where the company saw its future. All cars had independent suspension front and rear and all-round disc brakes.

The seven-bearing crankshaft 2.5-litre (153 cu in) engine was all-new; however, the 3-litre (183 cu in) unit was little different to the one used in the early 1950s. The 2.5-litre was replaced by the 2.8-litre (170 cu in) unit in 1968 (badged as the 280S/280SE) and there was a long-wheelbase version, the 280SEL.

The 3-litre (183 cu in) engined car was far more conservative than its predecessor, using coil springs instead of air suspension, although air suspension was used on the longer-wheelbase W109 300SEL. In 1968, the engine was downsized to 2.8 litres (170 cu in), while still retaining the same badging, and the glorious 3.5-litre (214 cu in) V8 arrived in 1969. Only the US market was offered the big 4.5-litre (275 cu in).

The range also spawned the ultimate in 'wolf-in-sheep's-clothing' – the 300SEL 6.3 – which, despite the extra weight of its power disc brakes, offered buyers high performance.

Engine: 2778cc (170 cu in), 6-cylinder
Power: 95–186kW (128–250bhp)
0–96km/h (60mph): 9.8 secs
Top speed: 206km/h (129mph)
Production total: 56,092

MERCEDES-BENZ PAGODA

1963–71

This particular Mercedes received its name from the shape of the roof on the hardtop model, which formed an obvious concave profile. Based on the existing 220 floorpan, but with a shorter wheelbase, it featured double wishbone suspension at the front and swing axles at the rear. The car's styling was by the sculptor and painter Paul Bracq.

The coupé and convertible were both available with either a four-speed manual or an automatic transmission option. The 230SL had front disc brakes, while the bigger-engined 250 (which was introduced in 1966) had all-round disc brakes and the option of an extra gear.

Both the 250 and the 280 that were to follow in 1968 had much improved torque over the earlier version of the car.

As Mercedes offered both a coupé and a convertible, cars were available with a hood only, a hardtop and hood, or a hardtop alone, which made room for back-seat passengers – one in the 230SL and two, on a bench seat, in the 250 and 280SL. Being more of a tourer than a sports car, this machine was to set the tone for all future Mercedes performance cars, single-handedly taking over from both the magnificent 300SL and the 190SL.

Engine: 2778cc (170 cu in), 6-cylinder
Power: 127kW (170bhp)
0–96km/h (60mph): 9.3 secs
Top speed: 204km/h (127mph)
Production total: 48,902

MERCEDES-BENZ W114/115

1968–76

Prized by taxi drivers around the globe, the new range of smaller-sized entry-level Mercedes proved both durable and highly successful throughout its eight-year production lifespan. The shape was all-new, distinguished by vertical headlight units in the wings, which incorporated the sidelights and indicators; however, the unitary construction body, semi-trailing link suspension and the ubiquitous upright Mercedes grille were conventional.

A confusing range of engines included the entry-level 2-litre (122 cu in), several diesel options and an all-new twin camshaft straight-six petrol unit. Automatic transmission and power-assisted steering were options on all cars.

A limousine version, with an extra long wheelbase, was also available, called the 220D, 240D and 230.6, as well as an attractive two-door pillarless coupé version. This was slightly shorter and lower than the saloon, as well as being significantly more expensive. The coupé was initially available with a 2.5-litre (153 cu in) engine and

then a twin camshaft 2.8-litre (170 cu in) unit after 1971.

CE versions of the range had fuel injection and more power, and power-assisted steering became standard from 1975.

This range had traditional unitary construction and a bewildering array of engine options – including a five-cylinder diesel. Rugged and reliable, it became a favourite among taxi drivers the world over.

Engine: 2778cc (170 cu in), 6-cylinder
Power: 138kW (185bhp)
0–96km/h (60mph): 13.7–24.2 secs
Top speed: 198km/h (124mph)
Production total: 1,326,099

MERCEDES-BENZ W107 SL

1974–89

The W107 SL Mercedes enjoyed a production lifespan that lasted almost 15 years and drew heavily on the success of the Pagoda, but with new US safety regulations forcing it to become bigger and

subsequently more refined. At first there was the choice of either a 3.5-litre (214 cu in) or 4.5-litre (276 cu in) V8 engine, but these were joined in 1974 by the 280SL with the sporting twin-camshaft fuel-

injected six-cylinder engine from the 280SE. It was this car that continued in production until 1985.

The car also featured an improved suspension system with semi-trailing arms at the rear, and

power steering came as standard. There was also the option of automatic transmission. Like its Pagoda predecessor, the removable hardtop had a distinctive concave dip in the centre.

The range was revised in 1980 to become the 280SL/380SL, 500SL and later the 560SL. Despite its huge 5.6-litre (342 cu in), 169kW (227bhp) engine and low fuel economy, this actually became the biggest selling car in the range. Production of these cars finally ceased in 1989.

Definitely a classic in its own lifetime, the W107 SL had a production life that spanned two decades. The optional removable hardtop had a dip in the centre reminiscent of its 'pagoda roof' predecessor.

Engine: 4520cc (276 cu in), 8-cylinder
Power: 168kW (225bhp)
0–96km/h (60mph): 8.8 secs
Top speed: 214km/h (134mph)
Production total: 107,038

MERCEDES-BENZ SLC

The SLC models were mechanically identical to the two-seater SLs, but had considerably longer wheelbases and were judged to be less attractive. A large production run means these cars are unlikely to become collectors' items.

Like the SL, the 280SLC arrived in 1974 with a twin-camshaft engine, and it gained mechanical fuel injection from 1975. Although arguably not quite as attractive as the SL, the SLC was in fact an unrivalled grand tourer, and it was able to transport its occupants at speed and in both style and comfort. Its wind-down side windows gave it a pillarless effect and a charm all its own, and many well-kept examples still exist today. Like the SL, the range was revised in 1980, although the 280 lasted until 1981.

Launched soon after the coupé and convertible, the SLC range of fixed-head coupés had a longer wheelbase and was designed to accommodate four in comfort. Mechanically, there was little difference between the SL and the SLC, except that the latter weighed significantly more; however, this did little to dent performance, which was formidable – especially from the powerful 4.5-litre (276 cu in) V8, which produced a very impressive 168kW (225bhp) and enormous amounts of torque. Again, it was in this guise that the SLC met with the most success, with more than 30,000 cars sold.

Engine: 4520cc (276 cu in), 8-cylinder
Power: 168kW (225bhp)
0–96km/h (60mph): 7.4 secs
Top speed: 214km/h (134mph)
Production total: 56,330

MERCEDES-BENZ W116 S-CLASS

Some described the astonishing new Mercedes-Benz W116 S-class as the best car in the world at its launch, the only competition worthy of note being Rolls-Royce. Indeed, it was a formidable car, gaining Mercedes the reputation for peerless build quality that has stayed with it ever since.

Other key qualities were performance, superb handling, comfort and unheard-of levels of refinement. Styling was best described as stately, rather than stunning, although its mere presence on the road demanded attention wherever it went.

The semi-trailing rear suspension came from the SL and, because of its size, power-assisted steering was mandatory. Automatic transmission was also a standard feature, although some 280s were offered with a manual option. The SEL had an extended wheelbase for further rear passenger legroom.

The ultimate model in this class was the ultra-luxurious 450SEL, which twice as expensive as a Jaguar XJ12 at the time. A bored-out version of the 600 V8 engine gave this vast car fantastic performance (0–96km/h [60mph] in 7.3 seconds), while still retaining its trademark superlative levels of comfort.

Excellent engines, peerless build and unsurpassed levels of comfort and refinement made this one of the best cars in the world in the early 1970s. Most had the six-cylinder 2746cc (168 cu in) engine, but the 350 and 450 V8s performed best.

Engine: 2746cc (168 cu in), 6-cylinder
Power: 115kW (155bhp)
0–96km/h (60mph): 9.2 secs
Top speed: 189km/h (118mph)
Production total: 437,240

MERCURY MONTEREY

1952–72

Plugging the gap between its low-cost V8 range of Ford cars and the luxury Lincoln K-series of the 1930s, and in order to provide competition for Oldsmobile and Buick, came the all-new Mercury Eight in 1938, masterminded by Edsel Ford.

By the late 1940s, Mercury was moving towards the Lincoln end of the US car spectrum, which eventually resulted in the launch of the Monterey in 1952. Gone was the company's archaic flathead V8 and in came an all-new Y-block unit that produced 120kW (161bhp).

The car was an immediate success, promoted no doubt by its association with youthful Hollywood star James Dean – it was the car famously driven over the edge of a cliff in the film *Rebel Without a Cause*. Other Hollywood film stars were also drawn to the Monterey, and Gary Cooper was also a proud owner of the car.

The Monterey was available as either a convertible, a pillarless

coupé, a four-door sedan, or a station wagon (estate) version. Customers could also choose from 35 different colour schemes. Despite its enormous proportions and elephantine weight, the Monterey had drum brakes fitted both front and rear, which didn't help matters.

Ford created Mercury as a middle-class marque in the late 1930s to rival its competitors for the mass market, Oldsmobile and Buick. The strategy worked to an extent, and Mercury continued to make big, thirsty cars like the Monterey, with its eight-cylinder engine, into the 1950s and 1960s.

Engine: 6502cc (397 cu in), 8-cylinder
Power: 120kW (161bhp)
0–96km/h (60mph): 14 secs
Top speed: 161km/h (100mph)
Production total: 174,238

MERCURY COMET

1960–70

Under the leadership of Henry Ford II, Mercury set about widening its appeal, launching the compact model, the Comet, in 1960. Derived from the Ford Falcon, it originally borrowed its 2360cc (144 cu in) six-cylinder engine but, in 1961, the car was made available with a more conventional V8 powerplant.

The Comet's styling was broadly on the same lines as the bigger Mercury cars, and there were three

body styles, the two and four-door saloons and the station wagon. The cars sold well, and especially intriguing was the sporty S-22 model from 1963 with its 2785cc (170 cu in) engine, 122kW (164bhp) power output and 11.5-second 0–96km/h (60mph) ability. The car also featured bucket seats at the front.

The Comet was renamed the Caliente (which means 'hot' in

Spanish) in 1964, by which time Mercury had fitted a 149kW (200bhp) V8 engine with optional power steering and power-assisted brakes. Buyers could choose between cars with sporty bucket seats or the conventional front bench seat of the time. Unlike most other American saloons at the time, the Comet's suspension was firm, yet comfortable, with little body roll.

Engine: 2785cc (170 cu in), 8-cylinder
Power: 122kW (164bhp)
0–96km/h (60mph): 11.5 secs
Top speed: 150km/h (94mph)
Production total: n/a

The Comet 'compact' was Mercury's first car to be sold with anything other than a V8 engine. The Luxury Caliente of 1966 (below) had a longer wheelbase than the standard car.

MERCURY METEOR

The Meteor was described as being the 'in-between' sized car in Mercury's line-up, and was available as a two-door saloon. It shared the same basic shell as the Ford Fairlane, but with a slightly longer wheelbase, and bore a strong resemblance to the other cars in the Ford family with its clean, smooth lines.

Performance was only average for its class, mostly because it shared the same engine as the Ford Falcon and the Comet, although the unit was set back from the front of the car to provide better balance and less front-end dive under braking.

The Meteor used Mercury's 'Cushion Link' suspension, comprising independent coils at the front and a rigid axle with a five-leaf semi-elliptic spring set-up at the rear. This quirky device allowed the front and rear wheels

to move rearwards as well as up and down over bumpy terrain, thus further ironing out bumps and providing a smoother ride.

Build quality and panel fit was particularly good on Mercury cars and the Meteor was no exception in this respect.

The unmemorable-looking Meteor introduced a number of complex technical innovations including 'cushion-link' suspension which was designed to give its occupants a smoother ride over rough road surfaces. Build quality was always particularly high.

Engine: 3645cc (222 cu in), 6-cylinder
Power: 108kW (145bhp)
0–96km/h (60mph): 15.2 secs
Top speed: 152km/h (95mph)
Production total: n/a

MERCURY CYCLONE

Mercury decided to give the Comet range a sporting image in 1963 with the launch of the Cyclone, which was offered initially as a convertible and then, in 1968, as a fastback coupé. There was also a notchback version with bucket seats and an optional fibreglass roof with simulated air scoops, a feature designed for grabbing the attention of onlookers. It also had an odd aluminium visor in the screen designed to reduce radio interference from the ignition system.

Capacity of the Cyclone's engines rapidly increased in a quest for more power, finally reaching 317kW (425bhp) on the 1967 model. In 1969, the Cyclone CJ featured the Ford 428 cu in Cobra engine and sported spoilers and bonnet scoop with Ram Air induction fitted. The Cyclone suffered severe rear axle hop, even with the performance handling kit option fitted, although sharp steering made it an extremely fun car to drive.

Based on the compact theme of the Comet, Mercury's Cyclone was something of a muscle car in its time. The stacked headlight version here originates from 1965, but later cars got more aggressive in appearance and more power to match their looks.

The 1970 Cyclone Spoiler was targeted at the youth market and featured prominent air dams front and rear. A contemporary report flirtatiously described it as 'Long of

Engine: 7030cc (429 cu in), 8-cylinder
Power: 317kW (425bhp)
0–96km/h (60mph): 8.8 secs
Top speed: 213km/h (133mph)
Production total: 90,023

hood, short of rump, firm in the curves and hot off the line.'

Sadly, production of the Cyclone drew to a close at the beginning of the 1970s after a little over 90,000 cars had left the Mercury production line in less than a decade.

MERCURY COUGAR

1966–73

Engine: 4736cc (289 cu in), 8-cylinder
Power: 156kW (210bhp)
0–96km/h (60mph): 10.2 secs
Top speed: 168km/h (105mph)
Production total: 90,236

With Mercury wanting their own Mustang to sell, the company decided to launch its own version – the Cougar – which first appeared as a sporty two-door hardtop. Slightly bigger than Ford's offering, and with slightly better specification, Mercury's 'personal car' sold for around 10 per cent more money.

A three-speed manual gearbox was standard, with a four-speed manual and either a three-speed automatic or four-speed Borg Warner gearbox listed as optional items. All cars had V8 engines, though capacity grew from 4736cc (289 cu in) to a staggering 7030cc (429 cu in) during its lifetime. 1960s examples were crisply styled, with concealed headlights and fared-in bumpers, bridging the gap between Ford's Mustang and Thunderbird. However, as production entered the 1970s, the car became over-elaborate with an odd waterfall grille and tacky exterior adornments.

The luxurious XR7 with its 276kW (370bhp) engine and plush

Resembling the same basic design as the Ford Mustang, the Cougar became longer and less sporty with time. A facelift after 1970 made matters worse, so brutish 1960s cars remain the most desirable.

hide trim (especially in convertible form), the GT-E with its sporty handling package and the 1969 Eliminator are all becoming desirable among collectors.

MESSERSCHMITT KR200

1955–64

The idea of a bubble car might seem absurd today but, in the 1950s, a basic, inexpensive and no-frills means of transport made a lot of sense.

The 'Kabinroller', as it was known, was the brainchild of German aircraft engineer Fritz Fend, and his idea was taken up by the Messerschmitt aeroplane factory in 1953.

The KR200 appeared in 1955 and featured a one-piece perspex canopy through which the cabin was accessed. Just like a plane's cockpit, passengers sat in tandem, while steering was via a pair of motorcycle-style handlebars.

The model was powered by a 191cc (12 cu in) single-cylinder engine, developing 7kW (10bhp). But because of the car's minimal weight and tubular spaceframe construction, this engine was enough to propel it to 100km/h (62mph).

With cable-operated brakes and a rudimentary swing-beam suspension set-up, this was fast enough for most, while those requiring hood-down motoring could opt for a convertible version.

Kabinrollers were popular thanks to their simple construction and ease of maintenance, while a high survival rate means they're not too difficult to find.

Engine: 191cc (12 cu in), 1-cylinder
Power: 7kW (10bhp)
0–96km/h (60mph): n/a
Top speed: 100km/h (62mph)
Production total: 41,190

Based on the design of an aircraft cockpit, the lightweight Kabinroller seated two passengers in tandem and used a single-cylinder 7kW (10bhp) engine.

MESSERSCHMITT TG500

Although most people refer to the TG500 as the Tiger, the car never actually bore the name. The German truck maker Krupp had patented it, but that didn't stop the minutive two-seater from becoming a microcar legend.

With four wheels, it had more stability than three-wheeled Schmitts, while a 493cc (30 cu in) Sachs air-cooled two-cylinder engine was enough to give it a top speed of 121km/h (75mph) – faster than many contemporary saloon cars and quicker than most off the mark.

The hot hatch of microcars, the Tiger came with hydraulic brakes and an improved steering and suspension set-up compared to the KR200. Tandem seating and handlebars remained features, meaning that it took a while to learn how to master driving the car at speed. A low-roof coupé version was also available, and became the most collectable variant.

Despite the car prompting an enthusiastic response from the public, few were made and although no official figures are available, it is believed that less than 500 left the factory.

Engine: 493cc (30 cu in), 2-cylinder
Power: 15kW (20bhp)
0–96km/h (60mph): 18.7 secs
Top speed: 121km/h (75mph)
Production total: 450 approx

The 'Tiger' was the hot hatch of bubblecars, with a frightening top speed of 121km/h (75mph) and entertaining handling, although the skinny wheels meant there wasn't much grip.

MG 14/40

While the very first MGs appeared in the early 1920s, they were nothing more than special-bodied Morris Oxfords built at Cecil Kimber's 'Morris Garages' workshop in Oxford, England.

Kimber's cars, which wore the now famous octagon logo on their running boards, proved popular and inspired him to design and build his own sporting models, supported by Morris.

A new factory was built in 1927 near the Morris works in Cowley, Oxfordshire and the first production MG, the 14/40, appeared later in the same year, mostly using Morris mechanical components.

Aimed at enthusiastic drivers, the 14/40 had a respectable top speed of 96km/h (60mph) from its old-fashioned side-valve engine, while good roadholding and servo-assisted brakes meant it steered and stopped much better than any of its contemporaries – although MG's claim that it was, 'The car that cannot skid' was a little ambitious and over-enthusiastic.

As the first independently built MG, the 14/40 was a historically important car. Compared to most cars of the 1920s it had impressive handling capabilities.

The popularity of the MG marque prompted Kimber to open the Pavlova Works in Abingdon in 1929. It remained the home of MG until British Leyland tried to kill off the name in 1981.

Engine: 1802cc (110 cu in), 4-cylinder
Power: n/a
0–96km/h (60mph): n/a
Top speed: 96km/h (60mph)
Production total: 900 approx

MG 18/80

William Morris had high hopes for the Light Six saloon when it was shown for the first time at the Olympia Motor Show in 1927, with a new Woollard and Pendrel-designed straight-six overhead camshaft engine and the promise of excellent performance. But he was let down badly by his engineers, and the result was a car that went quickly, but demonstrated ponderous handling characteristics.

Morris turned in desperation to MG to develop a new frame for the car, and the 18/80, which made its debut at the 1928 London Motor Show badged as the MG Six, was a much better package than the Light Six.

The 18/80 was a true sporting saloon with excellent road manners and elegant coachbuilt bodywork. A Mark II model was introduced in 1929 and had twin carburettors and

uprated brakes, meaning it could theoretically cruise at over 130km/h (80mph).

Five racing 18/80s were built in 1930 for the Morris Garages works team, and with lightweight bodywork and the smooth, torquey straight-six, these were capable of over 160km/h (100mph) and enjoyed a moderate degree of competition success.

Despite being primarily a large and elegant touring car, the 18/80 still had quite a turn of pace. Morris Garages took five examples racing to prove, quite successfully, the model's sporting pedigree.

Engine: 2468cc (151 cu in), 6-cylinder
Power: 45kW (60bhp)
0–96km/h (60mph): n/a
Top speed: 126km/h (78mph)
Production total: 736

MG Midget

Until the move to Abingdon, MG had specialized in large sporting saloons and racing specials. But with room for more production in the new factory, the company embarked upon a small sports car project, using the 847cc (52 cu in) overhead camshaft engine developed for the Morris Minor.

The Midget's trump card was its low purchase costs – this was a sports car for the masses.

The Midget's chassis also came from the Morris Minor, but with lowered suspension, while weight was kept to a minimum by using fabric instead of metal for the body panels.

The original Midget was replaced in 1932 by the D-Type Midget, which lost some of the original's cute looks, but came with four seats, metal bodywork and a proper folding hood.

The two-seater layout returned for the J-Type Midgets of 1932, which again used the same engine and underpinnings. The J2 was a two-seater open top only, while the larger J1 could have four seats and a metal roof.

The C-Type Midget of 1931 with engine capacity reduced to 746cc (46 cu in) was built specifically for racing in the 750cc racing series. A supercharged variant was available with 39kW (53bhp) and 160km/h (100mph) capability.

Engine: 847cc (52 cu in), 4-cylinder
Power: 24kW (32bhp)
0–96km/h (60mph): n/a
Top speed: 105km/h (65mph)
Production total: 5992

Midget by name and midget by nature – MG's baby showed just how much fun could be had by making a car as basic as possible. The Midget became a popular car with racers, as the engines were easy to tune.

MG MAGNA

Slightly bigger than the Midget and more geared for comfort, the Magna was aimed at a more mature buyer. But that didn't stop it competing, as this participant in a time trial proves.

By the early 1930s, the MG range had started to get very confusing, with a wide choice of models, engine types and styling variations. The Magna was targeted at a more mature and sophisticated market than the Midget and used a straight-six overhead camshaft engine developed for the Wolseley Hornet, yet despite having two more cylinders than most rivals it was still only available in either a 1-litre (67 cu in) or 1.3-litre (79 cu in) capacity.

It was also a disappointing car to drive compared to other MGs, with clumsy handling caused by a long wheelbase and narrow track, and a fussy crash gearbox that required patience and concentration.

The first Magna was known as the F-Type and was replaced after just a year by the L-Type, which had wider bodywork and a more

powerful engine, thanks to the addition of twin SU carburettors. It was a much better-looking car, too, with flared front wings, a cutaway door line and a larger front scuttle, although it still had the same

compromised driving characteristics. The prettiest, and rarest, Magna variant was the L-Type Continental Coupé, which closely resembled the Bugatti Type 57 in appearance.

Engine: 1087cc (66 cu in), 6-cylinder
Power: 28kW (37bhp)
0–96km/h (60mph): n/a
Top speed: 113km/h (70mph)
Production total: 1826

MG MAGNETTE

Engine: 1271cc (78 cu in), 6-cylinder
Power: 36kW (48.5bhp)
0–96km/h (60mph): n/a
Top speed: 121km/h (75mph)
Production total: 1351

A selection of body styles was offered to Magnette buyers. This one is a two-seater sports-bodied example with a performance exhaust system, but saloons and coupés were also available.

Even more confusing than the Magna range, the Magnette was designed to be all things to all owners. A four-seater, four-door saloon, a two-door saloon, a four-seat open tourer or a two-door sports body were offered, with a mind-boggling myriad of power and capacity variations on the

small-block six-cylinder engine, that it shared with the Magna.

Of these variants, the most attractive was the Magnette K2 – a pretty two-seater sports car with separate mudguards and a neatly stowed roof.

The entire range was given a facelift in 1933 and became known

as the KN Magnette, with better equipment levels, more streamlined bodywork and a power boost taking it to 42kW (56bhp). Apart from the awkward gearbox, it was a fine car to drive, with accurate steering and above-average brakes.

A more modern-looking N-Type Magnette appeared at the 1935 Olympia Motor Show in London and had more sculpted bodywork, a stiffer chassis and a firmer ride.

The Magnette was also the basis for the record-breaking K3. This supercharged competition special was one of the most successful MG racers of all time, winning the 1933 Tourist Trophy with Tazio Nuvolari at the wheel. The car also won the 1933 British Racing Drivers' Club 500-mile (800km) challenge, at an average speed of over 171km/h (106mph).

MG P-TYPE

1934–36

Replacing the Midget wasn't easy for MG, and the company decided to play for safety with the PA. A marginally longer wheelbase and a stronger, three-bearing crank appeared, as well as the option of unusual airline coupé bodywork.

Steering response was also improved, but MG very sensibly left the Midget's distinctive exhaust note and characterful handling unchanged.

One of the P-Type's more unusual features was a combined rev counter and speedometer, which had two needles and two sets of numbers – a novel idea, but one which was irritating and misleading to use.

The PA was replaced by the PB in 1935, which was even more

A relatively safe option, the P-Type replaced the Midget. Nevertheless, it hinted at what was to come from MG in the future, with flared wings and styling that resembled a scaled-down TC.

entertaining to drive thanks to a larger-capacity engine. Using the same block as the PA, it displaced 939cc (57 cu in) and offered 32kW (43bhp).

MG also took the opportunity to equip the PB with separate speedometer and rev counter gauges, consigning the PA's bizarre combined unit to the history books. A smoother gearbox appeared on the PB as well, answering a criticism that was often levelled at MGs of the era.

Engine: 847cc (52 cu in), 4-cylinder
Power: 30kW (40bhp)
0–96km/h (60mph): n/a
Top speed: 121km/h (75mph)
Production total: 2526

MG SA

1936–39

Harking back to the MGs of old, the SA was an extremely elegant grand-touring coupé that made absolutely no pretensions to being a sports car.

A range of different bodies was available, but all were elegant, avant-garde designs with smooth, sweeping curves and a low bonnet and roofline. All were four-seaters with excellent legroom and rear access, while an open tourer option was offered in time for the summer of 1937.

As with the smaller MGs, the SA's pushrod engine came courtesy of Wolseley and offered excellent torque but sluggish acceleration, although a comfortably smooth ride and excellent steering made it a pleasant machine to drive, especially if it was fitted with the synchromesh gearbox offered from late 1937 onwards.

One of the SA's idiosyncracies happened as a result of engineers and body designers failing to communicate properly; the 2.3-litre (140 cu in) straight-six engine was originally far too tall to fit into the car's cramped engine bay. MG got around the problem by ingeniously

designing horizontal dashpots for the twin downdraught carburettors, so just allowing the bonnet to close with less than 2.5cm (1in) of space to spare.

One of very few MGs not to be marketed as a sporting vehicle – the SA was, instead, an elegant tourer built with comfort and elegance in mind.

Engine: 2288cc (140 cu in), 6-cylinder
Power: 46kW (62bhp)
0–96km/h (60mph): n/a
Top speed: 129km/h (80mph)
Production total: 2738

MG VA

he SA's popularity prompted MG offer a smaller-engined and eaper variant based on the same atform.

Like the SA, it was available as open or closed tourer with enty of room for four, although clusive coachbuilt bodywork as not offered as an option. Even , the asking price of £280 made e VA an attractive proposition er similarly-priced, but much ss impressive rivals.

The 1548cc (95 cu in) engine me from the Wolseley 12 and, hough slightly outdated ngside other units in the MG nge, it offered performance most identical to that of the SA, eit at the expense of refinement.

Built-in hydraulic jacks were ted as standard to avoid the oblem of drivers jacking the car in the wrong place – with long d heavy bodywork and wood-med panels, such a practice uld prove disastrous. Indeed, dy flex was a criticism often

levelled at the SA and VA series, as well as heavy steering thanks to the weighty coachwork and sliding trunnion suspension.

Despite these faults, however, the VA was one of the finest cars in its class and proved to be popular with buyers.

The VA was the SA's successor and was aimed at a similar market. Its heavy bodywork and ash-frame made for awkward handling and very heavy steering. Built-in hydraulic jacks prevented drivers from destroying the bodywork when using a manual jack.

Engine: 1548cc (94 cu in), 4-cylinder
Power: 39kW (53bhp)
0–96km/h (60mph): n/a
Top speed: 129km/h (80mph)
Production total: 2407

MG WA

ere it not for the outbreak of orld War II, the WA might have ne down in motoring history as e of the finest touring cars of its y. But MG unfortunately chose wrong time to launch its gship car, which appeared in 38, and only 369 were built fore the Abingdon factory pped car production to help with e British war effort.

Effectively, the car was an updated and improved SA, but with all of the earlier car's problems ironed out thanks to some intelligent engineering.

The sluggish performance was partially rectified by increasing the engine's compression ratio, while a dual circuit hydraulic braking system gave the WA stopping power to rival most racing cars,

making it an enjoyable car to drive.

Again, a range of stylish coachbuilt bodies was offered and all were elegant and spacious inside, while MG added lots of luxury extras.

Leather trim, thick carpets and wooden door cappings made the WA a relaxing car in which to travel, while neat touches included unusual octagonal ivory-backed

dials and a comprehensively equipped toolkit that was so nice to look at, it would have been a shame to use it.

Engine: 2561cc (156 cu in), 6-cylinder
Power: 52kW (70bhp)
0–96km/h (60mph): n/a
Top speed: 137km/h (85mph)
Production total: 369

soon as MG had got its large car range finally sorted, r broke out and production was stopped. The WA was a e car, but only 369 were ever made.

MG T-Series

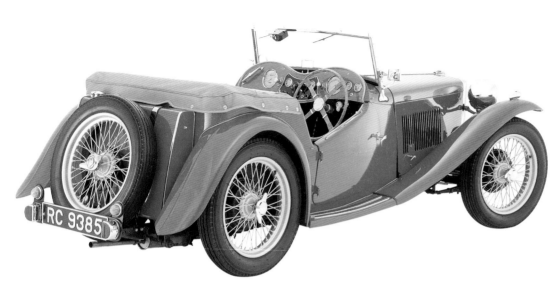

**With tiny proportions and the lin«
of a grand tourer, the TC was one
of the most attractive sports cars «
its day.**

The first T-Series cars appeared in 1936, but the start of World War II saw production halted after less than three years.

With no funds and the need to restart production straight after the end of the conflict, MG had to resurrect their old model in order to revive the company, and while the TC had a bigger cabin and partial synchromesh on the gearbox, it was little different from the TB it had superseded.

Launched in 1945, the car made do with archaic ash frame construction and semi-elliptic leaf springs underneath, but it was still a popular car, especially with American servicemen who were stationed in Britain.

The distinctive engine note and entertaining handling marked it out as a traditional sports car, and a firm ride and heavy steering made it an involving machine to drive.

Nevertheless, driving a TC was never an easy experience. Despite synchromesh on second, third and fourth gears, gear changes could not be hurried, while hydraulic drum brakes were only slightly more effective than earlier cars' cable brakes.

Despite most sales being to the United States, all TCs were right-hand drive, and many have since been imported back to Britain by MG enthusiasts.

With the TC rapidly restoring its reputation, MG knew it couldn't rest on its laurels, and despite selling more than 10,000 cars in just four years, the Abingdon-based concern knew it had to refine and update the car if its revival was to continue apace.

Funds and materials were still severely limited, so the TC's 1949 replacement, the TD, had to make do with the same chassis and XPAG engine, but MG also fitted the independent front suspension, uprated braking system and rack-and-pinion steering from the Y-Type saloon. These modifications made the TD a much easier car to drive, while the steering was a lot lighter and more direct than in the earlier cars.

The TD retained the look of the TC, albeit with slightly softer lines and heavy chrome bumpers front and rear, while steel wheels replaced the earlier cars' wire ones in a bid to cut production costs. A higher compression engine appeared in 1952 and gave the TD a top speed of 137km/h (85mph), making it even more popular wit enthusiastic drivers and ensuring that nearly 30,000 units were sol again mostly to export markets.

It also became a popular car with amateur motorsport enthusiasts and tuning companie« offered conversions to boost the XPAG engine's modest output. With a Shorrock supercharger fitted, the TD could top 160km/h (100mph) and produced 74kW (99bhp).

The final incarnation of the T-Series of cars was the TF of 1953. Reflecting a shift towards more streamlined shapes across th entire motor industry, the TF had its headlights fared into the bodywork and gained a sloping front radiator grille, as well as longer, lower flanks. Inside, separate front seats replaced the TC and TD's bench seats and, at the same time, wire wheels made welcome comeback.

But the TF was again lacking i« performance and, with more weig on board but the same engine, it was actually slower than the car i« replaced, producing 43kW (57.5bhp) and offering a top spee« of just 127km/h (79mph).

A 1500cc (92 cu in) engine, fitted from 1954, gave the TF the performance the range had always really needed and, today, the 195< model is the most desirable of the TF breed. Its rarity is assured, as only 3400 were built before the range was replaced by the unitary construction MGA. Traditionalists prefer the early TC cars, with thei« uncompromising styling and crud« driving characteristics.

Engine: 1250cc (76 cu in), 4-cylinder
Power: 40kW (54bhp)
0–96km/h (60mph): 22.7 secs
Top speed: 126km/h (78mph)
Production total: 51,000 approx

The TC was originally available only with bench seats, but the version in this photograph has be« fitted with separate front seats. It was a tricky car to drive, and the tiny interior dimensions meant th« cabin was extremely cramped and the gear lever difficult to reach.

MG Y-TYPE

order to keep costs down, MG's st postwar sporting saloon made with several parts already ailable from the Nuffield group's ble. The main hull, rear panels d doors were all lifted from the orris 8, while the model was ted with the 1250 XPAG engine st seen in the T-Series sports car. But new developments derneath signalled its intention be a sporting saloon, with dependent front suspension using il springs, and rack-and-pinion ering. The latter was designed Alec Issigonis, who would later on to father the Morris Minor, e Mini and BMC (British Motor rporation) 1100/1300 Series.

All Y-Series models were xuriously appointed, with wood d leather interiors and an tricate dashboard, while later B models had a more powerful

engine and simpler rear axle layout. Yet despite claiming to be sporting saloons, the Y-Type cars were never very fast – even the YB could muster only 114km/h (71mph).

As a footnote, a YT open-top model was available for a short time for the US market, offering four seats and twin carburettors. Fewer than 900 were made.

It might have been rushed into production, but the Y-Type was advanced. It had independent front suspension using coil springs and rack-and-pinion steering, designed by Alec Issigonis.

Engine: 1250cc (76 cu in), 4-cylinder
Power: 36kW (48bhp)
0–96km/h (60mph): 27.7 secs
Top speed: 115km/h (71mph)
Production total: 7459

MG MAGNETTE ZA/ZB

dge engineering might appear a latively modern phenomenon, but e first MG to be based on another anufacturer's car appeared almost lf a century ago. The Magnette A took its bodywork from the olseley 4/44, but looked more

attractive thanks to its fluted MG grille, chrome embellishments and straight front bumper.

The car also marked the first appearance of the venerable BMC B-Series engine in an MG car. This was significant because the unit

would later go on to power the company's two world-famous and most successful sports cars – the MGA and MGB.

The Magnette also had an uprated platform, with rack-and-pinion steering and improved

Although it took its bodywork from the Wolseley 4/44 and, therefore, resembled it, the Magnette was – and looked – a much sportier car. It had revised suspension, rack-and-pinion steering and a snappy close-ratio gearbox.

suspension, while 45kW (60bhp) made it a lively performer. A close-ratio gearbox not only gave it better acceleration than the Wolseley, but had a pleasant, snappy action, while buyers who valued luxury and a hint of sophistication found it in the Magnette's wood and leather-equipped cabin.

A more powerful ZB variant replaced the ZA in 1956 and was offered with optional Varitone two-colour paintwork and a wrap-around rear screen. A few cars also appeared with manumatic semi-automatic transmission – a novel, but not, in fact, hugely effective attempt at creating a clutchless manual set-up that, despite being quite unpleasant to use, was many years ahead of its time.

Engine: 1489cc (91 cu in), 4-cylinder
Power: 51kW (68bhp)
0–96km/h (60mph): 22.6 secs
Top speed: 129km/h (80mph)
Production total: 36,600

MGA

1955–62

Clean, modern lines and excellent aerodynamics made the MGA a popular choice in the United States and Europe. It offered two versions of the standard BMW B-Series engine, plus a specially made Twin Cam unit.

The stylish MGA ushered in a new era of modernity for the Abingdon-based manufacturer, with mechanical parts borrowed from across the BMC range, including independent front suspension and rack-and-pinion steering – the first appearance of these on an MG sports car.

But it was the car's lines that were its most modern aspect. Derived from a special 1954 Le Mans car, based on the MG TD and built on a strengthened box-section chassis, the car was designed from the outset to have a slippery, aerodynamic appearance.

The chassis was heavy, however, and meant the agile-looking MG was difficult to steer and stop, especially as early models had only drum brakes all round.

The earliest MGAs had the ubiquitous 1489cc (91 cu in) BMC B-Series engine, and while this didn't offer huge performance, it was enough to make the car lively and entertaining to drive, while a range of tuning accessories was

available to make it quicker. In standard tune, 0–96km/h (60mph) was possible in 15 seconds, which was quick for a car of its era, although gear engagement could be difficult and downchanges often required double-declutching, even with synchromesh fitted.

A fixed-head coupé model joined the line-up in 1956 and offered better aerodynamics, but the trade-off was an uncomfortably cramped and rather claustrophobic cabin. This irritating problem was not significantly relieved until 1960

with the introduction of proper sliding windows.

Both cars shared similar driving characteristics and had impressive handling for their era, which brought the MGA modest competition success and made it a popular car on the amateur rallying scene.

BMC recognized this and, in 1959, both the coupé and roadster got a power boost, with an increase in engine size from 1489cc (91 cu in) to 1588cc (97 cu in), giving 60kW (80bhp), while front disc brakes were also fitted.

Drive one of these later cars today and it's easy to appreciate why the model proved popular with motorsport enthusiasts – the steering and gears may feel cumbersome compared to more modern machines, but the car's chassis felt sharp and the raspberry-blowing exhaust note was full of character.

The 1588cc (97 cu in) unit also became the basis for the quickest-ever production MGA. Racing car builder Harry Weslake developed a new twin-camshaft head for the B-Series engine, and it was available as an option on the range for two years in the late 1950s. Only 2111 MGA Twin Cams were made and they were impressively quick, with 80kW (108bhp) on tap

A huge speedo and rev counter dominated the MGA's dashboard to make sporty motorists feel at home. Other dials included oil pressure and temperature.

and a top speed of 177km/h (110mph). But the engine quickly acquired a reputation for piston damage, and due to their fragility, few survive. The Twin Camshaft model was distinguished by its lightweight wheels with centre-spinners, all-round disc brakes and a slightly modified bonnet.

The standard MGA continued unchanged until 1961, when a more modern Mk II model was announced for its final two years of production. Visual changes were minor, limited to different rear light clusters and a recessed radiator grille, but under the bonnet the B-Series block had been bored out to 1622cc (99 cu in), upping power to 64kW (86bhp), while all-round discs brakes were optional on De Luxe specification cars.

While arguably not quite so pretty as the Mk I, the Mk II was much more flexible in terms of in-gear performance and tractability, and was hailed as the car for the better driver, although no MGA is ever disappointing from behind the wheel.

The final MGA rolled off the production line in 1962 to make way for Britain's most successful sports car ever – the MGB. Although a far more modern design, the MGB never managed to emulate the MGA's design purity.

Engine: 1489cc (91 cu in), 4-cylinder
Power: 54kW (72bhp)
0–96km/h (60mph): 15 secs
Top speed: 160km/h (100mph)
Production total: 101,081

MG MIDGET

Under the skin, the Midget was essentially the same as the Austin-Healey Sprite. Earlier cars, such as this one, had chrome bumpers and squared-off wheelarches.

n today's competitive motor industry, names are important. If a manufacturer saddles its new model with the wrong image, it could lose millions of dollars and in hours of development work.

These days, the big carmakers pay billions for a tag that sums up everything the car stands for and captures the public's imagination. This was exactly what happened with the diminutive MG Midget, which enjoyed an impressive 18-year production run as the world's favourite baby sports car.

You know from the name that this car isn't going to offer acres of interior space, or room for more than a few bags of shopping in its luggage area. But that cheeky name means you forgive it everything. By simply driving a Midget, you immediately become at one with the car.

Launched in 1961, the smallest MG was based entirely on the underpinnings of the Austin-Healey Sprite – one of the first fruits of the merger between Austin and Nuffield Motors, which owned the Morris and MG brands. The fact that Austin-Healey and MG had been such deadly rivals in the past meant it was quite odd to see their cars sharing components, and while it was the cute Austin-Healey 'Frogeye' that was first on the market, it was the MG that would go on to be the true sales success story.

By late 1961, the Frogeye was dead, and while badge-engineered Austin-Healeys continued, they

were identical to the Midget in everything but name.

Only the earliest Midgets were identical underneath to the Frogeye Sprite, with quarter-elliptic leaf springs and an eager but somewhat breathless 948cc (58 cu in) A-Series engine. By mid-1962, the Midget had been improved and gained a more powerful 42kW (56bhp) 1098cc (67 cu in) engine and front disc brakes, while further improvements in 1964 saw larger semi-elliptic springs aimed at aiding ride comfort and making the back end less twitchy in the wet. Added to these was a more rounded windscreen, wind-up windows in place of simple sliding

ones and – for the first time – lockable doors.

A Mk III model appeared in 1966 which this time had the performance the Midget had always craved, with a 48kW (65bhp) 1275cc (78 cu in) A-Series engine under the bonnet and the ability to almost reach 160km/h (100mph). Practicality was improved too, with a proper folding hood instead of a removable hardtop – no longer did Midget owners need to check the weather forecast before going out for a drive.

When British Leyland took control of MG in 1968, the brand was seen as important for the

company's image and the plan was not to interfere too much with the Midget; it continued largely unchanged until 1974. A matt black grille and sills, and slimmer bumpers appeared in 1969 and, by 1972, the squared-off rear arches were swapped for round ones to make wheel changes easier, but any car from the 1966–74 era is enjoyable to drive, with the purity of the original Midget design still fully intact.

But there were dark clouds on the horizon. New environmental and safety legislation in its most popular market, the United States, meant changes had to be made. First to go was the lively but polluting A-Series engine, to be replaced by a 1493cc (91 cu in) overhead valve unit from sister company Triumph. The 48kW (65bhp) unit offered good performance and, had it been fitted to earlier Midgets, may well have been a popular engine option.

But new laws also meant visual changes which did little to enhance its appeal. Regulations on headlamp height meant the ride had to be jacked up by almost 8cm (3in), while huge polyurethane impact bumpers were attached front and rear, completely ruining the original car's good looks. Inexplicably, the square wheelarches also made a comeback at this time.

Although the Midget remained a fun car to drive, its ungainly new appearance, coupled with the introduction of new, exciting and more practical sports cars from other manufacturers meant that by 1979 sales had almost completely dried up and the car finally went out of production.

The Midget's cabin was comfortable but not very practical, with no storage space and a distinct lack of weather protection.

Engine: 948cc (58 cu in), 4-cylinder
Power: 34kW (46bhp)
0–96km/h (60mph): 20 secs
Top Speed: 140km/h (87mph)
Production total: 226,526

MGB

The MGB is without doubt the world's most popular classic car. Adored in Europe and the United States alike, a whole industry has built up around its continued survival. But why did the humble B, which shares its platform with mundane vehicles such as the BMC Farina saloon and Sherpa van, become such a roaring success?

Their appeal lay in the fact that they were cheap to buy and run, great to look at and involving to drive, despite their less than glamorous underpinnings.

First to appear, in 1962, was the Roadster. It was the first MG sports car to boast unitary construction, while other advantages over the MGA (which it replaced) included proper wind-up windows, an easy-fold hood and a relatively spacious interior. Rear-wheel drive and a simple yet effective suspension set-up meant the B was also a pleasure to drive, with lively performance from the latest generation B-Series engine, which offered 71kW (95bhp).

A coupé version, dubbed MGB GT, appeared in 1965 and claimed to be a practical 2+2. Certainly, the side-opening rear hatch added extra versatility to the B and some would argue it's a prettier car, but the rear seats are really only suitable for very small children, due to lack of legroom in the back. Improvements across the range in 1967 meant all Bs got a tougher five-bearing

crank, full-synchromesh gearbox, an improved rear axle and different gear ratios, allowing for better high-speed cruising, while overdrive was offered as an option across the range.

As the 1970s drew nearer, timely modifications included a revised radiator grille, a more sumptuous interior and Rostyle polished steel wheels, all of which continued until 1974.

The most powerful factory-built MGB, born after the unsuccessful MGC failed to sell, was the MGB V8, which used Rover's ex-General Motors 3.5-litre (214 cu in) alloy unit, developed 102kW (137bhp) and had a top speed of almost 225km/h (140mph), but high prices and compromised handling meant only 2600 were sold.

The same American safety legislation that finished off the MG Midget threatened to do the same to the MGB as well, and cars from

1974 onwards underwent the same modifications; the ride height was increased to raise the headlamp aim, while thicker rear bumpers and a huge polyurethane beak became standard fittings.

The first examples were dreadful, with ponderous handling, an unresponsive ride and rather incongruous looks, although the GT looked better than the Roadster after the enforced modifications.

The only Bs from this era that are at all desirable are the limited edition GT Jubilees, finished in British Racing Green and sporting gold alloy wheels, a triple gold coachline and a one-off interior scheme. Just 751 examples were made, to celebrate the 50th anniversary of the marque.

British Leyland, who by now owned MG, realized the B needed to be a better car to drive. Because it was still a strong seller, especially in the United States, the company

Perhaps the world's most famous sports car? The MGB sold for two decades in five continents.

extensively revised the car for 1976, with a thick anti-roll bar addressing the handling issues and with revised interiors which were better equipped, but often finished in gaudy colour schemes.

Ultimately, the changes weren't good enough. The Datsun 260Z took over as the United States' (and the world's) best-selling sports car, and patriotic British buyers could keep the flag flying only until 198 when BL chairman Michael Edwardes demanded the closure of the Abingdon plant. The last 1000 MGBs, badged LE, were all finished in silver and black and marked the end of an era.

The MG badge was revived for sporting models in the Austin range, while a limited edition RV8 using the MGB shell, appeared briefly in 1993. Buyers had to wait until 1995 and the introduction of the MGF before MG became a proper sports car maker again.

Engine: 1798cc (110 cu in), 4-cylinder
Power: 71kW (95bhp)
0–96km/h (60mph): 12.2 secs
Top speed: 166km/h (103mph)
Production total: 513,272

Later cars from the 1970s came with a large dashboard and garish stripy seats.

MGC

On paper, the MGC should have been a great car. An all-new engine, designed for the Austin 3-litre (183 cu in) saloon, plus the MGB's good looks meant the high-performance successor to the legendary Austin-Healey 3000 should have been – and could have been – a big hit.

However, despite a moderate level of competition achievement at Daytona, Sebring and Le Mans, the MGC was too much of a

compromise. The heavy engine upset the MGB's natural balance and gave it a very twitchy rear end, especially on damp roads, while performance was meek compared to that of Healeys it was meant to replace.

The C wasn't helped by the successful V8 conversions being offered by outside companies, which used a Rover 3.5-litre (214 cu in) V8 to give the MGB

blistering performance and far better weight distribution than the straight-six MGC. In the end, MG gave up on the C and made its own V8s instead.

The C did find one famous owner, however, thanks to the British Royal family. HRH The Prince of Wales had a 1968 model which he drove well into the 1970s, and the car has recently been restored.

Engine: 2912cc (178 cu in), 6-cylinder
Power: 108kW (145bhp)
0–96km/h (60mph): 10 secs
Top speed: 202km/h (125mph)
Production total: 8999

The MGC was a missed opportunity. The six-cylinder engine was heavy and many agreed BMC should have used a V8 for better handling.

MG Magnette III/IV

With so many different brand names under its belt, BMC felt the need to offer Austin, Morris, Wolseley, Riley, Vanden Plas and MG versions of almost everything it produced, and the Magnette III and IV were the supposedly sporty versions of the humble but worthy 'Farina'

saloons of the 1960s.

That meant MG versions got an extra carburettor to give a minimal performance boost, a rudimentary anti-roll-bar set-up and a leather and wood interior to suggest superiority.

Magnette IIIs had a 1489cc (91 cu in) engine, while later IVs had a

1622cc (99 cu in) unit, plus optional automatic gearbox and two-tone paint. Visual differences included a trademark, if somewhat incongruous, MG grille, plus different indicator lamp lenses. The Magnette was inexpensive but largely unloved compared to what

the car-buying public considered to be 'proper' MGs.

Engine: 1622cc (99 cu in), 4-cylinder
Power: 51kW (68bhp)
0–96km/h (60mph): 20.2 secs
Top speed: 142km/h (88mph)
Production total: 30,996

MG 1100/1300

It might have been yet another recycled BMC product, but at least the 1100/1300 Series could replicate some of the traditional MG spirit.

Fine handling, sharp steering and willing engines, even in the earliest 1098cc (67 cu in) models, meant that these small MG saloons

could be driven flat out almost all the time.

The last versions, made from 1968, were the best, with a 1275cc (78 cu in) twin-carburettor version of the popular A-Series engine under the bonnet, giving true 145km/h (90mph) performance and

a characterful exhaust note, while all versions were far better appointed inside than their more humble Austin and Morris siblings. Although cheap to buy and run, they had an unenviable reputation for rusting. Four-door models were sold across Europe, but two-door

versions were destined solely for the United States.

Engine: 1275cc (78 cu in), 4-cylinder
Power: 52kW (70bhp)
0–96km/h (60mph): 15.6 secs
Top speed: 145km/h (90mph)
Production total: 157,409

MIDAS BRONZE

1978–94

Kit car or classic? It's difficult to label the Midas as either, as several of them left the factory fully built, while many of the components were shared with well-regarded British cars of the era.

The Midas can be regarded as a classic, however, because it's such a gem to drive. Conceived by McLaren production manager Harold Dermott and fine-tuned by Gordon Murray, who went on to create the sensational McLaren F1, it's no surprise that the Midas was a highly entertaining machine to drive, with accurate steering, wonderful chassis balance and a clever under-car aerodynamics set-up on later models which provided brilliant cornering.

The Midas looked very similar to the Mini-based Mini Marcos, but was a completely different car. Construction was by a clever glassfibre monocoque, similar to that of the Lotus Esprit, while the use of a Mini front subframe meant almost any A-Series engine could

be fitted. Versions fitted with a turbocharged unit from an MG Metro could outperform many pedigree sports cars – and, for that matter, outhandle them as well.

Designed with fun in mind, the Midas Bronze might have looked like a kit car but it drove like a racing car with accurate steering and superb cornering.

Engine: 1275cc (78 cu in), 4-cylinder
Power: 57kW (76bhp)
0–96km/h (60mph): 11 secs
Top Speed: 161km/h (100mph)
Production total: n/a

MINERVA AK

1927–37

For a company that originally built bicycles in a small factory in Antwerp, Belgium, it was quite extraordinary that, for a short while at least, Minerva also became known for creating the finest European luxury cars.

For an entire decade, the enormous AK was the transport of choice for kings, queens, movie stars and anyone with pretensions to grandeur, all over the world, with sales in the early 1930s mostly going to Hollywood.

Indeed, it was the stars of the United States' silver screen and their desire to buy enormous, sumptuous motor cars that eventually killed Minerva, as American companies recognized the market and started to make their own.

The AK is perhaps the finest of all Minervas, with a choice of grandiose body styles, crushed velvet interiors and a smooth, effortless 5.9-litre (363 cu in) straight-six under the bonnet.

But the combination of political unrest in Europe and flagging sales in the USA saw Minerva drop the AK in 1937. The company carried on trading thanks to a merger with fellow Belgian manufacturer Imperia, and surpassed all expectations by surviving two more decades, finally going bankrupt in 1958; by then it was building Land Rovers under contract from the British government.

Engine: 5954cc (363 cu in), 6-cylinder
Power: 112kW (150bhp)
0–96km/h (60mph): n/a
Top speed: 145km/h (90mph)
Production total: n/a

For a short time the Minerva was the most exclusive and luxurious car in the world and the favourite of the rich and famous, but it was ousted by the likes of Cadillac and Packard, which targeted wealthy American buyers.

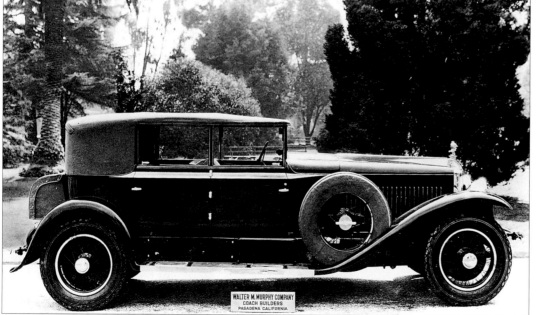

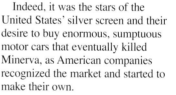

MINI

Dubbed 'Wizardry on Wheels' by BMC's marketing department, the Mini is perhaps Britain's most famous four-wheeled export. The baby saloon was designed by Alec Issigonis, who also created the Morris Minor and BMC 1100/1300 series, and was a masterpiece of packaging. In 1959, small cars and practicality didn't mix, and the impact of the Mini was consequently huge, especially considering its launch price of just £496 – almost £50 cheaper than a Ford Anglia.

Its front-drive, transverse engine layout was innovative, and was soon adopted by car manufacturers across the globe, while clever use of interior room, thanks to tiny wheels and massive door bins, made it a perfectly adequate proposition for family motoring. Practicality was boosted by the addition of a Countryman estate version in 1960.

Mechanical space-savers included a sump-mounted four-speed gearbox, plus an unusual rubber cone suspension system developed by Dr Alex Moulton, who would also create the unusual fluid and gas-filled Hydrolastic and Hydragas systems fitted to later BMC products.

But it wasn't just the clever layout and low pricing that made the Mini a big hit. The car was also fantastic fun – cute looks, a sporty exhaust note and a hard and bumpy ride gave it immense character. Driven hard, even the

most humble of Minis could be made to move a lot more quickly than the performance figures would suggest. Wonderfully communicative steering, superb grip and incredible handling meant the miniature marvel could show a clean pair of heels to all of its rivals, as well as many more exotic machines.

Initially sold as either the Austin Seven or Morris Mini Minor, the car was known simply as 'Mini' from 1961, when the legendary Cooper models (detailed below) also first appeared.

By 1967, after one million cars had already been sold, the Mini received its first facelift, although this was limited to a different radiator grille, larger door handles, a bigger rear window and all-synchromesh gearchange, while the floor-mounted starter button was swapped for a key-start mechanism. An automatic gearbox was also offered as an option, but was frustrating and not very efficient in use.

The biggest changes were under the bonnet, where a 1-litre (61 cu in) A-Series engine joined the range on the top specification cars, upping power to 31kW (42bhp) and offering a 137km/h (85mph) top speed.

British Leyland, as Britain's biggest carmaker was now known, unwisely tried to update the Mini in 1969 by adding a squared-off snout and flat bonnet based on a scaled-down Austin Maxi, but the

Mini Clubman sold in smaller numbers than the standard car and was withdrawn in 1980, leaving the original Mini to continue in production throughout the 1980s.

Despite newer and more practical designs, including BL's own Metro, the British public were still in love with the Mini, and customer demand kept production figures high.

Basic City and luxury Mayfair specifications were offered throughout the 1980s, plus a host of special editions using both 1-litre (61 cu in) and 1.3-litre (79 cu in) A-Series engines, the latter having joined the range in 1980 after the 1275GT (detailed below) was pensioned off.

In a bid to create a practical small saloon car, BMC inadvertently created one of the finest driver's cars ever – the Mini.

Although sales dwindled during the last decade of the 20th century, demand remained strong enough to make Mini production worthwhile. Even when BMW took over the Rover Group (which replaced BL) in the mid-1990s, the car remained in the range, eventually being declared 'Car of the Century' in 1999. A replacement for the Mini was already on the drawing boards at the time of the BMW takeover, and after the two companies split acrimoniously in 2000, BMW kept the rights and introduced its own interpretation of the car, called MINI, in 2001.

But it is the Issigonis-designed saloon that remains close to the hearts of British motoring enthusiasts, and many sentimental tears were shed when the last Mini rolled off the production line at Longbridge, Birmingham, England, on 31 October 2001.

621 AOK was the first ever Mini – Mk 1 cars had tiny rear light clusters, pronounced body seams, rounded radiator grilles and a floor-mounted starter button.

Engine: 848cc (52 cu in), 4-cylinder
Power: 25kW (33bhp)
0–96km/h (60mph): 27.1 secs
Top Speed: 116km/h (72mph)
Production total: 5,400,000 approx

MINI COOPER

1961–71

First and last – an original Cooper S hides behind a 1998 Rover model for a publicity shot.

Angered by the decision, BMC competed in the Rally again in 1967 – this time with headlights inspected before the start – and won again. A car originally designed to meet the family-carrying needs of budget-conscious British drivers had graduated to become a motorsport legend, and the Cooper had earned its place as an all-time great.

As well as being a successful competition car, however, the Cooper S was a fine road car, with the same famed racing handling and lively performance passed on to enthusiastic road users. The standard car's finest hour came in 1969, when a trio of patriotically painted red, white and blue Minis, loaded with gold bullion, made a dramatic escape through the sewers of Turin in the cult heist movie, *The Italian Job*.

By 1971, however, BMC had become British Leyland, and the new company had its own ideas about what a performance Mini should be. It severed its links with Cooper Garages to cut costs, and attempted to replace a legend with the 1275GT (detailed below), which had a standard 1275cc (78 cu in) engine lifted from the BMC 1300 saloon.

It wasn't until 1990 that the Cooper name reappeared on a Mini, after the ghost of BL had been exorcised and the new Rover Group's marketing department recognized the importance of past glories. The Rover Mini Cooper, complete with 30.5cm (12in) Minilite alloys and bonnet stripes, made a comeback, again developed by John Cooper and fitted with a tuned 1275cc (78 cu in) engine, this time with fuel injection. It, too, enjoyed a decade of popularity, outliving John Cooper himself.

The best thing about the Cooper was its handling – the power output was modest but you didn't have to slow down for corners.

It didn't take long for the Mini's incredible handling to catch the attention of motorsport enthusiasts, so when racing driver and engineer John Cooper approached BMC in 1960 with the idea of creating a performance Mini, BMC was quick to agree. Initially using a 997cc (61 cu in) A-Series engine, Cooper increased its bore and stroke so that the new car could reach almost 145km/h (90mph) with lively acceleration.

In order to enter the British Saloon Car Racing Championship, John Cooper asked the factory to build 1000 of the new cars quickly to satisfy homologation regulations, and their efforts were rewarded in 1962 when, in the hands of Sir John Whitmore, the early Cooper won nine of the championship's 11 rounds, although an unusual handicap and classification system meant the overall championship winner was Jack Sears in a Ford Galaxie.

But it would be the Cooper S, introduced in 1963, that would go on to achieve legendary status. Initially built with a choice of 970cc (59 cu in) 1071cc (65 cu in) engines, the now familiar 1275cc (78 cu in) unit was offered from 1964, with twin carburettors, 57kW (76bhp) and an impressive top speed of 154km/h (96mph).

By this time, BMC had already achieved some rally success with the Cooper, while it was also a regular performer on club circuits across the country. It was still putting in strong appearances in the British Saloon Car Racing Championship in the hands of famous drivers such as Sir John Whitmore, John Rhodes and Barrie Williams.

But the British company's works motorsport division pulled off the ultimate coup in 1964, when the Cooper S stormed to a shock victory in the prestigious Monte Carlo Rally. Despite being underpowered compared to some

more exotic competitors, the diminutive Cooper proved ideal for the tight corners of the Rally, while the icy conditions suited the car's front-wheel drive set-up against its rear-wheel drive rivals.

And to prove this rallying success wasn't just a one-off, BMC went back the following year and did it again. In 1966, Minis finished an impressive first, second and fourth, before being disqualified by officials over a technicality. Allegedly, the headlights on the Minis were set too brightly, and the French organizers instead awarded Monte Carlo victory to a Citroën...

Engine: 1275cc (78 cu in), 4-cylinder
Power: 57kW (76bhp)
0–96km/h (60mph): 10.1 secs
Top speed: 156km/h (96mph)
Production total: 144,910

MINI 1275GT

British Leyland's attempt to replace the Cooper wasn't a huge success. Buyers weren't keen on the front-end styling, which resembled that of the deeply uninspiring Austin Maxi.

With plans already in progress to stop production of the Cooper, British Leyland launched its intended replacement in 1969. Based on the Mini Clubman and sharing the same awkward squared-off nose, the Mini 1275GT was billed as the next-generation performance Mini, but potential and actual buyers were rather less than impressed.

While its miniature Rostyle wheels, triple side stripes and 1275GT badging looked sporty and impressive, the GT was missing one essential thing – power.

Exactly why BL chose to use a standard-tune 44kW (59bhp) engine and single carburettor is unclear (apart, of course, from the cost savings achieved by lifting the engines straight off the 1300 saloon production line), but the move proved to be a counter-productive one.

Looking back, the 1275GT wasn't a bad car. It was lively enough, had the Mini's famous

handling characteristics and the cabin was better laid out than in standard cars, with the instruments in a pod behind the steering wheel rather than in the centre of the dashboard. But with a livelier engine, it could have been much better – as many enthusiasts found out for themselves by adding aftermarket tuning products.

Engine: 1275cc (78 cu in), 4-cylinder
Power: 44kW (59bhp)
0–96km/h (60mph): 13.3 secs
Top speed: 145km/h (90mph)
Production total: 117,949

MINI MOKE

Motoring at its most minimal, the Moke was originally designed as a military vehicle but soon became a cult, if fleeting fashion icon in the Swinging Sixties.

The Mini Moke was BMC's attempt to build a military vehicle and was extremely unsuccessful. After they had invested a very considerable amount of money in creating a basic, low-maintenance Mini variant to use for ferrying army personnel, the armed forces immediately dismissed it because of its lack of ground clearance and mediocre performance.

In desperation, BMC tried to sell it to the public as the cheapest, most basic form of transport on the road. The purists loved its spartan appeal and open roof, but it was never a huge sales success – at least not in Britain with its wet and unreliable climate and crowded, polluted roads. It enjoyed a limited period of cult status, almost as a fashion accessory

Production shifted to the warmer climes and more open expanses of Australia in 1966, where the Moke

enjoyed more success as a basic carry-all, while a factory opened in Portugal in 1980 to build Mokes under licence. In southern Portugal, it is still possible to get one as a budget hire car.

The Mini Moke is a curiosity, certainly, and an icon of the brief heyday of 'Swinging London' in the 1960s, but not a particularly pleasant machine to drive, with booming noise levels and an uncomfortable driving position.

The strangest variant, built as a prototype to try and win another military contract, was the four-wheel drive Moke of 1966. It had two engines – one to power each axle.

Engine: 848cc (52 cu in), 4-cylinder
Power: 25kW (34bhp)
0–96km/h (60mph): 27.9 secs
Top speed: 135km/h (84mph)
Production total: 14,518 (UK production)

MITSUBISHI COLT LANCER 2000 TURBO

1979–87

Here's where it all started – fans of the Mitsubishi Lancer Evo rally cars should look at the original Lancer Turbo to learn where the legend was born.

Were it not for its alloy wheels and subtle side stripes, the Mitsubishi Lancer 2000 Turbo wouldn't have warranted a second glance. Its conventional looks mirrored most of the cars in the Japanese firm's line-up, but its blandness was partly its biggest appeal.

But beneath the staid exterior was a powerful motor. The 2-litre (122 cu in) overhead camshaft engine was capable of producing 125kW (168bhp) – enough to propel the Lancer from 0–96km/h (60mph) as quickly as a Jaguar XJS and on to a top speed of almost 210km/h (130mph). Controlling this power was difficult, however. Turbo lag was

excessive and, when the power did arrive, it did so aggressively, making the front tyres burn and leaving the driver struggling to rein in the large amount of torque steer.

The Lancer Turbo was never intended as a mass-market car but was designed to demonstrate Mitsubishi's new engine

technology. It also marked the dawn of Mitsubishi's World Rally Championship ambitions – now far advanced thanks to the spectacular Lancer Evo models. But it's with the original Lancer Turbo that it all started – a seminal sports saloon, even if few people have heard of it.

Engine: 1997cc (122 cu in), 4-cylinder
Power: 125kW (168bhp)
0–96km/h (60mph): 8.6 secs
Top speed: 205km/h (127mph)
Production total: n/a

MITSUBISHI STARION

1982–90

Mitsubishi's answer to the Nissan-Datsun 300ZX and Mazda RX-7 was the Starion, launched in 1982. The unusual name is rumoured to have come from a confused telephone conversation between Mitsubishi and its UK importer, where the name suggested by the Japanese company was 'Stallion'. Name aside, the Starion was an

impressive machine. Its brilliant, communicative rear-wheel drive chassis, hard ride and well-weighted steering made it a thrilling driver's car.
The same 1997cc (122 cu in) engine as used in the Lancer Turbo was fitted, but power was increased to 132kW (177bhp), making the Starion a very fast car. The turbo

lag problems associated with the Lancer were still there, however, which made it unpredictable. Mitsubishi tried to address this issue in 1989 by increasing the engine capacity, boosting torque and reducing power output. The last 2.6-litre (159 cu in) EX models are easier to drive than the original cars, but they lack the thrilling

performance that made the original Starion such fun.

Engine: 1997cc (122 cu in), 4-cylinder
Power: 132kW (177bhp)
0–96km/h (60mph): 6.9 secs
Top speed: 215km/h (133mph)
Production total: n/a

Strange name, but great to look at and drive. The Mitsubishi Starion was a finely balanced and brutally powerful coupé, but suffered from heavy turbo lag.

Monica GT

When French railway tycoon Jean Tastevin couldn't find a grand tourer to suit his every need, he decided to build his own. Employing the expertise of British engineer, Chris Lawrence, Tastevin built a four-door coupé using a unique tubular spaceframe chassis, with bodywork made of hand-rolled steel. De Dion rear suspension provided adequate handling given the car's immense size, while all-round disc brakes meant it could stop well enough.

Lavishly expensive, only 10 cars were sold, all to private buyers, while a further 25 development cars were made.

But despite being admirably ambitious, the project collapsed after just a year due to a pan-European recession and massive cutbacks across the engineering industry. The Monica project was

With a massive saloon centre section and a sports car-like front end, the Monica GT was nothing if not distinctive.

bought by Panther Cars in the UK, but never again saw production.

Those that did make it were impressive machines, with a sumptuously well-appointed cabin and excellent, smooth performance from the Chrysler-sourced (but

heavily modified) 5.6-litre (339 cu in) V8 engine.

Its strange looks drew on the Jaguar XJ6 and Lotus Elan +2, but were nevertheless elegant, if somewhat incongruous.

Engine: 5560cc (339 cu in), V8-cylinder
Power: 227kW (305bhp)
0–96km/h (60mph): n/a
Top speed: 234km/h (145mph)
Production total: 35

Monteverdi 375

If you can't find a car that suits you, then build your own… That was certainly the mantra of Swiss businessman Peter Monteverdi when he created the 375.

While few people have heard of Monteverdi, the range of cars it produced throughout the 1970s were spectacularly beautiful, hand-crafted machines to rival the style of marques such as Ferrari. The company was founded by Swiss car dealer Peter Monteverdi, who had always harboured a desire to run his own car company, and the elegant 375 series was the first of the breed.

With styling by Frua and engines from Chrysler, the cars made perfect grand tourers. Initially, two different coupé body styles were offered, a two-seater and a 2+2.

Later variants included a convertible and the 375/4, which was stretched by 61cm (24in) to create a strange four-door limousine aimed at buyers who wanted something more exclusive than a Rolls-Royce.

All 375s could be ordered with either a 6.9- (421 cu in) or 7.2-litre (439 cu in) Chrysler V8. All offered good performance, although the big, heavy tubular chassis, soft rear suspension and standard automatic transmission meant the car was a true grand tourer with few sporting pretensions. Monteverdi's sports car, the Hai, would come later.

Engine: 7206cc (440 cu in), V8-cylinder
Power: 279kW (375bhp)
0–96km/h (60mph): 6.9 secs
Top speed: 250km/h (155mph)
Production total: n/a

MONTEVERDI HAI

1970–72

After the success of the 375 Series, Peter Monteverdi decided to pursue another dream – to create a car to rival the Ferrari 250 and Lamborghini Miura, and this time to design it himself.

Given that Monteverdi's only motor industry experience had been in sales and servicing, albeit on exclusive cars, the Hai was a remarkable achievement. The

stunning bodywork was beautifully styled by his own hand, and had been created with such attention to detail as to be relatively easy to turn from blueprint to prototype. This took just 12 months.

Unlike its Italian rivals, the Hai was exceptionally well equipped, with leather trim and air conditioning, but it was still an aggressive sports car.

With 335kW (450bhp) powering relatively narrow rear tyres, the Hai could be difficult to control, especially when cornering in the wet.

Peter Monteverdi made no secret that the Hai was created entirely for himself, and while he was happy to sell them to interested customers, they were hugely expensive. Only two are said to have been built.

Nobody knows how many Monteverdi Hais were built, but it rumoured that only two examples of the Lamborghini Miura rival le the Swiss factory.

Engine: 6974cc (426 cu in), V8-cylinders
Power: 335kW (450bhp)
0–96km/h (60mph): 5.4 secs
Top speed: 290km/h (180mph)
Production total: 2

MONTEVERDI SIERRA

1977–84

In the mid-1980s, an acrimonious courtroom battle erupted between global giant Ford and minor British kit-car-maker Dutton over the Sierra name. Dutton claimed it had used the name first in 1979, and that by calling its new mid-size

hatchback the same, Ford was infringing on Dutton's copyright.

In fact, Monteverdi had been using the name for longer than either of them. The Monteverdi Sierra made its debut at the 1977 Geneva Motor Show and was the

most conventional car Monteverdi made. Based on the platform of the American Plymouth Volare, the car had hand-crafted panels and a well-equipped interior, with looks that drew on the Fiat 130 Coupé and the Ford Granada.

Engine: 5210cc (318 cu in), V8-cylinder
Power: 134kW (180bhp)
0–96km/h (60mph): n/a
Top speed: 210km/h (130mph)
Production total: n/a

MORETTI 1000

1960–62

Of all the strange and wonderful car companies to have ever existed, Moretti was one of the best. The marque was created in 1945 and originally built motorcycles to its own design, before switching to exclusive small cars.

Morettis were expensive and no better than their mass-produced contemporaries, but Italians valued the cars' individuality enough to

ensure the company remained independent throughout its life.

Until 1957, the company designed and built its own overhead camshaft engines and fitted them to platforms, also designed in-house. It then exclusively used Fiat chassis, and while engines also came from the Turin manufacturer, these were significantly re-engineered.

The Moretti 1000 was one of the company's prettiest designs. Based on the underpinnings of a Fiat 1100 saloon, an angular two-door coupé was first to appear, followed by a saloon, a convertible and an estate. Moretti went on to create a range of Fiat 500- and 126-based city cars, plus an oddball hatchback based on the 127. The company finally closed

its doors in the mid-1980s after widespread globalization across the motor industry destroyed hundreds of small manufacturers throughout Europe.

Engine: 980cc (60 cu in), 4-cylinder
Power: 31kW (41bhp)
0–96km/h (60mph): n/a
Top speed: 123km/h (76mph)
Production total: 1000 approx

MORGAN SUPER SPORTS AERO

Engine: 1098cc (67 cu in), V-twin
Power: n/a
0–96km/h (60mph): n/a
Top speed: 153km/h (95mph) approx
Production total: 18,000 approx

In 1919, the Morgan Motor Company moved from its founder's garage into a small factory in Malvern Link, Worcestershire, England. This was a pivotal moment in the company's history, as the new premises finally gave company founder, HFS Morgan, enough space to design and build a four-wheeled car.

But until the 4/4 appeared 17 years later – nothing ever happens quickly with Morgan – the company continued successfully to build a range of three-wheelers, the most famous of which were the 'Aero-bodied' models introduced the year the company moved to Malvern Link.

Unlike the standard cars, Aero-bodied models had a streamlined cover over the rear wheel, plus a rounded 'Bullnose' front end. The Super Sports Aero, introduced in 1927, had brilliant handling, and with a choice of Ford, JAP, Matchless and Blackburne motorbike engines, was ideal for tuning and modification. It spawned its own one-make racing series and led Morgan to competition success in other national trialling and racing events.

An unusual cross between a car and a motorcycle, the vehicle's accelerator was a lever on the steering wheel and the car had two-speed chain-driven transmission.

Three-wheeled cars were Morgan's speciality for years – they were quick and hugely entertaining to drive.

MORGAN PLUS 4

The Standard Vanguard-engined Plus 4, introduced in 1950, was Morgan's attempt to try and replace the evergreen 4/4, but this resulted in falling sales, and so the budget 4/4 was reintroduced after a five-year absence.

Similar in appearance to the 4/4, the Plus 4 had separate mudguards and bolt-on headlights. The wheelbase was four inches longer and the track was two inches wider – and there was more room in the cabin.

Mechanical differences, apart from the 2088cc (127 cu in) four-cylinder engine, included a full synchromesh gearbox and hydraulic brakes, both of which were fitted to the 4/4 when it returned from its enforced lay-off.

The original Plus Four used a two-litre four-cylinder engine plucked from the Standard Vanguard, but it was a much more sporting package. Despite the anachronistic driving position the Plus 4 could still be excellent fun on country roads.

A four-seater version of the Plus 4 was offered from 1951, while cars from 1953 onwards got a 4/4-style curved radiator grille, and disc brakes from 1960.

The Vanguard engine unit stayed until 1958, although the smaller, but livelier, TR2 2-litre (122 cu in) unit was offered as an option from 1954.

Both engines were dropped in 1961 in favour of the 77kW (104bhp) 2138cc (130 cu in) unit from the new TR4, meaning the Plus 4 was capable of 169km/h (105mph) flat-out.

The ultimate Plus 4, however, is the highly-tuned Super Sports, of which 101 were built between 1962 and 1968. With light-alloy panels and twin Weber carbs, it could hit a frightening 193km/h (120mph).

Engine: 1991cc (121 cu in), 4-cylinder
Power: 67kW (90bhp)
0–96km/h (60mph): 17.9 secs
Top speed: 155km/h (96mph)
Production total: 4542

MORGAN 4/4

The Morgan 4/4 can claim the longest production run of any car ever made, with the latest versions available to order today, fitted with Ford Zetec engines.

However, the earliest cars weren't quite so fast as the 4/4s made today. Launched in 1936, the new model realized HFS Morgan's dream of producing a four-wheeled car. Traditional Morgan features, such as ash-frame construction, live rear axle and semi-elliptic leaf springs, were present, as was the tubular chassis on which even today's 4/4s are built.

Production temporarily ceased in 1939 to concentrate on Britain's war effort, but resumed in 1945 almost unchanged, other than the introduction of a 1.3-litre (79 cu in) Standard engine in place of the original's primitive Climax unit.

In this format, the 4/4 continued until 1950, when again production was interrupted to concentrate on satisfying demand for the new Plus 4 (detailed below).

But the model made a glorious return in 1955, with a few visual changes. These included wider, more flared wings and running boards, and a more aerodynamic grille. Nevertheless, the 4/4 still looked dated compared to streamlined offerings from MGB and Austin-Healey.

The new 1955 models were breathlessly slow thanks to an 1172cc (72 cu in) Ford side-valve engine, lifted from the Popular 100E. This was rectified in 1959 by the introduction of the Ford Anglia's far livelier 997cc (61 cu in) overhead valve four, followed by the 1340cc (82 cu in) and 1498cc (91 cu in) engines developed for the Ford Classic and Cortina throughout the 1960s. The 4/4's Ford connection still remains, although a Fiat Twin Camshaft was offered briefly in the 1980s.

By 1968, the 4/4 had become a proper sports car, thanks to the launch of Ford's Crossflow series of engines, which offered tuning potential and a potent 71kW (95bhp). This meant the 4/4 could hit 160km/h (100mph) for the first time. Crossflow engines remained the mainstay of the 4/4 range until

the early 1980s, when Ford's new CVH (Compound Valve Hemi) units were fitted, initially with carburettors and later with the fuel-injection system lifted from the Escort XR3i. The switch to Zetec engines came in 1998, but no other concessions to modernity were made apart from a tamper-proof digital odometer.

A four-seater Morgan was available from 1969, and although it added extra practicality to the model, the car was nowhere near so attractive or pure-looking as the two-seater, especially with the hood up.

However, driving a Morgan with the hood up is almost unthinkable. Ask any Morgan owner what to do when it starts raining and they'll tell you to do up your top button, put on your goggles and drive as fast as you can until the rain eases.

Launched in 1936 and still being built today, the 4/4 has the record of the longest ever production run.

However, driving a Morgan quickly in the wet demands a high level of concentration. Even the latest cars, with their Zetec powerplants, are built on the same tubular chassis and ash frame as their forebears, and if anything, are even harder to drive as there's more power to control. The archaic construction, hard ride and unnerving body flexing can also produce erratic handling in dry weather conditions.

Yet the 4/4 remains an adorable motoring anachronism, with its brave disregard for the pressures of technological development. This approach works, too, because the company is thriving, with a queue of enthusiasts waiting up to five years to take delivery of Morgan's built-to-order cars. Indeed, the company's waiting list is longer than that of either Aston Martin or Rolls-Royce.

Early versions of the 4/4 had flat radiators.

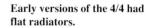

Engine: 1498cc (91 cu in), 4-cylinder
Power: 58kW (78bhp)
0–96km/h (60mph): n/a
Top speed: 163km/h (101mph)
Production total: 8000 approx

MORGAN PLUS 4 PLUS

1963–67

If the management at Malvern Link ever needed convincing that the key to its cars' appeal lay in their antiquity, the Plus 4 Plus was it.

In a bid to create a genuine contender in the grand tourer market, the Plus 4 Plus had an elegant closed body, a drooping MGA-style nose, a bubble-shaped hardtop and graceful rear-end styling, while technological developments included glassfibre body construction and gas-filled suspension dampers. The Plus 4 Plus was also the first Morgan to get wind-up windows.

Enthusiasts of the marque were horrified by the car, which they felt compromised everything Morgan stood for and was far too refined, while buyers of other marques snubbed the Plus 4 Plus because of its bumpy ride, flimsy construction and archaic chassis.

Production ceased after just 26 cars had been built and the company lost a lot of money on the project – but today, the Plus 4 Plus is a curiosity. Only a handful survive, and despite being a flop, it helped shape Morgan's future.

Morgan tried to go modern with the Plus 4 Plus, but buyers hated it. It lacked the traditional Morgan character and only 26 were made.

Engine: 2138cc (130 cu in)
Power: 78kW (105bhp)
0–96km/h (60mph): 14.9 secs
Top speed: 177km/h (110mph)
Production total: 26

MORGAN PLUS 8

1968–PRESENT

The success of this car lay in Morgan's foresight to buy up lots of ex-General Motors 3.5-litre (214 cu in) V8 engines. By fitting the all-alloy unit in the 4/4's light-weight body, Morgan had created its own AC Cobra. Erratic handling, especially in the wet, incredible performance and an unforgiving ride mean the Plus 8 is only for experienced drivers, as its oversteer can be dramatic.

The option of aluminium body panels from 1977, in place of the original steel, made the very quick Plus 8 even faster and even more difficult to control, but rather than stop here, Morgan kept increasing the car's power. 1990 saw the introduction of a high-compression version of the V8 borrowed from the Range Rover, with a displacement of 3.9-litre (238 cu in) and a power output of 142kW (190bhp). More recent versions have been offered with 4-litre (244 cu in) and 4.6-litre (281 cu in) developments of the engine, producing as much as 179kW (240bhp).

Engine: 3528cc (215 cu in), V8-cylinder
Power: 142kW (190bhp)
0–96km/h (60mph): 5.6 secs
Top speed: 202km/h (125mph)
Production total: 5000 approx

With a Rover V8 engine and ash-frame bodywork, the Plus 8 was an unforgiving and difficult car to drive, but devastatingly quick.

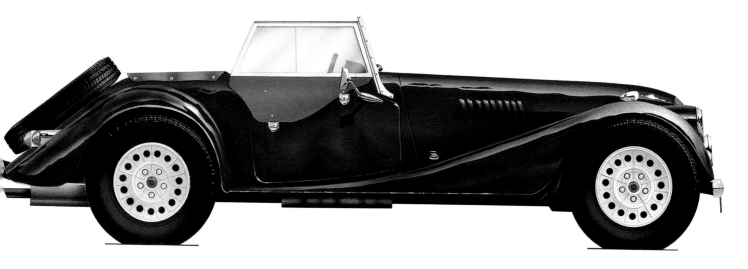

MORRIS BULLNOSE

1919–20

The Bullnose title was a generic term for early Morris Oxfords and Cowleys fitted with the characteristic attractive curved radiator surround, said to be the same profile as a bullet.

William Morris, later to become Viscount Nuffield, started out repairing bicycles, then making motorcycles in his native city of Oxford, England. By 1912, he had built his first car in nearby Cowley, and Morris the motor company came into existence.

These first efforts had a distinctive curved radiator surround, the top resembling the appearance of a bullet. This earned them the 'Bullnose' nickname. Two variants were available, the cheaper Cowley and the more upmarket Oxford, but both were designed to cater for the mass-market and be highly affordable. This meant buying in components at very cheap prices, and the eventual acquisition of component manufacturers by Morris itself. The public took the Bullnose to its heart, and bought as many as the firm could make.

Oxfords used British parts, but to make the price of the Cowleys cheaper, Morris bought in mechanical equipment from the United States. The engine, gearbox, steering and axles all came from there and were considerably cheaper than their British equivalents.

World War I caused a hiatus in production, but when hostilities were over, supplies from across the Atlantic became unavailable. The anticipated boom for light cars in America never materialized, so manufacture of components ceased. The last Anglo-American Bullnoses were made in 1919, with one solitary example in 1920.

Engine: 1495cc (91 cu in), 4-cylinder
Power: 18kW (24bhp) at 2350rpm
0–96km/h (60mph): n/a
Top speed: 89km/h (55mph)
Production total: 282

MORRIS COWLEY

1927–35

Named after the factory where they were built, Cowleys of the 1920s and 1930s were among Britain's biggest-selling cars of the era. After sporting a Bullnose, then Flatnose radiator surround, the cars ended with the elegant design seen here.

The Bullnose became a Flatnose in 1927. With the original Cowley design beginning to look antiquated, it was updated with a new chassis, suspension and brakes. The trademark radiator surround disappeared, to be replaced by a more modern-looking item, although one with less character than the original. The mechanics remained

unchanged from previous models, but new bodies were introduced, including all-steel ones built to an American design. Despite this strong transatlantic influence, the Cowley still kept its traditional British appearance.

The Flatnose look had a short run compared to the Bullnose. It was replaced in 1932 by a more elaborate design, with new bodies

and much-improved hydraulic brakes. By this time, sales of the Cowley were beginning to fall, and it was renamed the 12/4 in 1935. For just two years (1934 and 1935), there was also a six-cylinder 1938cc (118 cu in) Cowley Six which, as usual, was the poorer cousin of the Oxford model. Like the four-cylinder Cowley, this too was renamed in 1935, becoming

the 15/6. The final change in designation marked the end of the long-established Cowley name, at least until it was revived in the 1950s.

Engine: 1550cc (95 cu in), 4-cylinder
Power: 20kW (27bhp) at 3400rpm
0–96km/h (60mph): n/a
Top speed: 92km/h (57mph)
Production total: 256,236

MORRIS MINOR

1929–32

ustin brought out its Seven in 923, a move that revolutionized ritish motoring by opening up car wnership to the masses. It could e described as the UK's version of e Ford Model T. Other British manufacturers struggled to match it, and it wasn't until 1929 that Morris finally caught up. In the process, it introduced the name that would later go on to star on its most famous model.

The postwar Minor was a very different machine from the vehicle launched in 1929. The original Morris baby boasted simple styling and an overhead camshaft engine courtesy of Morris's takeover of Wolseley. By acquiring one of the oldest British carmakers, Morris bought much-needed capacity to build the Minor. Fabric saloons, two-seater tourers, sports coupés and several coachbuilt creations were among the bodies available.

In 1931, the 847cc (52 cu in) overhead camshaft-engined Minor was joined by a side-valve version with the same capacity. It was introduced so Morris could build a £100 ($150) two-seater Tourer, for those who enjoyed open-topped motoring, but didn't have much money to spend. The other body styles were also available.

Engine: 847cc (52 cu in), 4-cylinder
Power: 15kW (20bhp)
0–96km/h (60mph): n/a
Top speed: 89km/h (55mph)
Production total: 86,318

The Minor was introduced as a depression buster, to tide Morris over when sales of its larger cars fell. It was a well-regarded small car, and the two-seater open tourer was a cheap and cheerful model with some sporting pretensions.

MORRIS OXFORD

1930–35

Morris introduced its elegant six-cylinder Isis model in 1929, with a 2468cc (151 cu in) overhead camshaft engine and very advanced styling. However, the company didn't forget its traditional customers, and so launched a less powerful, less expensive side-valve six, bearing the Oxford name.

The Oxford Six, with its 1938cc (118 cu in) engine and hydraulic brakes, was very popular. More than 15,500 were sold in the first year alone. For 1932, an attractive sports Coupé joined the line up, and the same year, both the engine and chassis were modified and a four-speed gearbox appeared. A bigger 2062cc (126 cu in) engine was adopted in 1933, which solved the overheating problems that had plagued the original.

The Oxford Six was revamped again for 1934, with another new chassis and similar styling to the Cowley Six. As well as the all-synchromesh four-speed transmission, there was an automatic clutch option, although

this was really rather more of a gimmick than a reliable alternative to the manual gearbox.

In 1935, the Oxford name was rested and the Six was renamed the Morris 16 (complemented by a bigger-engined Morris 20 variant), but returned on the Oxford MO just over a decade later.

The posh brother to the Cowley was the Oxford. In return for spending a little more money, buyers got better-appointed interiors and a more impressive performance. These cars were among the last of the 'upright' Morrises. After 1935, styling became more aerodynamic.

Engine: 1938cc (118 cu in), 6-cylinder
Power: n/a
0–96km/h (60mph): n/a
Top speed: 95km/h (59mph)
Production total: 38,590

MORRIS EIGHT

Much of Morris's success in the 1930s came from its Eight model, one of the most popular cars of its era on the home market. Its outstanding sales figures helped save Morris from the economic depression which bankrupted several of its competitors.

The Morris was clearly influenced by Ford's products, both its styling – which looked like Ford's 6kW (8hp) Model Y – and its side-valve engine. However, unlike Ford, Morris offered two- and four-seater Tourer versions, which added some excitement to the range.

A short-lived Series II emerged in 1938 with just a few superficial changes, but there was a more dramatic restyle later that year with the Series E which featured a plunging waterfall grille and – rather weak – headlights in the wings. For Morris, this new look was quite revolutionary, although none of the mechanicals changed, except for the introduction of a four-speed gearbox.

With the end of World War II, production of the Eight restarted in 1945, continuing until 1948, when the new Minor replaced the old Eight.

Engine: 918cc (56 cu in), 4-cylinder
Power: 22kW (29.5bhp) at 4400rpm
0–96km/h (60mph): n/a
Top speed: 93km/h (58mph)
Production total: 120,434

The cascading grille and the wing-mounted headlamps of the Morris Eight were considered quite avant garde in the 1930s. By the time the Eight went out of production in 1948, it was seen as dated.

MORRIS MINOR

A very early 'low light' Morris Minor leads two younger models in this short parade of one of the world's best-loved cars.

America had the Model T Ford, Germany had the Volkswagen Beetle, France had the Citroën 2CV and Italy had the Fiat 500. Britain's entry into the 'people's car' hall of fame was the ubiquitous Morris Minor. The curvaceous, friendly looking Moggy (as it was affectionately nicknamed) stayed in production for almost a quarter of a century, and became as much an icon of Britain as red telephone boxes, Big Ben and London's black taxi cabs.

Plans for a new, postwar small Morris were drawn up during World War II, although it had to be done covertly, as development was against wartime rules. The car was the brainchild of Alec Issigonis, a gifted young engineer from Turkey who had joined the firm in 1936. The new Morris took shape quickly; by 1943, a recognizable prototype was running, patriotically named Mosquito after a British combat aircraft. The shape was very rounded, utilizing monocoque construction (in those days a very novel approach) and it was originally planned to use two different new flat-four engines.

In the end, finances dictated the use of the old side-valve Morris Eight engine instead, something Issigonis was against. Development carried on right up to the October 1948 launch date. At a very late stage, the whole car was widened (resulting in the strip down the centre of the bonnet and split bumpers) and the Mosquito name

was also dropped, replaced by the old Minor name that had last been used in the 1920s.

The Minor was just one of three new Morris models at the 1948 London Motor Show, yet it eclipsed its bigger Oxford and Six sisters, and almost threatened to upstage the other star of the show, the new Jaguar XK120. There was much praise from both press and public, one magazine lapsing into over-the-top hyperbole by saying it 'approached perfection'.

Almost the only person who didn't like the new Minor was boss William Morris, by now, Lord Nuffield. He disparagingly referred to it as looking like a poached egg. His customers though, disagreed with him, and bought well over 1.2 million vehicles (making it the first British car to reach the magic million mark) over its 23-year production life.

The Minor was initially available both as a two-door saloon and a convertible tourer, with a four-door saloon appearing in 1950. Criticisms about the lighting resulted in the headlights being moved higher up to the top of the front wings in 1951, although, for US cars, this change happened in 1949.

The merger of Austin and Morris to form the British Motor Corporation in 1952 resulted in the replacement of the weak side-valve engine with Austin's better 803cc (49 cu in) overhead valve A-series unit, much to the understandable annoyance of Morris engineers, who didn't want their car powered by a 'rival' engine. In 1953, the range of bodies was increased, with a Traveller estate, van and pick-up joining the existing saloon and convertible.

The Minor changed name to become the Morris 1000 in 1956 when the styling was also changed (the split-windscreen making way for a single item) and the engine increased to 948cc (58 cu in). Another capacity increase followed in 1962, to 1098cc (67 cu in).

By the time production ended in 1971, the Minor had become a British institution, part of the social landscape. Like its Beetle and 2CV contemporaries, it was reliable, cheap, pleasant to drive and well-designed. Most of all though, it seemed to have a 'big personality' that somehow endeared it to everybody. It was truly classless, the very definition of a real people's car.

Engine: 1098cc (67 cu in), 4-cylinder
Power: 36kW (48bhp) at 5100rpm
0–96km/h (60mph): 24.8 secs
Top speed: 124km/h (77mph)
Production total: 1,293,331

MORRIS OXFORD MO

1948–54

Engine: 1476cc (90 cu in), 4-cylinder
Power: 30kW (40.5bhp) at 4200rpm
0–96km/h (60mph): 41.4 secs
Top speed: 113km/h (70mph)
Production total: 159,960

If you wanted a Minor, but also wanted more power, luxury and pace, the next step up from the small Morris was the Oxford MO. Except for the grille, which was slightly more elaborate than on the Minor, the Oxford was almost an exact enlarged facsimile of its smaller relation. It was far less interesting though, and went on to have a much shorter production life, lasting just six years to the Minor's 23.

Power came from a 1476cc (90 cu in) side-valve engine, which was only just able to power the car to 113km/h (70mph), although the column-mounted gear change was not intended for performance use. Independent front suspension (by torsion bars) was fitted, but its effectiveness was questionable, forcing Morris to fit telescopic shock absorbers in 1950.

Changes to the Oxford MO were minimal. In 1952 a two-door Traveller estate appeared. A new grille was also fitted and van and pick-up versions were made.

The Oxford MO should have been called a Major, since it looked exactly like an enlarged Minor, complete with estate, van and pick-up versions too. Despite the resemblance, it failed to have the same enduring appeal as the smaller model and its production life was 17 years shorter than that of the Minor.

MORRIS SIX

1948–54

Wolseley was one of the other companies owned by the Morris group and it was used by its parent company to sell more luxurious and, of course, more expensive products, while Morris continued to

manufacture for the mass-market. In the late 1940s, a policy of standardization was introduced by the company, which included sharing body styles between Morris and Wolseley.

Thus, when the Wolseley 6/80 appeared in 1948, there was also a Morris Six lookalike, with a less comfortable interior, a distinctive Morris grille and a detuned version of the Wolseley 2215cc (135 cu in)

six-cylinder engine. The overhead camshaft unit was fitted with just one carburettor (the Wolseley had two) and was a smooth but uninspiring performer, with doubts over its reliability. The curvaceous body, from the long nose back to the rear of the car, was the same as the Oxford MO – itself just a bigger version of the Minor.

While the Wolseley became popular with police forces, and so some excitement was associated with it, there was no such drama surrounding the Morris Six. It sold poorly, overshadowed by its more luxurious sibling, before going out of production in 1954.

The Morris Six was related in style to the Oxford MO and the Minor, but accommodating a bulky engine resulted in a disproportionate nose being grafted on to the front.

Engine: 2215cc (135 cu in), 6-cylinder
Power: 49kW (66bhp) at 4800rpm
0–96km/h (60mph): 22.4 secs
Top speed: 138km/h (86mph)
Production total: 12,464

MORRIS OXFORD/COWLEY

1954–60

1954 saw the revival of the Cowley name, last used in the 1930s. It appeared as a downmarket version of the Oxford, Morris's new mid-sized saloon, and the first all-new model to be built since Morris and Austin merged in 1952 to form the

British Motor Corporation (BMC). This was, in all but name, a takeover by Sir Leonard Lord who was in charge of Austin, and problems were compounded by Lord Nuffield's declining interest in the company. Despite this unifi-

cation of the two main British manufacturers, both companies continued initially with a policy of building distinctly different models, albeit with some standardization.

The Oxford/Cowley was designed by Alec Issigonis, with

unitary construction. The more luxurious Oxford had more ornamentation than the Cowley and was powered by the new B-series 1489cc (91 cu in) engine. The more basic Cowley had a smaller 1200cc (73 cu in) engine.

Both received a facelift for 1956, with the Cowley getting the 1489cc (91 cu in) engine as well. Confusingly, in 1957, there was another restyle for the Cowley, to turn it into a Traveller estate. After the new Farina saloons were introduced in 1959, only this estate model remained in production, to fulfil the need for a load-carrying Morris model. When the Farina estate appeared in 1960, it superseded the Cowley Traveller which was then dropped.

Engine: 1489cc (91 cu in), 4-cylinder
Power: 30kW (40.5bhp) at 4200rpm
0–96km/h (60mph): 29 secs
Top speed: 122km/h (76mph)
Production total: 167,494

MORRIS ISIS

1954–5

The Morris Isis replaced the Six in 1954. A product of BMC's policy of standardization, it was a more upmarket version of the Oxford, fitted with Austin's C-series 2639cc (161 cu in) six-cylinder engine. Much of the bodywork was borrowed from the Oxford, but the bonnet was stretched for

the bigger engine, and stronger suspension and better brakes were fitted.

The Traveller estate version was an early version of a people carrier, thanks to its extra row of seats which allowed it to accommodate eight people. Extra character was added by the wood

panelling around the load area. Performance was reasonable, but the Isis's downfall was its clumsy handling, which did not help sales figures.

When the Oxford was restyled in 1956, the Isis followed suit, and the wood-lined estate version was dropped. The engine also

received a higher compression ratio which took power up to 67kW (90bhp).

Engine: 2639cc (161 cu in), 6-cylinder
Power: 64kW (86bhp) at 4250rpm
0–96km/h (60mph): 17.8 secs
Top speed: 142km/h (88mph)
Production total: 12,155

MORRIS OXFORD FARINA

1959–71

The badge may have said Morris, but other versions of the Farina were badged as Austin, MG, Riley or Wolseley. The car took its odd-sounding name from the Italian Pininfarina styling house, which had been employed to modernize BMC's range of family cars for the forthcoming decade.

The Oxford Farina (Series V/VI) was the Morris version of BMC's 1960s core model mid-sized saloon. Except for a different grille, there was virtually nothing to distinguish it from its Austin counterpart, but BMC sold it in order to satisfy its loyal Morris customer base.

From 1959 to 1961, the Oxford had prominent rear fins and a B-series 1489cc (91 cu in) engine. The four-door saloon was complemented by the practical Countryman estate from 1960. In 1961, a slight restyle reduced the size of the fins, and engine capacity was increased by fitting a

1622cc (99 cu in) B-series unit. The models stayed almost unchanged until replaced in 1971.

Engine: 1622cc (99 cu in), 4-cylinder
Power: 45kW (61bhp) at 4500rpm
0–96km/h (60mph): 21.4 secs
Top speed: 130km/h (81mph)
Production total: 296,255

MORRIS 1100/1300

1962–73

MC's badge-engineering policy reached its high point with this successful, best-selling range. The Morris variant was launched first in August 1962, soon followed by Austin, MG, Wolseley, Riley and Vanden Plas examples, all almost exactly the same except for the levels of trim.

Alec Issigonis was behind the 1100, which was, in essence, simply a bigger version of his successful Mini, with the ubiquitous A-series engine mounted transversely and driving the front wheels. Its all-independent suspension was a novel gas/fluid Hydrolastic system.

The Mk II 1100 appeared in 1971, the same year as the 1300 version which featured a 1275cc (78 cu in) unit. A sporty version of the car, the Morris 1300GT, appeared in 1969. The Mk III version of the Morris was available only as a Traveller estate, from 1971 to 1973.

Engine: 1098cc (67 cu in), 4-cylinder
Power: 36kW (48bhp) at 5100rpm
0–96km/h (60mph): 22.2 secs
Top speed: 126km/h (79mph)
Production total: 801,966

MORRIS 1800/2200

1966–75

Another attempt by Morris to reuse the Mini formula on a larger scale, the 1800 was launched two years after its almost identical Austin counterpart, but several years before the more luxurious Wolseley version.

The same familiar mechanical components were used, with a transverse 1798cc (110 cu in) B-series engine, front-wheel drive and Hydrolastic suspension. The 1800 was very spacious inside, although sparsely equipped and clumsy-looking. It soon earned the nickname 'Landcrab' thanks to its appearance and tendency to go around corners sideways.

The Mk II version of 1968 tidied up the styling and the interior, and from 1969 to 1972, a twin-SU carburettor 1800S version was offered. All 1800 models were replaced in 1972 by the smoother, more powerful 2200 (using the same body), powered by a six-cylinder 2227cc (136 cu in) engine.

Engine: 1798cc (110 cu in), 4-cylinder
Power: 60kW (80bhp) at 5000rpm
0–96km/h (60mph): 17.4 secs
Top speed: 148km/h (92mph)
Production total: 105,271 approx

MORRIS MARINA

1971–80

The Marina was one of the most derided vehicles of the 1970s, although replacing a much-loved British institution like the Morris Minor (as well as the 1100/1300 and mid-sized Farina ranges) was never going to an easy task. The car was not quite so bad as was supposed, but it didn't have many selling points, either.

Everything about the Marina was utterly conventional, with rear-wheel drive and suspension based on that of the Minor, which was hardly advanced when it first appeared decades earlier.

Two body versions were initially available, a saloon and a coupé. An estate appeared in 1972. Power was from a 1275cc (78 cu in) A-series unit or a 1798cc (110 cu in) B-series version. The 'hot' versions using the latter were faster than an MGB, but suffered from severe understeer on corners, limiting their performance potential.

In 1978, the Marina was reworked inside and out, although it kept the same bodyshell. The 1275cc (78 cu in) engine continued, but the 1798cc (110 cu in) unit was replaced by a 1695cc (103 cu in) overhead camshaft one.

The Marina was replaced by the Ital in 1980, which looked almost exactly the same as the old model, despite being restyled by the famous Italian designer, Giugiaro.

'When British Leyland sets out to build a beautiful car...you get the Morris Marina!' That slogan was used to launch Morris's new saloon for the 1970s, but few agreed that it was quite so aesthetically pleasing as claimed.

Engine: 1798cc (110 cu in), 4-cylinder
Power: 71kW (95bhp) at 5500rpm
0–96km/h (60mph): 12.3 secs
Top speed: 161km/h (100mph)
Production total: 953,576

MORRIS 1800/2200 PRINCESS

1975–81

Morris's last big car was also one of its most striking, controversial and short-lived. It was only badged as a Morris (and Austin and Wolseley) for a mere six months before its name was changed to the more regal Princess.

The range was distinctively styled by British Leyland's Harris

Mann, who produced a dramatic wedge-shaped saloon quite unlike any other previous Morris family product. Its unconventional looks divided critics, but it was at least totally different from its rivals. The layout created lots of interior space, and the ride from the Hydragas suspension was smooth.

The Morris, with a 1798cc (110 cu in) four-cylinder or 2227cc (136 cu in) six-cylinder engine, had its own individual grille and quad headlights to distinguish it from the Austin and the more luxurious Wolseley.

All models lost their marque identities in late 1975, becoming

simply named as Princesses until the car was dropped six years later in 1981.

Engine: 2227cc (136 cu in), 6-cylinder
Power: 82kW (110bhp) at 5250rpm
0–96km/h (60mph): 13.5 secs
Top speed: 169km/h (105mph)
Production total: 225,842

MOSKVICH 400

1946–56

The official name for Moskvich is Avtomobilny Zavod Imeni Leninskogo Komsomola – 'Youth Communist League Automobiles'.

Moskvich, which means 'Muscovite', became a nickname and eventually a brand name for the company in 1939, when it launched its first car. The Moskvich 10 was based on a 1920s

Opel and the connection with the German company continued for the 400-Series cars, launched in 1946.

The 400 was based on the 1937 Opel Kadett and was ideal for the Russian market, with basic side-valve engines, rugged unitary construction and low running costs. A four-door version also appeared on the orders of Joseph Stalin, but

this model – dubbed the 420 – was poorly conceived and badly built, with big gaps between the panels and frightening body flex over rough surfaces.

By the time production stopped in 1956, Moskvich had sold over half a million 400s, but with its technology rooted in the 1930s, the car was completely out of date.

Thanks to a good relationship with Opel, Moskvich was able to launch its own version of the Kadett to sell to Russian buyers.

Engine: 1074cc (66 cu in), 4-cylinder
Power: n/a
0–96km/h (60mph): n/a
Top speed: n/a
Production total: n/a

MOSKVICH 402

1956–58

With no investment money to spend and no tooling with which to build an all-new car, Moskvich's attempts to modernize what they already had were bound to fail. The 402, which appeared in 1956, looked relatively fresh with unitary construction and contemporary 1950s styling, but underneath it was archaic, using the platform of

the 400/Opel Kadett and the same old beam axle suspension.

An even older engine was used, a 1930s Opel side-valve unit developing 26kW (35bhp), while a three-speed gearbox, wayward steering and a harsh ride made driving an unpleasant experience. One good thing about the 402 was its indestructibility, regardless of

the poor quality of Soviet fuels and road surfaces.

With buyers issued with cars, Moskvich had no trouble selling to its home market, but export sales were impossible until 1958, when the government-developed and vastly improved 407 appeared, with an aluminium cylinder head, adequate performance and a

serious European sales programme that would see the marque enjoy moderate success as a budget brand well into the 1970s.

Engine: 1288cc (79 cu in), 4-cylinder
Power: 26kW (35bhp)
0–96km/h (60mph): n/a
Top speed: 96km/h (60mph) approx
Production total: n/a

Muntz Jet

When eccentric American engineer Frank Kurtis decided to build his own car in 1948, the resulting prototype was an interesting production prospect. With the curves of an inverted bathtub and a huge four-seater interior, the concept was an unusual but highly practical car, but deemed too strange-looking to attract any attention from the US car industry's major manufacturers.

Instead, Kurtis sold the project to wealthy car dealer Earl Muntz on the understanding the prototype would make it into production – and it did just that.

Launched in 1950, the Muntz Jet was fitted initially with a Cadillac 5.4-litre (330 cu in) overhead valve V8, although later models had a slightly less powerful (and much cheaper) 5.5-litre (336 cu in) Lincoln-derived side-valve V8.

Aluminium body panels and a glassfibre bonnet kept weight to a minimum and ensured the Jet didn't rust like most mainstream cars, but these production specifications also made it expensive and construction labour-intensive. Sales were respectable for a small-scale car builder, however, with almost 400 Jets sold before Muntz lost interest in 1954 and went back to selling other people's cars.

You either really love or completely loathe its idiosyncratic looks, but there can be no denying the Muntz Jet's presence. It was undoubtedly interesting and proved highly practical, although it was, inevitably, rather expensive. With a choice of V8 engines it was fast, too.

Engine: 5424cc (331 cu in), V8-cylinder
Power: 119kW (160bhp)
0–96km/h (60mph): n/a
Top speed: 180km/h (112mph)
Production total: 394

Napier 18hp

The world of motorsport and the motor industry itself owe much of their progress and success to men like the eccentric Selwyn Francis Edge. Instead of copying other manufacturers, Edge was an innovator. A man who believed in progress through experiment, he would do whatever it took to fund his thirst for engineering knowledge. He also appeared to have a strong belief in his own

The 4.9-litre (302 cu in) Napier 18hp was the first six-cylinder production car and the first to wear distinctive British Racing Green paint – but reliability was, unfortunately, poor.

immortality, often racing in hugely overpowered and minimally constructed competition cars, winning the prestigious 1902 Gordon Bennet trophy in a colossal 17-litre (1037 cu in) four-cylinder monster of his own design. Its major contribution to motoring history, however, was its paint, because the Napier became the first car to wear British Racing Green.

Such cars never appeared in mainstream production, but that didn't stop Edge introducing new ideas to the market. The 4.9-litre (299 cu in) 18hp was the first production six-cylinder car, although it was very unreliable. Vibrations from the unit often caused the crankshaft to break, despite Edge's dismissing the noise to customers as 'power rattle'. Napier persisted with six-cylinder technology, and later units were smoother and more reliable.

Engine: 4942cc (302 cu in), 6-cylinder
Power: n/a
0–96km/h (60mph): n/a
Top speed: n/a
Production total: n/a

NAPIER 40/50

1919–24

Napier also introduced one of the most commonly seen engine components to the motor industry. The 40/50, launched in 1919, was the first car to feature SU carburettors – a design that would go on to appear on nearly every British car and would net the company hundreds of thousands of pounds over the coming decades.

Otherwise, the 40/50 was unremarkable. With a six-cylinder engine, the 40/50 marked the company's new one-model strategy. Designed by the very highly regarded coachbuilder AJ Rowledge, who left to work for Rolls-Royce in 1920, it was a smart but unadventurous design, with steel hulls built by the shipbuilder Cunard.

The Napier was an expensive car and one which failed to fire the imagination, falling well short of its intended 500 sales. It lacked the social cachet of other luxury cars, such as Rolls-Royce. This sales shortfall lead the company to cease car production overall and concentrate instead on engineering developments. Its only four-

wheeled device thereafter was the Mechanical Horse, designed as a light articulated tractor unit, put into production by Scammell and popularized by British Railways.

The 40/50 was marketed as a luxury car, but sales were slow as monied buyers preferred the grandeur of such marques as Rolls-Royce. Production lasted five years.

Engine: 6150cc (375 cu in), 6-cylinder
Power: 29kW (39bhp)
0–96km/h (60mph): n/a
Top speed: 96km/h (60mph)
Production total: 187

NASH EIGHT

1930–39

There were, incredibly, no fewer than 102 different variants of Nash Eight offered throughout the 1930s, from the original, upright-looking Town Sedan to the swish 1939 Streamlined Roadster.

Yet despite these permutations, all Eights were built around the same theme. All came with huge and quite powerful straight-eight engines and were built on smooth-riding chassis frames.

Launched in 1930, the Eight initially came with a side-valve engine, switching to overhead valve units for 1933, while smaller-engined Sixes used scaled-down versions of the Eight's bodywork.

The biggest change to the range came in 1934, when the previous boxy shape was ditched in favour of a much more elegant, avant garde design that included a pointed 'shark-nose' bonnet and fared-in wings and running boards

The most common model was the Ambassador, a six-seater saloon, while the most bizarre was the 1935 Aeroform Fastback, which had a torpedo-shaped rear end and 'Speedstream' styling, incorporating chrome flashes on the bonnet, a V-shaped windscreen an aggressive radiator grille and aerodynamic wheel spats.

Built on the same chassis as Hudson and Railton cars, the Nash Eight was available in many body styles. This example is a four-door coupé.

Engine: 4834cc (295 cu in), 8-cylinder
Power: 67kW (90bhp)
0–96km/h (60mph): n/a
Top speed: n/a
Production total: n/a

NASH HEALEY

With excellent performance and distinctive looks, the Nash Healey was a highly regarded car in its day. However, it lacked the sporty appeal of some rivals.

Long before he formed an alliance with Austin, Donald Healey joined up with Nash to build a sporting car primarily destined for the American market.

The engine and chassis came from the Nash Ambassador and offered lively performance, although the heavy steering and poor brakes made the Healey a ponderous car if driven too hard.

Its looks were not very sports-like either so, in 1952, Nash commissioned a Pininfarina restyle, which resulted in curvaceous wings, bulbous rear arches and a notchback rear end – not one of the Italian designer's best creations, but smooth and inoffensive nonetheless.

While most Nash Healeys were sold in the United States with a 3.8-litre (235 cu in) engine of US origin, a few were built and marketed in Britain with a more

lethargic 2-litre (122 cu in) Alvis engine (that had some tuning potential) under the bonnet.

Sales were always fairly slow, and production ceased altogether after Donald Healey signed a contract with Austin at the 1953

Motor Show in England to build his next sports car.

While the Austin-Healey marque would go on to become a legend, Nash, on the other hand, became just a rare and interesting piece of motoring history.

Engine: 3848cc (235 cu in), 6-cylinder
Power: 93kW (125bhp)
0–96km/h (60mph): 14.6 secs
Top speed: 168km/h (104mph)
Production total: 506

NASH METROPOLITAN

The Nash Metropolitan, which was also sold as a Hudson in the United States and an Austin in mainland Europe was the result of a collaboration between Nash and Austin, that had been effected by Donald Healey.

On paper, the Metropolitan sounded like a winner. Nash president, George Mason, had a vision of a small and economical car that would appeal to the US market, and the new car promised to combine US styling with the

A tendency to rust, poor handling and a lack of practicality didn't seem to deter buyers of the Nash Metropolitan, especially in the United Sates – over 100,000 of the quirky convertibles were sold in an eight-year period.

British company's long-standing small car expertise.

Sadly, it was a disaster. The Metropolitan was very prone to rust, while its high-sided and truncated body was at odds with its 1950s Austin underpinnings, resulting in handling that was, at best erratic and, at worst, downright dangerous. It wasn't very practical either – despite its boxy styling, an opening boot wasn't offered until 1960.

Yet despite these major deficiencies, the Metropolitan was a surprising sales success, especially in the United States. Over 100,000 Metropolitans found homes in a seven-year production life, fitted with a variety of Austin-sourced engines, including the venerable A-Series and B-Series units.

Engine: 1489cc (91 cu in), 4-cylinder
Power: 35kW (47bhp)
0–96km/h (60mph): 24.6 secs
Top speed: 121km/h (75mph)
Production total: 104,368

NSU PRINZ 4

1961–73

Germany's equivalent of the Hillman Imp had a lot in common with the popular Rootes Group car. Stubby styling, a rear-mounted engine and entertaining handling were hallmarks of both.

The German car was first to go on sale and was a successful model for one of Europe's smaller manufacturers, proving especially popular in its home market. The air-cooled twin-cylinder engine wasn't very advanced, but it was durable and, thanks to the car's light weight, never felt lacking in performance.

Indeed, the Prinz was a pleasant car to drive, with nimble road manners, a slick synchromesh gearbox and effective disc brakes on all but the earliest versions. It was surprisingly well planned, too, and despite its minuscule external dimensions had a spacious cabin and a useful amount of boot space at the front.

NSU was absorbed by the VW-Audi group in 1969 and the Prinz range was sidelined. Sales continued until 1973 but the car was no longer actively marketed

by the parent company, which unwisely saw greater value in developing its adventurous but ultimately unsuccessful rotary engine experiments.

With the engine adrift of the rear axle and lightweight bodywork, the Prinz had remarkably entertaining roadholding. It was extremely well-engineered, too.

Engine: 598cc (36 cu in), 2-cylinder
Power: 22kW (30bhp)
0–96km/h (60mph): 32.2 secs
Top speed: 121km/h (75mph)
Production total: 576,023

NSU SPORT PRINZ

1958–68

If the Prinz 4 could be criticized for its awkward looks, the Sport Prinz redeemed its saloon stablemate. The pretty two-door coupé bodywork was the work of esteemed stylist Franco Scaglione, who, at the time, was working for Bertone.

The sleek car was tiny in its dimensions, but could be pushed along as quickly as some much

Despite the German name, the Sport Prinz was built in Italy by styling house Bertone for the first seven years. Later cars were made in Heilbronn, Germany.

larger and more mature sports cars. It wasn't powerful – with just 22kW (30bhp) available from the standard Prinz's air-cooled twin – but quick steering and a

surprisingly well-balanced chassis meant it held the road brilliantly in the hands of an expert driver. Like the saloon, however, it had a tendency to snap into oversteer if driven too hard through corners, especially in wet conditions.

Despite being marketed as a German model, all Sport Prinzs

were actually built by Bertone for the first seven years, only moving to Heilbronn in Germany for the last three years of production.

Despite its remaining popular and still looking fresh, NSU's parent company killed off the Sport Prinz in 1968 to concentrate on developing rotary engines.

This 1964 Sport Prinz was capable of 137km/h (85mph), and the company claimed it could match the 16l/100km (45mpg) economy of the Prinz 4. It retailed at £699 7s 6d.

Engine: 583cc (36 cu in), 2-cylinder
Power: 22kW (30bhp)
0–96km/h (60mph): 31.7 secs
Top speed: 123km/h (76mph)
Production total: 20,831

NSU WANKEL SPIDER

Three years before the controversial Ro80 appeared, NSU was experimenting with rotary technology. The Wankel Spider looked like a Sport Prinz but had a revolutionary new engine.

The Wankel Spider can claim a place as one of the most important cars in motoring history, even though few have heard of it. This unassuming little cabriolet was the first production car to use a rotary engine, although it wouldn't be until 1967 and the introduction of the NSU Ro80 that rotary cars became a sales success.

Based on the pretty Sport Prinz coupé, but with the roof chopped off to create an even more stylish design, the car was a desirable, if slightly overpriced offering, with an all-new Felix Wankel-designed 497cc (30 cu in) rotary engine mounted ahead of the rear axle.

It was a good performer, too, capable of a top speed of 161km/h (100mph) thanks to the light weight of the engine. Prinz's already impressive chassis

provided good roadholding, too. It could have been, and should have been, a great success, but like all early rotaries, the Wankel Spider was hampered by reliability problems that put off buyers and

investors alike. NSU should be admired for being adventurous enough to build the car, but given its great looks and performance, the Wankel Spider was really a missed sales opportunity.

Engine: 497cc (30 cu in), rotary
Power: 37kW (50bhp)
0–96km/h (60mph): 16.7 secs
Top speed: 148km/h (92mph)
Production total: 2375

NSU 1000/110/1200

NSU's family-orientated version of the Prinz had more spacious bodywork and a bigger engine, this time with four-cylinders but still reliant on air cooling.

Unusual oval headlights were a distinctive, but ugly, feature, while the elongated wheelbase and plastic cooling fins gave the 1000 a strange appearance. An even longer

version, named 110 (surprisingly not 1100, given the rest of NSU's model derivations), joined the range in 1965 with a larger 1.1-litre (67 cu in) engine, while the

1.2-litre (73 cu in) 1200 appeared in 1967, with the option of semi-automatic transmission from 1970. Despite their relatively small dimensions and small engines, the 1000-Series cars all enjoyed a much bigger car feel.

The 1000 also spawned the strange TT sports saloon, which shared the same bodywork as the standard 1000 saloon. With lively acceleration and a 161km/h (100mph) top speed, the TT was a popular car among keen drivers and enjoyed some racing success, but the rear engine, rear-wheel drive layout, coupled to the car's featherweight body and increased power could be lethal in the wrong or inexperienced hands.

Basically enlarged Prinz 4s, the 1000 and its derivatives were unusual family transport.

Engine: 996cc (61 cu in), 4-cylinder
Power: 30kW (40bhp)
0–96km/h (60mph): 20.5 secs
Top speed: 129km/h (80mph)
Production total: 423,704

NSU Ro80

Much was praised about the Ro80 when it was launched, but a series of quality control problems and high running costs were the key to its eventual downfall.

Dynamically brilliant, technologically advanced and immediately crowned European Car of the Year at its launch in 1968, the NSU Ro80 promised to be one of the most successful and important cars of its era. But within a year, the Ro80 had fallen into a mire of quality control problems, excessive fuel consumption, warranty claims and broken rotary engines.

Unfortunately, NSU had left its customers to do the development work, and the twin rotary engine, although sensational in concept, was an engineering disaster, with most units needing replacement within the first 48,000km (30,000 miles).

Yet time has now shown that the rotary experiment needn't have been anything like so shambolic,

and thanks to a network of specialists finishing the job that NSU started, Ro80s can now be made reliable. However, this unfortunately came too late in the day for NSU, whose landmark car became a laughing stock in the motor industry.

When it worked, it was a truly great machine – swift, smooth and with handling that was light years

ahead of its rivals, the Ro80 also sported such technological innovations as semi-automatic transmission and class-leading aerodynamics.

Engine: 2 x 497cc (30 cu in), rotary
Power: 86kW (115bhp)
0–96km/h (60mph): 13.1 secs
Top speed: 181km/h (112mph)
Production total: 37,398

Ogle SX1000

Ogle Design created the Reliant Scimitar and a special-bodied Riley One-Point-Five, but it was the SX1000 that became the company's most popular and, ultimately, fateful machine.

Based on a Mini van platform and with unusual bulb-shaped

plastic bodywork, SX1000 could be specified with any variant of the BMC A-Series engine – the twin-carburettor 1275cc (78 cu in) version, with Mini Cooper S mechanical components, giving it impressive acceleration and a top speed of 177km/h (110mph).

Tragedy marred the life of the Ogle SX1000. Shortly after its launch, project founder David Ogle died in a high-speed accident driving one of his cars. Hardly surprisingly, the public lost confidence in the car and production ceased after only two years.

The SX1000 was luxuriously equipped and interiors could be tailor-made to the customer's own specifications, while Ogle also offered to convert customers' Mini into their own creations if they could afford the relatively expensive production costs.

But the project collapsed when company owner David Ogle lost control of his SX1000 and was killed. Understandably, customers lost confidence and the concept died in its infancy.

The bodyshell was briefly revived by boatbuilder Norman Fletcher, but just four of the renamed Fletcher GTs were ever completed before the SX1000 disappeared forever. Another great and imaginative idea became just one more footnote in the history of motoring.

Engine: 1275cc (78 cu in), 4-cylinder
Power: 57kW (76bhp)
0–96km/h (60mph): 11 secs
Top speed: 177km/h (110mph)
Production total: 66

OLDSMOBILE EIGHT

1935–39

The elegant streamlined styling of this Oldsmobile Eight mark it out as a post-1938 facelifted model. It had identical styling to the Pontiac De Luxe and Buick Special.

Oldsmobile was one of the first manufacturers in the American car industry, although the man after whom the company was named, Ransom Eli Olds, had left in 1904 to set up his own carmaking concern known as REO. Oldsmobile became a constituent company of General Motors (GM) and, like all GM's bread-and-butter products, Oldsmobiles were touted as value for money machines.

This was certainly true of the Eight, which offered elegant styling and excellent levels of passenger space for a modest price. Two side-valve straight-eight engines were offered in either 3.9- (238 cu in) or 4.2-litre (256 cu in) capacities, the larger of which could reach 145km/h (90mph).

Both versions were also offered with a fully automatic gearbox – General Motors was the first company to successfully bring this new technology to the car market.

A radical restyle in 1938 saw a completely different front end, with stylish streamlined looks, while the 4.2-litre (256 cu in) engine became the only size available. The later car shared its bodywork with the Pontiac De Luxe and Buick Special, but was aimed at slightly more upmarket buyers.

Engine: 3936cc (240 cu in), 8-cylinder
Power: 60kW (80bhp)
0–96km/h (60mph): n/a
Top speed: 137km/h (85mph)
Production total: 155,618

OLDSMOBILE 88

1949–99

The 88 name lasted the life of Oldsmobile. This car dates from 1960 and shows all the frills and chrome associated with the era – later 88s were bland and uninspiring by comparison.

With a production life of an amazing 50 years, it's hardly surprising that the Oldsmobile 88 is an American legend.

The original 1949 models bore little resemblance to the last 88s, with their streamlined 1930s-style styling, but the model's target market remained the same throughout its production life. Powerful engines in compact, family-sized cars meant the 88 was always a quick car, and it went on to prove this by becoming the dominant car on the NASCAR racing circuit throughout the 1950s and 60s. Perhaps its greatest achievement was winning the first ever Daytona 500 in 1959, piloted by stock car legend Lee Petty.

Also significant was the 1953 88 Starfire concept car, shown at that year's Detroit Motor Show. The prototype was inspired by the Lockheed Starfire fighter jet and came with glassfibre bodywork, a wraparound windscreen and sinister-looking wheel spinners. A production Starfire appeared in 1961 and was quite different from the concept, with conventional styling and a host of luxury extras that included power steering, electric windows and automatic transmission.

By the mid-1970s, however, the 88 had become nothing more than a name that was applied generally to powerful versions of standard Oldsmobiles, and these boxy four-door saloons can't begin to match the stylish cars of the first two decades of production. The 88 name finally died in 1999, when General Motors decided to end the Oldsmobile marque.

Engine: 6551cc (400 cu in), V8-cylinder
Power: 257kW (345bhp)
0–96km/h (60mph): 8.5 secs
Top speed: 181km/h (112mph)
Production total: approx 10,000,000

OLDSMOBILE CUTLASS

1961–74

Despite being sold as a compact car, the Cutlass continued to grow throughout its life, as can be seen by the dimensions of this 1970 convertible model.

The fins and chrome excesses of the 1950s saw American cars get bigger and bigger, and by the end of the decade it was impossible to buy a compact vehicle.

General Motors realized this, and introduced a car for buyers on a budget. The F-85 Cutlass shared its platform and many body panels with models from Pontiac and Buick, although unique to the Oldsmobile range were the Cutlass Supreme notchback coupé and Cutlass S fastback, which later formed the basis for the 4-4-2 detailed below.

Yet despite marketing the Cutlass as a compact car, it, too, began to grow rapidly and, by 1964, had become as large as anything offered by the United States' 'Big Three' manufacturers.

There was also a bewildering range of engine options, from the base model's 4-litre (244 cu in)

Chevrolet-sourced straight-six, through to a 291kW (390bhp) 7.4-litre (452 cu in) V8. A five-speed manual gearbox was also made available as an option in the 1972 Hurst Oldsmobile.

Like the Oldsmobile 88, the

Cutlass name lasted out to the end of the life of the marque and was only withdrawn in 1999. By this time, however, it had lost all claims to being unique and become yet another characterless modern car.

Engine: 4184cc (255 cu in), 6-cylinder
Power: 155kW (208bhp)
0–96km/h (60mph): 10.9 secs
Top speed: 177km/h (110mph)
Production total: n/a

OLDSMOBILE TORONADO

1966–70

Front-wheel drive might not seem to be the most appropriate way of transferring 287kW (385bhp) of power to the road, but that's exactly what Oldsmobile achieved with the Toronado.

And an achievement it certainly was – the big Olds was one of the fastest and most desirable super coupés of its day with sensational styling, massive panelwork and a great engine note.

Automatic transmission came as standard and was fed through a huge torque convertor to stop the 287kW (385bhp) destroying the gearbox and driveshafts, while the front-wheel drive meant handling was more agile and predictable than most 1960s muscle cars.

The unfortunate thing for GM, which had invested millions of dollars developing front-wheel drive, was that most American

buyers didn't notice the differences in the driveline and many thought the Toronado too adventurously styled for it to sell really well.

Other minus points included high fuel consumption, heavy tyre wear and, like most big American cars of the era, inefficient drum brakes. Nevertheless, it remains an icon in US motoring history, and was hugely important for its technological advances.

Fitting the Toronado with front-wheel-drive was a brave move, but with a 7446cc (454 cu in) engine it could outperform most muscle car rivals. It was one of the fastest super coupés of its time.

Engine: 7446cc (454 cu in), V8-cylinder
Power: 287kW (385bhp)
0–96km/h (60mph): 8.7 secs
Top speed: 210km/h (130mph)
Production total: 143,134

OLDSMOBILE 4-4-2

here the Toronado was futuristic
d technologically highly
vanced, the 4-4-2 was a much
ore conventional muscle car.
unched in 1967 with a Plymouth
arracuda-style fastback body, the
4-2 name stood for 400 cubic
ches, four-barrel carburettor and
o exhausts.

As well as the fastback, a
nvertible was introduced in
68, followed by a more
nventional hardtop coupé with
aditional three-box styling.

Power output varied from
2kW (190bhp) to a massive
8kW (400bhp), with the range-
pping 455 cu in version using a
assive 7.4-litre engine, the same
that in the Toronado.

An ultra-conventional rear-wheel
ive chassis, essentially that of an
ldsmobile Cutlass saloon but with
ffer springs, meant the 4-4-2 had
pical brawny American car
ndling, making it quick in a
aight line but hard to control if
shed through corners too quickly,
pecially in higher output
rsions.

Like all cars of its type – and
quite a few others, too – the
4-4-2 was killed off by the 1970s
energy crisis and new American
emissions legislation, which led
to power outputs being very
drastically reduced.

**4-4-2 stood for 400 cubic inches,
four-barrel carburettor and two
exhausts – Oldsmobile certainly
wasn't shy about the model's
performance aspirations. It was
typically fast in straight lines, but
could be a problem on corners.**

Engine: 6551cc (400 cu in), V8-cylinder
Power: 216kW (290bhp)
0–96km/h (60mph): 10.3 secs
Top speed: 194km/h (120mph)
Production total: 86,883

OPEL OLYMPIA

ter World War II, Germany
uggled economically, and its
eviously successful carmaker,
pel, was forced to make do with
chaic designs until it could raise
ough money to develop new

models. Also, the tooling for its
Kadett small car had been sold to
the Russians to become their new
Moskvich, meaning the only car the
German firm could offer was a
reworked version of the Olympia.

**With independent suspension,
monocoque bodywork and an
overhead valve engine, the Olympia
was advanced for its era. However,
it was slow and felt heavy and
awkward to drive.**

Luckily, it was an advanced car
when it first appeared in the late
1930s, with a monocoque body,
overhead valve engine and
aerodynamic styling, as well as
quite surprisingly effective
independent suspension.

The Olympia wasn't a great car
to drive, with lazy power delivery
and wayward steering, but it did an
important job for Opel and for the
German economy, with low
production costs meaning it could
be sold cheaply.

By the time the Olympia was
dropped five years later in 1952,
Opel had done enough to start
developing new and exciting
models, while financial backing
from General Motors meant the
firm's future was now secure. The
model's replacement, the Olympia
Rekord, looked like a scaled-
down Chevrolet.

Engine: 1488cc (91 cu in), 4-cylinder
Power: 28kW (37bhp)
0–96km/h (60mph): 31.4 secs
Top speed: 110km/h (68mph)
Production total: 187,055

OPEL KAPITAN

1953–58

Engine: 2473cc (151 cu in), 6-cylinder
Power: 56kW (75bhp)
0–96km/h (60mph): 21.4 secs
Top speed: 142km/h (88mph)
Production total: 154,098

Opel's flagship model had obvious Detroit influences, with vast metalwork, an intricate (and wholly unnecessary) chrome grille with shining 'teeth', whitewall tyres and polished metal side flashes.

However, it was an impressive piece of engineering, with a tough, solid body, independent coil and wishbone suspension at the front and semi-elliptic leaf springs at the back.

The 2.4-litre (151 cu in) straight six was smooth and surprisingly

lively, while the three-speed column change transmission was easy to use and aided by the engine's excellent torque, which meant, in fact, that changes were frequently unnecessary.

A facelift in 1955 saw the Kapitan's grille replaced by a much less ornate affair, while an all-synchromesh gearbox and better trimmed interior were also offered.

The Kapitan was replaced in 1958 by a new model that had even more American influences, including a wraparound windscreen on which unsuspecting passengers could easily hit their knees when they were trying to get out of the car. A more powerful engine, which produced 67kW (90bhp),

four-speed gearbox and automatic transmission were also offered on the new model, which continued unchanged until 1964.

American in its styling, but truly European in character, the Kapit[a] used an efficient six-cylinder engi[ne] and three-speed manual gearbox.

OPEL OLYMPIA P1

1957–6[3]

By the time the Olympia P1 appeared, Opel freely admitted that the United States was influencing its styling – perhaps as an excuse to justify the P1's ungainly looks. While the wraparound screens, tailfins and chrome adornments might have worked on larger cars, on a small two- or four-door saloon the size of the British Vauxhall Viva, the effect simply looked

confused. The stubby bodywork looked at odds with the curved front and rear screens, while the huge radiator grille made the Olympia P1 look like a cheap caricature of some of the United States more impressive models.

But that didn't stop the Opel from being a roaring success, with over 1.5 million cars sold in six years. A 'Caravan' estate car was

offered from 1958, which looked even stranger, while P1 buyers could also choose from a range of engines, including the earlier Olympia's 1488cc (91 cu in) overhead-valve unit, a new 1205cc (74 cu in) overhead-valve engine or a more lively 1680cc (103 cu in) car, known as the Rekord P2.

Both the Olympia and Rekord survived until 1963, when Opel

embarked on a completely new styling direction that much more closely reflected that of other European manufacturers (see below).

Engine: 1488cc (91 cu in), 4-cylinder
Power: 34kW (45bhp)
0–96km/h (60mph): 28 secs
Top speed: 116km/h (72mph)
Production total: 1,611,445

OPEL REKORD A/B

1963–6[5]

The Rekord A had a much more European look after the chromed US copies Opel had been producing. Squared-off, boxy lines, a spacious passenger compartment

and rectangular headlights meant the Opel looked clean and modern.

A more interesting-looking coupé option appeared in 1964, followed by the Rekord B in 1965,

which replaced the original overhead-valve engines with modern overhead camshaft engines of 1.5-, 1.7- and 1.9-litre (92, 103, 116 cu in) capacities. The Kapitan's 2.6-litre (159 cu in) six-cylinder unit was also offered in the Rekord B, coupled to a new four-speed floor shift transmission or a three-speed

GM automatic. With full unitary construction and front disc brakes (from 1965) the Rekord was technologically advanced compared to Opels of old, but it still had a live rear axle and leaf springs at the back.

The Rekord was a big success story for Opel, with over a milli[on] sold in a relatively short producti[on] life. It was replaced by the simila[r] looking, but much more modern, Rekord C/Commodore in 1966.

The Rekord was a larger car than the Kapitan, but the family influences were evident.

Engine: 1680cc (103 cu in), 4-cylinder
Power: 41kW (55bhp)
0–96km/h (60mph): 21 secs
Top speed: 147km/h (91mph)
Production total: 1,152,824

Opel Kadett B

The limited edition Kadett Rallye (above) was instantly recognizable by its black stripes and spotlamps.

The Kadett was Opel's answer to the vast numbers of small cars proving popular in Europe, such as the Ford Anglia, Renault 8 and VW Beetle.

The original Kadett appeared in 1962 and was built at a brand new factory. It used a 993cc (61 cu in) engine, but it was considered underpowered and sported looks that were old-fashioned right from its launch. The replacement Kadett B, launched in 1965, was a much more attractive proposition, with the same competent chassis as the first Kadett, but a wider choice of engines, ranging from 1-litre (61 cu in) to a high compression 1.5-litre (92 cu in) twin-carburettor unit, capable of over 160km/h (100mph).

It was the larger engine that powered the best-loved Kadett,

the Rallye Coupé, introduced in 1967. The Rallye had the appearance of a scaled-down American muscle car, with pressed steel wheels, twin coachlines and a matt black anti-glare bonnet, plus dual circuit disc brakes as standard.

But even the standard Kadetts were well made and fun to drive, with over 2.5 million sold across Europe during an eight-year production life.

The Kadett was also the first Opel to be a successful seller in Britain, despite GM's large presence in the market with Vauxhall.

Engine: 1492cc (91 cu in), 4-cylinder
Power: 67kW (90bhp)
0–96km/h (60mph): 12.6 secs
Top speed: 165km/h (102mph)
Production total: 2,649,501

Standard Kadetts like this four-door version were much plainer than the Kadett Rallye.

OPEL OLYMPIA

1967–7(

For 1967, Opel took the Olympia name but instead of applying it to a completely new model, the company decided instead to use it on upmarket Kadetts.

Available as a two- or four-door saloon, the Olympia came better equipped than the Kadett with a well-trimmed cabin, fake wood and a rev counter. External differences included neat chrome wheeltrims, whitewall tyres and a vinyl roof, plus a distinctive two-bar radiator grille that curved around into the front wings.

All came with twin-carburettor engines, even in the most basic 1.1-litre (66 cu in) form, and all were free-revving and sporty, complemented by tidy handling and a supple ride from Opel's best chassis to date.

The Olympia's biggest problem was the price – buyers weren't prepared to pay a huge premium for an Opel Kadett with extra trim. Despite being a good car, the Olympia would account for only one in 30 of the company's small saloon car sales, and the model name was unobtrusively dropped in 1970, never to be seen again. Upmarket trim was carried over t(the Kadett LS.

Engine: 1078cc (66 cu in), 4-cylinder
Power: 45kW (60bhp)
0–96km/h (60mph): 19.3 secs
Top speed: 145km/h (90mph)
Production total: 80,637

OPEL DIPLOMAT

1964–68

A fleeting return to American-influenced styling appeared on both the Admiral and Diplomat, launched in 1964, with lines that were almost identical to GM's (US) Buick Special.

These Opels looked very much smarter than the Opels of the past, however, as the new emphasis from Detroit was on clean-cut, three-box styling instead of the previous decade's hallmark fins and chrome.

The Admiral, an inexpensive and spacious big saloon, used the 2.6-litre (159 cu in) engine from the old Kapitan, but it was the luxurious Diplomat that proved to be the most desirable.

Under the bonnet a 4.6-litre (283 cu in) or 5.3-litre (323 cu in) engine was fitted, taken from the Chevrolet Chevelle, meaning that the Diplomat was a quick and refined cruising machine. This, therefore, made it absolutely ideal for driving on Germany's recently constructed autobahns.

The good points included a cossetting ride and excellent standard equipment, but the Diplomat was very prone to rust, used a lot of fuel and handled badly at speed.

Also worthy of note is the ultra-rare Diplomat Coupé, built in 1967 only by coachbuilders Karmann. It was extremely elegant but very expensive, so just 304 were built.

Engine: 4638cc (283 cu in), V8-cylinder
Power: 171kW (230bhp)
0–96km/h (60mph): 10.3 secs
Top speed: 210km/h (130mph)
Production total: 89,277

American car fans could be forgiven for mistaking the Diplomat for a Buick Special, but it was smaller and aimed at more upmarket buyers. It was more popular than the Admiral of the same period.

OPEL KAPITAN

The Kapitan name reappeared for the next range of big Opel saloons, which replaced the Admiral and Diplomat in 1969.

The Kapitan came with a 2.8-litre (170 cu in) straight six, which offered strong performance for its era, while the rather more luxurious Admiral shared the same engine. The Diplomat retained its US-derived 5.4-litre (330 cu in)

V8 engine and had GM's Hydramatic auto transmission as standard, although the car could also be ordered with a six-cylinder engine and four-speed manual gearbox instead.

Distinctive stacked headlights aped the big Mercedes saloons of the late 1960s, but the car had the same slab-sided bodywork of smaller Opels, a thick C-Pillar and

a rear end appearance that was a cross between a saloon and fastback coupé. Handling and performance were similar to the previous generation Admiral and Diplomat, on which the new model was based.

The Kapitan was dropped in 1971 because of slow sales, the name dying with it, but the Admiral and Diplomat continued

until 1977 when they were replaced by the Rekord and Senator, which were also sold in Britain as the Vauxhall Carlton and Senator until the mid-1980s.

Engine: 2784cc (170 cu in), 6-cylinder
Power: 96kW (129bhp)
0–96km/h (60mph): 10.9 secs
Top speed: 176km/h (109mph)
Production total: 61,019

OPEL GT

The first genuinely sporting Opel, the GT was produced to illustrate exactly how good the Kadett's underpinnings were. The car started life as a styling exercise at the 1965 Frankfurt Motor Show, but proved so popular that GM gave it the green light for production.

Neat mini-Corvette styling was done in-house at Opel, but franchised out to coachbuilders Brissoneau and Lotz to build in

France. Unusual features included headlights which hydraulically rotated out of the bonnet, and a distinctive Kamm tail, but under the pretty bodywork it was an utterly conventional Opel.

Not that this was in any way a bad thing, as the lightweight body made the GT a quick and surprisingly agile car, while front discs and a quicker steering rack made handling reassuring.

More than 80 per cent of the cars built were shipped to the United States, where buyers loved the Opel's compact Corvette looks. All cars in Europe were left-hand drive, although a handful were officially imported to Britain. Many American purchases have since found their way back across the Atlantic as European fans of the Opel have repatriated rust-free dry state cars.

Europe's answer to the Chevrolet Corvette? The Opel GT was built to improve the company's rather boring image – and it worked a treat.

Engine: 1897cc (116 cu in), 4-cylinder
Power: 67kW (90bhp)
0–96km/h (60mph): 12 secs
Top speed: 185km/h (115mph)
Production total: 103,373

OPEL ASCONA

1970–75

Launched at the 1970 Turin Motor Show, the Ascona was completely conventional, but it was also an extremely important car for Opel. Intended as a replacement for the smaller Olympia, it offered considerably more interior space and a larger boot, making it a serious rival in Europe to cars such as Ford's Taurus and Cortina ranges.

The car used a unitary construction bodyshell, which was by now the industry-accepted norm, with either a 1.6- (98 cu in) or 1.9-litre (116 cu in) overhead camshaft engine in a choice of two-door, four-door and estate body styles. A strong four-speed manual gearbox had a slick operation, while a three-speed auto was offered as an option.

Although pleasant enough to drive thanks to light steering, coil springs all round and front disc brakes, somehow the Ascona still never quite managed to excite the imagination, despite some moderate rallying success.

A big seller for Opel and, significantly, the basis for the Manta sports coupé, the mid-size saloon was a pivotal car in the

company's growth until its 1975 replacement, which would also become the new Vauxhall Cavalier in the United Kingdom.

Engine: 1897cc (116 cu in), 4-cylinder
Power: 67kW (90bhp)
0–96km/h (60mph): 12.5 secs
Top speed: 158km/h (98mph)
Production total: 641,438

OPEL MANTA A-SERIES

1970–75

Directly after the highly successful Ford Capri came the coupé Manta, which, like the Ford, was based on conventional saloon car underpinnings – in this case, the Ascona. Other common themes included a confusing engine range, from a tiny 1.2-litre (73 cu in) four-cylinder to a 75kW (100bhp)-plus 1.9-litre (116 cu in), although there was never a Capri-rivalling V6 option.

The Manta was neatly styled, using Ascona panels as far as the windscreen pillars and entirely new two-door notchback styling for the rest of the car, plus Ferrari-style round separate tail-lights.

Fastest and most desirable was the 1973 Manta GT/E, which acquired Bosch fuel injection, Rostyle wheels, auxiliary driving lamps and a matt black bonnet.

Like the Ascona, it was pleasant to drive, but lacking in driver involvement, although the supple ride and slick gearbox made it a comfortable cruising car. The

Another sporty Opel, the Manta was the German firm's answer to the Ford Capri. It never matched its rival's success, but was a strong seller nonetheless.

Manta nevertheless won the hearts of enthusiasts who didn't like the Capri, and its image was always considered more upmarket than that of Ford's offering.

Engine: 1897cc (116 cu in), 4-cylinder
Power: 78kW (105bhp)
0–96km/h (60mph): 9.8 secs
Top speed: 189km/h (117mph)
Production total: 498,553

OPEL COMMODORE

Links between Opel of Germany and Vauxhall in Britain started to become closer in the early 1970s, when GM saw fit to introduce platform- as well as component-sharing to its two European representatives.

The first fruit of the platform-sharing alliance was the 1972 Rekord, which shared its floorpan with the Vauxhall Victor FE,

although at this stage, Vauxhall and Opel were still keen to differentiate between their respective ranges. Of the two, it was the Opel line-up that was the more interesting, in particular the imposing coupé Commodore, which came with either 2.5- (153 cu in) or 2.8-litre (170 cu in) straight-six engines borrowed from the Diplomat. Top of the range GS/E models were

very well equipped, with a 119kW (160bhp) fuel-injected engine, distinctive body stripes, power-assisted steering and an automatic gearbox fitted as standard – although a few manual variants are

A large and elegant coupé (below) or an executive saloon, the Commodore was popular among wealthy European buyers.

rumoured to have left the factory. It sold well in Germany, where coupés were fashionable in the 1970s, but only enjoyed limited success elsewhere in Europe.

Engine: 2784cc (170 cu in), 6-cylinder
Power: 119kW (160bhp)
0–96km/h (60mph): 8.9 secs
Top speed: 194km/h (120mph)
Production total: 140,827

OPEL KADETT

Another Opel that eventually became a Vauxhall, the Kadett became the Chevette, although with an ugly drooping snout. The Opel was a much better-looking and better-equipped car, although the new economy-level 993cc (61cu in) version was slow and had a spartan interior.

A massive range, as buyers had come to expect from Opel, encompassed saloon, hatchback, estate and coupé models, as well as a limited edition targa-roofed convertible, available for one year only in 1976.

Other models of interest include the lively fuel-injected GT/E, which offered 86kW (115bhp) and 190km/h (118mph) from its 2-litre (122 cu in) engine, as well as surprisingly entertaining handling. Also worthy of note was the earlier Rallye, launched in 1974, which had drilled steel wheels and a matt black bonnet, available only as a fastback coupé. The Rallye replaced the Ascona as Opel's rallying flagship and enjoyed moderate success.

It was replaced, in turn, in 1979 by a newer, larger front-wheel drive Kadett which not only shared its platform with Vauxhall's new Astra, but looked identical too. The days when Opels were original designs were finally over.

The 1973 Kadett was sold in Britain as the Vauxhall Chevette, but the German-built model was more attractive, with far neater front-end styling instead of the Chevette's drooping snout, better equipped and with a wider range of models.

Engine: 993cc (61 cu in), 4-cylinder
Power: 30kW (40bhp)
0–96km/h (60mph): 23.9 secs
Top speed: 123km/h (76mph)
Production total: 1,701,075

OPEL MANTA B-SERIES

Opel's replacement for the Manta A-Series was a much bigger and more mature car, based on the platform of the second-generation Ascona/Vauxhall Cavalier.

Engines varied from a weak 1.2-litre (73 cu in) entry-level unit which, hardly surprisingly, did not sell at all well, to a 1.9-litre (121 cu in) powerplant. A 1981 update saw new 1.8-litre (110 cu in) and 2-litre (122 cu in) units added.

A hatchback model, also sold as the Vauxhall Cavalier Sportshatch, appeared in 1978 and the Manta enjoyed a long production run, outliving its Vauxhall sister car by seven years.

It was more of a driver's car than the previous Manta,

Early B-Series Mantas were offered as two-door coupés only.

especially in 1981 GT/E form, where it was capable of 194km/h (120mph) and rapid acceleration.

The most interesting Manta was the limited production 400, built as a Group B rally homologation special. It came with a 2.4-litre (146 cu in) 16-valve Cosworth-developed engine and sported lightweight body panels, puffed-out wheelarches and additional cooling vents. It was very fast, but the handling was slightly suspect when driven flat out.

All B-Series Mantas had an enthusiastic group of fans, which kept the range alive until 1988 when Opel successfully silenced those who said coupés had become unfashionable by unveiling the stunning Opel Vectra/Vauxhall Cavalier-based Calibra.

A hatchback version appeared in 1978 and was also sold as the Vauxhall Cavalier Sportshatch in Britain. The German Manta's production run, however, was much longer than that of the British model.

Engine: 1979cc (121 cu in), 4-cylinder
Power: 82kW (110bhp)
0–96km/h (60mph): 8.5 secs
Top speed: 194km/h (120mph)
Production total: 603,000

OPEL MONZA

The Monza was a big and very practical hatchback coupé based on the Opel Senator, with a 3-litre (181 cu in) engine and a choice of five-speed manual or four-speed automatic gearboxes.

Despite its bulk, the Monza was a surprisingly agile performance car, with tenacious grip and fine handling, although the rear end could slide dramatically if pressed too hard.

Equipment levels were high, but this was reflected in the relatively high prices. Nonetheless, the Monza was a successful niche market car for GM and was sold for a limited period as the Vauxhall Royale, which accounted for an extra 7000 sales in the UK between 1978 and 1984.

The 3-litre (181 cu in) straight-six engine was fantastic, with 179lb ft (243Nm) of torque at a relatively low 4800rpm. This meant it had flexible in-gear performance, while remaining very refined when cruising at high speeds.

Although reliable and well made, early Monzas rotted dramatically, especially in damp climates. Sales of all coupés slumped across Europe in the early 1980s, and by the time production ended in 1986, Monza sales were almost zero.

Thanks to its torquey engine, agile performance and lavishly equipped interior, the Monza enjoyed a long production run even though it was relatively expensive. This is a 1983 model, with a facelifted front end. By the mid-1980s, however, coupés were becoming unfashionable.

Engine: 2968cc (181 cu in), 6-cylinder
Power: 134kW (180bhp)
0–96km/h (60mph): 215km/h (133mph)
Top speed: 8.5 secs
Production total: 43,500

OSCA 1600

Engine: 1568cc (96 cu in), 4-cylinder
Power: 104kW (140bhp)
0–96km/h (60mph): 8.2 secs
Top speed: 210km/h (130mph)
Production total: n/a

The Maserati brothers, who had sold their own company to the Orsi family in 1937 to avoid bankruptcy, only returned to small-scale performance car production at the start of

the 1960s. Their biggest commercial success was the OSCA 1600, based on the floorpan of the Fiat 1600S, which boasted superb handling and lively

performance from its twin-camshaft engine. OSCA tuned the engine to deliver as much as 104kW (140bhp) – very impressive for a 1.6-litre (96 cu in) unit even today – but the units were extremely fragile, with peak power at a valve-bending 7200rpm.

Buyers could choose their own body styling, although most opted for the cheapest and arguably prettiest option of a Zagato-designed two-door coupé, reminiscent of Pininfarina's Ferrari 275GTS. Other stylists included Fissore and Vignale, and a handful of convertible OSCAs were also made. All were quality, hand-built cars with an exclusive price tag, and despite the small engines, were considered a genuine alternative to a Ferrari or Porsche.

Production ceased in 1967 when the Maserati brothers went into retirement and sold the OSCA factory to MV Augusta.

The Osca is like a baby Maserati, and was created by the same family as the legendary sports cars. This is a Zagato-styled coupé.

PACKARD TWIN-SIX

Legend has it that James Ward Packard was so disappointed with his new Winton Phaeton that he returned it to the factory with some suggestions for improvement. Alexander Winton was dismissive to say the least, so he set out to design and develop a much better car of his own from his home in Warren, Ohio, USA. It helped that he was a graduate in engineering.

The first Packard appeared in 1899 and was considered so well engineered that prominent businessman Henry B. Joy invested in the company, taking control completely in 1903.

Packard soon earned a reputation for technical innovation, and introduced the first commercially viable V12 engine in 1915. The Packard Twin-Six was a luxury model aimed at wealthy owners, and was a huge success, earning itself a reputation for image and build quality.

The company received a huge boost when US President Warren Gamaliel Harding – later notorious for his extraordinarily lavish lifestyle – decided to use a Twin-Six for official duties, and his was the first presidential inauguration in which the newly elected head of state travelled to the ceremony by car.

Despite labour-intensive build methods, Packard managed to construct over 35,000 Twin-Sixes in eight years, before eventually replacing the model with the in-line Single Eight in 1923.

Not even Cadillac could compete with the luxury offered by the Twin-Six. It was designed entirely in-house and came with the first production V12 engine. Packard received excellent publicity when President Harding rode to his inauguration in one.

Engine: 6950cc (424 cu in), V12-cylinder
Power: n/a
0–96km/h (60mph): n/a
Top speed: n/a
Production total: 35,046

PACKARD STANDARD 8

1930–36

An iconic luxury car, the Packard Standard 8 was a beautifully built, finely engineered and sumptuously equipped motor car.

Power came from a 5.3-litre (326 cu in) side-valve straight eight, which offered good performance for its era, while the mechanical layout was utterly conventional. Built on a separate chassis, the 8 used a spiral bevel final drive unit and semi-elliptic leaf springs all round. Inside, wood and leather prevailed, with very comfortable seats and vast rear legroom, as many Packard owners preferred to be driven rather than drive themselves. The tradition of presidential patronage, for example, continued for some time.

Initially available with an upright grille and individual mudguards, a bigger and more streamlined model replaced the successful original car in 1932, with the option of a longer wheelbase and split-folding roof, along with a chrome-plated radiator mounting and wider running boards.

The final incarnation of the Standard 8 appeared in 1935 and was in production for just over a year. It featured a more aerodynamic sloping grille and

could be ordered as an elegant drophead coupé for the few users who preferred to drive without a chauffeur. It was replaced by the smaller and more economical Eight/120.

Photographs don't begin to convey the sheer size of the Standard Eight. It was almost 6m (18ft) long and so became a prestigious symbol for kings, presidents and other politicians.

Engine: 5342cc (326 cu in), 8-cylinder
Power: n/a
0–96km/h (60mph): n/a
Top speed: 121km/h (75mph)
Production total: 64,871

PACKARD EIGHT/120

1938–39

A Packard for the masses? The Eight marked a highly significant move downmarket for the company, but over 40,000 were sold in two years.

A move downmarket for Packard, the 120 was nevertheless a successful and desirable car. Initially launched as the Eight, the name was changed to 120 after just six months in a bid to distance the car from Packard's more luxury-orientated cars. Styling was neat, with fared-in mudguards, a sloping grille and V-shaped windscreen.

The 120 offered legendary build quality and technical supremacy to the middle classes and was keenly priced, making it a popular seller against more mainstream Oldsmobiles, Chevrolets and Fords, which were less luxurious but had similar prices.

Several coachbuilt body styles were available, the most popular

being a four-door touring saloon. But buyers could also have a two-door sporting coupé, a drophead convertible saloon, a shorter coupé-shaped convertible or a stretched limousine. All were good, solid cars to drive, while the addition of overdrive for the 1939 model year

made them more economical than many of their contemporaries. But the cheapening of the Packard name and the subsequent effect on its image would have serious ramifications for the company in later years, despite initially boosting sales.

Engine: 4620cc (282 cu in), 8-cylinder
Power: n/a
0–96km/h (60mph): n/a
Top speed: 135km/h (84mph)
Production total: 40,271

PACKARD CARIBBEAN

Packard's descent into the mass market saw the company lose ground to prestige marques such as Cadillac, while the resultant loss of status saw many previous clients swap their allegiance for fear that their Packards were no longer regarded as upper class.

Few postwar cars ever revived the firm's 1930s glory days, but there was one that came very close. Launched in 1952, the Caribbean was a stunning machine that posed a serious threat to Cadillac's equally enormous Eldorado convertible. Designed by Richard Teague, the soft-top Packard had

Unfortunately, the interior of the Caribbean was austere and luxury car buyers preferred the comfort and trimmings offered by Cadillac. The Caribbean finally proved to be a sales disaster.

an imposing chrome snout, a massive wheelbase and continental-style rear wheel carrier, although it still used an old side-valve straight-eight engine.

A Deliberately limited production run kept the Caribbean desirable, but the Packard brand couldn't compete with the glamour of Cadillac in the early 1950s and

The Caribbean was a huge and impressive motor car, and its ornate styling by Richard Teague was years ahead of rival manufacturers.

had already lost much of its earlier prestigious image. In a desperate bid to move back upmarket, Packard bought ailing carmaker Studebaker in 1954, but the massively debt-ridden company proved to be instrumental in Packard's own downfall. Despite an exciting new range of cars launched in 1956, sales continued to waiver, and Packard was forced to close in 1958.

Engine: 5358cc (327 cu in), 8-cylinder
Power: 156kW (210bhp)
0–96km/h (60mph): 12 secs
Top speed: 174km/h (108mph)
Production total: 1150

PANHARD DYNA

The Dyna was a fascinating and truly innovative car, despite its ugly, bug-eyed looks. Designed before World War II, it didn't appear until 1946 when it became a popular choice for motorists on a tight budget.

Power came from a front-mounted 610cc (37 cu in) flat-twin engine that was so simple to take in and out that most repairs resulted in a new engine. It was cheaper and less labour intensive to replace the whole unit rather than repair it, and many specialists used to offer exchanges on reconditioned units taken from other examples.

Drive was via a four-speed overdrive gearbox – at a time when most rivals made do with non-synchromesh three-speed ones – while other modern features included a hydraulic braking system, lightweight unitary construction bodywork with light alloy panels, and fully-independent suspension.

Later cars had a choice of 745cc (45 cu in) or 850cc (52 cu in) versions of the flat-twin engine, the larger of which could reach 130km/h (80mph). The Dyna was technologically brilliant, but not sold in sufficient numbers to have the fan-base it deserved.

The Dyna, Panhard's budget car, was a genuine alternative to other innovative small cars, especially the highly successful Citroën 2CV, and was advanced for its time with hydraulic brakes and a synchromesh gearbox. It deserved a far greater level of recognition.

Engine: 610cc (37 cu in), 2-cylinder
Power: 18kW (24bhp)
0–96km/h (60mph): n/a
Top speed: 100km/h (62mph)
Production total: 55,000

PANHARD DYNA 54

The 1946 Panhard Dyna was a modern car, with fully independent suspension, four gears and hydraulic brakes, but it would be the Dyna 54 that really established Panhard as a maker of technically advanced but quirky cars – with a rather unusual appearance.

Despite having a tiny air-cooled twin-cylinder engine, the Dyna 54 was a lively performer, while keeping the engine and drivetrain ahead of the cabin meant interior space could be maximized; six people could travel in a Dyna 54, albeit somewhat uncomfortably squashed together.

The strange bug-eyed body was made from light alloy to keep weight to a minimum, while the superb aerodynamics meant the Dyna 54 was economical, too. Later Dyna 57 and Dyna 58 had increased power output and front coil springs instead of torsion bars.

dramatic change of policy after World War II saw Panhard develop a new range of air-cooled twin-cylinder engines and shift its marketing strategy to a more mainstream audience. Panhards

were now perceived as affordable cars for the masses, but offered more in the way of luxury and innovation than equivalent machines from Citroën, Renault and Peugeot.

Even more than the 1946 Dyna, the looks of Dyna 54 were an acquired taste – and many did acquire it – but the technology underneath was enough to impress visitors to the 1953 Paris Motor Show.

Engine: 851cc (52 cu in), 2-cylinder
Power: 37kW (50bhp)
0–96km/h (60mph): 24.3 secs
Top speed: 148km/h (92mph)
Production total: 155,000

PANHARD PL17

The Dyna 54's successor kept costs to a minimum by using the platform and central body panels of the earlier car, although this time the body was all-steel rather than lightweight alloy, which meant it had a tendency to rust quickly.

Challenging, futuristic styling, the norm for a Panhard, was married to class-leading aerodynamics and economy and the same six-person seating capacity as its predecessor.

The PL17 Tigre of 1961 is perhaps the most interesting, with its twin-choke 45kW (60bhp) engine and 145km/h (90mph) cruising potential, although a Panhard in any guise is never a boring car, especially if you value alternative designs. All-synchromesh gearbox from 1962 made the PL17 a much

It was always pleasant to drive and technologically brilliant but, unfortunately, the PL17 was often riddled with rust.

PL17 convertibles were a rare sigh as they were very expensive – almost twice the price of saloons – but it was one of the first open-top cars where the roof folded flush with the rear scuttle panel.

nicer machine to drive, while hydraulic brakes and supple suspension made it a good, if underpowered, touring car.

It was also offered as a two-doo convertible, with a roof that folde almost flat against the rear tonnea – one of the first cars with this feature. The drop-top was well designed, but its cleverness came a price and sales were quite limite – convertibles were almost twice the price of saloons and rusted even more badly.

Engine: 851cc (52 cu in), 2-cylinder
Power: 45kW (60bhp)
0–96km/h (60mph): 22.6 secs
Top speed: 145km/h (90mph)
Production total: 130,000

PANHARD 24-SERIES

1963–67

While carmakers across Europe were busy making money out of nondescript mass market cars, the French decided to throw away the entire rule book. At the time of the car industry's fastest growth, throughout the 1950s and 1960s, Gallic car manufacturers were busy trying out startling new ideas that challenged the conventional – and, in the process, they created some of the world's oddest, yet most beautiful, classics.

One such example is the Panhard 24CT. Loosely based on the PL17, the CT had an unusual but effective trapezoidal roofline, angular rear end, fared-in headlight lenses and a sharp aerodynamic snout.

The engine was taken from the PL17, but like the earlier car, the 24 always felt a lot quicker than its performance on paper would suggest. However, despite being one of the most technologically advanced and strikingly styled cars on the market, the 24CT never sold in great numbers. But this is not surprising, as for the same price as the tinny flat-twin coupé, buyers could invest in an equally unusual, but much more practical, Citroën DS22.

Engine: 848cc (52 cu in), 2-cylinder
Power: 37kW (50bhp)
0–96km/h (60mph): n/a
Top speed: 145km/h (90mph)
Production total: 23,245

Even more striking designs from Packard – the 24-Series cars were angular and dramatic, but were also expensive and impractical.

PANHARD CD

1963–65

Engine: 848cc (52 cu in), 2-cylinder
Power: 45kW (60bhp)
0–96km/h (60mph): 10 secs
Top speed: 169km/h (105mph)
Production total: 92

In a determined bid to prove just how effective Panhard's air-cooling and aerodynamic designs were, director Charles Deutsch decided to commission a racing project that would take the small French manufacturer to Le Mans.

The Packard CD was a truly surprising success, winning its class in the 1962 24-hour race with comparative ease, proving remarkably reliable when run at consistently high speeds.

To celebrate, Panhard put the CD into limited production as a road car, although its price matched that of some much more expensive exotica. The oddball glassfibre bodywork was mounted on a tubular steel backbone chassis, keeping weight to a minimum and offering phenomenal acceleration from such a small power unit.

The CD wasn't a comfortable car, with seating strictly for two (small) people. But it was immense fun to drive, with tactile handling, a fantastic exhaust note and the ability to embarrass many more powerful cars in competition. Just 92 cars were built over three years, before Panhard was bought by Citroën and the CD was dropped. The Panhard marque died in 1967.

The CD racer took its name from Panhard director Charles Deutsch's initials.

PANHARD ET LEVASSOR

Réné Panhard, financier, and Emile Levassor, designer, the pioneers of motoring and renowned industrial engineers, produced their first car in 1891.

The first example had a 566cc (35 cu in) V-twin engine designed and developed by Gottlieb Daimler in Germany and used in his cars as early as 1889. The Panhard et Levassor was similar in concept to

Daimler's cars, too, with the small engine mounted below the car, aft of the rear axle. The rear wheels were driven by a simple chain arrangement, while rudimentary cart springs, solid rubber tyres on wood rims and tiller steering were also used.

Panhard was the first manufacturer to successfully complete a long-distance drive

when, in 1892, the company's founders drove the 'Hippolyte' horseless carriage from Paris to Nice to demonstrate the birth of a new age in mobility. The journey, which would take about seven hours today, took nine days, although this included a break to rebuild the engine.

Development of the Panhard et Levassor continued apace, and by

1895 the Daimler engine had been replaced by a vertical twin of Panhard's own design, while the company's first four-cylinder engine appeared in 1898.

Engine: 566cc (35 cu in), V-twin
Power: n/a
0–96km/h (60mph): n/a
Top speed: 32km/h (20mph) approx
Production total: n/a

PANTHER J72

The brainchild of the British businessman Bob Jankel, Panther was a car company that based its appeal on nostalgia fitted into a modern package. It worked – up to a point – but the cars were very ostentatious and overpriced so that they appealed only to the extrovert rich. Indeed, one of Panther's first customers was actress and film star Elizabeth Taylor.

Jankel's first project, the J72, looked like an amateurish replica of the fabulous Jaguar SS100, albeit with modern Jaguar running gear, a choice of straight-six or V12 engines, also from the Browns Lane Jaguar factory in Coventry, and a unique tubular frame. Thanks to minimal weight, the J72 had astonishing acceleration, but top speeds were restricted by poor

aerodynamics, meaning the six-cylinder cars could muster only 185km/h (115mph).

They were dramatic to drive, too, with a crude ride thanks to rigid front and rear axles, heavy steering with a very direct linkage and brutal power delivery. High build quality and exclusivity were the appeal but, in 1972, a J72 cost as much as a new Jaguar E-Type V12.

It might have looked like a thirties Jaguar, but the J72 came with a modern 5.3-litre V12 engine. Low weight and impressive acceleration made it a handful to drive.

Engine: 5343cc (326 cu in), V12-cylinder
Power: 198kW (266bhp)
0–96km/h (60mph): 6.4 secs
Top speed: 219km/h (136mph)
Production total: 300

PANTHER FF

1974–75

Although the Panther FF was a uniquely interesting project, it was quite clearly doomed to failure from the outset. Under orders from the Swiss coachbuilder Willy Felber, Panther was to create a car that looked like the classic Ferrari 375 using contemporary Ferrari running gear.

This meant that not only did the finished product exhibit terrible handling characteristics, a complete lack of practicality and an exorbitant price tag, but a Ferrari had to be butchered in order to provide its engine and transmission.

Most cars were powered by engines from the Italian company's 330GTC, but Felber himself is rumoured to have driven one that used a broken Ferrari 365GTB Daytona as a base. This unique hybrid was sprayed metallic purple. Official production figures were never released, but it's rumoured there were seven production cars and five prototypes.

Engine: 3967cc (242 cu in), V12-cylinder
Power: 223kW (300bhp)
0–96km/h (60mph): n/a
Top speed: 258km/h (160mph)
Production total: 12

PANTHER DEVILLE

1974–85

Not content with trying to replicate the Jaguar SS100, Panther turned its attentions to creating a pastiche of another globally renowned classic. The 1974 Deville was loosely based on the Bugatti Royale and featured a tubular chassis, all-round disc brakes, power steering, an exquis-itely trimmed cabin and, bizarrely, the doors from an Austin Maxi. The rarer two-door convertible looked less awkward, and in this format, the Panther came with doors from an MGB.

Again Panther turned to Jaguar for the engine, either a 4.2-litre (256 cu in) six or 5.3-litre (326 cu in) V12. While there's no denying the Deville had presence on the road, it cost as much as a Rolls-Royce Silver Shadow and was sold in strictly limited numbers throughout its 11-year production life.

The convertible cost even more, and enjoyed the dubious accolade of being Britain's most expensive car.

Engine: 5343cc (326 cu in), V12-cylinder
Power: 168kW (266bhp)
0–96km/h (60mph): 8.8 secs
Top speed: 221km/h (137mph)
Production total: 60

PANTHER RIO

1975–77

After the oil crises of the mid-70s hit luxury car sales so severely, Panther decided to offer a fuel-efficient model in its line up. The Panther Rio was based on the Triumph Dolomite and shared its floorpan, running gear and engines, although with electric windows and power steering, and the interior was completely retrimmed, with deep pile Wilton carpets and Connolly leather. The design was squared off and finished with a Rolls-Royce style grille, flanked by the headlights of a very much more humble Ford Granada.

As a concept, the Rio wasn't a wholly bad idea, but in practice it failed miserably. The extra weight, coupled with the Dolomite Sprint's high-compression 16-valve engine, meant fuel consumption struggled to top 8l/100km (23mpg), performance was too slow for Panther fans and the asking price of £8,995 (enough to buy three Dolomite Sprints) alienated buyers.

Engine: 1998cc (122 cu in), 4-cylinder
Power: 96kW (129bhp)
0–96km/h (60mph): 9.9 secs
Top speed: 185km/h (115mph)
Production total: 34

PANTHER LIMA

1976–82

By far Panther's most successful model, the Lima was the most affordable way to own one of Bob Jankel's idiosyncratic nostalgia cars. The Lima was developed on a Vauxhall Magnum platform, which gave it far more compliant handling than Panthers of old, while the lightweight GRP bodywork took most of its strength from an MG Midget tub, doors and windscreen.

Although cramped, bumpy to travel in and lacking in refinement compared to the previous Panthers, the Lima had the advantage of being affordable and, for a short time at least, was offered as an unusual special edition in a few hand-picked Vauxhall dealerships in the UK. Financial problems caused by low sales and mounting debts forced Bob Jankel to sell Panther to a conglomerate of Korean enthusiasts in 1981, and the Lima was developed further. Reborn and renamed Kallista, the last version of the car dropped the Vauxhall floorpan and suspension in favour of a unique tubular chassis and Ford Cortina wishbones, while GM engines were swapped in favour of straight-four and V6 Ford units.

Although superbly built throughout its life, the Lima always lacked the necessary refinement to become a true success.

Engine: 2279cc (139 cu in), 4-cylinder
Power: 133kW (178bhp)
0–96km/h (60mph): 8.9 secs
Top speed: 202km/h (125mph)
Production total: 918

Panther's most successful car, the Lima, was initially offered through Vauxhall dealerships. Later cars, badged Kallista, used Ford engines and running gear.

PANTHER SOLO

1989–9(

The Panther Solo could have been a brilliant success, but was sadly marred by underdevelopment and a lack of investment.

The stunning aluminium composite and glassfibre bodywork was designed by respected designer Ken Greenley and won many plaudits when it was unveiled at the 1989 Earls Court Motor Show, while incredible handling, thanks to a Ferguson Formula four-wheel drive set-up, won plenty of admirers.

Power came from a 152kW (204bhp) Ford Cosworth engine based on that of the Sierra RS Cosworth and, while it offered potent acceleration, all-out speed and refinement were lacking. The

unit proved noisy at high revs, while further hindrances included lack of luggage space and a cramped cockpit.

From the outset, Panther said it would build only 100 Solos and was determined the model would become a lasting testament to its engineering abilities, marking the way forward for future expansion. But financial difficulties, largely caused by the Solo's development costs, saw production cease after just 12 had been built.

Engine: 1993cc (123 cu in), 4-cylinder
Power: 152kW (204bhp)
0–96km/h (60mph): 6.8 secs
Top speed: 232km/h (144mph)
Production total: 12

Britain's stillborn supercar had the looks and the handling, but the engin was bought in from Ford and Panther hit financial difficulties.

PEERLESS

1958–6(

The Peerless was an interesting project, but like so many 1950s specials, it never fulfilled its early promise. Based on Triumph TR3 mechanicals and using the same 75kW (100bhp) 1991cc (121 cu in) engine, the car was built on a unique spaceframe chassis and had glassfibre bodywork, making it much quicker than the Triumph on which it was based.

The two-door coupé body was fairly spacious and comfortable and although the stiff ride was really quite uncomfortable on bumpy roads, a De Dion rear end meant that handling was both safe and predictable.

A Phase Two model appeared in 1959 and featured recessed headlights and a simpler one-piece body, but despite modern, elegant

lines and a realistic price tag, a lack of corporate investment saw Peerless go the way of so many small manufacturers of the period and, eventually, bankruptcy forced the company to close its doors in 1960.

The car was briefly revived in 1961 under the name Warwick, this time with a different grille, tailfins and the option of the Buick

3.5-litre (213 cu in) V8 that later went on to power countless Rove However, once again, slow sales meant production ceased after another 45 cars were made.

Engine: 1991cc (121 cu in), 4-cylinder
Power: 75kW (100bhp)
0–96km/h (60mph): 12.3 secs
Top speed: 189km/h (117mph)
Production total: 290

PEGASO Z102

1951–5(

As founder of the most famous Italian sporting brand, Enzo Ferrari developed a reputation for speaking his mind and – not uncommonly – upsetting other industry movers and shakers. Perhaps the most famous was when he pulled out of a deal with Ford that prompted the Blue Oval to build the GT40 in 1965 in order to get its own back and beat Ferrari at Le Mans.

But five years before that, another manufacturer was busy getting even. Ferrari had said Pegaso chief Don Wilfredo Ricart wore thick rubber-soled shoes to stop his brain from getting any shocks, and in response to the insult, the Spanish truck maker

Pegaso normally made lorries – but there was nothing at all truck-like about the beautiful styling of the Z102 coupé.

decided to make a very fast coup that would be able to beat Ferrari at its own game.

The Z102 appeared in 1951 an came with a specially designed quad camshaft V8, with power outputs ranging from 142kW (190bhp) to as much as 268kW (360bhp).

Built entirely at the Pegaso factory in Barcelona, Spain, it als had a five-speed gearbox, a state-of-the-art pressed platform chassi and a very complicated steering linkage. Apart from a high noise level, its greatest problem was the high price. A brutally fast car, it was surprisingly agile to drive.

Engine: 3178cc (194 cu in), V8-cylinder
Power: 205kW (275bhp)
0–96km/h (60mph): 7 secs
Top speed: 258km/h (160mph)
Production total: 112 (inc Z103)

PEGASO Z103

More stylish than the Z102 and with a new, even more powerful engine, the Z103 was touted as the most advanced performance car ever. But strangely, the technology used was archaic compared to that put into its predecessor. While the engine put out higher power figures – as much as 298kW (400bhp) was rumoured in tuned cars – it used simple overhead-

valve technology instead of the Z102's complex but fascinating quad camshaft set-up.

The Z103 used the same steel bodywork construction methods as the Z102, but used less metal and was subsequently lighter, making it a faster but very much scarier car to drive, with an extremely unstable back end and severely limited grip.

Despite the immense power output and Formula One-style production technology, neither the Z102 nor Z103 enjoyed much competition success, and by the late 1950s, Don Wilfredo Ricart had lost interest and dropped Pegaso's sports car projects, concentrating instead on the firm's core output of trucks and buses. In eight years, Pegaso had built just

over 100 sports cars – Z102 and Z103 – and had certainly proved its point, albeit at phenomenal expense to both itself and those who bought them.

Engine: 3988cc (243 cu in), V8-cylinder
Power: 261kW (350bhp)
0–96km/h (60mph): 5.5 secs
Top speed: 274km/h (170mph)
Production total: 112 (inc Z102)

PEUGEOT 190

Peugeot has a history that other manufacturers can only feel envious about, with continuous car production since 1889, despite a merger with former rivals, Citroën, in the mid-1970s.

The most popular Peugeot of the prewar period was the unusual but inexpensive Quadrilette, a bizarre two-seater small car in which the passenger was seated directly behind the driver.

The 190, which first appeared in 1928, was slightly more sophisticated, with conventional flat-nosed styling, disc wheels and a familiar drop-away rear end. Based on an improved version of the Quadrilette chassis, the 190

was limited by the original car's dimensions, and while the two passengers could now sit side-by-side, conditions were still exceptionally cramped. For all that, it was inexpensive and popular.

Not bad to drive by the standards of the era, the 190 had an effective gear linkage direct to the rear axle and a surprisingly compliant three-speed gearbox. However, the archaic four-cylinder side-valve engine was very unresponsive.

Engine: 719cc (44 cu in), 4-cylinder
Power: n/a
0–96km/h (60mph): n/a
Top speed: 94km/h (58mph)
Production total: 33,674

Not an exciting car, but bread-and-butter motoring for thousands of French families. The 190 was Peugeot's first mass-produced saloon and had a pleasant gearbox, but the engine was old-fashioned even when new.

PEUGEOT 402

Regular Peugeot buyers weren't quite ready for the 402 when it appeared in 1939. In place of the

familiar upright, conventional Peugeot look came something that was altogether different.

The 402 took streamlining to the point of excess, with the headlights concealed inside an art-deco radiator grille, horizontal bonnet cooling fins and stylized rear wheel spats.

The car was intended as the answer to the technologically innovative Citroën Traction Avant, although underneath its rather futuristic skin it was a standard machine, with cantilever suspension (independent at the front) rear-wheel drive, a three-speed synchromesh gearbox and a

Weird streamlined looks and concealed headlamps gave the 402 a menacing air, but the driving experience didn't match the cutting-edge styling. It would have been a big seller, but the outbreak of World War II meant production ended prematurely.

very conventional four-cylinder overhead-valve engine.

In other circumstances, the 402 could have been a massive success for Peugeot. The company sold almost 80,000 in its first year, but then World War II broke out and production was shelved.

Interesting variants of the 402 included the 402L, which used the smaller bodyshell of the 302 coupled to the 402's engine and transmission, as well as the stunning 402DS racing coupé, of which 200 were built. It could top 150km/h (95mph), and had styling reminiscent of contemporary coachbuilt Delahayes.

Engine: 1991cc (121 cu in), 4-cylinder
Power: n/a
0–96km/h (60mph): n/a
Top speed: 129km/h (80mph)
Production total: 79,862

PEUGEOT 202

1938–48

Launched alongside the 402, the 202 was, in effect, a scaled-down version of the bigger car, with an all-new overhead-valve four-cylinder engine, quarter-elliptic rear leaf springs in place of cantilever suspension and a much shorter wheelbase.

The transmission worked in much the same way, with a three-speed all-synchromesh change making it a pleasant, if somewhat leisurely, car to drive.

The same futuristic styling as the 402 hinted at Citroën's then secret 2CV project, with integral wings and a swooping bonnet.

Fortunately for Peugeot, all the 202's factory tooling survived the war and production of the car was restarted following a six-year break in February 1945, before the conflict had, in fact, officially ended.

Peugeot sold another 40,000 cars between 1945 and 1948. The 202's replacement, the 203, featured up-to-the-minute styling, an excellent new engine and rack-and-pinion steering, plus a four-speed gearbox. A durable car, it went on to sell over 600,000 units across Europe, before it was withdrawn in 1960.

Engine: 1133cc (69 cu in), 4-cylinder
Power: 22kW (30bhp)
0–96km/h (60mph): n/a
Top speed: 96km/h (60mph)
Production total: 104,126

PEUGEOT 403

1955–5(

Initially planned as a replacement for the popular 203, the 403 instead complemented the smaller car in Peugeot's line-up for its first five years. Similar in concept, but featuring larger Pininfarina-styled bodywork, the 403 was a spacious and well-built machine.

Basic models came with the 203's 1290cc (79 cu in) engine, although a bored-out 1468cc (90 cu in) version was also offered and, from 1959, buyers in France and Spain could choose a sluggish but highly economical 1.8-litre (110 cu in) diesel.

An estate model was offered from 1956 onwards and could be

The 403 was offered as an eight-seat estate (above) from 1956.

specified with eight seats arrange(in three rows – suggesting the 40: was significantly ahead of its time given the current popularity of people carriers and SUVs.

A Décapotable cabriolet model was also offered between 1956 an(1963, although this accounted for only 2000 of the 403's seven-figu(production run.

In most other respects, the 403 was a very conventional machine, but the huge sales and successful exports were instrumental in bringing Peugeot – and the Frencl economy – back from the brink o(postwar bankruptcy.

Although very popular, the 403 (left) was a conventional saloon.

Engine: 1290cc (79 cu in), 4-cylinder
Power: 40kW (54bhp)
0–96km/h (60mph): 29.5 secs
Top speed: 121km/h (75mph)
Production total: 1,119,460

PEUGEOT 404

1960–75

Another Pininfarina-designed saloon, the 404 bore more than a passing resemblance to the Austin Cambridge/Morris Oxford saloons offered in Britain, also styled by the Italian design house.

The 404 was an elegant and well-finished machine, with compliant handling thanks to its independent front suspension and sharp, well-weighted steering. Entry-level models came with the 403's 1.5-litre (90 cu in) engine, although a new 1.6-litre (98 cu in) model, based on the old unit, was also offered with a lively 63kW (85bhp) on tap. Some cars were fuel injected, pushing the power output up to a class-leading 72kW (96bhp) and giving the 404 genuine 160km/h (100mph) cruising ability.

Like the 403, Peugeot offered estate versions, as well as an eight-seater Familiale model, while an improved 39kW (53bhp) 2-litre (122 cu in) diesel unit was introduced to satisfy the growth in popularity of this fuel in France.

Peugeot also offered coupé and

cabriolet versions of the 404, although these looked completely different from the saloon and were available only with the 1.6-litre (98 cu in) engine, with or without fuel injection.

BMC's lawyers might have had something to say about the 404 – its Pininfarina-styled bodywork was almost identical to the Morris Oxford and Austin Cambridge saloons, styled by the same designer.

Engine: 1468cc (90 cu in), 4-cylinder
Power: 48kW (65bhp)
0–96km/h (60mph): 22 secs
Top speed: 135km/h (84mph)
Production total: 2,769,361

PEUGEOT 504

1968–82

All-round independent suspension, all-round disc brakes and a new range of powerful engines marked out the 504 as an impressive car, with a supple ride, informative handling and Peugeot's usual high

standards of finish. 504 saloons almost immediately replaced the 404, but the former car sold in small numbers until 1975, primarily in estate form. The estate version of the 504 didn't appear

The beautiful convertible was a far cry from the ugly-duckling 504 saloon and later estate models. However, they were all really great to drive and had well-packaged interiors.

until 1971, but was truly massive. The usual eight-seat Familiale option and fold-flat rear bench made them immensely useful, and they're still on sale new in emerging markets such as North Africa, where they make ideal, tough and easy-to-fix runabouts.

Petrol engines were either 1.8-litre (110 cu in) or 2-litre (120 cu in) fours, both with ample performance and a fuel-injection system offered as an option from launch. 2-litre (120 cu in) diesels were also available, initially borrowed from the 403 until a much-improved 2.1- (128 cu in) and more powerful 2.3-litre (140 cu in) unit appeared from 1977 onwards.

European sales ceased in 1982 when the 505 came out, although the 504's frontal bodywork and engines continued until 1993 in the 504 delivery van or pick-up.

Engine: 1971cc (120 cu in), 4-cylinder
Power: 72kW (97bhp)
0–96km/h (60mph): 12.4 secs
Top speed: 166km/h (103mph)
Production total: 2,836,837

PEUGEOT 304

1969–80

The 304 was based to a large extent on the 204 and shared the original car's excellent overhead-camshaft engines, which had been introduced in 1965, front-wheel drive, independent suspension and servo brakes, although the 204's column-shift gearchange was switched to the floor for the new model.

Diminutive but lively engines, with the exception of the bad, but very economical 1.3-litre (79 cu in) diesel, were offered in mainland Europe. A sporty S model had a 1.3-litre (79 cu in) petrol unit and anti-roll bars, plus a 160km/h (100mph) top speed.

A confusing myriad of models was offered, consisting of a conventional four-door saloon,

five-door and three-door estates, a neat but severely impractical two-door coupé and a very attractive, but seldom seen, two-seater convertible.

All 304s were well equipped and had entertaining handling, making them a far more interesting and exciting alternative to their contemporary European rivals,

By far the most attractive 304 was the two-seater convertible, but most of the 1.25 million cars built were saloons. Buyers could also choose an estate or an unusual, but impractical, two-door coupé.

such as the Ford Escort, Austin Allegro and Renault 12. The 304's only real weakness was a rust problem, meaning few cars survived past the 1980s. It was replaced by the neat but less attractive 305, with no convertible or coupé option.

Engine: 1127cc (69 cu in), 4-cylinder
Power: 34kW (45bhp)
0–96km/h (60mph): 14.7 secs
Top speed: 158km/h (98mph)
Production total: 1,292,770

PEUGEOT 205GTi

1984–94

Engine: 1905cc (116 cu in), 4-cylinder
Power: 97kW (130bhp)
0–96km/h (60mph): 7.8 secs
Top speed: 195km/h (121mph)
Production total: n/a

It was the hot hatch darling of the 1980s – the 205 GTi was a fine handling, great-looking and phenomenally quick little car. The 1.6-litre version had better balance than the 1.9 pictured (left).

It might have been expensive, but the GTi had a basic interior almost identical to standard 205s, although the sports seats were comfortable and supportive. Its demise in 1994 was a disappointment to its many young fans.

It might not have started the GTi craze – that accolade belongs to the VW Golf – but the 205 quickly became a much-loved icon of the GTi generation.

The original 1984 engine wasn't, in fact, that good, producing just 78kW (105bhp) but, by 1986, two models were offered that handled and performed brilliantly – an 86kW (115bhp) 1.6-litre (98 cu in)

and a 97kW (130bhp) 1.9-litre (116 cu in).

The GTi proved just how effective Peugeot's popular supermini could be with these more powerful engines and it quickly established itself as the best 'hot hatch' of the 1980s, with grin-inducing handling, a firm ride and a popular image, especially with younger drivers. On the limit,

handling could be a real test of driver skill, however, as the car, particularly the 1.9 version, had a twitchy rear end.

Spiralling insurance premiums and new emissions legislation killed off the 205 GTi in 1994, much to the disappointment of its many fans, although the car's spirit lived on in the equally thrilling 106 GTi, launched in 1992.

PIERCE-ARROW SILVER ARROW

1933

struggling American manufacturer Pierce-Arrow, which was under the wing of the ailing Studebaker company, was bought out by a conglomerate of Buffalo, NY businessmen in 1933.

Their first project was to create a car that would steal the show at the 1933 Chicago World's Fair – which they achieved. Designed by stylist Philip Wright, a close friend

of Pierce-Arrow vice-president Roy Faulkner, the Silver Arrow was billed as, 'The car built in the 1930s for the 1940s'.

It was, quite simply, stunning, with handcrafted teardrop-shaped bodywork, an odd raised rear 'dormer' window and a pair of spare wheels stashed imaginatively behind 'secret panels' in the front wings.

Inside, plush velour seats and maple veneer made it very luxurious, while rear seat passengers had their own set of instruments – apparently to make sure the chauffeur was obeying the law – plus their own radio set built into a floor-mounted pod.

But while it was widely regarded as a forward-thinking and brilliantly conceived concept, the

Silver Arrow never made it into full-scale production, although 10 cars were built to order for wealthy buyers who loved the prototype – at a cost of over $7500 each.

Engine: 7030cc (429 cu in), V12-cylinder
Power: 175kW (235bhp)
0–96km/h (60mph): n/a
Top speed: 185km/h (115mph)
Production total: 10

PLYMOUTH PA

1931

Engine: 3213cc (196 cu in), 4-cylinder
Power: n/a
0–96km/h (60mph): n/a
Top speed: n/a
Production total: n/a

Conceived as an attempt to make Chrysler-built cars appeal to buyers on a budget, the Plymouth brand made its debut in 1928.

Its first own design was the PA, launched in 1931. An upright two-door saloon, coupé or convertible, the PA offered seating for four and a spacious, if somewhat spartan, interior.

Surprisingly advanced for a budget car, the PA also came with a three-speed floor-mounted gearbox, freewheel device and a Lockheed hydraulic braking system. Easy to drive and a lively performer, it also had limited success in the UK market, although it proved nowhere near so popular as in the United States, where it reached third place in the country's sales charts.

The PA was replaced by the near-identical looking PB for 1932, although this car had a stronger chassis, semi-elliptic leaf springs and a higher price tag. The PA and

PB set the precedent for a whole range of P-Series Plymouths, which grew increasingly more aerodynamic and more expensive until well into the 1950s.

There was nothing sensational about the PA's styling, but it was surprisingly modern underneath, with hydraulic brakes and a pleasant to use gearbox. Early Plymouths were marketed as budget cars with roomy, but hardly luxurious interiors. They sold well in the United States and also had some success in Britain.

PLYMOUTH P-19

1950

The last of the P-Series Plymouths which could trace its roots directly back to the company's birth in 1928, the P-19 symbolized all that was conventional about the Plymouth marque.

More advanced than previous P-Series models, it featured electric windscreen wipers in place of vacuum-operated units, but had ordinary, albeit curvaceous, styling

and the company's by-now familiar bull nose radiator grille.

It was also the last car to feature Plymouth's award-winning, but particularly irritating 'Safety Signal' speedometer, which would flash a green light on the dashboard at speeds of up to 48km/h (30mph), then start flashing amber up to 80km/h (50mph), before flashing red at

speeds over that. Most owners removed the fuse.

Other innovations in the P-Series that were evident on the P-19 were an interior light that came on and went off when the doors were opened and closed – a first – plus an ignition that worked by simply turning the key, a development that Plymouth quite falsely claimed it had invented.

Restyled and renamed Plymouths appeared for 1951, with the Concord, Cambridge and Cranbrook names replacing the 'P' designations.

Engine: 4260cc (260 cu in), V8-cylinder
Power: 124kW (167bhp)
0–96km/h (60mph): n/a
Top speed: n/a
Production total: n/a

PLYMOUTH FURY

1956–74

An all-American legend was born in 1956 in the form of the two-door Plymouth Fury, which went on to become one of the most popular models in American motoring history. With over 200 derivatives of Fury, the model was all things to all buyers.

The most spectacular examples were the late-1950s cars, which featured huge tailfins, twin headlights and a wraparound radiator grille to distinguish them from contemporary Chryslers and Dodges. Indeed, it was a 1958 Plymouth Grand Fury two-door coupé that achieved immortality – literally – in the Stephen King book and horror movie *Christine* as a car possessed by the devil.

Four-door models were offered soon after launch, although unlike many rivals, there wasn't a pillarless option.

The Fury remained distinctively styled well into the 1960s, before it became absorbed into Chrysler's characterless range of badge-

engineered three-box saloons and was robbed of its identity. The last interesting Furys were built in 1974, before all of Chrysler's saloons lost their style and became too fuel thirsty for the post-oil crisis market.

Engine: 5212cc (318 cu in), V8-cylinder
Power: 168kW (225bhp)
0–96km/h (60mph): 10.8 secs
Top speed: 169km/h (105mph)
Production total: n/a

This is the 1958 Fury, immortalize in the Stephen King book and movie *Christine*. With its hooded headlamps and big fins, it is regarded as the ultimate version.

PLYMOUTH ROAD RUNNER

1968–71

Built with the permission of Warner Brothers, the Road Runner featured the cartoon maker's fictional bird on the front wings to show it was more than a modified Belvedere sedan.

Cashing in on popular culture, Plymouth paid $50,000 to Warner Brothers for permission to use the eponymous cartoon bird on its budget muscle car. The Road Runner also came with the cartoon character's trademark 'meep-meep' horn, and also, like Wyle E Coyote's famous adversary, it was very fast.

Alloy wheels were offered on the options list, along with various styling tweaks, while the standard bonnet-mounted air scoops were merely cosmetic and did nothing to aid induction.

The Road Runner was offered as either a coupé or convertible with standard four-speed manual transmission or an optional three-

speed self-shifter. A new three-speed manual transmission appeared for 1970, when the engine acquired increased torque and Plymouth deemed the extra ratio unnecessary.

New emissions legislation killed the Road Runner's awesome performance in 1970 and the last cars saw their power output drop

by as much as 56kW (75bhp). The model name continued until 1974, but the last 'proper' cars were made in early 1971.

Engine: 6276cc (383 cu in), V8-cylinder
Power: 250kW (335bhp)
0–96km/h (60mph): 7.1 secs
Top speed: 182km/h (113mph)
Production total: 125,904

PLYMOUTH BARRACUDA

Later 'Cudas lacked the styling purity of earlier cars and were characterized by their stubby notchbacks and small rear quarterlights.

Ford's Mustang might have been the original and most successful 'Pony Car', but Plymouth wasn't far behind, unveiling its Barracuda the same year. In fact, the Plymouth appeared a fortnight before the Ford, but it couldn't offer the same combination of performance, value, sporty appearance and versatility.

The car was based on the Valiant saloon and shared its frontal styling, as well as its lower bodywork, while the conventional interior allowed seating for six on two benches. It featured distinctive styling, especially from the rear with its upright lamp clusters and huge curved screen, which wrapped round into the D-pillars. These would later appear on Chrysler (Europe) Sunbeam Alpine and Rapier models, which were almost identical to the Plymouth but in a scaled-down format.

The Barracuda's only innovation was its clever folding rear seat, which could almost disappear into the floor, allowing plenty of room for carrying loads.

A 'Formula S' performance option was introduced in 1965 with about 10 per cent more power, but the Barracuda was still unable to compete with the fastest Mustangs, or the newer offerings from Chevrolet and its sister company, Pontiac. The S-pack also helped the car's handling by needing firmer suspension bushes and anti-roll bars, which helped to reduce the standard model's bad handling when cornering at speed.

In 1967, an all-new Barracuda replaced the original and was a much more competitive proposition in the pony car market, thanks to a longer wheelbase and bigger engine range, lead by a 6.3-litre (384 cu in) V8, plus potent smaller units, although the base 5-litre (305 cu in) model still delivered a very modest 108kW (145bhp).

The wraparound rear screen had gone and three different body styles were now offered – a fastback coupé, a notchback coupé, or two-door, six-seat convertible.

Again, a Formula S pack was offered and came with suspension modifications, fatter tyres and a rev counter, plus Formula S decals.

The original Barracuda coupé looked remarkably similar to the Sunbeam Alpine Fastback, sold by Chrysler UK.

Power steering and a 246kW (330bhp) engine introduced in 1969 helped boost the 'Cuda's appeal, but it wasn't until 1970 that Plymouth got really serious about performance.

The Barracuda for the new decade was introduced in late 1970 and was almost unrecognizable when compared to the bland original model. Body panels, engines and transmission were shared with the equally muscular Dodge Challenger and, at last, Chrysler had created a brace of muscle cars that could match the might of Ford and GM.

Styling was almost a deliberate copy of the Chevy Camaro, with barrel sides, a four-headlight snout and pillarless coupé panels on hardtop models.

A poor 108kW (145bhp) entry-level engine was still on offer, later replaced by a 3.7-litre (226 cu in) straight-six, but the V8s were more potent than ever, especially when equipped with the tuned 7.2-litre (440 cu in) Hemi engine lifted from the Plymouth Superbird. This gave the Barracuda a sensational 0–96km/h (60mph) sprint ability of 5.2 seconds and a top speed of 233km/h (145mph).

Hemi-engined cars also came with a large bonnet scoop and, unlike most American cars with this feature, it was actually essential to the engine's induction efficiency; the additional air intake was routed directly to the carburettor housing.

Between 1970 and 1972, the Barracuda achieved considerable success both in the showroom and in competition, although it still remained a slow seller compared to the mighty Mustang.

The introduction of strict environmental legislation on emissions in 1972 saw the Hemi engines dropped and once again there was no 'Cuda available with more than 179kW (240bhp). That, combined with the energy crisis of the 1970s and economy and safety campaigns, marked the end of the Barracuda and it slipped away quietly in 1974, along with the gradual but inevitable demise of the muscle car era.

Engine: 4490cc (274 cu in), V8-cylinder
Power: 175kW (235bhp)
0–96km/h (60mph): 8.8 secs
Top speed: 181km/h (112mph)
Production total: 391,887

PLYMOUTH SUPERBIRD

1970

Despite both being part of the Chrysler Corporation, Plymouth and Dodge were keen rivals on America's national stock car tracks. After Dodge won the 1969 NASCAR championship with its Daytona, Plymouth's response was to design and develop the stunning Superbird, based on the Road Runner.

The huge rear wing and long sculpted snout might have looked dramatic, but Plymouth insisted that they were there purely for aerodynamic reasons.

NASCAR regulations meant that, in order to compete, at least one car had to be sold by each of the manufacturer's dealers, so in

the end Plymouth built 1,920 Superbirds, each with a huge rear aerofoil and sculpted shark nose styling, plus trademark fluorescent green paint. The aerodynamic nose added 48cm (19in) to the Road Runner's overall length and made the car difficult to park, as the first metre (3ft) of bodywork were invisible from the driver's seat.

The 7-litre (426 cu in) engine gave amazing performance – the Superbird had a top speed of 234km/h (145mph).

Inside, it was standard Road Runner, with a standard front bench, although bucket seats and harnesses could be fitted as an option, while extra dials included oil pressure and oil temperature.

Awesome performance meant the Superbird quickly became America's most revered muscle car

Engine: 6974cc (426 cu in), V8-cylinder
Power: 317kW (425bhp)
0–96km/h (60mph): 5.1 secs
Top speed: 234km/h (145mph)
Production total: 1920

PLYMOUTH VALIANT

1972–74

Plymouth's post-energy crisis offering still seems very big by European standards, but the Valiant's 5.2m (17ft) length and 2.8-litre (170 cu in) slant-six engine were considered compact by Americans used to V8 dinosaurs.

Surprisingly pleasant to drive and capable of over 9l/100km (25mpg) if driven gently, the Valiant made for sensible yet oddly stylish family transport, and was offered as either saloon, coupé or split-tailgate station wagon.

Four body styles were offered on the Valiant – this example is a two-door fastback with optional high-back seats. The Valiant sold well in the United States and achieved moderate success in Europe, including the UK.

The slant-six engine could trace its roots back to the original Valiant of 1960, and as well as the economy 2.8-litre (170 cu in) version, 3.2- (195 cu in) and 3.7-litre (226 cu in) versions of the six-cylinder were offered. The in-line engined cars were sold with a fair amount of success by Chrysler's European operation, including a few right-hand drive engineered cars for the UK, although British sales couldn't begin to compete with those in the United States.

American buyers were also offered four V8 units of 4.5-, 5.2-, 5.6- and 5.9-litre (274, 317, 341, 360 cu in) capacity, all with three-speed 'Torqueflite' automatic transmission. In coupé form, they made good junior muscle cars.

Engine: 2789cc (170 cu in), 6-cylinder
Power: 104kW (140bhp)
0–96km/h (60mph): n/a
Top speed: 161km/h (100mph)
Production total: 900,000 approx

PONTIAC EIGHT

1935–38

Pontiac's mainstream model of the mid-1930s, the Eight was a pleasantly styled and comfortable car that was always a pleasant machine to drive. Power came from a 3.8-litre (232 cu in) side-valve V8 which had a distinctive exhaust note, but was never particularly quick.

A vast model range included two- and four-door saloons, a stretched Deluxe saloon, two- and four-seater soft tops and sports coupé body styles. A conventional chassis was supported by independent front suspension and a live rear axle, while all versions came with hydraulic brakes.

Three- and four-speed manual gearboxes were offered, but lacked synchromesh on lower gears and could prove awkward to drive in traffic, although the light steering and supple ride made the Eight a good touring machine.

A larger 4.1-litre (250 cu in) engine was added for 1937, along with more rounded frontal styling, a new radiator grille and repositioned headlights. Later cars also came with a much more useful all-synchromesh gearbox.

The smaller-engined Pontiac Six used a 3.6-litre (220 cu in) side-valve straight-six unit, but shared the larger car's chassis and bodywork, although it was the more powerful Eight that accounted for most sales.

One of America's staple cars of the 1930s, the Pontiac Eight was a pleasantly styled saloon with a lazy but great sounding side-valve V8 engine. The later cars (above) from 1937 were the best, with all-synchromesh gearboxes.

Engine: 3801cc (232 cu in), V8-cylinder
Power: n/a
0–96km/h (60mph): n/a
Top speed: 137km/h (85mph)
Production total: n/a

PONTIAC CHIEFTAIN

1953–58

Styling was everything throughout the 1950s, and with the Chieftain Pontiac proved that even the most ordinary cars could be made to look dramatic and exciting.

The 1953 Chieftain was an all-new design, with a curved one-piece windscreen, stepped rear wings and aerodynamic rear wheel covers, plus a choice of two-

tone paint schemes, whitewall tyres and ornate chrome side flashes.

The same theme continued inside, with multi-coloured fabrics, an intricately detailed and colour-coded dashboard and a panoramic

The Chieftain was one of the finest-looking cars of the early 1950s, with lots of stylish chrome. The look continued inside, with an ornate dashboard and panoramic instrument panel.

instrument panel that allowed every one of the car's occupants to view the gauges.

Options and body styles were almost endless. Buyers could choose from ordinary two- or four-door saloons, a striking two-door 'Catalina' coupé – which proved to be a massive hit with collectors in later years – an odd-looking four-door station wagon, two- and four-door convertibles and a 'Custom Sedan', which came with a lower roofline and extra chrome trim.

A choice of six or eight-cylinder engines was offered, but with petrol prices so low during this period, more than 85 per cent of buyers opted for the larger units.

Engine: 4638cc (283 cu in), V8-cylinder
Power: 91kW (122bhp)
0–96km/h (60mph): n/a
Top speed: n/a
Production total: 379,705

PONTIAC BONNEVILLE

During the era of fins and chrome adornments, the Bonneville was very much Pontiac's 'trophy' car. The brainchild of the company's chief stylist, Semon 'Bunkie' Knudsen, it featured enormous rear fins and an unusual rear bumper that appeared to have downward-pointing overriders and incorporated horizontal tail-lights.

Touted as a family car, the Bonneville was available as a two- or four-door saloon, a huge split-tailgate station wagon, coupé or convertible.

Power came from the engine of the existing Pontiac Star Chief, but bored-out to 6063cc (370 cu in) and offering 190kW (255bhp), although some fuel-injected versions could produce over 224kW (300bhp).

As big as contemporary Cadillacs, the Bonneville weighed in at over 2000kg (2 tons) and was 538cm (17ft 8in) long, meaning it struggled in tight spaces and proved unwieldy if driven quickly.

Power steering and automatic transmission were fitted as standard, while convertible models also came with electric windows and a power folding roof. The Bonneville sold in relatively low numbers, which was just as GM intended, as it was by far the most upmarket and expensive Pontiac offered at the time.

Engine: 6063cc (370 cu in), V8-cylinder
Power: 190kW (255bhp)
0–96km/h (60mph): 10.1 secs
Top speed: 161km/h (100mph)
Production total: 180,531

By the time the Bonneville appeared in 1957, fins and chrome were at the peak of their popularity. The vast rear deck of the car meant it had an enormous luggage area.

PONTIAC TEMPEST LE MANS

For buyers who wanted a GTO but couldn't afford one, the Tempest Le Mans was the next best thing.

Based on the standard Tempest coupé or convertible (or saloon, if you wanted one, although few buyers did), the car came with GTO-style wheels, air intakes on the front wings, front bucket seats with foam padding, electric windows and a 10 per cent power boost over standard Tempest models. External differences included distinct 'Le Mans' badging, a vinyl-covered roof (or an electric folding top on convertible models) and chrome side flashes. A completely unsporting Le Mans Station Wagon was also offered, with fake wood panelling replacing the side flashes.

For 1969, the model had an ill-advised facelift which saw the frontal styling picked out in an odd

chrome-plated frame, while fake wood was applied to the interior.

Always a strong seller, Le Mans was a popular model name for Pontiac, lasting into the 1990s.

For buyers wanting a GTO on a budget, the Tempest Le Mans offered the looks and the sporty interior – but it couldn't match the performance of its bigger brother.

Engine: 4638cc (283 cu in), V8-cylinder
Power: 145kW (195bhp)
0–96km/h (60mph): n/a
Top speed: n/a
Production total: 831,331

PONTIAC GTO

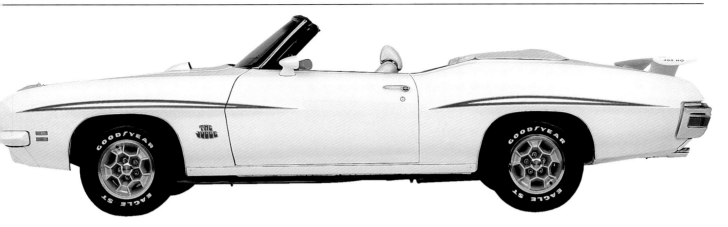

Both coupé and convertible versions of the GTO were offered – this example is a Mk 2 soft-top introduced for the 1968 model year. The roof could be retracted electronically.

erceived by many as the first real muscle car, the Pontiac GTO bucked trends in the motor industry. While most American manufacturers were looking at developing ever larger and more luxurious cars, Pontiac instead dropped a big block power plant into the relatively compact body of the Tempest coupé.

By doing so, it broke GM protocol. In 1963, the company had decreed that no more performance cars were to come from the company's constituent marques, as driving fast was considered socially unacceptable.

But Pontiac's chief engineer John Z. De Lorean, who later went on to create the infamously ill-fated sports car bearing his name, persevered and the Pontiac GTO was created via a loophole in GM's company strategy – by offering the high-performance engine as an option package on the Tempest model line-up. As well as the 6555cc (400 cu in) engine, the GTO option gave buyers quicker steering, firmer suspension, twin exhausts and wider tyres for a $300 premium over the standard Tempest.

With the GTO name lifted straight from the eponymous Ferrari, where GTO stood for 'Gran Turismo Omologato' in reference to its racing exploits, it was obvious that comparisons would be made between the two cars. Although any collector would immediately choose the Ferrari, performance-wise the Pontiac came close, with the ability to sprint from 0–96km/h (60mph) in less than seven seconds, and as little as 5.9 seconds on later, more potent models. Owners joked that the GTO initials on the Pontiac

stood for 'Gas, Tyres and Oil', as the overpowered car copiously consumed all three.

Strong sales in the first year prompted Pontiac to make a few changes for 1965, such as stacked twin headlights to resemble larger models, while a 'Ram-Air' option was offered over-the-counter, with an effective bonnet-mounted 'street scoop' that would channel air into the engine bay and feed it directly to three carburettors.

A year later, GM gave up trying to stop its associated companies from making performance models, as it was obvious this was a growing market in the United States and GM could not afford to lose sales to Ford and Chrysler.

To celebrate, John De Lorean decided the GTO would become a model in its own right. The 1966 GTO was similar to the earlier cars, but its profile was tweaked to give a more elegant, flowing appearance, with contoured 'Coke-bottle' styling along the flanks, plus different rear lamps and a more menacing radiator grille. However, the triple-carburettor set-

The earlier GTOs were the most distinctive, with stacked headlamps and a prominent fluted radiator grille. Performance was stunning, but the soft suspension and live rear axle meant handling could be tricky.

up of the 1965 model was dropped after GM banned multiple carburettors in the face of stringent new emissions legislation.

Pontiac's answer was to increase the engine size of the top models for 1967, and the flagship GTO now had a massive 7457cc (455 cu in) unit, giving it 276kW (370bhp) and 209km/h (130mph) performance, plus the ability to sprint from 0–96km/h (60mph) in six seconds. It might have had just the one carburettor, but the GTO could still fly.

An all-new bodyshell was introduced for the 1968 model year which brought the car up to date. One of the main new features was the 'Endura' front bumper, which satisfied new safety legislation by being made of deformable polyurethane, yet at the same time was cleverly disguised not to look like a bumper, wrapping round the entire front of the car and housing the mesh radiator grille. De Lorean

proved the efficacy of the new bumpers by appearing on US television repeatedly bashing one with a sledgehammer to absolutely no effect.

Another new development was the introduction of hidden headlights, which later appeared on rival machines such as the Mercury Cougar. The lights were concealed behind plastic grilles, which revolved out of the way when the lights were switched on.

The new style body lost some of the original car's elegance, but was still fresh and modern-looking, with pillarless coupé styling and traditional GTO add-ons, such as Mag wheels, subtle striping and twin air vents on the bonnet.

The ultimate version of these second-generation GTOs was the 'Judge', offered as an option pack. Its power output was nearly 298kW (400bhp), thanks to a quad-carburettor 'Ram Air' set-up, and also had large front and rear spoilers, bright paint schemes, a three-speed manual shift transmission and 'Judge' decals.

Sales of the GTO as a model in its own right died in 1971 after a huge drop in muscle car popularity and a trend towards less powerful, more luxurious cars in the United States. The GTO remained as an option pack on the Pontiac Le Mans until 1974, but couldn't recall the spirit of the glory days.

Engine: 6555cc (400 cu in), V8-cylinder
Power: 257kW (345bhp)
0–96km/h (60mph): 6.8 secs
Top speed: 200km/h (124mph)
Production total: 486,591

PONTIAC FIREBIRD

This 1968 Firebird 350 H.O. wa
a huge hit with drivers wh
wanted the perfect compromis
between power and econom

Pontiac's compact sports coupé, the Firebird, was launched to take on the might of the Ford Mustang, which had rapidly become America's best-selling car.

The Firebird was part of a double-fronted attack by General Motors to beat the Blue Oval, and shared many of its components – including chassis and body panels – with the Chevrolet Camaro, with GM correctly hoping that brand loyalty would see both the Pontiac and the Chevrolet account for sales of more than a million units.

The Firebird appeared half a year later than the Camaro, giving Pontiac time to develop its car further, adding Ram Air power, extra chrome and a new twin-headlight nose, as well as distinctive cooling fins in the rear quarter panel to feed a stream of air to the rear brake drums.

Top models also got the 7.5-litre (455 cu in) V8 from the Pontiac

GTO – an option never offered in the Chevrolet, which had a 6.5-litre (397 cu in) engine in its most powerful model.

The Firebird was also better equipped than the Camaro, with a choice of four-speed manual or three-speed automatic gearboxes over the standard three-speed heavy-duty unit, plus free-flow exhausts, a performance rear axle and the option of front disc brakes.

The trade-off was, of course, a higher asking price, with Firebirds costing between $200 and $600 more than the equivalent Chevrolet. The Camaro outsold the Pontiac by a ratio of over two to one over the course of the next decade and a half, but loyalty, plus perceived better quality, meant the Firebird was still a strong seller.

The first facelift came in 1969, when the Firebird got a new front end and revised interior, although the new look was spurned by

customers, who preferred the simple lines of the original. 1969 also saw the introduction of the first Trans Am models, sold initially as a special edition in white with blue racing stripes. Less than 700 were built.

The biggest shake-up came in 1970 when, along with the Camaro, a completely new body was offered. A new quad-headlight nose made from Endura plastic appeared, attached to longer, wider bodywork. The convertible option offered on earlier cars was also deleted, although a T-top roof could be ordered as an option. At the same time, the Trans Am became a standard addition to the range and could be ordered in either blue with white stripes, or

Sharing its bodywork with the Chevrolet Camaro, the Firebird was marketed as a rather more upmarket offering.

vice-versa. Two heavy-duty gearboxes were introduced to cope with the Trans Am's extra power, either a four-speed manual Hurst unit or a three-speed 'Turbo-Hydramatic' automatic.

Power outputs were reduced drastically the following year to comply with new emissions legislation, and sales plummeted as a result. In fact, the Firebird very nearly ceased production altogether in 1972 when the Pontiac factory went on a six-month strike, and serious question about the model's future were asked at GM's headquarters.

Luckily, the car's future was secured by the introduction of a new high-performance 7.5-litre (455 cu in) engine marking the return of a genuine performance offering in the Trans Am. A facelif in 1974 wasn't a success, however although buyers welcomed the introduction of a larger rear screen to aid visibility.

Any performance aspirations were killed altogether the following year as power outputs were again cut to cope with the introduction of mandatory catalyti converters, although sales remaine strong enough to keep the Firebird in production. The last cars using the Camaro platform were built in 1981, and the Firebird name went on to be used on Pontiac's future flagship coupés, a trend which continues today.

Engine: 7457cc (455 cu in), V8-cylinder
Power: 257kW (345bhp)
0–96km/h (60mph): 5.5 secs
Top speed: 210km/h (130mph)
Production total: 1,339,100

PORSCHE 356

While Porsche's first project was to design the Volkswagen Beetle before World War II, it was the 356 that was the first machine to bear the company's name. Launched in 1948, it was initially available with a 1131cc (69 cu in) flat-four VW engine. The car's distinctive styling, which can still be seen in Porsche's current output, was derived from a design created by the company in 1939 for a racing VW, called the Type 64 coupé.

Complex aluminium construction and Porsche's patented all-independent torsion bar suspension meant the 356 wasn't a cheap car, but it still proved popular with those who could afford one.

For its era, the 356 was dynamically brilliant. Its light weight and technologically advanced suspension made it entertaining to drive, with compliant handling and superb balance. Performance in standard cars was fairly ordinary, with just 3kW (44bhp) on offer in the earliest models, but a variety of different performance and tuning options meant most were fast and enthralling machines to drive.

From 1950, production moved from Porsche's spiritual home in Austria to a new factory in Stuttgart, Germany, where Porsche is still based, and bodies were made out of steel in order to cut production costs. To cope with the extra weight of the steel bodywork, the engine capacity was upped to 1286cc (78 cu in), and then again

to 1488cc (91 cu in) for 1952.

A year later, Porsche unveiled the 356 Speedster, designed to meet the demands of the booming American market. Buyers in hot weather 'dry' states, such as California, wanted open-top cars, so Porsche cut the roof off the 356 coupé, fitted a rudimentary hood and sports seats and dubbed the newcomer 'Speedster'. Although it was an attractive car, the Speedster was crudely finished, and in 1958 Porsche commissioned coachbuilders Drauz of Heilbronn to create a custom-made cabriolet with a better hood and greater all-round visibility.

The first significant change for the 356 came in 1955, with the launch of the 356A. While still immediately recognizable as a 356, the A had a higher ride, new front indicator lenses, larger rear lights, different wheeltrims and a

Thanks to timeless styling and entertaining road manners, the 356 enjoyed a long career. This 1961 model has the rare Karmann Hardtop bodywork.

one-piece panoramic windscreen, while the interior was made more user-friendly. Two new engines were offered – both air-cooled flat-fours with a choice of 1290cc (79 cu in) and 1582cc (97 cu in) capacities.

The same year also saw the launch of the 356 Carrera, which came with an 83kW (112bhp) race-tuned 1498cc (91 cu in) engine, with four overhead camshafts and a top speed of over 120mph.

The 356A and Carrera continued until 1959, when the updated 356B was launched, using just the 1582cc (97 cu in) engine from the A. It would remain in production for three years until the more modern 356C took over, again using the same engine but with a new suspension set-up and four-

wheel disc brakes.

The Carrera's successor, the Carrera 2, appeared in 1960 and had a 1966cc (120 cu in) development of the four camshaft engine which, in race-tuned format, was capable of producing 115kW (155bhp) and giving the car an impressive top speed of over 209km/h (130mph).

All 356s were fine-handling cars, but with the engine mounted behind the rear axle, they could be very unpredictable if pushed to their limits.

Also worthy of note is the 356-based 550 Speedster, developed by Porsche to compete at Le Mans in 1953. It used an early version of the Carrera's 1.6-litre (98 cu in) engine and was available as a road-legal machine, with thrilling but tricky handling characteristics. Despite its competition successes, it is perhaps best remembered as being the car movie icon James Dean was driving when he crashed and died.

Engine: 1582cc (97 cu in), 4-cylinder
Power: 56kW (75bhp)
0–96km/h (60mph): 11.2 secs
Top speed: 169km/h (105mph)
Production total: 77,509

Later 356s used four-wheel disc brakes, a new suspension set-up and a 1.6-litre (97 cu in) engine, plus a larger one-piece windscreen.

PORSCHE 911

Launched in 1964, the 911 soon earned a reputation as a fantastic driver's car. Its horizontally opposed air-cooled engine was mounted at the rear, making for near-perfect weight distribution.

Cars don't come more legendary than the Porsche 911, which even in its current water-cooled form can trace its roots back to the 356 of 1948. The original 911 was launched in 1964 as a replacement for the 356 and maintained the early car's horizontally opposed air-cooled engine set-up, although this time it had an extra bank of cylinders and was targeted at a more sporting, and wealthy, sector of the market.

Designed by Ferdinand Porsche's sons. Ferry and Butzi, the 911 was engineered to iron out the 356's unpredictable on-limit handling characteristics, and had a more forgiving all-new rear suspension. Even so, the car still had a strong tendency to oversteer and needed expert handling at high speeds.

From its launch, all 911s came with a five-speed gearbox, with a dog-leg first gear, and all-round disc brakes, while quick steering and a clever torsion bar suspension set up at the rear made the 911 a particularly agile and encouraging car for a competent driver to drive quickly. Two bodyshells were offered – the standard two-door coupé, or a targa-roofed model which had detachable panels in the hardtop.

The first cars used a 1991cc (121 cu in) flat-six, which

Even today, the current 911 can trace its roots back to the first cars. The engine is still a flat six, but traction aids have calmed its notorious twitchy rear end.

developed 97kW (130bhp) and gave a top speed of 210km/h (130mph). By 1967, three power outputs were available, with the quickest cars boasting 127kW (170bhp), while engine capacity increased to 2.2-litres (134 cu in) for 1969, with a more even spread of torque and flexible in-gear performance.

Engine capacities again rose in 1971, with a 2.4-litre (146 cu in) unit, while 1972 saw the return of the Carrera name with the 2.7 RS (165 cu in). Built for just one year, the Carrera RS had a stripped-out bodyshell and stiffer suspension for all-out performance and was easily capable of 250km/h (155mph).

For 1973, the 2.7-litre (165 cu in) engine was standardized, with power outputs ranging between 112 and 156kW (150 and 210bhp). The most powerful example acquired the Carrera name, which was no longer

the preserve of competition-developed special editions.

The same year, the 911 acquired some visual changes to satisfy new safety legislation in its biggest market – the United States. This meant the addition of new impact bumpers front and rear, plus the adoption of the car's trademark 'tea-tray' rear spoiler, while a two-pedal semi-auto Sportomatic transmission was offered as an option on all examples.

Answering criticisms of weak performance in smaller-engined models, Porsche unveiled the Turbo for the 1974 Paris Motor Show. The Turbo model was initially very expensive, but offered a 0–96km/h (60mph) time of just 5.1 seconds and a top speed of 257km/h (160mph). However, power delivery wasn't smooth – turbo lag would initially keep the car very quiet, then it would lurch forward dramatically.

Despite being an aged design, the 911 continued to sell strongly into the 1980s as the economic boom in both Europe and America saw demand for sports cars rise, while its user-friendliness and superb build quality saw it become the ultimate expression of wealth.

1983 saw the ultimate non-turbo Porsche, the 3.2-litre (195 cu in) Carrera 911 Club Sport, which had super-firm suspension and low-profile tyres, stunning acceleration and very little in the way of passenger comfort.

A new convertible appeared in 1987 which continued for just two years until the debut of the all-new Carrera 2 and Carrera 4 models in 1989, which used an entirely new bodyshell for the first time. Porsche hadn't altered the shape too much, but handling, especially on the four-wheel drive Carrera 4, was much more forgiving – much to the annoyance of some Porsche purists. But the purists would become even more frustrated in 1998, when the German firm unveiled the next generation 911, codenamed 996. While the engine was still sited behind the rear axle it used a water-cooled engine for the first time.

However, Porsche cars are still raw, thrilling and beautifully styled, and the legend of the 911 looks set to live forever.

Engine: 2993cc (183 cu in), 6-cylinder
Power: 171kW (230bhp)
0–96km/h (60mph): 5.5 secs
Top speed: 250km/h (155mph)
Production total: n/a

PORSCHE 912

Because of the 911's high purchase price, Porsche introduced the entry-level 912 in order not to alienate the buyers who would previously have chosen a standard 356C. Externally, the 912 looked absolutely identical to the 911, with the same pretty bodyshell, chrome wheeltrims and combined indicators and air vents.

Under the rear bonnet, however, was the 356's old 1582cc (97 cu in) engine, meaning the 912 was much less powerful than its six-cylinder sibling. The 911's five-speed gearbox was absent, too, although it was offered as an option for those who didn't want the 912's standard four-speed one. The interior was also significantly different from the 911, with a stark dashboard and vinyl seats.

However, the 912 was still a fun car to drive and the lighter four-

For people who wanted the 911 but without the high running costs, Porsche introduced the 912. Early cars used a 356 engine, later versions had VW power.

cylinder engine meant that the rear end of the car was lighter and easier to control.

Production of the 912 ceased in 1969 as a result of failing demand, although the concept was briefly revived during the oil crisis years of the 1970s, when the VW-powered 912E was launched for the United States market. It lasted a mere 18 months between 1975 and 1976.

Engine: 1582cc (97 cu in), 4-cylinder
Power: 67kW (90bhp)
0–96km/h (60mph): 11.8 secs
Top speed: 177km/h (110mph)
Production total: 30,300

PORSCHE 914

Positively loathed by Porsche traditionalists and disregarded by sports car fans, the 914 is a forgotten and most unfairly maligned machine. Developed and sold in conjunction with Volkswagen, the car used a tuned version of the engine from VW's quirky 411 saloon.

The striking bodyshell was built round a mid-mounted engine, making it strictly a two-seater, with pop-up headlights and a removable targa roof panel. The mid-engined

layout made for safe handling, while in more powerful examples, the 914 was a suprisingly competent sports car, with great balance and a strong spread of torque throughout the rev range.

Five-speed gearboxes came as standard in the 914, although Porsche's two-pedal Sportomatic semi-auto could be specified as an option. The engine size was upped from its original 1.7 litres (104 cu in) to 1.8 litres (110 cu in) in 1972, and then to 2 litres

(120 cu in) with fuel injection for 1973.

One of the most interesting derivatives of the 914 concept was the 1969 914/6, which used the air-cooled flat-six engine from the base 911 model, the 911T, which offered 82kW (110bhp), although the heavier engine and far less subtle power delivery made it a much less agile car than the four-cylinder versions. Fewer than 3500 examples were built before it went out of production.

A tie-in with Volkswagen led to the 914 – Porsche's attempt at an economy sports car. Purists hated it, but it was always a fine car to drive. Over 100,000 were sold, mostly in the United States.

Engine: 1971cc (120 cu in), 4-cylinder
Power: 75kW (100bhp)
0–96km/h (60mph): 8.2 secs
Top speed: 192km/h (119mph)
Production total: 115,646

PORSCHE 924

1976–89

The Porsche that was never meant to be – the 924 was originally developed as a tie-in with Audi and should have worn the saloon car maker's badge. Astonishingly, it shared its engine with the VW Transporter van!

If the 914 caused an outcry among Porsche's more traditional buyers, then the 924 caused outrage. The stylish 2+2 coupé was originally designed by Porsche for Audi, which wanted to create a more sporty image to market alongside its solid but uninspiring saloons.

But the collapse of the European economy in the mid-1970s scared the Ingolstadt-based firm away from anything adventurous, so Porsche decided it would market the car itself. Audi was used to build it, while under the bonnet came a 2-litre (121 cu in) water-cooled four-cylinder engine. Purists were shocked at the appearance of a water-cooled Porsche, but were even more horrified to find the engine was taken directly from the VW Transporter van.

Porsche's persistence paid off, however, and an affordable way into owning the exclusive Porsche badge was all most potential buyers needed. The 924 was a good car to drive, with safe and predictable handling and a fair spread of performance. More exciting versions included the 1978 Turbo, which could touch 240km/h (150mph), and the 156kW (210bhp) Carrera GT. Last-of-the-line cars, built between 1985 and 1989, used a detuned 2.5-litre (153 cu in) engine from the 944 and were badged 924S.

Engine: 1984cc (121 cu in), 4-cylinder
Power: 93kW (125bhp)
0–96km/h (60mph): 9.5 secs
Top speed: 203km/h (126mph)
Production total: 138,586

PORSCHE 928

1977–95

The 928 was intended to be a replacement for the 911, but since demand for the 911 continued unabated, the 928 instead became an expensive supplementary model, which would sell, in limited numbers, alongside its more legendary stablemate.

Expensively developed, the car featured an all-new 4.7-litre (285 cu in) water-cooled V8 engine, which was incredibly smooth and flexible. Interesting styling features included trapezoid side windows and unusual revolving headlights, plus a

Porsche thought the 928 would be a replacement for the 911 – but it was not to be. While the car was stylish and stunningly quick, traditional buyers hated the front-mounted water-cooled V8 engine and the lack of heritage in the car's styling.

curvaceous rear end with individual housings for the tail lamps, rear indicators and reversing lights.

Most examples had a four-speed automatic gearbox as this coped best with the car's large torque, although a handful of five-speed manuals were also offered.

The fastest 4.7-litre (285 cu in) car was the 231kW (310bhp) 928S of 1979, which used an uprated induction system, while the even more potent 5-litre (305 cu in) 928S4 became the performance flagship in 1989. From then on, outputs and performance figures continued to grow, and by the time production ceased in 1995, the 928 was available with a 5.4-litre (330 cu in) 261kW (350bhp) engine, could hit 257km/h (160mph) and stormed from 0–96km/h (60mph) in 5.1 seconds.

Engine: 4664cc (285 cu in), V8-cylinder
Power: 231kW (310bhp)
0–96km/h (60mph): 6.3 secs
Top speed: 250km/h (155mph)
Production total: 39,210

PORSCHE 944

To prove to buyers that the 924 had been developed for sporting drivers, Porsche introduced the 944. The 2.5-litre (151 cu in) straight-four gave admirable performance and impressive refinement.

After the criticism levelled at the 924 when it first appeared, Porsche was determined to prove a compact water-cooled model could be made desirable to the purists.

Its answer was the 944. Similar in profile to the 924 and effectively using the same bodyshell, the 944 was fatter, lower and had a much more sporting temperament thanks to a firm chassis, sharp steering and wider tyres. The newcomer was well received by the press, which complemented its prodigious grip and great engine, albeit at the expense of an over-firm ride.

Under the bonnet, a new 2.5-litre (151 cu in) four-cylinder engine made its debut, with a specially developed balancer shaft system to overcome uneven running problems often associated with large capacity fours.

The engine was the car's most fascinating facet. Extensively redesigned and developed, it was actually the 928's V8 unit cut in half, with a single overhead camshaft. At its launch in 1981, it was available in 121kW (163bhp) output only, although the unit size grew steadily over the next few years.

Conventional McPherson struts at the front and Porsche's trademark torsion bar set up at the rear meant the 944 enjoyed superb handling and quickly established itself as one of the most entertaining cars of the 1980s, proving that a water-cooled Porsche needn't sell its soul in the switch to a more conventional powerplant and engine layout.

The fastest 944 made its debut in 1985 and came with a turbocharger attached, as well as a softer front end style after the bonnet line was raised slightly to accommodate the turbo. It was quick, hitting 96km/h (60mph) from standstill in just six seconds, but power delivery was far from subtle, with immense turbo lag. However, the 944's incredible handling abilities made up for this, and providing the turbo pressure could be kept up, the 944 Turbo was a thrilling machine.

S2 versions of the 944 (below) were introduced in 1989 and had larger engines and higher power outputs, plus smoother lines.

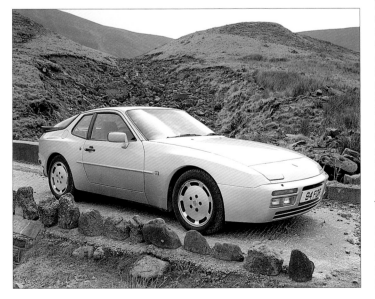

It was at the time of the Turbo's launch that Porsche decided to further distance the 944 from the 924 by completely reworking the interior, giving the more powerful car a much better quality fascia and more impressive levels of standard equipment as the Porsche keyring became the one to flaunt in trendy wine bars.

Standard cars had their engine capacity upped to 2.7 litres (165 cu in) in 1987 when a new twin-camshaft 16-valve head was introduced, offering more torque and in-gear flexibility, and then again to 3 litres (183 cu in) in 1988, when a 944 cabriolet also joined the range.

The final versions of the 944, called S2, were launched in 1989 and continued until 1993, developed 157kW (211bhp) and had a top speed of nearly 257km/h (160mph).

Styling changes for the new models included a rounder nose, although the distinctive pop-up headlights remained, while the chassis was modified to provide a more comfortable ride (always a weakness in the 944) without compromising handling abilities. Coupé and cabriolet versions of the S2 were offered, although the standard 944 continued to sell alongside it until 1992.

After an impressive production run, which saw over 110,000 sales in 12 years, the 944 was discontinued, but didn't disappear completely. The 'new' 968, which had 928-style rotating headlights and larger bodywork, was little more than a heavily reworked variant of the 944. Potential customers weren't impressed and that, combined with a global downturn in sports car popularity, had serious implications for the Stuttgart-based company. With sales only a mere fraction of those forecast, the 968 struggled to make a name for itself and Porsche was forced to postpone future model launches until it had written off the model's debts. The 968 was quietly dropped in 1995.

Engine: 2479cc (151 cu in), 4-cylinder
Power: 142kW (190bhp)
0–96km/h (60mph): 6.7 secs
Top speed: 226km/h (140mph)
Production total: 112,550

PORSCHE 959

1987–88

For a short while, the 959 was the world's fastest production car with a top speed of 318km/h (197mph). Its air-cooled engine was derived from that of the 911.

When it first appeared, the Porsche 959 was the world's fastest production car. It was developed specifically for the company's motorsport aspirations as a homologation special for Group B rallying, immediately proving its pedigree when a pre-production model stormed to victory in the 1986 Paris-Dakar rally.

Based on the 911, the 959 retained the air-cooled flat-six engine layout with the engine behind the rear axle, but better handling came from a pioneering four-wheel drive system that later appeared on the 911 Carrera 4.

Unusual construction methods saw the 959 appear with aluminium doors, bonnet and boot

panels attached to a monocoque formed from incredibly strong plastic that is normally used in aircraft manufacture.

These construction methods, coupled with the impressive grip offered through the car's electronically controlled driveline, made the 959 an incredibly fast car while the twin turbos were set up so as to deliver their power as low down the rev range as possible, minimizing turbo lag.

In spite of its supercar performance, the 959 was an extremely easy car to drive, with light controls and a tactile six-speed gearbox, making it a far more practical machine than the similarly potent Ferrari F40.

The 959 was developed for rallying, winning the 1986 Paris-Dakar event. Desert-going versions had jacked up suspension and light-weight bodywork.

Engine: 2994cc (183 cu in), 6-cylinder
Power: 302kW (405bhp)
0–96km/h (60mph): 3.7 secs
Top speed: 318km/h (197mph)
Production total: 200

PUMA GT

1967–85

Brazil doesn't have much of a reputation for producing stylish, pretty two-seater sports cars, yet the Puma was just that. Launched in 1967, the glassfibre machine was the brainchild of Italian engineer Genaro 'Rino' Malzoni, who emigrated to South America in the late 1950s.

Despite its diminutive proportions, the GT resembled a

Lamborghini Miura, with similar slatted B-pillars and large oval headlights. Underneath the bonnet, however, it was more conventional. Power came from a variety of Volkswagen air-cooled engines, which were built for the South American market in a factory close to Malzoni's São Paulo premises.

It wasn't just the engines that came from VW, either, as the GT

was constructed on a Karmann Ghia platform and was even sold in some smaller VW dealerships in Brazil, while all agreed to service it. Later cars were built on standard Beetle platforms after the Karmann Ghia ceased production. During 1973, 357 cars were also produced in South Africa by Bromer.

Other cars built by Puma included a Fissore-designed two-

door coupé and the GTB, which looked similar to the GT but was much larger, using a locally built Chevrolet platform and front-mounted engine.

Engine: 1493cc (91 cu in), 4-cylinder
Power: 54kW (72bhp)
0–96km/h (60mph): 11.7 secs
Top speed: 161km/h (100mph)
Production total: 30,000 approx

RAILTON TERRAPLANE

Terraplane was the name of a chassis successfully used by American manufacturer Hudson as well as the UK firm, Railton. Both companies also combined to develop a new range of straight-eight machinery.

Most Hudson cars were elegant touring machines, but it was the Railtons that were the more exciting cars, marketed as cheaper alternatives to Lagondas, Alvises and even Bentleys.

The Terraplane was crude but effective, while the range of bodies available was quite bewildering – tourers, saloons, convertibles, limousines and even racing specials were available.

Performance was sensational for its era. Even in standard form, the Railton was quick, accelerating from 0–96km/h (60mph) in just 13 seconds and on to a top speed of 161km/h (100mph) depending on the weight of the coachwork. Race-tuned examples of the Railton were even faster.

The huge straight-eight engines were very smooth and reliable, but were high on fuel consumption – 17l/100km (16mpg) was the best

figure, even if driven gently – while the mechanical gearbox was difficult to master.

Sadly, Railton, like many great British manufacturers, was totally crippled by World War II and never reopened in peace time.

The Terraplane chassis was all things to all buyers with a bewilderingly wide range of bodies available – from a luxury limousine to a stripped-out racing car. This one has a two-seater sporting body.

Engine: 4010cc (245 cu in), 8-cylinder
Power: 92kW (124bhp)
0–96km/h (60mph): 13 secs
Top speed: 161km/h (100mph)
Production total: 1379

RAMBLER REBEL

With an all-new body and quite controversial angular styling, the 'full-size' Rambler marked a dramatic change in approach from parent company AMC, which had previously been respected for building well-engineered but dull

cars under the Nash and Hudson names. The new cars certainly weren't dull; indeed, the rakish front end and huge fins were for extroverts only.

The Rebel was the flagship model in the range, using a 160kW

To say the least, distinctive styling was definitely the Rebel's unique selling point – but for many buyers it was 'more unique' than they required. Contemporary motoring journalists went as far as to call it 'plain ugly'.

(215bhp) V8 engine in place of standard cars' six-cylinder units. Two body styles were offered – a four-door 'Country Club' sedan, with an unusual pillarless profile and a glass area that cut deep into the car's waistline, and an even more challenging estate version, with an odd luggage rack over the rear area of the roof.

Optional extras included 'Flash-O-Matic' push-button overdrive, power steering, electric windows, a radio, record player and reversing floodlights, which were guaranteed to blind following motorists if activated in public.

Rebels were distinctive for their torpedo-shaped badging, ornate hub caps and excess chrome. Otherwise, they looked identical to lesser Ramblers.

Engine: 4704cc (287 cu in), V8-cylinder
Power: 160kW (215bhp)
0–96km/h (60mph): n/a
Top speed: 169km/h (105mph)
Production total: n/a

RELIANT REGAL

1951–73

Is it a car or is it a tricycle? The Regal was sold as a trike in order t avoid heavy taxation on new cars, but it was unstable at speed.

The beauty of Reliant's legendary Regal was that no full driving licence was needed to drive it; because it was a three-wheeler, it was officially classed as a tricycle, yet offered car- (and even van-) like passenger and load carrying capabilities.

The first bubble-shaped Regal appeared in 1951 and was crudely built using a pressed-steel chassis, with semi-elliptic leaf springs at the rear and a single torsion bar and stub axle arrangement for the single front wheel.

Power came from a 747cc (46 cu in) Austin Seven engine, although concessions to modernity included surprisingly effective hydraulic brakes and a four-speed gearbox. Early models came with aluminium bodywork attached to an ash frame, but later cars gained glassfibre bodywork.

The second generation Regal, immortalized by Del Trotter in the British comedy TV series *Only Fools and Horses*, appeared in 1962 and had an all-new 592cc (36 cu in) alloy engine, designed by Reliant and based on the old Austin Seven unit. Saloon versions featured a sharp reversed rake rear window similar to that of the Ford Anglia. Reliant persisted with three-wheeled cars right up until 2001, when the Regal's replacement, the Robin, finally ceased production.

Engine: 747cc (46 cu in), 4-cylinder
Power: 12kW (16bhp)
0–96km/h (60mph): n/a
Top speed: 96km/h (60mph)
Production total: n/a

RELIANT SABRE

1961–66

Reliant's range of cars was curious, so it came as no surprise when the company decided to complement its line-up of quirky three-wheeled microcars and delivery vans with, of all possible choices, an... open-top sports car.

The Sabre's development had effectively already been paid for, as Reliant had built a similar car called the Sabra for limited sales in the Israeli market, so only a few minor changes were needed before production could start at its factory in Tamworth, England.

Complex construction included a strange leading-arm front suspension, which was never very effective, as well as expensive glassfibre bodywork supplied by Ashley Engineering. The car's distinctive styling included a kamm tail and ugly, horned overriders, which did little to boost its appeal to potential buyers.

The standard Sabre used a 1703cc (104 cu in) Ford Consul engine and wasn't very fast, but the

With beautiful styling that loosely resembled that of 1960s Ferraris, the Sabre was a classy car. But it was expensive to buy, as the glassfibre body made it very costly to build.

more expensive Sabre Six, which came with the Ford Zephyr Six's 2.6-litre (159 cu in) straight-six engine and more conventional Triumph TR4 suspension, could reach 177km/h (110mph) along with much more assured handling. The Six also had more fluent body styling, with a neater front end and rounded rear arches.

Neither Sabre was a great sales success for the company, but their development and production would set the precedent for future sports machines.

Engine: 1703cc (104 cu in), 4-cylinder
Power: 54kW (73bhp)
0–96km/h (60mph): 14.1 secs
Top speed: 145km/h (90mph)
Production total: 285

RELIANT SCIMITAR GT

1964–70

With styling from respected designers at Ogle Engineering and power units from Ford, the Scimitar GT was a guaranteed success. It established Reliant as a respected sports car maker.

Were it not for Reliant's sheer persistence, the Scimitar might never have been produced. The car originally started life as a styling exercise by Ogle Design and was built on a Daimler SP250 'Dart' platform, but the Tamworth-based company liked the shape so much that it bought the rights.

A truncated version of the car appeared on the platform of the Sabre Six and became Reliant's first genuine sports car success, using traditional glassfibre bodywork and engines lifted from Ford, initially the 2.6-litre (159 cu in) Zephyr Six unit, then later, the V6 that had been developed for the Capri.

Early cars could be difficult to handle at speed, but the addition of trailing arm rear suspension in

1965 reversed this defect significantly, making the later versions genuine performance cars, with excellent handling, potent acceleration and surprisingly good build quality.

Were it not for the huge or even disproportionate amount of time required to hand-build the cars, Reliant could easily have sold more Scimitars, but the company and Ogle were already working on a larger and more powerful successor which became a serious player in the sports car market of the late 1960s and early 1970s.

Engine: 2994cc (183 cu in), V6-cylinder
Power: 101kW (136bhp)
0–96km/h (60mph): 8.9 secs
Top speed: 195km/h (121mph)
Production total: 1005

RELIANT REBEL

1964–73

Experienced drivers who liked the style of the Reliant Regal but had full driving licences could always opt for the four-wheeler Rebel, which used the same engines, gearbox and rear end set-up as the three-wheeler version.

The glassfibre bodywork was

uninspiring but the car was surprisingly useful, especially the estate version; ultimately, however, the car never really posed a threat to more conventional compact cars, such as the Ford Anglia, Mini or Hillman Imp.

Its best facet was its entertaining handling, although the trade-off was a bumpy ride and large amounts of interior noise from the aluminium engine. It was very slow, even with the largest capacity 748cc (46 cu in) unit installed, but non-metal bodywork meant that it

didn't rust and it was surprisingly tough and durable.

Engine: 700cc (43 cu in), 4-cylinder
Power: 23kW (31bhp)
0–96km/h (60mph): 35.9 secs
Top speed: 110km/h (68mph)
Production total: 700

RELIANT SCIMITAR GTE

1968–86

The GTE gained Royal approval from Britain's Princess Anne. She was so fond of it that she bought more than 10 examples over the years. This is an early SE5 model.

The Scimitar proved that it was perfectly possible to combine a sports car and estate car to amazingly good effect.

Although the GTE wasn't very well built and relied on parts from several different British manufacturers for its engines, suspension and switchgear, it was quick, lightweight and entertaining to drive. It was also very practical, with a useful load bay, comfortable seating for four people and a choice of manual overdrive or automatic gearboxes.

A unique British achievement from an independent firm, the car gained approval from the highest quarters, with Princess Anne

having owned more than 10 over the years. To this day, one is kept for the occasional journey.

Earliest cars, dubbed the SE5, were the prettiest. The later SE6 was both longer and wider, but couldn't quite match the same overtly sporting character as the original.

Final versions cars came with a German-built 2.8-litre (171 cu in) Ford V6 as used in the Capri 2.8 Injection Special. The GTE, which was also available as a GTC convertible, was dropped in 1986, but was briefly revived in 1988 by small independent carmaker Middlebridge, which sold a further 80 examples.

Engine: 2996cc (183 cu in), V6-cylinder
Power: 103kW (138bhp)
0–96km/h (60mph): 10.7mph
Top speed: 189km/h (117mph)
Production total: 10,425

RELIANT SS1

1984–90

It was a fine handling car, but the SS1's build quality and controversial wedge-shaped styling meant it had limited appeal.

The unfortunately named SS1 was designed by Reliant to fill the gap left by small sports cars, such as the MG Midget and Triumph Spitfire, which disappeared early in the 1980s.

Unusual styling was partially completed by Michelotti, but its transition from drawing board to production wasn't a great success, as the car had awkward looks and a flimsy finish. Cheapest examples came with a choice of Ford engines, from the Escort L's 52kW (70bhp) 1296cc (79 cu in) unit to the 1596cc (97 cu in) carburettor engine of more upmarket models. However, design complications meant Reliant was unable to fit the motor it wanted – the Escort XR3i's 86kW (115bhp) unit –

under the SS1's bonnet, so it searched in vain for an engine powerful enough to give the car proper sports performance.

The answer came from Japan in the form of the 1.8-litre (110 cu in) turbocharged Nissan Silvia unit, which was coarse and unrefined, but offered 101kW (135bhp) and

thrilling power delivery. The SS1 could storm from 0–96km/h (60mph) in less than seven seconds, but delicate throttle control was needed to prevent the turbo from kicking in while cornering. Driven carefully, however, the model displayed competent and reassured handling.

If it hadn't been so poorly conceived and built, the SS1 could have been a huge success.

Engine: 1809cc (110 cu in), 4-cylinder
Power: 101kW (135bhp)
0–96km/h (60mph): 6.9 secs
Top speed: 203km/h (126mph)
Production total: n/a

RENAULT MONASIX

1930–32

The Monasix was typical of Renault's prewar designs, with an angled radiator grille and Michelin disc wheels distinguishing it from

other contemporary saloon cars. In all other ways, it was utterly conventional, with a small-capacity six-cylinder side-valve engine

offering lots of torque but little performance, mounted on a simple steel chassis. Transverse leaf springs on both axles made for a

reasonably comfortable ride, but handling was very poor, with wayward steering and a tendency to drift if driven at speed. A three-speed central control gearbox, which made down changes difficult, was much the same as that offered by its rivals. However, the mechanical brakes were also very poor.

But dynamic ability was hardly the point. The Monasix was built to satisfy the needs of ordinary motorists as an easy-to-own, reliable and inexpensive means of transport, and in that context, it fulfilled its brief. A variety of different body styles was offered, from two-door coupés and convertibles up to seven-seater limousines. It was France's best-selling car in its era.

Durability and ease of maintenance were the key to the Monasix's appeal. It was a cumbersome machine to drive, but offered legendary reliability.

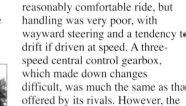

Engine: 1474cc (90 cu in), 6-cylinder
Power: n/a
0–96km/h (60mph): n/a
Top speed: n/a
Production total: n/a

RENAULT JUVAQUATRE

Being a surprisingly modern offering when new meant the Juvaquatre was able to go straight back into production after World War II. Its strong sales were vital for Renault's postwar success.

offered impressive interior space. Under the bonnet was an old-fashioned 1-litre (61 cu in) side-valve engine, but it was economical and simple to maintain, which was exactly the requirement of the majority of postwar owners.

Otherwise, the Juvaquatre was fairly modern, with transverse leaf springs at the rear, independent front suspension, hydraulic brakes and a smooth gearbox.

Saloon models were dropped in 1950 as they were no longer needed alongside the 4CV, but the van and estate models continued up to 1960, with engines taken from the 4CV and Dauphine. The Juvaquatre was an important and successful model for Renault's postwar recovery at a time when the French car industry needed it most.

Because the Juvaquatre had entered production just 18 months before the outbreak of World War II, it was still a relatively modern car by the time the conflict ended in 1945.

That meant Renault was in the fortunate position of being able to put the car straight back into production and so could offer a means of cheap transport that was

significantly more advanced than many of its rivals.

The car was available as a four-door saloon, van or commercial-based shooting brake, which

Engine: 1003cc (61 cu in), 4-cylinder
Power: 18kW (24bhp)
0–96km/h (60mph): n/a
Top speed: 90km/h (56mph)
Production total: 40,681

RENAULT 4CV

France's answer to the VW Beetle had a lot in common with the German car, with a four-cylinder engine mounted adrift of the rear axle, bathtub curves and a distinctive engine note. It is curious, and interesting, that it had been developed in secret during the German occupation of France.

Initial cars could be difficult to operate, with a clumsy three-speed constant mesh gearbox, irritating floor-mounted mixture control and underpowered 13kW (18bhp) engine, but as the industry moved on, Renault's policy became one of constant improvement.

By the mid-1950s, the 4CV was a common sight on European roads and had gained extra power from a new 747cc (46 cu in) engine, which replaced the earlier cars' 760cc (46 cu in) unit. Particularly desirable was the R1052 Sport

variant, which offered a respectable 31kW (42bhp) and enough flexibility to cruise at over 130km/h (80mph), while the car's nimble chassis and short wheelbase meant it even enjoyed minor competition success.

Yet despite the 4CV's strange styling, rear engine layout and front 'suicide' doors, the French firm decided to play safe with the 4CV's successor, the 4, and with enormous success. It was a sensible idea, as despite its superior quality and better levels of equipment, the 4CV was never able to match the popularity of rival Citroën's 2CV.

Engine: 747cc (46 cu in), 4-cylinder
Power: 31kW (42bhp)
0–96km/h (60mph): n/a
Top speed: 140km/h (87mph)
Production total: 1,105,543

Styling flair was evident on the 4CV, which looked like a scaled-down American sedan. Renault sold over a million before concentrating on the more conventionally-styled R4.

RENAULT DAUPHINE

1956–68

Cuddly looks and a sensible interior disguised the fact that the Dauphine had a great chassis. There was even a 'Rallye' version.

Although the Renault 4 took over from the 4CV in 1961, the earlier car's spirit continued in the Dauphine, which made its debut in 1956. Despite much more spacious bodywork and a lengthened chassis, the Dauphine was effectively an uprated 4CV, with an enlarged 845cc (52 cu in) version of its engine, identical gearbox and braking system.

However, the suspension set-up was different, with independent coil springs and wishbones at the front and the option of 'Aerostable' semi-pneumatic springing – introduced to rival Citroën's impressive ride comfort – available as an option from 1959.

The clumsy three-speed gearbox was swapped for a much better four-speed version for the 1960s, while all-round disc brakes were an important innovation for the last four years of production.

The most interesting variant of the Dauphine was the Gordini,

which despite its sporty name, was never a particularly fast car in standard form, struggling to reach 130km/h (80mph). However, in the hands of tuners, Gordinis could easily be turned into 160km/h (100mph) racers.

There was one factory version built to be a quicker car, though. The 1093 Rallye, which was only offered in France and Spain, had 41kW (56bhp), came with garish body stripes and could top 170km/h (105mph).

Engine: 845cc (52 cu in), 4-cylinder
Power: 36kW (49bhp)
0–96km/h (60mph): 28.2 secs
Top speed: 119km/h (74mph)
Production total: 2,120,220

RENAULT FREGATE

1951–60

As France started to put the events of the war and the first post-war years behind it, demand for larger, prestige cars started to trickle through once again. Renault's answer was the Fregate – a large unitary construction design that offered plenty of passenger space and reasonable levels of luxury, although it wasn't so well built as the majority of its contemporary rivals.

It was pleasant to drive, however, with a soft ride thanks to

Although it was similar in appearance to the Dauphine, the Fregate was a much larger car, built to satisfy new demand for luxury vehicles as the French economy underwent a post-war resurgence.

all-round fully independent suspension and an all-synchromesh four-speed gearbox with a column mounted remote change. Two-pedal transmission was offered on the options list, initially as a full automatic and subsequently Renault's patented 'Transfluide' semi-automatic set-up.

The original 2-litre (122 cu in) engine was replaced by a new and more flexible 2.1-litre (131 cu in) unit for 1955. An estate car, called the Domaine, made its debut at the same time and offered a choice of six or eight seats, plus an enormous load bay.

Like many large saloons of its era, the Fregate was extremely prone to rust and by the mid-1970s survivors were rare – and largely forgotten.

Engine: 2141cc (131 cu in), 4-cylinder
Power: 45kW (60bhp)
0–96km/h (60mph): 18.5 secs
Top speed: 145km/h (90mph)
Production total: 177,686

RENAULT COLARE PRAIRIE

1951–55

An exotic-sounding name, but not actually a particularly exotic car. The Renault Colare Prairie was introduced as a stop-gap estate to complement the large Fregate saloon until an estate version of the Fregate appeared in 1955.

Front end styling was almost a facsimile of the Austin A40, but from the windscreen pillars back, the Colare Prairie's commercial vehicle origins were obvious; the standard Colare model was offered as either a panel van or pick-up truck. In profile, the Prairie's styling looked strange, as the bodywork had been hastily redesigned to incorporate an extra pair of rear doors, and it was also considerably wider than most contemporary rivals.

An antiquated suspension set-up, designed for load carrying rather than comfort, was another serious

Renault's stop-gap estate car offered massive load-carrying ability, but the Colare Prairie was heavy, awkward to drive and had a very harsh ride. It also had an unpleasantly noisy engine.

problem as was the very noisy 2.4-litre (146 cu in) side-valve engine, which could trace its roots back to 1936.

Matters improved, but only to a limited extent, in 1952 when the Colare Prairie got the Fregate's 2-litre (131 cu in) overhead valve unit, but even this felt underpowered trying to move the bulky station wagon bodywork.

Engine: 2383cc (145 cu in), 4-cylinder
Power: 42kW (56bhp)
0–96km/h (60mph): 43.8 secs
Top speed: 100km/h (62mph)
Production total: n/a

RENAULT FLORIDE

1959–63

The Floride was a great-looking car and made best use of the Dauphine platform on which it was based, but the hand-built bodies had a tendency to rot.

'Transfluide' semi-automatic were offered as options. The Floride looked best as a convertible, although the high ride height appeared somewhat at odds with the low-cut panelwork.

Nevertheless, the Floride was a fun car to drive, with light steering and a bumpy ride, although grip was questionable when cornering quickly, and the tiny engine always felt faster than it actually was.

Performance improved slightly in 1956 with the introduction of the S model, which came with a bored-out 956cc (58 cu in) engine offering 38kW (51bhp).

All Florides were built externally by coachbuilders Brissoneau and Lotz and suffered from extensive rust problems. Production was discontinued in 1963, with a total of nearly 200,000 cars sold during its four-year life.

With absolutely stunning coupé or convertible styling, tactile controls and quite a high price tag, the only thing that prevented the Renault Floride from being a true sports car was, ironically, its notable lack of performance.

The pretty rear-engined machine, styled by Frua, was effectively a standard tune Dauphine Gordini underneath, which meant it came with the same 845cc (52 cu in) engine and temperamental three-speed column-change gearbox, although a four-speed box and

Engine: 845cc (52 cu in), 4-cylinder
Power: 28kW (38bhp)
0–96km/h (60mph): 28.7 secs
Top speed: 127km/h (79mph)
Production total: 177,122

RENAULT CARAVELLE

The lineage is evident – the Caravelle looked like the Floride, but had a more modern interior and different styling features, such as the chrome hubcaps on this example.

Essentially an uprated and facelifted Floride, the Caravelle took the name already used by its predecessor for the American market. Styling differences from the Floride included smaller chrome strips, no trim around the air vents, a larger rear cooling grille, bigger bumpers, heater vents under the front bumper and Caravelle badging across the front panel, as well as larger wheels and revised wheeltrims. The roof was also raised on coupé models to counter criticisms of poor rear headroom in the Floride.

The earliest models used the 956cc (58 cu in) engine of the Floride S, derived from that of the Renault 8 and, like the Floride, the unit was mounted behind the rear axle.

From 1963, the engine capacity was increased to 1.1 litres (67 cu in) and it's these later models that show the coupé's performance potential to its best advantage, although they also show some serious handling concerns if driven hard.

Other modifications for 1963 included an all-synchromesh gearbox and larger petrol tank, while convertible models came with a detachable hardtop as standard. The Caravelle was always something of a curiosity – never a brilliant seller.

Engine: 1108cc (68 cu in), 4-cylinder
Power: 40kW (54bhp)
0–96km/h (60mph): 17.6 secs
Top speed: 144km/h (89mph)
Production total: n/a

RENAULT 4

The Citroën 2CV might be an icon of rural France, but it was the Renault 4 that was the country's best-seller. Over eight million were sold in a production run that topped 30 years.

Only the Volkswagen Beetle and Ford Model T have generated more sales than the Renault 4, which attracted more than eight million buyers during more than three decades of production.

Perhaps no one was more surprised at this success than Renault itself, as it launched the 4 to act as a rival to the Citroën 2CV, which had rapidly become France's best-selling car.

Like the Citroën, the 4 had a bouncy ride, super-soft suspension, unpredictable handling and a strange push-pull gearchange, but it was clothed in flimsy bodywork that looked even more like corrugated iron than that of its fiercest rival.

However, a simple mechanical layout, reliability and extremely low running costs made the 4 an inexpensive and highly popular choice for French buyers, with exports proving to be particularly successful in developing markets. The car became a best-seller.

Early cars came with a 603cc (37 cu in) straight-four, although capacity grew on numerous occasions throughout its life, borrowing units from the 4CV, Dauphine and Caravelle and, later, the 1.1-litre (67 cu in) motor from the Renault 5.

As well as a five-door hatchback body style, the 4 could also be ordered as a delivery van, crew cab, pick-up truck and even a beach buggy.

Engine: 1108cc (68 cu in), 4-cylinder
Power: 25kW (34bhp)
0–96km/h (60mph): 25.7 secs
Top speed: 116km/h (72mph)
Production total: 8,135,424

RENAULT RODEO

1973–81

Anything Citroën could do, Renault reckoned it could do just as well, if not better, and as if to prove it, the 4 was dismantled and turned into the Rodeo, which was marketed as a direct rival to Citroën's Mehari.

The Rodeo was made at a time when fun vehicles were very much in vogue in southern Europe and was built along similar principles to the Mini Moke, with little in the way of passenger comfort and no roof, although a canvas canopy could be ordered as an option. Like the Citroën Mehari, it came with reinforced plastic bodywork and despite its rugged 4x4 looks, was nothing more than a two-wheel drive standard 4 platform, with the same 845cc (52 cu in) engine and push-pull gearchange.

Two versions were offered – the 4 Rodeo, which used round headlights, a raised bonnet and truncated chassis, and the 6 Rodeo, which was based on the slightly larger Renault 6 and had square headlights, a flatter bonnet and larger 1108cc (68 cu in) engine, which gave it the ability to reach 130km/h (80mph).

If you wanted a real four-wheel drive Rodeo, conversion firm Sinpar would build one for you – but there were plenty of more competent off-roaders for the same amount of money.

Engine: 845cc (52 cu in), 4-cylinder
Power: 25kW (34bhp)
0–96km/h (60mph): n/a
Top speed: 100km/h (62mph)
Production total: n/a

RENAULT 5

1972–97

The 5 was another massive success and best-seller for Renault, combining the chic simplicity of the 4 with the gearbox-ahead-of-engine layout and practical hatchback of the 16.

Among its many attributes were a superb ride, thanks to torsion bar independent suspension, and cute styling that would see it outlive most contemporary rivals.

A masterpeice of packaging, the 5 had a spacious interior and a useful boot. Its wheel-at-each-corner layout made it a fun car to drive, with predictable handling and surprising levels of grip.

Faster versions were badged Alpine in Europe and Le Car in the United States, although the old Gordini name was revived in Britain because the Alpine name was already in use by Chrysler. A five-door option was introduced in 1981, followed by a completely new model for 1994 – although the original lines were still so stylish they were left mostly unchanged until the last one left the production line in 1997. It was often imitated, but never bettered until the appearance of the Peugeot 205 in 1982.

Engine: 1397cc (85 cu in), 4-cylinder
Power: 47kW (63bhp)
0–96km/h (60mph): 12.2 secs
Top speed: 155km/h (96mph)
Production total: 5,471,709

Chic styling and excellent packaging meant that the Renault 5 still looked relatively fresh when production ceased in 1997 – after a 25-year innings.

RENAULT 5 TURBO

1978–86

Not to be confused with the conventional 5, the 5 Turbo was a road-going rally car developed for homologation purposes.

Renault's all-alloy 1.4-litre (85 cu in) engine underwent some major surgery and emerged sporting a turbo and intercooler – enough to give it 119kW (160bhp) – and was mounted right in the middle of the car to ensure near-perfect weight distribution.

Mid-engined balance and a lively 119kW (160bhp) turbocharged powerplant meant the Renault 5 Turbo enjoyed immense rallying success.

Visually, it was unmistakably a Renault 5, although the flared rear arches, which served more than just cosmetic purposes by sucking much needed air into the engine, added 60cm (24in) to its width.

Weight was kept to an absolute minimum by a spartan cabin and aluminium doors, bonnet and tailgate, while other modifications included heavy duty racing suspension, massive brake discs and fat tyres. Turbo 2, launched in 1983, was marginally slower thanks to its all-steel bodywork.

Unlike most rally specials, however, the 5 Turbo was simple to drive, with fairly light controls

and a great five-speed gearbox, although noise levels in the cabin were almost deafening. Incredible grip and forgiving handling characteristics made the car a performance motoring icon.

Engine: 1397cc (85 cu in), 4-cylinder
Power: 119kW (160bhp)
0–96km/h (60mph): 7.7 secs
Top speed: 218km/h (135mph)
Production total: 5007

RENAULT 18 TURBO

1978–87

Following Renault's success with turbocharged motorsport engines in the 5 Turbo and its first Formula One car, the company decided to make its new technology available to the mass market in the shape of the 18 Turbo.

The standard 18 was a dull car, but the Turbo version was far from it. Taking the virtues of the ordinary saloon, which included decent handling and a supple ride, plus a practical cabin and useful boot, Renault added a set of rather

odd-looking alloy wheels, a spongy rear boot spoiler and decals that emphasized the extra power under the bonnet.

It was justified in doing this, too, because behind the bland nose was a 1.6-litre (96 cu in) all-alloy engine

assisted by a Garrett T3 turbocharger. On paper, it didn't sound that fast, with 93kW (125bhp) and a 0–96km/h (60mph) sprint time of just under 10 second – but the first 3½ seconds were spent waiting for the turbo lag to disappear. After that, power delivery was brutal, with tyre-squealing and understeer the norm under hard acceleration. The car enjoyed only moderate success, but Renault persisted with turbo technology throughout the 1980s, with 'hot' versions of the 9, 11 and 21.

Turbo performance for the masses
The Renault 18 was one of the first commercially successful turbocharged saloons.

Engine: 1565cc (96 cu in), 4-cylinder
Power: 93kW (125bhp)
0–96km/h (60mph): 9.9 secs
Top speed: 195km/h (121mph)
Production total: n/a

RENAULT GTA

It wore Renault badging, but the A610 GTA was designed and built for Renault by styling house Matra In Dieppe. The V6 sports car was enormous fun to drive with great balance on cornering and truly amazing acceleration.

uilt for Renault by Matra in ieppe, the A610 GTA was a urprisingly affordable alternative a supercar, with really stunning erformance and distinctive edge-shaped styling. Despite its

conventional profile – and that was the only thing that was conventional about the car – the A610 had a rear-mounted engine, available as a 2.8-litre (171 cu in) normally aspirated unit, which

delivered an impressive 119kW (160bhp), or as a turbocharged 2.5-litre (150 cu in) motor with 149kW (200bhp) available.

Yet despite the power being fed through the rear wheels, the A610

was surprisingly good when it came to high-speed cornering, with impeccable balance and a huge amount of grip available thanks to the fat rear tyres. Lightweight plastic bodywork meant no rust, and fantastic acceleration.

Low pricing and seating for four weren't enough to convince people the A610 was a genuine sports coupé, however, and the Renault name failed to impress those in the market for either a grand tourer or all-out sports machine, meaning the GTA never enjoyed the sales success it so obviously deserved.

Engine: 2458cc (150 cu in), V6-cylinder
Power: 149kW (200bhp)
0–96km/h (60mph): 5.7 secs
Top speed: 266km/h (165mph)
Production total: 17,450

REO ROYALE

EO was founded by Ransom i Olds in 1904 after he left ldsmobile, which he had also thered. The marque was created offer luxurious, well-constructed rs at an affordable price and it tained success in its early years, buyers perceived an REO to fer much more than a Ford, hevrolet or even Oldsmobile, ithout having to pay too much of price premium.

However, the years of the epression affected sales badly and EO never really recovered despite e 1930s seeing the best cars the mpany had ever produced.

The Royale made its debut in 931 and came with a torquey 9-litre (358 cu in) eight-cylinder ne-bearing side-valve engine, hich offered impressive celeration, but proved to be ther noisy at speed.

A fluted aerodynamic radiator ille marked the Royale out from sser cars, while interiors were ell equipped. The 1932 model as the most desirable, with

elegant and simple styling and a vacuum-operated clutch. 1933 versions had bulkier bodywork and wider wings, but still looked attractive alongside most large saloons of the era.

REO made its final car, a Flying Cloud, in 1936, before it eventually

switched its attentions to the manufacture of trucks.

Engine: 5866cc (358 cu in), 8-cylinder
Power: n/a
0–96km/h (60mph): n/a
Top speed: n/a
Production total: n/a

Photographs do little to illustrate the Royale's vast bulk. It was an enormous vehicle for its day, with acres of interior space and top levels of luxury. However, the economic hardship of the Great Depression was to have a deleterious effect on sales.

RILEY 17/30

1913–22

As one of the pioneers of motoring in Great Britain, Riley quickly established itself as a maker of high quality, luxury vehicles, far removed from the bicycles that were the company's initial product. Indeed, the car company was kept completely separate from Riley's other ventures, which as well as bicycles included engine, bearing and wheel manufacture for other carmakers.

Its advertising boldly proclaimed that Riley cars were 'As old as the industry; as modern as the hour'. This claim was spurious when applied to the 17/30 – its first offering after World War I. Effectively identical to the prewar Riley, except for its oblong radiator grille and elaborately styled front mudguards, the 17/30 was practically obsolete at launch.

It was a reliable machine, however, with an all-new large capacity four-cylinder side-valve engine that employed technology pioneered on Riley's prewar Sixes. It also had a clever three-speed gearbox, with a constant mesh top that allowed for quiet and refined cruising. Riley offered the 17/30 in its price lists as late as 1926, but no cars were actually built after 1922.

Engine: 2951cc (180 cu in), 4-cylinder
Power: 16kW (21bhp)
0–96km/h (60mph): n/a
Top speed: n/a
Production total: n/a

RILEY NINE

1930–37

The first Riley Nines were built in the late 1920s, but it was the second generation car of 1930 that would prove to be a major success for the company, based in Coventry, England. It used a similar chassis to the original machine, but with extra bracing and strengthened side members to offer more confident handling, while the introduction of cable-operated brakes meant a significant improvement in stopping power compared to the earlier cars.

A power boost arrived in 1933, but any performance increase was negated by larger, more weighty bodywork, available in a variety of styles ranging from two-door convertibles to full four-seater saloons, although the tiny engine struggled to cope with some of the more bulky offerings.

A second facelift took place in 1936, when the range was

Riley's first true sporting car, the Nine, boasted an agile chassis and free-revving engine among its many attributes. This is a 1933 model, with larger bodywork than the original.

rationalized. These last-generation cars used a brand new chassis frame which employed tubular crossmembers to cut down on weight and thus improve performance. These were the best Nines to drive, as they could cruise at over 96km/h (60mph) and had more effective rod-type brakes as well as a three-speed synchromesh gearbox. The Riley family had created a winner with the Nine.

Engine: 1087cc (66 cu in), 4-cylinder
Power: 18kW (24bhp)
0–96km/h (60mph): n/a
Top speed: 96km/h (60mph)
Production total: n/a

RILEY BROOKLANDS

1929–32

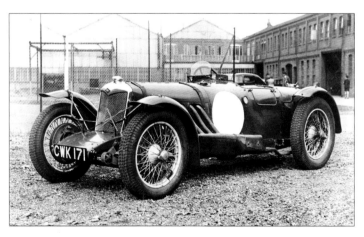

Named after Britain's first motor racing circuit in Weybridge, Surrey, the Riley Brooklands was sold as a competition vehicle. It won the 1932 Tourist Trophy.

Perhaps the most famous pre-World War II Riley, the Brooklands was a stripped-out racer based on the Nine, although it came with an all-new chassis developed for racing by contemporary competition drivers Reid Railton and Parry Thomas.

Significantly shorter and lower than the Nine, the Brooklands was one of the neatest handling racers of its era, while extra performance was added to further boost its race-winning potential.

Modifications included the addition of high compression pistons, twin exhaust camshafts, a four-branch manifold, racing oil pump and dual carburettors. Top speed was rumoured to be in the region of 145km/h (90mph), although some cars were timed at much higher speeds. The Brooklands could leave its driver feeling vulnerable, however, with little in the way of cabin protection, no roof and a tiny wind deflector in place of a front screen.

The car enjoyed numerous race victories, the most notable of which was overall victory in the 1932 Tourist Trophy against many much more powerful and larger-engined machines.

Engine: 1087cc (66 cu in), 4-cylinder
Power: n/a
0–96km/h (60mph): n/a
Top speed: 145km/h (90mph)
Production total: n/a

RILEY IMP

The Imp used a shortened version of the Riley Nine chassis and was offered as a two-door sports car only. Although it wasn't that quick, it was great to drive.

It might have used the engine of the ubiquitous Riley Nine, but the Imp had little else in common with the more family-orientated machine. It was designed specifically as a sports car, with stunning low-slung bodywork that looked even more attractive than an MG TC, thanks to its flowing wings, upright headlights and pretty chrome radiator grille.

In addition, it was a fun car to drive, with an all-new short chassis that provided great handling, as well as the choice of either an effective ENV pre-selector transmission or a racy four-speed close-ratio gearchange.

Riley's staple 1087cc (66 cu in) side-valve four only just fitted under the narrow bonnet, although access was difficult for servicing, while a pair of twin SU carburettors gave it a power boost over its humbler Nine stablemates.

However, the Imp wasn't actually that fast – struggling to top 115km/h (70mph) – but the chassis was so well-balanced and the steering so communicative that it could be driven flat out at all times. A true classic of its era.

Engine: 1087cc (66 cu in), 4-cylinder
Power: n/a
0–96km/h (60mph): n/a
Top speed: 121km/h (75mph)
Production total: n/a

RILEY MPH

Building on the success of the beautiful Imp, Riley tried even harder to impress with the six-cylinder MPH, whose name made no attempt to hide its performance aspirations.

Visually, the car was truly stunning, with a racing-style rounded rump and similar flowing wings to the Imp, as well as the same ornate grille and large, dished headlights.

The chassis was based on Riley's 1933 Tourist Trophy racer and was just as effective at grabbing attention as the stylish bodywork. Underslung at the rear, it sloped upwards to the front of the car and offered tremendous grip and great driver feedback from its lively rear end.

Under the bonnet, there was a choice of overhead-valve straight sixes developed for the 12/6 and 15/6 saloon models, but in the case of the MPH, they were uprated to include magneto ignition, twin SU carburettors and a six-branch exhaust, which also gave a glorious engine note.

Other performance updates included massive brake drums with built-in cooling fins, plus a choice of pre-select transmission or a close-ratio three-speed gearbox.

It was unquestionably one of the most stylish British sports cars of its era – and it was devilishly quick as well. The MPH was a true great, but was expensive to buy.

Engine: 1726cc (105 cu in), 6-cylinder
Power: n/a
0–96km/h (60mph): n/a
Top speed: 145km/h (90mph)
Production total: n/a

RILEY RM SERIES

1945–54

Despite a takeover by the Nuffield organization, Riley cars remained traditionally produced in the years immediately after World War II, with the same separate chassis and ash-frame construction that had been employed on the company's earlier offerings.

The first postwar model from the company was the RMA, which had an elegant streamlined body, while torsion bar independent front suspension and semi-elliptic leaf springs at the rear provided reasonable handling.

Unusually for a fifties saloon car, the RMA (left) used a twin-cam engine and had a surprising turn of speed. Later cars had bigger long-stroke units, but they lacked the RMA's character.

An impressive car for its era, the RMA's 1.5-litre (91 cu in) twin-camshaft engine was ahead of its time and offered an impressive power output for such a small capacity unit.

The RMA was the basis for a host of other RM-type Rileys. The RME used the same engine but had hydraulic brakes and better all-round visibility, while the RMB, RMC, RMD and RMF came with long-stroke four-cylinder 2443cc (149 cu in) engine, a two-door convertible option and the ability to reach 161km/h (100mph) in full 75kW (100bhp) tune. The RM was a true and traditional British touring saloon that became vastly underrated by collectors.

Engine: 1496cc (91 cu in), 4-cylinder
Power: 40kW (54bhp)
0–96km/h (60mph): 25.1 secs
Top speed: 121km/h (75mph)
Production total: 22,909

RILEY PATHFINDER

1953–57

Riley traditionalists were horrified by the appearance of the Pathfinder, which shared its bodywork with the almost identical Wolseley 6/90. The 2.5-litre (149 cu in) straight-six from the RM range was carried over, however, and was exclusive to the Riley, giving an impressive power output of 82kW (110bhp).

However, driving a Pathfinder quickly was not a good idea. It might have looked similar to contemporary unitary construction cars, but the Pathfinder still employed a separate chassis and front torsion bar suspension, coupled to old-fashioned 'cam-and-roller' type steering, which gave it a strong tendency to understeer. This earned it the cruel nickname of 'Ditchfinder' from Britain's notoriously critical motoring press.

Despite these shortcomings, it offered a luxurious interior and a supple ride, while the servo-assisted hydraulic brakes worked well. The right-hand gearlever,

fitted even on right-hand drive cars, took getting used to, meaning the big Riley was an easier car to drive in two-pedal semi-automatic form, offered from 1955.

Luxury and elegance came as standard with the Pathfinder, but it was never a great car to drive. At speed the handling was tricky, as many unlucky drivers found out.

Engine: 2443cc (149 cu in), 6-cylinder
Power: 82kW (110bhp)
0–96km/h (60mph): 16.7 secs
Top speed: 165km/h (102mph)
Production total: 5152

RILEY 2.6

1957–59

Oddly, the 2.6 looked like it came from an earlier era than the car it replaced. It drove better, but still wasn't an inspiring choice.

Riley was absorbed by the BMC empire in 1958. Its replacement for the Pathfinder appeared retrograde, but was introduced purely on economic grounds. By dropping the old – and much lamented – RM engine, BMC could use the same 2.6-litre (159 cu in) six as it fitted in the Wolseley 6/90, with a slight power boost to placate traditionally sporting Riley drivers.

The only notable advantage over the Pathfinder was the use of semi-elliptic leaf springs at the back instead of the previous model's unsteady Panhard rod and coil spring arrangement, which partially, but never fully, countered the Pathfinder's understeer.

The car was never much-loved and not a great success – hardly a surprise considering the ethos behind its production – most 2.6s rotted away, and few people ever tried to preserve them.

Engine: 2639cc (161 cu in), 6-cylinder
Power: 76kW (102bhp)
0–96km/h (60mph): 17.8 secs
Top speed: 153km/h (95mph)
Production total: 2000

RILEY ONE-POINT-FIVE

1957–65

Engine: 1489cc (91 cu in), 4-cylinder
Power: 46kW (62bhp)
0–96km/h (60mph): 17.4 secs
Top speed: 135km/h (84mph)
Production total: 39,568

The One-Point-Five was a badge-engineered Riley that could at least revive some of the brand's sporting spirit. Still applying BMC's policy of developing Riley and Wolseley models together and making the former sporty and the latter luxurious, the car was at least an obedient and lively driver's machine, although Riley purists must have been disappointed by what lay underneath the pretty four-door bodywork. The One-Point-Five was really nothing more than a Morris Minor, which accounted for its awkward, short-looking wheelbase. It came as little comfort that the Minor was regarded as one of the most entertaining small cars on Britain's roads at the time of the new model's launch.

However, a boost was provided by the ubiquitous BMC B-Series engine, in 1489cc (91 cu in) twin-

carburettor form. This meant the car had almost the same performance as an MGA, and could be tuned to offer 160km/h (100mph) performance if desired. The only downsides were very average brakes and, like many cars of the era, terrible rust problems.

Badge engineering might have put off the purists, but the One-Point-Five had a genuinely sporting feel and a luxury cabin.

RILEY 4/68–4/72 'FARINA'

1959–69

By the time the 'Farina' range of saloons made its debut in 1959, BMC had completely given up on the idea of developing Rileys and Wolseleys separately from other BMC models and opted for the much less expensive (and far less adventurous) approach of badge-engineering them.

In the case of the Riley 4/68 – and latterly the 4/72 – this meant taking a standard Morris Oxford, removing its nose, replacing it with Riley's traditional 'grille and whiskers' style and adding two-tone paintwork.

The sporting Riley variant got a few performance enhancements, including front and rear anti-roll bars and a twin-carburettor engine, shared with the equally badge-engineered MG Magnette. The 4/72 replaced the 4/68 in October 1961, and featured front and rear anti-roll bars, wider track and optional automatic transmission – a Riley first – along with a 1622cc (99 cu in) engine to replace the earlier car's 1489cc (91 cu in) unit.

Engine: 1622cc (99 cu in), 4-cylinder
Power: 51kW (68bhp)
0–96km/h (60mph): 19.5 secs
Top speed: 147km/h (91mph)
Production total: 25,011

RILEY ELF

1961–69

When BMC asked the Mini's creator, Alec Issigonis, to create a booted version of his miniature marvel, he refused. Instead, BMC employed Australian designer Dick Burzi to add a notchback to the popular small car, thus creating a

The doors, wings, roof and glass areas were all shared with BMC's miniature marvel, but the Elf had a more mature feel.

vehicle that had the same great handling, lively performance and clever packaging, but a more mature feel.

Developed alongside the Wolseley Hornet, the finished article was surprisingly attractive, sharing the Mini's wings, doors and windows, but with an entirely new shell and a choice of traditional Riley or Wolseley radiator grilles.

Inside, the Riley model came with an impressive wood veneer dashboard and deep pile carpets to mark it out as an exclusive model. Later versions, from 1963, saw the engine capacity increased from 848cc (52 cu in) to 998cc (61 cu in), along with the contemporary Austin and Morris Minis. Mk III models, from 1966, got winding windows and hidden door hinges.

Surprisingly successful given its origins, the Elf appealed largely to older drivers who wanted the luxury and build quality of a larger car, but preferred the light steering and gearbox of a smaller machine.

Engine: 998cc (61 cu in), 4-cylinder
Power: 28kW (38bhp)
0–96km/h (60mph): 24.1 secs
Top speed: 124km/h (77mph)
Production total: 30,912

RILEY KESTREL

1965–69

BMC took badge engineering to new heights with the 1100/1300 series of cars, which were available with no less than six different marque names. Riley versions were named the Kestrel and came with a traditional Riley grille and a sumptuous interior, which boasted

walnut veneer, circular dials (including oil pressure and rev counter, and the twin-carburettor 1098cc (67 cu in) engine from the MG 1100, although without the MG's sports exhaust.

Initially only available with this engine, a 1275cc (78 cu in) variant

was introduced for 1967, along with the option of automatic transmission. The last models were the best – from 1968, the 1.3-litre (78 cu in) engine was fitted with twin carburettors and produced 52kW (70bhp), giving genuine 160km/h (100mph) capability. The

Kestrel was fun to drive, but suffered from serious corrosion.

Engine: 1098cc (67 cu in), 4-cylinder
Power: 41kW (55bhp)
0–96km/h (60mph): 17.3 secs
Top speed: 144km/h (89mph)
Production total: 21,529

ROCHDALE OLYMPIC

1959–68

While some place names seem to lend themselves naturally to cars, such as Monte Carlo, Capri, Daytona and even Caterham, the small Lancashire mill town of Rochdale, England doesn't quite have the same stylish flair. Nevertheless, the small independent sports car maker survived for almost a decade, building a pretty two-seater coupé that employed complex glassfibre monocoque construction.

The earliest cars were two-door versions with no boot opening, while those from 1963 onwards came with a proper hatchback. Running gear came from a variety of BMC sources, with either A-Series, B-Series or Triumph-based engines, although some

examples used Ford Cortina or even side-valve Anglia units.

Later cars were better than early examples, with improved build quality and Triumph Spitfire front suspension. A Rochdale could take any engine that fitted – and the glass-reinforced-plastic body could handle it, too, with tight handling, a twitchy rear end and a bumpy ride. It was fun to drive and much better than anyone realized, although its kit car feel did little for its reputation among fans of 'genuine' sports cars.

Engine: 948cc (58 cu in), 4-cylinder
Power: 33kW (44bhp)
0–96km/h (60mph): 14.9 secs
Top speed: 134km/h (83mph)
Production total: 400

The Rochdale Olympic was an agile and entertaining little sports car. Refinement, however, wasn't its strong point, and the cabin was lacking creature comforts.

ROLLS-ROYCE TWENTY

1922–29

The first entirely new Rolls-Royce model since 1907, the Twenty was a compact alternative to the Silver Ghost and was a more economical ownership proposition thanks to its smaller, more fuel-efficient engine. However, it was still very expensive compared to most cars of the era – a price discerning owners were prepared to pay for the knowledge that they were buying a supremely well-engineered and hand-crafted motor car.

Traditional looks, with Rolls-Royce's by this time traditional upright radiator grille and Spirit of Ecstasy mascot sitting proud on the filler cap, were married to modern developments for the Twenty. Early cars had a centrally positioned gearchange, although this was moved back to the right-hand side of the steering wheel in a seemingly retrograde move in the mid-1920s, halfway through its production life.

Other innovations included servo braking on all four wheels from 1924, plus vertical radiator shutters that prevented debris from getting caught up in the cooling system.

Interior space was massive, especially in the rear of the car, although the Twenty was designed primarily with owner-drivers in mind, rather than for chauffeurs and passengers, as in the case of the larger models in the company's line-up.

Engine: 3127cc (191 cu in), 6-cylinder
Power: n/a
0–96km/h (60mph): n/a
Top speed: n/a
Production total: 2940

Most Twenty owners chose not to have a chauffeur and the car was designed with owner-drivers in mind. However, judging by his smart peaked hat and demeanour, this gentleman is on his way to collect his wealthy employer…

ROLLS-ROYCE SILVER GHOST

A chance meeting between a young car dealer from London and a Peterborough-born electrical engineer might not have been the likeliest basis on which to build 'The Best Car in the World', yet this is the basis of the formation of the Rolls-Royce Motor Company.

Royce Ltd, a manufacturer of electric generators, started making petrol-engined cars in Manchester in 1904. Frederick Henry Royce, who preferred to be known as Henry, was a meticulous engineer, but he felt happier designing and improving his cars than he did trying to sell them. He needed an outgoing salesman to convince potential buyers of the engineering excellence he had built into his vehicles.

Charles Stewart Rolls, the youngest son of Lord Llangattock, was selling Panhard et Levassor cars to London's aristocracy from an exclusive dealership in Mayfair. A well-known racing driver and aviation pioneer, Rolls was also an astute businessman – and the engineering excellence of Henry Royce's motor cars appealed to him as he believed it would become a major selling point among his upmarket buyers.

He travelled to Manchester in 1904 to visit Royce and a deal was struck that would see Rolls investing in new premises in Manchester and later Derby and Crewe (where Rolls-Royces were still produced until production transferred to Sussex in 2002 under new owner BMW). According to the arrangement, Royce and his workforce would build the cars under the jurisdiction of Claude Johnston, who was Royce's top engineer and designer, and often regarded as the 'hyphen' in Rolls-Royce. Indeed, Johnston was more important in the shaping of the company than Charles Rolls himself, who was killed in a flying accident in 1910 at the age of 32.

Up to 1906, Rolls-Royce had built several different models with four- and six-cylinder engines, and even a V8. For 1907, they decided on a one-model policy for the

Attention to detail extended under the bonnet – Rolls-Royce engines were as finely engineered as the rest of the car.

company. This would permit them to concentrate all efforts on developing it, rather than wasting their resources building several different ones.

The Silver Ghost was launched at the Olympia Motor Show in London in November 1906. It was a large car, weighing over 1,500kg (1.5 ton). Power came from a 7.4-litre (453 cu in) side-valve six-cylinder engine with amazing refinement and smoothness, while tall gearing gave it a much higher top speed than most cars of the era. In 1911, a special aero-bodied

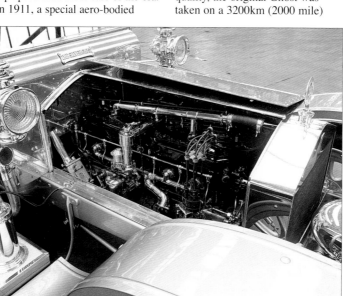

example was clocked at over 163km/h (101mph) at the Brooklands race track.

The 'Silver' part of its name came from the silver-plated metal trim parts of the car while the 'Ghost' implied its quiet operation – a tradition which continues in Rolls-Royce folklore to this day. The Silver Ghost models were officially known as the 40/50 Series, but the more common name, 'Ghost', is frequently used by enthusiasts.

To demonstrate the new model's quality, the original Ghost was taken on a 3200km (2000 mile)

AX201 was Rolls-Royce's own car, and can now be seen at Britain's National Motor Museum in Beaulieu, Hampshire.

reliability run, which included driving from the south coast of England up to Scotland in top gear, under the strict scrutiny of the motoring organization, the RAC. It completed the distance effortlessly. In order to prove its hardiness further, the company immediately sent it out on a 24,000km (15,000 mile) test, with Charles Rolls as one of the drivers. This, too, was completed without involuntary stops (except for tyre changes) and it broke the world record for reliability and long-distance driving.

The Ghost was then stripped down by engineers to determine how much wear it had suffered. There was no deterioration in the engine, transmission, brakes or steering, and the model quickly established itself as the finest car in the world. Incredibly, the original Silver Ghost test car is still running today, and has now covered over 800,000km (500,000 miles).

Engine: 7428cc (453 cu in), 6-cylinder
Power: n/a
0–96km/h (60mph): n/a
Top speed: n/a
Production total: 7876

ROLLS-ROYCE 40/50 NEW PHANTOM

1925–29

A huge six-cylinder engine and expensive hand-built coachwork made the New Phantom one of the most desirable sporting cars of the 1920s. The exact power output was never disclosed – another Rolls-Royce tradition – although standard production examples were tested at speeds in excess of 144km/h (90mph). Elegant saloon, open tourer or coupé body styles were available, while the excellent performance was complemented by servo-assisted hydraulic brakes and gas-filled shock absorbers, giving the car ride and handling abilities that were significantly ahead of their time. Right-hand gearchange and a non-synchromesh gearbox remained, meaning that changing gear smoothly required some forward planning.

The only drawback of the New Phantom was its archaic chassis, designed along the same principles as the Silver Ghost and utilizing a very basic cantilever-type suspension.

The New Phantom was also built in the United States, at a factory in Springfield, Ohio. The American cars differed from those built in Britain by having a central gearchange, left-hand drive and more extravagant bodywork. Production ceased in Britain in 1929, but carried on in the United States until 1931.

Engine: 7668cc (468 cu in), 6-cylinder
Power: n/a
0–96km/h (60mph): n/a
Top speed: n/a
Production total: 3453

A traditionally-minded company with traditionally-minded customers, Rolls-Royce made few changes to the Silver Ghost chassis when it produced the New Phantom, later named the Phantom I.

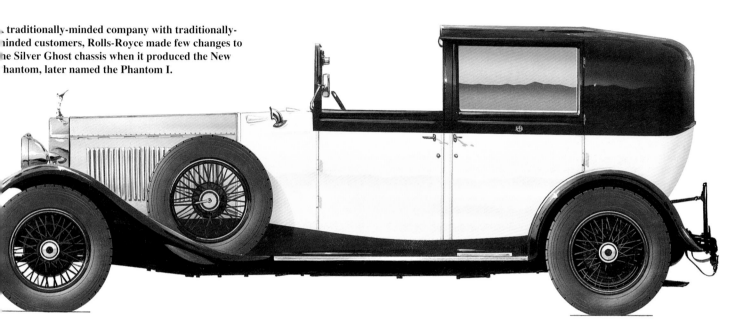

ROLLS-ROYCE 40/50 PHANTOM II

1929–35

The New Phantom was often criticized for its old-fashioned chassis which, although offering compliant handling, featured overly-heavy steering and little in the way of lateral stability. This was corrected for the second generation 40/50 Phantom II, unveiled in 1929 to replace the New Phantom. It had semi-elliptic leaf springs front and rear, which gave much more assured road-holding, far lighter steering and an even more supple ride – as demanded by all of Rolls-Royce's upper-class clients.

The earlier car's right-hand gearchange remained, however, and was not improved upon until 1932, when synchromesh was added to the top three ratios. The same engine was used as in the earlier New Phantom, which meant the Phantom II was an equally lively machine to drive, while modifications that coincided with the new synchromesh gearbox saw the car's weight drop significantly. That, coupled to an altered gear ratio, gave standard-bodied Phantom IIs the ability to pass the 161km/h (100mph) barrier – quite a feat for its era.

Visually, it was very little different from the New Phantom, but the Phantom II had a much better chassis and was far more pleasant to drive. Its lighter steering and more assured road-holding were noticeable improvements.

Engine: 7668cc (468 cu in), 6-cylinder
Power: n/a
0–96km/h (60mph): n/a
Top speed: n/a
Production total: 1767

ROLLS-ROYCE 20/25

1930–37

20/25 was the 'baby' Rolls-Royce for the Depression era. Although never a bad car, in Rolls-Royce terms it was far from the company's best. Its good points included a compact, economical engine, flexible performance and a surprisingly agile chassis, but some of the body styles offered were at odds with the fine quality of the engineering, while in later years, as

One of the smallest Rolls-Royces of its era, the 20/265 was pleasant, but lacked passenger space.

the notion of a Rolls-Royce for the owner-driver became absurd, the compact and cramped 20/25 was largely undesirable.

Early cars, especially with Barker or Gurney-Nutting Coupé de Ville bodywork, were the best,

while later cars grew heavier, slower and too ornamental to be considered tasteful.

Despite most manufacturers opting for a conventional gearchange layout, Rolls-Royce still, irritatingly, favoured the right-hand gearchange. Although a tactile car to drive, the 20/25 felt big and unwieldy and any high-speed manoeuvres required careful

forward planning. Unrest in Europe prior to World War II signalled the 20/25's demise, and no subsequent effort was ever made to build a compact Rolls-Royce again.

Engine: 3669cc (224 cu in), 6-cylinder
Power: n/a
0–96km/h (60mph): n/a
Top speed: n/a
Production total: 3827

ROLLS-ROYCE SILVER WRAITH

1946–59

Rolls-Royce's first postwar car was actually a prewar design, based on the short-lived 1939 Wraith. Initially for export only in a bid to boost Britain's shattered economy (most cars went to the United States), the Silver Wraith was offered on the domestic market from 1948.

Power came from a new inlet-over-exhaust valve six-cylinder engine, and although no official power output was ever quoted in keeping with Rolls-Royce tradition, it is estimated the unit developed around 97kW (130bhp).

Very few Silver Wraiths looked the same, as no standard body style was offered by Rolls-Royce and it was up to the individual buyer to select a coachbuilder's design from those offered by dealerships or, alternatively, to have a car tailored to specific requirements.

As with all of the company's products, it was supremely refined

and well engineered, although the model was unresponsive to drive and performance was fairly uninspiring. Despite this, elegant and spacious long wheelbase variants became popular with heads of state. Automatic gearboxes were offered from 1952 – a Rolls-Royce

first, yet commonplace on all subsequent models.

Engine: 4527cc (276 cu in), 6-cylinder
Power: n/a
0–96km/h (60mph): 24 secs
Top speed: 137km/h (85mph)
Production total: 1783

There's something quintessentially British about a Rolls-Royce, and it was this ethos that made the Silver Wraith an export success. Most were sold to the United States and the long-wheelbase variants achieved a measure of popularity with foreign heads of state.

ROLLS-ROYCE SILVER DAWN

By acquiring Bentley, Rolls-Royce had access to shared resources. The Silver Dawn was effectively a badge-engineered Bentley Mk VI, but was still a luxurious means of transport, although never particularly inspiring to drive.

Not so much a Rolls-Royce as a badge-engineered Bentley, the Silver Dawn was aimed primarily at European export markets.

Based on the Bentley Mk VI, the Silver Dawn wasn't a tremendous success. It was a quality car nonetheless, with a well-equipped wood and leather trimmed interior, plus a larger version of the engine from the Silver Wraith. Compact dimensions and a column-change Hydramatic gearbox made the Dawn a simple car to drive, while it was more driver-orientated than most Rolls-Royce offerings thanks to its Bentley origins. Performance was uninspiring – again, the manufacturer never revealed the engine's power output – but handling was reasonably tight and it was lighter than most of the company's other cars.

Almost all of the 761 Dawns built were left-hand drive and only a handful were sold in Britain, where larger models were much more popular.

Not so well built as some Rolls-Royces, the pressed steel bodywork was quite prone to rust, making the Dawn a rarity today – and, as a result, a highly desirable car among collectors.

Engine: 4566cc (279 cu in), 6-cylinder
Power: n/a
0–96km/h (60mph): 16.2 secs
Top speed: 140km/h (87mph)
Production total: 761

ROLLS-ROYCE PHANTOM V

The first Rolls-Royce to use the by-now-familiar 6.3-litre (380 cu in) V8 engine was also one of the biggest cars ever to emerge from the manufacturer's workshops in Crewe.

Tipping the scales at almost 3000kg (almost 3 tons), the Phantom V had a 3.6m (12ft) wheelbase and enormous passenger space in the rear, where its occupants were often royalty, the gentry or multi-millionaire businessmen. Under the bonnet, the pushrod V8 resembled that of units built by Chrysler and GM in America and used an aluminium block and cylinder heads.

Power steering was standard – it needed to be – as was automatic transmission, while underneath the imposing bodywork was a lengthened version of the Silver Cloud's chassis. A choice of coachwork was offered, although most buyers opted for the HJ Mulliner six-light styling, usually painted black. Performance was spirited, not that this was a consideration to most buyers, but fuel consumption was very high. It was replaced by the even more extravagant but visually similar 6.7-litre (409 cu in) Phantom VI for 1968, which remained available on special order into the 1990s.

Engine: 6230cc (380 cu in), V8-cylinder
Power: n/a
0–96km/h (60mph): 13.8 secs
Top speed: 163km/h (101mph)
Production total: 793

Rolls-Royce's venerable all-alloy V8 made its debut in the Phantom V and went on to power generations of the company's models. Its excellent refinement and 'adequate' power output were ideal for Rolls-Royce customers.

ROLLS-ROYCE SILVER CLOUD

Traditional styling cunningly concealed the Silver Cloud's many attributes. It was an impressively quick and surprisingly agile motor car, with incredible luxury inside.

The Silver Cloud was the first Rolls-Royce to have its body made in-house, although it still retained a separate chassis. The company's thinking was that, unlike most unitary construction rivals' cars, buyers could have a special body fitted if they wanted one without too much re-engineering.
It also meant that the chassis could be used for other projects within Rolls-Royce, perhaps the most highly regarded of which was the beautiful Bentley Continental S, launched in 1955. It also formed the basis of more conventional Bentleys, including the S1 and S2 saloons. With a successful export programme swelling Rolls-Royce's coffers, chief engineer Harry Grylls commissioned the Cloud as an entirely new vehicle, which would use steel bodywork and enjoy typical levels of luxury.

The new cars were announced in April 1955 and were initially available with the 4887cc (298 cu in) inlet-over-exhaust valve six-cylinder engine originally found in the Bentley Mk VI and Rolls-Royce Silver Dawn.

The car retained the traditional interior, with a veneered dash and deep leather chairs, while further luxury adornments included GM's Hydramatic automatic transmission as standard, plus power steering and optional air conditioning.

With heavy-gauge steel and impressive bodywork 5.4m (17.6ft) long, the Cloud was an imposing and heavy car, and although the six-cylinder engine was smooth, quiet and refined, it lacked the necessary power to propel the huge hull with ease.

This was corrected in 1959 by the introduction of the Silver Cloud II, which used Rolls-Royce's new aluminium V8, initially available in a 6.2-litre (380 cu in) capacity. The unit was chosen instead of a 7-litre (427 cu in) straight eight, as engineers believed this would add unnecessary length to the car.

The new engine transformed the Cloud's character, and although it remained serenely quiet and supremely refined, it was now quick enough to cruise at high speeds in well-damped silence. As ever, Rolls-Royce never revealed the unit's power output, although at an estimated 149kW (200bhp) it was more than adequate compared to the previous six-cylinder, which produced somewhere in the region of 112kW (150bhp). It also enjoyed better fuel economy, although a leap from 19l/100km (12mpg) to 17l/100km (15mpg) hardly made the Silver Cloud an inexpensive car to run.

A 1962 facelift, called the Silver Cloud III, saw the car gain twin headlights similar to those on the Phantom VI, a lower grille, a new power steering arrangement and a higher compression ratio, although the engine's true power output remained a closely guarded secret.

As well as the standard saloon, buyers could choose a Park Ward-bodied limousine, with an extended wheelbase and even more sumptuous interior, a striking two-door coupé or an HJ Mulliner-designed drophead convertible (from 1962), which offered incredibly stylish looks and an even more exotic price tag.

But in an era of rapid technological development in the motor industry, the Silver Cloud started to struggle into the 1960s. It might have been acceptably modern when it was launched in 1955, but by the time production ceased a decade later, cheaper rivals were offering unitary construction, disc brakes and fully-independent suspension. It was time for the company to unveil a new plan of attack, and it would do so with its most successful model ever – the Silver Shadow.

Engine: 6230cc (380 cu in), V8-cylinder
Power: n/a
0–96km/h (60mph): 11.5 secs
Top speed: 182km/h (113mph)
Production total: 7374

A drophead version of the Cloud appeared in 1962, styled by HJ Mulliner. Its looks were sensational – but so was the price tag!

ROLLS-ROYCE SILVER SHADOW

1965–80

Side by side the styling differences between the 1965 Shadow I and 1977 Shadow II are obvious. The later car (left) has rubber bumpers and a front spoiler.

switches for the driver to operate all of them.

A long-wheelbase option, along with a new safety-padded dashboard, were introduced for 1969, while 1970 models saw the engine displacement increased to 6750cc (412 cu in), although Rolls-Royce still refused to reveal the power output. A two-door coupé and convertible version were also unveiled, although these would become a model in their own right – the Corniche – by 1974.

Following a turbulent start to the 1970s, which saw Rolls-Royce declared bankrupt and split into several separate constituent companies, sales of the Silver Shadow continued to be strong and highly profitable, ensuring the car division's future.

Sales were strong enough, in fact, to justify investing in a considerable improvement programme to see the Shadow through its final years until the Silver Spirit appeared. So, in March 1977, Rolls-Royce unveiled the Shadow II at the Geneva Motor Show.

Instantly recognizable by its polyurethane front spoiler and matt black bumpers, the newcomer featured more than just visual changes, while the Silver Wraith name was revived for long-wheelbase models. In what might seem a retrograde step, the four-speed automatic box was swapped for a three-speed one, although it was so smooth and the engine so flexible that Rolls-Royce's reasoning could be understood. That, coupled to a tauter suspension, sharper steering and an even more luxurious cabin, made the car a worthy update and would make certain that it was sorely missed by purists when replaced by the angular Silver Spirit in late 1980. A true great and a very successful car for Rolls-Royce.

If the Silver Cloud was archaic in its construction methods, then the Silver Shadow proved Rolls-Royce could build a car as up to the minute, if not more so, than the most technologically advanced in the world.

The Tibet project, which was the Shadow's factory codename, was commissioned by chief engineer Harry Grylls in 1958 – a whole seven years before it would appear and just three after the Cloud had entered production. In the face of stiff competition, Rolls-Royce wanted to prove unequivocally that it was still worthy of the 'Best Car in the World' title.

By the time the Shadow arrived in showrooms in October 1965, it appeared the company had realized its ambition, as here was a car that offered supreme ride comfort, a wonderfully serene driving experience and a design that managed to brilliantly combine up-to-the-minute three-box styling with traditional Rolls-Royce cues such as the upright radiator grille, twin headlights and chrome trim.

Beautifully finished burr walnut veneer, Wilton carpets and Connolly leather – it could only be a Rolls...

Unitary construction saw the car being built mostly out of heavy gauge steel, although weight was kept down by using aluminium for the doors, bonnet and bootlid, while a lower floor and clever rear axle arrangement meant the Shadow enjoyed better rear legroom than its predecessor despite being considerably shorter.

Initially, the car used the Silver Cloud's 6.2-litre (380 cu in) V8 engine, along with a four-speed automatic gearbox with a column change, although this had been re-engineered to allow smoother, almost seamless changes. Further

comfort for occupants was guaranteed by the use of Citroën's hydropneumatic technology for the back suspension although, unlike the French firm's cars, the Rolls's system was constantly pressurized, rather than just when the engine was running.

Luxury – always a Rolls-Royce byword – was assured thanks to the usual high veneer dashboard, Wilton carpets and sumptuous high-quality leather, while further additions included split-level air conditioning, electrically adjustable seats, a Motorola radio and electric windows, with a separate bank of

Engine: 6750cc (412 cu in), V8-cylinder
Power: n/a
0–96km/h (60mph): 9.4 secs
Top speed: 192km/h (119mph)
Production total: 27,915

ROLLS-ROYCE CORNICHE

Convertible versions of the Silver Shadow had been available since 1965, but the Corniche did not become a model in its own right until 1971. A coupé was offered, too.

but this was only to be expected on Britain's most expensive car. Leather and walnut was standard, while cruise control and a radio-cassette were introduced for 1974 models, and split-level air conditioning for 1976. Second generation models, called the Corniche II, came with the Shadow's new and less attractive safety bumpers, plus a new range of colours and trim, a revised fascia and improved suspension set-up.

The car lasted until 1994, when it was replaced by an all-new model based on the Bentley Azure/ Continental.

Coachbuilder Mulliner Park Ward, which by the late 1960s was a constituent company of Rolls-Royce Motor Cars, had been offering coupé and convertible versions of the Silver Shadow from the model's inception back in 1965, but it was not until 1971 that the Corniche became a model in its own right.

All cars with the Corniche name used the 6.7-litre (412 cu in) engine from the later version of the Shadow (some earlier conversions had the 6.3-litre [384 cu in] unit), with power estimated to be around 149kW (200bhp).

Standard equipment was lavish,

Engine: 6750cc (412 cu in), V8-cylinder
Power: n/a
0–96km/h (60mph): 9.6 secs
Top speed: 194km/h (120mph)
Production total: 6350

ROLLS-ROYCE CAMARGUE

With an asking price of £29,250, the Camargue was Britain's most expensive car when it went on sale in 1975, costing as much as a large house. It was also a commercial flop, with controversial Pininfarina-styled lines, which made it look like a bloated and over-garnished Fiat 130 Coupé. It also rusted badly, too.

Under the skin. the Camargue used a Silver Shadow floorpan and engine, while inside it was as luxurious as any Rolls-Royce, with traditional wood, leather and split-level air conditioning.

It was more powerful than the Shadow, too, with four-barrel carburettors. Most commentators estimate it developed around

164kW (220bhp), which was relatively modest for the 6.7-litre (412 cu in) V8 pushrod unit under the bonnet.

Sales were slow, mostly because the Corniche was just as luxurious, almost as quick and arguably far better to look at, although some owners liked the Camargue for its curiosity value.

Engine: 6750cc (412 cu in), V8-cylinder
Power: n/a
0–96km/h (60mph): 10 secs
Top speed: 190km/h (118mph)
Production total: 531

Traditional buyers weren't ready for the controversial Camargue. The striking Pininfarina bodywork was too edgy for most buyers.

ROLLS-ROYCE SILVER SPIRIT

Although intended as a complete replacement for the Silver Shadow, the Spirit was in effect a Shadow with a major facelift. It looked totally different but used essentially the same engine, transmission and platform as its forebear.

Later in its life, concessions to modernity included fuel injection,

This example (below) is a Silver Spur – note the extra length in the rear doors and chrome finished alloy wheels. Extra rear space meant it was ideal for wedding use.

which increased the famously undisclosed power output to about 171kW (230bhp), as well as anti-lock brakes and improved air conditioning. A 1989 facelift saw the interior revised and brought right up to date, with a deeper, wider dashboard and a chunky, leather-bound steering wheel in place of earlier cars' old-fashioned, thin-rimmed examples.

Longer wheelbase versions were called Silver Spur and offered improved rear accommodation for those who preferred to be driven

It might have looked fresh and modern, but the Silver Spirit used the same platform, engines and transmission as the Silver Shadow that it was designed to replace.

rather than drive. Handling was ponderous, with excessive body roll and little feedback through the steering, but then most Rolls-Royce owners tended not to be enthusiastic drivers. Those who were could opt instead for the identical-looking, but far better honed, Bentley Mulsanne and

Turbo R, which offered incredible performance and similar levels of luxury.

The Silver Spirit enjoyed an even longer life than the Shadow, remaining in production until it was eventually superseded by the BMW-powered Silver Seraph in 1997.

Engine: 6750cc (412 cu in), V8-cylinder
Power: n/a
0–96km/h (60mph): 9.5 secs
Top speed: 215km/h (133mph)
Production total: n/a

ROVER EIGHT

Simplicity was the order of the day with the air-cooled Rover Eight. It was a very basic car, and those hot cylinder heads sticking out from each side of the bonnet were hardl the most safety conscious features.

An individual feature of the Eight was the way the cylinder heads stuck out of the side of the bonnet, and glowed red whenever the Eight was driven hard. It may have looked dramatic but it wasn't the most practical of designs.

For its time, the Eight was a successful light car. Its chassis was re-engineered in 1924 to accept a four-cylinder engine with water-cooling, that model being launched as the 9/20hp. The original Eight was dropped a year later.

Rover started production in 1884 as a bicycle manufacturer and started building cars in 1905. It made a variety of models, with varying levels of success, gradually moving its cars upmarket.

One of its cheaper models was the Rover Eight, introduced in 1919. It was an individual little car, and what it lacked in creature comforts, it more than made up for in character.

The idea for the basic-looking vehicle, with its lively air-cooled, horizontally opposed two-cylinder engine, was bought from designer Jack Sangster. Rover also bought a factory in Birmingham to build it.

Engine: 998cc (61 cu in), 2-cylinder
Power: 10kW (13bhp) at 2800rpm
0–96km/h (60mph): n/a
Top speed: 72km/h (45mph)
Production total: 17,700

ROVER SIX

A six-cylinder Rover first appeared at the 1923 London Motor Show, but although three prototypes were built, the experiment was shelved and the 3.5-litre (214 cu in) engine disappeared.

That was until 1927, when a new Rover Six, christened the 2-Litre, was unveiled, sporting the firm's first production six-cylinder engine. Its capacity was smaller, at 2023cc (123 cu in), but it was a more impressive and advanced pushrod overhead-valve design, by Peter Poppe. In both original and enlarged form, it would subsequently go on to power other models in the Rover range.

Several different body styles were offered for the Six, and there were two different wheelbases, too. One of the more expensive options was the upright fabric-bodied Weymann saloon, but for those customers wanting more sporting performance, the Rover Light Six was the vehicle of choice, especially if fitted with the semi-streamlined Sportsman's coupé body. One of these models raced the luxury high-speed Blue Train express across France in January 1930, and won.

Initially, a three-speed gearbox was offered on all models, but a four-speed version became an option in 1930 and servo-assisted brakes could also be specified from 1931.

Engine: 2023cc (123 cu in), 6-cylinder
Power: 34kW (45bhp) at 3600rpm
0–96km/h (60mph): n/a
Top speed: 97km/h (60mph)
Production total: 8000 approx

The Six's most famous exploit was to race one of Europe's premier express trains across France. The car came first, the train was second. It was a foretaste of the future of transport.

ROVER SPEED 20 1931–34

uge headlamps, an imposing rille and the general upmarket ppearance of the Rover Speed 20 aarked it out as important in over's prewar catalogue.

eter Poppe's 2023cc (123 cu in) x-cylinder overhead-valve engine as first seen in the Rover Six of 927. It had the potential to be nlarged, and a 2565cc (157 cu in)

unit duly appeared in the Meteor, the largest car in the Rover line-up for many years.

The engine was then used in the new Speed 20 model of 1931. The aptly-named car had Rover's biggest engine fitted in the company's smallest chassis, making the car fast and agile and capable of almost 137km/h (85mph) flat out. As usual, customers could choose from several

different bodies including a Weymann fabric body, a sportsman's coupé and the distinctive notchback Hastings coupé.

Although fitted with Rover's premier engine, power output was compromised by the single down-draught carburettor, which led to the adoption of three SU carburettors in 1934. This move boosted power to a credible 54kW

(72bhp). Servo brakes complemented this higher power output. The Speed 20 was discontinued in 1934, although the name was re-used in 1937.

Engine: 2565cc (157 cu in), 6-cylinder
Power: 54kW (72bhp)
0–96km/h (60mph): n/a
Top speed: 134km/h (83mph)
Production total: n/a

ROVER P3 1948–49

over restarted production llowing the end of World War II ith its prewar 10, 12, 14 and 16hp 2 models, having moved to olihull after its old factory in oventry had been destroyed by e Luftwaffe.

Its first 'new' postwar model ppeared in 1948, although there as little to distinguish it visually om its immediate predecessors.

The P3 was wider and was built on a new, shorter chassis with an all-steel body instead of the ash frame of the P2. Two new inlet-over-exhaust engines, one a four-cylinder, the other a six, were fitted, along with all-independent front suspension. Much thought was given to the look of the front end with styling following American fashions. Initial designs

were quite radical, but Rover's conservatism resulted in the P3 eventually looking strictly conventional.

Two different bodies were offered, a four-light saloon (two windows per side) and a six-light (three windows per side). There were also a couple of special models made by coachbuilders including Tickford and Graber,

who built a stylish tourer on the same chassis.

The P3 stayed in production for just 18 months before being replaced by the fresher P4.

Engine: 2103cc (128 cu in), 6-cylinder
Power: 54kW (72bhp) at 4000rpm
0–96km/h (60mph): 29.4 secs
Top speed: 121km/h (75mph)
Production total: 9111

ROVER P4

The upright and distinguished looking P4 established Rover as a manufacturer of dignified but unexciting cars for the middle classes. It became the favourite of 'professionals'. The design echoed American styles of the late 1940s.

At last, in 1949, Rover put a completely new saloon on sale. The P4's chassis was developed from the P3, but the look of the solid new car was completely different, strongly influenced by the Studebaker designs of Raymond Loewy and Virgil Exner.

The first P4s (known as Rover 75s) had 2103cc (128 cu in) engines carried over from the P3, and earned the nickname 'Cyclops', thanks to the single auxiliary driving light mounted in the centre of the grille. This distinctive feature eventually disappeared in 1952, when the front end was restyled.

In various guises, the P4 lasted for 15 years, helping to create Rover's friendly 'Auntie' image. The original Rover 75 was joined by the 2.6-litre (159 cu in)

Rover 90 in 1953 and in the same year, four-cylinder models in the forms of the 1997cc (122 cu in) Rover 60 and 2286cc (140 cu in) Rover 80 entered the catalogue.

After a slight facelift in 1954, the 75 got a new 2.2-litre

(136 cu in) engine and two years later, the Rover 105 appeared, featuring twin carburettors. The final P4s were the 95, 100 and 110, fitted with an improved 2625cc (160 cu in) engine. Manufacture ended in 1964.

Engine: 2230cc (136 cu in), 6-cylinder
Power: 60kW (80bhp) at 4500rpm
0–96km/h (60mph): 20.8 secs
Top speed: 140km/h (87mph)
Production total: 114,746

ROVER P5

The P5 of 1959 took Rover upmarket, gaining the firm a new reputation. This handsome, luxurious and robust car became a favoured vehicle of the British government, with examples being used by Prime Ministers into the 1980s. What better publicity for a car firm than to have its product

consistently appearing on the television news?

The P5 was Rover's first monocoque construction vehicle, with the bulky but crisp look designed by David Bache. The traditional interior was finished in wood and leather. Initially, the model was available with just one

By the simple expedient of lowering the roofline a few inches, in 1963, Rover managed to transform its P5 from luxury saloon to robust grand tourer. The V8-powered version of the model remains one of the most sought-after Rover models by today's collectors.

engine, a 2995cc (183 cu in) straight-six unit developed from the earlier P3.

In 1962, more power arrived, with the 'Weslake Head' (a modified cylinder head developed by performance expert Harry Weslake) version of the engine, taking power from 86kW (115bhp to 100kW (134bhp).

More significant, however, was the introduction of a coupé version for 1963. In reality, it may have been little more than a saloon with a lower roofline, but it somehow made the bulky car look a lot more sporting.

Rover put its newly acquired 3.5-litre (214 cu in) V8 engine in the P5 in 1967 to create the P5B, which transformed both performance and low-down power This variant lasted until 1973.

Engine: 2995cc (183 cu in), 6-cylinder
Power: 86kW (115bhp) at 4500rpm
0–96km/h (60mph): 16.2 secs
Top speed: 157km/h (98mph)
Production total: 69,141

ROVER P6

In 1964, the Car of the Year award was introduced, and the inaugural recipient of the accolade was Rover, for its brand new P6. It was a worthy winner.

Compared to the conservative offerings of the past, the new Rover was a smart car, with modern square-cut styling and a capable new overhead camshaft 2-litre (121 cu in) four-cylinder engine. Servo-assisted disc brakes

were fitted all round. The P6's method of construction was unusual, effectively a steel skeleton onto which the body panels and mechanicals were attached.

Initially, just the 1978cc (121 cu in) Rover 2000 was available at the launch in 1963. Three years later an automatic transmission option was offered, as well as more power in the shape of the twin-carburettor TC model.

1968 saw the appearance of the powerful Rover 3500, created by using the company's alloy V8 engine to make a superb cruiser. Initially, this was only available as an automatic, but the manual 3500S was offered in 1971.

Meanwhile, at the lower end of the P6 power spectrum, the 2000 was supplanted by the 2200 in 1973. All models were replaced by the advanced SD1 in 1977.

The P6 had enough extra room under the bonnet for a gas turbine engine. This never materialized, but Rover did drop its V8 engine in, five years after the launch of the four-cylinder original model.

Engine: 1978cc (121 cu in), 4-cylinder
Power: 67kW (90bhp) at 5000rpm
0–96km/h (60mph): 15.3 secs
Top speed: 163km/h (101mph)
Production total: 439,135

ROVER SD1

Stand far enough away, close your eyes a bit, and the Rover SD1 does look like a Ferrari Daytona… slightly! Nevertheless, the distinctive wedge profile of the SD1 was an exotic shape for a saloon car when launched in 1976.

Rover's traditional rather staid image had started to fade with the introduction of the P6. When the revolutionary SD1 appeared in 1976, it disappeared once and for all. Like the P6 before it, the SD1 was Car of the Year, but Rover's new executive saloon was even more of an eye-opener to potential buyers than its predecessor.

The hatchback SD1 – the name signified the first vehicle from British Leyland's Specialist Division – was a striking shape for the time, allegedly influenced by the exotic Ferrari Daytona. It was futuristic inside and out, without the usual wood, chrome and leather

that were usually associated with a Rover product.

The first variant was the Rover 3500, powered by the firm's versatile V8 engine. It was quickly followed by straight-six engined versions, the 2351cc (143 cu in) 2300 and 2597cc (158 cu in) 2600. Less powerful models arrived in 1982, with the four-cylinder 2000, and the diesel 2400SD.

Build problems had blighted the early cars, but these were largely solved by the time the entire range received a slight facelift in 1982. Some of the more exciting models, like the high-powered Vitesse and luxurious Vanden Plas, appeared about this time. The end for the last 'true' Rover came in 1986.

Engine: 3528cc (215 cu in), V8-cylinder
Power: 115kW (155bhp) at 5200rpm
0–96km/h (60mph): 8.4 secs
Top speed: 203km/h (126mph)
Production total: 171,946

LAND ROVER

Go anywhere, do anything. That was the philosophy behind the utilitarian but utterly unstoppable Landie. Thousands of the Jeep-like creatures have found their way all over the world, seeming at home in any climate and on any terrain.

With manufacturing almost completely destroyed in Europe during World War II, the postwar years saw severe shortages of all products, from food to cars. Many ex-military vehicles consequently found their way into civilian hands, simply because they were the only forms of motorized transport that were available.

Maurice Wilks, Rover's chief engineer, had one of these 'demobbed' motors, a Willys Jeep, for use on his Welsh estate. He was impressed by its on- and off-road abilities. When it started to wear out, there was nothing else on the market to replace it. Why not, he reasoned, build a British version, to sell to the public? Not only would it appeal to agricultural users but, as a temporary measure, it would bring in some badly needed revenue for Rover.

That 'temporary' vehicle went on to become the 4x4 Land Rover, one of motoring's biggest success stories. Wilks's stop-gap, basic and austere Jeep copy became a surprise legend, with its descendants still in production today.

For Land Rover fans, the early models are still the favourites. The headlamps set alongside the grille mark this out as a pre-1951 version. The move to lights on the wings was more practical, but made it less distinctive.

It took just a year to produce the Land Rover, from its conception in the spring of 1947. In order to by-pass the shortage of steel and other raw materials, it was decided to build the body out of readily available aluminium. The body was primitive, the simple alloy panels mounted on a basic box-section chassis. As many standard car parts as possible were incorporated to keep costs down, including the 1595cc (97 cu in) inlet-over-exhaust petrol engine and gearbox from the P3 saloon. Four-wheel drive was permanently engaged. The new highly utilitarian Rover

wasn't the sort of vehicle that was expected to excite anybody, particularly not Rover's usual customer base.

So Rover was totally astonished but thoroughly delighted when it did. The Land Rover received a sensational reception when launched at the 1948 Amsterdam Motor Show. The media and public alike loved the practical 'go anywhere' vehicle, many customers believing that the corrosion-proof aluminium body would be tougher than steel and easier to repair. Orders from all over the world started to flood in within just a few

weeks. Soon, Rover was building more off-roaders than cars.

Two body styles were offered originally, a pick-up version with a canvas roof, and a station wagon model. The former was the most versatile though, and proved by far the more popular.

Having rushed the 'Landie' into production, Rover started to improve it gradually but consistently. In 1950, the provision to engage two-wheel drive in top gears was introduced and the grille-mounted lights were moved to the wings in 1951. The engine grew to 1997cc (122 cu in) the same year. Two longer wheelbases became available in 1953, and again in 1956, just in time for the arrival of Rover's new 2052cc (125 cu in) diesel engine, which was fitted one year later.

A wider, more curvaceous look was unveiled with the Series II in 1958, which lasted for only three years before the mostly unchanged IIa superseded it. By this time, 250,000 vehicles had been sold worldwide, many for military purposes, which added a delightful touch of irony to the Landie's Jeep influenced beginnings.

The Series III, with its all-synchromesh gearbox, new grille and safety-conscious updated interior arrived in 1970, and a long overdue overdrive feature appeared during the energy crisis in 1974.

Perhaps the most significant development since the birth of the Land Rover itself occurred in 1970 when the Range Rover's 3.5-litre (214 cu in) V8 engine was fitted in its less glamorous ancestor.

The original Land Rover concept lives on today in the Defender, a more sophisticated vehicle but one still clearly related to that original accidental success of more than half a century ago.

Engine: 1997cc (122 cu in), 4-cylinder
Power: 39kW (52bhp) at 4000rpm
0–96km/h (60mph): n/a
Top speed: 97km/h (60mph)
Production total: n/a

RANGE ROVER

It's square, it's boxy, and the styling is hardly beautiful. Yet the original timeless Range Rover design endured for 24 years without major change, creating a niche in the market place that others have since rushed to fill.

But it was also refined enough to make it acceptable as an everyday vehicle, albeit an expensive one.

All models were two-door only, until a much-needed four-door version arrived in 1981, adding extra versatility to the design. Two years later, a five-speed gearbox appeared. Previously, the transmission had been four-speed, although with overdrive as standard. The first move away from V8 petrol power came in 1986, when a diesel option in the form of a 2393cc (146 cu in) four-cylinder engine emerged, marketed specifically at customers who loved the Range Rover's style and practicality, but were put off by its high fuel consumption.

The simple but timeless elegance of the original design lasted almost unchanged for half a century until replaced by a revised version in 1994. The overall businesslike theme of the original was kept but the new model was completely updated with a new body, more powerful engines and a better level of interior specification. Another more radical re-design appeared in 2001, to take the Range Rover well into the 21st century.

Engine: 3528cc (215 cu in), V8-cylinder
Power: 97kW (130bhp) at 5000rpm
0–96km/h (60mph): 14.3 secs
Top speed: 161km/h (100mph)
Production total: n/a

.'s difficult to imagine the motoring world today without luxury off-roaders. Few major manufacturers can consider its sales catalogue complete without at least one upmarket 4x4 for sale.

But prior to 1970, if you wanted to go cross-country, you had to accept austerity and an extreme lack of comfort as part of the experience. The closest thing to comfort in an off-roader was a cushion on the rear bench seat of a Land Rover.

And then came the Range Rover. When Rover purchased Buick's lightweight 3.5-litre (215 cu in) V8 engine for use in its road cars, it started to look at using it for other applications as well. Early tests were carried out in 1964 with a view to creating a higher-powered Land Rover. A Buick V6 was fitted in an adapted vehicle, but the project was dropped. Meanwhile, surveys carried out in the United States had suggested that, with the leisure activity vehicle market taking off, there was enormous potential for a more refined version of the utility off-roader. Rover decided to investigate further.

By 1994, the Range Rover had become more luxurious and the styling was updated to keep it competitive alongside newer clones from other manufacturers. Yet so good was the original design that the alterations were little more than a makeover.

Like the Land Rover before it, the Range Rover seems to have been a short-term project, designed to help the company through a financial slump caused by a drop in orders from the military. The concept that gradually evolved called for a Land Rover-type vehicle that was capable of coping with the roughest terrain, but with road car levels of comfort and suspension set-up.

The box-like Range Rover body was the result of a collaboration between engineers Spen King, Gordon Bashford and Phil Jackson. It was made of aluminium, and was designed with a large interior and a hatchback for versatility. A slightly detuned 3.5-litre (215 cu in) V8 provided the power for the permanently engaged four-wheel drive, and coil springs and self-

levelling suspension provided a much more relaxed ride than the Land Rover. Disc brakes were fitted all round.

The first prototype was running by the end of 1967, and was then worked on by Rover stylist David Bache for the production version. Prototypes were tested in an assortment of climates, from Norway to the Sahara desert, before its launch in 1970.

Designing an off-roader that came with luxury was a big gamble for Rover. Nothing like it had been done before and it could have failed spectacularly. Instead, it turned out to be one of motoring's landmarks.

A resounding success from the start, it was just as happy on the road as off it and was capable of going anywhere and tackling all environments with little trouble.

SAAB 92

1949–56

Engine: 764cc (47 cu in), two-stroke, 2-cylinder
Power: 19kW (25bhp)
0–96km/h (60mph): n/a
Top speed: 105km/h (65mph)
Production total: 20,128

The 92 was Saab's first production car, which flouted all conventional engineering and design principles. When the first prototypes were shown it looked like nothing else on the market – the cars were incredibly aerodynamic.

With all-round independent suspension and a strong monocoque, Saab acquired a reputation from the outset for quality and safety – even if there were a few shortcomings. There was no bootlid until 1953 – up until then, the boot had to be accessed via the rear seats. In the same year, the tiny split rear window gave way to a much larger single unit and Saab also decided the car could be used for overnight accommodation and a bed unit was then advertised.

1954 saw the car updated with lots of detail changes. Two years later, it was replaced by the 93.

More than two decades after Volvo started car production, Saab became the second major Swedish car manufacturer with the amazingly styled 92 It celebrated production of its 10,000th car in 1954.

SAAB 96

1960–80

The 96 arrived in 1960 with a 28kW (38bhp), 841cc (51 cu in) two-stroke three-cylinder engine, mated to a three-speed gearbox (with a fourth speed as an option until 1966 when it became standard). An estate version, the 95, was also offered. Safety was very important from the outset – the car was not only very strong but, from 1962, seatbelts were fitted and, from 1964, the car featured dual-circuit brakes.

Also making its debut in 1962 was the triple-carburettor Sport,

successor to the Gran Turismo 750 which had been introduced in 1960 for the Swedish market only. In 1966, the Sport became the Monte Carlo to celebrate Erik Carlsson's outright win of the famous rally – although his first Monte victory had actually been four years earlier.

In 1965, a new 96 arrived,

without the characteristic bullnose front. Two years later, the two-stroke engine was replaced by a 48kW (65bhp) 1498cc (91 cu in) V4 and front disc brakes were fitted as standard. 1968 saw the

introduction of a facelifted bodyshell, and apart from a revised dash in 1970 there was little new about the car. Impact-absorbing bumpers arrived in 1975.

Engine: 1498cc (91 cu in), V4-cylinder
Power: 48kW (65bhp)
0–96km/h (60mph): 17.1 secs
Top speed: 147km/h (92mph)
Production total: 547,221

Whether it's fitted with a two-stroke or a V4 engine, the 96 is one of the most characterful of postwar cars.

SAAB SONETT II

1966–70

This early Sonett II has much purer lines at the front than post-1967 examples thanks to the more flowing bonnet line.

Only six examples of the first Sonett (also known as the 94) were built because of the high purchase cost, so Saab needed something much more successful the second time around, pinning its hopes on the Sonett II, or 97. Launched at the 1966 Geneva Motor Show, the Sonett II was enthusiastically received but its $3500 price tag was still too high. This forced Saab to revise its production plans – just 455 were built in 1967 instead of the forecast 3000.

Although the prototype was made of steel, production cars were glassfibre, helping to keep weight down to 740kg (1630lb). As a result, the car was lively, able to reach 100mph (161km/h) with just a 45kW (60bhp) two-stroke three-cylinder engine under the bonnet.

The 96's 54kW (73bhp) V4 unit was fitted from 1967, with an ugly bulge in the bonnet to make room for the bigger engine. By fitting the larger engine and increasing demand for the car as a result of doing so, Saab managed to boost production to 846 units for 1968, but this was still well below the figures that had been envisaged at the outset. It was apparent that the car still needed a considerable amount of development, so production was stopped to make way for the Sonett III.

Engine: 1498cc (91 cu in), V4-cylinder
Power: 54kW (73bhp)
0–96km/h (60mph): 12.5 secs
Top speed: 165km/h (102mph)
Production total: 258 (two-stroke), 1609 (V4)

SAAB SONETT III

1970–74

A new design was called for if the Sonett was ever to sell in acceptable numbers, so Italian styling house Coggiola was commissioned to style an all-new car, which Saab completed in-house. Although the Sonett name was retained, it was known as the Sonett III to show that it had little in common with its predecessor – at least from the outside.

Slightly longer than the Sonett II, the new car was heavier but much sleeker. Pop-up headlights made it look much more modern and there was also a new fascia. First shown at the 1970 New York Motor Show, the car was instantly seen as an improvement over the old model and when the 1.7-litre (104 cu in) V4 unit replaced the previous 1.5-litre (92 cu in) powerplant in 1971, it became even better.

However, it was clear that the Sonett was just a distraction from Saab's main product line of saloon cars so, although bumpers were added in 1972 to allow the car to be sold in America and small detail changes were made to wheels, interior trim and grille, there was no substantial further development.

Engine: 1699cc (104 cu in), V4-cylinder
Power: 54kW (73bhp)
0–96km/h (60mph): 12 secs
Top speed: 171km/h (106mph)
Production total: 8368

The Sonett III was Saab's last attempt at a proper sports car – after this the company decided that it would concentrate on sports saloons.

SAAB 99

The 92 to 96 series had been extremely successful for Saab and showed that the company was both innovative and unconventional. However, repeating this success wasn't going to be at all easy, especially considering that a completely new approach was needed to take the company forward into the future, as buyers' expectations had changed radically since that car's introduction nearly 20 years previously.

The new approach resulted in the 99, first seen at the end of 1967 and on sale from 1969. Front-wheel drive was chosen from the outset but Saab needed a new engine to power the car.

Since it couldn't afford to develop a new powerplant on its own, one was developed in partnership with Triumph, although Saab spent time and money further developing the unit to make sure that its version didn't

suffer the reliability problems that Triumph's engines soon became notorious for.

With two- or four-door saloons and three- or five-door hatches (known as Combis) available, there was no shortage of choice, but the main attraction was the 99 Turbo, which went on sale in 1978. This car introduced the idea of a family saloon which could be designed without having to sacrifice practicality for performance.

The 99's predecessors were going to be a tough act to follow, but in the hands of such luminaries as Per Eklund and Stig Blomqvist, the 99 managed to win rallies throughout Europe during the late 1970s.

Engine: 1709cc (104 cu in), 4-cylinder
Power: 60kW (80bhp)
0–96km/h (60mph): 15.2 secs
Top speed: 150km/h (94mph)
Production total: 588,643

SAAB 900

Developed from the 99, which was over a decade old when the 900 appeared in 1978, the 900 upheld Saab's reputation for innovation. Under the skin, the 900's basic structure was closely related to the 99's, but it was lengthened to make room for more effective crumple zones and energy-absorbing bumpers.

The basic car was the GL, with a manual four-speed gearbox, while GLS models had twin carburettors and the option of automatic transmission. An EMS badge denoted fuel injection but at the top of the range was the turbocharged

Always seen as the sensible choice, the 900 was one of the safest cars available when it was first produced in 1979.

900 which, from 1986, was fitted with an intercooler to increase power and performance.

The 130kW (175bhp) 16S made its debut in 1985 and the following year a convertible version was offered – a car which proved extremely popular as there were few four-seater prestige convertibles available in Europe at the time.

Production of the car ended in 1993, and despite the fact that it was perceived as a small car manufacturer, Saab had managed to sell nearly one million 900s.

Engine: 1985cc (121 cu in), 4-cylinder
Power: 75kW (100bhp)
0–96km/h (60mph): 13.3 secs
Top speed: 161km/h (100mph)
Production total: 908,810

SALMSON S4

1946–52

In common with most of its rivals, Salmson's first postwar car, the S4, featured distinctly prewar styling.

The Salmson company was first known for making aero engines in World War I. The first Salmson S4s were cyclecars, based on the well-known GN models. During the 1920s, these cars were popular as people needed budget mobility but, by the 1930s, a demand for rather more sophisticated transport meant that cyclecars were no longer so fashionable, so Salmson moved upmarket. Its cars proved popular and the company even set up a factory in Britain for a while, but in the post-World War II period, all its cars were built in France.

In 1946, Salmson's first postwar model was introduced, in the form of the S4. With a 2218cc (135 cu in) four-cylinder twin-camshaft engine, the car was aimed at the more expensive end of the market and there was no shortage of innovation under the bonnet. The con rods were made from Duralumin, the aluminium cylinder heads incorporated hemispherical combustion chambers, the crankshaft was nitrided to make it last longer, the valves incorporated chrome and the valve springs featured vanadium to increase their lifespan.

But the most innovative engineering was saved for the transmission, which was a Cotal pre-selector unit. This allowed gearchanges to be made as quickly as the driver could execute them, without the need to use the clutch once the car was on the move – a system that proved very effective.

Engine: 2218cc (135 cu in), 4-cylinder
Power: 51kW (68bhp)
0–96km/h (60mph): n/a
Top speed: 130km/h (81mph)
Production total: n/a

SALMSON RANDONÉE

1950–53

Salmson was dependent on the same basic long-stroke twin-camshaft engine design for almost all the cars it ever made, but for the Randonée, it attempted something more exclusive. The result was a powerplant which made extensive use of lightweight alloy castings and components, allowing 50kg (110lb) to be shed in the process.

The car itself was a reworked version of the range-topping Salmson S4E first seen in 1937 and under the skin, the mechanicals were carried over in their entirety. The car therefore featured independent front suspension by longitudinal torsion bars, telescopic front dampers and rack-and-pinion steering along with hydraulic

brakes. A ladder frame provided the chassis and the rear axle was located by a torque tube and a pair of diagonal radius arms suspended on cantilevered semi-elliptic springs.

There was a choice of ZF manual or Cotal electromagnetic transmissions but since the engine developed just 53kW (71bhp),

performance was mainly irrelevant. This proved to be somewhat disappointing, in the light of the car's high price tag.

Engine: 2218cc (135 cu in), 4-cylinder
Power: 53kW (71bhp)
0–96km/h (60mph): n/a
Top speed: n/a
Production total: 539

SALMSON 2300 SPORT

1953–56

Probably the best car ever to come out of Salmson's Billancourt factory was also its last. With just 227 cars produced between 1953 and 1957, the 2300 Sport's styling was redolent of cars from Pegaso, Facel Vega and Ferrari.

The 2300 used a version of the double-overhead-camshaft four-cylinder engine first seen in 1921 in the first car ever produced by Salmson. When it was used in the 2300 it was used with a higher displacement, meaning the car was just able to achieve the 161km/h (100mph) mark.

However, when production of the 2300 began in 1953, France was still recovering from World War II and cars of any kind were

hard to find, so something as luxurious as Salmson's sportster was too profligate for most. The car was fitted with an all-steel coachbuilt body which was seen as unnecessary and something that only added to production costs without being of any real benefit. More bizarrely, no fewer than seven body styles were tried before a definitive range was chosen in 1954. But few could afford the cars and, within two years, the Salmson factory was forced to close.

Engine: 2312cc (141 cu in), 4-cylinder
Power: 78kW (105bhp)
0–96km/h (60mph): n/a
Top speed: 168km/h (105mph)
Production total: 227

The luxurious 2300 Sport was at the opposite end of the scale from the very basic GN-based cars first built by Salmson.

SEAT 600

1957–73

Seat's 600 was the car that gave Spain mobility. First presented at the 1955 Geneva Motor Show, here was an affordable car which was not only cheap to buy but also cheap to run. Closely based on Dante Giacosa's design for Fiat,

the 600 finally went on sale in May 1957, powered by a rear-mounted 633cc (39 cu in) engine. The first cars were imported from Italy, but it wasn't long before a Barcelona-based factory was mass-producing them in large quantities.

More than 800,000 examples of the Seat 600 rolled off the production lines during its 16-year lifespan. As well as the Fiat-derived 600 two-door model, the company also offered commercial derivatives, a convertible and, later,

a four-door version called the 800.

Engine: 633cc (39 cu in), 4-cylinder
Power: 16kW (21.5bhp)
0–96km/h (60mph): n/a
Top speed: 95km/h (59mph)
Production total: 800,000 approx

SIATA DAINA

1950–58

Having used Fiat parts extensively for years, Siata officially linked up with Fiat in 1950 to put the Daina into production. It was an arrangement which suited both parties very well since Fiat themselves did not want to produce cars which would only sell in small numbers and Siata could get help in developing the car.

Fiat 1400 running gear was used for the Daina, which was available as a closed coupé or an open-top

roadster. If the 1.4-litre (85 cu in) engine wasn't potent enough, the company also offered a 1.5-litre (92 cu in) unit instead. All models had a five-speed gearbox and the bodywork was constructed by Stabilimenti Farina.

From 1951, the Rallye 1400 received a new body design, influenced by the MG TD, and the range was increased with the addition of a six-seater limousine and an estate, thanks to the

development of a stretched chassis. The following year the Daina Sport (coupé) and Gran Sport (cabriolet) were launched, the former fitted with a 1500cc (92 cu in) 56kW (75bhp) engine.

Engine: 1393cc (85 cu in), 4-cylinder
Power: 48kW (65bhp)
0–96km/h (60mph): n/a
Top speed: n/a
Production total: 200 approx

Despite body styles as diverse as a cabriolet, limousine or estate, very few examples of the Siata Daina were built. Prices were high and the 1.4-litre engine didn't endow the car with particularly impressive performance.

SIATA 208S

1952–54

Based on perhaps the most collectable Fiat ever – the 8V – the Siata 208S carried a Vignale bodyshell with pop-up headlights and was officially available as either a coupé (initially built by Stabilimenti Farina, then Carozzeria Balbo) or a convertible, although there were numerous other variants built.

In fact Siata had been involved with the 8V from the outset, as it had built the prototype for Fiat. The car had all-round independent suspension mounted on a tubular chassis to which was added a steel body.

When Fiat stopped production of the 8V, only 114 cars had been built but 200 examples of the

double-overhead camshaft 16-valve engine had been produced – which were then sold to Siata. With so few of these engines available production of the 208S was necessarily limited, but that didn't stop Siata offering other variants, such as the long-wheelbase 208SC. The engine was developed as well with the

introduction of an eight-port head to make it more efficient – although only about eight of these were built.

Engine: 1996cc (122 cu in), V8-cylinder
Power: 95kW (128bhp)
0–96km/h (60mph): n/a
Top speed: 205km/h (128mph)
Production total: 32 approx

SIATA AMICA 1955–56

Until the Amica arrived, Siata hadn't managed to sell many cars. This didn't matter a great deal to the small company, as it wasn't really attempting to be a mass-producer – instead its expertise lay in tuning cars and selling performance equipment. In fact, the Societa Italiana Applicazione Transformazione Automobilistiche was a tuning company set up by amateur racing driver Giorgio

Ambrosini in 1926 with a view to making Fiats go faster. Understandably, because of the focus on Fiats until now, it was no surprise that the Amica used mainly Fiat parts.

Launched in 1950, the Amica was a two-seater available as either a coupé or a roadster. Suspension was courtesy of Fiat but the tubular chassis was developed by Siata. At the front was independent

suspension with a transverse leaf spring and lower wishbones, while at the back, there was a live axle suspended by quarter-elliptic springs.

Power was also provided by Fiat, its 500 engine being available in various states of tune including a 19kW (26bhp) 750cc (46 cu in) version. By the early 1950s, however, everyone was very keen to find a product for the extremely

lucrative American market, so an Amica was built with a 720cc (44 cu in) Crosley engine – Crosley was an American carmaker – but, in fact, it turned out that only a few buyers were interested.

Engine: 596cc (36 cu in), 4-cylinder
Power: 16kW (22bhp)
0–96km/h (60mph): n/a
Top speed: 100km/h (62mph) approx
Production total: n/a

SIMCA ARONDE 1951–62

The Aronde transformed Simca from a company which simply reconstituted Fiat's spare parts into France's largest and most

successful privately owned car maker. But the path the company took was unconventional in European terms as its cars were

heavily inspired by contemporary American designs.

The first Aronde was seen in May 1951, with conventional

engineering under the skin. The car had a unitary construction and at the front there was coil and wishbone suspension while at the rear there were semi-elliptic springs. Initially, build quality was poor and it took some time for the car to regain its credibility.

Only a four-door saloon was offered to start with but, by 1953, only two years later, there was an estate (the Chatelaine) and a two-door pillarless coupé (the Grand Large). Later came a small van (the Commerciale) and a panel van (the Messagère) along with a pick-up (the Intendante). A one-off convertible was made in 1954 while constant revisions to the range made sure sales remained strong until 1962.

It looks rather like something that might well have rolled off the Austin production line, but Simca's Aronde was actually a Gallic production.

Engine: 1221cc (75 cu in), 4-cylinder
Power: 34kW (45bhp)
0–96km/h (60mph): 28.6 secs
Top speed: 118km/h (74mph)
Production total: 1,274, 859

SIMCA OCEANE 1957–62

Although it was a two-seater, Simca's Aronde Oceane wasn't a particularly sporting car. Available as a convertible or coupé, the Oceane was equipped with a big-valve version of Simca's 1290cc (79 cu in) four-cylinder engine, rated at 42kW (57bhp). From 1961, a revised engine appeared with five main bearings and developing

46kW (62bhp). The following year, further tuning produced another 6kW (8bhp).

Although on paper the Oceane lasted just five years, in reality, its lifespan was double this as it was just an updated Simca 9, first seen in 1951. That car was facelifted almost annually so, by the time the Oceane badge was put on it in

1957, it didn't seem to be as old as it really was.

When the Oceane was first displayed, it resembled a Ford Thunderbird in appearance – but then Simca had often drawn the inspiration for the styling of its cars from the United States. However, in 1959, Simca just looked to Britain for its ideas and

used an Aston Martin-like grille for the final version of the car before it finally went out of production three years later.

Engine: 1290cc (79 cu in), 4-cylinder
Power: 42kW (57bhp)
0–96km/h (60mph): n/a
Top speed: 139km/h (87mph)
Production total: 11,560

SIMCA VEDETTE

1954–61

Ford France had been selling a car called the Vedette since 1949, with little success. So when Simca bought Ford in 1954, Simca's own version of the Vedette shared little except for the name and flathead V8 with its predecessor. Unlike its predecessor, the new car had monocoque construction but it retained rear-wheel drive and leaf spring rear suspension. It may not have seemed very innovative at the time but it certainly worried Simca's rivals at Citroën.

When the cars were first seen in 1954 they carried Ford badges and came in three trim levels. Trianon was the base model, followed by the Versailles and the top model, the Regence. There was also an estate called the Marly.

With just over 63kW (84bhp) on offer from its 2353cc (144 cu in) side-valve engine, the car had poor performance, but it was reliable and relaxing to drive, although the three-speed gearbox should have had an extra ratio. Although

French Vedette production came to an end in 1961, the tooling was shipped to Brazil where the car continued to be made until the end of the 1960s.

With its V8 engine, the Simca Vedette had more in common with contemporary American cars than its French rivals. It did cause Citroën some concern, however.

Engine: 2353cc (144 cu in), V8-cylinder
Power: 63kW (84bhp)
0–96km/h (60mph): 18.4 secs
Top speed: 146km/h (91mph)
Production total: 166,895

SIMCA 1000

1961–78

By the time the 1000 was introduced, Simca had become France's largest privately owned car manufacturer. As it had been producing conventional front engine/rear-drive saloons for many years, it came as quite a surprise when the company chose to launch a rear-engined, rear-wheel drive car in 1961.

The rearward weight bias meant handling was strange and with just 30kW (40bhp) coming from the 944cc (58 cu in) cast-iron powerplant, performance can only be described as leisurely.

The car featured all-round drum brakes and worm-and-roller steering, so was lacking in much engineering innovation, but it was cheap to buy and run which was what the majority of French drivers wanted at the time.

In 1962 Abarth launched the 1136cc (69 cu in) Simca-Abarth 1150 version of the 1000, which sported between 41kW (55bhp) and 63kW (85bhp) depending on tuning and by 1965, major changes had been made to the interior so it could compete with Renault's R8.

However, it wasn't until 1969 that heavily overdue brake, steering and suspension changes were finally introduced, along with an exterior redesign. By 1970, Simca had been bought by Chrysler but the 1000 still managed to last another eight years.

With simple engineering, the Simca 1000 is basic family transport, and was inexpensive to buy and economical to maintain and run. However, it can be made to really fly with straightforward tuning modifications.

Engine: 944cc (58 cu in), 4-cylinder
Power: 26kW (35bhp)
0–96km/h (60mph): 27 secs
Top speed: 118km/h (74mph)
Production total: 1,642,091

SIMCA 1100

When the 1100 was introduced by Simca in 1967, it was genuinely ground-breaking. With front-wheel drive and independent suspension, here was a five-door hatchback – and also, until 1969, a three-door hatchback – that was totally unlike anything else currently available even if a number of other manufacturers, such as Renault with its 16, did start to catch up fairly soon afterwards.

With front disc brakes and rack-and-pinion steering, the car was easy to drive, and with the 1118cc (68 cu in) engine – rather than the 944cc (58 cu in) version that was available only in France – it offered good performance, too.

By the time the 1100 had been launched, Chrysler had taken control of Simca and in the summer of 1970 Simca became Chrysler France. Nevertheless, in 1972, the 1100 was still France's best-selling car and the model continued to be developed with updates to the interior as well as specification improvements.

From 1980, the car carried a Talbot badge, after Simca was again swallowed up, this time by Peugeot-Talbot, before finally going out of production in 1982. The last 1100 commercial vehicles were built in 1985.

The innovative 1100 was incredibly successful for Simca, with French buyers being far more eager to appear unconventional than those from overseas.

Engine: 1118cc (68 cu in), 4-cylinder
Power: 37kW (50bhp)
0–96km/h (60mph): 19.6 secs
Top speed: 134km/h (84mph)
Production total: n/a

SINGER TEN

Introduced as an economy car to mobilize the masses, Singer's Ten was uncomplicated transport with the focus being on reliability above all other considerations.

Underneath the skin, there was little to distinguish the postwar Singer Ten from its prewar counterpart. With the exception of electric headlights as standard, the major change was in the car's appearance, as a new range of body styles was made available.

The two-seater Sports Coupé offered 80km/h (50mph) capability while the standard Phaeton configuration could manage just 72km/h (45mph). When Autocar tested the 10 Sports it commented on how good the engine was along with the amount of practicality the car offered – especially in Phaeton form when a dickey seat was fitted. For 1923, a cut-price version was offered called the Coventry Premier, with less equipment and a smaller choice of body styles.

Mechanically the car was very conventional, with a three-speed gearbox, semi-elliptic springs all round and brakes on the rear wheels only. Its four-cylinder engine had its combustion chambers cast in pairs and the car's simplicity and light weight meant it was ideally suited to privateer motorsport thanks to its tunability. As a result, Singer 10s were regularly seen being raced at hillclimb, trial and circuit venues around the UK.

Engine: 1096cc (67 cu in), 4-cylinder
Power: n/a
0–96km/h (60mph): n/a
Top speed: 80km/h (50mph) approx
Production total: 6000 approx

SINGER NINE

Engine: 972cc (59 cu in), 4-cylinder
Power: 7kW (9hp)
0–96km/h (60mph): n/a
Top speed: n/a
Production total: n/a

Replacing the Junior, the Singer Nine was one of the most easily recognized small cars in Britain during the 1930s. Its appearance quite deliberately mimicked the design of its predecessor in order to capitalize on that model's enormous popularity, but by 1932 sales of the Junior had begun to fall, as larger and more powerful cars became more desirable and available from numerous other manufacturers.

When the Nine was launched in 1933 it was equipped with the same overhead camshaft engine seen in the Singer Junior Special but its coachbuilt saloon body was larger than the Junior it replaced. It was unusually well equipped for such a small and affordable car, with opening windows all round, ashtrays, a clock, a fuel gauge and leather seat trim. For many, it represented real value for money.

In 1933 an all-new engine arrived, still with 972cc (59 cu in) but of tougher construction. At the same time, the chassis was lengthened and widened to improve both handling and

stability. Extra body styles were offered to increase the car's appeal, including a four-seater sports model called the Sports Nine.

Priced at just £185, the car was much cheaper than rivals such as the Riley Lynx, which cost over £100 more.

Despite its low price of just £185, the Singer Nine offered both modern engineering and beautifully sporty looks.

SINGER LE MANS

Produced to cash in on Singer's racing successes in the Le Mans 24-hour, the Le Mans model has become one of the most collectable prewar classics, despite its rather modest performance.

After Singer's success with a works Nine in the 1933 Le Mans 24-hour race – no mean achievement – it was only natural that the company would capitalize on the resultant publicity with a 7kW (9hp)-based car named after the famous circuit. As a result, the Singer Le Mans first went on sale in September 1933, just three months after the race. It was built to compete with MG's TA.

Although the front end was similar to the original model, the rear end was completely new with twin spare wheels fixed behind a

slab fuel tank. The engine was also more highly tuned with a high-lift camshaft, raised compression ratio, a higher capacity aluminium sump and a counter-balanced crankshaft. The gearbox was also changed with closer ratios, and the chassis was lowered.

The cars originally had rear-hinged doors, but an unfortunate and deeply worrying tendency for them to fly open on corners – and this was a car intended for competition – meant that the design was reversed with many of the earlier cars being converted to the later specification.

Engine: 972cc (59 cu in), 4-cylinder
Power: 30kW (40bhp)
0–96km/h (60mph): 27 secs
Top speed: 120km/h (75mph)
Production total: 500

SINGER SUPER TEN

1938–40

Announced in August 1938, the new Singer Ten and Super Ten featured a bored-out version of the engine fitted to the updated Bantam, the Ten's smaller sister. The Ten was a mid-range saloon that was spacious and airy thanks to its four-door, six-window saloon body. For added refinement, the powerplant was isolated on rubber mountings, which was still uncommon at the time and showed the high-quality engineering that Singer put into its cars.

Two versions of the Ten were available, the De Luxe (or Super Ten) and the Popular. The Popular had a three-speed synchromesh gearbox whereas the De Luxe version had an extra ratio, also fitted to the Twelve, the next car up in the range. The De Luxe was also equipped with a sliding sun roof and two windscreen wipers – the Popular had to make do with just a single wiper. A minor facelift in 1939 saw changes to the radiator grille as well as to the dashboard and interior trim, but the car was dropped in 1940.

Engine: 1194cc (73 cu in), 4-cylinder
Power: 28kW (37bhp)
0–96km/h (60mph): n/a
Top speed: 100km/h (62mph)
Production total: 11,595

SINGER SM1500

1949–54

The first true postwar Singer was the SM1500, which was a saloon influenced by contemporary American styling. Competing with cars such as the Jowett Javelin and Standard Vanguard, the Singer was never seen as desirable as these rivals, although a facelift in 1954 did allow it to gain some character, when it became the Hunter.

When the SM1500 first went on sale in October 1948, it was only available for export, but by the summer of 1949, cars were available for UK buyers. The four-door saloon offered seating for six and the column-mounted gearshift and independent coil-spring front suspension were pure Americana – indeed the suspension design was licensed from Packard.

Under the skin there was a four-speed three-synchromesh gearbox which was mated to a 1506cc (92 cu in) four-cylinder overhead camshaft engine. Features such as a variable-speed fan heater and spring-loaded door check links to hold the doors open were

Perhaps one of the least inspired of the immediate postwar designs, the Singer SM1500 was nevertheless well built and loaded with neat touches that its rivals couldn't offer.

characteristic Singer touches –-- just like the unusual viewing chamber on the side of the engine that negated the need to use a dipstick for checking the engine's oil level.

Engine: 1506cc (92 cu in), 4-cylinder
Power: 36kW (48bhp)
0–96km/h (60mph): 33.7 secs
Top speed: 114km/h (71mph)
Production total: 17,382

SINGER SM ROADSTER

1951–55

Singer launched its Singer SM Roadster (also known as the 1500 Roadster) in 1951 to compete with MG's dominant TD. Fitted with hydromechanical brakes and a

short-stroke single-overhead camshaft engine displacing 1497cc (91 cu in), the powerplant was available from 1953 with a twin-carburettor option to boost power

from 36kW (48bhp) to a more impressive 43kW (58bhp). This engine was thoroughly modern and gained Singer further credibility after its competition success with the Nine Le Mans.

However, the SM Roadster was really nothing more than a revamped Nine Roadster, which had first been seen in 1939, so the overall package was a little disappointing. Independent front suspension with telescopic dampers was an advance over the Nine's set-up but the worm-and-peg steering was so imprecise that it spoiled the driving experience.

Nowadays it's far easier to buy an MG TD than a Singer 4AD. Rarest and most valuable of all the postwar Singer 4ADs are the Bertone-bodied examples, constructed on behalf of the American Singer importer, though these rarely come up for sale.

Singer's SM Roadster was like many postwar cars which were little more than prewar bodyshells with updated mechanicals and so it was quite disappointing.

Engine: 1497cc (91 cu in), 4-cylinder
Power: 36kW (48bhp)
0–96km/h (60mph): 23.6 secs
Top speed: 117km/h (73mph)
Production total: 3440

SINGER GAZELLE

1956–67

When the Singer company became part of the Rootes Group in 1956, a new car was quickly produced for the end of that year. The new model was the Gazelle, really a Minx with a new 1494cc (91 cu in) overhead-valve engine, different front-end styling and a different dashboard. There was a choice of two- or four-door saloons and a convertible, all with a four-speed gearbox activated by a column-mounted gearchange. In 1957, the Gazelle became the Mk II when an estate was added to the range and overdrive became available.

From its launch until the end of production in 1967, model changes came annually. Between 1958 and 1961, the Mk IIA, Mk III, Mk IIIA and Mk IIIB were all almost identical. The biggest change was the fitting of a 1494cc (91 cu in) overhead-cam engine but when the Gazelle Mk IIIC arrived in 1961, this became a 1592cc (97 cu in) powerplant.

Next came the Mk V (there was no Mk IV) in 1963. Available only

as a four-door saloon, the new car had smaller wheels, better brakes and adjusted styling. The final derivative was the 1965 Mk VI, with a 1725cc (105 cu in) engine and a slightly restyled nose.

Engine: 1494cc (91 cu in), 4-cylinder
Power: 37kW (49bhp)
0–96km/h (60mph): 23.6 secs
Top speed: 125km/h (78mph)
Production total: 83,061

The open-top Gazelle was an unusual alternative to more common four-seater convertibles such as the highly successful Triumph Herald.

SINGER VOGUE

The Vogue was bigger and more expensive than the Gazelle, though initially it was intended to be a replacement for it, having started out as the Mk IV derivative missed out in the Gazelle's line-up. Instead, the two cars sold alongside each other.

Sharing much with the Hillman Super Minx, the Vogue had four headlights and a more luxurious interior than the Gazelle. There was a choice of automatic or manual/overdrive transmissions and the front drum brakes were uprated to disc brakes in 1962.

The Mk III of 1964 featured styling changes, larger rear doors, an alloy cylinder head and an all-synchromesh gearbox along with better interior trim. The final version, the Mk IV, came in 1965. Apart from the adoption of the 1725cc (105 cu in) engine seen

elsewhere in the Rootes Group's cars, there were no other changes.

Engine: 1592cc (97 cu in), 4-cylinder
Power: 46kW (62bhp)
0–96km/h (60mph): 20.9 secs
Top speed: 133km/h (83mph)
Production total: 47,769

SINGER CHAMOIS

Building on the Gazelle's four-footed theme, the Singer Chamois, launched in 1963, was nothing more than a rather more upmarket version of the Hillman Imp. This meant higher quality interior trim with walnut veneer, more equipment fitted as standard and

wider wheels to make it look as sporty as possible. In 1965, a Mk II car arrived and the following year the Chamois Sport appeared, which was a better equipped version of the Sunbeam Imp Sport, but with absolutely identical mechanicals.

In 1967, the suspension on the standard car was fettled and in the same year the Chamois Coupé went on sale. This was the same as the Hillman Imp Californian but again, had a better interior. In 1968, the fascia of the Chamois was changed and twin headlights added, but the

cars were all dropped in 1970 when the Singer marque died.

Engine: 875cc (53 cu in), 4-cylinder
Power: 38kW (51bhp)
0–96km/h (60mph): 16.3 sec
Top speed: 144km/h (90mph)
Production total: 49,798

SKODA 1101

The first postwar Skoda was rather more conventional than Czechoslovakia's other postwar car, the Tatra. Clean lines and straightforward engineering guaranteed that it was popular.

Although the Skoda factory was all but destroyed in the last few weeks of World War II, the company did manage to resume car production very quickly once hostilities were over.

The first car to be built by Skoda in the postwar period, after the company had been nationalized, was the 1101. Based on the 1933 420 Popular, the new car was longer, wider and more powerful as well as being better equipped. On sale from the autumn of 1945, the 1101 had a four-speed gearbox mated to a 1089cc (66 cu in) overhead-valve engine. Only one body style was available – a two-door four-seater saloon which was called the 1101 Tudor (for two-door).

Soon after the car's introduction, more body styles were offered, but these were not intended for general sale as they were mostly ambulances and vans. Indeed, the most interesting derivative was the 1101P, an all-terrain version built specially for military and police use. An estate and four-door saloon were launched in 1949 then, in 1952, the 1101 was replaced by the 1200.

Engine: 1089cc (66 cu in), 4-cylinder
Power: 24kW (32bhp)
0–96km/h (60mph): n/a
Top speed: n/a
Production total: n/a

SKODA OCTAVIA

1959–71

Although the Skoda Octavia first appeared in 1959, it was actually no more than a development of the earlier 440, which had been launched in 1954. The Octavia was so called because it was the eighth in a line of small cars made by the Czech manufacturer.

The Octavia Super was also offered alongside the standard car,

Although the Octavia lagged behind its competitors from the west, it still proved popular, especially on the home market where cars were scarce.

although this, too, was based on an old car – the 445.

If neither the standard nor Super models were enough, buyers could specify the Octavia TS (Touring Sport), with the 37kW (50bhp) twin-carburettor engine taken from the Felicia soft top. Other than this, the car in all forms was essentially a standard machine, although buyers of the Super did get a little extra performance thanks to a higher lift camshaft, new inlet and exhaust manifolds, twin carburettors, bigger valves and a higher compression ratio.

At first, the engine used was the familiar 1089cc (66 cu in) unit but from 1961, this was uprated to a 1221cc (75 cu in) powerplant, which also appeared in the Felicia.

Engine: 1089cc (66 cu in), 4-cylinder
Power: 30kW (40bhp)
0–96km/h (60mph): 36.6 secs
Top speed: 120km/h (75mph)
Production total: 279,724

SKODA FELICIA

1959–64

The original Skoda Felicia may not have been the most capable car of its time, but in Communist Czechoslovakia, the waiting list to own one was years long. Based on the Octavia saloon, the Felicia could muster just 39kW (53bhp) and the swing axle suspension mounted on to a separate chassis didn't make the car handle very well, but it was still fun to drive.

When the Felicia was introduced into the UK market in 1961, buyers weren't so keen to own one, despite the fact that the car was reliable and very well built, if not particularly highly specified. Perhaps potential customers were just unfamiliar with the Skoda name, because the Felicia's 135km/h (84mph) top speed was no worse than that of UK-produced

cars such as the Triumph Herald. Also, with the low fuel consumption figure of 9.5l/100km (30mpg) the car was cheap to run.

However, equipment levels weren't very impressive, with

Although the Felicia didn't offer especially good value in some markets, it did offer stylish looks with durability.

rubber mats in place of carpeting and plastic instead of leather seats, but they were still acceptable, with a heater, a radiator blind and sun visors.

Engine: 1221cc (75 cu in), 4-cylinder
Power: 39kW (53bhp)
0–96km/h (60mph): 27.5 secs
Top speed: 135km/h (84mph)
Production total: 15,864

SKODA 1000MB
1964–69

The launch of the 1000MB marked the start of Skoda's decline from being a manufacturer of desirable cars to an international joke.

The beginning of the end of Skoda's reputation was instigated by the launch of the 1000MB in 1964. Seen as outdated, very ugly and basic, the car's reliability and practicality were all far too easily overlooked.

Mounted at the back was an overhead-valve 988cc (60 cu in) engine, using an aluminium cylinder block to help keep weight down, something that was necessary with the powerplant hanging over the rear axle. The low compression ratio of 8.3:1 helped the engine to run on poor quality fuel, but it didn't do anything at all for the car's power output, which was a miserly 32kW (43bhp).

From the outset, only a four-door saloon was available, but from 1966, a twin-carburettor two-door pillarless coupé was offered. Called the 1000MBX, very few were built as the cars were absurdly expensive to buy. The next version was the 1000MBG, a twin-carburettor version of the standard four-door saloon and in 1967 the car became the 1100MB. For this model, the engine was enlarged to 1107cc (68 cu in) which offered a much more useful 40kW (54bhp). Even so, the damage to Skoda's reputation was done.

Engine: 988cc (60 cu in), 4-cylinder
Power: 32kW (43bhp)
0–96km/h (60mph): 30.8 secs
Top speed: 120km/h (75mph)
Production total: 419,540

SKODA S100
1967–77

The S100 was a major development of the 1000MB, hence the name change. The same 988cc (60 cu in) engine was mounted at the back and the swing axle rear suspension was also carried over. In fact, the only significant changes to the mechanicals were the adoption of disc brakes at the front and a twin-circuit hydraulic braking system.

It may have looked substantially different on the outside, but underneath the S100 shared much with its vilified predecessor, the 1000MB.

However, the bodyshell was substantially redesigned, along with the interior. There was also the option of a larger, 1107cc (67 cu in) engine in the 110L model, this being a development of the 1100MB which superseded the 1000MB. A year after the launch of the 100, a two-door coupé was introduced, which was only available with the larger engine. Called the S110R, the car had a 46kW (62bhp) version of the 1107cc (67 cu in) powerplant.

At the same time as the launch of the S110R, Skoda embarked on its rallying programme, generally using four-door saloons with 1144cc (70 cu in), 75kW (100bhp) engines. Despite the publicity generated by racing, the company's reputation did not gain very much benefit.

Engine: 988cc (60 cu in), 4-cylinder
Power: 32kW (43bhp)
0–96km/h (60mph): 30.8 secs
Top speed: 120km/h (75mph)
Production total: n/a

SS1

In 1922, William Lyons, the man who founded Jaguar cars, teamed up with William Walmsley and set up a coachbuilding company in Blackpool. Initially, they were producing motorcycle sidecars, but by the end of the 1920s, they were building special car bodies, the company having adopted the Swallow Sidecar and Coachbuilding Company name, with the car-producing offshoot becoming known simply as SS Cars Ltd. In 1928, the company moved to Coventry and a decade after Swallow Sidecars had been formed, the company introduced the SS1.

Lyons had struck up a business relationship with John Black, head of the Standard Motor Company, and it was this association that allowed Lyons to take the SS upmarket. Until then, the focus had been on rebodied Austin Sevens, but through Standard, he was able to secure a steady supply of chassis with six-cylinder side-valve engines of either 2054cc (125 cu in) or 2552cc (156 cu in) capacity. These engines had seven

main bearings and were mated to a four-speed manual gearbox while suspension was by semi-elliptics at both the front and rear.

The SS1 was launched at the 1931 Olympia Motor Show in London. As Grand-Tourers were becoming increasingly common during the 1930s, the SS looked more flamboyant than most – but with a price tag of just £310, it was far more affordable than anybody expected it to be. This was because the engineering was of poor quality compared to its fantastically designed body. So despite its being greeted with considerable enthusiasm, it soon became apparent that the car hadn't been properly developed, so the company returned the following year with something that wouldn't ruin the company's reputation before it had even got proper production underway.

Within a year of the SS1's debut, a new version was unveiled which was quite different from the original. The looks were still dramatic – perhaps even more so – but this time, the car featured

One of the most sought-after classic cars of all time, the SS1 doesn't actually offer that much performance. But the styling is simply exquisite.

running boards, more flowing front wings, a lower roofline to make it even sleeker and improved engine manifolds to allow it to 'breathe' better. This last piece of development ensured a bit more power which in turn improved the car's performance, something that was desperately needed as the first cars had a top speed of only 112km/h (70mph).

This time, the whole car was beautifully made, had adequate room for four people to travel in comfort and was a real delight to drive thanks to its excellent handling and roadholding – helped by an extra 18cm (7in) added to the wheelbase. Whereas just 502 examples of the first SS1 were built, the addition of a tourer to the range in 1933 meant that the second generation car was much more popular with 1249 cars built in the first year.

The final development came in 1934, when a new chassis was introduced but with the same 302cm (119in) wheelbase. This heralded the arrival of the Airline saloon, which was fashionable but controversial, with its streamlined styling. Still, there was always the option of a more conventional saloon or a drophead coupé if the Airline was too flamboyant for customers' liking. The new model also had a synchromesh gearbox and by now there were larger 2143cc (131 cu in) or 2663cc (163 cu in) engines available – both still side-valve straight-sixes. But to ensure the cars were as powerful as possible the camshafts were reprofiled to give more power and the compression ratios raised. The SS1 had always looked much faster than it really was, and this was Lyons' attempt at redressing the balance.

Engine: 2054cc (125 cu in), 6-cylinder
Power: 34kW (45bhp)
0–96km/h (60mph): 31 secs
Top speed: 112km/h (70mph)
Production total: 4254

SS90

The car from which the more famous SS100 was derived, the SS90 was more suited to competition thanks to its far greater agility.

front axle on semi-elliptic springs was still used but the 2.7-litre (163 cu in) side-valve six-cylinder engine was tuned slightly – enough to give the car a top speed of around 144km/h (90mph).

By the time the SS90 went on sale the company already had a good reputation, and with a price tag of just £395, SS should have been struggling to cope with demand. But just 23 examples of the SS90 were produced because, in 1936, the engine was developed with an overhead-valve cylinder head and its displacement rose to 3.5 litres (214 cu in) and it became the SS100.

he SS100 is one of the most ought-after classics of all time, but efore it came a car which looked ist as breathtaking, but is largely orgotten, perhaps because so few

of them – a total of 23 – were made. However, the SS90 of 1935 certainly has at least as much presence as its more famous younger brother.

The SS90 was itself a derivative of the SS1, and was based on its chassis, but with 38cm (15in) removed from the wheelbase to make it more nimble. The beam

Engine: 2663cc (163 cu in), 6-cylinder
Power: 52kW (70bhp)
0–96km/h (60mph): 17.5 secs
Top speed: 144km/h (90mph)
Production total: 23

STANDARD 9.5HP

gine: 1328cc (81 cu in), 4-cylinder
wer: n/a
-96km/h (60mph): n/a
p speed: n/a
oduction total: 1750

he first Standard Model S was itroduced in 1913, and proved an nmediate success thanks to its ffordability; with prices starting at 195 it was within reach of more rdinary people than many other irs. Both closed and open cars ere offered and with its 1087cc 6 cu in) engine, the car was liable as well as being very conomical to run.

But in the years following World Var I it was clear that something ew was needed to keep sales boming. The answer was an pdated version, which was unched in 1919. Called the SLS, e new model used a longer-stroke ersion of the original engine, this me displacing 1328cc (81 cu in). lthough the price of this two-eater had gone up to £350, the car as still much cheaper than many f its competitors.

However, even at its launch the SLS was almost out of date, so again, a replacement model was urgently needed. The result was the

11.6hp, launched in 1921 and complete with overhead valves in place of the side valves seen on every Standard until that time.

At a time when the supply of cars easily outstripped demand, the Standard 9.5hp tempted customers with its low price.

STANDARD NINE

1927–30

Although it was developed quickly the Standard Nine's simple mechanicals meant it was a very reliable car.

Things were looking bleak for Standard in 1927, as the 1926 General Strike in the UK had left carmakers vulnerable. Although Standard's cars weren't luxurious, most people still couldn't afford them, so the answer was a smaller, lighter, cheaper car.

Launched at the 1927 Olympia Motor Show, the Nine was the answer to the company's problems. Two prototypes had been tested in the Cotswold Hills in England over a one-month period and when they had passed their rigorous testing, the car was passed for production. In fact, this new model had been taken from initial drawings to full production in just six months. With conventional engineering, the powerplant reverted to a side-valve design and construction was simple.

When introduced, a four-seater fabric-bodied saloon cost just £198 and it was an immediate success. The following year, a new range of body styles was offered along with the option of a supercharged engine. In 1928, the unit was bored out to produce 9.9hp instead of the previous output of 8.9hp, and racing success at Brooklands followed. Two years later, the car was replaced by the Big Nine.

Engine: 1155cc (70 cu in), 4-cylinder
Power: n/a
0–96km/h (60mph): n/a
Top speed: 80km/h (50mph)
Production total: 10,000 approx

STANDARD VANGUARD

1948–52

Announced in July 1947, the Vanguard was Britain's first post-war all-new British car. With a 51kW (68bhp), 2088cc (127 cu in) four-cylinder engine and a three-speed gearbox, the Vanguard was capable of 120km/h (75mph) and 10.9l/100km (26mpg), while carrying five people in comfort.

Government regulations meant most cars produced in the immediate postwar years had to be exported, which is why many Vanguards found their way to the United States. These regulations had clearly been taken into account when the car was being designed, as not only was the exterior styling American-influenced, so was the column-change gearshift. Despite massive steel shortages, between 1000 and 2000 Vanguards were produced each week, few of which stayed in the UK.

In 1948, an estate and pick-up joined the range and, in May 1950, coachbuilder Tickford began offering a full-length sunroof. The car was not developed any further until the end of 1951, when a larger back window and a revised radiator grille heralded the arrival of the Phase Ia, which itself was replaced in March 1953 by the Phase II Vanguard.

Engine: 2088cc (127 cu in), 4-cylinder
Power: 51kW (68bhp)
0–96km/h (60mph): 22 secs
Top speed: 123km/h (77mph)
Production total: 184,799

The sheer size of the Vanguard suggests that it's a luxury car, but it was far more basic than the American rivals it was mainly up against. Most of the Vanguards produced were for export.

STANDARD EIGHT

1953–59

When the Eight was replaced, few mourned its demise thanks to its complete lack of redeeming features compared to its major rivals.

Launched in 1953 with an 803cc (49 cu in) engine, the Eight was automotive transport at its most basic. With no bootlid and a second windscreen wiper as optional extra, the car didn't prove popular. This no-frills idea had been borrowed from the Beetle and Citroën 2CV, but they had style – the Eight didn't.

In May 1954 the Eight was made less basic, with a 948cc (58 cu in) engine, winding windows and more trim inside and out when it was rebadged the Ten. The price rose from £481 to £538, but the austerity of the postwar era was almost over and people expected – and could afford – more.

In May 1955, the Family Eight replaced the basic model while from October that year, the range-topping Super Eight arrived. But by the end of 1956, the Phase II arrived to supersede all previous models. With a much-improved interior, it was more desirable and was further improved when the Gold Star arrived in 1957, featuring an opening boot and the option of overdrive. The Eight finally disappeared in 1960 despite some successes in international rallies, and was replaced by the Herald.

Engine: 803cc (49 cu in), 4-cylinder
Power: 19kW (26bhp)
0–96km/h (60mph): n/a
Top speed: 98km/h (61mph)
Production total: 136,317

STANDARD PENNANT

1957–60

Almost forgotten now, the Standard Pennant was an upmarket version of the Standard Ten which, in turn, was a development of the Standard Eight. The Ten was launched in 1954 to address the problem that the Eight was so basic and limited that it was deterring customers. By offering a De Luxe variant called the Ten, the original, sparsely equipped model could sell alongside as a separate range.

However, despite the fact that the Ten was slightly more upmarket, it still didn't go far enough to be an attractive purchase, so Standard needed yet another model and another name – the Pennant.

The new car featured a more powerful 28kW (37bhp) version of the 948cc (58 cu in) engine, two-tone paintwork, hooded headlights and longer front and rear wings. A larger rear window and a more flamboyant, three-bar grille were also part of the package and extra chrome strips along the car's flanks made sure your neighbours knew your car wasn't a mere Eight or Ten.

The Pennant was not much more than a badge-engineered Standard Ten, which also featured a little more equipment.

Engine: 948cc (58 cu in), 4-cylinder
Power: 28kW (37bhp)
0–96km/h (60mph): 34.9 secs
Top speed: 106km/h (66mph)
Production total: 42,910

STANGUELLINI

Between 1947 and 1966, Stanguellini produced very small quantities of hand-built sports cars, mainly using Fiat mechanicals. Although the company had been producing racing cars since 1938, its efforts following the end of World War II focused on building road cars. This shift of direction was based on a successful racing campaign in 1947 which the company attempted to translate into success on the road.

The first car was a four-seater Berlinetta with an 1100cc (67 cu in) – or optionally, a 1500cc (92 cu in) – Fiat engine in a Bertone body mounted on a tubular chassis. Because these road cars were often built with competition in mind, and contemporary Italian roads were in a poor state, the suspension was built for reliability rather than ultimate handling. This meant a transverse leaf and lower wishbone suspension was used at

the front and a live rear axle suspended by coil springs appeared at the back.

Stanguellini developed its own 750cc (46 cu in) engine for the 1950 Bialbero Sport and in 1954, the 1100 Berlinetta made its debut, but just nine were built. A 750cc (46 cu in) Formula Junior car arrived in 1958 but between then and 1966 one failed project followed another and the company went bankrupt.

Although Stanguellini is best known for its racing cars such as this one, it also produced tiny numbers of road cars over two decades.

Engine: 750cc (46 cu in), 4-cylinder
Power: 27kW (36bhp)
0–96km/h (60mph): n/a
Top speed: 180km/h (112mph)
Production total: n/a

STAR COMET

A handsome car and, with its six-cylinder engine, the Comet's performance was strong as well, but it just wasn't profitable.

After truck manufacturer Guy acquired Star in 1928, the Comet was an attempt by Guy to take Star downmarket in the wake of the Depression. Introduced in 1931, the Comet was competitively priced at just £345 in saloon or coupé form, but since the car was hand-built in relatively small numbers it was quite apparent that its profitability was negligible.

A four-speed gearbox built in-house was backed up by Bendix cable brakes and Marles steering – all high-quality equipment. To entice as many buyers into the

showrooms as possible the range was expanded with the addition of various styles of coupé and saloon, but still the cars weren't profitable.

Although the Comet used quality components, there were just too many cars competing in the same market and, rather than inject a large amount of money into the company to keep it going, the decision was made to close it down in 1932. This was despite Star introducing the Comet Fourteen in 1932 to take the car even further downmarket with a smaller engine.

Engine: 2470cc (151 cu in), 6-cylinder
Power: 10kW (14hp)
0–96km/h (60mph): n/a
Top speed: 112km/h (70mph) approx.
Production total: n/a

STEYR 50 AND 55

1936–40

Extremely innovative with boxer engine and unitary construction, the 50 and 55 were leagues ahead of most European small cars.

Looking very similar to the contemporary Fiat 500, the 50 was the final car to be designed by Steyr's Karl Jenschke before he left to join Adler. He had worked for the company since the early 1920s and his last design was the smallest-engined car ever to have come out of the Steyr factory. With a 984cc (60 cu in) side-valve flat-four, the car was an economy model – and a departure from the more exclusive models Steyr had become known for. Just 16kW (22bhp) was on offer.

Brakes were cable-operated, despite Steyr having used hydraulic systems on its previous cars, but there was all-round independent suspension and a monocoque construction for its two-door coupé bodyshell. Although the car proved popular it

was clear that a bigger engine and more power would help sales. As a result, an 1158cc (71 cu in) powerplant was fitted towards the end of 1938 which developed just 2kW (3bhp) more, but did help the car's performance. Following a facelift, the model was rebadged Typ 55 but there were no further changes to the engine capacity.

Engine: 984cc (60 cu in), 4-cylinder
Power: 16kW (22bhp)
0–96km/h (60mph): n/a
Top speed: 97km/h (60mph)
Production total: 13,000

STEYR PUCH 500

1957–69

Although tuned versions were to follow later, the first Steyr Puch 500s were no more than Fiat 500s built under licence in Graz, Austria.

After Steyr's factory was all but destroyed during the course of World War II, a decision was initially made not to return to car production. However, in 1948, a deal was signed with Fiat to start producing its cars in Austria and, by 1957, a Steyr version of the Nuova 500 was being made at the Puch factory in Graz. Using a Fiat bodyshell and a 493cc (30 cu in) two-cylinder Steyr powerplant developing just 12kW (16bhp), the car was automotive transport at its most basic.

To add more performance, in 1964 the Steyr-Puch 500 equivalent of the Mini Cooper was introduced, in the form of the 650 TRII. Based on the 500 bodyshell, a 660cc (40 cu in) horizontally opposed twin-cylinder engine was fitted, pushing power output up to 30kW (40bhp) and top speed up to 128km/h (80mph).

Engine: 493cc (30 cu in), twin-cylinder
Power: 12kW (16bhp)
0–96km/h (60mph): n/a
Top speed: 100km/h (62mph)
Production total: n/a

STUDEBAKER PRESIDENT

1930–38

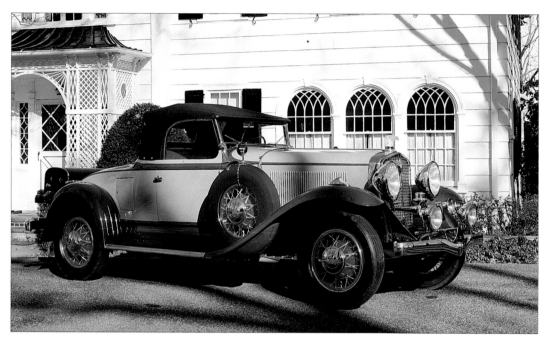

Although the President was Studebaker's most expensive car and was aimed at the rich, it was still very well priced compared with its competitors. Buyers could choose from various body styles including coupé, saloon, roadster or limousine – the latter option being the most expensive.

Buyers at the luxury end of the market had come to expect high levels of specification from cars like the President and, by 1932, such refinements as synchromesh transmission were being offered. A year later, power-assisted brakes and an automatic choke were added. Independent front suspension arrived in 1935 and radio speakers were put in the headlining of the car – something that other carmakers wouldn't incorporate for many more years to come.

The President was first seen in 1927 and was only available with a six-cylinder engine – not the opulent car it would later become. However, a straight-eight powerplant replaced the six-cylinder unit just a year later and the car was restyled between 1928 and 1930 with sleeker bodies and a longer wheelbase.

The President had the looks of a Cadillac or Lincoln but was more affordable, although it was still an exclusive car intended for the wealthy end of the market.

Engine: 5522cc (337 cu in), 8-cylinder
Power: 86kW (115bhp)
0–96km/h (60mph): n/a
Top speed: n/a
Production total: 67,372

STUDEBAKER COMMANDER

1935–39

Studebakers had always been premium cars offered at very competitive prices, and when the 1935 Commander was introduced it sat between the range-topping President and the entry-level Dictator. There was the option of a six- rather than eight-cylinder engine and across Studebaker's three-model range there were no fewer than 50 different variations on offer. The Commander was available as a roadster, saloon or coupé in a variety of constantly changing specifications. Having been launched with a 305cm (120in) wheelbase in 1930, the eight-cylinder Commander received a shorter wheelbase of 297cm (117in) in 1932 only to get an increase to 302cm (119in) in 1934.

From 1933, only the larger eight-cylinder unit was available – a 75kW (100bhp) unit that gradually became more powerful each year, so that by the time production ceased in 1939 it was developing 80kW (107bhp). In 1936, the Commander was dropped, but reappeared once more in 1938 as a six-cylinder car before being replaced with an all-new model in 1939.

Engine: 4064cc (248 cu in), 6-cylinder
Power: 56kW (75bhp)
0–96km/h (60mph): n/a
Top speed: n/a
Production total: n/a

A 38-model range in 1935 led to the Commander being dropped for three seasons while Studebaker tried to return to profitability. It was finally replaced in 1939.

STUDEBAKER CHAMPION

1939–57

The Champion was launched to appeal to the mass-market customer. At first, the company offered the model as a saloon, a three-passenger coupé or a five-passenger coupé. With relatively little development the model lasted until 1947, when it was replaced by an all-new car with modern styling.

Although the Champion was more expensive than its direct competitors, there weren't enough cars to meet demand in the years immediately following World War II, so Studebaker was able to sell every car it could build. Sales were also helped by the fact that Studebaker launched an all-new Champion in 1946 whereas its competitors didn't have their new designs ready until part-way through 1948.

Both the prewar car and its 1947 postwar successor were powered by a 60kW (80bhp) six-

The Champion was amazingly frugal for a prewar American car and was very advanced too, with a monocoque construction and no running boards.

cylinder engine, with the option of a 63kW (85bhp) unit in the later car. Like its predecessor, the 1947 Champion was styled by Raymond Loewy.

By the time Studebaker launched its 1953 range the Champion name had become little more than a trim level, rather than a separate and distinct model, as the Commander and President were now the same car but with higher levels of specification.

Engine: 2692cc (164 cu in), 6-cylinder
Power: 60kW (80bhp)
0–96km/h (60mph): n/a
Top speed: n/a
Production total: 450,000 approx.

STUDEBAKER AVANTI

1962–63

Although a second incarnation of the Avanti – the Avanti II – survived into the 1990s, the original model was far less successful. In fact, it lasted just a single season, having been rushed into production by an ailing Studebaker in a failed attempt to inject some sort of life into the marque before it finally disappeared completely.

When it was unveiled in 1962, the car was considerably better than anything else on the market, but Studebaker's South Bend factory was so far away from its component suppliers that productivity could never match that of its competitors.

Innovative features included disc brakes at the front, which had never been specified on an American mass-produced car before, and the styling was distinctive, too, designed by Raymond Loewy, who also penned the famous Coca-Cola bottle.

Power was supplied by a 4.7-litre (291 cu in) V8 engine and a four-speed manual gearbox. If this standard power output wasn't enough, tuning options were available which saw outputs rise to over 224kW (300bhp) through to the use of a supercharger.

Engine: 4763cc (291 cu in), V8-cylinder
Power: 156kW (210bhp)
0–96km/h (60mph): n/a
Top speed: 200km/h (125mph)
Production total: 4643

The Avanti featured styling which could, somewhat euphemistically, be called distinctive. Most would go further and complain that it is downright ugly.

STUTZ BEARCAT

The early 20th-century equivalent of the Caterham Seven, the Stutz Bearcat offered no-frills driving for those who prized performance above all else.

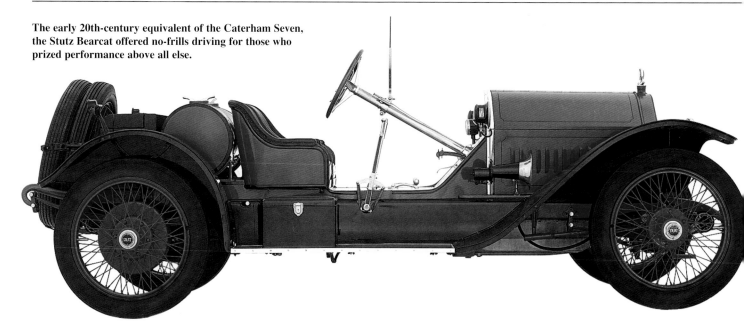

Harry C Stutz was the man behind the Stutz Car Company, but the first of his cars, produced from 1911, were actually made by the Ideal Motor Car Company of Indianapolis. At that time, the cars were only built as racers, but when the first road cars appeared in 1913, the Ideal name was seen as over-confident and the company changed its name to Stutz.

The first sports car built by the newly named company was the Bearcat, which made its debut in 1914. The car offered nothing in the way of interior comforts since it was really a road-going racer. It was conventionally engineered throughout, with the exception of its transmission. Drawing its inspiration from the contemporary Mercer Raceabout, the Bearcat featured the same type of basic bodywork as its major rival.

The car's bodywork was deliberately kept to a minimum because the key to maximum performance was keeping weight as low as possible. And with just 45kW (60bhp) on offer from the 6388cc (390 cu in) four-cylinder engine, any extra mass would upset the power-to-weight ratio very easily. The T-head engine was supplied by powerplant manufacturer Wisconsin and thanks to its large size was not built for

The Stutz Bearcat could easily cruise at 96km/h (60mph), making it the supercar of its day.

high revs. In fact, maximum power was generated at just 1500rpm. For those who wanted an engine with a greater rev range, the company also offered a 6.2-litre (378 cu in) six-cylinder engine, but very few cars were ever ordered with this unit.

To allow the Bearcat to handle well, the chassis was low-slung and featured a beam axle at the front suspended by semi-elliptic springs. At the rear there was a live axle, which was also suspended on semi-elliptic springs. As was customary, there were no brakes at the front, just drum brakes at the rear.

The three-speed manual transmission was mounted in unit with the rear axle, driving it via a prop shaft, something which at the

time was seen as innovative. Rather more conventional though was the exposed right-hand gearchange. With the exception of a monocle windscreen for the driver there was no protection from the weather for either of the car's two occupants. Two armchair-style bucket seats, positioned in front of the fuel tank, and a steeply raked steering column poking through the scuttle comprised the car's total level of interior trim. There were no doors.

The popularity of the Bearcat was due to the car's motorsport success. In 1915, the White Squadron racing team won all sorts of competitions in Bearcats, but these featured 16-valve overhead-

camshaft engines displacing 4.8 litres (293 cu in) – units which had nothing in common with those fitted to the factory-supplied models. However, this didn't stop those rich enough to be able to afford one from buying one, perhaps impressed by the exploits of 'Cannonball' Baker. In 1916, he'd managed to smash the time record for driving across the United States, a feat accomplished in a Bearcat and one which gained Stutz a huge amount of publicity.

Engine: 6388cc (390 cu in), 4-cylinder
Power: 45kW (60bhp)
0–96km/h (60mph): n/a
Top speed: 129km/h (80mph) approx.
Production total: 4000 approx.

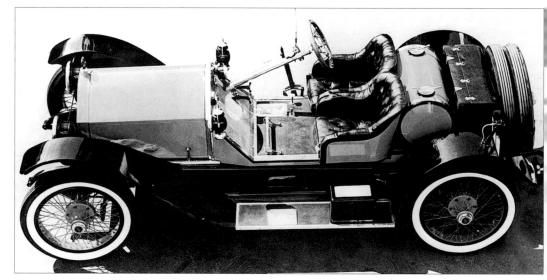

STUTZ BLACKHAWK

1929–30

Stutz had focused on expensive cars; the Blackhawk aimed to change that – but then came the 1929 Wall Street Crash.

In the mid-1920s, the Stutz company was making money. Demand for its cars was high and its Vertical Eight, otherwise known as the Safety Stutz, was also selling well. Although all its cars were seen as glamorous, an even more exclusive model was introduced to maintain this perception. Called the Black Hawk Speedster, the car became very fashionable.

So when business fell away at the end of the decade, Stutz decided to introduce another car called the Blackhawk, to cash in on the magic of the earlier name. This model was marketed as a separate marque to distance it slightly from Stutz, as it was cheaper than the cars produced by the parent company.

On offer were six- or eight-cylinder engines offering 63kW (85bhp) or 71kW (95bhp) and a choice of open or closed body styles. But the Wall Street Crash in 1929 put an end to production, as although the cars were priced lower than the contemporary Stutz models, still not enough people could afford them.

Engine: 3957cc (241 cu in), 6-cylinder
Power: 63kW (85bhp)
0–96km/h (60mph): n/a
Top speed: n/a
Production total: 1590

STUTZ SV16

1931–34

The SV16 was so called because it featured a 16-valve engine with single valves arranged as one inlet and one exhaust valve for each of its eight cylinders. Similarly, there was a DV32 alongside it in the range, the designation DV32 being short for dual-valve 32, as the model was equipped with four valves per cylinder. A derivative of the ill-fated Blackhawk, the SV16 was equipped with a 5277cc (322 cu in) straight-eight engine. This produced an impressive 84kW (113bhp) but prices were very high – $5775 for the short-wheelbase car and $7495 for the long-wheelbase version.

Throughout the car's lifetime there was little development, although in 1933 the option of a three-speed gearbox in place of the usual four-speed Warner unit was offered. This cut the price by $400, but in the years of the Great Depression, this simply wasn't enough to save Stutz, which produced just six cars in 1934. By 1937, the Stutz company had become bankrupt.

Engine: 5277cc (322 cu in), 8-cylinder
Power: 84kW (113bhp)
0–96km/h (60mph): n/a
Top speed: n/a
Production total: n/a

SUBARU 360

1958–71

The 360 was the first car made by Subaru and appeared in 1958. Designed with affordability as its key selling point, the car was a typical late 1950s Japanese economy car, with an air-cooled twin-cylinder engine mounted at the back of the car, driving the rear wheels.

The car was barely 3m (9.8ft) long, and its 356cc (22 cu in) two-stroke engine developed just 12kW (16bhp). Power output was later increased to 15kW (20bhp) until a 422cc (26 cu in) engine was introduced, developing 16kW (22bhp). Called the Maia or K212, the uprated car had a three-speed gearbox and independent

With few survivors, the first production car from Subaru is now perhaps the only collectable model.

suspension on all four wheels. By 1969, a four-speed gearbox was fitted as well as torsion-bar independent suspension all round.

An estate version of the 360, called the Custom, was also offered, alongside a pick-up and a beach car, which drew its inspiration from Fiat's Jolly model.

Engine: 356cc (22 cu in), twin-cylinder
Power: 12kW (16bhp)
0–96km/h (60mph): n/a
Top speed: 90km/h (56mph)
Production total: 5000 approx.

SUBARU LEONE

1971–79

The introduction of Subaru's Leone in 1971 was significant because it was the first all-wheel drive mass-market car. Although cars such as the Jensen FF had all-wheel drive, they were all expensive machines. The Leone, however, made this capability affordable.

At first, the company only made a saloon available but, from September 1972, an estate was added to the range, in an effort to boost the car's popularity. Few people had ever thought of needing four-wheel drive for everyday use, so initially the car was bought by people, such as farmers, who needed mobility in adverse conditions. However, as the car became more comfortable and the specifications improved, it appealed to a wider market and more road users bought it.

By the end of the 1970s, the Leone had become the world's best-selling four-wheel drive, helped greatly by the appearance of a pick-up version in 1977. Still to be seen on farms all over the world, this car – also known as the Brat in some countries – has ensured that Subaru's reputation for building reliable cars is now well known.

Engine: 1595cc (97 cu in), 4-cylinder
Power: 48kW (65bhp)
0–96km/h (60mph): 16.7 secs
Top speed: 139km/h (87mph)
Production total: 1,269,000

SUNBEAM 3-LITRE

1925–30

When you're charging a lot for your car, buyers expect something special. When Sunbeam sold its 3-litre (or Super Sport) for £1125 at a time when a Morris Bullnose was just £170, owners expected a sensational driving experience. They didn't get it.

What they got was a detuned racing powerplant producing 69kW (93bhp), but mated to a chassis which couldn't cope with this power. A narrow track and a long wheelbase made the car unstable and it was also nose-heavy due to the heavy engine being mounted too far forward. There was also cantilever leaf spring rear suspension – primitive even by mid-1920s standards.

If the chassis was disappointing, the engine was anything but, with a seven-bearing crankshaft, dry-sump lubrication and a pair of overhead camshafts. In fact, the car's powerplant was so ground-breaking that the 3-litre (178 cu in) was the first car to be sold in the UK with a twin-camshaft engine. In 1928, a supercharged 3-litre was introduced, but this was even more difficult to control than the standard car. Sales dwindled and the last car was built in 1930.

Engine: 2916cc (178 cu in), 6-cylinder
Power: 69kW (93bhp)
0–80km/h (50mph): 24 secs
Top speed: 145km/h (90mph)
Number made: 305

It may have been groundbreaking, but the chassis of the 3-litre did not match the huge engine.

SUNBEAM TWENTY-FIVE

1934–35

After its heyday in the 1920s, Sunbeam struggled to be profitable during the early 1930s, with very little money available for investment in new models. The Sunbeam Twenty-Five had its roots in the earlier Sixteen of 1929, but with an exclusive price tag of £875.

With upgrades and facelifts the only option, the Sixteen was upgraded to become the Twenty in 1933, which in turn was upgraded to become the Twenty-Five in 1934. However, the cars featured very elegant bodywork and adequate engines and suspension layouts. The problem was that Sunbeam couldn't make any money out of building them.

With a 3317cc (202 cu in) straight-six engine and a four-speed all-synchromesh gearbox, the cars were very pleasant to drive and despite a weight of over 2000kg (4400lb), it was possible to drive at 128km/h (80mph). The brakes were strong and the steering was very accurate but profitability continued to prove elusive to Sunbeam and the company eventually became part of the Rootes Group in 1935.

Engine: 3317cc (202 cu in), 6-cylinder
Power: n/a
0–96km/h (60mph): n/a
Top speed: 128km/h (80mph)
Production total: n/a

SUNBEAM-TALBOT 90

1948–54

Sunbeam-Talbot's 90 sold alongside the 80, which was a cheaper, lower specification version of the same car.

concerted effort by the factory to compete in motorsport to demonstrate the new car's considerable abilities.

The Mk II was a major development over its predecessor because of its all-new chassis with coil spring and wishbone front suspension, as well as a larger version of the four-cylinder powerplant fitted to the Mk I – this time with 2267cc (138 cu in). At the same time, the inset driving lights were abandoned in favour of extra cooling grilles and when the Mk IIa arrived in 1952, the rear wheel spats were also dropped, to help cool the now larger rear brake drums.

When the Sunbeam-Talbot 90 went on sale in July 1948, it had a beam front axle and half-elliptic springs all round. It wasn't exactly cutting edge design, but the 1944cc (119 cu in) overhead-valve engine did produce enough power to allow quite respectable performance.

As well as the saloon, a drophead coupé was offered, both cars representing the start of a new line of rather smarter and faster Sunbeam-Talbots. The cars were so capable that when the Mk II was launched in 1950, there was a

Engine: 1944cc (119 cu in), 4-cylinder
Power: 48kW (64bhp)
0–96km/h (60mph): 22.5 secs
Top speed: 128km/h (80mph)
Production total: 20,381

SUNBEAM ALPINE

1953–55

Engine: 2267cc (138 cu in), 4-cylinder
Power: 60kW (80bhp)
0–96km/h (60mph): 18.9 secs
Top speed: 152km/h (95mph)
Production total: 3000 approx.

Based on the Sunbeam Talbot 90 Mk II saloon, the original Sunbeam Alpine was a two-door, two-seater version of the more mundane family runabout, complete with a reinforced chassis to make up for the open top.

The mechanicals were also taken from the 90 Mk II, which meant there was independent suspension at the front by coil springs, and power was supplied by a 2.3-litre (138 cu in) four-cylinder engine, first seen in the Humber Hawk. With just 60kW (80bhp) available in what was a heavy car, performance was poor, although the machines enjoyed much rally success – particularly an outright win of the 1955 Monte Carlo Rally at the hands of a privateer.

The car was really designed with the American market in mind, with both the engine and the suspension being uprated to distance the car from the machine on which it was based. This meant stiffer springs at the front, more direct steering and freer-breathing cylinder heads. But prices were much higher than rivals such as the Triumph TR2, which meant sales were disappointingly slow. After just two years, the car was dropped.

The original version of the Sunbeam Alpine was a stylish car, but it was too expensive, compared with its rivals, so lasted just two years before being dropped.

SUNBEAM RAPIER

1955–67

Although the Rapier's engineering wasn't advanced, its toughness made it popular for racing.

Essentially a tuned two-door Hillman Minx, the first of the Sunbeam Rapiers was launched in 1955 as a four-seater sports saloon. Under the skin, the car closely resembled the Minx, with its coil spring and wishbone front suspension and overhead-valve 1390cc (85 cu in) engine, although the gearbox and standard overdrive were based on the unit seen in the Humber Hawk.

From 1958, the Series II received a 1494cc (91 cu in) powerplant and the column gearchange gave way to a floor-mounted unit along with minor steering and suspension changes.

When the Series III arrived in 1959, everyone assumed this would be the final version, with some crossover between the Rapier and the then-new Alpine. An alloy cylinder head, front disc brakes and closer-ratio gears made the car better but, in 1961, there were further improvements when the Series IIIa was unveiled. This had a 1592cc (97 cu in) engine but no other changes – these were reserved for the final version, the Series IV of 1963. The main changes were smaller wheels and an all-synchromesh gearbox.

Engine: 1494cc (91 cu in), 4-cylinder
Power: 51kW (68bhp)
0–96km/h (60mph): 20.2 secs
Top speed: 144km/h (90mph)
Production total: 68,809

SUNBEAM TIGER

1964–67

To create the Sunbeam Tiger a 4261cc (260 cu in) Ford V8 was planted in the engine bay of an Alpine Series IV. The structure of the car was barely altered, although rack-and-pinion steering was fitted and the rear suspension was modified with the addition of a Panhard rod.

Sales began in 1964 with the car proving more popular in the United States than in the UK, with British buyers more bothered by the car's poor braking and undersized wheels and tyres. US buyers were also much happier with its soft ride but trouble already lay ahead.

In late 1964 Chrysler took a financial stake in the Rootes Group and the US company didn't want a rival manufacturer's engine under the bonnet. A Mk II version was marketed for a short period in 1967 (including just 12 right-hand drive cars), with a 4727cc (288 cu in) Ford engine producing 164kW (220bhp). Top speed rose to 196km/h (122mph) but the whole project was dropped before the year was out with just 6495 Mk Is and 571 Mk IIs being built.

Engine: 4261cc (260 cu in), V8-cylinder
Power: 122kW (164bhp)
0–96km/h (60mph): 9.5 secs
Top speed: 188km/h (117mph)
Production total: 7,066

Performance had never been the main focus of the Alpine, so the Tiger was built to change all that. A Ford V8 soon fixed the horsepower deficit but the chassis struggled to cope.

SUNBEAM ALPINE SERIES I–V

By the time the Alpine went on sale in July 1959, the Rootes Group had earned itself a reputation for building cars which put comfort, style and quality of finish above all else. While Triumph, MG and Healey were building cars which put the driving experience to the fore, Sunbeam worried less about ultimate performance.

After Sunbeam's in-house design team didn't come up with a look that was exciting enough, Englishman Ken Howes was given the brief of coming up with something quite radical. He'd worked with Studebaker and Ford in America, so it's no surprise to see American influences in his final sketches, which were immediately given approval.

First on sale in July 1959, the Series I Alpine was slow, with just 58kW (78bhp) on offer from its 1494cc (91 cu in) four-cylinder powerplant. This was the overhead-valve engine that had first been seen in 1954, in a smaller capacity 47kW (63bhp) 1390cc (85 cu in) guise. The Alpine's engine also had a four-branch manifold and an alloy cylinder head, which helped to increase the power output.

The car itself was based on a Hillman Husky floorpan and had a top speed of just 163km/h (101mph), which was as fast as any

production Alpine ever got, although the engines were easy to tune. The transmission was the same as that found in the Rapier, but with closer gear ratios and the option of a Laycock overdrive.

In October 1960, after 11,904 Series Is had been built, the Series II appeared. With a larger, 60kW (80bhp) 1592cc (97 cu in) engine, the new update kept the fins and detachable aluminium hardtop of its predecessor but the seating was made more comfortable. By the time it gave way to the Series III in March 1963, 19,956 had rolled off the production lines.

The third-generation Alpine brought with it a new option – the

GT. This car strangely had no folding hood, to keep weight and costs down, although the interior was much better with wood trim for the dash and a wood-rim steering wheel. Even more perversely, the GT is now the least sought-after Alpine unless it's been converted to have a folding roof – in which case it's one of the most desirable thanks to its wooden trim and steering wheel.

The optional detachable hardtop on the Series III onwards was steel instead of aluminium (and was more angular) and twin fuel tanks replaced the single item fitted to earlier cars, which meant the boot space was increased. Just 5863

Competing squarely with the MGB, the Sunbeam Alpine was nicely built if not as exciting to drive. Now it's often overlooked as an affordable roadster.

Series IIIs were made, making it the rarest Alpine (except for the Harrington fixed-roof Alpines), and one of the most desirable too, as it's the most refined of the big-finned models.

When the Series IV was launched in January 1964, it had almost lost its tailfins and the grille had become a single chrome bar in place of the previous four-bar unit. 12,406 Series IVs were built before production gave way to the final version of the Alpine, the Series V, in September 1965. With a five-bearing engine for the first time, the Series V sported a 1724cc (105 cu in) engine and a pair of Stromberg carburettors producing 69kW (92bhp) – still only enough to push it to 161km/h (100mph). By the time the Alpine went out of production in January 1968, a total of 19,122 Mk Vs had been built.

Engine: 1494cc (91 cu in), 4-cylinder
Power: 58kW (78bhp)
0–96km/h (60mph): 13.6 secs
Top speed: 161km/h (100mph)
Production total: 59,251

SUNBEAM VENEZIA

1963–65

Although the Sunbeam Venezia had an exotic name, it was nothing more than a prettier version of the Hillman Super Minx. This didn't deter Sunbeam from charging almost as much money for its car as required for a Jaguar, despite its 1592cc (97 cu in) four-cylinder engine. Unsurprisingly, the company struggled to sell the Venezia, which was launched in September 1963 and lasted less than two seasons.

Apart from the standard overdrive and a slightly more powerful version of the engine that was normally fitted to the more mundane cars in the Rootes line up, there were no mechanical differences between the Venezia and the more ordinary models in the range.

You had to want a Venezia really badly to pay the high asking price, although it was very stylish with its Touring design.

Built by Touring of Milan, the Venezia stuck to the Superleggera (superlight) principles of a tubular steel frame over which aluminium panels were stretched. Convertible and V8 versions were suggested, but were never built. Unexciting mechanicals and a high purchase price ensured demand was low and in the two seasons of production just 145 cars were built.

Engine: 1592cc (97 cu in), 4-cylinder
Power: 66kW (88bhp)
0–96km/h (60mph): n/a
Top speed: 161km/h (100mph) approx.
Production total: 145

SUNBEAM IMP SPORT

1966–76

When the Rootes Group decided to make a sporty Hillman Imp, they decided to put a Sunbeam badge on it, along with the Imp Sport name. The car was closely related to the Imp and both the bodyshell and mechanicals were carried over, although the Sunbeam got a pair of carburettors in place of the single unit fitted to the Hillman. This produced more power and thanks to wider wheels, handling was improved, as was engine bay cooling as a result of the use of a slatted engine bay cover. In 1970, when the Rootes range was rationalized, the Imp Sport became simply the Sport, at which time it also received a few trim and styling detail changes to mark it out from its older brother.

Engine: 875cc (53 cu in), 4-cylinder
Power: 39kW (51bhp)
0–96km/h (60mph): 16.3 secs
Top speed: 144km/h (90mph)
Production total: 10,000 approx.

SUNBEAM STILETTO

1967–63

Now the most collectable of all the Imp derivatives, the Sunbeam Stiletto took the coupé bodyshell of the Hillman Imp Californian and mated it to the Imp Sport's mechanicals. The interior treatment was unique to the range with reclining front seats and a bespoke dashboard, while the car also got a four-headlight front in place of the previous two-headlight look.

To help the Stiletto handle a bit better than its siblings, the camber on the front suspension was reduced which turned the car into a real racer with superb handling capabilities. But sales of the car never took off, and when Chrysler rationalized its range in the early 1970s, the Stiletto was one of the first cars to be dropped.

Engine: 875cc (53 cu in), 4-cylinder
Power: 38kW (51bhp)
0–96km/h (60mph): 17.6 secs
Top speed: 139km/h (87mph)
Production total: 10,000 approx.

UNBEAM RAPIER AND ALPINE

obody's product range was mplete in the 1970s without a upé, and this was Sunbeam's o-door version of the much more undane Hillman Hunter.

lthough the Sunbeam Rapier oked sporty with its pillarless oupé construction, it was little ore than a prettier Hillman unter. By the time the car was unched, Sunbeam had become rt of Chrysler, and there were any who suggested that the car oked too much like the Plymouth arracuda for it to be just a oincidence. But Roy Axe, the an who designed it, denied that ere was any link.

With 66kW (88bhp) available om the 1725cc (105 cu in) agine, performance was ceptable, especially linked to the ose-ratio gearbox and overdrive, oth standard. The ultimate version the Rapier was the Holbay-ned H120, with a breathed-on linder head, a pair of twin-choke carburettors and styling changes such as Rostyle wheels and a bootlid spoiler to make it stand out.

The other option was to buy the Alpine, a more downmarket, affordable version of the Rapier.

With a single-carburettor engine, less equipment and lower performance it allowed buyers to drive a car that looked like a Rapier but without the high purchase cost.

Engine: 1725cc (105 cu in), 4-cylinder
Power: 57kW (76bhp)
0–96km/h (60mph): 12.8 secs
Top speed: 165km/h (103mph)
Production total: 46,204

UZUKI SC100 'WHIZZKID'

Japanese K-class car, the original uzuki SC100 was built with strict les in mind. This meant a 660cc 0 cu in) capacity limit and strictions on the car's size. The Japanese market cars were fitted with either a two-stroke three-cylinder engine or a twin-camshaft 574cc (35 cu in) four-stroke unit, rear-mounted.

Although the car, styled by Giorgetto Giugiaro, made its debut in 1971, it wasn't until seven years later, in 1978, that it actually entered production. By the time it arrived in Europe, it had a 970cc (59 cu in) alloy-headed four-cylinder powerplant which allowed it to cruise at 128km/h (80mph) and made it far more palatable for the market.

Although the car wasn't particularly well packaged, with little luggage space, room for only two people to travel comfortably, despite being 15cm (6in) longer than a Mini, it was still a great success. Fun to drive and amazingly capable, there were just 2000 SC100s (nicknamed Whizzkid in Britain) available each year in the UK. All were quickly sold and when the car was replaced by the front-wheel drive Alto, things were never the same.

Despite a prolonged gestation period of seven years, the SC100 was popular for its whole lifespan of just four years. Now it is extremely collectable.

Engine: 970cc (59 cu in), 4-cylinder
Power: 35kW (47bhp)
0–96km/h (60mph): 17.3 secs
Top speed: 131 km/h (81 mph)
Production total: 894,000 (all models)

SWALLOW DORETTI

The Triumph TR2-based Swallow Doretti is now sought-after thanks to its rarity – brought about by a high purchase cost.

With a bodyshell built in-house by Swallow themselves, the Doretti's mechanicals were taken from the Triumph TR2. This meant reliable and well-proven engines and gearboxes, with plenty of torque even if some of the engineering was unrefined.

Swallow had been sold to Tube Investments by William Lyons when he moved into car production with Jaguar. When the sidecar market went into terminal decline in the mid-1950s Tube Investments decided to create its own car – the Doretti.

A tubular frame was clothed by a hand-made sheet steel skin with aluminium panels hung off it and a leather-trimmed interior. Boot space was limited but the car was great to drive with near-160km/h (100mph) potential thanks to the TR2's 1991cc (121 cu in) four-cylinder engine developing a healthy 67kW (90bhp) and 117lb of torque.

But production costs were high and with the TR2 itself selling for over £250 less, buyers chose the more familiar Triumph. It was clear the company could never make money from building bespoke sports cars in such small numbers so production was halted in 1955 with no attempt to produce a follow-up car.

Engine: 1991cc (121 cu in), 4-cylinder
Power: 67kW (90bhp)
0–96km/h (60mph): 13.4 secs
Top speed: 156km/h (97mph)
Production total: 276

TALBOT 14/45

When the 14/45 was launched by Talbot in 1926, the company was part of the Sunbeam-Talbot-Darracq group. But unlike the other parts of the group Sunbeam was doing very badly – in fact it was making large losses. Designed by Georges Roesch and with a 1665cc (102 cu in) six-cylinder overhead-valve engine developing 34kW (45bhp), the 14/45 was just what was needed for the group to start making a profit. Even more remarkable was the fact that the car was developed in just six months and racing successes soon gained the car a reputation for durability.

Top speed was only around 96km/h (60mph), but the car's touring abilities were what distinguished it from its rivals. Superbly refined and with excellent handling thanks to its over-engineered chassis, the 14/45 was more comfortable than anything else available for the money. The handling was helped by well set-up suspension that used semi-elliptics at the front and quarter-elliptics at the rear, and a large range of body styles made sure that there was something to suit everyone. Alongside the cabriolet and tourer there were saloons, coupés and even a landaulette.

Engine: 1665cc (102 cu in), 6-cylinder
Power: 34kW (45bhp)
0–96km/h (60mph): n/a
Top speed: 96km/h (60mph)
Production total: 11,851

The 14/45 was the car that brought Talbot back from the brink of financial disaster. Despite its being very innovative, the car proved extremely reliable and the comfortable ride made it especially popular. At the same time, it also returned a much-needed healthy profit for the parent company.

ALBOT-LAGO

albot-Lago was one of the ompanies that resulted from the ollapse of Sunbeam-Talbot-arracq in 1935. Founded by nthony Lago, the new venture as set up to produce a range of xclusive (and expensive) sports ars. Initially, these were all six-cylinder machines, including the 1947 Grand Sport which had a 4482cc (274 cu in) engine. In its day this car was the ultimate grand tourer with three carburettors, centre-lock wire wheels and independent front suspension. Whereas the immediate postwar period marked the end of other manufacturer's exotic designs, Talbot-Lagos were incredibly stylish with designs by flamboyant designer Saoutchik which were especially impressive.

In 1950, the cheaper 2.7-litre (165 cu in) Baby was introduced to increase sales, but even with a complete redesign in 1952 it wasn't a success. A final attempt at making the company work was made in 1957 with the America which used a 2.6-litre (159 cu in) BMW engine. But although the cars produced by Talbot-Lago were very desirable and well-respected, the company struggled to survive and in the end it was taken over by Simca in 1959.

Engine: 2491cc (152 cu in), 4-cylinder
Power: 89kW (120bhp)
0–96km/h (60mph): n/a
Top speed: 174km/h (109mph)
Production total: 80 approx.

Talbot-Lago suffered from the classic problem of building a low-volume car while trying to make a profit. Its cars were popular but were sold at a loss.

ATRA TYPE 11

atra started car production in 897 and was originally called esselsdorf, the name of the Czech own in which the cars were built. /hen this town was renamed oprivnice in 1918 the company as renamed the more easily ronounced Tatra after a nearby ountain range. By 1923 a new ar was launched, designed by lans Ledwinka.

A new type of light car, the Type 11 as it was called, used a backbone chassis in place of the previously specified conventional chassis. The body was supported on outriggers from the central tube and at the rear there was independent suspension using swing axles while the front of the car was supported by a transverse leaf spring.

The 1036cc (63 cu in) air-cooled flat-twin powerplant was front-mounted and, thanks to the swing axle suspension, the Type 11 could cope rather better with Czechoslovakia's roads than most of its contemporaries. As a result, the car was an instant success. It was also cheaper than its rivals.

Over the next three years, around 3500 examples of the T11 were produced, before the T12 arrived. This car was essentially a T11 but with brakes on all four wheels and with a number of additional minor improvements.

Engine: 1036cc (63 cu in), twin-cylinder
Power: 10kW (13bhp)
0–96km/h (60mph): n/a
Top speed: 90km/h (56mph)
Production total: 3500 approx

ATRA TYPE 77

ype 77 was amazingly futuristic but it was also out of reach for all but e most important government officials.

Compare the Tatra Type 77 with its contemporaries and it seems very advanced. Even Citroën's Traction Avant looked dated alongside this Czech marvel. With full-width styling and masses of interior space the Type 77 was truly a car ahead of its time, so it's a shame that the car was out of reach for everyone except Communist Party leaders.

Designed by Hans Ledwinka, the Type 77 was unlike anything else available because of its exterior styling and the engineering that went underneath it. Although its backbone chassis was a standard Ledwinka design, Type 77 was unique in having an air-cooled 2970cc (181 cu in) V8 mounted at the back.

With swing axle suspension and all the weight at the back, the handling was terrible, but despite the car's 1678kg (3,700lb) bulk it could still manage 137km/h (85mph), or another 8km/h (5mph) more with the optional 3400cc (207 cu in) powerplant which became available in 1935. However, the car's weight meant that acceleration was poor and once the car was travelling quickly, the front end lifted – an unpleasant driving experience.

Engine: 2970cc (181 cu in), V8-cylinder
Power: 45kW (60bhp)
0–96km/h (60mph): n/a
Top speed: 137km/h (85mph)
Production total: n/a

TATRA T57B

1938–49

The first car in the T57 range was introduced in 1931, with a 1150cc (70 cu in) front-mounted air-cooled overhead-valve engine that generated just 13kW (18bhp). As was traditional with Tatra designs, the car also featured a tubular chassis with swing axles at the rear. The T57 became the first Tatra to be officially imported into Britain –

by a Captain Fitzmaurice – but with a purchase price of £260 it was just too expensive to compete successfully against its rivals. In addition to this, a unique Fitzmaurice version was created which cost £595, complete with a 1484cc (91 cu in) engine, extra instrumentation and a more luxurious interior.

The car became the T57a in 1936 when the power output was increased to 15kW (20bhp) and further changes were made in 1938 when it became the T57b, with a 1256cc (77 cu in) version of the same engine, generating 19kW (25bhp).

Models included a closed saloon and an open tourer and all versions

had a ride quality which was far ahead of anything else available in the car's market, but once again, high prices deterred customers.

Engine: 1256cc (77 cu in), flat-four
Power: 19kW (25bhp)
0–96km/h (60mph): n/a
Top speed: n/a
Production total: 22,000 (of all T57 types)

TATRA TYPE 87

1937–50

With many lessons learned from the Type 77, the Type 87 utilized an aluminium engine which was both lighter and quieter than the unit it replaced. In fact, the car was 24 per cent lighter than its predecessor largely because of the alloy engine and this allowed the car to be driven with more confidence thanks to better weight distribution.

The car's design and construction was just as unconventional as the car it replaced, designer Hans Ledwinka simply fine-tuning the lines of the Type 77. Curved glass was still not a possibility so there was a three-piece windscreen with small windows where the A-posts would normally be.

To cope with poor quality fuel, the compression ratio was just 5.6:1, but the car could still manage 161km/h (100mph) on the

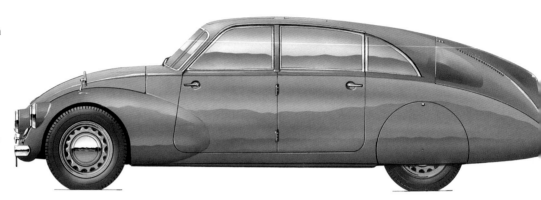

56kW (75bhp) available thanks to a drag co-efficient of just 0.36cd – still better than many of today's cars. But the handling was still unpredictable; indeed, many German Army officers were banned from driving the T87 as they were having too many

accidents and the Army's fleet was being wrecked in the process.

Engine: 2968cc (181 cu in), V8
Power: 56kW (75bhp)
0–96km/h (60mph): n/a
Top speed: 161km/h (100mph)
Production total: n/a

The Type 87 was equally as unattainable as its predecessor, which was probably just as well because its handling was so unpredictable. It was also equally unconventional in its design and construction, although it was considerably lighter.

TATRA T600 TATRAPLAN

1948–54

The convertible version of the T600 is extremely unusual, with the four-door saloon being more typical of the breed.

Work on the T600 Tatraplan began during the winter of 1945 and by early 1946 the first prototype was ready. Dubbed Ambroz, the car's design was uncompromising, with a very slippery shape, a tailfin, enclosed rear wheels and a split windscreen.

The aim was to get the car ready for the 1947 Prague Autosalon, where the first six models went on display. At that stage, the car carried the T107 name, but it was renamed the T600 Tatraplan when it went into production.

Launched in 1948, the T600 was available alongside the T57, T87 and T97 and, although it is now over half a century old, it still looks futuristic. When first announced, it must have looked very unusual. With a body based on that of the T97, the car was unusually aerodynamic and by the time production was halted, all sorts of special versions had been made. Examples include the diesel-engined T600D, the aluminium-bodied Monte Carlo T601 and ambulance and pick-up models.

Engine: 1950cc (119 cu in), 4-cylinder
Power: 39kW (52bhp)
0–80km/h (50mph): 25 secs
Top speed: 130km/h (81mph)
Production total: n/a

TATRA 603

After a three-year gap in passenger car production, Tatra revealed its amazing 603 in 1957. Able to trace its heritage back to Ledwinka's first T77 with its trademark rear-mounted air-cooled V8 and room inside for six passengers, the 603 used a hemi-head 2.5-litre (151 cu in) V8. To ensure the powerplant didn't overheat, there were air scoops in the rear wings and a thermostatically operated air vent in the front bumper.

Although the engine was reasonably light thanks to its all-alloy construction, its low compression ratio of just 6.5:1 meant power was a mere 75kW (100bhp). In a car that weighed nearly 1500kg (3300lb) this meant performance was relatively poor although thanks to its slippery shape, it could very nearly break the 161km/h (100mph) barrier if it

was driven in a straight line for long enough.

The four-speed gearbox was operated by a column-mounted gearshift and early cars featured drum brakes all round, although discs were fitted later. Changes throughout production were gradual, the biggest ones being reserved for the 603-2 of 1967. This had headlights further apart in a new grille, and many earlier cars were upgraded by owners who fitted these later panels.

The last of the really curvy Tatras, the 603 was as unconventional as all those that came before it.

Engine: 2472cc (151 cu in), V8-cylinder
Power: 78kW (105bhp)
0–96km/h (60mph): 15.2 secs
Top speed: 158km/h (99mph)
Production total: 20,422

TATRA 613

By the time the 613 was launched by Tatra in the mid-1970s, rear-engined cars were almost extinct. Although the Fiat 126, Porsche 911 and VW Beetle were still in production, there were very few other cars with their engines mounted in this way. Nevertheless, Tatra had built rear-engined cars for decades and saw

no reason to change this policy just to follow fashion.

However, Tatra had learned that a large powerplant positioned so far back resulted in poor handling. So when the 613 was engineered to accept the long-standing quad-camshaft air-cooled V8, the unit was located much further forward than it had been in previous cars.

The four-door saloon layout stuck but the swoopy, curvy bodywork was replaced by a new, far more angular Vignale design. Demand was always low as few

In production for two decades, the 613 was the last car made by Tatra before the company's sad demise in 1998.

people could afford such a large car, but despite this, the T613 carried on until 1998, built as the T700 from April 1996.

Engine: 3495cc (213 cu in), V8-cylinder
Power: 123kW (165bhp)
0–96km/h (60mph): 12 secs
Top speed: 184km/h (115mph)
Production total: n/a

TERRAPLANE SIX

1932–37

Hudson started making cars in 1909, and when it decided in 1919 to produce a small, inexpensive car, it carried the Essex name to distance it from the more upmarket parent company's cars. (The name was chosen from a map and the car was nearly called a Kent.) Then in 1932 the Essex-Terraplane was launched, a cheaper (but more

refined) car than the Essex. In light of the dire economic conditions that prevailed in the early 1930s it was essential that Hudson took this course of action if it was to survive as people could no longer afford the more expensive cars that Hudson was building.

Powering the car was a 52kW (70bhp) 3164cc engine. With six

cylinders and a side-valve design the Six was sprightly thanks to its lightweight chassis which Hudson claimed endowed the car with the greatest power-to-weight ratio of any car in its class. Moreover, as a result of very competitive pricing the Six was also able to take on the best that Ford, Chevrolet and Plymouth had to offer, and its

success meant the English country name of Essex was dropped in 1933 so that the car became known simply as the Terraplane Six.

Engine: 3162cc (193 cu in), 6-cylinder
Power: 52kW (70bhp)
0–96km/h (60mph): n/a
Top speed: 144km/h (90mph)
Production total: n/a

THURNER RS

1969–74

Using parts from the NSU 1200TT, the Thurner RS is one of the least-known German cars, even though production lasted for half a decade. Produced in glassfibre, the low-volume hand-built sports car had a front end reminiscent of the Porsche 904, partly dictated by the fact that the windscreen was taken from the 904 GTS.

Rudolf Thurner's aim had been to build a sports car for the masses, and thanks to his RS being affordable, it was successful for the few years it was in production, although sales figures were still low, with just 121 built.

Based on a shortened NSU 1200TT chassis, Thurner's grand plan was to give the car Porsche

power and, therefore, great performance. However, the Porsche powerplant didn't arrive, although with a kerb weight of just 570kg (1250lb), the car was still fast, even with the replacement NSU engine fitted. The four-cylinder air-cooled engine could be tuned to give 93kW (125bhp) and the sleek lines of the design, complete with

gull-wing doors, helped to minimize drag and so provide performance well over and above that of the 1200TT.

Engine: 1177cc (72 cu in), 4-cylinder
Power: 48kW (65bhp)
0–80km/h (50mph): 7.1 secs
Top speed: 180km/h (112mph)
Production total: 121

TOYOTA SPORTS 800

1965–70

When the Toyota Sports 800 went on sale in 1967 it was produced by Japan's largest car manufacturer. But Toyota was too inward-looking to sell the car outside Japan, so

neither the United States nor Europe got to sample this diminutive yet delightful sports car.

Derived from the Publica saloon, the Sports 800 was powered by an

air-cooled 790cc (48 cu in) horizontally opposed twin-cylinder engine which delivered just 37kW (49bhp). But the car's light weight, 580kg (1276lb), meant 154km/h

(96mph) was attainable and reliability also came as standard.

With a carburettor to feed each of the engine's two cylinders the engine was lively, but roadholding was limited. A live rear axle with semi-elliptic springs was not very sophisticated, but double wishbones and an anti-roll bar at the front helped to keep things in check.

The removable aluminum targa top was something not seen before, except on Triumph's TR4, and the all-synchromesh four-speed gearbox was a delight to use. As the car was cheaper than its main rival, the Honda S800, it was disappointing that Toyota chose not to export any examples.

Engine: 790cc (48 cu in), twin-cylinder
Power: 37kW (49bhp)
0–96km/h (60mph): n/a
Top speed: 155km/h (97mph)
Production total: 3131

All but forgotten nowadays, the Toyota 800 is always overshadowed by its more popular and common rival, the Honda S800. With considerable short-sightedness, Toyota marketed the car only in Japan, thus missing out on promising export markets.

Toyota 2000GT

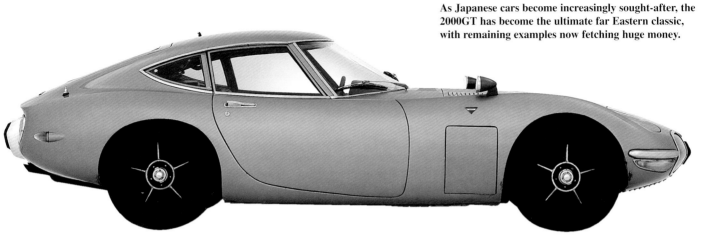

As Japanese cars become increasingly sought-after, the 2000GT has become the ultimate far Eastern classic, with remaining examples now fetching huge money.

The 2000GT made its first appearance in 1967, after four years of development. Toyota's engineers had looked at the best sports cars on offer at the time and decided they could make their own.

The Crown's 1998cc (122 cu in) six-cylinder block was used, with a new double-overhead camshaft cylinder head, producing a substantial 112kW (150bhp) –

enough to give a top speed of 219km/h (137mph) and to get to 96km/h (60mph) from a standstill in less than 10 seconds.

Helping to make the 2000GT a true driver's car was a backbone chassis, built on the same principles as Lotus's Elan, which was the contemporary benchmark for dynamic ability. With disc brakes and unequal-length

wishbones all round, the chassis set-up allowed the car to excel. Unfortunately, over-elaborate styling and Toyota's somewhat lacklustre image ensured that despite the car's very real ability, buyers looked elsewhere for their driving thrills.

Just 337 examples of the 2000GT were sold and despite the appearance of a specially built

convertible example in the James Bond film, *You Only Live Twice*, the car's sales didn't improve and after just three years, the 2000GT was dropped.

Engine: 1998cc (122 cu in), 6-cylinder
Power: 112kW (150bhp)
0–96km/h (60mph): 8.4 secs
Top speed: 219km/h (137mph)
Number made: 337

Toyota Corona

The Corona was launched in 1957 and although the car changed radically during the following three decades, there was always a Corona model in Toyota's line-up well into the 1980s. Always intended to be a staid family saloon, by the mid-1960s, it had become Toyota's most successful car, earning it valuable income to develop other models.

When the third-generation Corona went on sale in 1964 it represented a big leap forward in terms of engineering, with monocoque construction and a new 69kW (92bhp) 1591cc (97 cu in) four-cylinder engine. The car immediately became a bestseller in its home market with great overseas success as well. The American magazine *Road & Track* voted it Imported Car of the Year in 1969 and in 1971 went a stage further, awarding the fourth-generation Corona the Car of the Year accolade.

The fourth generation car had been launched in 1970, with a new 1707cc (104 cu in) engine rated at 71kW (95bhp) or 78kW (105bhp)

depending on compression ratio. To maximize sales, a range of body styles was offered, extending from a saloon, a coupé and a hatch to an estate.

Engine: 1591cc (97 cu in), 4-cylinder
Power: 69kW (92bhp)
0–96km/h (60mph): 17.2 secs
Top speed: 150km/h (94mph)
Production total: 1,788,000

The Corona was a car for the masses, which meant fairly unexceptional styling married to conventional engineering. It was, however, very successful.

TOYOTA CROWN

Engine: 1988cc (121 cu in), 6-cylinder
Power: 93kW (125bhp)
0–96km/h (60mph): 12.7 secs
Top speed: 163km/h (102mph)
Production total: n/a

When Toyota launched its third-generation Crown in 1967 it featured an all-new chassis designed to meet tough new safety regulations in the United States. It was produced with the American market in mind, because Toyota had realized that its largest, most luxurious mass-produced car would do well in a country where size was considered important.

With its 93kW (125bhp) 1988cc (121 cu in) straight-six engine the car was relaxing to drive and supremely comfortable over long distances. To increase desirability, it was also made available as a coupé as well as a saloon. For Japanese buyers, there was the option of an all-new 1994cc (122 cu in) four-cylinder engine, which was cheaper to buy and run, and in 1968, an estate was released to further widen the range.

In 1971, the fourth-generation Crown was unveiled with such

innovations as an electronic anti-skid braking system as well as an electronically controlled automatic transmission. If the 2-litre (122 cu in) engine wasn't powerful enough, there was now the option of a 2.6-litre (159 cu in) powerplant, ideal for effortless cruising on US highways. The car is now one of the most desirable Japanese classics.

With ample power, very good build quality and inbuilt innovation, the Crown was guaranteed to win in the important American market.

TOYOTA CELICA

Toyota's first Celica was unveiled at the 1970 Tokyo Motor Show. Using the floorpan and mechanicals of the Carina, there was a choice of engines but there was only one body style available – a two-door coupé. A new five-speed gearbox was developed for the car and although the Celica had the lines of a sports car, it wasn't built for speed or handling; smoothness, reliability and comfort were considered more important.

Front suspension was by MacPherson struts with coil springs and an anti-roll bar, while rear suspension was by a live rear axle suspended by coil springs. Brakes were disc at the front and drum at the rear, while under the bonnet there was either a 1.4- (85 cu in) or 1.6-litre (97 cu in) engine for the home market in Japan or a 1.6- (97 cu in) or 2-litre (122 cu in) powerplant for cars intended for export.

Unusually, there was also a choice of single or twin-camshaft units, the former cars carrying ST badges and the latter ones a GT tag. Competing against the Ford Capri, the Celica was Toyota's pony car, and even the smallest engine could take the car to 168km/h (105mph).

Engine: 1588cc (97 cu in), 4-cylinder
Power: 54kW (73bhp)
0–96km/h (60mph): n/a
Top speed: 170km/h (106mph)
Production total: 1,210,951

The name survives into the 21st century, and the first Celica was just as stylish while delivering an excellent driving experience.

TOYOTA MR2 MK I

1984–89

Affordable two-seaters were almost extinct when the MR2 was first shown. This car kick-started a whole new generation of budget sportsters.

Having showed its SV-3 concept car at the 1983 Tokyo Motor Show, there was an overwhelmingly positive response to Toyota's proposal for a budget mid-engined sports car and, within a year, the production version of the Midship Runabout Two-Seater (MR2) was born.

Powerplants were either a double-overhead camshaft 1588cc (97 cu in) unit or a 1453cc (89 cu in) single-overhead camshaft one. Sitting over the driven wheels near the middle of the car, these free-revving powerplants offered up to 107kW (143bhp) (as seen in the supercharged version available in some markets), giving sparkling performance thanks to a fairly low weight of just 1050kg (2300lb).

The engine could rev from its 800rpm idle to its 7500rpm redline in less than a second, which helped the car sprint from a standstill to

96km/h (60mph) in less than eight seconds before reaching over 193km/h (120mph).

Disc brakes and Macpherson struts were fitted all round, and the MR2 was comfortable with the

same levels of trim and refinement normally associated with Toyota's rather more mundane offerings. The result was a very popular car which sold successfully from when it was first introduced.

Engine: 1588cc (97 cu in), 4-cylinder
Power: 91kW (122bhp)
0–96km/h (60mph): 7.7 secs
Top speed: 193km/h (120mph)
Production total: 166,104

TRABANT 601

1965–91

When East and West Germany were re-unified, one car captured the imagination – the Trabant 601. Seen everywhere, it became obsolete (and almost worthless) overnight, yet was seen as the ultimate in chic.

Developed from its predecessor the 600, the 601 entered production in 1964 with virtually no development over the 600. Various 601s body styles were on offer, the most popular being the saloon, known, amazingly, as the

Although the Trabant was cruelly mocked when the Berlin Wall came down in 1989, for years it had served up reliability and economy – if not much excitement. It also acquired an ironic reputation for being chic.

Limousine. There was the option of a military version, an estate (the Universal) or a cabriolet, constructed by Osnabruck-based coachbuilder Osterman.

During 26 years of production there was little development. From 1965, an automatic gearbox was offered as an option and in 1969 an extra 2kW (3bhp) was added to the engine. 12-volt electrics arrived in 1983 and from May 1990 a 1.1-litre (67 cu in) VW Polo engine was used, although 601 production ended just a year later.

But the Trabant's strongest point was its reliability, based on its simplicity. The cars were entered in rallies worldwide, ranging from the 1000 Lakes to the RAC in Britain winning the Acropolis Rally in Greece along the way.

Engine: 594cc (36 cu in), two-stroke 4-cylinder
Power: 19kW (26bhp)
0–96km/h (60mph): n/a
Top speed: 100km/h (62mph)
Production total: 3,000,000 approx.

TRIDENT CLIPPER

1967–78

Spiritual successor to the Sunbeam Tiger, Trident's Clipper offered plenty of power in a crude chassis.

By the time Trident showed its first car at the 1966 Racing Car Show in England, its development period had become a story in itself. What began as a TVR prototype became part of the demise of specialist car builder Grantura

Engineering and the fact that it achieved even limited production was a miracle. The car didn't go into full production until 1969, and although the car first shown was based on a TVR Grantura Mk III chassis, the first production examples used a 291kW (390bhp) 4.7-litre (287 cu in) Ford V8 mounted in an Austin-Healey 3000 chassis.

However, it wasn't long before the Austin-Healey went out of production, so the car was then based on a Triumph TR6 frame, but at £1923 in kit form, the Clipper cost more than a Jaguar E-type and not much less than an Aston Martin DB5.

The company went bankrupt in 1972, having replaced the 4.7-litre (287 cu in) V8 with a 5562cc (339

cu in) one, but when the project was revived briefly in the mid-1970s, this became a 6-litre (366 cu in) Chrysler unit.

Engine: 4727cc (287 cu in), V8-cylinder
Power: 291kW (390bhp)
0–96km/h (60mph): n/a
Top speed: 219km/h (137mph)
Production total: 225 (including Venturer and Tycoon)

TRIDENT VENTURER AND TYCOON

1969–78

Mounted on a modified Triumph TR6 chassis, the Venturer and Tycoon used the same basic style as the Clipper, with a Ford six-cylinder engine instead of a V8. The Venturer used the 103kW (138bhp) 2994cc (183 cu in) Essex

V6 engine from the Ford Capri while the Tycoon used the 112kW (150bhp) 2498cc (152 cu in) fuel-injected straight-six usually seen under the bonnet of a TR6.

It is estimated that only around seven Tycoons were built, the

Both the Venturer and the Tycoon borrowed heavily from the Clipper, with the same outward appearance. But underneath was a much less powerful engine, yet it was still more costly than far more prestigious rivals.

company focusing instead on the more saleable Venturer. However, since this car was more expensive than an E-type, it wasn't easy to sell – especially when *Motor* tested one and claimed the car had dangerously poor handling. It is quite surprising that Trident managed to sell any cars at all.

An attempt to boost interest by entering the 1970 London to Mexico Rally came to nothing when the entry retired with suspension problems but, in 1976, four years after Trident went bankrupt, there was a revival. By now the cars were using a live rear axle in place of the previously specified Triumph independent rear suspension, but nobody noticed Trident had returned and the following year the company disappeared for good.

Engine: 2994cc (183 cu in), V6-cylinder
Power: 103kW (138bhp)
0–96km/h (60mph): n/a
Top speed: 192km/h (120mph)
Production total: 225 (including Clipper)

TRIUMPH SUPER-SEVEN

1927–32

Cashing in on the success of Austin's Seven, Triumph's Super-Seven was a success on a smaller scale. This is one of the saloon versions, but many other (more exciting) styles were available.

Triumph started life as a bicycle manufacturer. It was set up by a German, Siegfried Bettman, in 1890, and moved into making motorcycles in 1902.

It was more than 20 years before its first car appeared, the 10/20 of 1923. The diminutive Super-Seven which followed four years later was its first model to appeal to the mass market, pitched against competitors like the Austin Seven, although the Triumph was a more expensive machine.

The 832cc (51 cu in) Super-Seven was available in several different styles, such as the Popular Tourer, Tourer de Luxe, Two-Seater de Luxe, Fabric Saloon and the streamlined Gordon England Fabric Saloon. There was

also the elegant Coachbuilt Saloon, which looked like a much larger car in miniature. Other coachbuilders soon started offering their own styles for the chassis.

1929 saw the introduction of the aluminium-bodied Special Sports

with a Cozette supercharger, which enjoyed some success, but the tough little Seven was more successful as a rally car. It was superseded by the Super Eight in 1933, which used the same engine but a bigger body.

Engine: 832cc (51cu in), 4-cylinder
Power: 16kW (21bhp) at 4000rpm
0–96km/h (60mph): n/a
Top speed: 85km/h (53mph)
Production total: 17,000 approx.

TRIUMPH GLORIA

1934–37

Triumph started its move upmarket with the Gloria. The company was justifiably proud of this extremely good-looking car, marketing it somewhat extravagantly as the 'smartest car in the land' or the 'queen of cars'.

Although this was an exaggeration, the various Gloria models were handsome creations, low-slung and rakish. The Gloria was offered with four- and six-cylinder Coventry Climax engines of 1087cc (66 cu in) and 1476cc

(90 cu in) respectively, and with a variety of saloon and open bodies, including the sporting Monte Carlo Tourer which had its own special 1232cc (75 cu in) twin-carburettor engine. This was the brainchild of competition driver Donald Healey.

For 1935, Triumph dropped its other models to concentrate on the Gloria alone, offering new body styles and engine options, including the exotic-looking Flow-free model with its aerodynamic, art deco styling. It was the Gloria Six which was most developed, sporting a 1991cc (121 cu in) engine. A new Gloria radiator mascot – a winged lady slightly reminiscent of the Rolls-Royce Spirit of Ecstasy – characterized the updated range.

Despite good sales – or so Triumph claimed – the company itself was in trouble, which led to a less impressive selection of Glorias for 1936. Production finally came to an end in 1937.

Engine: 1991cc (121 cu in), 6-cylinder
Power: 41kW (55bhp) at 4500rpm
0–96km/h (60mph): 22 secs
Top speed: 120km/h (75mph)
Production total: 6000 approx.

Gloria by name, glorious by nature. The open-top, sporting versions of the Gloria were handsome creations, and enjoyed considerable success in motorsport.

TRIUMPH DOLOMITE STRAIGHT EIGHT

1934–35

An undeserved failure, Triumph's Dolomite Straight Eight was intended to compete against foreign sports cars and prevent them stealing British glory. Had Triumph's fortunes not been so precarious, more than just three would have appeared.

The supercharged Dolomite Straight Eight was a glorious failure. It was the most spectacular vehicle built by Triumph to date, and has since become recognized as one of the company's most notable models ever. Yet it was put together by a company in serious financial difficulties so unfortunately only three were made.

The mastermind behind the Dolomite Straight Eight was Donald Healey, who had joined Triumph in 1933 as experimental manager. He jingoistically saw a need for a large-engined British sports car to compete against the best of the foreign opposition, such as the Alfa Romeo 2300, the racer on which the Straight Eight was based.

Apparently with a flattered Alfa Romeo's full approval, Triumph set about creating a practical carbon copy of the eight-cylinder Alfa engine, although with a lower capacity. Even the supercharger was retained, and the beautiful open sports body was very Italian in style.

Despite the lofty ideals, Triumph's perilous fortunes meant that the Straight Eight was a luxury it couldn't afford. Production was halted in April 1935.

Engine: 1990cc (121 cu in), 8-cylinder
Power: 89kW (120bhp) at 5500rpm
0–96km/h (60mph): n/a
Top speed: 177km/h (110mph)
Production total: 3

TRIUMPH DOLOMITE

1937–39

Engine: 1767cc (108 cu in), 4-cylinder
Power: 46kW (62bhp) at 4500rpm
0–96km/h (60mph): 32.2 secs
Top speed: 117km/h (73mph)
Production total: 7200 approx.

The 1937 Dolomite range was a last effort by the company to stop losing money. New bodies, by stylist Walter Belgrove, updated the Gloria look, while the first Triumph-designed and built engines (masterminded by Donald Healey again) went into production to power this car.

As with the Gloria, the new Dolomite could be specified with four-cylinder engines of 1496cc (91 cu in) or 1767cc (108 cu in), or a bigger six-cylinder unit with 1991cc (121 cu in). The Triumph engines were advancements on their predecessors, featuring overhead valves and a 'crossflow' cylinder head.

Cosmetically, the cars were modern, too, featuring a stylized 'waterfall' grille which aped American trends. As charismatic as the grille was, it still shocked many of Triumph's more traditionally minded buyers, so a conventional grille was offered on the Dolomite Continental model in order to appease them.

An increasingly desperate Triumph expanded the Dolomite range in 1938 to attract more customers, introducing drophead and open versions. For 1939, there was also the very luxurious Dolomite Royal.

However, the Dolomite failed to save the company. On 7 June 1939, Triumph declared itself bankrupt and all production ceased.

Decades before the Dolomite name was used on a 1970s Triumph saloon, it had featured on a handsome range of late-thirties models. Triumph pinned its hopes on the car saving the firm but, unfortunately, it was unable to halt the financial decline and the company was declared bankrupt.

TRIUMPH ROADSTER

1946–49

Engine: 1776cc (108 cu in), 4-cylinder
Power: 48kW (65bhp) at 4500rpm
0–96km/h (60mph): 34.4 secs
Top speed: 128km/h (80mph)
Production total: 4501

Although many of Triumph's physical assets were badly damaged during bombing raids on Coventry during World War II, the name and enthusiasm for the old company survived. In 1944, it was purchased by the Standard Motor Company, which was looking for a way to increase its sporting profile. A new Triumph tubular chassis was designed, intended to be capable of taking two different bodies, one a luxury saloon, the other a sporting open tourer.

The 1800/2000 Roadster made its debut in 1946. The new Standard-Triumph concern tackled the design in-house, producing a curvaceous, elegant, but unconventional, design. The Roadster could seat three abreast up front, thanks to the bench front seat, as well as another two passengers tightly squeezed in the rear dickey seat.

Initially the Roadster was powered by a prewar Standard 1776cc (108 cu in) side-valve engine, but this was changed in 1948 to a 2088cc (127 cu in) unit which used the new Standard

Vanguard overhead-valve unit, as well as other shared parts. Unable to compete in the vital export market, it was discontinued.

The reborn Triumph company put the Roadster into production one year after the war ended. Novel features were the rear dickey seat, (the cover of which could be used as an additional glass screen), and triple wipers at the front.

TRIUMPH RENOWN

1949–54

Sister vehicle to the Roadster was the Triumph 1800/2000 Saloon. It shared the same engine and mechanics as its sportier stablemate, as well as a slightly altered chassis, but the body was totally different, as it was intended to appeal to a completely different kind of customer.

Triumph initially asked coachbuilders Mulliners of Birmingham to produce a design. However, the new head of the Standard-Triumph body engineering department, Walter Belgrove, came up with his own blueprint, and it was his ideas that were chosen. The outcome was a rather grand and stately looking saloon with razor-edged styling, a look that company boss Sir John Black liked.

Complementing the Roadster was the Renown saloon and limousine. Despite its completely contrasting look – staid, as opposed to sporting – it shared most of the same mechanical components and chassis. It was built from aluminium panels mounted on an ash frame.

Launched at the same time as the Roadster in 1946, the 1800/2000 Saloon went on to have a longer and more successful career than the Roadster. The bigger 2088cc (127 cu in) Vanguard engine was fitted in 1949, and soon afterwards the car was renamed the Renown, when it received the Vanguard's chassis and independent front suspension as well.

Production continued until 1954, with a longer-wheelbase limousine option for 1951, which became the new standard wheelbase size for the model one year later.

Engine: 2088cc (127 cu in), 4-cylinder
Power: 51kW (68bhp) at 4200rpm
0–96km/h (60mph): 28.4 secs
Top speed: 120km/h (75mph)
Production total: 12,000

TRIUMPH MAYFLOWER

1949–53

Every so often, car companies produce some strange models – and the Mayflower was Triumph's effort. No other Triumph model, up until the TR7 almost 30 years later, has generated such hugely divided opinion about its styling as the curious-looking small saloon unveiled in 1949.

The idea behind the Mayflower was that it was to be an economy model for the US market. The theory at least was sound, but its execution was poor. Sir John Black insisted on retaining the razor-edged styling of the bigger Triumph saloons, despite the fact that it looked odd on the much shorter wheelbase as the proportions were completely wrong. It didn't help that one designer, Leslie Moore, styled the

basic body, while another, Walter Belgrove, styled the front. On the plus side though, it did feature unitary construction.

Unsurprisingly, the Mayflower wasn't a success. Although it was spacious, well-equipped and well-built, buyers didn't like the awkward looks, weak 1247cc (76 cu in) side-valve engine, three-speed gearbox and perilous handling no matter how cheap the car was. Despite improvements and the introduction of a drophead coupé, it lasted just four years until 1953.

Engine: 1247cc (76 cu in), 4-cylinder
Power: 28kW (38bhp) at 4200rpm
0–96km/h (60mph): 30 secs
Top speed: 101km/h (63mph)
Production total: 35,000

The Mayflower was styled by two different designers...and it shows. The idea of an economy model for America was sound in theory, but Triumph's attempt to shrink down its big car styling doomed the car from the start.

TRIUMPH TR2

1955–62

Engine: 1991cc (121 cu in), 4-cylinder
Power: 67kW (90bhp) at 4800rpm
0–96km/h (60mph): 12.2 secs
Top speed: 166km/h (103mph)
Production total: 8628

The Triumph marque will always be best known for its highly successful range of TR sports cars introduced in 1953. If it hadn't been for the TR series – and most notably, the TR2 that started it all off – Triumph as a marque might have died out, instead of becoming the dominant partner of the Standard-Triumph concern. TRs were popular throughout the world, but it was in the United States that the cars were really successful, becoming among the most popular of the sporting European imports.

The TR2 was born from Sir John

Black's desire to steal some of MG's glory in the United States. The MG TD was selling well across the Atlantic and developing quite a reputation. If MG could be successful abroad, reasoned Black, so could Triumph.

The first car to wear the TR badge was the TRX, an abandoned replacement for the Roadster shown at the 1950 Paris Motor Show, but never put into production. The TRX, however, did donate some of its features to what would become the new TR2, including its twin-SU carburettor four-cylinder Vanguard engine, albeit with some development. The chassis, however, was modified from the Standard Flying Nine frame. This model, which went out of production in

1939, was hardly at the cutting edge of modern motoring technology, even with the addition of independent front suspension. It was chosen primarily because there were several hundred surplus Flying Nine frames lying around unused, and production costs could be kept to a minimum if these were utilized.

Triumph's new sports car, known initially as the 20TS, was unveiled at the 1952 London Motor Show. It had been developed very quickly to get it ready in time, and when it came to testing, the flaws were very obvious. Ken Richardson, formerly involved with the BRM Grand Prix project, was invited to drive the 20TS and called it 'a death trap'.

His words were taken to heart by the company, and he was invited to join Triumph to help develop the car. Much of the work centred around stiffening up the chassis to improve handling, but work was also carried out on the styling, especially around the rear end, which was not aesthetically particularly pleasing.

By the end of 1952, the old car

From small acorns grow mighty oaks: the TR2 was the mother of Triumph's sporting range. It may have been initially rather slow to catch on, but it was fast on the road, setting the theme for the TRs that followed it.

(which would become retrospectively known as the TR1, although it never bore this name officially) had been reworked into the TR2, with a completely new chassis. It was unveiled – again – to the world at the 1953 Geneva Motor Show. As well as the new look and the new underpinnings, the power of the 2-litre (121 cu in) engine had also been upped to 67kW (90bhp).

The TR2 was better received than its predecessor, but still needed to prove itself. It had its chance in the summer of 1953, when a modified car was taken to Belgium for a high speed run on the Jabbeke motorway. With Ken Richardson at the wheel, a speed of almost 201km/h (125mph) was achieved. Other valuable racing laurels followed, including Le Mans, the Mille Miglia and an outright win on the 1954 RAC Rally.

Yet the TR2 wasn't a strong seller. Despite performance superiority over its MG TF rival, early cars had teething problems with brakes and noise levels. They were initially slow to catch on in the United States as well, even after the introduction of a hardtop option in 1954, which made the TR2 a nicer car to drive in bad weather. Triumph started a policy of continuous improvement, which culminated in the visually similar but improved TR3 introduced in late 1955.

TRIUMPH TR3

Visually, there was very little to distinguish the TR3 from its TR2 forerunner. Apart from the different name, the most obvious change was the egg-crate grille covering the radiator cooling intake. Underneath though, was a more powerful engine, developing 3.5kW (5bhp) more than its previous incarnation, thanks to its having bigger SU carburettors. There was also a Le Mans-type head available, which developed 75kW (100bhp).

A major development – not just in TR terms, but for motoring technology in general – came with the TR3 revealed in 1956. The fitment of Girling disc brakes on the front wheels made the TR3 the first British production car to boast this feature. Sales of the TR3 started to accelerate as a result of the improvement, and customers in the United States finally started to pay attention to the small but vigorous British sports car.

Further improvements weren't long in coming. For 1957, there was a styling update, which included a full length grille and door handles on the outside of the car. This model was known as the TR3A, and continued in production until 1962.

There was also a short-lived US market TR3B in 1962 with a 2138cc (130 cu in) engine designed to overlap with the new TR4 for more traditional buyers, and lasting less than a year.

Engine: 1991cc (121 cu in), 4-cylinder
Power: 75kW (100bhp) at 4800rpm
0–96km/h (60mph): 12 secs
Top speed: 169km/h (105mph)
Production total: 74,944

One of the most traditional features of the TR3 was its cutaway doors, shown to good effect below. As of 1954, the doors had become 'short doors' to help them clear high pavements.

Triumph answered criticisms about the primitive nature of the TR2 by launching the updated TR3. The photo above shows a TR3A model, identifiable by its full-length grille, plus door handles on the outside.

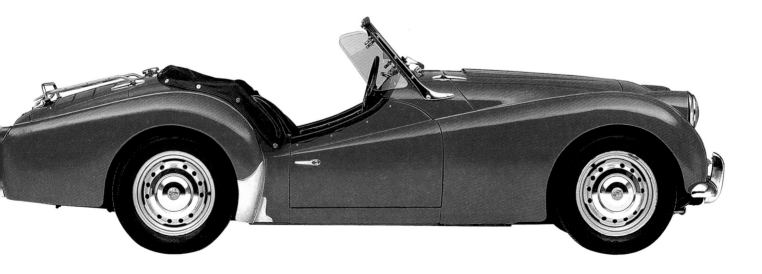

TRIUMPH ITALIA

1959–63

As the 1950s wore on, it became obvious that the TR3 would need to be updated to stay competitive in the sports car market. A British businessman, Raymond Flower, introduced the company to Italian stylist Giovanni Michelotti, who came up with some alternative Triumph-based sports car designs in 1957.

Michelotti was given a TR3 chassis to work with, and within three months, offered Triumph a flamboyant-looking machine in return, built by Vignale of Turin. That car didn't go into production,

Just to show what could be done with a TR chassis, Giovanni Michelotti created the beautiful and typically continental-looking Italia for European sale. It was prettier than a standard TR3, but also more expensive to buy, and production remained strictly limited. It is, perhaps, no surprise that the largest market was Italy.

but Michelotti was given a contract to style future models for the company, including the next TR.

One of the ideas he came up with was a pretty-looking fixed-

head coupé on a TR3A frame. It appeared at the 1958 Turin Show, with a streamlined front end, and was so well-received that Vignale put it into limited manufacture as

the Triumph Italia. The production version came with a conventional nose and chrome wire wheels, plus the standard TR3A 1991cc (121 cu in) 75kW (100bhp) engine up front.

Sales of the Italia were confined to mainland Europe, most of them finding homes with prosperous Italians. Today, they're not only rare, but very desirable too.

Engine: 1991cc (121 cu in), 4-cylinder
Power: 75kW (100bhp) at 5000rpm
0–96km/h (60mph): 11.4 secs
Top speed: 174km/h (108mph)
Production total: 329

TRIUMPH TR4

1961–67

The Triumph Italia had been one of the by-products of Triumph's quest for a replacement for the TR3. However, as attractive as it looked, the management at Standard-Triumph felt that it wasn't quite the right image for Triumph in the 1960s, and Italian stylist Giovanni Michelotti was asked to keep producing ideas for the new TR.

Along the way, he came up with two other prototype examples, both of which showed clear signs of the future TR4 shape. In 1958, the Zest prototype was completed on a TR3A chassis, which showcased many of the design cues that would later characterize the TR4, especially around the front, with its hooded headlights and long grille. The different-looking Zoom exercise, which

followed it, had a longer wheelbase, and front styling that would later go on to be modified for the Triumph Spitfire. However, the Zoom did include an innovative two-piece hardtop, a future TR4 feature. One of the more significant characteristics about this car was its 20X 'Sabrina' 112kW (150bhp) racing engine, derived from Triumph's recent, but unsuccessful exploits at Le Mans.

In 1960, Triumph finally made up its mind about what it wanted, and Michelotti was asked to combine the shape of the Zoom with the shorter wheelbase, nose, bonnet and hardtop of the Zest, to create the definitive TR4 shape. The car was announced in September 1961, with deliveries beginning almost immediately.

As well as crisper, more modern lines, one major benefit of the TR4 was the size of the boot, which was considerably larger than on previous models.

Compared to the very traditional previous TR offerings, the TR4 was very modern. Although based on the chassis of the old car, there were few reminders of this heritage. The crisp lines were just right for the new decade, and the car was more comfortable, practical and spacious than many of its contemporaries. Although much of the original TR3 remained underneath, it was updated with rack-and-pinion steering and servo brakes as well as an all-synchromesh manual transmission. An enlarged 2138 cc (130 cu in) 75kW (100bhp) engine was the standard unit, although the old 1991cc (121 cu in) engine could be specified. Few customers wanted the old unit, though.

Sales were good, certainly strong enough to worry Triumph's rivals, and competitors like MG and Austin-Healey were put under pressure. Apart from a few detail updates (new seats for the end of 1962 and the adoption of twin Zenith-Stromberg carburettors in place of the SU ones for 1963), the TR4 remained untouched until 1965, when it became the TR4A. The change was made mainly as a response to the MGB, which had started taking sales away from Triumph from 1962.

This time, the body stayed the same, but the underpinnings were

updated in response to complaints about the car's handling. Sports car standards had moved on since the chassis was born in the mid-1950s, but the TR hadn't. It also had a harsher ride than its rivals. A new frame was developed, and onto it was fitted an all-independent suspension based on that of the new Triumph 2000 saloon, a move which considerably improved the dynamics of the TR4.

However, US dealers demanded that a version with the old live beam rear axle be made available too, as a cut-price alternative. Triumph complied, and modified the new frame to take the old TR4 axle.

Apart from the different badging, a subtly modified grille and sidelights moved to the wing tops, there was little to visually distinguish between the old and the new TR4 models. The TR4A was a little heavier than its immediate predecessor, but the engine manifold was slightly revised to add more power as compensation, the four-cylinder unit now capable of producing 77kW (104bhp).

The TR4A stayed in production until 1967, by which time Triumph had something very special planned for the next TR model.

Engine: 2138cc (130 cu in), 4-cylinder
Power: 75kW (100bhp) at 4600rpm
0–96km/h (60mph): 10.9 secs
Top speed: 167km/h (104mph)
Production total: 68,718

TRIUMPH TR5/250

Once again, it was MG who provided the impetus for the six-cylinder update of the TR range. Triumph's fiercest competitor had launched a 3-litre (183 cu in) version of the MGB (known as the MGC) in 1967, and Triumph followed suit the same year with the six-cylinder TR5.

The power unit for the TR5 was based on that used in the Triumph 2000 saloon, albeit with the stroke lengthened to bring capacity up to 2498cc (152 cu in) and with Lucas fuel injection fitted to increase power. Triumph thus became the first British company to use fuel injection on a production car.

Other changes included larger brakes, a stronger rear suspension and a safety-conscious interior, but the body stayed exactly the same as the TR4A. Even though the TR4As bonnet bulge was no longer needed, it was kept, just for appearance's sake.

Unfortunately for Triumph, the Lucas system failed to meet American emission laws, so cars bound for the States were fitted with reworked Zenith carburettors instead, a set-up which produced a paltry 78kW (105bhp) instead of 112kW (150bhp). To distinguish them, these less powerful models were named TR250s instead.

With fuel injection and a powerful engine, these cars were all about performance. Top speed of 195km/h (121mph) was reached quickly, and the ride was hard and aggressive.

Engine: 2498cc (152 cu in), 6-cylinder
Power: 112kW (150bhp) at 5500rpm
0–96km/h (60mph): 8.8 secs
Top speed: 195km/h (121mph)
Production total: 11,431

The TR5's styling may have been the same as the TR4A, but its power output definitely wasn't. The TR5 featured a six-cylinder engine and fuel injection, which added half as much power again compared to the TR4. The bonnet bulge wasn't needed, but Triumph kept it anyway. The American version, which lacked Lucas fuel injection, was known as the TR250.

TRIUMPH TR6

Triumph turned from Italy to Germany for the next generation of TR models. With Michelotti unable to find time to do the TR6, Karmann was instead responsible for remodelling the front and rear ends in record time.

In the United States, the TR5/250 was a big disappointment. It may have had a smoother six-cylinder engine, but it was no faster and no more powerful than its TR4A forerunner and didn't look any different either. Triumph was going to have to try harder if it was to hold onto its position of eminence in the US.

By this time, the Triumph group had merged with the British Motor Corporation to form British Leyland (BL), a move which made it part of the same family as MG. The six-cylinder MGC hadn't been a success (and was due to be dropped in 1969 after just two years), which left the way clear for Triumph to try again with another six-cylinder TR for the United States. And this time, the car looked different.

However, Triumph's styling guru, Giovanni Michelotti, was already busy with other BL projects so, instead of Italy, Triumph went to Germany, to the newly expanded Karmann coachbuilding firm.

Karmann was given a tough task by the budget-conscious Triumph: to transform the appearance of the TR5 without altering the basic structure of the vehicle. Wheel-arches, floorpan, scuttle, windscreen, doors and even the inner panels all had to stay the same, the styling had to get

approval from all the various BL committees, and Karmann were expected to manufacture the new tooling as well. And it all had to be done within a mere 14 months.

Somehow, Karmann managed the practically impossible. By just remodelling the front and rear ends of the TR5, it produced a much more modern-looking sports car. The radiator grille was raised, and a blunt, Kamm-type tail was fitted, which had the beneficial side-effect of increasing luggage space as well. And at last, the redundant carburettor-clearing bulge on the bonnet disappeared as well. Other new TR6 features included an improved soft top, a new-look hard-top and redesigned seats.

The purposeful-looking body did a good job of masking the ageing underpinnings. Apart from wider wheels (which required flared wheel-arches) and an anti-roll bar to improve handling (the TR6 was heavier than the old TR5), there were no other technical changes. The American market cars still didn't get fuel injection like the

Compared to the TR2 of almost 20 years earlier, the TR6 offered drivers and passengers a far more inviting environment inside. Instrumentation was better, and there was far more emphasis on safety, with lots of soft padding.

rest of the world, having to make do with the twin-carburettor set-up once again. This time though, cars destined for the United States did have the same TR6 designation as their European counterparts, albeit with the 'Carb' suffix tacked on to create the TR6 Carb model. The TR6 proved to be the longest-lived of all the TR sports cars. And although it didn't sell so quickly as previous models, it was a consistently good performer in the market place, especially in the United States.

Its successful formula meant that there was little incentive to change it during its eight-year production life. A stronger gearbox was fitted

from 1971 (the same unit as used in the Triumph Stag) and other small details were altered. However, in the United States, the TR6 had to contend with increasingly stringent laws on both safety and emissions and more pollution control equipment was fitted as the 1970s progressed. 1974 saw unattractive black rubber over-riders appearing on the front and rear bumpers to meet impact regulations, but at least it escaped the ignominy of growing complete rubber bumper mouldings as the MGB and other European sports cars were forced to do.

The TR6's modern looks attracted many new converts to the sporting Triumph cause, despite handling remaining equivalent to the previous TR5 (with the same chassis of course), although a front anti-roll bar made it a better proposition on fast corners. By now though, it was all feeling a bit ancient compared to what else was around. Almost 95,000 TR6s were built before the car was dropped in July 1976, to be replaced by a radically different – and very controversial – TR model.

Engine: 2498cc (152 cu in), 6-cylinder
Power: 106kW (142bhp) at 5700rpm
0–96km/h (60mph): 8.2 secs
Top speed: 195km/h (121mph)
Production total: 94,619

TRIUMPH HERALD

1959–71

Mechanically, the Herald was antiquated when it appeared in 1959, yet the sharp styling did a good job of disguising that fact and ensuring it a prosperous career. The three main variants – saloon, convertible and rare coupé – are pictured here.

When the Standard company took over Triumph, the word 'standard' meant 'excellence'. But by the 1950s, the word had come to mean 'basic', so when it became time to replace the small Standard 8 and 10 models in 1959, it would be Triumphs which succeeded them.

The Herald range became one of the most successful small British cars of the 1960s, yet it was strictly conventional in all but look. The crisp and angular modern body came from Michelotti, allegedly drawn in five minutes, but underneath it, Triumph stayed very traditional. The Herald had an anachronistic separate chassis, drum brakes and was powered by improved versions of the old Standard engine. All-independent suspension was fitted, but the elementary rear set-up was poor.

The success of the Herald inspired many variations. As well as the saloon, there was a convertible, a short-lived but good-looking coupé, an estate and a van.

A bigger 1147cc (70 cu in) engine was added in 1961, expanded to 1296cc (79 cu in) in 1967 when a revised 'slanted look' front end was adopted as well.

Engine: 1147cc (70 cu in), 4-cylinder
Power: 29kW (39bhp) at 4500rpm
0–96km/h (60mph): 28.6 secs
Top speed: 122km/h (76mph)
Production total: 544,210 approx.

TRIUMPH VITESSE

1962–71

No-one could mistake the Herald origins of the Vitesse. However, the four angled headlamps gave it a more aggressive persona to match the extra six-cylinder engine performance. The open-air versions were most popular.

The Herald was a versatile vehicle and very popular with the car-buying public. Its separate chassis meant that it could be adapted for a variety of different vehicles, and it proved to be a good basis for building specials.

Triumph also saw the potential for a family of Herald-based offshoots. In 1962, it launched the Vitesse, really just a more powerful six-cylinder version of the Herald, with a strengthened chassis, disc brakes up front, a sportier gearbox

and overdrive as an option. The Vitesse could be distinguished from its less powerful sister by its slanted quad-headlamp front styling, another example of Michelotti's art. It could be bought in both saloon and convertible

versions, with the latter being a competent budget sports car, packed with character.

A 2-litre (122 cu in) engine and all-synchromesh gearbox came in 1966, but handling problems caused by the rear swing axle independent suspension weren't addressed until 1968, with the Vitesse Mk II. As well as revised suspension, there was more power as well with this update. Like the Herald range on which it was based, the Vitesse was dropped in 1971.

Engine: 1998cc (122 cu in), 6-cylinder
Power: 77kW (104bhp) at 5300rpm
0–96km/h (60mph): 11.9 secs
Top speed: 164km/h (102mph)
Production total: 51,212

TRIUMPH SPITFIRE

1962–80

The Spitfire was another Herald-based offering, designed to compete with MG's Midget. There had been plans for a sports version of the Herald since it took shape on the drawing board, but these were shelved until Triumph chiefs saw a sketch Michelotti had prepared for a pretty little roadster in 1960.

This Bomb project, as it was known, emerged as the nostalgically named Spitfire in 1962, to much acclaim. The finished car was built on a shortened chassis, with the Herald's 1147cc (70 cu in) engine fitted with twin carburettors to produce 47kW (63bhp). Front disc brakes were standard, and the car was capable of 145km/h (90mph) – although the Herald rear suspension made the Spitfire's handling suspect on fast corners.

The Spitfire outlasted the Herald by eight years, receiving continual updates. In 1963, the Mk II version added more power, a new grille and a nicer interior. For 1967, the Mk III had the new Herald 1296cc (79 cu in) engine, plus higher bumpers to meet new US safety regulations. Michelotti redesigned the front and rear for the Mk IV of 1970, and the final major update came in 1974, when the Spitfire received a 1493cc (91 cu in) engine, ironically the same as used in the 'rival' MG Midget.

The patriotically named Spitfire was Triumph's budget sports car, an entertaining alternative to the MGB. It lasted the same length of time, too, being launched in 1962 and staying in production, albeit with modifications, for the next 18 years.

Engine: 1296cc (79 cu in), 4-cylinder
Power: 56kW (75bhp) at 6000rpm
0-96km/h (60mph): 13.6 secs
Top speed: 161km/h (100mph)
Production total: 314,332

TRIUMPH GT6

1966–73

During the period Triumph was making the six-cylinder Vitesse and the four-cylinder Spitfire, the logical progression was to combine the two, to create a more potent version of the Spitfire.

The marriage occurred in 1966, and the new car was called the GT6, boasting the Vitesse's 2-litre (122 cu in) engine. Unlike the Spitfire, the GT6 was only available as a hardtop coupé, and its name clearly signalled its rivalry with the MGB GT. The fastback styling was 'borrowed' from competition Spitfires which had run previously at Le Mans and on rallies, but the GT6 was given greater practicality thanks to its hinged rear window.

Because of its ancestry, the GT6 suffered from the usual handling problems as the rest of the Herald family, at least until the Mk II revamp of 1968 improved matters considerably by reworking the

The GT6's looks and impressive performance earned it the name of 'the poor man's E-type'. It was effectively a Spitfire with a hard top grafted on and hatchback added for practicality. The styling contrasts between the versions are illustrated by this picture.

car's rear suspension. The Mk III version of the GT6 appeared in 1970, showing the same top and tail Michelotti styling alterations as seen on the Spitfire and flared wheel arches to add a more aggressive sporting look.

The Mk IV model proved to be very short-lived indeed, as it was introduced in 1973, the same year that the GT6 was dropped.

Engine: 1998cc (122 cu in), 6-cylinder
Power: 71kW (95bhp) at 5000rpm
0-96km/h (60mph): 12 secs
Top speed: 174km/h (108mph)
Production total: 40,926

TRIUMPH 2000

The 2000 was the mainstay Triumph saloon for almost 15 years. Michelotti's effective design meant that it needed only a minor restyle to keep it looking fresh during that time. This is a Mk I version, built from 1963 to 1969.

When Triumph was not trying to beat MG with its sporting range, it was taking on Rover in the executive saloon market. Rover produced its elegant 2000 model in 1963, and Triumph launched its own equally impressive 2000 in the same year.

Although the Rover was probably slightly better-looking than the Triumph, the Triumph had the mechanical advantage of a smooth six-cylinder engine lifted from the outgoing Standard Vanguard. As usual, Michelotti was responsible for the handsome styling, with the model featuring unitary construction and all-independent suspension.

An estate joined the line-up in 1965, and the 2000 was updated for the 1970s in 1969, when it became the Mk II, with a longer, restyled nose and tail. One of the major changes to the range had happened a year earlier, however, when the 2.5PI was created, by fitting a fuel-injected TR5 engine under the 2000 bonnet. The Lucas injection system proved to be unreliable, though, so a twin-carburettor version was introduced alongside it in 1974. This allowed Triumph to drop the PI model in 1975. The whole range disappeared in 1977, ironically to make way for Rover's new SD1.

Engine: 1998cc (122 cu in), 6-cylinder
Power: 67kW (90bhp) at 5000rpm
0–96km/h (60mph): 13.5 secs
Top speed: 150km/h (93mph)
Production total: 219,816

TRIUMPH DOLOMITE

The Dolomite family became large and confusing. In 1965, Triumph launched its only front-wheel drive car, the 1300. Michelotti's styling closely emulated his larger 2000 saloon. Then, in 1970, the car was re-engineered to take rear-wheel drive, becoming the Toledo, although the 1300 carried on, albeit with a larger 1493cc (91 cu in) engine and renamed the 1500. Cosmetically, both these cars had redesigned front and rear ends as well. Finally, in 1973, the 1500 became rear-wheel drive, too.

Meanwhile, 1972 saw the arrival of the rear-wheel drive Dolomite 1850, with its new slanted four-cylinder overhead-camshaft engine, using the 1500 shell, but with more luxury inside. A 'hot' version of the Dolomite, called the Sprint, was launched for 1973. Its reworked two-litre (122 cu in) engine featured 16 valves, novel for the time. The Sprint was an excellent performer when it worked properly, but unfortunately was often unreliable.

In 1976, the Toledo (which had remained in production alongside these other cars) was renamed as a Dolomite too. The range continued to be built until 1980.

Engine: 1854cc (113 cu in), 4-cylinder
Power: 68kW (91bhp) at 5200rpm
0–96km/h (60mph): 11.6 secs
Top speed: 166km/h (103mph)
Production total: 177,237

The Dolomite was a revival of an old 1930s Triumph name. Top model was the Dolomite Sprint, usually finished in a garish 1970s colour scheme. Its 16-valve engine would have guaranteed success if it had not been so troublesome.

TRIUMPH 1300 FWD

1965–70

The Triumph 1300 was intended as a replacement for the Herald. In the end, it went into production alongside the car it was meant to supersede, and the original version was dropped a year before the Herald.

With the success of front-wheel drive cars such as the Mini and 1100, Triumph decided to make one itself. The company's front-wheel drive 'Ajax' project adopted a mechanical arrangement where the gearbox was situated behind the engine, a format that made it easier to incorporate possible four-wheel drive in the future. Power came from an adapted Herald engine, bored out to 1296cc (79 cu in), and all-independent suspension was adopted.

The evergreen Michelotti was given the task of styling 'a junior 2000' and designed a car that was attractive in its own right, yet kept the Triumph family resemblance. 'Ajax' emerged as the Triumph 1300 in October 1965, selling well immediately. After two years, a twin-carburettor 1300TC was added, effectively a 1300 with a Spitfire engine installed.

The 1300 grew into the 1500 and the Toledo in 1970, by which time Triumph had become part of the British Leyland empire, which had a different view of the value of front-wheel drive.

Engine: 1296cc (79 cu in), 4-cylinder
Power: 45kW (61bhp) at 5000rpm
0–96km/h (60mph): 19 secs
Top speed: 138km/h (86mph)
Production total: 148,350

Triumph's only foray into the world of front-wheel drive was the 1300. Styling was influenced by the bigger 2000 model. Despite the front-wheel drive configuration, a variant of the rear-wheel drive Herald engine provided power.

TRIUMPH STAG

1970–77

The Triumph Stag could have been a world-beater. The car was a novel design that produced a very attractive four-seater convertible blessed with great performance and well-behaved, compliant handling. Unfortunately, by the time it appeared, Triumph was part of British Leyland, a name that had come to mean unreliability and poor build quality.

The Stag's origins stretched back to 1963, when Giovanni Michelotti decided to amuse himself by attempting to design a sporting open-top version of the 2000. Triumph did not see the vehicle until 1966, when chief engineer Harry Webster visited Michelotti and 'discovered' the concept car he had built for motor shows. Webster immediately made arrangements to have the car taken back to Britain for appraisal, where Triumph management realized that there would be a market for sales of around 12,000 a year. The Stag was scheduled for introduction in 1968, but did not reach showroom floors until 1970 thanks to commercial and production problems.

Although a rollover T-bar had been added (to satisfy US safety law requirements) and the original hidden headlights were dispensed with, the finished car still looked much like Michelotti's original concept. The four-seater convertible idea was inventive, and Triumph had a new and seemingly impressive 2997cc (183 cu in) V8 unit, developed from the forthcoming Dolomite 1854cc (113 cu in) four-cylinder engine, to put under the bonnet. An optional removable hardtop was available to turn the car into a coupé, and the Stag could be ordered with either manual or automatic transmission.

Hopes were high, and sales of 500 cars a week were anticipated.

Despite a promising start, however, serious problems soon manifested themselves with the V8 engine, which was prone to overheating and distorting the cylinder heads. The Stag started to earn a reputation for being troublesome. Another blow was struck to the Stag by the 1973 energy crisis, and its sales dropped even further. Eventually, it was withdrawn from sale in the United States – three-quarters of all US Stags had problems with their valve gear. With the car's main market gone, the Stag was doomed, and it was dropped in 1977.

Perhaps if it had been fitted with British Leyland's other V8, the Rover/Buick 3.5-litre (214 cu in) unit, the Stag might have been more successful. Today, its engine problems have been solved, and it has a devoted enthusiast following.

Engine: 2997cc (183 cu in), V8-cylinder
Power: 108kW (145bhp) at 5500rpm
0–96km/h (60mph): 10.1 secs
Top speed: 188km/h (117mph)
Production total: 25,939

The Stag was a great 'what might have been' car. It was a lovely looker and, on paper, it offered exciting performance. But British Leyland's lack of quality control killed a true classic.

TRIUMPH TR7

With its thoroughly modern, dramatic, wedge-shaped styling and pop-up headlights, the TR7 was bound to divide critics. Those weaned on traditional 'hairy-chested' Triumph sports cars loathed it, but the 'unloved' TR7 still managed to sell more than any other TR model.

Rarely has any new model from an established sports car manufacturer prompted so much controversy and debate as the TR7 did when it appeared in 1975. The sporty new Triumph was completely different to any previous TR model. Indeed, it was a complete contrast to anything the firm had built in the past. Some people loved it because of that, but many others were not at all convinced.

By the 1970s, the TR range was badly in need of an update. The TR6 may have looked modern, but it was running on a very antiquated chassis, and it was felt by many that it was being left behind by more modern products from other manufacturers. The trouble for Triumph was that, as part of British Leyland, it was affected by the financial turmoil and management problems going on in the rest of the diverse empire, and it had to wait in line for permission to start work on a new TR.

It was in this climate of restraint and desperation that, eventually, Triumph was asked to start work on two new front-engined sports cars, codenamed 'Bullet' and 'Lynx'. The former was a two-seater coupé, the latter a longer 2+2 fastback. The Lynx was dropped after six prototypes had been built, but Triumph continued with the Bullet. Mechanically, the monocoque construction coupé

was based on the Dolomite; however, getting the shape right proved to be more of a challenge.

Harris Mann, stylist for Austin-Morris, was brought in from Longbridge to work on the intended TR. Mann was going through a 'wedge' phase at the time (as were many other designers), and his idea was for a radical, dramatic-looking sports car based on this design principle. The Bullet/TR7 concept looked more like a mid-engined supercar in miniature than a front-engined budget sports car. Despite being a complete contrast to accepted TR practice, the styling was given approval by management, and they even considered building an MG version to replace the MGB.

As development continued, though, the TR7 shape became compromised, losing some of its original cutting-edge style in the process. When it was launched in 1975, its distinctive wedge shape, with pop-up headlights and sharply angled rear window, was certainly a talking point. Many chose to criticize it, perhaps too harshly.

The TR7's small cockpit could be claustrophobic, and extensive use of cheap plastic did not make the car look like a quality bit of engineering. Tartan seats were the sort of thing manufacturers could get away with only in the 1970s!

The famous Italian designer Giorgetto Giugiaro (a man not unknown for his own radical wedge-shaped creations) was alleged to have walked around the vehicle and remarked: 'My God, they've done the same on this side as well …'

Powering the TR7 was an eight-valve version of the Dolomite Sprint 1998cc (122 cu in) four-cylinder engine, which also provoked much comment at the time. Compared to the rest of the macho TR range, the TR7 was a more sophisticated, user-friendly machine, and TR traditionalists naturally hated it just for that reason alone.

However, the car was initially well received by most buyers, but

soon started to develop a reputation for poor build quality. The Liverpool factory where it was made was at the time a hotbed of industrial unrest, which led to severe manufacturing delays. The factory was closed in May 1978, and production of the TR7 was shifted to Coventry, where build standards improved.

For 1979, the TR7 received a five-speed gearbox and a good-looking convertible was launched. If this had been available from the start, critics might well have been kinder about the TR7's styling. The TR8 offshoot (a TR7 with a V8 engine for the US market) was to appear soon after.

Tarnished by its unenviable reputation, the TR7 lasted just a few years more before being dropped in 1981. By that time, it had matured into a usable, reliable sports car. And whatever its detractors may say about it, there's no denying that the TR7 was the most successful of all of Triumph's TRs, managing to sell a total of well over 100,000 units in just six short years.

Engine: 1998cc (122 cu in), 4-cylinder
Power: 78kW (105bhp) at 5500rpm
0–96km/h (60mph): 9.1 secs
Top speed: 177km/h (110mph)
Production total: 112,368

TRIUMPH TR8

Engine: 3528cc (215 cu in), V8-cylinder
Power: 102kW (137bhp) at 5000rpm
0–96km/h (60mph): 8.4 secs
Top speed: 193km/h (120mph)
Production total: 2497

A V8-engined TR7 had been planned right from the start. Some of Harris Mann's styling sketches clearly showed a V8 bonnet bulge, and space was allowed in the engine bay for the lightweight Rover/Buick 3.5-litre (215 cu in) V8 engine.

Yet it took four years from the launch of the TR7 for the TR8 to appear and, even then, it was for the US market only. Its timing coincided with another energy crisis which made big-engined cars unattractive. Triumph, it seemed, just could not win.

The TR8 released the untapped potential of the TR7. It was fast, powerful, fun and more reliable than its smaller-engined sibling. Fuel was fed through twin Stromberg carburettors or, for California, Lucas/Bosch K-Jetronic fuel injection, which gave it even more power. Most examples were convertibles, but some fixed-head coupés were also completed.

The TR8 deserved better than its short-lived production run of just two years. There are now far more TR8s in existence than were ever built by Triumph, thanks to enthusiasts converting TR7s to V8 power, a popular and relatively easy task.

Available only in the United States, the TR8 was a TR7 with a V8 heart. Had it been available everywhere from the start of TR7 production, the painful story of Triumph's final sports car may have been different.

TUCKER TORPEDO '48'

1948

If ever a car deserved to succeed, it was Preston Tucker's Torpedo '48'. With both imaginative styling and engineering, the car was first shown in 1948 and, alongside the predictable offerings from the more familiar American carmakers, the Torpedo 48 was very much a breath of fresh air.

Tucker had worked in the motor industry for years, and he was well connected enough to secure millions of dollars to set up a new car company. He employed the forward-thinking Alex Tremulis to design the car, and such innovations as a curved front windscreen, disc brakes and rubber springing for the suspension were all promised.

Despite the fact that there was neither the time nor the money to deliver all these promises, however, the Torpedo 48 was nonetheless bursting with fresh ideas. The central headlight which turned with the front wheels was something not seen before, and the doors which were cut into the roof to ease entry and exit were also a new concept.

The Torpedo's interior featured seat cushions which were interchangeable between the front and rear, so that wear could be evened out. The engine was positioned below the rear seat line to ensure that noise, heat and fumes inside the cabin were kept to a minimum, and the aerodynamic design (the drag coefficient was just 0.30cd) allowed the car to travel incredibly quietly.

Safety was also inherent in the Torpedo's design, with recessed or protected controls inside the car, huge bumpers to protect the bodywork, windscreen glass that popped out on impact and a safety chamber into which front-seat passengers could dive if a collision were imminent.

The engine was positioned at the back of the car, rather than the front, and it was not like any powerplant fitted to any other car at the time. At launch, it was going to be a 9.7-litre (592 cu in) engine developed from a helicopter unit. Although the original unit as used in helicopters was air-cooled, a sealed water-cooling system was

devised for the powerplant's new application – something that had never been done before on a production car. Furthermore, a bespoke automatic transmission was promised, to be named the Tuckermatic and, with such an advanced specification on offer, 300,000 orders were soon waiting to be fulfilled.

But making everything work was proving more of a challenge than Tucker had anticipated, and as a result he had to substitute the originally specified 9.7-litre (592 cu in) engine with a 124kW (166bhp) 5491cc (335 cu in) flat-six unit sourced from Air Cooled Motors. Not only that, but the Tuckermatic transmission was also dropped, to be replaced by an off-the-shelf version from Cord.

All these new features added to the car's bulk, and the Torpedo weighed in at an enormous 1909kg (4200lb). Despite this, it could still sprint from standstill to 96km/h (60mph) in 10 seconds and also reach 193km/h (120mph), thanks in part to the car's aerodynamic shape. It could even achieve 14.2l/100km

Probably the most impressive and far-sighted car that never was. If the Tucker had succeeded, it would have made all the cars produced by the big American manufacturers look out of date overnight.

(20mpg) at a steady 89km/h (55mph) – something the saloons produced by other American corporations could never do.

Even though the final car was ahead of its time, it still was not the car that Tucker had promised his investors or his customers, and the whole project was brought to a halt when he was indicted on fraud charges. Although he was eventually acquitted, it was too late. His investors had lost confidence and so had most of his potential customers. The dream was over, with just 37 cars made, although a further 14 were built from the parts which remained.

Engine: 5491cc (335 cu in), 6-cylinder
Power: 124kW (166bhp)
0–96km/h (60mph): 10.1 secs
Top speed: 193km/h (120mph)
Production total: 51

TURNER SPORTS

A very pretty and capable car, the Turner suffered from the same problems that faced so many other low-volume sports cars – high production costs which led to a high asking price, thus making it uncompetitive on the market.

a price. Despite being costly, the Turner Sports appealed to those who saw the cars being campaigned successfully by the Turner works racing team, which operated between 1960 and 1963.

The Mk II Sports arrived in 1960, with a better interior, an optional hardtop and Triumph Herald suspension in place of the A35 set-up previously used. Ford engines were then used and, in 1963, the final version appeared, the Mk III. Changes were slight but the company folded after founder Jack Turner died.

Although the Turner 950 Sports cost a third more than an Austin-Healey Sprite when it was launched in 1959, it was more basic and not as well built. It was therefore no surprise that fewer than 400 cars were built during its seven-year production run.

Using a glassfibre bodyshell on a tubular steel chassis, the Turner was very light. If a customer chose the 67kW (90bhp), 1220cc (74 cu in) Coventry Climax engine option, the car was very fast – and actually much faster than the Sprite – but at

Engine: 948cc (58 cu in), 4-cylinder
Power: 45kW (60bhp)
0–96km/h (60mph): 12 secs
Top speed: 152km/h (95mph)
Production total: 400 approx.

TVR GRANTURA

Engine: 1216cc (74 cu in), 4-cylinder
Power: 62kW (83bhp)
0–96km/h (60mph): 10.8 secs
Top speed: 163km/h (101mph)
Production total: 800 approx

Although Trevor Wilkinson founded TVR Engineering in 1947, it was not until 1958 that he produced his first production car, the Grantura. Using Beetle trailing arm rear suspension, the first Granturas had hard springing to reduce roll, and serious oversteer meant that the car was only suitable for enthusiasts. Buyers could specify the engine, typically a Coventry-Climax overhead-camshaft four-cylinder unit. With 62kW (83bhp) and a weight of only 660kg (1455lb), performance was good. Other popular options were the 1.5-litre (92 cu in) MGA unit, the side-valve Ford 100E engine or the new 105E 'Kent' engine as used in the Ford Anglia.

In mid-1960, the Mk II arrived, unchanged except for a single engine option, the 1.5-litre (92 cu in) MGA unit, and a few detail design changes. Although the factory could not cope with demand, the car was barely profitable. The Mk III was to arrive in 1962, with a new tubular chassis with independent suspension all round. Most cars were still fitted with the MGA engine, but from 1964 the MGB 1800cc (110 cu in) engine was used, and the car became the Mk IV. The interior was also improved and detail changes such as new tail lights distinguished the Mk IV from its predecessor.

It took TVR more than a decade to build its first series production car, having built nothing more than a run of different specials in that time. The Grantura was the result, and its handling meant that it was definitely a car for enthusiasts.

TVR VIXEN

1967–73

The TVR Vixen was very closely related to the Grantura. A larger rear window, a bonnet scoop and different rear styling with new rear light clusters were the most obvious differences, and there was also a change to a Ford-built 1599cc (98 cu in) engine. The four-speed gearbox was also sourced from Ford and, with 66kW (88bhp) available, the car was entertaining to drive thanks to its light weight. The Ford parts and a switch to steel wheels also helped to keep the purchase price down to a very competitive £998 in kit form.

To improve things even further, a longer-wheelbase chassis, originally developed for the Tuscan SE, was used for the Vixen S2, which was launched in 1968. This helped ride quality, and the addition of a brake servo meant that the performance on offer could be better exploited. The body was practically the same as the S1, but

with a distinctive bulge on the bonnet and, after 1969, the addition of two air intakes. By now, the body panels were bolted, rather than bonded, to the chassis and, in 1970, the S3 Vixen was launched, with a 69kW (92bhp) Capri engine. The last 23 Vixens were Series 4 cars, using the then-new 'M' chassis under the bodyshell.

Engine: 1599cc (98 cu in), 4-cylinder
Power: 66kW (88bhp)
0–96km/h (60mph): 11 secs
Top speed: 170km/h (106mph)
Production total: 746

Although TVR used essentially the same bodyshell for a series of high-power cars, the early cars were to feature much smaller, less powerful engines. The Vixen had just 66kW (88bhp) on offer from its four-cylinder engine, but the car's light weight meant that it was still able to crack 160km/h (100mph).

TVR GRIFFITH

1963–65

This particular car took its name from its creator, Jack Griffith. TVR's high-performance Grantura had a Ford 4.7-litre (288 cu in) V8 unit fitted in a car which originally had an engine less than half the size. Hair-raising performance was guaranteed.

Jack Griffith was an American motor trader who first fitted the V8 engine in a TVR in 1962, after seeing the works cars race at the

American Sebring race circuit. He negotiated a deal with TVR to sell the uprated Granturas with his own name on them, and these were initially known as the Griffith 200. The car was based on the Mk III Grantura, and it came with manual or automatic transmission. Suspect engine cooling and poor brakes, however, meant that development work was needed quickly. The result was the 400, which was

The Griffith was the first of the seriously powerful TVRs, although the chassis had not been developed enough to cope with the huge amount of power on offer.

based on the Mk IV Grantura and introduced in 1964.

But there was an insurmountable hurdle in the transformation from MGB-engined sportster to a V8-engined beast – weight distribution.

With the smaller engine, it was easy to drive the car hard; however, in the TVR Griffith, it was virtually impossible. Really not such a good idea when it comes to a high-performance sports car.

Engine: 4727cc (288 cu in), V8-cylinder
Power: 202kW (271bhp)
0–96km/h (60mph): 5.7 secs
Top speed: 248km/h (155mph)
Production total: 300 approx.

TVR TUSCAN

1969–71

The first Tuscans were TVR's attempt to produce the car that the Griffith should have been. Build quality improved dramatically, and the cars were essentially updated Griffith 400s. A better chassis, blistering performance and a competitive price should have made the car a success. Yet everyone remembered the Griffith, and few people wanted the new car.

TVR's solution was to produce something more usable than the V8-engined Tuscan, but which still offered strong performance – something to slot between the four-cylinder Vixen and the V8 Tuscan.

The answer was to fit Ford's 3-litre (183 cu in) Essex V6 into the Vixen's bodyshell to produce the Tuscan V6. The four-speed gearbox was also Ford-sourced, with the option of overdrive, and the rear axle was the Salisbury limited-slip unit used on the original V8-engined cars.

The Tuscan was aimed at the kit car market, and most buyers were happy with the standard four-cylinder offering. Also, when emissions regulations in the United

States became tighter in the early 1970s, the V6 became too polluting for the US market. With the much cleaner Triumph 2.5-litre (153 cu in) straight-six used instead, the Tuscan V6's fate was sealed.

Engine: 2994cc (183 cu in), V6-cylinder
Power: 95kW (128bhp)
0–96km/h (60mph): 8.3 secs
Top speed: 201km/h (125mph)
Production total: 156

With buyers frightened off by the Griffith's lack of driveability, TVR opted for a better developed chassis, along with a big reduction in power – although performance was still plenty strong enough.

TVR M-SERIES

1972–79

Although the M-series, launched in 1972, was supposedly a new car for TVR, it was really just an evolution of the Grantura and Vixen models that had been around for more than a decade. The backbone chassis was basically the same as that

found in earlier TVM cars; however, for the M-series, it was strengthened significantly.

Under the bonnet there were four- or six-cylinder engines to choose from, from the 1599cc (98 cu in) Ford four-cylinder in the

Even though the silhouette of the M-series looked very much like the earlier cars brought out by TVR, the car's bodyshell was completely new – although there was still no opening boot and only slightly more space for luggage.

1600M to the 2994cc (183 cu in) V6 in the 3000M. Alternatively, there was the 2500M, with Triumph's 2498cc (153 cu in) straight-six – an option that was to prove especially popular in the American market.

Apart from the doors, and front and rear windscreens seen on previous TVRs, the M-series featured an all-new body. Although it was inspired by the Tuscan V8 SE of the late 1960s (and it inspired the S-series of the 1980s), the bodyshell was a great improvement over what had gone before. There was still no real boot, with luggage space accessed behind the seats; however, the spare wheel was relocated to under the bonnet, which created more space for luggage.

Engine: 2498cc (153 cu in), 6-cylinder (2500M)
Power: 79kW (106bhp)
0–96km/h (60mph): 9.3 secs
Top speed: 174km/h (109mph)
Production total: 1749 (all types)

TVR TAIMAR

It took TVR nearly three decades to build a car with an opening boot, and the Taimar was it. Although the huge glass hatch looked little different from previous TVRs, it was much more practical than those seen on previous models.

was the company's first production convertible. Using a conventional boot, the Taimar drop-top was all-new from the windscreen frame back, although wind-up windows were not available despite being featured in the fixed-head car. Instead, sliding windows in detachable frames were used in the Taimar convertible.

If the standard 3-litre (183 cu in) V6 did not offer enough power, TVR offered a turbocharged version, produced in conjunction with Broadspeed. Sub-14l/100km (20mpg) fuel consumption put most potential buyers off, and, as a result, just 30 examples were built. But with 171kW (230bhp) available, performance was strong, with a top speed of 224km/h (139mph) and a 0–96km/h (60mph) time of just 5.8 seconds.

The Taimar was a hatchback 3000M, with power for the car supplied by the familiar Ford 2994cc (183 cu in) V6 mated to a four-speed all-synchromesh Ford gearbox. The car's layout and interior were carried over from the M-series, and performance was exactly the same as well. The Taimar ran concurrently with the 3000M, but the extra practicality ensured that more buyers were to choose the Taimar.

The Taimar also marked an important milestone for TVR, as it

Engine: 2994cc (183 cu in), V6-cylinder
Power: 106kW (142bhp)
0–96km/h (60mph): 7.7 secs
Top speed: 193km/h (121mph)
Production total: 395 (plus 30 turbos)

TVR 3000S

The 3000S was never marketed with this name, it is only since the car went out of production in 1979 that it has retrospectively become known as the 3000S. Sold simply as the TVR Convertible, the 3000S was a drophead version of the 3000M on which it was based. However, the bodyshell was almost all new from the windscreen back, to allow for a separate boot and folding roof.

The 3000S also had a new cabin and a redesigned tail. But the backbone chassis was not altered, which necessitated a space-robbing transmission tunnel. At least the chassis carry-over meant that there was wishbone suspension on each wheel to ensure decent handling for those who wanted to make the most of the car's 103kW (138bhp). Like

the Taimar, there was a Turbo version available with output boosted to 171kW (230bhp) for the ultimate wind-in-the-hair experience. With just 63 TVR Turbos built during the 1970s, however, it is hard to find one now.

Engine: 2994cc (183 cu in), V6-cylinder
Power: 103kW (138bhp)
0–96km/h (60mph): 7.7 secs
Top speed: 200km/h (125mph)
Production total: 258

Looking very much like the TVRs of the early 1990s, the TVR 3000S, or TVR Convertible, as it was badged when new, had excellent handling and performance, even if only a few cars were produced.

TVR Tasmin

From the 1957 Grantura through to the last 3000M produced in 1979, TVR had always followed a discernible styling theme. The 1980 Tasmin was to take a different route, however, with straight edges replacing the old curves. But the chassis was still the same as that found under the 3000M, albeit with a longer wheelbase.

First seen at the January 1980 Belgian Motor Show, the Tasmin had been developed in less than two years, using Ford 2.8-litre (170 cu in) V6 power mounted in a tubular space frame chassis. There were disc brakes all round, and the 119kW (160bhp) output was enough to give the car 201km/h (125mph) performance.

Initially, there was just a two-seater hatch available, but in 1980 a convertible was launched alongside a Plus 2 car, which had

The start of a completely new look for TVR: suddenly the curves were gone, to be replaced by angles and straight lines – although the chassis was carried over from the 3000M.

token rear seats. The following year, a Ford 2-litre (122 cu in) engine became available in the Tasmin 200 to make TVR ownership more affordable, which also coincided with the arrival of

the Series 2. But TVR also launched a bigger-engined model in 1983 when the 3.5-litre (215 cu in) V8 Tasmin made its debut – which would prompt the demise of the Tasmin name.

Engine: 2792cc (170 cu in), V6-cylinder
Power: 119kW (160bhp)
0–96km/h (60mph): 7.7 secs
Top speed: 201km/h (125mph)
Production total: 2563

TVR 350i

Originally the 3.5-litre (215 cu in) V8 from the Tasmin range, the 350i was to outlast the other Tasmin derivatives to become a model in its own right. Although the Ford V6-engined 280i also outlasted the name, it was the TVR 350i which was to continue in production all the way to 1990, along with other

outlandish versions such as the 390SE, 420SEAC and the 450SEAC.

Using the familiar 3528cc (215 cu in) Rover V8 engine, the TVR 350i was a very quick car, thanks to its lightweight glassfibre bodyshell and 142kW (190bhp) power output. Build quality was

still sometimes suspect; however, for the money, there was not really anything else that could compete with it. Rover supplied the five-speed manual gearbox (although a few automatics were produced). Most 350is were convertibles, but about five per cent of the production total were 2+2 coupés.

As soon as the 350i became established, all the other products available from TVR simply paled into insignificance. It therefore came as no surprise that the V6-engined models were sidelined so that the production lines could focus on the V8-powered supercar.

In 1985, a Series 2 version was introduced. This version had softer contours around the front and modified suspension to improve the car's handling.

Engine: 3528cc (215 cu in), V8-cylinder
Power: 142kW (190bhp)
0–96km/h (60mph): 6.6 secs
Top speed: 218km/h (136mph)
Production total: 955

To compensate for the relatively weak performance of the first Tasmins to be produced, the classic Rover 3.5-litre (215 cu in) V8 engine was slotted into the engine bay of the 350i and the Tasmin name was dropped.

TVR 450SEAC

The 450SEAC was the third in a hat-trick of wild 350i-derived roadsters from TVR, following on from the 400SE and 420SEAC. The name was short for Special Equipment Aramid Composite, which was a technical way of saying that the car's construction was of Kevlar, instead of glassfibre, to allow for a stronger bodyshell while still keeping the weight down and improving the car's power-to-weight ratio.

Using a heavily uprated 4.5-litre (271 cu in) version of Rover's V8, traditional tuning modifications such as a strengthened block, bigger valves, gas-flowed cylinder heads, stronger valve springs and a better camshaft were used to distance the 450SEAC from its lesser stablemates. That meant there was 241kW (324bhp) on offer – enough to guarantee incredible performance such as a top speed of 265km/h (165mph) and a 0–96km/h (60mph) time of less than five seconds. But using the performance was not always easy, and the car could be difficult to handle, especially in the wet.

Pitting the 450SEAC against more established rivals, TVR found it difficult to sell what was an expensive car, although, for the money, no other car could offer performance like this one.

The ultimate incarnation of the Tasmin theme, the 450SEAC combined lightweight materials with huge power to give blistering performance. Build quality and reliability were still patchy.

Engine: 4441cc (271 cu in), V8-cylinder
Power: 241kW (324bhp)
0–96km/h (60mph): 4.7 secs
Top speed: 265km/h (165mph)
Production total: 18

TVR S

When the Tasmin arrived and the older, more curved TVRs went out of production, the cars became too expensive for many potential buyers. The answer was to build a model which captured the essence of the M-series, but which was available only as a convertible.

Badged simply as the S, the car used Ford's 2.8-litre (170 cu in) V6 engine and five-speed gearbox. The basis was a backbone chassis with semi-trailing arm independent rear suspension, and disc brakes on the front wheels helped to provide braking performance.

In 1988, the car became the S2 when a 2.9-litre (177 cu in) engine replaced the earlier unit; however, the very basic hood fitted to the first cars was retained. Catalytic converters were available from 1989 (on the S2C cars) and, in 1990, for the S3 and S3C versions, the car's doors were lengthened and driving lights were fitted under the front bumper.

By 1993, the car was known as the S4C and had catalytic converters fitted as standard but it was overshadowed by the V8S launched in 1991. Using a 179kW (240bhp) 3.9-litre (238 cu in) Rover V8, the car was incredibly fast.

Engine: 2792cc (170 cu in), V6-cylinder (S1)
Power: 119kW (160bhp)
0–96km/h (60mph): 7.6 secs
Top speed: 205km/h (128mph)
Production total: 2600

After the straight lines of the 1980s, the S marked a return to the classic TVR look. Initially engines were V6s, but eventually a V8 was fitted instead.

Unipower GT

1966–70

Inspired by Carlo Abarth's tiny GTs, Ford engineer Ernie Unger sketched designs for a Mini 850-powered sports car of his own during the mid-1960s. A mid-engined prototype was built and tested; however, when more investment was needed, forklift manufacturer Universal Power Drives stepped in, in an attempt to boost its image by being associated with a GT car.

Development continued with the Mini engine retaining its transverse location, but positioned behind the driver and turned through 180 degrees. The car made its debut at the 1966 Racing Car Show and orders flooded in, although the first cars were not delivered until 1968. By this time, a 41kW (55bhp) 998cc (61 cu in) Cooper engine was used with a four-speed gearbox, although, for an extra

£200, buyers could have a 1275cc (78 cu in) engine and even a five-speed gearbox.

In 1968, Universal Power Drives lost interest and the project passed to Unger's new company, UWF. A revised model was unveiled, and a motorsport campaign began. Development proved too costly, however, and the company closed after only 15 of the cars had been produced. Although its life was

brief, the car's influence on the specialist motor industry was far-reaching and it had many unusual features for a car of its era, including a right-hand gear change and front disc brakes.

Engine: 998cc (61 cu in), 4-cylinder
Power: 41kW (55bhp)
0–96km/h (60mph): 12.6 secs
Top speed: 153km/h (96mph)
Production total: 75

Vanden Plas Princess 4-litre Limousine

1952–68

Around 1250 examples of the Austin A135 had already been built when the model evolved into the Vanden Plas Princess 4-litre in 1959. The A135 had been introduced in 1952; however, as the 4-litre (244 cu in) was the largest car in the British Motor Corporation (BMC) stable, it made sense to visibly distance it from its more

affordable siblings by putting a more prestigious badge on its bonnet.

With a choice of saloon or landaulette body styles, the 4-litre was not affordable to many, but it was still less expensive than many of its competitors. With seating for six in three rows of two (including a pair of forward-facing occasional seats in the middle), the car was

not really aimed at the owner/driver – it was for the man who expected to be chauffeured from one place to another.

Although the 4-litre was a big car, it could still manage nearly 161km/h (100mph) from its 91kW (122bhp) 3993cc (244 cu in) six-cylinder engine. And the chauffeur's life was made much

easier by the provision of a four-speed automatic transmission, servo-assisted brakes (drums all round) and power-assisted steering.

Engine: 3993cc (244 cu in), 6-cylinder
Power: 91kW (122bhp)
0–80km/h (50mph): 11.5 secs
Top speed: 158km/h (98mph)
Production total: 3350 approx.

Using traditional coachbuilding methods of construction, such as a separate chassis, the Vanden Plas Princess 4-litre limousine featured a split windscreen.

Vanden Plas Princess IV

1956–59

Descended from the Austin Sheerline and Princess saloons of the 1950s, the Princess IV was a limited-production grand tourer. The chassis was produced by Austin, and the bodyshell was built by Vanden Plas, which by now was part of BMC.

With a length of 510cm (16.6ft) and a weight of more than 2200kg

(4850lb), the Princess IV had to use its 112kW (150bhp) engine to its full extent, although, with typical fuel consumption of little more than 28l/100km (10mpg), few people could afford to run one.

Automatic transmission and power-assisted steering were standard and, when *Autocar* reviewed a Princess IV in 1958,

the testers were very impressed with the level of refinement. Not only was the car extremely quiet, even at high speed, but the lack of vibration and smoothness of the transmission were something to be savoured as well. With a price of £3376, however, there were few people who could actually afford to buy a Princess IV, never mind run

one with its high fuel consumption. Unsurprisingly, there were not many examples built and, of those, few survive today.

Engine: 3993cc (244 cu in), 6-cylinder
Power: 112kW (150bhp)
0–96km/h (60mph): 16.1 secs
Top speed: 161km/h (100mph)
Production total: n/a

VANDEN PLAS PRINCESS 3-LITRE

1959–64

The Princess 3-litre was simply a badge-engineered version of the Austin A99. Selling alongside the Austin and Wolseley versions, the Vanden Plas was the most exclusive A99, with a special grille, extra soundproofing and more upmarket interior. Although the car's roots were patently clear, it sold well thanks to its high-quality build and, when the Mk II version was launched in the autumn of 1961, the Princess 3-litre was improved still further.

Now a genuine 161km/h (100mph) car, the Mk II featured a more highly tuned 2.9-litre (178 cu in) straight-six engine, a longer wheelbase and changes to the suspension to make it more comfortable. For those who chose to drive rather than be driven, power-assisted steering became optional in 1962. In 1964, the car was discontinued in favour of the Vanden Plas 4-litre.

Engine: 2912cc (178 cu in), 6-cylinder
Power: 77kW (103bhp)
0–96km/h (60mph): 17.9 secs
Top speed: 156km/h (97mph)
Production total: 12,703

VANDEN PLAS 4-LITRE R

1964–68

The most luxurious version of the Westminster ever built, the Vanden Plas 4-litre R was beautifully built, refined and sumptuously trimmed.

When Rolls-Royce and BMC decided to collaborate on a relatively affordable luxury saloon, the Vanden Plas 4-litre R was the result. Based on the 3-litre (183 cu in) A110 Westminster, the Vanden Plas used a 4-litre (239 cu in) Rolls-Royce six-cylinder engine mated to a Borg-Warner automatic gearbox. With seven main bearings, the 130kW (175bhp) all-alloy engine offered both refinement and torque; however, it also consumed a lot of fuel and the car's running costs were high.

The body shape was close to the Westminster's, but with reduced fin size and new tail-lights. More steeply raked front and rear windscreens increased headroom inside. The interior was also suitably upgraded with Connolly leather seats and walnut veneer on the dash and door cappings.

From the outset, the aim was to produce 100 cars a week, but the 'affordable' luxury car was simply not affordable enough. By 1968, production was halted after just 6555 cars had been built – in fact, production had never risen above 60 cars a day throughout the car's production run. A Bentley-badged version was also planned; however, Rolls-Royce saw trouble ahead and pulled out.

Engine: 3909cc (239 cu in), 6-cylinder
Power: 130kW (175bhp)
0–96km/h (60mph): 12.7 secs
Top speed: 179km/h (112mph)
Production total: 6555

VANDEN PLAS PRINCESS 1100 & 1300

1963–74

Fred Connolly, maker of the famous Connolly leather, requested that an 1100 be given the full luxury treatment for his personal use; however, when the BMC management saw, and liked, the result, the Connolly car became a standard production model.

The production car arrived in 1963, available with four doors only, and it was an instant success. It appealed very much to drivers who wanted a small car, but a luxurious one. Mechanically, the Vanden Plas Princess 1100 was identical to all the other 1100s put on sale by the BMC empire. In 1967, a 1275cc (78 cu in) engine became available, as did an automatic gearbox and a Mk II version of the 1100, complete with chopped-down fins. The following year the 1100 was dropped, but the Mk II 1300 – with a more powerful twin-carburettor engine – continued to be made until 1974.

Engine: 1098cc (67 cu in), 4-cylinder
Power: 41kW (55bhp)
0–96km/h (60mph): 21.1 secs
Top speed: 136km/h (85mph)
Production total: 43,741

VANDEN PLAS 1500

1974–80

The Austin Allegro was one of the most reviled cars ever made in the United Kingdom, so, when a version was sold with a Vanden Plas badge on the front and a grille that was completely out of all proportion to the rest of the car, it was clear that not only were

Vanden Plas's days numbered, but also the name did not really mean anything any more.

All examples of the Vanden Plas 1500 were four-door saloons, initially with the 1485cc (91 cu in) engine that had already been seen in the Allegro 1500, but later with

a 1748cc (107 cu in) powerplant, in line with the introduction of the Allegro 1750.

As with the standard Allegro, Hydragas suspension was used; however, the Vanden Plas 1500 also gained a five-speed gearbox and an incredibly lavish level of

interior trim, including veneered picnic tables in the back.

Engine: 1485cc (91 cu in), 4-cylinder
Power: 51kW (69bhp)
0–96km/h (60mph): 16.7 secs
Top speed: 144km/h (90mph)
Production total: 11,842

VAUXHALL PRINCE HENRY

1910–15

Until 1908, Vauxhall had no sporting heritage at all, but in that year the engine from the company's 3-litre (186 cu in) 15kW (20hp) model was developed to produce 45kW (60bhp). This engine was then installed in the three team cars entered for the 1910 Prince Henry of Prussia tour, which gave the new model its name.

The C-type, as it was officially originally called, was first shown at the 1910 London Motor Show and, in 1911, the car was officially listed as a Vauxhall model, with four seats, but no doors, the

emphasis being on speed and handling. Indeed, it soon gained a reputation for being one of the best sporting cars of its day thanks to a top speed of 120km/h (75mph) and excellent engine flexibility.

Within two years of the car going into production, it received a larger, 3964cc (242 cu in) engine, which developed 64kW (86bhp) and was rated at 19kW (25hp). This change meant even better performance and, to cater for 'ladies', small doors were fitted to offer some protection from the elements – a further 133 of these later cars were built.

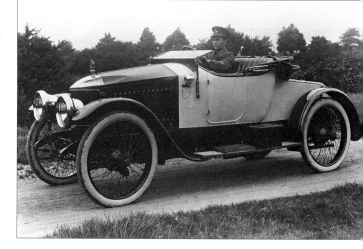

The great success of the Prince Henry in the Russian Reliability Trial from St Petersburg to Sevastopol led to the car going into production. Few, however, could afford such a sporting car.

Engine: 3054cc (186 cu in), 4-cylinder
Power: 45kW (60bhp)
0–96km/h (60mph): n/a
Top speed: 120km/h (75mph)
Production total: 58

Until the Prince Henry arrived, Vauxhall was known for its rather pedestrian cars. The introduction of this model was extremely important because it changed Vauxhall's image for the better, and it also marked a change of direction for the company towards more sporting vehicles.

VAUXHALL 30/98

Even with four passengers, the 30/98 had plenty of power to compete successfully in motorsport. Although the car was dated during the postwar years, when first introduced it was very modern and able to compete with the best available elsewhere.

Vauxhall's 30/98 is regarded as one of the benchmarks for early sporting cars – a car which initially could compete on equal terms with the best that Bentley, Alvis, Talbot and Sunbeam could offer. Throughout much of its life, it was overshadowed by Bentley's 3-litre (183 cu in) model, although the 30/98 was significantly faster. Until 1926, the car had rear-wheel brakes only – this was the norm when the car was launched.

The 30/98 was essentially a development of the Trials Car that Vauxhall had built to compete in reliability trials in 1908. Although durability was more important than outright speed, the trials car was still able to attain 137km/h (85mph) and, in streamlined form, reached 174km/h (108mph) at Brooklands. For those who wanted speed above all else, a stripped-out version of the trials car was offered

Even more expensive than the pricey Prince Henry, the 30/98 was out of reach for all but the most wealthy. With such low production numbers, Vauxhall's new parent, GM, discontinued the model.

which was guaranteed to reach 161km/h (100mph) – exceptional performance at the time. But it was not until 1912 that the first cars were competing in motorsport, regularly enjoying success and, by the summer of 1913, the first road versions were being built for their wealthy owners. But with a chassis listed at £900 when a Prince Henry could be bought complete for £580, the car was too expensive for all but the very wealthy. In the event,

just a dozen chassis were produced before World War I.

In 1919, the 30/98 became a properly catalogued model, although it was still prohibitively expensive for most buyers. At £1675 with Velox coachwork, this was a car that few could afford. Over the next three years, however, 274 cars found owners who were won over by the car's reputation as the finest sporting machine of the early 1920s. The postwar car was

significantly developed over its prewar counterpart, with both lighting and starting being operated electrically, as well as a much stronger cylinder block being incorporated into the design.

Fast, heavy and with excellent roadholding, the 30/98 suffered as a result of its high price so, in 1921, the cost of buying one was reduced to £1300. Even though this was a substantial reduction, it was still expensive, and the 3-litre (183 cu in) Bentleys were now competing against it – cars which had also been proving themselves in motorsport.

For 1922, a redesigned 30/98 appeared, with a shorter stroke engine that allowed it to be revved more freely and an overhead valve layout. With 86kW (115bhp) available, along with a stiffened chassis, the car had even better performance, helped by the addition of cable-operated brakes on the front wheels in 1923.

Vauxhall was taken over by General Motors in 1925, and the American company's policy was to turn Vauxhall into a mass-market car manufacturer. Nevertheless, in 1926, an updated 30/98 appeared, with hydraulic brakes all round and an 89kW (120bhp) engine – enough to take it to 152km/h (95mph) and give it a 128km/h (80mph) cruising speed. But prices were still high at £950 for the chassis alone. Not only that, but the car was now well over a decade old as well, and both Sunbeam and Bentley were offering much more modern cars for the same price.

By the time the car went out of production in 1927, just 598 30/98s of various types had been produced, an unacceptable figure for the new General Motors management.

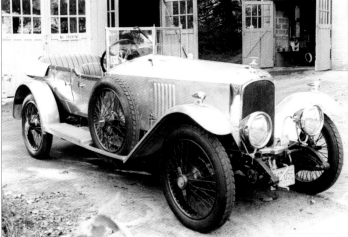

Engine: 4525cc (276 cu in), 4-cylinder
Power: 67kW (90bhp)
0–96km/h (60mph): n/a
Top speed: 136km/h (85mph)
Production total: 598

VAUXHALL 20/60

In 1925, Vauxhall was bought by General Motors, after the US giant had failed in its initial bid to acquire Austin. The first car to be developed and launched under General Motor's stewardship was the Vauxhall 20/60 in 1928.

Because of Vauxhall's new owners, some people were suspicious of the 20/60, claiming that it was simply too American.

Certainly innovations such as the 12-volt electrics, central gearshift and single-plate clutch did not seem very British. The 20/60's styling also appeared to have been influenced by contemporary Buicks. Vauxhall was quick to defend the car, however, claiming that the project had been instigated before the company's acquisition by General Motors.

But whoever had developed the car, there was no denying that it was a very good one. The Vauxhall 20/60's cable and rod brakes were more effective than those to be found on the car's predecessors, and the traditional Vauxhall worm-and-wheel steering was dropped in favour of more modern Marles gears – a definite improvement. One of the biggest innovations,

however, was the adoption of wooden artillery wheels in place of the previously fitted wire items, which allowed for far greater reliability and smoothness.

Engine: 2762cc (169 cu in), 6-cylinder
Power: n/a
0–96km/h (60mph): n/a
Top speed: 108km/h (67mph)
Production total: 4228

VAUXHALL 10

When Vauxhall launched a new version of its family car in 1946, it was not much different from the car which had first been seen in 1938. But in the postwar seller's market, that simply did not matter, as almost every car was guaranteed to be sold on the export market – and the model was nearly as advanced in 1946 as it had been in 1938, as car design had been mostly halted by the war.

The Vauxhall 7.5kW (10hp) was innovative because it used semi-monocoque construction, a unique feature at the time. This, along with a longer wheelbase than its predecessor, meant that there was much more interior space, and four windows on each side ensured the

cabin had a more spacious feel than those of its competitors.

Because only low-quality petrol was available in the immediate postwar years, the 1203cc (73 cu in) engine was detuned slightly to allow it to run on the low-octane fuel that was available, making the car affordable to run.

Engine: 1203cc (73 cu in), 4-cylinder
Power: 23kW (31bhp)
0–96km/h (60mph): n/a
Top speed: 97km/h (60mph)

Although it did not differ that much from the car first seen in 1938, Vauxhall's first postwar car was still innovative with its semi-monocoque construction.

VAUXHALL VELOX E-TYPE

When the Wyvern appeared in 1951, Vauxhall's new parentage became obvious. The car's basis was a 1949 Chevrolet, and the large grille and lots of chrome were pure Americana, just like the full-width styling and fluted bonnet.

The years of postwar austerity were coming to a close, and car buyers were expecting more from their vehicles. As a result, much more attention was being paid to comfort and a better driving experience. In the case of the Velox E-type, extra cabin space was a

key selling point, and the car was big enough to carry six passengers in comfort – an improvement over its predecessor, the Velox LIP, which had been sold between 1948 and 1951. With a choice of four- or six-cylinder engines, the Velox E-type was also much more comfortable than the car that it replaced, thanks to independent coil-sprung suspension at the front.

The car was further developed throughout its life, with upgrades to the exterior and interior trim, as well as an increase in the window size to make the cabin airier. Tax-busting short-stroke engines were also introduced.

Many British mass-produced cars of the 1950s, such as those from BMC, Ford and Vauxhall, were taking their styling influences from across the Atlantic. The E-type Velox was no exception to this, with Vauxhall's GM parentage obvious in its lines.

Engine: 2275cc (139 cu in) 6-cylinder
Power: 41kW (55bhp)
0–96km/h (60mph): 20.9sec
Top speed: 129km/h (80mph)
Production total: 545,388 (incl. Wyvern)

VAUXHALL CRESTA PA

1952–67

Vauxhall's parent company was US-owned – something that was apparent in the design of some of its postwar cars. Large fins, wraparound windscreens and heavy, chrome-laden bumpers front and rear were all styling cues inspired by the American cars of the time.

Also taken from its US cousins was the concept of a large, unstressed engine, although in the Cresta it had six cylinders in place of the favoured American V8. It initially displaced 2262cc (138 cu in) and, although there was just 56kW (75bhp) on offer, there was plenty of torque, so there was no need to use the three-speed column-mounted gearshift too much. The ride was supreme, helped by the bodyshell's huge bulk, and the boot was also very large – but, despite an oversized cabin, there was not actually much passenger space.

Extremely rot-prone, which has not helped the car's survival rate, the Cresta PA looks madly outlandish with its fins, imposing bulk and bright colour schemes.

The aspect that drew the most attention, however, was the colour schemes – bright pinks and greens were out of step with the norm.

In 1960, a 2651cc (162 cu in) engine replaced its smaller.

predecessor, and, with an extra 15kW (20bhp) available, the Vauxhall Cresta PA became even more enjoyable to use, especially if the optional Hydramatic automatic gearbox was specified.

Engine: 2262cc (138 cu in)
Power: 61kW (82bhp)
0–96km/h (60mph): 16.8 secs
Top speed: 145km/h (90mph)
Production total: n/a

VAUXHALL VICTOR FB

1961–64

The Victor FB was the second version of the earlier FA (or F-series) model, which had been launched in 1957. That original car's styling dated very quickly, so, when the FB was introduced, the dogleg A-pillar and flutes in the doors and wings were dropped.

Ensuring that the car appealed to as wide an audience as possible, Vauxhall offered four-door saloons or five-door estates and a choice of either 41kW (55bhp) 1.5-litre (92 cu in) or 44kW (59bhp) 1.6-litre (97 cu in) engines. The car was a resounding success, especially with its crisp, modern styling that looked far better than the earlier car.

The car's comfort levels were also improved, thanks to an increase in interior space and large bench seats (which could be swapped for bucket seats instead). The more generous exterior

proportions helped greatly and, overall, the Victor FB was much more refined. The standard three-speed gearbox was poor, however, so most customers specified the optional all-synchromesh four-speed unit instead.

Engine: 1508cc (92 cu in), 4-cylinder
Power: 41kW (55bhp)
0–96km/h (60mph): 22.6 secs
Top speed: 122km/h (76mph)
Production total: 328,640

With 100,000 vehicles being churned out each year, the Victor FB was a very successful car for its manufacturer, Vauxhall. Its popularity was helped along by a wide range offering plenty of choice to potential car buyers.

VAUXHALL CRESTA PB

Looking very much like its smaller brother, the Victor FB, the Vauxhall Cresta PB was essentially a six-cylinder version of the smaller car. As well as having the same basic structure, the doors were carried over from the other car, which meant that the basic look of the two was much the same.

Launched as a four-door saloon in 1962, a five-door estate, built by Martin Walter, arrived a year later.

Using a saloon as its basis, but with the roof chopped off and replaced by a bespoke glassfibre shell, the estate was a luxurious carry-all built at a time when estates were not seen as anything other than workhorses.

The only engine initially on offer was a 2651cc (162 cu in) straight-six, but there were no fewer than three different transmission options. The basic car came with a

Much less ostentatious than the PA that it replaced, the Cresta PB's sober styling was ultra-modern when it was introduced in the early 1960s. But it was still a luxury car with its six-cylinder power.

three-speed manual gearbox, with overdrive as an option. The alternative was a Hydramatic self-shifting transmission, although, from 1965, this became the two-

speed Powerglide. At the same time that the transmission choice changed, so, too, did the engine, becoming a 3294cc (201 cu in) straight-six – with a consequent increase in performance.

Engine: 2651cc (162 cu in), 6-cylinder
Power: 71kW (95bhp)
0–96km/h (60mph): 19.5 secs
Top speed: 149km/h (93mph)
Production total: 87,047

VAUXHALL VICTOR FC

Although the Vauxhall Victor FC (also known as the Victor 101) looked significantly different from its FB predecessor, underneath the skin, little had changed. The engine was the familiar 1594cc (97 cu in) unit seen before, and there were still wishbones and coil springs at the front, along with a live axle and semi-elliptic springs at the rear.

To distance it from the FB, the Victor FC had much sleeker styling, with thinner pillars, more curvy panels and a slightly concave rear window – a trend which did not catch on. The choice of transmission was either a three- or four-speed manual, along with a two-speed Powerglide automatic gearbox, available from 1966.

Thanks to the car's bold new styling, the Vauxhall Victor FC offered one of the largest boots in its class, more interior space and a class-beating ride. There was a choice of six cars across the saloon and estate bodyshells, including the range-topping VX4/90.

This last version had a four-speed all-synchromesh gearbox as standard, with no automatic option. It also produced 63kW (85bhp), compared to the standard car's 57kW (76bhp).

Engine: 1594cc (97 cu in), 4-cylinder
Power: 45kW (60bhp)
0–96km/h (60mph): 17.1 secs
Top speed: 137km/h (85mph)
Production total: 219,814

To make it more spacious than its FB predecessor, the Vauxhall Victor FC was both longer and wider. It was also thirstier than its rivals, however, which meant that many potential buyers bought elsewhere, rather than put up with the higher running costs.

VAUXHALL VISCOUNT PC

1966–72

Although it was supremely comfortable, the Viscount PC cost £400 more than the standard Cresta on which it was based. That and the high running costs because of the extra fuel consumption due to its increased weight meant that sales would always be limited.

The most luxurious Vauxhall in its day, the Viscount PC was the most expensive car available in the Cresta range. It was powered by a 3294cc (201 cu in) straight-six engine and had high equipment levels fitted as standard. This included lots of sound insulation, bigger wheels, power steering, electric windows, a vinyl roof and wooden cappings.

An automatic gearbox was also included in the price – although a four-speed manual gearbox was available on the Viscount PC for £85 less. Few cars were specified with the manual gearbox, however, especially after 1970, when the GM-built three-speed automatic was fitted in place of the previous two-speed unit.

The engine had just four main bearings, and this was evident when it was driven hard because the unit did not have the refinement of some of its better-engineered competitors. But performance was strong (if slightly blunted by the weight of all the standard equipment) and the ride was supremely comfortable.

Engine: 3294cc (201 cu in), 6-cylinder
Power: 89kW (120bhp)
0–96km/h (60mph): 15.5 secs
Top speed: 157km/h (98mph)
Production total: 7025

VAUXHALL VICTOR FD

1967–72

Not only was the Victor FD incredibly stylish with its Coke bottle design, but it was also technically advanced with its hemi-head overhead-camshaft engine, supposedly safe to 9000rpm.

For the first time, Vauxhall moved over to a four-headlight layout and, thanks to careful design of the rear axle, handling and road-holding were better than most of its competitors. But the seating was criticized for being uncomfortable, the gearchange was poor and, until the three-speed automatic was introduced in 1970, the early self-shifting transmissions were poor.

From May 1968, there was the option of an estate, which sold alongside the four-door saloon seen at the car's launch. From 1970, the four-cylinder cars were renamed Victor Supers.

The Vauxhall Victor FD was launched at the 1967 London Motor Show, in Vauxhall's 60th year of car production. At first there was a choice between a 1599cc (98 cu in) or a 1975cc (121 cu in) four-cylinder engine; however, from 1968, there was also the option of the familiar 3294cc (201 cu in) six-cylinder engine in a version badged as the Ventora (Ventora II from 1970). The four-cylinder engines were the new 'slant four' overhead-camshaft powerplants as used in the Viva, and there was coil-sprung suspension all round, along with rack-and-pinion steering.

Engine: 1975cc (121 cu in), 4-cylinder
Power: 77kW (104bhp)
0–96km/h (60mph): 14 secs
Top speed: 153km/h (95mph)
Production total: 198,085

VAUXHALL VENTORA FE

1972–76

The fifth incarnation of the Victor was also the biggest, with an increase in both length and wheelbase over its predecessor to make it more comfortable inside. In fact, the Victor FE was so spacious, that none of Vauxhall's competitors could compete.

Based on the same floorpan as the Opel Rekord, this was an early example of platform-sharing to save development time and cost. As well as a four-door saloon, a five-door estate was also offered.

The Victor range was introduced in March 1972, and initially the

Nothing more than a Victor FE with a big engine, the Ventora was so named to distance itself from the common or garden variety car on which it was based. It had comfort on its side, but running costs were high.

range topper was the Victor 3300. From 1973, however, this became the Ventora, in an effort to distance this Chevrolet-powered derivative from its lesser siblings. With power steering, dual-circuit brakes, vinyl roof and wood trim as standard, the Ventora was luxurious; however, it was expensive to run, thanks to its thirsty 3.3-litre (201 cu in) engine.

For those who found even the high standards of the Ventora not luxurious enough, a VIP special edition was launched in 1973, available with black paintwork only. By 1976, the Ventora had been dropped, and it was replaced by the Victor 2300 SL.

Engine: 3294cc (201 cu in), 6-cylinder
Power: 92kW (124bhp)
0–96km/h (60mph): 12.6 secs
Top speed: 166km/h (104mph)
Production total: 7984

VAUXHALL VIVA

1963–79

In the early 1970s, the HA Viva was Vauxhall's first car to achieve a six-figure production run, thanks to over 100 different derivatives being offered across three generations.

The car was introduced in 1963 with a 33kW (44bhp) 1057cc (65 cu in) engine and, in 1965, the sporty Viva SL was launched with 49kW (66bhp). The following year the Viva HB arrived with a bigger, all-new body, improved suspension,

The Viva HA was perhaps one of the most unspecial cars of its time, if not ever. It did not take anyone long to notice this, so it was replaced as quickly as possible by the HB, which was a big leap forward.

uprated brakes and a 42kW (56bhp) 1159cc (71 cu in) engine – a bored-out version of the 1057cc (65 cu in) powerplant. In 1970, the Viva HC was unveiled with a

choice of two- or four-door saloons, a coupé or three-door estate, and it had engines ranging from 1159cc (71 cu in) to 1599cc (98 cu in). The HC was mechanically much like the HB, but did feature a restyled bodyshell.

In 1971, the Firenza made its debut with 1159cc (71 cu in), 1599cc (98 cu in) or 1975cc (121 cu in) engines. A luxury Viva, the Magnum, appeared in 1973, with

1759cc (107 cu in) or 2279cc (139 cu in) engines available, wrapped in saloon, coupé or estate shells. All had four headlights instead of two, to distinguish them from lesser Viva models.

Engine: 1057cc (65 cu in), 4-cylinder
Power: 33kW (44bhp)
0–96km/h (60mph): 22.1 secs
Top speed: 123km/h (77mph)
Production total: 321,332

VAUXHALL FIRENZA DROOP SNOOT

1973–75

The Vauxhall Firenza Droop Snoot was an example of how to take a very ordinary car and transform it into something special. Modified bodywork, stronger mechanicals and a breathed-on engine turned the Viva coupé into the Droop Snoot – or the Firenza HP as it was officially known.

In the early 1970s, Vauxhall decided that it wanted to capture the youth market, and the result was a Firenza coupé with a tweaked Magnum 2.3-litre (139 cu in) engine, beefed-up transmission and a wind-cheating glassfibre nosecone which cut drag by 30 per cent and increased the car's top speed to 193km/h (120mph).

The plan was to produce at least 1000 examples each year, with the potential for up to 50,000 to be made in total. But two years after its introduction the Firenza HP (for 'High Performance'), otherwise known unofficially as the Droop Snoot, was dropped. Just 204 had been produced – all painted silver.

This left Vauxhall with lots of nosecones, which the company needed to put to some use. The answer was to produce the Sportshatch – an estate version of the Firenza Droop Snoot. This car had the stock 82kW (110bhp) motor which was normally found under the Magnum's bonnet, albeit with a few minor head and carburation tweaks to produce an extra 6kW (8bhp).

And while the Sportshatch was never officially listed as a production model, 197 were made – just seven fewer than the officially listed Droop Snoot.

Engine: 2279cc (139 cu in), 4-cylinder
Power: 98kW (131bhp)
0–96km/h (60mph): 9.4 secs
Top speed: 193km/h (120mph)
Production total: 204

VAUXHALL CHEVETTE

1975–84

Engine: 1256cc (77 cu in), 4-cylinder
Power: 44kW (59bhp)
0–96km/h (60mph): 16.7 secs
Top speed: 141km/h (88mph)
Production total: 415,608

As General Motors spread its corporate tentacles during the 1970s, its aim was to produce a global car – a vehicle which could be sold in dozens of different countries with as few modifications as possible. Whether an Opel in Germany, an Isuzu in Japan or a Vauxhall in Britain, underneath the skin the basic cars were the same, but on the outside there were significant differences.

Taking its engine and transmission from the 1300 Viva, the Chevette was available as just a three-door hatch when it went on sale in 1975. The following year an estate joined the range, along with a four-door saloon and, between them, the three models helped Vauxhall back to profitability – the promise of 80km/h (50mph) and 5.5l/100km (50mpg) was too much

for many buyers to resist.

But the big news came in 1976 with the launch of the Chevette 2300HS. Conceived to take on Ford in motorsport, the 2300HS was reasonably successful as a racing car, although the 450 road cars produced were not especially appealing to most ordinary drivers, able though they were.

The Chevette was good at helping with the family chores, rather than being thrashed along twisty back roads. To inject some spice into the range, a driver's version was added.

VAUXHALL CAVALIER

In two-door coupé form, the Mk I Cavalier was quite stylish, although the more usual configuration was as a four-door saloon. Little was offered in the way of innovation, but it was a good driver's car.

Seen throughout Europe as the Opel Ascona, the Vauxhall Cavalier was introduced into Britain without General Motors actually telling anyone about it. That is because the cars had already been sold in the United Kingdom wearing Opel badges and through Opel dealers, so to then publicize the same car with different badges would have been strange.

With a diverse range being offered, however, Vauxhall need not have worried. The car was an instant hit, with a choice of 1.3- (79 cu in), 1.6- (97 cu in) or 1.9- litre (116 cu in) engines and four different body styles – two-door saloon or coupé, a three-door 'sportshatch' or a four-door saloon. Produced to slot in between the Viva and the Victor, the Cavalier was a thoroughly modern-looking car, even if it retained a rear-wheel drive layout. In coupé or 'sports-hatch' form, the Cavalier was little more than an Opel Manta with different badges, which meant impeccable German engineering and superb rust-proofing. Few cars of the time could claim 11-stage anti-rust treatment, zinc plating of some panels and wax injection into the sills. Not only that, but the car was great to drive as well.

Engine: 1584cc (97 cu in), 4-cylinder
Power: 51kW (69bhp)
0–96km/h (60mph): 14.8 secs
Top speed: 157km/h (98mph)
Production total: 238,980

VAUXHALL LOTUS CARLTON

Although ultra-fast saloons are common now, when the Vauxhall Lotus Carlton was launched in 1990, its only rival was BMW's M5. With 281kW (377bhp) available and rear-wheel drive with no electronic road holding aids, the Carlton could be quite a handful if it were driven hard, but nothing could challenge its 285km/h (177mph) top speed.

It was this huge potential speed that caused outrage at the time, with the press questioning the point

Hardly the last word in understatement, the Lotus Carlton was definitely not a case of all show and no go. Crushing performance was virtually unbeatable by all but the most capable of cars from the established supercar makers.

of a car which could attain such high speeds while carrying five adults in comfort – Ferrari never received such criticism.

The reason that the Lotus Carlton could reach such high speeds was that it had a twin-turbocharged Chevrolet Corvette ZR-1 V8 unit under its bonnet, matched to a six-speed gearbox through which 419lb ft (561Nm) of torque was transmitted.

Lotus, now part of the General Motors empire, set up the brakes, steering and suspension. The standard Carlton's McPherson strut front suspension and multi-link rear unit were developed by lowering and stiffening them, ensuring that handling and road-holding were the best available for the money. However, at £48,000, the car was still a lot of money.

Engine: 3615cc (221 cu in), 6-cylinder
Power: 281kW (377bhp)
0–96km/h (60mph): 5.1 secs
Top speed: 283km/h (177mph)
Production total: 440

VERITAS COMET

The Veritas Comet was one of a family of three cars which had made their debuts at the 1949 Paris Salon, the other two being the Saturn and the Scorpion.

Although all three used the same mechanicals, the different names were allocated to the different body styles available, the Saturn being a two-door coupé, while the

Scorpion was a cabriolet version of the same car. The Comet was the least glamorous of the trio, being the all-purpose model.

All three were powered by a seven-bearing 1988cc (121 cu in) straight-six unit, although, as this level of sophistication made the car very expensive, it was possible to specify a short-stroke 1.5-litre

(92 cu in) engine taken from the BMW stable.

It was also possible to have a BMW 328 engine fitted, which meant that power outputs ranged between 73kW (98bhp) and 110kW (147bhp), all of which were fed through a five-speed manual gearbox – something which was especially unusual at the time.

The Comet, the Saturn and the Scorpion were all based on a BMW chassis, but a de Dion rear axle was fitted along with uprated brakes.

Engine: 1988cc (121 cu in), 6-cylinder
Power: 75kW (100bhp)
0–96km/h (60mph): n/a
Top speed: n/a
Production total: n/a

VERITAS DYNA-VERITAS

In the late 1940s, Lorenz Dietrich of specialist carmaker Veritas was offered the chance to distribute the Panhard Dyna in Germany, with a view to using the chassis and engine from the car in a special of his own.

The result was the Dyna-Veritas, produced in tiny numbers between 1950 and 1952, as a hand-built special which very few Germans

could afford to buy. There was a choice of coupé or cabriolet body styles; however, the majority of the cars built were cabriolets. Whichever type was chosen, the bodies were designed by Veritas and built to order by the Stuttgart-based coachbuilder, Baur.

The car's construction was straightforward, as a hand-made bodyshell was mounted on a

tubular steel chassis. But the engineering beneath the body was less conventional, with a Panhard-sourced 744cc (45 cu in) flat-twin engine driving the front wheels through a gearbox also from the same company.

Although there was only 25kW (33bhp) available, performance was good thanks to the car's light weight. Financing the project,

however, had always been a problem, and the combination of the cars' high cost and tiny production numbers meant that, by 1952, Dyna-Veritas was dead.

Engine: 744cc (45 cu in), V-twin cylinder
Power: 25kW (33bhp)
0–96km/h (60mph): n/a
Top speed: n/a
Production total: 200 approx.

VESPA 400

Although the scooters which carry the Vespa name are very much an Italian tradition, the cars which bore the famous badge were

actually produced in France. This was due to an agreement with Fiat that no motorcycle producer would challenge Fiat's market domination

by producing cars in Italy – but producing them in another country was considered acceptable. As a result of this agreement, the

decision was taken to make the Vespa 400 at Nievre in France.

One of the better-built microcars of the time, the Vespa 400 had a monocoque construction with a roll-back cloth sunroof. Although sold as a 2+2 coupé, only two passengers could be comfortably accommodated.

The air-cooled vertical twin engine was mounted at the rear of the car, making space at the front for carrying luggage and, although it was not fast, the car could cruise quite happily at 65km/h (40mph).

There was independent suspension all round, a three-speed gearbox and hydraulic brakes, meaning that this was definitely no crudely engineered backyard special. By the time production of the Vespa 400 ended in 1961, around 34,000 had been built.

Engine: 393cc (24 cu in), twin-cylinder
Power: 11kW (15bhp)
0–96km/h (60mph): n/a
Top speed: 80km/h (50mph)
Production total: 34,000 approx.

Manufactured for economy motoring, the Vespa 400 was one of the few truly charming microcars of the late 1950s.

VIGNALE-FIAT 850

1965–70

Great fun, but a poor investment thanks to its lack of decent rustproofing, the Fiat 850-based Vignales were built in small numbers. Of those, the Spider is the most desirable, but few survive.

After Fiat had launched its 850 in 1964, various Italian styling houses were commissioned to produce their own interpretations of the car. Bertone's Spider went into production as a Fiat; however, when Vignale came up with a trio of designs, the company decided to put them into production with a Vignale badge on.

The three variants of the Vignale-Fiat 850 were the four-seater 850 Special Coupé, the 2+2 850 Special saloon and the 2+2 850 Special Spider, each of which carried over all the Fiat parts, with the exception of the bodyshell itself. That meant that the floorpan, suspension, steering, brakes, engine and transmission were all taken from the 850.

Inside the cabin there was fake leather, plenty of standard equipment and extra chrome for

the controls, as well as metallic paint for the exterior bodywork.

The engine was rear-mounted, just like in the donor car and, with just 26kW (35bhp) available, there

was not much performance. There was also a lot of scuttle shake thanks to a lack of rigidity in the chassis. Very few examples of this car survive today.

Engine: 843cc (51 cu in), 4-cylinder
Power: 26kW (35bhp)
0–96km/h (60mph): n/a
Top speed: 136km/h (85mph) approx.
Production total: n/a

VIGNALE-FIAT SAMANTHA

1966–70

Out of all the Vignale-Fiats produced, the Samantha must surely rate as the prettiest by far, even if its 125 base was less than adequate. When sold new, the car

was marketed as 'the most beautiful four-seater in the world'. In fact, the car's height made the car look unbalanced so, in an effort to counter this, the sills were

painted black – this apparently made the car look slimmer.

The car's Fiat 125 roots were all too obvious in the car's construction, with the floorpan,

front bulkhead, dashboard, rear lights and all the underbonnet panels carried over.

The Porsche 928-style bug-eyed headlights were a bit of an acquired taste and, like most of the Vignale-Fiats, build quality was atrocious. Thanks to the Samantha weighing more than the Fiat 125 saloon on which it was based, performance was sluggish, although later cars did get more power with a choice of 67kW (90bhp) or 75kW (100bhp) engines.

Engine: 1608cc (98 cu in), 4-cylinder
Power: 67kW (90bhp)
0–96km/h (60mph): 12.6 secs
Top speed: 165km/h (103mph)
Production total: n/a

It had looks on its side, but sadly for the Vignale-Fiat Samantha there was precious little else. It was expensive to buy, had poor performance thanks to its humble Fiat 125 roots and was badly made. No wonder very few people were tempted to buy one.

VIGNALE-FIAT EVELINE

1966–70

The Eveline did not have the charm of other cars in Vignale's range, although it was far better put together. Meagre performance and the usual high production costs meant that hardly any were built.

Although in the 1960s Fiat was renowned for its sporty coupés with sweet handling and good performance, the Fiat 124-based coupé built by Vignale had neither – at least the Fiat 124 whose floorpan it used did win the Car of the Year award, so it must have had half-decent mechanicals. With just 1197cc (73 cu in) generating 45kW (60bhp), the car needed more power to exploit a chassis which could easily have coped with it.

Like the other Vignale-Fiats, under the skin everything was carried over from the Fiat 124, which also supplied the floorpan and a four-speed manual gearbox. One thing that was not carried over

was the fascia, a plastic unit being specially constructed for the car.

Unlike all the other Fiats which received attention from Vignale, the Eveline was well constructed

with good panel fit. Equipment levels were also high, although the leather that lined the interior was not real and the car's reliability was questionable.

Engine: 1197cc (73 cu in), 4-cylinder
Power: 45kW (60bhp)
0–96km/h (60mph): n/a
Top speed: 144km/h (90mph) approx.
Production total: 200 approx.

VIGNALE GAMINE

1967–70

Looking as though it has been taken straight out of a book of toy cars for children, the Gamine was in fact sold with Vignale-Fiat badges on. The work to turn an

ordinary 500 into a retro-style roadster was carried out by Vignale, with Fiat's only involvement being as the supplier of 500s for conversion. The aim of the

Gamine was to recall the lines of the prewar Balilla roadster; however, with the exception of the radiator grille, it did not really manage to do this, although the

end result certainly looked unconventional.

With a 500cc (30 cu in) engine fitted at the back of the car, performance was not very good, but later models had a more powerful 650cc (40 cu in) engine.

Most Gamines were built for the British market after Greek tycoon Frixos Demetriou spotted a Gamine and decided that it was the perfect car to start a new business venture with – selling them to British buyers. Shoddy build quality and high prices, however, meant that few were sold. With its rust-prone bodywork, even fewer are left today.

Engine: 500cc (30 cu in), twin-cylinder
Power: 25kW (34bhp)
0–96km/h (60mph): n/a
Top speed: 120km/h (75mph) approx.
Production total: 2000 approx.

The Vignale Gamine frequently prompts comparisons with Noddy's car. It might have had the mischievous charm of its namesake, but lack of practicality meant it could never be more than a toy.

Voisin 32-140

As amazing now as it would have been when new, Voisin's creation combined imposing bodywork with meticulous engineering. But such innovation always has a high price attached to it.

Gabriel Voisin had a reputation for being wildly innovative and did not seem capable of compromising in the design or construction of any of his cars, leading to amazing machines such as the Laboratoire

Grand Prix racer. His cars were not only amazing to look at, but also fantastically well engineered. Unfortunately, however, hardly anybody could afford to buy one of these unique creations.

In 1930, Voisin launched one of the most daring designs to come out of France during the prewar years, the 32-140. With swooping, wind-cheating lines, the car looked like nothing else available at the

time, and it was big, heavy and very expensive. The limousine cost £1900, although there was also a saloon, two-door coupé, four-door coupé and drophead coupé available. All versions of the car were powered by Voisin's refined 5830cc (356 cu in) overhead-valve straight-six engine with a four-speed gearbox.

Engine: 5830cc (356 cu in), 6-cylinder
Power: n/a
0–96km/h (60mph): n/a
Top speed: n/a
Production total: n/a

Volga M21

The Volga M21 was launched in 1955 as a successor to the popular M20 Pobjeba model. Although the body design was completely new, under the skin many of the parts found in the Volga M21 were carried over from the M20, the mechanics of which were proven to be reliable.

The first cars, which are known retrospectively as the Series 1, used the side-valve engine from the M20, but enlarged to 2432cc (148 cu in). By 1957, an all-new overhead-valve powerplant was developed, displacing 2445cc (149 cu in); the following year, the Series 2 M21 was unveiled. But

changes were very minor, with just small alterations to the grille and the dashboard. Perhaps the most noteworthy model during the life span of the M21 was the estate, launched in 1962, although this was seen as a completely different model, so was known as the M22. The final version, the Series 3,

arrived in 1962, but changes were once again very slight, being restricted to minor trim alterations.

Engine: 2445cc (149 cu in), 4-cylinder
Power: 71kW (95bhp)
0–80km/h (50mph): 18 secs
Top speed: 137km/h (85mph)
Production total: 638,875

Volga M24

Looking heavily influenced by the early 1960s Chevrolet Impala, the Volga M24 was the car that replaced the Volga M21. With a longer wheelbase and lower height, the M24 was an attempt at offering better packaging and a sleeker design. Although the same 2445cc (149 cu in) engine was used in the M24 as in its predecessor, the car's top speed rose as a result of better aerodynamics and a higher compression ratio of 8.2:1, which increased the power output while still allowing the car to run on relatively poor-quality fuel.

The M24 saloon did not go into production until 1970, with a taxi version following soon after. This had an engine with a lower

Looking like something from the early 1960s, the Volga M24 was not introduced until the end of that decade. And if it looked dated on the outside, it was positively ancient underneath, with greasing points galore.

compression ratio to allow it to run on even lower-quality fuel, but at least for all M24s the driving experience was improved over the M21, as it adopted servo-assisted brakes and a floor shift replaced the previous column shift.

Also, a four-speed gearbox replaced the previous three-speed unit; however, perhaps the greatest sign that the Volga was coming into the modern age was the reduction in lubrication points in the M24 from 37 to just nine.

Engine: 2445cc (149 cu in), 4-cylinder
Power: 83kW (112bhp)
0–96km/h (60mph): n/a
Top speed: 144km/h (90mph)
Production total: n/a

VOLKSWAGEN BEETLE

1945–PRESENT

The profile of the Beetle is unmistakable, although this classic to end all classics also ultimately spawned another car that's just as evergreen – the Porsche 911.

Possibly the popular car of all time, Volkswagen's Beetle nearly never went into production at all. But more than half a century after production began, it's still being made. By 1981, 20 million had been produced and, so far, more than 22 million have rolled off the production lines, this despite the fact that Volkswagen never called the car the Beetle at all – it was simply a nickname which stuck.

The Beetle started out as a pet project of Ferdinand Porsche, who set up a design studio in the early 1930s. He designed rear-engined cars for Zundapp and NSU, but neither could afford to tool up for production. In 1934, however, the Nazi government requested that a people's car (the German translation is *Volkswagen*) be designed and built. By 1937, 30 prototypes had been made by Mercedes-Benz, and the following year their car was ready for production, until the outbreak of World War II delayed manufacture.

The first examples of the Beetle, which at the time was simply called the Volkswagen, were built in 1945. The first year of manufacture produced just 1785 units, with each car fitted with an 1131cc (69 cu in) four-cylinder

There is little hope of any car ever catching up with the production tally of the original Beetle – unless it's several generations of a car with nothing but the name carried over.

engine, cable-operated brakes and a transmission with no synchromesh.

In spite of its lowly specification, the Beetle was popular as it was cheap and reliable, and postwar Germany was starved of new cars. Production continued throughout the 1940s and, by the start of the 1950s, major exports began – although the first had taken place in 1947, to the Netherlands. This led to continuous development of the car and ever greater popularity. Its affordability and reliability were always major selling points, but roadholding was always poor, just like its performance, carrying capacity and interior space.

In 1954, the engine grew to 1192cc (73 cu in) and, in 1960, the car received a full-synchromesh gearbox, along with a small but welcome power increase to 25kW (34bhp). Similarly, the move in 1962 to hydraulic brakes in place

Until the start of the 1960s, the Beetle was Volkswagen's only product, which is why it received so much internal development. Probably the most significant external change was the move from a split rear window to a single unit in 1953, although under the skin there were other changes such as an improved transmission and better brakes.

of the previous cable-operated system made the car much better to drive – although such a change was well overdue in its home market as export models had been equipped with the new brakes since 1950.

In 1965, a 1285cc (78 cu in) powerplant was installed, and the arrival of the 1500 Beetle the following year meant that the car was finally able to compete on equal terms with many of its competitors – especially as disc brakes were also now part of the package. By 1968, the car was beginning to lose its character, as the bumpers grew in size along with the rear light clusters.

In 1972, the 1300cc (79 cu in) 1302 and 1600cc (98 cu in) 1302S were launched with MacPherson strut front suspension. These models were superseded by the curved windscreen 1303 and 1303S a year later.

Production in Volkswagen's Wolfsburg factory was phased out in 1977, but continued in Mexico, where Beetles are still made, featuring a fuel-injected 1.6-litre (98 cu in) engine. And if the original rear-engined car is not to your taste, there is always the Golf-derived water-cooled car which arrived in 1998.

Engine: 1131cc (69 cu in), 4-cylinder
Power: 19kW (25bhp)
0–96km/h (60mph): n/a
Top speed: 101km/h (63mph)
Production total: 22,000,000

VOLKSWAGEN BEETLE HEBMÜLLER

1949–53

Produced at the same time as the Karmann-built Beetles, the Hebmüller Beetle had much cleaner lines with the roof down. But disaster cut production short.

Hebmüller was a small coach-builder formed in 1889. In 1919, the founder died and his four sons took over – and it was they who decided to produce a roadster version of the VW Beetle. Like the Karmann-built Beetle, the Hebmüller was a full convertible, but with much cleaner lines thanks to its flush-fitting stowed hood.

Unlike the Karmann car, the Hebmüller carried VW badges and was sold as a Volkswagen Cabriolet and, after much testing, the VW management was so impressed with the car's build quality that it ordered 2000 to be sold through its agents.

The first cars were ordered at the start of July 1949, but by the end of that month disaster had struck, with fire destroying almost the entire Hebmüller factory. Hardly anything was left to save, and, although a few more cars were

built in 1950 and 1951, it was clear the company could not survive. By the middle of 1952, it was declared bankrupt, and the Hebmüller coupé which had been planned for production alongside the Hebmüller roadster disappeared with it.

Engine: 1131cc (69 cu in), 4-cylinder
Power: 19kW (25bhp)
0–96km/h (60mph): n/a
Top speed: 101km/h (63mph)
Production total: 700 approx.

VOLKSWAGEN BEETLE KARMANN

1949–80

All Beetles are highly sought-after, but one derivative is particularly highly coveted – the Karmann-built Cabriolet. Having built its first drophead prototypes in 1946, Karmann unveiled the production version of its Beetle Cabriolet in 1949. Thousands of miles of testing showed that the car was up to the standards that were expected of a Volkswagen, so 2000 were ordered.

During a life span of more than three decades, changes to the Karmann Beetle mirrored those of the standard car, with engine, brake and suspension upgrades, as well as improvements to the interior and electrical systems – essential as prices were much higher than the standard car's.

The Karmann's roof was also upgraded along the way, as initially

it offered almost no rear visibility when raised, thanks to a back window the size of a letterbox.

The most valuable of the normal production Beetles, Karmann's Cabriolet was extremely well built, but had a price tag to match. Despite this, it was successfully produced for more than 30 years and is still a desirable car today.

Although visibility was never as good as that in the saloon, however, the multi-layered hood made the car incredibly refined. It is still a gem today.

Engine: 1131cc (69 cu in), 4-cylinder
Power: 19kW (25bhp)
0–96km/h (60mph): n/a
Top speed: 101km/h (63mph)
Production total: 331,847

VOLKSWAGEN KARMANN GHIA

Karmann started negotiations with Volkswagen in 1950 with regard to building a sports car for the company. It was not until 1955, however, that the car first appeared, after the design house Ghia had been approached to design and build a prototype.

As soon as the car went on sale it was a hit, despite a high purchase price and standard Beetle mechanicals underneath the stylish body. In fact the car was not a sports car at all – it may have looked like one, but performance was far too low. The Beetle did, however, have an excellent reputation for reliability and low running costs, which must have meant more to buyers than outright dynamic ability.

Initially, only a 1200cc (73 cu in) coupé was offered but, from 1965, buyers could specify a 1300cc (79 cu in) version and, in 1970, a 1.6-litre (98 cu in) model was introduced. But the most sought-after Karmann Ghias are the cabriolets, launched in 1957 with 1200cc (73 cu in) engines, later upgraded to 1300cc (79 cu in) units before the final versions, with the familiar 1600cc (98 cu in) powerplants, arrived in 1970.

Engine: 1192cc (73 cu in), 4-cylinder
Power: 22kW (30bhp)
0–96km/h (60mph): n/a
Top speed: 115km/h (72mph)
Production total: n/a

Looking far more sporty than they really were, the Beetle-based Karmann Ghias were built for two decades. They may not have had much performance, but there was definitely plenty of style.

VOLKSWAGEN KARMANN GHIA TYPE 34

1961–69

Otherwise known as the Type 34, the Karmann Ghia 1500 and 1600 were part of the Type 3 family (see next entry), and they followed on from the saloon, convertible and estate that had already been introduced. As the name suggests, the car was designed by Ghia, but built by Karmann and sold by Volkswagen alongside its other cars, including the now-coveted Karmann Ghia 1200.

Wider, longer and higher than the 1200, the 1500 and 1600 were based on a wider floorpan so that the car could more usefully serve its purpose of being an all-round family car. And it seemed that the car had it all – comfort, reliability, chic styling and good performance. A high purchase price and an insatiable thirst (as low as 15.8l/100km [18mpg]) if used at high cruising speeds, however, meant that many potential buyers simply could not afford to buy or run one.

The car made its debut in 1961, but it did not arrive in the United Kingdom until 1963 and was never exported to the United States. By 1967, automatic transmission and fuel injection were available, but by 1969 the car was obsolete.

Effectively an overgrown version of the Beetle-based Karmann Ghia, the Type 34 used parts from the larger VW Type 3 for performance.

Engine: 1493cc (91 cu in), 4-cylinder
Power: 34kW (45bhp)
0–96km/h (60mph): n/a
Top speed: 144km/h (90mph)
Production total: 42,563

VOLKSWAGEN TYPE 3

1961–73

First seen at the 1961 Frankfurt Motor Show, the VW 1500, or Type 3, was only the second passenger car from Volkswagen. The basic principles of the Type 3 followed those of the Beetle, with a rear-mounted air-cooled engine. Despite the position of the engine, there was still a luggage compartment at the rear of the car, as well as another at the front.

Initially, a Karmann-built cabriolet was shown alongside the two-door saloon. It never went into production, but an estate was to arrive in 1962, and the following year the 1500S was launched with twin carburettors. By 1965, the 1493cc (91 cu in) engine was complemented by a 1584cc (97 cu in) unit after the introduction of the 1600TL. This heralded the launch of the TL-badged fastback saloon – a car that looked like a modern hatchback, but with a conventional boot and just two doors.

By 1966, the 1500cc (91 cu in) engine was dropped, and all Type

3s used 1584cc (97 cu in) units instead. Apart from detail design changes, there was no further development of the car, which finished production in 1973.

Engine: 1493cc (91 cu in), 4-cylinder
Power: 34kW (45bhp)
0–96km/h (60mph): n/a
Top speed: 130km/h (81mph)
Number produced: 1,542,342

Based on the same design principles as the Beetle, the Type 3 was much bigger and never caught on in the same way as VW's iconic first car.

VOLKSWAGEN 411

Following the same layout as its predecessor, the Type 3, the VW 411 (also known as the Type 4) marked a first for Volkswagen – a car with more than two doors. Although there was the usual rear-mounted air-cooled engine, the chassis was changed significantly, with transverse links and MacPherson struts in place of the trailing link front axle and torsion bars of the Beetle.

The 411 was long overdue. By the time it was launched, the Beetle was becoming old, and a car that offered more space, comfort and practicality was needed. By the time the 411 arrived, it was seen as being too close in concept to the cars which came before it (the Type 1 and Type 3), and many potential buyers were deterred by what was seen as an outdated layout. In 1974, the VW 411 was replaced by a heavily redesigned car – the VW 412. Although under the skin it was closely related to the 411, the changes to the car were far-reaching enough to warrant a change of name.

With Volkswagen used to life cycles for its cars that are measured in decades, rather than years, the short production span of the 411, and later the 412, was something of a disappointment for the company.

Engine: 1679cc (102 cu in), 4-cylinder
Power: 51kW (68bhp)
0–96km/h (60mph): 13.8 secs
Top speed: 155km/h (97mph)
Production total: 355,300 (incl. 412)

VOLKSWAGEN 181

Also known as the *Kurierwagen*, Volkswagen's 181 was an update of the classic Kubelwagen troop carrier seen during World War II. Using the Type 14 Karmann Ghia floorpan, the 181 had no fixed roof and not only could the doors be easily removed, but the windscreen could be folded flat for maximum exposure to the elements as well.

To emphasize the car's utilitarian nature, the VW 181 did without interior trim or sound insulation – it was meant to be able to be hosed out after a drive.

When the car went on sale in 1969, it was equipped with a reinforced crossmember to stop it buckling on manoeuvres, while the front suspension and steering were also strengthened. Initially, the 1.5-litre (91 cu in) Beetle powerplant was used; however, from 1971, this became the 1600cc (98 cu in) engine seen in the 1302S. Although it looked like a four-wheel drive, power was only transmitted to the rear wheels. But despite the lack of any equipment and weight, fuel consumption was poor – just 14l/100km (20mpg). In 1975, production of the VW 181 moved to Mexico, before it stopped altogether in 1978.

Engine: 1493cc (91 cu in), flat-four
Power: 33kW (44bhp)
0–96km/h (60mph): n/a
Top speed: 115km/h (72mph)
Production total: 70,395

VOLKSWAGEN K70

By the time Volkswagen bought NSU in 1969, the design of the K70 was well under way. Before the NSU version of the K70 could be released in 1969, Volkswagen had taken control of NSU as part of its takeover of Auto-Union. The NSU Ro80 had been losing huge amounts of money, as it was too far ahead of its time, and its rotary-engine technology had not been properly developed.

The K70 was intended to change that, with its four-cylinder, four-stroke water-cooled engine mounted at the front and driving the front wheels. When NSU was bought by VW, the Wolfsburg company received the K70 as part of the deal. Although VW was actually close to launching its own car in the same market sector – the Passat – there is no doubt that the company was very interested in the car's water-cooled engine and front-wheel drive. Still, the result was a short life span for the K70.

Like the Ro80 before it, the K70 was very modern to drive, with superb refinement and excellent dynamics. There was a choice of 1605cc (98 cu in) or 1807cc (110 cu in) overhead-camshaft four-cylinder engines, the latter unit producing a useful 75kW (100bhp), propelling the car to 161km/h (100mph). It had excellent road-holding and safety, with a spacious interior and good luggage space. However, because the car had been developed as an NSU, it was impossible for VW to interchange parts with any other of its own cars, which made the car's production very inefficient.

Developed as an NSU, the K70 was actually launched as a Volkswagen. The mechanical specification of the car was a completely different one for Volkswagen and led to production inefficiencies, although it would not be long before all the company's production cars followed the same principles.

Engine: 1605cc (98 cu in), 4-cylinder
Power: 56kW (75bhp)
0–80km/h (50mph): 10.5 secs
Top speed: 147km/h (92mph)
Production total: 211,100

VOLKSWAGEN GOLF MK I

1974–83

One of the most popular cars ever made, VW's Golf has become a permanent fixture on the road and has appeared as five different generations so far. The car first appeared in 1974, launched to bring Volkswagen up to date so it could compete with cars such as the Renault 5 and Peugeot 104. Styled by Giugiaro, the car was indeed modern, but continued the

Beetle's concept of simple transport with basic equipment levels.

The VW Golf proved incredibly popular, with more than one million cars being built in less than three years. Within a year of launch, a 1588cc (97 cu in) engine was fitted, and this paved the way for the introduction of the Golf GTi in 1976 – one of the first 'hot hatches' ever and the one which

sparked the launch of dozens of imitations. By the time the Mk II Golf arrived in 1983, a diesel, a cabriolet and a booted version, the Jetta, were on sale.

Engine: 1272cc (78 cu in), 4-cylinder
Power: 45kW (60bhp)
0–96km/h (60mph): 13.2 secs
Top speed: 147km/h (92mph)
Production total: 6,000,000 approx.

It has grown over the years, but the original Golf was cheap to run, mechanically simple and utterly reliable. It is no wonder that huge numbers were built, which were eagerly snapped up by buyers who wanted durability and practicality above all else.

VOLKSWAGEN SCIROCCO

1974–81

When Giugiaro initially designed the Mk I Golf, it was also suggested that the car would provide the perfect basis for a 2+2 coupé. VW was not interested, so Giugiaro decided to go direct to Karmann to see if it would become involved in such a project. The success of the Karmann Ghia suggested that the proposal could be profitable, so Giugiaro's Italdesign company and Karmann collaborated on the project that would become the Scirocco.

When the prototype was shown to VW, the company said that it could not afford to develop it, so Karmann engineered the bodyshell and VW helped with the mechanicals. The Scirocco went into production before the Golf, initially available with 1.1- (67 cu

A classic case of a car that is more than the sum of its parts, the Scirocco was far more stylish than it had any right to be, as it was based on the Golf.

in) and 1.5-litre (92 cu in) engines when it was launched in 1974.

By 1975, the Golf's 1588cc (97 cu in) engine was fitted, and a year later it followed in the footsteps of the Golf when it received fuel injection to become the Scirocco GTi. A facelift in 1977 tidied up the exterior, and in 1981 the car was replaced by the Mk II.

Engine: 1588cc (97 cu in), 4-cylinder
Power: 82kW (110bhp)
0–96km/h (60mph): 9 secs
Top speed: 185km/h (115mph)
Production total: 504,200

VOLVO PV444

The PV444 was the car which put Volvo on the global map. Indeed, it was the car which put the country of Sweden itself on the automotive global map because it was the first model to be exported in significant numbers. Developed during World War II, the PV444 did not go on sale until 1947.

Until the 1930s, Volvo had focused on side-valve six-cylinder engines; however, fuel shortages and the need for affordable cars led the company to rethink its output and move into four-cylinder cars.

Although the car's unitary construction was inspired by the 1939 Hanomag, the styling was much more trans-Atlantic in its inspiration. The integrated front wings mimicked 1942 Ford cars, and the coil and wishbone suspension and hydraulic brakes also had a distinct US flavour.

Despite the four-cylinder overhead-valve engine being just 1.4 litres (86 cu in), the car's reasonably light weight of 968kg (2128lb) meant that a speed of more than 115km/h (70mph) could be achieved.

When the Amazon's 1582cc (97 cu in) engine was fitted from 1957 the car became even better, before being replaced in 1958 by the broadly similar PV544.

Engine: 1414cc (86 cu in), 4-cylinder
Power: 30kW (40bhp)
0–96km/h (60mph): 24.9 secs
Top speed: 118km/h (74mph)
Production total: 196,004

Volvo's first postwar car, the PV444, took the company downmarket from what it was used to in the wake of a war which left relatively few people able to afford to buy a new car.

VOLVO PV544

Just when everybody thought Volvo would replace its ageing PV444 with a completely new model, the company reintroduced it with a few minor changes and a small amendment to the name.

The Volvo PV544 superseded the PV444 in 1958, using almost the same bodyshell as its predecessor, although there was now room for five in the back and larger front and rear windscreens. Whereas the PV444's windscreen had been split and made of flat glass, the PV544's was a single, curved unit.

To make the car as popular as possible, Volvo offered it in four separate specifications, with different trim levels and a choice of standard or Sport engines. The Sport was fitted with an 63kW (85bhp) 1.6-litre (96 cu in) unit which up to that point had been reserved for cars intended for the US market only. When sold outside the United States, however, this made the car too expensive. To

counter this, Volvo added extra equipment to make the model better value for money.

In 1960, a 1.8-litre (110 cu in) engine was offered which had up to 67kW (90bhp) available if twin carburettors were specified. Not only that, but a four-speed gearbox was offered alongside the three-speed standard unit as well.

The last Volvo PV544 was built in 1965, nearly a decade after the introduction of the Amazon – the car which had been introduced to supersede the PV range.

Engine: 1580cc (96 cu in), 4-cylinder
Power: 63kW (85bhp)
0–96km/h (60mph): n/a
Top speed: 136km/h (85mph)
Production total: 243,995

VOLVO PV445

As carmakers moved to monocoque construction for their cars, one-off and bespoke bodies became much harder. Volvo solved the problem by introducing a separate-chassised 'car' which used the tried and tested mechanics of the PV444.

development allowed new variants to be developed very quickly, easily and cheaply, the first of which were light commercial vehicles capable of carrying around 500kg (1100lb).

Introduced in 1949, it was not long before ambulances, hearses and even convertibles were being built by independent coachbuilders. One of the most popular conversions was an estate, and this prompted Volvo to develop its own estate car launched in 1953.

Engine: 1414cc (86 cu in), 4-cylinder
Power: 30kW (40bhp)
0–96km/h (60mph): 24.9 secs
Top speed: 118km/h (74mph)
Production total: n/a

After the PV444's introduction, Volvo realized that the car's monocoque construction meant that producing one-off bodies for special customers was difficult. Developing other variants was also not easy, so a PV444 with a separate chassis was introduced.

This version used the PV444's engine, electrics, transmission, brakes and front suspension. The rear suspension was changed to semi-elliptic leaf springs and double-acting hydraulic dampers, all of which was attached directly to the chassis to make bespoke bodywork much easier to fit. Known as the PV445, this

VOLVO P1900

In 1953, Volvo boss Assar Gabrielsson visited the United States and saw how popular European sports cars had become in that country. He resolved to build one of his own and commissioned the California-based company, Glasspar, to design, engineer and build such a car.

Designs were duly developed, using the 1.4-litre (86 cu in) B14 engine from the PV444. A pair of SU carburettors was installed to increase the car's power to 52kW (70bhp), and the powerplant was mated to a standard Volvo three-speed gearbox.

Having debuted the car in September 1954 – and still without a name – Volvo announced that the car would be going into production later that autumn, at the rate of a car a day. But it was not until 1956 that the first cars were delivered and, even then, only 44 were built in that year. The following year, just 23 cars were produced, and it was clear that the P1900, as it was now called, was never going to make any money, as the hand-built

bodyshells meant high production costs. It also used glassfibre panels, which were still a new and largely untested construction material, so production standards were not high enough. Volvo had no option but to drop the car from its range.

Engine: 1414cc (86 cu in), 4-cylinder
Power: 52kW (70bhp)
0–96km/h (60mph): n/a
Top speed: n/a
Production total: 67

Volvo's first attempt at a sports car, the P1900 was not manufactured to the high quality that had come to be expected of a car of this particular marque. Coupled to this problem was that fact that it was expensive to build as well.

VOLVO 120

Like all Volvos, the 120 was not a range that featured built-in obsolescence. There was gradual evolution of the model, but the final cars were not that different from the first ones.

By the early 1950s, Volvo was thinking about a replacement for the PV series, knowing that it would take several years to design and engineer something that would maintain the company's reputation for longevity and dependability. After considerable testing and development, the 'Amason' was ready for launch in 1956. However, the moped manufacturer Kriedler also produced a product with this name and claimed that the trademark belonged to them. After much negotiation, Volvo was allowed to use the Amason badge on its new car, but only for the Swedish market. All exported cars carried the 120-, 130- and 220-series names instead, with the launch car being the 121. Despite this, enthusiasts around the world have adopted the more familiar Amazon tag for the car.

The first cars were equipped with a single-carburettor 1583cc (97 cu in) version of the three-

bearing engine fitted to the PV444. With just 45kW (60bhp) available, performance was poor, partly due to the three-speed gearbox carried over from the PV444.

In March 1958, the next development arrived – the 63kW (85bhp) 122S complete with an all-synchromesh four-speed gearbox. In October 1961, the two-door car, known as the 131, was introduced, and the estate version was to arrive in February 1962.

More improvements were promised for 1965, the most significant of which was to be the introduction of disc brakes as standard at the front wheels of all cars. Estate versions also had servo assistance, and a more affordable Amazon, known as the Favorit, was introduced. This had a lower specification, such as less external chrome trim, a more austere interior and a three-speed all-synchromesh gearbox in place of

the standard four-speed unit. By now, the Amazon was being built in large numbers, and it looked as though the car would remain in production despite the car's supposed successor (the Volvo 140) going on sale in 1966.

Instead of taking the car out of production, a new sports version of the Amazon was unveiled. Badged as the 123GT (or the 120GT in some export markets), the new car mated the 1.8-litre (110 cu in) engine from the 1800S with the two-door bodyshell of the 122. With 86kW (115bhp) available and a four-speed gearbox with overdrive, the car was more practical than the 1800S, as well as being more affordable.

At the end of 1967, the four-door Amazon was taken out of production, as the 144 had become the more popular car – although, for the first half of the year, the 121 was still the bestselling car in Sweden. But the two-door and estate versions continued to be built, and in autumn 1968 it was announced that the cars would be available with the B20 2-litre (122 cu in) engine, which was a bored-out version of the B18 powerplant. Rated at either 67kW (90bhp) or 88kW (118bhp) depending on the state of tune, the car's extra power was less important than the greatly improved torque. At the same time, the cars were fitted with the dual-circuit braking system that had been fitted to the 140-series right from the start.

In 1969, the Amazon estate was discontinued, superseded by the 145 and leaving just the 122 in production. It was clear that the car would not be built for much longer, so changes for the 1970 model year were very minor, restricted to front-seat head rests and the provision of rear seat belts. The last car was built in the summer of 1969.

Although the four-door 120-series was generally much more popular than the two-door, it was the latter shell on which the sportiest derivative was based – the 123GT.

Engine: 1583cc (97 cu in), 4-cylinder
Power: 49kW (66bhp)
0–96km/h (60mph): n/a
Top speed: 144km/h (90mph)
Production total: 667,323

VOLVO 140

After the curvy PV-series and 120-series cars, the square-cut, angular 140-series was a bit of a shock. But it was incredibly safe and durable, and soon proved to be a hit.

The suspension was also carried over from the Amazon (with a few modifications), and, at launch, the car was fitted with a 1.8-litre (109 cu in) engine. In 1968, a five-door estate version joined the range, then, six months later, a two-door saloon arrived. The next change was the introduction of a 2-litre (122 cu in) engine with up to 158kW (118bhp) on offer if buyers specified the twin-carburettor option.

The final amendments to be made to the Volvo 140 came in 1972, when a Mk II version appeared. Changes were restricted to a new dash, minor cosmetic exterior updates and new 8km/h (5mph) impact bumpers.

Few people ever bought a Volvo 140 because of its looks, but safety was a different matter entirely. Ever since the 120 series had been launched, Volvo had been studiously cultivating its reputation as a maker of safe cars, and the Volvo 140 reinforced this image.

Most of the mechanicals had already been seen on the Amazon that preceded it, including the 260cm (102in) wheelbase.

Innovations that made the car safer in a crash included a collapsible steering column, rear seat belt mountings and stronger locks to prevent the doors flying open in the event of an accident.

Engine: 1778cc (109 cu in), 4-cylinder
Power: 63kW (85bhp)
0–96km/h (60mph): 12.5 secs
Top speed: 163km/h (102mph)

VOLVO 164

Volvo started production with six-cylinder cars, so it made sense to offer them once again in the more affluent 1960s. The result was the 164, effectively a six-cylinder 144 with a longer wheelbase to allow for an extended engine bay. But although the 164 was much like its four-cylinder sibling from the A-pillars back, it was conceived as a more exclusive car with more equipment as standard and a more ostentatious front end. This allowed Volvo to retain customers who were thinking about trading up from a Volvo to a Mercedes, unable to find anything in the Swedish company's range to suit their needs.

Interior space in the Volvo 164 was the same as the 144's, but the straight-six engine gave the car performance that was far ahead of its smaller brother. This engine was essentially a 144 unit increased in size by 50 per cent. Many of the components were shared with the 144 and, with its seven-bearing crankshaft, the cylinder block was really just a B20 engine with a pair

of cylinders added. Twin Zenith-Stromberg carburettors were fitted to the car, and either automatic or manual/overdrive gearboxes could be specified.

With all the classic Volvo virtues of solidity, safety and conservative styling, the 164 was a true luxury express for those who might have been tempted to leave Volvo.

Engine: 2979cc (182 cu in), 6-cylinder
Power: 97kW (130bhp)
0–96km/h (60mph): 11.3 secs
Top speed: 170km/h (106mph)
Production total: 155,068

VOLVO P1800

Despite Volvo's P1800 provoking interest the day it was introduced, the car's engineering was completely conventional, and it promised rather more excitement than it actually delivered. And, despite the company's reputation for solid build quality, the early cars were not very well made.

The poor build quality was because the P1800's manufacture was outsourced due to Volvo's lack of factory capacity. An agreement had been reached for Jensen to put

the cars together once the Pressed Steel Company had built the bodyshells at its Scottish Linwood factory.

In 1963, production was moved to Sweden, and the car was rebadged the 1800S. At the same time, the engine was uprated with higher compression and a better camshaft to increase power, but there were few other changes. It was not until 1968 that engine capacity was increased to 2 litres (122 cu in), but this unit was just a

Despite the ropey build quality of early cars, the Volvo P1800 is one of the most usable and stylish classic cars available for relatively affordable sums of money. It is also a pleasure to drive, if not as sporty as perhaps its looks would suggest.

development of the B18 engine seen in the Amazon. The following year saw the introduction of fuel injection (when the car became the 1800E, 'E' for *Einspritz*, or fuel injection) and, in 1971, just one year before production ended, an automatic gearbox was made available.

Engine: 1780cc (109 cu in), 4-cylinder
Power: 75kW (100bhp)
0–96km/h (60mph): 13.2 secs
Top speed: 166km/h (104mph)
Production total: 39,407

Penned by Italian design studio Frua, the P1800's suave shape was chosen to star alongside Roger Moore in the TV series *The Saint*.

VOLVO 1800ES

In 1971, Volvo unveiled the 1800ES. Using the same concept as Reliant's Scimitar GTE, the car gave the 1800 a new lease of life – albeit for just two more years. Until the launch of Radford's shooting-brake conversions of the Aston Martin DB5 in 1964, estate cars were seen as practical boxes on wheels designed to ferry people or goods around, and combining such utilitarianism with a sports car seemed absurd – but the concept actually proved popular.

When the 1800ES went on sale it cost £2650 ($4000), for which you could have had a sports estate from Reliant or BMW. Disc brakes were fitted all round, and overdrive was standard, which the car's competitors could not claim. When it came to dynamics, however, the

Looking less sporty than its coupé stablemate, the 1800ES sports estate is an even better bet thanks to even greater practicality, but without the driving experience.

1800 was well behind its rivals. The 1800ES went out of production in 1973 when US safety regulations meant that the car would have had to be re-engineered with 8km/h

(5mph) impact bumpers from the 1974 model year onwards. This would prove too costly, so the 1800's largest market was also the one which killed it off.

Engine: 1986cc (121 cu in), 4-cylinder
Power: 83kW (112bhp)
0–96km/h (60mph): 9.7 secs
Top speed: 181km/h (112mph)
Production total: 8077

WANDERER W50

Wanderer catered for the same market as Volvo, which meant its cars were conservatively styled both inside and out, but could be depended upon to give faithful service for years and years.

The W50 was a typical Wanderer product, with high-quality engineering, but a predictable design. Available as a Pullman limousine, a four-door saloon, a four-seat cabriolet or a two-seat cabriolet, the W50 was powered by a Ferdinand Porsche-designed straight-six engine. This featured pushrod-operated overhead valves, along with seven main bearings and an alloy block with cast-iron wet cylinder liners. This was mated to a four-speed all-synchromesh gearbox. Under the chassis, the Wanderer W50 had independent suspension all round, with swing axles at the rear and a transverse leaf spring at the front.

Wanderer was part of the Auto-Union group in the 1930s, along with Audi, Horch and DKW. Helped by state funding, the group was one of the major German manufacturers

of the time, aiming to offer something for everyone thanks to its different brands having clear prestige levels. Lowest was DKW, with Wanderer above them, but

below Audi and Horch. As a result, the company was charged with building cars for professionals, but their products were seen as staid and conventional, albeit dependable.

Engine: 2255cc (138 cu in), 6-cylinder
Power: n/a
0–96km/h (60mph): n/a
Top speed: n/a
Production total: n/a

WARSZAWA M20

The Warszawa M20, launched in 1951, was a redundant Soviet car, the Pobieda, first seen in 1945. Although production was slow to start (just 75 cars were built in the first year), things gradually speeded up so that, by 1956, the M20 was a completely Polish product.

To mark the occasion, a new engine was fitted to replace the ageing side-valve unit. Featuring an overhead camshaft, the new powerplant generated 52kW (70bhp) – enough to give the car a top speed of 105km/h (65mph).

In 1957, an estate version was produced in prototype form, and the following year another facelift was undertaken, the main change being a less ornate grille. In 1960, Ghia designed a saloon version of the Warszawa M20; however, during the rest of the decade, there was little development and production ended in March 1973.

By that time, more than 250,000 examples of the car had been built, many of which were being used as taxis. The car's heavy construction and design simplicity ensured reliability – and, as a result of this, the Warszawa M20s are now increasingly sought after in their home country.

Engine: 2120cc (129 cu in), 4-cylinder
Power: 52kW (70bhp)
0–96km/h (60mph): 30 secs approx.
Top speed: 104km/h (65mph)
Production total: 254,470

WARTBURG 311 & 312

The Wartburg 311 was launched at the 1956 Leipzig Spring Fair, and it was a well-engineered (if slightly old-fashioned) car with a superbly designed body. Redolent of Borgwards of the same era, the Wartburg 311 was at first available as either a four-door saloon or two-door estate (known as the Kombi), although later, a cabriolet and a coupé were also introduced (covered below).

Transverse leaf springs at both front and rear were antiquated even when the car was first seen and, in 1964, the model was superseded by the Wartburg 312, complete with a new chassis and gearbox. The bodyshell was carried over from the Wartburg 311, but now there was independent coil-sprung suspension all round. Service intervals for the car rose to an incredible 48,200km (30,000 miles) – although many owners in what was then East Germany probably still went over these!

With very little money to invest in a new model, engineers worked on a replacement for the 312, trying out various mechanical configurations; however, when the car was finally superseded by the Wartburg 353 in 1967, the mechanicals were carried over and only the bodyshell was updated.

With two-tone paintwork and plenty of chrome trim, the early Wartburgs looked far more upmarket than they really were, with their crude engineering and relatively low price.

Engine: 900cc (55 cu in), 3-cylinder
Power: 28kW (37bhp)
0–96km/h (60mph): n/a
Top speed: 115km/h (72mph)
Production total: n/a

WARTBURG COUPÉ AND CABRIOLET

1957–66

Looking like a Borgward Isabella coupé, the Wartburg Coupé was a superbly stylish car that was crying out for a more potent powerplant than the 900cc (55 cu in) three-cylinder unit with which it was equipped.

output was increased from 22kW (30bhp) to 28kW (37bhp). The non-synchromesh four-speed gearbox and front-wheel drive layout were also carried over – front-wheel drive was innovative at the time. The mechanical specifications were barely changed between the old model and the new, so almost all the differences between the two cars were in the bodyshell, especially in the case of the coupé. This particular model offered relatively little passenger space, but a huge bonnet, under which was housed not just the engine, but also a longitudinally mounted gearbox.

Although Wartburgs are now thought of as noisy, smelly, slow two-strokes (mainly thanks to the Knight of the 1970s), the first cars were actually quite stylish, even though they were outdated in terms of engineering. The first postwar Wartburgs were built by the state-owned IFA company in 1950, badged as the F9. When a new car was needed, it was decided to revive the Wartburg name which had been used for cars built at Eisenach in East Germany until production had ceased in 1904. Using the same DKW-inspired 900cc (55 cu in) three-cylinder two-stroke engine used in the F9,

Engine: 900cc (55 cu in), 3-cylinder
Power: 28kW (37bhp)
0–96km/h (60mph): n/a
Top speed: 115km/h (72mph)
Production total: n/a

WARTBURG SPORT

1957–60

Although the Wartburg Sport was listed as a separate model, in reality it shared almost everything with its more common 311-based Coupé and Cabriolet counterparts. The transverse leaf springs all round were carried over from these versions, and the three-cylinder 900cc (55 cu in) engine still drove the front wheels via a four-speed gearbox. The flowing lines and wraparound window glass front and rear were also retained – these were cars which were genuinely good-looking vehicles.

The Wartburg Sport was first announced in 1957, with its major selling point being a powerplant that had been tuned slightly to give more power – 37kW (50bhp) instead of the standard car's 28kW (37bhp). This significantly improved performance, and the car was now able to travel at 140km/h (87mph), as opposed to the standard model's top speed of 115km/h (72mph).

From 1958, in common with the rest of the Wartburg range, the

four-speed gearbox received synchromesh on all the forward gears; however, by 1960, the Sport version had been dropped from the Wartburg range.

Engine: 900cc (55 cu in), 3-cylinder
Power: 37kW (50bhp)
0–96km/h (60mph): n/a
Top speed: 140km/h (87mph)
Production total: n/a

The name 'Sport' was something of a misnomer, although the car was uprated by Wartburg to offer more sparkling performance than the coupé on which it was based.

WARTBURG 353 (KNIGHT)

1966–68

First shown in 1966, the 353 (or Knight), was a new body mounted on the chassis of its predecessor, the 312. Although build quality was poor, there had been some attention to detail. To help reduce injuries in the event of a collision, the steering column was collapsible, and much of the switchgear was placed safely under the dash. Panels were bolted on, rather than welded on, so they could be easily replaced if the car

were involved in an accident,and, on the estate version, known as the Tourist, the rear wings and tailgate were glassfibre to reduce manufacturing costs and weight.

There was almost no development of the car throughout its life span, although LED instrumentation was adopted in 1984 along with a new carburettor and cooling system. A two-stroke engine powered the 353 from beginning to end. As a result,

the last cars were sold in Britain in the mid-1970s when new emissions legislation outlawed them. As other countries followed suit, export markets dried up, but the Wartburg 353 survived until 1988 for the undemanding home market.

Engine: 991cc (60 cu in), 3-cylinder 2-stroke
Power: 34kW (45bhp)
0–96km/h (60mph): 22.8 secs
Top speed: 118km/h (74mph)
Production total: n/a

This was the car that ensured Wartburg was finished outside its homeland. Other than East Europeans, few people would accept the pollution produced by its three-cylinder two-stroke engine or the crude build quality of the car in general.

WILLYS MODEL 38

1938–39

A direct descendant of the Willys Model 77, the Model 38 had just one key selling point in its home market – an incredibly competitive price. By the time the car was brought to Europe, however, it was looked on as less competitive and was overshadowed by its European counterparts. The problem was that

the Willys company needed all the sales it could muster, as it had spent the whole of the 1930s lurching from one crisis to another. For example, in 1938, the company was geared up to build 125,000 cars; however, in the end only 12,000 were made, despite various body styles being available.

Even the 77 was outdated when it was introduced in 1933, so to try to revive the old model by simply renaming it the Model 38, giving it servo-assisted brakes and a synchromesh gearbox was an extremely optimistic move on the company's part. The Model 38's side-valve four-cylinder engine was

harsh, although the 'floating power' rubber engine mounts were innovative at the time.

Engine: 2200cc (134 cu in), 4-cylinder
Power: 36kW (48bhp)
0–96km/h (60mph): n/a
Top speed: 112km/h (70mph)
Production total: n/a

WILLYS STATION WAGON

The United States' first estate car with an all-steel bodyshell, the Willys Station Wagon was launched in 1946. Willys had built a reputation during World War II for incredible reliability with the Jeep – it now had to match that with a civilian car.

The initial proposal had been to build a two-door saloon to launch the company into the postwar years; however, it was thought that, having gained a reputation for building trusty workhorses, it made more sense for the company to produce a more functional vehicle. The result was a two-door estate (and later a two-door van) that proved popular with the public, and the first cars had two-tone paintwork that hinted at the 'woody' look which was then popular.

Although the Jeep was only available with four-wheel drive, the

It is clear what inspired Toyota to build its first Land Cruiser, as the Willys Station Wagon looks just like it. But, unlike Toyota, Willys had a reputation for building tough vehicles that could go anywhere.

first Station Wagons – which were also designated Model 463 – were rear-wheel drive, and it was not until 1949 that an all-wheel drive version was offered.

By the end of 1946, more than 6000 Willys Station Wagons had been sold and, by the end of the following year, the sales figures for the vehicle were more than five times this amount.

Engine: 2199cc (134 cu in), 4-cylinder
Power: 47kW (63bhp)
0–96km/h (60mph): n/a
Top speed: 104km/h (65mph)
Production total: 350,000 approx.

WILLYS JEEPSTER

1948–51

As the Jeep was such a success for Willys, the company decided to cross over into the civilian market with a car that was clearly related to the military version, but which was more comfortable to use every day. The intention was to build an open-top car which was immediately identifiable as a Jeep, but with creature comforts that would make it more saleable.

The stumbling block, however, was a ridiculously high price. Willys had decided that it wanted to recoup its development costs as quickly as possible, thus ensuring that the Jeepster would always be made in small numbers. However, more than 20,000 cars were sold in just three years – although, by setting the price at a more affordable level, the company

Looking almost like a parody of the real thing, the Willys Jeepster was amazingly popular considering its very high selling price. However, at least the vehicle's durability was guaranteed.

could have easily achieved a much larger figure.

From 1949, the Jeepster was available with a 2433cc (148 cu in) six-cylinder engine – up until this point, it had been available only with the four-cylinder powerplant found under the bonnet of the Willys Station Wagon.

Engine: 2199cc (134 cu in), 4-cylinder
Power: 47kW (63bhp)
0–96km/h (60mph): n/a
Top speed: 112km/h (70mph)
Production total: 19,132

WOLSELEY STELLITE

1913–28

The Wolseley Stellite was a joint venture between Wolseley and Birmingham-based Electric and Ordnance Accessories, which was a subsidiary of Vickers. A third partner, Crayford, was also involved in the project, the prime object of which was to produce a cheaper, reduced specification Wolseley which more people could afford to buy.

Although the 12/16 and 16/10 which preceded the Stellite were both very popular, with 7500 sold in total, Wolseley wanted to expand. The result was announced in 1913, complete with an 1100cc (67 cu in) monobloc four-cylinder engine featuring overhead inlet valves, an armoured wood frame and a two-speed gearbox in unit with the back axle. Within a year,

1500 had been built; however, the outbreak of World War I in 1914 meant that production of the car was halted until 1919.

Although the original Stellite went out of production in 1920, the name was revived the following year and put on a cheaper version of the 10. Able to cruise at 40km/h (25mph) while returning 6.3/100km (45mpg), this later Stellite directly

competed with cars from Austin and Morris – something which caused Wolseley major problems, as most buyers chose to purchase from the competition.

Engine: 1100cc (67 cu in)
Power: n/a
0–96km/h (60mph): n/a
Top speed: n/a
Production total: n/a

WOLSELEY HORNET

1930–36

Mixing good and bad in equal measure, Wolseley's Hornet was available in an amazingly large variety of guises during its six-year production run, which saw more than 30,000 examples produced.

Because Wolseley was bought by William Morris (later Lord Nuffield) in 1927, the company's cars after this date often shared their components with their Morris counterparts. The first major new car to come from the new company was the Wolseley Hornet, which was launched in 1930 and was available with tiny six-cylinder engines. The first unit displaced just 1271cc (78 cu in), and within six years more than 30,000 vehicles had been sold.

Mechanically, the Hornet was both good and bad, with modern hydraulic dampers and brakes, but a terrible chassis and poor steering and handling.

At a time when traditional coachbuilders were going out of business as mass-production

methods improved, Wolseley offered a chassis-only version of the Hornet with bespoke bodyshells in mind. As a result, there were more than 20 different variations of the Hornet available by 1931, and more than 2500 of these cars were specials.

The introduction of a 34kW (45bhp) twin-carburettor engine meant that the number of options for potential buyers increased still further and, by the time the last cars were made in 1936, there were also 1378cc (84 cu in) and 1604cc (98 cu in) derivatives available.

Engine: 1271cc (78 cu in), 6-cylinder
Power: n/a
0–96km/h (60mph): n/a
Top speed: 104km/h (65mph)
Production total: 32,000 approx.

WOLSELEY WASP

Engine: 1069cc (65 cu in), 4-cylinder
Power: n/a
0–96km/h (60mph): n/a
Top speed: 96km/h (60mph)
Production total: 5815

For buyers who did not want six cylinders but fancied a Wolseley in their garage, an overhead-camshaft four-cylinder option called the Nine was introduced in 1934. This car lasted only one year, as in 1935 it was replaced by a new model called the Wasp – which in turn lasted just one year. Unlike the Hornet, which was the basis of the Nine, only closed saloon versions of the Wasp were offered – this was no sports car.

Although the car had a new name, it was not much different from the car it replaced, the main changes being a bigger engine – with a displacement of 1069cc (65 cu in) in place of the earlier car's 1018cc (62 cu in) unit – and the adoption of Easiclean wheels in place of the Nine's spoked items. The powerplant retained its overhead-camshaft configuration, and the four-speed synchromesh gearbox that had been fitted to the Nine was also carried over.

Also in common with the earlier car, the Wasp featured hydraulic

brakes all round and semi-elliptic suspension front and rear, although 12-volt electrics and coil ignition were a welcome addition to the specification.

In the period prior to World War II, the Wolseley was aimed at conservative buyers who did not mind having relatively low-tech engineering along with staid styling. The Wolseley Wasp was a perfect example of this, even though, like the Wolseley Nine that had been introduced just a year previously, it lasted only one season.

WOLSELEY EIGHT

Once World War II was over, it soon became clear that Wolseley and Morris cars were going to share more components than they had done in prewar days. So when the postwar Wolseley Eight appeared, it was certainly no surprise to see that the four-door, four-seater car was essentially a Morris Eight with a distinctive Wolseley bonnet and grille grafted on.

However, some changes made beneath the skin were actually more significant than they first appeared, and these were to take the Wolseley Eight upmarket. With

Once World War II had finished, the Wolseleys became little more than badge-engineered Morrises. The Wolseley was the upmarket option of the two, which is why sales were always overshadowed by more affordable Morris versions of the car.

a 25kW (33bhp) overhead-valve engine displacing 918cc (56 cu in) (derived from the side-valve unit seen in the Morris Eight), the Wolseley Eight was fitted with a four-speed gearbox and hydraulic brakes along with a beam front axle. It was the car's powerplant which was most noteworthy, as it was far smoother than the side-valve version.

A higher level of interior trim also distanced the car from its lesser Morris sibling. But although the car was much nicer to drive than its Morris counterpart, just over 5000 examples were made – set against figures of 120,000 for the Morris Eights.

Engine: 918cc (56 cu in), 4-cylinder
Power: 25kW (33bhp)
0–96km/h (60mph): n/a
Top speed: 96km/h (60mph)
Production total: 5344

WOLSELEY 25

Largest of all the prewar Wolseleys, the 25 was a seven-seater limousine that was first seen just before the outbreak of World War II. The model was revived in 1946 and went into limited production. Before the car was even officially available, it had proved itself with a win in the 1939 Monte Carlo Rally Concours de Confort. Thanks

to a price of £2568 it did not really matter that the 25 was offered only to government officials, as few private individuals could afford it.

Based on a cruciform chassis with a very long 358cm (141in) wheelbase (one of the longest in production anywhere in the world), this Wolseley limousine incorporated Luvax-Girling

hydraulic dampers. The car's bodyshell was made traditionally using steel panels tacked on to a wooden frame, and with a 3.5-litre (213 cu in) engine, the car was one of the most comfortable on the market. Being a limousine, however, the important part was the cabin, which offered seating for five, plush carpets and wood trim.

It is no wonder very few examples of the Wolseley 25 were built, as it was incredibly expensive. Only 75 vehicles were made.

Engine: 3485cc (213 cu in), 6-cylinder
Power: 77kW (104bhp)
0–96km/h (60mph): 20.4 secs
Top speed: 136km/h (85mph)
Production total: 75

WOLSELEY 4/50

The Wolseley 4/50 was the last of four post-World War II family saloons unveiled by the Nuffield Organization in 1948; however, unlike its top-of-the-range brother, the 6/80, the mid-range 4/50 did not prove popular. Even though the least prestigious of the four cars

was the Morris Oxford, buyers chose this over the 4/50, opting for the space the Morris offered rather than the higher level of refinement offered by the Wolseley.

The 4/50 had a plush interior, including leather upholstery with rubber cushions. The car was

effectively a four-cylinder version of the 6/80, rather than an upmarket version of the Oxford. It had a shorter wheelbase than its bigger brother, although the engine was also an overhead-camshaft unit. When the Wolseley 4/44 arrived in the autumn of 1952,

sales of the 4/50 dried up and the model was dropped from the range.

Engine: 1476cc (90 cu in), 4-cylinder
Power: 38kW (51bhp)
0–96km/h (60mph): 31.6 secs
Top speed: 118km/h (74mph)
Production total: 8925

WOLSELEY 6/80

When the Nuffield Organization unveiled its postwar saloon range in 1948, there was a choice of wheelbase lengths and four- or six-cylinder engines. The result of this was a pair of new Wolseleys – the 4/50 and 6/80, with the latter being essentially the same car as the Morris Six.

With monocoque construction, independent front suspension and single overhead-camshaft engine, the car was modern. Not only that, but it was more upmarket than its Morris sibling as well, thanks to an extra carburettor on its 2.2-litre (135 cu in) powerplant and a much more luxurious interior. Standard equipment included leather trim and a heater/demister unit. Build quality was high – this was a car for the middle classes.

Sales were also good, and the car's speed and reliability endeared it to many police forces, which used 6/80s throughout the late 1940s and 1950s. There was little development of the car throughout its six-year life span, with only minor engine and suspension modifications made. In 1954, the car was taken out of production and replaced by the 6/90.

Engine: 2215cc (135 cu in), 6-cylinder
Power: 54kW (72bhp)
0–96km/h (60mph): 24.4 secs
Top speed: 125km/h (78mph)
Production total: 25,281

Previous Wolseleys often featured more advanced engines than their Morris counterparts, but not this time – this car featured the same powerplant as the Wolseley 6/80.

WOLSELEY 4/44

The Wolseley 4/44 was closely related to the MG Magnette ZA – the Wolseley being the luxury option. The MG (which was not available until the 4/44 had already been on sale for a year) was the sports version. This meant that those who bought the Wolseley

4/44 sat a little higher off the ground than in the MG, behind the traditional distinctive Wolseley grille. They were also able to sit in relative luxury, especially from 1954, when wood veneers could be specified for the plain but well-equipped dash.

The new saloon received coil and wishbone front suspension, making it much more modern than its predecessor (although there was still half-elliptic leaf spring suspension at the back), while the steering was updated with a rack-and-pinion unit. But, by 1956, the

car was obsolete and was replaced by the 15/50.

Engine: 1250cc (76 cu in), 4-cylinder
Power: 34kW (46bhp)
0–96km/h (60mph): 29.9 secs
Top speed: 117km/h (73mph)
Production total: 29,845

WOLSELEY 6/90

Wolseley's 6/90 was closely related to the Riley Pathfinder, sharing the same basic chassis and suspension units. This meant torsion bar independent front suspension with a rear axle located by coil spring and damper units, semi-trailing arms and a Panhard rod.

When the Wolseley 6/90 was launched, it used the then-new BMC straight-six 2639cc (161 cu in) C-series engine, which produced 71kW (95bhp). A column gearchange, twin carburettors and four speeds were also featured. Strong performance allied to good

build quality meant that several police forces used 6/90s.

In October 1956, the Series II arrived, with half-elliptic rear suspension and a move to a floor-mounted gearchange. Just eight months later, however, the Mk III appeared, with servo-assisted

brakes, but few other changes over its predecessor.

Engine: 2639cc (161 cu in), 6-cylinder
Power: 71kW (95bhp)
0–96km/h (60mph): 18.1 secs
Top speed: 150km/h (94mph)
Production total: 11,852

WOLSELEY 1500

1957–65

The Wolseley 1500 was basically the same car as Riley's 1.5, both of which were developed from an aborted project to replace the Morris Minor. The project car was going to use a 1.2-litre (73 cu in) engine; however, the final car, which became the Wolseley 1500, was equipped with a 1489cc (91 cu in) version of the old BMC B-series powerplant.

Planned to feature a 1.2-litre (73 cu in) engine, the 1500 was eventually launched with a 1489cc (91 cu in) powerplant – except for cars made for the Irish Republic, which did retain the 1.2-litre configuration.

The Minor's suspension was carried over and, with compact dimensions (it was just 386cm (152in) long with a 218cm (86in)

wheelbase), the 1500 was sold as a small luxury car. As the Riley was marketed as the sporting version, the Wolseley could not even claim to be quick. With just 32kW (43bhp) available, performance was poor.

In 1960, a Mk II version arrived, with hidden bonnet and boot hinges, along with some minor engine modifications which did nothing to boost power or torque

outputs. A Mk III version appeared in 1961, with a new grille, tail-lights and lower suspension, but it is hard to distinguish between any of the three generations.

Engine: 1489cc (91 cu in), 4-cylinder
Power: 32kW (43bhp)
0–96km/h (60mph): 24.4 secs
Top speed: 125km/h (78mph)
Production total: 93,312

WOLSELEY 6/99

1950–61

The Nuffield Organization had badge-engineered Wolseley cars for 25 years; however, the 6/99 was a break with tradition in that it was a badge-engineered Austin A99. With the exception of a few minor changes to the styling, trim and equipment levels, the Wolseley 6/99 and Austin A99 were identical,

even though they were assembled at different factories.

With monocoque construction and far more interior space than its predecessors, the Wolseley 6/99 was a big step forward. There was coil-spring independent suspension at the front of the car while, at the rear, there were half-elliptic springs

and anti-roll bars all round. Front disc brakes and camshaft-and-lever steering were joined by a three-speed all-synchromesh gearbox (with overdrive), although it was possible to specify a Borg-Warner automatic if wished.

Power for the Wolseley 6/99 was provided by a 77kW (103bhp)

2912cc (178 cu in) version of the C-series overhead-valve six-cylinder engine.

Engine: 2912cc (178 cu in), 6-cylinder
Power: 77kW (103bhp)
0–96km/h (60mph): 14.4 secs
Top speed: 157km/h (98mph)
Production total: 13,108

WOLSELEY HORNET

1961–69

The original Wolseley Hornet had been a sporting car in the 1930s, but there was nothing sporting about its namesake launched at the beginning of the 1960s. Just like all postwar Wolseleys, the basis of the car was the same as another vehicle available from within the BMC empire, in this case, the Riley Elf.

From the outside, it was not easy to tell the pair apart, the grille being the most obvious difference. On the inside, however, the Wolseley had a more luxurious fascia with circular instrumentation along the

An object lesson in how to widen even further the already huge appeal of a car – in this case, the Mini, which was made even more popular by taking it upmarket as the Wolseley Hornet.

lines of that seen in the Mini Cooper. Sharing the Mini's rubber cone suspension, the Mk I Hornet also used the same 848cc (52 cu in) four-cylinder engine seen in the Mini.

In March 1963, the Mk II Hornet superseded the Mk I, which meant a 998cc (61 cu in) engine was shoehorned under the bonnet and Hydrolastic suspension appeared. There were no other significant

changes until the Mk III arrived in 1966. This new model had winding windows instead of sliding ones, better ventilation and the option of automatic transmission from 1967.

Engine: 848cc (52 cu in), 4-cylinder
Power: 25kW (34bhp)
0–96km/h (60mph): 32.3 secs
Top speed: 114km/h (71mph)
Production total: 28,455

WOLSELEY 1100 AND 1300

1965–73

Now a cult car, the Wolseley 1100 was mechanically identical to contemporary Rileys and MGs. With optional two-tone paint and extra brightwork, the 1100 sat in the middle of the trio, but did not last very long. In 1967, the 1300

joined the range and, the following year, the 1100 was dropped so that only the 1300 was available until the car's demise in 1973.

Just a few Mk II 1100s were made, the emphasis being on the 1300 by that point. Using the

famous 1275cc (78 cu in) version of the A-series engine – with twin carburettors from 1968 to give 48kW (65bhp) – the Wolseley 1300 was an upmarket shopping or family car for those who wanted a little individuality.

Engine: 1098cc (67 cu in), 4-cylinder (1100)
Power: 41kW (55bhp)
0–96km/h (60mph): 18.4 secs
Top speed: 137km/h (85mph)
Production total: 17,397 (1100); 27,470 (1300)

WOLSELEY 18/85

1967–69

An upmarket Austin 1800, the Wolseley 18/85 appealed to people who wanted an ordinary car with more than an ordinary reputation, as well as a prestigious badge. This time, BMC did not also offer Riley and MG variants.

The Austin 1800 was first seen in 1964, but the Wolseley 18/85 did not arrive on the scene until 1967. It brought with it the option of an automatic transmission, which had not previously been available, and power steering was standard. It also had distinctive rear headlights and the usual Wolseley grille to distinguish it visually from the Austin 1800 version.

Costing £1,040 (plus £95 for the automatic gearbox), when the Austin 1800 was just £883, the car had to be special in order to justify its price. And it was – leather trim, an upmarket grille, wooden dash and thicker carpet were enough to attract buyers. In 1969, a Mk II arrived with much improved

seating, a higher quality dash and the option of twin carburettors on the S model, for added performance.

Engine: 1798cc (110 cu in), 4-cylinder
Power: 63kW (85bhp)
0–96km/h (60mph): 18 secs
Top speed: 145km/h (90mph)
Production total: 35,597

WOLSELEY SIX

1975

The last Wolseley ever produced was the Six. It appeared just before the marque was quietly dropped in 1975. For years, Wolseley had been just a name on another manufacturer's cars, and it was clear that it was not worth supporting another project when so few cars were actually being sold.

The final cars were 18/22 Princesses with Wolseley badges and a transversely mounted six-cylinder powerplant. By 1976, the Princess brand was being marketed as a marque in its own right.

The car had front-wheel drive and extra equipment such as a more comprehensive instrument

display and plusher trim, including velour seating and reading lamps for rear-seat passengers, to differentiate it from lesser siblings, and it was hoped that keeping the Wolseley marque separate would still prove a worthwhile exercise. It even had an illuminated badge on its front grille.

However, although the cars were not bad, they simply were not cost-effective to produce.

Engine: 2227cc (136 cu in), 6-cylinder
Power: 82kW (110bhp)
0–96km/h (60mph): 13.5 secs
Top speed: 166km/h (104mph)
Production total: 3800 approx.

ZAGATO ZELE

1974–91

Faced with bankruptcy in the early 1970s, Zagato decided to produce an electric city car for commuters, which was both cheap to buy and cheap to run. It was meant to be an antidote to the world oil crisis. The car was 196cm (77in) long and, being made of plastic, it was

corrosion-proof. Made of two plastic mouldings joined in the middle, the car's light weight was good; however, the most it could manage with its quartet of 24-volt batteries was 69km (43 miles) before it needed recharging. Top speed was also poor, just 40km/h

(25mph) being available from the rear-mounted electric motor.

The Zele was first shown at the 1972 Geneva Motor Show, going on sale in 1974. Most were badged as Elcars and sold in the United States, although Bristol did import them into Britain, where small

numbers were sold – including a golf-cart derivative.

Engine: 1000-watt motor
Power: n/a
0–96km/h (60mph): n/a
Top speed: 40km/h (25mph)
Production total: 3000 approx.

ZAZ 965

1960–63

The ZAZ 965 has often been called the worst car ever conceived. There are those who say it was not even conceived at all, but that its development was just an accident! Whatever its origins, the 965, otherwise known as the Zaphorozhets, or Zaporogets, was poorly engineered with decidedly ropey build quality. Looking like a Fiat 600 with a boot, the 965 was powered –

unusually – by an air-cooled V4 engine.

The original powerplant was a 748cc (46 cu in) unit developing just 17kW (23bhp). But within a year of its introduction, the 965 gained an extra 200cc (12 cu in), increasing its engine capacity to 887cc (54 cu in). This also developed a bit more power, with 20kW (27bhp) available and, from this point on, the car became

known as the 965A. The ZAZ 965 was imported into the UK in 1961 and 1962 and appeared at the London Motor Show in both years.

Throughout production, the suspension was independent at the front with longitudinal trailing arms and transverse torsion bars while, at the back, there were semi-trailing arms with coil springs and lever arm dampers.

Drum brakes were fitted all round, and it was not until the 966 was introduced in 1967 that there were any major changes made to the car.

Engine: 748cc (46 cu in), 4-cylinder
Power: 17kW (23bhp)
0–96km/h (60mph): n/a
Top speed: 80km/h (50mph)
Production total: n/a

ZAZ 966

1967–68

Launched in 1967, the Russian-built ZAZ 966 resembled the NSU Prinz. With its rear-mounted engine, booted design and just two doors, it was produced at the rate of around 150,000 cars each year.

After a year of production, the engine was upgraded to a 1200cc

(73 cu in) unit, and the suspension was also altered to make it handle much better. A minor redesign in 1972 meant that the car was renamed the 968, but the changes were only cosmetic. There was also a version produced in Belgium which wore Yalta 1000 badges.

For sales outside Russia only, the car was powered by a Renault 1000cc (61 cu in) engine, and these cars were fitted with front disc brakes. The car was to remain in production in 968 form into the 1980s, with more than two million produced.

Engine: 1196cc (73 cu in), 4-cylinder
Power: 34kW (45bhp)
0–96km/h (60mph): n/a
Top speed: 120km/h (75mph)
Production total: 2,000,000 approx.

ZIL 111

In production between 1956 and 1967, the ZIL was the most prestigious limousine available in Russia. Reserved for top government officials and communist leaders, the 111 was unbridled luxury in what was a purely American body.

With a 149kW (200bhp) 5980cc (365 cu in) V8 engine, the ZIL had a push-button automatic gearbox, similar to the US Powerflite gearbox of the period. In fact, in a strange twist given the political climate of the time, the whole car was US-inspired throughout.

In 1962, the car was restyled, with a sleeker front and rear panelling. The styling was still heavily influenced by contemporary American designs, both inside and out and, for the first time ever on a Russian car, air conditioning was an option. There were also power windows and power steering.

If the standard cars were still too ordinary, there were some special developments available in the form of a super-stretch version (the 111A) or a convertible, wearing the 111V tag. The former weighed 2814kg (6205lb), while the convertible had an electrically operated hood.

Engine: 5980cc (365 cu in), V8-cylinder
Power: 171kW (230bhp)
0–96km/h (60mph): n/a
Top speed: 161km/h (100mph)
Production total: 112

ZIL 114

With a kerb weight of 3048kg (6720lb), the ZIL 114 really needed its 224kW (300bhp) power output to pull it along. The engine was made out of aluminium (ironically, to help keep the car's weight down), and it struggled to deliver fuel economy anything better than 18.9l/100km (15mpg).

Like its predecessor, the 111, the 114 plagiarized American designs, looking surprisingly modern when it was launched in 1967 – indeed, its looks had more in common with 1970s US cars than those from its own decade.

Equipment levels had grown steadily since the first postwar limousines had rolled out of the ZIL factory gates. By the time the 114 reached production, there were such luxuries as servo-assisted ventilated discs all round, while the VIPs being transported inside the ZIL 114 could enjoy electrically adjustable seats, vacuum-operated central locking, tinted glass, power windows, power mirrors and a stereo radio. With tiny production numbers, however, very few people ever had the pleasure of sampling such luxury.

Looking more like a 1970s car than something from the late 60s, the ZIL 114 was produced in small numbers for an exclusive clientele of VIPs and politicians.

Engine: 6962cc (425 cu in), V8-cylinder
Power: 224kW (300bhp)
0–96km/h (60mph): n/a
Top speed: 188km/h (118mph)
Production total: n/a

ZIM (12)

1950–59

Made by Gaz and known officially as the 12, or unofficially as the ZIM, this 5.5m (18ft) long, six-seater, four-door monster was made between 1950 and 1959.

Modelled on contemporary American designs, and thus huge in every dimension, the ZIM was completely unaffordable for most

Russians; however, it was still not as prestigious as a ZIL limousine, which was reserved for the most important VIPs and Communist Party officials.

The car was not very fast, although it could allegedly reach a top speed of 120km/h (75mph). It featured independent suspension at

the front and a live axle at the rear.

When the ZIM was launched, it was as modern as any contemporary American car; however, with a life span of nearly a decade, it was hopelessly archaic by the time production finished. Even small details such as the split front windscreen could not be updated

very easily, as there was not the technology to produce curved windscreens in Russia at the time.

Engine: 3.5-litre (214 cu in), 6-cylinder
Power: 66kW (89bhp)
0–96km/h (60mph): n/a
Top speed: 120km/h (75mph)
Production total: n/a

ZIS 110

1946–56

Developed during the last months of World War II, the ZIS 110 went into production in August 1945. Borrowing its undoubted good looks from the US Packards and Cadillacs of the early 1940s, the 110 was a completely unaffordable proposition for almost all Russians. In many ways it was similar to the 1942 Packard Super Eight, the model which had been given to Joseph Stalin by US president Franklin Roosevelt during the war.

With a 6-litre (366 cu in) engine generating 104kW (140bhp), the 110 could manage nearly 145km/h (90mph) and boasted such innovations as hydraulic valves, electric windows and independent front suspension. And, despite the fact that the car was designed to be a luxurious machine for VIPs, its large dimensions meant that it was also ideally suited to carrying patients on stretchers. As a result, many were used as ambulances

Looking as though it was produced by one of the big American carmakers, the ZIS 110 was beautifully designed and built. It's a shame that nobody could afford one in postwar Russia.

without any bodywork modifications – patients were simply slotted in through the boot.

In 1966 the ZIS 110 became the ZIL 110. The company had started out as ZIL (the 'L' standing for Ligachev factory), but had changed its name to ZIS when Stalin was in power, the 'S'

standing for Stalin. Once Stalin fell out of favour, the company reverted to being called ZIL.

Engine: 6-litre (366 cu in), V8-cylinder
Power: 104kW (140bhp)
0–96km/h (60mph): n/a
Top speed: 139km/h (87mph)
Production total: 1500 approx.

ZUNDAPP JANUS

1957–58

In 1955, German microcar maker Dornier unveiled its tiny new product, the Delta. An angular car which was symmetrical along its length and width, it featured two pairs of seats arranged back to back. Passengers accessed these seats via a door on the front or an identical one on the back.

Although the car's concept was somewhat odd, this did not stop the German motorcycle maker Zundapp from buying the rights to produce it. The result was the Janus, which went on sale in 1957 featuring several changes from the original Delta's design.

First, the doors were no longer hinged at the top and were instead conventionally hinged at the side. There were still no signs of side doors. Front-seat passengers entered by a door at the front of the car and the back-seat passengers by a door on the back of the car. Back-

Engine: 248cc (15 cu in), single-cylinder
Power: 10kW (14bhp)
0–96km/h (60mph): n/a
Top speed: 80km/h (50mph)
Production total: 6800

seat passengers also faced backwards when travelling – hence the name Janus. Still, the car's styling was changed to look slightly less strange; however, the centrally mounted engine remained – this was definitely still a car which defied all convention when it came to design and construction.

The Janus's engine itself – a 248cc (15 cu in) single-cylinder two-stroke – was less idiosyncratic, as it was similar to the powerplants installed in many microcars, a form of vehicle which had become very popular because of the Suez crisis. In 1958, however, the Janus was dropped, and Zundapp returned to focusing on motorbike production.

Although the Janus lasted just one season, an astonishing 6800 were built – snapped up by cash-strapped buyers who needed a car that was economical above all else.

Only a few examples of the Zundapp Janus survive today; many of the cars rotted or were stored in poor conditions, and it is very difficult to find spare parts.

GLOSSARY

A-pillar Angled roof supports each side of the front windscreen
ABS Anti-lock braking system
Acceleration Rate of change of velocity, usually expressed as a measure of time over a given distance such as a quarter of a mile, or from rest to a given speed, such as 0–96km/h (60mph)
Aerodynamic drag Wind resistance, expressed as a coefficient of drag (Cd); the more streamlined a vehicle, the lower the figure
Aeroscreen Small, usually individual, often semi-circular, windscreen fitted to early sportscars, sometimes hinged to enable them to lay flat

Aftermarket Accessory fitted to a vehicle after purchase, not always offered by the manufacturer
Airbag Secondary restraint device automatically inflated in the event of collision
Air cooled engine Where ambient air is used to cool the engine, by passing directly over fins on the cylinders and cylinder head
Air dam Device at the lower front of a car to reduce air flow underneath and thus prevent lift at higher speeds
Alternator Electrical generator using magnetism to convert mechanical energy into an electrical output (AC)

Aluminium block Engine cylinder block cast from aluminium, usually with cast iron sleeves or liners for the cylinder bores
Antique U.S. term for vehicles built before 1925
Anti-roll bar Transverse rod between left and right suspension at front or rear to reduce body roll
Atomizing carburettor Spray of fuel broken into a fine mist to aid combustion
Axle Rotating shafts or spindles forming the centre of rotation for one or more wheels
Axle tramp Bouncing when climbing a steep hill while exerting power in a low gear;

usually only occurs with leaf-spring suspension

B-pillar the roof and door frame support behind the driver
Backbone chassis Chassis consisting of a single central structure, usually tubular
Badge engineering Selling of similar models with different manufacturer's name badges
Baffle Metal plates inside an exhaust system to absorb and reflect noise
Ball joint Ball and socket device used in suspension and steering mechanisms
Beam axle Axle that is rigid along its length, not having independent suspension

The Riley Imp was a graceful and classic sports car which helped the Riley name become synonymous with British sporting success. Its 1087cc (66 cu in) engine could be tuned to produce something approaching 130 kW (180bhp). Many of the cars have survived to this day, and are highly sought-after.

Looking at first glance like an American muscle car, the aggressive styling of the Aston Martin DBS got a mixed reaction when it was unveiled in 1967. The car's huge weight meant that cornering was poor, and its high fuel consumption was not helped by the introduction of a new V8 engine in 1970.

Bearing Device that transmits a load to a support with the minimum of friction between the moving parts

Belt drive Transmission of power from one shaft to another by means of a flexible belt

Bench seat Single, full-width seat at the front of the car for driver and passenger(s)

Bendix Helical gear and spring device that causes a starter motor pinion to be thrown into mesh with the starter ring

Bevel gear Conical-shaped gear wheel used to transmit power between shafts at 90 degrees to each other

bhp Brake horse power; 1 bhp = raising 550 foot-pounds per second or 745.7 watts; 1 bhp = torque x rpm/5252 with torque measured in foot-pounds

Big end Crankshaft end of the connecting rod

Birdcage chassis Chassis made from a complex arrangement of fine tubing, used on racing cars

Blown engine or 'blower' Engine fitted with a system of forced air induction such as a supercharger or turbocharger

Boat tail Styling where the rear of the car resembles the front of a boat

Bore The diameter of an engine's cylinder in which the piston travels

Bottom dead centre (BDC) when the piston arrives at the bottom of its stroke

Bucket seat Seat with added support in leg and shoulder area to secure the driver while cornering, used in rally sport

Bulkhead Panel usually separating engine from cabin compartment

Bumper Rigid addition (usually) to bodywork front and rear to prevent panel damage in the event of collision, usually chrome-coated steel or plastic

C-pillar Side pillar to the rear of the rear seats supporting the roof

Cable operated Usually relating to brakes worked by a cable, not hydraulic pressure

Cabriolet Open-top car with a removable or folding roof; often abbreviated to 'cabrio'

Calliper Disc brake component in which hydraulic pistons move friction pads on and off the brake disc surface

Camshaft Engine component which controls the opening and closing of valves via lobes, either directly or indirectly

Capacity The volume displaced by every piston moving from BDC to TDC measured either in cubic centimetres (cc) or cubic inches (cu in); 1 cu in (CID) = 16.4cc

Carburettor Device for vaporizing fuel and mixing it with air in an exact ratio ready for combustion, via the inlet manifold

CC Cubic capacity, or cubic centimetres; the total volume of the displacement of the engine's pistons in all cylinders

Centrifugal clutch Clutch in which pressure is exerted on the drive plate only above a specific speed of rotation, so it engages and disengages according to engine speed

Chain drive Transmission of power via a chain passing between two sprockets

Chassis Component to which body, engine, gearbox and suspension are attached

Choke Narrowed section within a carburettor where airflow is accelerated, thus creating an increased vacuum and sucking in more fuel

CID Cubic Inch Displacement, U.S. measure of engine size

CIH Cam In Head, engine where the camshaft is in the cylinder head

Classic Specifically vehicles built after January 1, 1930 and

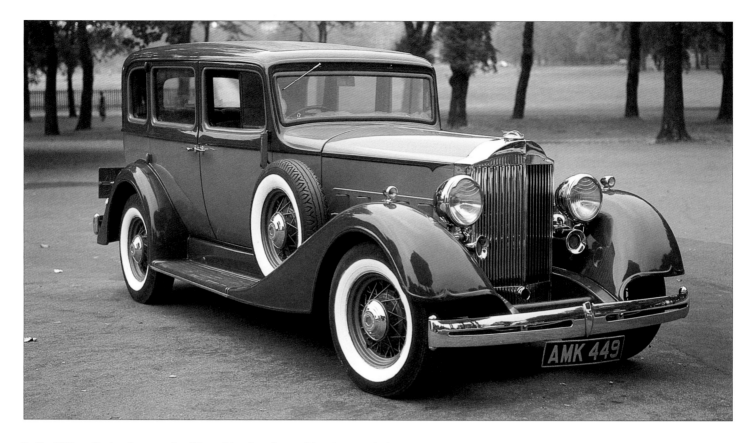

In the 1930s, a Packard was a splendid combination of everything that was desirable in a motor car – good looks, reliable engineering and high quality. The 1931 Packard Eight shown here offered plenty of status – and legroom – to the chauffeur-driven VIPs who were its prime market.

more than 25 years old. In U.S., relates to vehicles made during the years 1925–1948 inclusive

Close ratio Gearbox with closely spaced ratios, used in competition

Clunker U.S. and Australian slang for an older car in poor condition

Clutch Device for controlling the transmission of power from the engine to the gearbox, usually by means of friction materials

Coachbuilt Vehicle body built by hand, usually by a specialist company

Coil spring Helical steel alloy rod used for vehicle suspension

Column change Gearchange lever mounted on the steering column

Compact U.S. term for small saloon car with 2.83–3.11m³ (100–110 cu ft) of passenger and luggage space

Compression ratio The ratio of maximum cylinder and combustion chamber volume with the piston at top dead centre (TDC) to that at bottom dead centre (BDC)

Concours d'élégance Competition judged on a car's condition and originality

Con rod Connecting rod that links the piston and the crankshaft, the little end connecting to the piston and the big end connecting to the crankshaft

Con rod bearings Bearings upon which the connecting rod runs

Coupé Two-door cross between saloon car and sports car (coupe in U.S.) often with token seats in the back (2+2)

Crash gearbox Constant mesh gearbox without synchronization, name taken from noise made when gears are selected

Crossflow A cylinder head which has inlet and exhaust manifolds on opposite sides

Custom Personalized paint, body or mechanical modifications to a vehicle

Cylinder chamber in which piston travels, usually cylindrical in shape

Cylinder head Component which carries the sparkplugs, valves and sometimes camshafts

De Dion Axle/suspension system named after its inventor Count Albert de Dion, designed in 1894, where the driven axle is mounted on the chassis with universal joints at each end to keep the wheels vertical to improve handling, usually in conjunction with in-board disc brakes

DHC Drop-head coupé

Dickey seat Additional seat fitted to some vintage cars

which folds into the boot when not in use

Diesel engine Internal combustion engine which burns oil instead of petrol, without a spark ignition system, with the fuel/air mixture burning as result of high pressure

Differential Arrangement of gears in the drive axle which allows the drive wheel on the outside of a bend to travel faster than the one on the inside

Distributor Rotary switch which delivers the necessary charge to each of the sparkplugs at the correct interval

Disc brake System of braking by which friction pads are pressed against a flat, circular metal surface

Displacement Volume of the piston's swept area between BDC and TDC multiplied by the number of pistons

Dog clutch Simple method of engagement where one shaft has a square pin at the end, the other a square slot, requiring both shafts to be static or revolving at precisely the same speed

Dog leg first Gear selection layout where first and fourth gear are nearest the driver

DOHC Double overhead camshaft; where two camshafts are located in each cylinder head, one operating the inlet valves, the other the exhaust valves

Double wishbone Method of suspension where each wheel is supported by an upper and lower pivoting triangular framework, mainly used on sportscars

Downdraught carburettor Carburettor with a vertical barrel

Drag coefficient (Cd) Ratio demonstrating a vehicle's resistance while moving through the atmosphere divided by the flat area of an identical frontal silhouette with no axle length moving at the same speed

Driveshaft Shaft that transmits drive from the differential to the wheel, especially on front wheel drive cars with independent rear suspension

Drivetrain Entire power transmission system from the engine's pistons to its tyres

Drophead Open top car with a removable or folding hood (DH). Also drophead coupé (DHC)

Drum brake Braking system whereby friction materials (shoes) are moved radially against the inside surface of a metal cylinder (drum)

Dry sump Where lubricating oil is contained in a separate reservoir rather than being held in the crankcase; often used in competition to prevent oil surge/starvation

Dual circuit braking Braking system which uses two separate hydraulic circuits to reduce risk of failure

EFI Electronic Fuel Injection

Elliot axle Front axle design where ends of the axle are forked to hold the kingpin

EOI Engine with exhaust Over Inlet

Epicyclic gear An internally toothed drum containing 'planetary' gears which revolve around the main shaft, which carries a 'sun' gear wheel with which they mesh

Ergonomic Layout of controls in an easy-to-use configuration

Exhaust Device, usually of metal pipe construction, to conduct spent combustion gases away from the engine

The seven years during which Citroën had control of Maserati saw the development of the Citroën SM, a sophisticated, fast and technologically innovative car with a very respectable performance. It allied a Maserati V6 engine to a chassis inspired by the groundbreaking Citroën DS.

Fabric body Construction of bodywork where a lightweight waterproof fabric is stretched over a wooden frame; used on some veteran and vintage cars

Facia or fascia A car's dashboard or instrument panel

Fastback Body style of a car with a steeply sloping, aerodynamic rear end, similar to a coupé but usually with an opening hatch

Fender U.S. term for mudguard or wing

Fibreglass see glassfibre

Fin Styling element consisting of a angular 'fin' shape on the top of the rear wings

Fishtail When the rear of a rear-wheel drive car moves from side to side under power

Fixed head Hardtop version of a convertible car

Flathead Style of engine where the valves are mounted in the cylinder block, and the cylinder head has a flat surface

Flat-out At maximum speed, full throttle

Flat twin/flat four Boxer engine configuration where cylinders are horizontally opposed to each other, such as in the VW Beetle

Floorpan Structural floor to a car, part of the chassis

Fluid clutch Clutch using a fluid coupling, flywheel or torque converter

Fly-off handbrake Opposite operation to a conventional handbrake where a button is pressed to engage the ratchet; used for racing starts

Flywheel Rotating mass connected to the crankshaft assembly used to store energy and smooth power delivery

Four stroke Engine based on the Otto cycle (named after its inventor, Dr. Nicholas Otto) requiring four piston strokes for each power stroke

Forced induction Engine using a turbocharger or supercharger to pressurise the induction system to force air and hence more fuel, giving more power

Free-revving Used to describe an engine that responds quickly in terms of revs to accelerator pressure without a comparable increase in road speed at the wheels

Freewheel device Mechanism in the transmission to disengage the drive on the overrun

Freewheeling hubs Locked or free rotating front hubs on vehicles with selectable four-wheel drive, where the front transmission does not rotate when in two-wheel drive mode. Operated automatically via a traction control device, or manually by the driver

Fuel injection Direct metered injection of fuel into the combustion cycle by mechanical or electro-mechanical means, first devised in 1902

Glassfibre Strands of spun glass, either pressed or woven, set by a chemical process to form a rigid form. Used for bodywork construction, sometimes referred to as GRP (glass reinforced plastic) or fibreglass

Gearbox Component of the transmission system that houses a number of gears of different ratios that can be selected either automatically, or manually by the driver. Different gears are selected to suit a variety of road speeds throughout the engine's rev range

Gear ratio The revolutions of a driving gear required to turn the driven gear through one revolution, calculated by the number of teeth on the driven gear divided by the number of teeth on the driving gear

GP Grand Prix; race first run at Circuit de la Sarthe near Le Mans, France, in 1906

Grand Tourer Term originally used to describe an open top luxury car, now typically a high performance coupé

Grey import Vehicles imported privately, otherwise not available via an official manufacturer's source

Grille Metal or plastic protection for the radiator

Ground clearance Distance between the lowest point of a vehicle's underside and the ground when at its maximum kerb weight

GT Gran Turismo; Italian term used to describe a high performance luxury sports car or coupé

Gullwing Doors that open in a vertical arc, usually hinged along the centre of the roofline

H-pattern Conventional gear selection layout where first and third gear are furthest from the driver and second and fourth are nearest

Half shaft Shaft that transmits drive from the differential to the wheel, commonly used on cars with a live rear axle

Handbrake Brake operated manually by the driver when a vehicle is static, usually operating on the rear wheels via a cable

Hardtop Removable car roof; a pillarless coupe in the U.S.

Hatchback Car with an opening rear panel that provides direct access to the passenger compartment

Maserati turned to master designers Bertone to style the Khamsin. The result was angular and purposeful.

Helical gears Gear wheel with its teeth set oblique to the gear axis which mates with another shaft with its teeth at the same angle

Hemi engine An engine with a hemispherical combustion chamber

Hill climb Standing start uphill course timed against the clock

Hood Fabric covering on a convertible or open-top car, or U.S. term for engine cover

Hotrod A highly modified vehicle used for timed rest start acceleration races

Hubcap Decorative metal or plastic wheel cover, often with the car manufacturer's logo in the centre

Hydractive suspension Suspension system where ride height is automatically lowered to aid stability at speed, and raised over rough surfaces to increase ground clearance, developed by Citroën

Hydraulic Mechanism by which the pressure of a fluid is used to control movement of other components, such as brakes and suspension dampers

Hydraulic lifters System of valve operation that uses pressurized lubrication oil

Hydrolastic suspension System of suspension where compressible fluids act as springs, with interconnections between wheels to aid levelling

Hypoid gear Type of gear design where drive is transmitted between non-parallel shafts, where the gears slide instead of roll against each other resulting in high pressure between gear teeth. Used on hypoid rear axle as

well as many crownwheel and pinion gears, as well as worm and wheel

IFS Independent Front Suspension

Idler gear Gear interposed between two others to avoid using overlarge working gears

Ignition Process by which fuel is ignited to produce an expansion of gases

In-board brakes Brake discs positioned towards the centre of the vehicle at the inner end of each driveshaft to reduce

As well as being Britain's bestselling car during the 1960s, the Ford Cortina was also a force to be reckoned with on the racetrack and rally course. This photograph shows Roger Clark and Brian Melia in their Cortina GT during the 1966 Monte Carlo Rally.

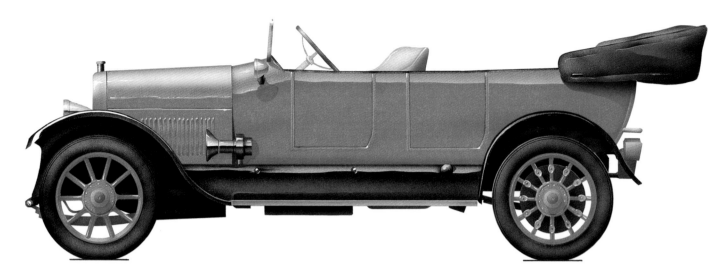

In 1914, General Motors introduced the world's first series-production V8 engine in its Cadillac range of luxury cars. The original V8 Cadillacs, available in a range of body styles, were sold from 1914 to 1927. The elegant example shown above is an original 1914 model.

unsprung weight, thus improving handling

Independent suspension System of suspension where all wheels move up and down independently of each other, thus having no effect on the other wheels and aiding stability

Intercooler Device to cool supercharged or turbocharged air before entering the engine to increase density and power

Internal combustion engine engine in which energy is transformed via the process of combustion in the engine cylinder and not in a separate chamber

IOE Inlet Over Exhaust; engine with overhead inlet valve and side exhaust valve

Kamm tail Type of rear body design developed by W. Kamm, where the rear end of the car tapers sharply over the rear window and is then cut vertically to improve aerodynamics

Kerb weight A vehicle's weight when unladen and without the driver but with tools and a full tank of fuel

Kickdown Shifts to a lower gear made to aid acceleration

with automatic transmission when the accelerator pedal is pressed sharply to the floor

Kilowatt (kW) the standard ISO measure of horsepower (1kW = 1.3596PS or 1.341bhp)

Kingpin Vertical post forming part of the front steering on older cars allowing the wheels to change in direction

Kit car Car supplied as a kit of (mainly body) components, with underpinnings often from a variety of different manufacturers. Introduced initially for those on a limited budget for construction at home, and not subject to VAT prior to 1973. Bodywork usually glassfibre

Km/h Kilometres per hour, used as a measure of speed

Ladder frame Tradition form of chassis with two constructional rails running front to rear with lateral members adding rigidity

Landau Large veteran car with a removable roof section over the front seats, a roof and window section in the centre and a folding hood over the rearmost pair of seats; named after the town in Germany where it was first constructed

Landaulette Smaller version of a landau without the centre saloon section, having just a removable roof over the front seats and a folding rear hood behind

Leaf spring Method of suspension comprising one of more narrow strips of spring steel, typically semi-elliptic, fitted on mainly older vehicles

Le Mans Race circuit in northern France famous for its 24-hour endurance races, the first of which took place in 1923

Lemon Car with a great number of inherent faults, unreliable

Limited edition Made in a limited quantity, with a specification that is different to the normal production model; usually collectable

Limited slip differential Device to control the difference in speed between left and right driveshafts so both wheels turn at similar speeds. Fitted to reduce the likelihood of wheel spinning on slippery surfaces

Limousine Luxury car typically having a lengthened chassis and bodywork to provide greater interior space, often with a glass panel

between the driver and passengers. Often abbreviated to 'limo'

Live axle Axle assembly patented by Louis Renault in 1899, where the axle contains shafts which drive the wheels

MacPherson strut System of suspension developed by Earle S. MacPherson in 1947, comprising a helical spring around a damper with a flexible upper mounting and a rigid mounting at the bottom, commonly used on the front though sometimes appearing at the rear

Magneto Type of electrical generator on some vintage and older cars

Manifold Pipe system used for gathering or dispersal of gas or liquids

Master cylinder Brake fluid reservoir and pump in a hydraulic braking system

Metric horsepower The power output of an engine expressed in metric units named *pferdestärke*, abbreviated to PS. 1PS = 0.75349875 kW or 0.98632 imperial horsepower

Mid engine Vehicle with its engine mounted just behind the driver and significantly ahead of the rear axle to provide even weight distribution, thus giving the car better handling characteristics

Monobloc An engine with all its cylinders cast in one piece

Monocoque Body design where the bodyshell carries the structural strength without conventional chassis rails (see 'unitary construction')

Monte Carlo rally Famous rally named after the town in Monaco, France, which hosts the finish; first held in 1911

mpg Miles per gallon, measure of a car's fuel consumption

Mud-plugger Vehicle suited to off-road use

Multiplex Wiring system using a central processor and local processors to reduce the amount of vehicle wiring

Muscle car U.S. term to describe a high-powered car, usually over 296kW (400bhp)

Normally-aspirated Engine charged by atmospheric pressure rather than by forced induction

Octane rating Measure of the anti-knock properties of fuel

Offset crankshaft Crankshaft layout where the crankshaft is not centrally below the cylinders, so that the con rod is more central to the piston during the power stroke to reduce wear

OHC Overhead Camshaft engine, where the camshaft is located in the cylinder head

OHV Overhead Valve engine, where the camshaft is located in the cylinder block, the valves are in the cylinder head operated by pushrods

Overheating A condition where the engine's coolant exceeds its maximum design temperature due to a fault or blockage in the cooling system or insufficient coolant/oil

Outrigger Extension to the chassis supporting the edge of the body or running boards

Overdrive Additional higher ratio gear(s), usually on the third or fourth gear selected automatically by the driver

Over-square Description of an engine in which the bore is greater than the stroke, as with most modern engines

Pagoda roof Car roof style that is concave in the middle and higher at the sides

Panhard rod Method of lateral location of a rigid axle to the chassis. Rod is mounted

at one end of the axle and extends to the chassis near the other end of the axle

Phaeton U.S. term for a luxury convertible with a very large trunk or boot

Pillarless coupé A coupé without a B-pillar where the door windows seal directly against the rear windows

Piston Moving plunger in a cylinder, accepting or delivering thrust

Planetary transmission See epicyclic gear

Poke Acceleration performance

Pop-up headlamps Headlamps that retract flush with the bonnet profile, used on sports cars to improve styling and aerodynamics

Power Rate of work, measured in kW, horsepower or PS

The sleek, composite-bodied TVR S was one of the few 1980s cars still built over a separate chassis. When it was introduced in 1986, the S was considerably less expensive than TVR's other convertibles, derived from the Tasmin, and soon deservedly became the company's best seller.

Although Ford have had a Thunderbird model continuously on sale for over fifty years, the most famous of all is the original two-seater sporting model produced from 1954 to 1957. A total of 53,166 examples were produced before the four-seater was introduced in 1958.

Pre-unit Description of a layout with separate engine and gearbox, opposite of 'in-unit'

Pre-selector transmission Gear selector system where a gear may be pre-selected before it is required, then later engaged by the driver by operation of a foot or hand control, common on buses

Prewar classic Term used for vehicles built between January 1, 1930 and September 2, 1939 inclusive

Prototype Full-size (usually) functional model of a new design

Pullman Luxury car or stretch limousine named after designer G.M. Pullman

Quarter light Small, often triangular window abutting an A or C pillar, usually opened by swivelling on its vertical axis

Rack and pinion System of gearing typically used in a steering box with a toothed rail driven laterally by a pinion on the end of the steering column

Radiator Device for dissipating heat, generally from the engine coolant

Reduction gearbox Gearbox positioned at the stub axles to reduce wheel speeds and increase torque, used to reduce weight and increase ground clearance

Retro design Styling which borrows design cues from an earlier model, typically with modern revisions

Rev counter (Tachometer) device for measuring rotational speed (revs per minute, rpm) of an engine

Rigid axle An axle or pair of stub axles where movement of one wheel has an effect on the other according to camber

Rocker arms Pivoting arm translating rotational movement of the camshaft into linear movement of the valves

Road car Vehicle meant for use on public roads as opposed to the racetrack

Roll bar Strong, usually curved bar either internally or externally across a vehicle's roof then secured to the floor or chassis to provide protection in the event of the car turning over. Used on some open-top sports cars

Rolling chassis Chassis complete with suspension, brake components and steering

– sometimes with an engine but never with a body

Rotary engine Internal combustion engine in which power is derived from a single rotor without reciprocating pistons, and very few moving parts. Pioneered by Felix Wankel in Germany, in 1956

rpm Revs per minute, measure of the crankshaft's rotational speed

Running gear General description of a vehicle's underbody mechanicals, including the suspension, steering, brakes and drivetrain

Saloon Traditional booted vehicle with a fixed roof, two rows of seats and either two or four doors

Scissor engine Type of rotary engine typified by the Tschudi engine where the pistons travel in a circular motion

Scuttle shake Vibration, or horizontal movement especially noticeable in the dashboard on convertible cars where there has been a reduction in structural integrity

Sealed beam Light unit with lens, bulb and reflection as one sealed unit

Sedan U.S. term for a saloon car having four doors, or a two-door having a minimum of 0.93m³ (33 cu ft) of interior space

Sedanca Two-door coupé in which the front seats are open or have a removable top and the rear seats are covered by a fixed roof

Sedanca de Ville Typically a larger chauffeur-driven veteran car where the driver remains exposed to the elements and the passengers ride in a closed saloon body behind

Semi-elliptic spring Leaf spring suspension used on the rear axle of older cars in which the spring conforms to a specific mathematical shape

Semi-independent suspension System on a front-wheel drive car where the wheels are located by trailing links and a torsioned crossmember

Separate chassis Where the body and chassis are separate components which are bolted together. All pre-World War II vehicles had this configuration, but today it is used only on trucks

Sequential gearbox Gear selection layout in which the selection is made by a linear movement rather than in the conventional H-pattern, used on some sports cars and rally cars

Servo assisted Powered by a vacuum, air, hydraulics or electrically to aid the driver, giving a powerful output from minimal input. Typically used on brakes, steering and clutch

Shock absorber Hydraulic device, part of the suspension system, typically mounted between the wheel and the chassis to prevent unwanted movement, to increase safety and aid comfort. More correctly known as 'damper'

Short stroke Markedly oversquare engine

Alfa Romeo's Alfetta derived its name from Alfa's postwar single-seater Grand Prix car. With a sporty feel and a finely-tuned chassis, the Alfetta was a real racer underneath its uninspiring bodywork. This is a 1976 2000cc (122 cu in) model.

Dr Ferdinand Porsche is pictured here with his most famous brainchild, the Volkswagen Beetle, designed at the request of Adolf Hitler. Production was due to start in 1940, but the outbreak of World War II meant that it was not until 1945 that the first cars rolled out of the Wolfsburg factory.

Sidevalve engine An engine where the camshaft is in the cylinder block and the valves are to one side below the cylinder head, mainly used on vehicles made prior to WWII

SOHC Single Overhead Camshaft Engine

Souped up Vehicle with an engine that has been tuned or increased in capacity to improve performance. Originally derived from 'suped', which referred to cars with a supercharger fitted

Spark plug Device for igniting combustion gases via the arcing of HT current between two electrodes

Spat Wheel arch extension commonly used to accommodate wider wheels

Spider Luxury open-top roadster, sometimes Spyder

'Split driveline' layout An extra set of epicyclic gears to provide a closer interval between the standard set of ratios, so an eight speed gearbox will actually have 16 gears

Spoiler Device fitted to the front of the car, low to the ground, to reduce air flow under the car and increase down-force, thus improving roadholding at higher speeds

Station wagon U.S. term for estate car

Straight 6, 8 An engine with six or eight cylinders in a single row

Suicide door A door hinged at its rearmost edge which opens

to the front; fitted to some vintage and veteran cars, dangerous if opened while moving

Supercharger Mechanically-driven air pump used to force air into the combustion cycle, thus improving performance

SU Carburettors Type of carburettor pioneered by a company called Skinners Union in 1905

SV Sidevalve engine

Swept volume Volume covered by the travel of a piston, cylinder displacement

Swing axle Type of independent suspension of a drive axle which pivots near the centre of the vehicle instead of at the wheel

Synchromesh Automatic synchronization using cone clutches to speed up or slow down the input shaft to smoothly engage gear, first introduced by Cadillac in 1928

Targa Removable roof panel and rigid roll bar, named after the Targa Florio race in Sicily

Tie bar Link or bar under tension or compression, used in the suspension and steering

Tonneau The rear seating area of a convertible, or a cover used to protect the passenger compartment of an open-top car against the elements

Torque The rotational twisting force exerted by the crankshaft, horsepower being the measure of torque over time

Torque steer Effect on the front wheels from the sudden delivery of power on powerful front-wheel drive cars

Touring car Luxury saloon car with a large luggage-carrying ability; also used for vintage models with a convertible body and two or four unglazed doors

Traction control Electronic system of controlling the amount of power to a given wheel to reduce wheelspin

Transmission General term for the final drive, clutch and gearbox. U.S. term for gearbox

Transverse engine Engine type where the crankshaft lies parallel to the axle

Transverse leaf spring Largely prewar suspension system in which a pair of leaf springs are mounted transversely, with one inverted, joined at their ends and mounted to the chassis and axle at their mid-points

Turbocharger Air pump for use in forced induction engines. Similar to a supercharger but driven at very high speed by exhaust gases, rather than mechanically to increase power output

Turbo lag Unwanted delay in response from the turbocharger when the accelerator is pressed

Two-stroke An engine cycle with a power impulse every other stroke. The fuel/air mixture is compressed beneath the piston before entering the combustion chamber via ports in the cylinder wall, hence no valves or timing gear

Unibody Monocoque construction in which the floorpan, chassis and body are welded together to form one single structure

Unitary construction Monocoque bodyshell

structurally rigid enough not to require a separate chassis

Unit construction Engine in which the powerplant and transmission are together as one, integrated unit

Unsprung weight The weight of components such as wheels, tyres, brakes and suspension lying roadside of the car's springs

Valve Device used for regulating the flow of a liquid or gas

Venturi principle Basis upon which carburettors work: gas flowing through a narrow opening creates a partial vacuum

Veteran Specifically a vehicle built prior to December 31, 1918

Vintage Specifically any vehicle built between January 1, 1919 and December 31, 1939

Wankel Rotary engine invented by Felix Wankel in 1956, operating on a four-stroke cycle but without reciprocating parts

Weight distribution Ratio describing the amount of a vehicle's weight placed on the front and rear wheels respectively

Wet liner The lining of a cylinder which is in direct contact with its coolant

Whale tail Very large rear spoiler, initially developed by Porsche

Wheelbase Distance between front and rear wheel spindles

Yaw The turning motion of a car's body around a vertical axis, particularly prevalent while cornering

The first American front-wheel-drive car since the 1930s, the Oldsmobile Toronado caused a stir when it was introduced in 1966. The front wheel drive made for excellent handling, but its adventurous styling and high fuel consumption meant that the Toronado never sold particularly well.

PICTURE CREDITS